OXFORD EC LAW LIBRARY

General Editor: F. G. Jacobs
Advocate General, The Court of Justice
of the European Communities

THE GENERAL PRINCIPLES OF EC LAW

OXFORD EC LAW LIBRARY

The aim of this series is to publish important and original studies of the various branches of European Community Law. Each work will provide a clear, concise, and critical exposition of the law in its social, economic, and political context, at a level which will interest the advanced student, the practitioner, the academic, and government and Community officials.

Other Titles in the Library

EC Company Law
Vanessa Edwards

EC Sex Equality Law
second edition
Evelyn Ellis

European Community Law of State Aid
Andrew Evans

EC Competition Law
third edition
Daniel G. Goyder

External Relations of the European Community Law
I. MacLeod, I. D. Hendry and Stephen Hyett

Directives in European Community Law
Sacha Prechal

EC Tax Law
Paul Farmer and Richard Lyall

The European Internal Market and International Trade
Piet Eeckhout

The Law of Money and Financial Services in the European Community
J. A. Usher

Legal Aspects of Agriculture in the European Community
J. A. Usher

Trade and Environmental Law in the European Community
Andreas R. Ziegler

The General Principles
of EC Law

TAKIS TRIDIMAS

OXFORD
UNIVERSITY PRESS

OXFORD

UNIVERSITY PRESS

Great Clarendon Street, Oxford OX2 6DP

Oxford University Press is a department of the University of Oxford.
It furthers the University's objective of excellence in research, scholarship,
and education by publishing worldwide in

Oxford New York

Athens Auckland Bangkok Bogotá Buenos Aires
Cape Town Chennai Dar es Salaam Delhi Florence Hong Kong Istanbul
Karachi Kolkata Kuala Lumpur Madrid Melbourne Mexico City Mumbai
Nairobi Paris Sao Paulo Singapore Taipei Tokyo Toronto Warsaw
with associated companies in Berlin Ibadan

Oxford is registered trade mark of Oxford University Press
in the UK and in certain other countries

Published in the United States
by Oxford University Press Inc., New York

British Library Cataloguing in Publication Data

Data available

Library of Congress Cataloging-in-Publication Data
Tridimas, Takis.
The general principles of EC law / Takis Tridimas.
p. cm. — (Oxford EC law library)
Includes bibliographical references and index.
1. Constitutional law—European Union countries.   2. Justice,
Administration of—European Union countries.   3. European Union.
I. Title.   II. Series.
KJE947.T75   1999   341.242´2—dc21   98–54610

ISBN 0–19–826012–1
ISBN 0–19–829932–X (Pbk)

Typeset in Bembo
by Hope Services (Abingdon) Ltd.
Printed and bound in Great Britain
on acid-free paper by
Biddles Ltd, www.biddles.co.uk

To Kristin, Emily and Beatrice

Καὶ μὴν τοῦτό γε αὐτό, ἡ εὐβουλία, δῆλον ὅτι ἐπιστήμη τίς ἐστιν· οὐ γάρ που ἀμαθίᾳ γε ἀλλ᾽ ἐπιστήμῃ εὖ βουλεύονται.

Plato, *The Republic*, Book δ, para 428a

General Editor's Foreword

Although Athene sprang fully armed from the head of Zeus, a new legal order—such as the European Community legal system—cannot emerge fully fledged from a treaty. The Treaties establishing the European Communities and the European Union, and the amending treaties, elaborate and complex as they now are, have never been sufficient to resolve many fundamental issues. To take an early example: was a Community measure invalid if it infringed fundamental rights, in the absence of any general requirement in the Treaty for the protection of such rights? Lacking the matrix of a fully developed legal system, Community law provided no express answer to such questions. Nor could the gaps be filled by the large and growing corpus of Community legislation—the regulations, directives, decisions and other measures adopted by the Community institutions. On the contrary, that legislation, which usually addresses the particular rather than the general, constantly raises new issues.

Faced very frequently with that situation, the European Court of Justice, which is given a general mandate to rule on all questions of interpretation of the Community Treaties and on the interpretation and validity of Community legislation, finds it necessary and appropriate to draw on general principles outside the formal sources of Community law.

In that task the Court of Justice—and now also the Court of First Instance—gain inspiration, naturally enough, from the legal systems of the Member States. Examples which by now may seem obvious, but which are none the less still of great practical everyday significance, are the principles of equality before the law, legal certainty, and the protection of fundamental rights. Such principles were not spelt out in the Treaties, in any event not as fundamental principles of general application. It seems clear however that all Treaty provisions should be construed so as to gives effect to such principles and that all Community legislation must have effect subject to them and, in case of conflict, be declared invalid. Thus the general principles rank alongside the Treaties as primary sources of Community law, prevailing over conflicting legislation. They have proved a particularly fertile and constantly evolving field for the judicial development of the law.

An understanding of these fundamental principles—often now called 'general principles of Community law' rather than 'general principles of law'—is therefore vital to any study of the Community legal system itself. Moreover the impact of these principles is pervasive: they are relevant in all branches and at all levels of Community law. They condition not only the actions of the Community institutions, but also those of the Member States wherever they implement Community law. In that respect the principle of proportionality plays a particularly important role.

The publication of this thorough examination of some of the most fundamental principles will therefore be of great value to scholar and practitioner alike. The principles are relevant in illustrating the development of a legal system and the interaction of Community law with national law. They provide what is perhaps the best example of judicial techniques in the construction of the Community legal order. But they are also of great practical importance in the everyday application of the law. As the author recognises, the role of general principles cannot be assessed in the abstract but only by reference to results reached in concrete cases: to be of any use, the study of such principles has to be a study of outcomes. This book will therefore be welcomed by students, scholars, practitioners and officials as a valuable addition to the Oxford EC Law Library.

Francis G. Jacobs

Author's Preface

In this book the term 'General Principles of Community law' is used as a shorthand for the general principles of law recognized in the Community legal order. The two terms are not synonymous. Strictly speaking, a book on the general principles of Community law may be expected to discuss the salient features of the Community legal system, introducing the reader to the constitutional and administrative law of the European Union, the internal market, and the various Community policies. This book has a different objective. It discusses selected underlying principles derived by the Court of Justice from the laws of the Member States and from the spirit of the founding Treaties and elevated in the case law to unwritten primary sources of Community law. Although it may be viewed as a solecism by the purist, the Court itself refers to equality, proportionality, effectiveness, etc. as general principles of Community law.

The case law on general principles is important in many respects. It provides a prominent example of judicial law-making, in particular, the contribution of the Court of Justice to the development of Community law as a new legal order. It is instructive of the Court's jurisprudential policy: the elaboration of general principles shows, perhaps better than any other area of the case-law, how the Court perceives its function and what it considers to be the ideological bases of judicial review. Finally, the evolution of general principles illustrates the interaction and dialectical relationship between the laws of the Member States and Community law.

This book is concerned primarily with the following principles: equality, proportionality, legal certainty and protection of legitimate expectations, fundamental rights, rights of defence, the principle of effective remedies in national courts and the principles governing liability in damages. The first chapter provides a typology of general principles, examines their origins, functions, and scope of application in the Community legal order. The second chapter discusses the principle of equal treatment in its diverse expressions. It focuses on the application of the principle on Community measures and examines also two more specific aspects: the affinity between the prohibition of sex discrimination and the general principle of equal treatment; and the prohibition of discrimination on grounds of nationality as enshrined in Article 12[6] EC. The third and fourth chapters discuss the application of proportionality on Community and national measures respectively. The fifth chapter is concerned with the principles of legal certainty and protection of legitimate expectations. That chapter also incorporates a relatively detailed discussion of retroactivity. Such discussion has been included for two reasons. First, because a large number of cases concerning legitimate expectations have arisen in relation to the retroactive application of Community acts. Secondly, because continental administrative law discourse tends to treat retroactivity as an integral part of legitimate expectations. Chapter 6 focuses on the development of the Court's case law on fundamental rights. It discusses, among others, the newly established right of access to documents held by the Community institutions. Although not fundamental in the sense of the rights traditionally recognized in the case law, the right of public access has given rise to interesting cases and illustrates the response of the Community judicature to a right in relation to the recognition of which the legislature has taken the initiative.

Chapter 7 discusses the rights of defence, a principle which, for historical reasons, is influenced by the common law tradition more than any other unwritten source of rights recognized in the Court's case law. Chapter 8 examines the so-called principle of effectiveness, i.e. the requirement imposed on national courts to provide full and effective protection of Community rights. Effectiveness is less the meeting point of national legal traditions and more the result of the Court's quest for minimum standards of judicial protection. The birth of the principle marks a fundamental shift in judicial policy from rights to remedies. Although the origins of effectiveness lie in primacy and direct effect, the principle has a close affinity with the right to judicial protection as a fundamental right. Chapter 9 discusses the principles governing the liability of Community institutions and national authorities. It focuses in particular on State liability as the culmination of the principle of effectiveness. It discusses also the liability of the Community as the elaboration of rules governing the latter provides an insight as to how the Court has used the mandate granted to it by Article 288(2)[215(2)] EC to develop a system of rules on the basis of principles derived from the laws of the Member States. Chapter 9 borrows from my work in Chapters 2 and 13 of Beatson and Tridimas, *New Directions in European Public Law*, Hart Publishing, 1998. The final chapter contains some concluding remarks.

Although at the time of writing the Treaty of Amsterdam has not yet entered into force, I thought it better to take account of renumbering for ease of reference in the future. References in the text to articles of the EC Treaty are to the consolidated version followed in brackets by the number of the article in the preconsolidated version.

In accordance with the general aim of the Clarendon series on European law, I have sought to present the law in its economic, political and social context and be useful to all those interested in the subject whether from a theoretical or a practical perspective. Law is stated as at the end of April 1998. Wherever possible subsequent developments have been taken into account.

T.T.

University of Southampton
July 1998

Acknowledgements

I would like to thank a number of people without whose assistance the completion of this book would not have been possible.

My special thanks go to Francis Jacobs. He was the first person to initiate my interest in the subject and was a steadfast supporter of this project throughout its completion. Without his guidance and eye for detail, the end result would have been much worse. But I owe him a lot more. During my years at the Court, I benefited enormously from his intellect, his power of reasoning, and his working ethos. I have been very fortunate indeed to have him as a mentor and a friend.

My thanks are also due to Jack Beatson who took the trouble to look at the manuscript, made valuable comments, and proved a constant source of inspiration. I had the opportunity to discuss aspects of my work with many others and I would like to thank in particular Professor Walter Van Gerven, Paul Craig and Dimitiris Gratsias, Member of the Greek Conseil d'Etat. I am grateful to the staff of the Press for their most valuable support throughout the writing and the production of this book. I am indebted in particular to Michaela Coulthard, John Louth, Chris Rycroft, and Nigel Sleight for putting up with my broken promises as to the date of completion and providing effective, efficient, first-class support. Last but not least, my thanks to Kristin without whose encouragement and unfailing patience I simply would not have been able to write this book. Needless to say, any mistakes, errors or inaccuracies remain entirely my own responsibility.

T.T.

Contents—Summary

Contents—Outline

Table of Cases

Court of First Instance

Opinions (chronological order)

European Court of Human Rights (alphabetical order)

Germany (chronological order)

International Court of Justice (alphabetical order)

United Kingdom (alphabetical order)

Table of Legislation

Regulations

Decisions

General EC legislation

1

The General Principles of Law in the Community Legal Order

1.1. Introduction

What is a general principle of law and how can it be distinguished from a specific rule? As a starting point, it may be said that a principle is a general proposition of law of some importance from which concrete rules derive.[1] Where reference is made to the general principles of law as a source of law in national or supranational legal systems, such reference usually connotes principles which are unwritten and which are derived by the courts from specific rules or from the legal system as a whole. Concrete rules, whether they are contained in legislation or judge-made law, can be viewed as specific expressions of underlying, more abstract, propositions of law on which the legal system is founded. Principles in that sense are derived by a process of abstraction and provide justification for concrete rules. In his Hague lectures on international law, Sir Gerald Fitzmaurice observed that a principle of law, as opposed to a rule, underlies a rule and explains the reasons for its existence. A rule answers the question 'what' whereas a principle answers the question 'why'.[2] The importance of general principles as reasons for specific rules is aptly demonstrated in Dworkin's analysis of rights.[3] Dworkin remarks that both principles and rules point to particular decisions about legal obligations but differ in the character of the direction that they give.[4] Rules, because of their specificity and concrete character, stipulate answers. Principles do not set out legal consequences that follow automatically from them. A principle states a reason which gives arguments in one direction but does not necessitate a particular result.[5] For example, the principle that the burdens imposed on the individual must not exceed what is necessary to achieve their objective (proportionality) does not mean that a charge imposed on a trader in specific circumstances is necessarily illegal. It does tell us something, however, about the values which the courts believe underlie the

---

[1] *The Shorter Oxford Dictionary* (edn.,1993) defines the term 'principle' as meaning 'a fundamental . . . proposition on which others depend; a general statement or tenet forming the basis of a system of belief . . . a primary assumption forming the basis of a chain of reasoning'. See also in the same sense, *Oxford Dictionary of English* (Second edn., 1989) entry 5a.

[2] Sir Gerald Fitzmaurice, 'The General Principles of International Law' (1957) 92 Collected Courses of the Hague Academy of International Law, p. 7.

[3] R. Dworkin, *Taking Rights Seriously* (1994) pp. 24 *et seq*.

[4] Op.cit., p. 24.   [5] Op.cit., p. 26.

legal system. In short, principles incorporate a minimum substantive content and guide the judicial inquiry on that basis. They provide strong arguments for a certain solution, they may even raise a presumption, but rarely do they dictate results in themselves. If that analysis is correct, a principle must be judged on the basis of two parameters: the intrinsic value of the right that it embodies, and how well it structures the judicial inquiry.

Continental authors tend to distinguish the following types of general principles in a legal system, according to their origin:[6]

- *Principes axiomatiques*, that is to say, principles which are inherent in the very notion of a legal order. Such principles are said to be so fundamental that a court may rely on them without need to have recourse to a specific legal basis. They are referred to as 'compelling' legal principles[7] because they represent 'les exigences suprêmes du droit et de la conscience collective'[8] and are considered to be a form of natural law. Which principles fall into this category depends on the society concerned and differs from State to State. A list of such principles is therefore hard to give.
- *Principes structurels*, that is to say, principles which derive from the distinct characteristics of a specific legal system. In Community law this category includes, for example, the principles of primacy and direct effect.
- *Principes communs*. This category is distinct to supranational legal systems and comprises principles common to the constituent parts of the legal system. The reference to 'the general principles common to the laws of the Member States' in Article 288(2)[215(2)] EC and to 'the general principles of law recognised by civilised nations' in Article 38(1)(c) of the Statute of the International Court of Justice belong to this category.

The above classification may be helpful in certain contexts, but overall, its value seems limited. In fact, the term 'general principle' has a relative character. It lacks any a priori specific legal meaning and, often, classifications raise more questions than they answer. The category of so-called *principes axiomatiques*, for example, seems to defy objective standards. Also, classifications by themselves tell us little about the implications of the principles involved on concrete cases especially where principles recognized by a legal order come to conflict with each other. The importance of general principles cannot be assessed in the abstract but only by reference to results reached in concrete cases. To be of any use, the study of general principles has to be a study of outcomes.

---

[6] Variations of this classification are accepted by a number of authors. See R. E. Papadopoulou, *Principes Généraux du Droit et Droit Communautaire* (Bruylant, 1996) p. 8 where further references are given. See also B. J. Boulois, *Droit Institutionnel des Communautés Européennes* (Paris 1984) pp. 153 *et seq.*; Schermers and Waelbroeck, *Judicial Protection in the European Communities*, p. 27; and further, P. Pescatore, 'Les objectifs de la CEE comme principes d'interprétation dans la jurisprudence de la Cour de justice', in *Miscellanea Ganshof van der Meersch* (Bruxelles, Bruylant, 1972) II, p. 325.

[7] Schermers and Waelbroeck, op.cit., p. 27.

[8] G. Issac, *Droit Communautaire Général* (3rd edn., Masson, 1992) p. 145.

In Community law, the term 'general principles' is manifold.[9] Depending on the criterion used, one may identify many such principles and draw various distinctions among them. A possible classification by subject matter is the following:

- Principles which underlie the constitutional structure of the Community. Such principles refer to the relationship between the Community and Member States, such as the principle of primacy, attribution of competences,[10] subsidiarity,[11] and the duty of co-operation provided for in Article 10[5] EC. They may also refer to the legal position of the individual, such as the principle of direct effect, or to relations between the institutions of the Community, such as the principle of institutional balance.[12] It is indicative of the extraordinary influence which the Court of Justice has had on the development of Community law that the main principles which define the constitutional structure of the Community are not provided for expressly in the Treaty but were 'discovered' by the Court by an inductive process. This applies in particular to the principles of primacy and direct effect, which in the Court's own language form the 'essential characteristics of the Community legal order'.[13]
- Principles which derive from the rule of law and pertain primarily to the relationship between the individual and the (Community and national) authorities. In this category belong for example, equality, proportionality, legal certainty, the protection of legitimate expectations, and fundamental rights.
- Principles of substantive Community law, such as those underlying the fundamental freedoms or specific Community policies, for example agricultural law.

In this book, the term 'general principles' is used to signify fundamental unwritten principles of law which underlie the Community law edifice. Such principles are derived by the Court of Justice primarily from the laws of the Member States and used by it to supplement and refine the Treaties. Their distinct features can be said to be the following:[14] (a) they derive from the rule of law and pertain to public law. They refer primarily to the relationship between the individual and the public authorities (both Community and national) but find diverse applications and, because of their all-embracing character, they may also be relied upon by Member States and Community institutions; (b) they are derived by the Court from the laws of the Member States but their content as sources of Community law is determined by the distinct characteristics and needs of the Community legal order; (c) they can

---

[9] For general works on the subject see J. A. Usher, *General Principles of EC Law* (Longman, 1998); R. E. Papadopoulou, *Principes Généraux du Droit et Droit Communautaire* (Bruylant, 1996); J. Schwarze, *European Administrative Law* (1992); A. Arnull, *The General Principles of EEC Law and the Individual* (1990).

[10] Article 5(1)[3b(1)] EC.   [11] Article 5(3)[3b(3)] EC.

[12] The principle was referred to by the Court in Case C–70/88 *Parliament* v. *Council* [1990] ECR I–2041.

[13] Opinion 1/91 *on Draft Agreement relating to the creation of the European Economic Area* [1991] ECR I–6079, para. 21.

[14] There is no attempt here to state exhaustively the requirements which a principle needs to have in order to be recognized as a general principle of law by the Court.

be said to pre-exist written law in that provisions of the Treaty which expressly provide for them are understood to be their specific expressions. The characteristics of those principles will now be examined in more detail.

1.2. The general principles of law derived from the laws of Member States: An overview

Among the sources of Community law, the general principles referred to above occupy a distinct position. They are unwritten principles of law extrapolated by the Court from the laws of the Member States by a process similar to that of the development of the common law by the English courts.[15] They derive from the legal systems of the Member States but their content as sources of Community law is determined by the distinct features of the Community polity. Thus, the Court may recognize a general principle as part of Community law although it is not recognized in the laws of all Member States. Also, the scope of a principle as applied by the Court may differ from that which it has in the law of a Member State. In short, the general principles of law are children of national law but, as brought up by the Court, they become *enfants terribles*: they are extended, narrowed, restated, transformed by a creative and eclectic judicial process. The importance of the general principles as a source of Community law lies primarily in two elements: as rules of law, they pose significant limitations on the policy-making powers of the Community institutions and of Member States; as judicially developed rules, they show eminently the creative function of the Court and, more generally, its contribution to the development of the Community from a supranational organization to 'a constitutional order of States'.[16]

The Court has recognized, among others, the following as general principles of Community law:

- the principle of equal treatment or non-discrimination;
- the principle of proportionality;
- the principle of legal certainty;
- the principle of the protection of legitimate expectations;
- the protection of fundamental rights; and
- the rights of defence.

Those principles have constitutional status. They are binding on the Community institutions and a measure, whether legislative or administrative, which infringes one of them is illegal and may be annulled by the Court. They are also binding on Member States.[17] A common characteristic of the principles referred to above is

---

[15] See de Smith, Woolf and Jowell, *Judicial Review of Administrative Action* (Fifth edn.) p. 833.
[16] The term is used by A. Dashwood, 'The Limits of European Community Powers' (1996) 21 ELRev. 113 at 114.
[17] See below 1.6.

that they have been derived by the Court from the laws of the Member States, sometimes with little assistance from the text of the Treaty. Respect for human rights was recognized by the Court as a general principle of Community law in the early 1970s[18] although there is no express reference in the Treaty to the protection of such rights. Various Treaty provisions prohibit discrimination on certain grounds but, according to the established case law, those provisions are merely specific illustrations of a general principle of non-discrimination which underlies the Community legal order.[19] Similarly, although a number of Treaty provisions can be said to incorporate the principle of proportionality, the case law has developed proportionality to a general principle of law transcending specific provisions. The same is true for the principles of legal certainty and protection of legitimate expectations. Some principles first developed in the case law were incorporated in the Treaty in subsequent amendments. The Treaty on European Union added Article 5(3)[3b(3)] to the EC Treaty which provides for proportionality as a general principle of law governing the exercise of Community competence. It also made express reference to the protection of fundamental rights.[20] Now, Article 6(1) of the Treaty on European Union, as amended by the Treaty of Amsterdam, makes express reference to the principles of liberty, democracy, respect for human rights and fundamental freedoms, and the rule of law as principles which are common to the Member States and on which the Union is founded. The Treaty of Amsterdam also makes a major innovation by providing for an enforcement mechanism in the event that a Member State fails to respect the principles referred to in Article 6(1).[21] Thus in relation to the general principles, the Court has followed a proactive approach. The case law showed the way, with subsequent Treaty amendments endorsing in many cases judicial developments. The fact that the case law has prompted law reform in that way is telling of the Court's contribution to the political process and the evolution of the Union. It shows that, despite what ephemeral political rhetoric may suggest, where the Member States acting in a sovereign capacity decide to amend the founding Treaties, they look on the Court as a source of inspiration rather than as an aberrant institution whose powers should be curtailed.[22]

The principles referred to above are principles of public law. They have been developed by the Court in order to protect the individual and, more generally, to ensure that Community institutions and national authorities act within the remit of the rule of law. It is pertinent to point out at this juncture the dual function of equality and proportionality. Those principles operate both in the sphere of public

---

[18] Case 11/70 *Internationale Handelsgesellschaft* v. *Einfuhr- und Vorratsstelle Getreide* [1970] ECR 1125.

[19] See e.g. Joined Cases 117/76 and 16/77 *Ruckdeschel* v. *Hauptzollamt Hambourg-St. Annen* [1977] ECR 1753, para. 7.

[20] See Article F(2) (now Article 6(2)) of the Treaty on European Union. See also Single European Act, Preamble, recital 3.

[21] See Article 7 TEU, added by the Treaty of Amsterdam.

[22] Judicial activism on the part of the Court of Justice attracted much criticism in the 1990s, especially in the UK. See further T. Tridimas, 'The European Court of Justice and Judicial Activism' (1996) 21 ELRev. 199.

law and in the sphere of substantive law. As principles of public law, they have been derived by the Court from the rule of law, with a view to protecting the individual vis-à-vis Community and national authorities. As principles of substantive law, they underlie the provisions of the Treaty on free movement, their function being to facilitate integration and promote the establishment of the internal market. As we shall see in subsequent chapters, the dual function of equality and proportionality underlies diverse trends in the case law.[23]

1.3. Origins and development of general principles

Recourse to general principles of law was first made by the Court in early cases decided under the Coal and Steel Community Treaty. The origins of non-discrimination and proportionality are to be found in the case law of the 1950s, where the Court invoked them to control the restrictive effects on economic freedom of market regulation measures introduced by the High Authority.[24] In that early case law the Court confronted in an embryonic form some of the problems which it was later to face much more acutely in the context of the common agricultural policy. Another area where the general principles were applied at an early stage was staff cases.[25] In the early years, disputes between the Communities and their employees accounted for a comparatively high percentage of the case law and provided fruitful ground for the development of Community administrative law.[26] As the Community evolved, the application of general principles expanded in other areas. The decade of the 1970s saw a proliferation of cases in a number of areas, including agricultural law. The basic features of equality, proportionality, and protection of legitimate expectations were laid down in the case law of that period. The recognition of fundamental rights as binding on the Community institutions also dates from that time.[27]

Subsequently, the case law of the 1980s established that the general principles bind not only the Community institutions but also the Member States where they

---

[23] See below 2.3, 3.1. and 4.1.

[24] See e.g. on proportionality, Case 8/55 *Federation Charbonniere Belgique* v. *High Authority* [1954–6] ECR 292, and on equality, Case 14/59 *Pont-à-Mousson* v. *High Authority* [1959] ECR 215.

[25] See e.g. for the rights of defence, Case 32/62 *Alvis* v. *Council* [1963] ECR 49.

[26] As the Community legal order developed and litigation in other areas increased, the importance of staff cases decreased correspondingly. Since 1989, jurisdiction to hear staff cases at first instance lies with the Court of First Instance (CFI). Since 1994, the judgments of the CFI on staff cases are published as part of the official court reports only where they are of general interest or establish principles of law. Otherwise, they are published separately in the Reports of European Community Staff Cases, the full text of the judgment being available only in the language of the case. In an effort to reduce the mounting workload of the CFI, consideration is currently being given to the possibility of establishing single-member chambers to hear staff cases.

[27] Case 11/70 *Internationale Handelsgesellschaft* v. *Einfuhr- und Vorratsstelle Getreide* [1971] ECR 1125; Case 4/73 *Nold* [1974] ECR 491; Case 44/79 *Hauer* v. *Land Rheinland-Pfalz* [1979] ECR 3727.

implement Community law.[28] The application of general principles to national measures further expanded in the 1990s.[29] The extension of general principles to action taken by national authorities had important repercussions as regards the powers of national courts and, more widely, the very structure of the national systems of administrative justice. This is because it enabled national courts to review, if necessary following a reference to the Court of Justice, the compatibility of a wide range of national measures with standards higher than those applicable ordinarily under national administrative law, thus opening the way for reverse discrimination against claims based purely on national law. This is particularly the case with the United Kingdom where the Diceyan tradition and the doctrine of parliamentary supremacy imposed strict limitations on the power of the courts to review the discretion of public authorities. The late 1980s saw a separate but related development in the sphere of constitutional law, namely, the gradual transformation of primacy from a general principle of constitutional law to a specific obligation on national courts to provide full and effective protection of Community rights, if necessary, by establishing new remedies.[30] This shift of emphasis from rights to remedies and the gradual inroads of Community law into the national systems of remedies triggered a trend towards some convergence of national public laws.[31]

Since its establishment in 1989,[32] the Court of First Instance also applies the general principles of law within the limits of its jurisdiction. Far from being merely a fact-finding tribunal, the CFI has made its own mark in the case law.[33] In some areas, it has applied a higher standard of scrutiny than hitherto applied by the Court of Justice, adopting in a number of cases a more critical stance towards the discretion of the Community institutions and requiring more exacting standards in their decision making.[34] Overall, however, in the sphere of general principles, the case law seems balanced. In some cases the Court of Justice has reversed decisions of the CFI taking a more restrictive view of the rights of the individual[35] but in others it

[28] See Joined Cases 201 and 202/85 *Klensch* v. *Secrétaire d'État à l'Agriculture et à la Viticulture* [1986] ECR 3477.

[29] See Case C–260/89 *ERT* [1991] ECR I–2925.

[30] See e.g. the obligation of national courts to grant interim measures: Case C–213/89 *Factortame and Others* [1990] ECR I–2433; and the development of Member State liability in damages for breach of Community law first introduced in Joined Cases C–6 and C–9/90 *Francovich* [1991] ECR I–5357. Those developments are discussed in Chs. 8 and 9.

[31] See further J. Schwarze (ed.), *European Influences in Administrative Law* (Sweet and Maxwell, 1998).

[32] See Council Decision 88/591/ECSC, EEC, Euratom of 24 Oct. 1988 establishing a Court of First Instance of the European Communities, OJ 1988 L 319, 1, as amended.

[33] For an initial assessment, see N. Brown, 'The First Five Years of the Court of First Instance and Appeals to the Court of Justice: Assessment and Statistics' (1995) 32 CMLRev. 743.

[34] See e.g. Joined Cases T–163 and T–165/94 *Koyo Seiko* v. *Council* [1995] ECR II–1381 where the CFI annulled an anti-dumping regulation of the Council. Upheld on appeal: Case C–245/95 P, [1998] ECR I–401. See also Joined Cases T–79/89 etc. *BASF AG and Others* v. *Commission* [1992] ECR II–315, rvsd. on appeal: Case C–137/92 *Commission* v. *BASF and Others* [1994] ECR I–2555.

[35] See e.g. on the requirement to give reasons, Case T–289/94 *Innamorati* v. *Parliament* [1995] ECR-SC II–393 rvsd. on appeal: Case C–254/95 P *Parliament* v. *Innamorati* [1996] ECR I–3423.

has reversed decisions of the lower court giving a broader definition to general principles.[36] The CFI has contributed not only by applying established principles of law but also by interpreting new principles recognized by the Community legal order such as the citizen's right of access to information held by Community authorities.[37] An area where the CFI has played a distinct role is in determining the requirements of the rights of defence in the context of competition law and other areas where natural and legal persons come to deal with the Commission either directly or through the intermediation of national authorities. The influence of the CFI in applying the general principles of law is aptly demonstrated in *Altmann and Casson* v. *Commission*.[38] There, the CFI reversed the earlier judgment of the Court of Justice in *Ainsworth*[39] and annulled on grounds of incompatibility with the general principle of equal treatment a provision of Community law which the Court of Justice had found to be lawful at the time of its adoption.[40] As far as the relationship between the two Community courts is concerned, *Altmann* is the most important decision delivered by the CFI so far. It demonstrates the considerable impact of the CFI in the application of general principles and more widely its contribution to the development of Community jurisprudence.

Two conclusions may perhaps be drawn from this brief historical survey. Although the general principles of law were initially invoked to cover gaps in the Treaty and the written law of the Community, their importance has not lessened as the Community legal order develops and more Community measures are adopted. The proliferation of such measures and, in some areas of law the resulting polynomy, has made recourse to general principles equally necessary. Also, the application of general principles has gradually expanded both with regard to the areas where they apply and with regard to the requirements that they impose. One area of law, for example, where equality, proportionality, and protection of legitimate expectations have increasingly been applied since the 1980s is the external relations law of the Community.[41] Also, recent years, saw moves towards the recognition of a new generation of human rights, both in the political sphere, such as the obligation of transparency and the cognate right of access to information held by public authorities, and the social sphere, such as the rights of transsexuals under the cover of sex discrimination.[42] Such developments are instructive of the general

---

[36] See in relation to the rights of defence: Case C–294/95 P *Ojha* v. *Commission* [1996] ECR I–5863 reversing the decision of the CFI in T–36/93; and Case C–404/92 P *X* v. *Commission* [1994] ECR I–4737 where the Court of Justice defined more broadly than the CFI the right to medical confidentiality.

[37] See below 6.2.7.

[38] Joined Cases T–177 and T–377/94 *Altmann and Others* v. *Commission* [1996] ECR II–2041.

[39] Joined Cases 271/83 and 15, 36, 113, 158 and 203/84 and 13/85 *Ainsworth* v. *Commission and Council* [1987] ECR 167.

[40] The judgments of the Court of Justice do not constitute binding precedent for the CFI except to the extent provided in Article 54 of the Statute of the Court of Justice or where the principle of *res judicata* applies. See also Case T–162/94 NMB [1996] ECR II–427.

[41] See e.g. Case C–24/90 *Werner Faust* [1991] ECR I–4905.

[42] See Case C–13/91 P v. *S and County Council* [1996] ECR I–2143.

principles as instruments of judicial methodology. They are flexible, lend themselves to an evolutive interpretation of the law, and make for a judiciary more responsive to social change.

1.4. The general principles as a source of Community law

1.4.1. The gap-filling function of general principles

Recourse to general principles as a source of law may be made by a court either as a result of an express reference contained in a legal text (renvoi obligatoire) or spontaneously by the court itself in order to fill a gap in written law (référence spontanée).[43] An example of an express reference is provided by Article 38(1)(c) of the International Court of Justice which mandates that court to apply the general principles of law recognized by civilized nations.[44] The EC Treaty contains two such references, an express one in Article 288(2)[215(2)] and a more oblique one in Article 220[164]. We shall return to those provisions in due course. For the time being, it is worth looking more closely at the function of general principles in judicial reasoning.

In any system of law a situation may arise where a lacuna exists in that a given situation is not governed by a rule of law, statutory or judicial. In such a case, the court having jurisdiction will resolve the case by deducing from the existing rules a rule which is in conformity with the underlying premises on which the legal system is based. This process is by no means peculiar to the Community legal order. It is practised by national courts, including in particular the French Conseil d'Etat on which the Court was modelled.[45] Lacunae are more likely to arise in Community law, especially in the early stages in its development, since it is a new legal order. Community law simply lacks the accumulated judicial experience, buttressed in case law, that national legal systems possess. The need to fill gaps is exacerbated by the distinct characteristics of the Community legal order. First, Community law is not only a new legal order but also a novel one in the sense that it has no historical precedent or indeed contemporary equivalent.[46] It represents a new development in the law of international organizations. Secondly, the EC Treaty is a traité cadre. It provides no more than a framework. It is rampant of provisions overpowering in their generality and uses vague terms and expressions

[43] See D. Simon, 'Y a-t-il des principes généraux du droit communautaire?' (1991) 14 Droits 73.

[44] See below 1.8.

[45] See, for example, to this effect the comments of commissaire du gouvernement Letourneur, quoted in D. Simon, op.cit., p. 73: 'à côté des lois écrites existent de grands principes dont la reconnaissance comme règles de droit est indispensable pour compléter le cadre juridique dans lequel doit évoluer la Nation, étant donné les institutions politiques et économiques qui sont les siennes'.

[46] Even if it is true that specific aspects of the legal and political system of the Community are found in other organizations, no organization combines all those aspects to such a degree of intensity and in such a way that they are combined in the European Community.

which are not defined. It bestows the Court with surprisingly broad powers to develop Community law. Thirdly, Community law seeks to supplement rather than to substitute the national legal systems. It is logical for the Court, in filling any gaps which arise, to resort to and gain inspiration from the laws of Member States. Fourthly, by its nature, the Community is a dynamic entity. The founding and amending treaties are moulded by teleology. The EC Treaty itself sets final objectives and intermediate goals, the notion of incremental integration being inherent in its provisions.[47] Recourse to general principles enables the Court to follow an evolutive interpretation and be responsive to changes in the economic and political order.

Those features peculiar to Community law explain why the Court is more 'active' than some national courts, i.e. why, as it is often said, it engages in judicial law-making.[48] The need to fill lacunae by recourse to national laws was expressly referred to in *Algera*, one of the early cases, where, faced with the problem of revocation of administrative acts granting rights to individuals, the Court stated:[49]

The possibility of withdrawing such measures is a problem of administrative law, which is familiar in the case law and learned writing of all the countries of the Community, but for the solution of which the Treaty does not contain any rules. Unless the Court is to deny justice it is therefore obliged to solve the problem by reference to the rules acknowledged by the legislation, the learned writing and the case law of the member countries.

Two points may be made in this juncture. First, it must be emphasized that the significance of general principles is not exhausted in their gap-filling function. They express constitutional standards underlying the Community legal order so that recourse to them is an integral part of the Court's methodology. The second point follows from the first. Once it is accepted that the general principles embody constitutional values, they may bear determinative influence on the interpretation of written rules, irrespective of the existence of gaps. In fact, the logical sequence may be reversed. Legislative provisions may be interpreted in the light of the underlying premises of the legal system in such a way as to leave gaps which then need to be filled by recourse to general principles. That is in effect what happened in *Chernobyl* where the Court, in order to avoid an openly *contra legem* interpretation of Article 173 (now 230) EC, established the existence of a procedural gap which it then filled by recourse to the principles of institutional balance and effective judicial protection.[50] There is no intention here to criticize, or indeed to commend, the Court in its use of general principles, rather to expose their function in judicial reasoning.

---

[47] In its reasoning, the Court sometimes inserts the proviso 'in the present state of Community law', see e.g. Case 81/87 *The Queen* v. *Treasury and Commissioners of Inland Revenue, ex parte Daily Mail and General Trust plc* [1988] ECR 5483. It will be noted, however, that the term 'integration' lacks a specific legal meaning. See further for a discussion of the term, G. Soulier, *L'Europe*, p. 271.

[48] See Tridimas, op.cit., n. 22.

[49] Joined Cases 7/56 and 3–7/57 *Algera* v. *Common Assembly* [1957–8] ECR 39 at 55.

[50] Case C–70/88 *Parliament* v. *Council* [1990] ECR I–2041, discussed below 1.7.2.

1.4.2. Article 220[164]

Article 220[164] charges the Court with the responsibility of ensuring that in the interpretation and application of Community law 'the law is observed'. This concise and seemingly innocuous article is arguably the most important provision of the founding Treaties. It assumes the existence of a legal order but tells us nothing about its substantive principles.[51] Its cardinal importance lies precisely in that it mandates the Court to work out a system of legal principles in accordance with which the legality of Community and Member State action must be determined. In assessing the compatibility of Member State action with the Treaty the Court is guided by the objectives and scheme of the Treaty, giving preference to a teleological interpretation of Community norms. Where it exercises judicial review of Community measures, the Court has less guidance. Article 220[164] establishes the principle of legality as a paramount and overriding principle of Community law. Also, since it contains no substantive principles of its own, it mandates the Court to have recourse to the legal traditions of the Member States and extrapolate principles of law found therein, with a view to developing a notion of the rule of law appropriate to the Community.[52] In effect, Article 220[164] does no less than to grant the Court jurisdiction to create 'constitutional doctrine by the common law method',[53] drawing inspiration from the liberal constitutional tradition. According to this model, the general principles of law as applied by the Court can be said to represent a common constitutional heritage. As Dutheillet de Lamothe AG put it:[54]

The fundamental principles of national legal systems . . . contribute to forming that philosophical, political and legal substratum common to the Member States from which through the case law an unwritten Community law emerges, one of the essential aims of which is to . . . ensure the respect for the fundamental rights of the individual.

In conclusion, the fundamental justification of judicial recourse to the general principles of law should be sought in the function which those principles fulfil in the Community legal order. They enable the Court to develop a notion of the rule of law appropriate to the Community polity and at the same time ensure conceptual and ideological continuity from the legal systems of the Member States.

---

[51] See T. Koopmans, 'The Birth of European Law at the CrossRoads of Legal Traditions' (1991) 39 AJCL 493, at 495.

[52] The Court has certainly understood Article 220[164] as giving it jurisdiction to gain inspiration from the laws of the Member States, see e.g. Joined Cases C–43 and C–48/93 *Brasserie du Pêcheur* v. *Germany and the Queen* v. *Secretary of State for Transport, ex parte Factortame Ltd*. [1996] ECR I–1029, paras. 27, 41.

[53] See R. Posner, Law and Legal Theory in the UK and USA, p. 14. The comparatist will find it difficult to resist the temptation to draw parallels with the US Supreme Court. See, *inter alia*, K. Lenaerts, *Le Juge et la Constitution aux États-Unis d'Amérique et dans l'Ordre Juridique Européen* (1988) and H. Rasmussen, *On Law and Policy in the European Court of Justice* (1986).

[54] Case 11/70 *Internationale Handelsgesellschaft* v. *Einfuhr- und Vorratsstelle Getreide* [1970] ECR 1125 at 1146.

1.4.3. The Court's evaluative approach

It has become obvious from what has been said so far that the search for principles in the legal systems of Member States is not a mechanical process. The Court does not make a comparative analysis of national laws with a view to identifying and applying a common denominator. Such an exercise would be as impractical as it would be futile. Rather, it makes a synthesis seeking the most appropriate solution on the circumstances of the case. The essence of the Court's evaluative approach was expressed by Lagrange AG as follows:[55]

. . . the case law of the Court, in so far as it invokes national laws (as it does to a large extent) to define the rules of law relating to the application of the Treaty, is not content to draw on more or less arithmetical 'common denominators' between the different national solutions, but chooses from each of the Member States those solutions which, having regard to the objects of the Treaty, appear to be the best or, if one may use the expression, the most progressive. That is the spirit . . . which had guided the Court hitherto.

In accordance with the tenor of the above quote, it has been said that the Court seeks such elements from national laws as will enable it to build a system of rules which will provide 'an appropriate, fair and viable solution'[56] to the legal issues raised, and the judicial inquiry has been referred to as 'free-ranging'.[57] The Court's approach can be illustrated by reference to two cases decided in the 1970s concerning respectively the protection of legitimate expectations and the rights of defence.

In the *Staff Salaries* case,[58] a dispute arose between the Commission and the Council regarding the formula to be used for the increase in the salaries of Community employees. Article 65 of the Staff Regulations provides that the Council shall review annually the remunerations of Community servants taking into account the rise in the cost of living and the increase in the salaries of public servants in the Member States. Following negotiations, the Council, the Commission, and staff representatives agreed a formula for adjusting salaries and by a decision of 21 March 1972 the Council decided to apply it on an experimental basis for a period of three years. Nine months after the adoption of the decision, however, when the next salary review occurred, the Council used a different formula. The Commission argued that the Council was bound by its undertaking to use the formula specified in the decision of 21 March. Warner AG made a comparative overview of the laws of the Member States and came to the conclusion that, in the national laws, a public authority may not fetter its discretion for the future where it exercises a legislative power. It may only, in exceptional circumstances, be bound in relation to an individual decision. The Advocate General con-

---

[55] Case 14/61 *Hoogovens* v. *High Authority* [1962] ECR 253, at 283–4.
[56] Kapteyn and Verloren van Themaat, *Introduction to the Law of the European Communities*, p. 161.
[57] Brown & Jacobs, *The Court of Justice of the European Communities* (Fourth edn.) p. 161.
[58] Case 81/72 *Commission* v. *Council* [1973] ECR 575.

cluded that, since the contested decision applied generally to all employees of the Communities, legitimate expectations could not arise. The Council's decision 'was, in law, no better than a rope of sand'.[59] The Court took the opposite view. It held that in adopting the decision of 21 March 1972, the Council had gone beyond the stage of preparatory consideration and had entered into the phase of decision making.[60] The principle of protection of legitimate expectations required the Council to be bound by its undertaking. The judgment may not be as far-reaching as it appears on first sight: the Council considered itself bound by the decision of 21 March 1972 and the decision was not incompatible with the Staff Regulations. It does illustrate, however, that the content of a general principle of law as recognized by the Court may differ from that which it has in the laws of the Member States. The *Staff Salaries* case established the principle of protection of legitimate expectations as a general principle of Community law which binds the Community not only in relation to administrative acts but also in relation to legislative measures.

In *AM & S v. Commission*,[61] the Commission required the applicant company to produce certain documents in the course of its investigation in a suspected violation of competition law. The company raised the objection that the documents in issue were covered by legal professional privilege. The problem was that neither Regulation 17,[62] which provides for the powers of the Commission to order inspections and carry out investigations, nor any other provision of Community law recognized the confidentiality of communications between lawyer and client. The Court started by pointing out that Community law derives not only from the economic but also from the legal interpenetration of Member States and must take into account the principles and concepts common to their laws concerning the confidentiality of lawyer–client communications. The rationale for such confidentiality is to ensure that a person is not inhibited from consulting a lawyer and obtaining independent legal advice. The Court noted that, although the confidentiality of lawyer–client communications is protected in all Member States, the scope of protection varies. It identified two tendencies. In some Member States, the protection against disclosure is seen as deriving from the very nature of the legal profession and serving the interests of the rule of law, whilst in others, it is justified on the more specific ground that the rights of defence must be respected. Despite those differences, the Court found that all national laws protect legal professional privilege subject to two criteria, namely, that communications are made in the interests of the client's rights of defence and that they emanate from independent lawyers, that is to say, lawyers who are not bound to the client by a relationship of employment. It concluded that Regulation 17 must be interpreted as protecting the legal professional privilege subject to those conditions and, on the facts, annulled in part the Commission's request for disclosure.

[59] Op.cit., 595.   [60] Para. 8.   [61] Case 155/79 [1982] ECR 1575.
[62] First Regulation implementing Articles 85 and 86 of the Treaty, OJ, English Spec.Ed., 1959–62, p. 87.

AM & S, in contrast to the *Staff Salaries* case, suggests a minimalist approach. The Court identified common criteria in the national laws and recognized a principle of Community law subject to those criteria. By contrast, in *Staff Salaries* the Court provided a higher degree of protection for the individual than that recognized in national laws. Two points may be made in this context. It is evident that the Court's function is *par excellence* a creative one. It borrows elements from the laws of Member States and may have particular regard to 'the best elaborated national rules'[63] but principles and solutions suggested by national laws are conditioned by the Community objectives and polity. This is of particular importance in the area of human rights which are protected in Community law but, according to the standard formula used by the Court, may be subject to limits justified by the objectives of the Community provided that their substance is left untouched.[64] The second point refers to comparative law as an aid to interpretation. In both cases discussed above, the Advocates General made ample references to the laws of Member States.[65] Although recourse to national laws was made more often at earlier stages in the development of Community law, it is by no means an exercise which has exhausted its usefulness.[66] A recent example is provided by *Van Schijndel* and *Peterbroeck*,[67] where Jacobs AG referred to the laws of the Member States concerning the powers of national courts to raise issues of national law *ex propriu motu*. In fact, a criticism which may be levelled against the Community judiciary is that it does not always take comparative law sufficiently seriously. For example, in the recent cases concerning the liability of Member States in damages,[68] the Court referred to the laws of the Member States with a view to establishing the conditions of liability, but did not make a serious attempt to derive truly common principles from the national legal systems regarding the right to reparation.[69]

---

[63] Case 5/71 *Zuckerfabrik Schöppenstedt* v. *Council* [1971] ECR 975, at 989 per Roemer AG.

[64] See e.g. Case 4/73 *Nold* [1974] ECR 491, para. 14.

[65] The Court incorporates a Research and Documentation Division which is staffed by experts in national laws. One of their tasks is to prepare at the request of the Court comparative accounts of the laws of Member States on specific topics. These are used for internal purposes and are not published. Occasionally, the Court may ask the Commission to produce information regarding the regulation of an economic activity in the Member States: see Joined Cases 60 and 61/84 *Cinéthèque* v. *Fédération Nationale des Cinémas Français* [1985] ECR 2605, para. 19.

[66] See T. Koopmans, 'Comparative Law and the Courts' (1996) 45 ICLQ 545.

[67] Joined Cases C–430 and C–431/93 *Van Schijndel and Van Veen* v. *SPF* [1995] ECR I–4705 and Case C–312/93 *Peterbroeck* v. *Belgian State* [1995] ECR I–4599.

[68] See Joined Cases C–43 and C–48/93 *Brasserie du Pêcheur* v. *Germany and the Queen* v. *Secretary of State for Transport, ex parte Factortame Ltd.* [1996] ECR I–1029; Case C–5/94 *The Queen* v. *Ministry of Agriculture, Fisheries and Food, ex parte Hedley Lomas (Ireland) Ltd.* [1996] ECR I–2553; Joined Cases C–178, C–179, C–188–90/94 *Dillenkofer and Others* v. *Federal Republic of Germany* [1996] ECR I–4845.

[69] See the criticism of W. Van Gerven, 'Taking Article 215 EC Seriously', in J. Beatson and T. Tridimas (eds.), *New Directions in European Public Law* (1998), p. 47.

1.4.4. The influence of national laws

The question which now arises is this: 'No doubt, the Court's approach is eclectic but the raw material is found, inevitably, in the laws of Member States. Have the laws of any particular State or States proved more influential?' Since in most cases it is not possible to trace the origins of Community solutions directly to concepts of national laws, this question can only be answered in more general terms by reference to principles, trends, and methodology. It may be said that two legal traditions have proved particularly influential in forming Community administrative law: the German and the French traditions. The reasons are, more than anything, historical.

The German influence is prominent in the development of the general principles, such as proportionality, legitimate expectations and protection of fundamental rights.[70] Why has German law proved so influential? It is arguable that, in the formative years of the Community, the Court of Justice found itself in a position similar to that of the German judiciary in post-war years.[71] In the aftermath of the Second World War, German legal thought experienced a resurgence of natural law thinking. The abuses of the Nazi regime had as a consequence the distrust of executive power and the search for constitutional principles constraining administrative discretion. Prevailing doctrine sought to give the concept of 'Rechtsstaat' a minimum substantive content. The principles of equality, proportionality, and protection of legitimate expectations which, in the pre-war era were recognized only in embryonic form and played only a limited scope in judicial reasoning, in the 1950s were developed by the judiciary as constitutionally mandated principles forming part of a wider substantive 'Rechtsstaat'. Those principles, together with the doctrine of limited administrative discretion, gradually led to the establishment of a body of administrative law founded on the new constitutional order. A parallel has been drawn between the emergence of general principles of administrative law in post-war Germany and the elaboration of general principles in the case law of the Court of Justice. In both cases, recourse to general principles has been in search of legitimacy. In the case of post-war Germany, it was imbued by considerations of substantive justice and was the result of a crisis of legitimacy. In Community law, recourse to general principles has been in an effort to assert the legitimacy and supremacy of Community law over conflicting national traditions.[72]

The French tradition has influenced Community law both directly and indirectly. Its direct influence is particularly prominent in the system of legal protection established by the Treaties. It has been decisive as regards the action for annulment (for example, Articles 33 ECSC and 230[173] EC) and as regards the organization of the Court of Justice which was modelled on the French *Conseil*

---

[70] See Schwarze, *European Administrative Law*, esp. Chs. 1, 2 and 8.

[71] See G. Nolte, 'General Principles of German and European Administrative law—A Comparison in Historical Perspective' (1994) 57 MLR 191.

[72] Op.cit., 200, 205–6.

d'Etat. French law also influenced Community law indirectly through its impact on the national laws of other Member States. The French public law tradition is the strongest in Europe and French administrative law provided a model for other continental countries already from the nineteenth century.

It should not be overlooked that the French and the German traditions were represented by the first two Advocates General of the Court, Lagrange AG and Roemer AG. They served during the most formative years of Community law fulfilling in effect the role of pathfinders. Their influence has been particularly instrumental in establishing the principles of Community administrative law, and in distilling, through a comparative method of interpretation, the elements of national laws most suitable for transposition in the Community legal order. Notable examples include *ASSIDER* v. *High Authority*,[73] where Lagrange AG made a comparative analysis of the notion of misuse of powers, and *Algera* v. *Common Assembly*,[74] where he considered the national rules governing the revocation of beneficial administrative acts.

English law, by contrast, has had comparatively less influence at least on the development of substantive principles of law. The reasons are not difficult to understand. The United Kingdom and Ireland being late entries, the common law tradition was absent in the early formative years of Community law. More importantly, English administrative law does not share the theoretical underpinnings of its continental counterparts. Bred in a Diceyan tradition, it developed subject to the constraints of parliamentary supremacy and the *ultra vires* doctrine. But its weakness has also been its strength: preoccupied as it has traditionally been with issues of procedure, it influenced decisively the development of procedural safeguards in the case law of the Court of Justice.[75]

If any conclusion may be drawn from this short survey it is that no national law can claim overriding influence to the development of Community public law. More importantly, perhaps, one must not be left with the impression that the flow of ideas has been only one way. Even legal systems which have proved particularly influential on the case law, such as the German and the French systems, have themselves been profoundly influenced by jurisprudential developments for which they provided the raw material in the first place.[76] Rather than dividing the national legal systems to 'borrowers' and 'lenders', one should celebrate the dialectical development of Community and national laws through which a *jus communae* may eventually evolve.

---

[73] Case 3/54 [1954–6] ECR 63.

[74] Joined Cases 7/56 and 3–7/57 [1957–8] ECR 39.

[75] See above *AM & S* and below Ch. 7.

[76] For the influence of the Court's case law on general principles of French law, see Y. Galmot, 'L'apport des principes généraux du droit communautaire à la garantie des droits dans l'ordre juridique français' (1997) 33 CDE 67. For its influence on German law, see Nolte, op.cit., 206–11. For the inter-relationship between Community law and English law, see D.Wyatt, European Community Law and Public law in the United Kingdom', in B. S. Markesinis, *The Gradual Convergence*, pp. 188–201.

1.5. The function of general principles in the Community legal order

In Community law, the general principles perform a threefold function. They operate as aid to interpretation, as grounds of review, and as rules of law breach of which may give rise to tortious liability. Each of those functions will now be examined in turn.

1.5.1. Aid to interpretation

Recourse to the general principles may be made as an aid to the interpretation of written law. According to a general rule of interpretation, which derives from the principle of hierarchy of norms, where a Community measure falls to be interpreted, preference must be given as far as possible to the interpretation which renders it compatible with the Treaty and the general principles of law.[77] Thus, the Court has interpreted agricultural regulations and other measures so as to comply with the principle of equal treatment,[78] the principle of protection of legitimate expectations,[79] the freedom to pursue a trade or profession,[80] other fundamental rights,[81] and the principle of proportionality.[82] In the same vein, it has been held that the Staff Regulations must be interpreted in such a way as to ensure that there is no breach of a superior rule of law, such as the principle of equal treatment.[83] The rule of consistent interpretation applies of course not only to regulations but to all provisions of secondary Community law.[84] One of its specific expressions, is the presumption against the retroactive application of laws.[85]

An obvious question which defies general answer is what are the limits of consistent interpretation. Clearly, general principles of law do not authorize a *contra legem* interpretation of Community measures[86] and there are dicta to the effect that the Court does not have a general power to supplement or amend legislation which

---

[77] See Case 218/82 *Commission* v. *Council* [1983] ECR 4063, para. 15; Joined Cases 201 and 202/85 *Klensch* v. *Secrétaire d'État à l' Agriculture et à la Viticulture* [1986] ECR 3477, para. 21; Case C–314/89 *Rauh* [1991] ECR I–1647, para. 17.

[78] *Klensch*, op.cit.

[79] C–314/89 *Rauh* [1991] ECR I–1647. See also for legal certainty: Case C–1/94 *Cavarzere Produzioni Industriali* v. *Ministero dell' Agricoltura e delle Foreste* [1995] ECR I–2363, para. 30.

[80] Joined Cases C–90 and C–91/90 *Neu and Others* [1991] ECR I–3617.

[81] See e.g. in relation to the rights of defence, Joined Cases 46/87 and 227/88 *Hoechst* v. *Commission* [1989] ECR 2859, para. 12.

[82] Case C–206/94 *Brennet* v. *Paletta* [1996] ECR I–2357.

[83] See e.g. Case T–93/94 *Becker* v. *Court of Auditors* [1996] ECR II–141.

[84] See e.g. for directives, Case C–392/93 *The Queen* v. *HM Treasury, ex parte British Telecommunications plc* [1996] ECR I–1631, para. 28, and for decisions, Case C–135/93 *Spain* v. *Commission* [1995] ECR I–1651, para. 37.

[85] See below 5.3.9.

[86] Case C–37/89 *Weiser* [1990] ECR I–2395 at 2415 per Darmon AG.

otherwise would be invalid.[87] The provision in issue must be reasonably capable of being interpreted so as to comply with the general principles. A parallel may be drawn here with the duty of *interpretation conforme* laid down by the Court in *Marleasing*.[88] In both instances, the purpose of consistent interpretation is the same, namely to ensure that in a hierarchical system of norms rules of the lower tier are interpreted in the light of rules in the higher tier.[89] It will be noted that, at least in one case, the Court adopted in the light of general principles a more liberal interpretation of the Treaty itself than it is normally prepared to adopt in relation to measures of secondary Community law.[90]

The limits of what can be achieved by interpretation are illustrated by *Mulder I* and *Von Deetzen*.[91] In those cases, the Court held that the contested regulation on milk quotas could not be interpreted in such a way as to guarantee a quota to producers who returned to the market after suspending production for a limited period, and found that the regulation was invalid for breach of the principle of protection of legitimate expectations. In borderline cases, there may be disagreement between the Court and the Advocate General. In *Diversinte*,[92] the Advocate General was prepared to follow a liberal interpretation of the provision in issue so as to ensure compliance with the principle of proportionality although he conceded that, in view of the text, such interpretation required 'goodwill'.[93] The Court took a different view and annulled the provision. In exceptional circumstances, the need to comply with the general principles may justify the analogical application of Community law. In *Krohn* v. *BALM*[94] it was held that traders may be entitled to rely on the application by analogy of a regulation which is not intended to apply to them if two conditions are satisfied: (a) the rules to which they are subject contain an omission which is incompatible with a general principle of Community law, and (b) those rules are very similar to the rules whose application they seek by analogy.[95] The general principles of law may be used also as an aid for the interpreta-

---

[87] Case C–85/90 *Dowling* [1992] ECR I–5305 at 5319 per Jacobs AG.

[88] Case C–106/89 *Marleasing* [1990] ECR I–4135. In that case it was held that, in applying national law, a national court is required to interpret it 'as far as possible' in the light of the wording and the purpose of the directive in issue, whether the national law was adopted before or after the directive (para. 8).

[89] In his Opinion in *Marleasing*, Van Gerven AG emphasized the limits imposed on the duty of national courts to interpret national legislation so as to comply with Community law by the principles of legal certainty and non-retroactivity. Also, in his Opinion in Case C–262/88 *Barber* v. *Guardian Royal Exchange Assurance Group* [1990] ECR 1889, at 1937, he stated that Community law may set limits to certain methods of interpretation applied under national law but it may not compel the national court to give a *contra legem* interpretation. The imperfect character of the interpretative duty laid down in *Marleasing* was implicitly recognized by the Court in Case 334/92 *Wagner Miret* [1993] ECR I–6911.

[90] See *Chernobyl case*, op.cit., discussed below 1.7.2.

[91] Case 120/86 *Mulder* v. *Minister van Landbouw en Visserij* [1988] ECR 2321; Case 170/86 *Von Deetzen* v. *Hauptzollampt Hamburg-Jonas* [1988] ECR 2355. Discussed below 1.7.2.

[92] Joined Cases C–260 and C–261/91 *Diversinte et Iberlacta* [1993] ECR I–1885.

[93] Op.cit., 1903 per Gulmann AG.   [94] Case 165/84 [1985] ECR 3997.

[95] Op.cit., para. 14. The omission of the regulation in issue infringed the principle of equal treatment. See for the same principle, Case 64/74 *Reich* v. *Hauptzollamt Landau* [1975] ECR 261, Case 6/78 *Union Française de Céréales* v. *Hauptzollamt Hamburg-Jonas* [1978] ECR 1675. Cf Case T–489/93 *Unifruit*

tion of national measures which implement Community law and, more generally, which fall within the scope of Community law. It follows that a national court must, as far as possible, interpret a provision of national law which falls within the ambit of Community law so as to comply with general principles and, if necessary, make a reference to the Court of Justice in order to ascertain the requirements of Community law in the case in issue.

1.5.2. Grounds of review

Most commonly, the general principles are invoked in order to obtain the annulment of a Community measure in proceedings under Article 230[173] or under Article 234[177]. As far as the grounds of review are concerned, indirect challenge under Article 234[177] is equivalent to direct challenge under Article 230[173].[96] A Community measure which infringes a general principle will be annulled by the Court or the CFI, depending on which court has jurisdiction.[97] It will then be up to the institution concerned to take the measures necessary to comply with the judgment, as provided by Article 233(1)[176(1)] of the Treaty. The Court, or the CFI, does not have jurisdiction to order the institutions to take such measures and may not issue directions to that effect.[98] In *AssiDomän Kraft Products and Others* v. *Commission (Woodpulp III)*[99] it was held that where the CFI or the Court of Justice annuls a Commission decision addressed to several undertakings, the Commission may be required under Article 233[176] to take measures in relation not only to the successful parties but also to the addressees of the decision who did not bring an action for annulment. This will only occur in exceptional circumstances but there may be scope for the application of the judgment in relation to general principles, as for example, where the Commission imposes a penalty or forfeits a deposit in relation to several undertakings in similar circumstances and one of those undertakings obtains the annulment of the decision imposing the penalty or forfeiture on grounds of breach of proportionality. In such a case, the Commission may be

---

Hellas v. *Commission* [1994] ECR II–1201, paras. 56 *et seq.*, where the CFI rejected an argument calling for the analogical application of a regulation in order to ensure the protection of legitimate expectations. Confirmed on appeal: Case C–51/95 P [1997] ECR I–727.

[96] For a detailed discussion of these articles, see T. Hartley, *The Foundations of European Community Law* (Third edn., 1994); Schermers and Waelbroeck, op.cit., Ch. 2.

[97] Since 1994, the CFI has jurisdiction to hear all direct actions brought by non-privileged applicants under Articles 230[173], 232[172], 235[178] and 238[181]. See Council Decision 94/149, OJ 1994 L 66/29.

[98] See e.g. Case T–346/94 *France-Aviation* v. *Commission* [1995] ECR II–2841, paras. 41–3; Case T–5/94 *J* v. *Commission* [1994] ECR II–391, para. 17; and see further Joined Cases 97, 99, 193 and 215/86 *Asteris* v. *Commission* [1988] ECR 2181 and Case T–224/95 *Tremblay* v. *Commission*, [1997] ECR II–2215.

[99] Case T–227/95 [1997] ECR II–1185. See also Joined Cases 42 and 59/59 *Snupat* v. *High Authority* [1962] ECR 53.

required to review the position of the other undertakings which are in the same situation, if the strict requirements provided for in *AssiDomän* are fulfilled.[100]

Article 231(2)[174(2)] provides that, in the case of a regulation, the Court shall, if it considers it necessary, state which of the effects of the regulation which it has declared void shall be considered as definitive. That provision applies not only on regulations but on any act of general application, including directives.[101] An example is provided by the *Staff Salaries* case.[102] It will be remembered that in that case the Court annulled the contested decision on the ground that the Council did not follow the formula which it had undertaken to use in subsequent salary adjustments. But to avoid a gap in the payment of salaries, the Court declared that the contested decision would continue to have effect until the measures taken so as to give effect to the judgment came into force. Article 231(2)[174(2)] is used in particular where a measure is annulled on procedural grounds. In recent years, the Parliament's tactical litigation policy, where successful, has supplied fruitful ground for its application.[103]

A ruling in proceedings under Article 234[177] that a Community provision is invalid produces vis-à-vis national courts comparable effects to a declaration of invalidity under Article 230[173].[104] By analogy with Article 231(2)[174(2)], the effects of the ruling may be restricted in time so as not to affect past transactions.[105] In exceptional cases, a finding of illegality may not lead to a declaration of invalidity. In the quellmehl cases,[106] Community regulations granted a subsidy for the

---

[100] In *AssiDomän*, the Court pointed out three material conditions: (a) the previous judgment in *Woodpulp* had annulled an act of the Commission which was made up of a number of individual decisions which were adopted on the completion of the same administrative procedure; (b) the applicants were addressees of the annulled act and had been fined for the alleged violation of Article 81[85] EC which the Court set aside in the *Woodpulp* judgment; (c) the individual decisions adopted in relation to the applicants were based, in their view, on the same findings of fact and the same economic and legal analyses as those declared invalid by that judgment (para. 71).

[101] Case C–295/90 *Parliament* v. *Council* (*Students' right of residence* case) [1992] ECR I–4193.

[102] Op.cit., n. 58.

[103] Since the seminal judgment in the *Chernobyl* case, op.cit., the Parliament tends to challenge measures of the other institutions if it considers that its prerogatives are infringed even where it agrees with the substantive provisions of the measure. In cases where the Parliament is successful, the Court usually declares that the annulled measure shall continue to produce effects until a new measure, following the correct procedure, is adopted. See e.g. Case C–65/90 *Parliament* v. *Council* (*Cabotage* case) [1992] ECR I–4593; Case C–271/94 *Parliament* v. *Council* (*Telematic networks*) [1996] ECR I–1689.

[104] This follows from Case 66/80 *International Chemical Corporation* v. *Amministrazione delle Finanze dello Stato* [1981] ECR 1191, para. 13, where the Court held that although a judgment given in proceedings for a preliminary ruling declaring a Community act to be void is directly addressed only to the national court which made the reference, it is sufficient reason for any other national court to regard the act as void for the purposes of a judgment which it has to give. However, the effects of a declaration of invalidity under Article 234[177] may be different from a finding of invalidity under Article 230 [173] as regards national authorities: see Case C–127/94 *R* v. *MAFF, ex parte Ecroyd* [1996] ECR I–2731, per Léger AG at 2753 *et seq.*

[105] See Case 4/79 *Providence Agricole de la Campagne* v. *Office National Interprofessionnel des Céréales* [1980] ECR 2823; Case 109/79 *Maiseries de Beauce* v. *Office National Interprofessionnel des Céréales* [1980] ECR 2883; Case 145/79 *Roquete Frères* v. *France* [1980] ECR 2917.

[106] See Joined Cases 117/76 and 17/77 *Ruckdeschel* v. *Hauptzollamt Hambourg-St. Annen* [1977] ECR 1753; Joined Cases 124/76 and 20/77 *Moulin Pont-a-Mouson* v. *Office Interprofessionnel des cereals* [1977] ECR 1795.

manufacture of quellmehl, a product derived from maize, and for the processing of starch. A subsequent regulation provided for the grant of subsidy for starch but not for quellmehl. The Court held that the abolition of the subsidy infringed the principle of non-discrimination on the ground that quellmehl was in a comparable position with starch. It stated, however, that the finding of illegality did not necessarily involve a declaration of invalidity of the contested regulation. Equal treatment could be restored in several ways and it was for the Community institutions responsible for administering the common agricultural policy to take into account economic and political considerations and to select the appropriate course of action.[107] The effect of the judgments was to maintain provisionally in force the subsidy but to apply it without discrimination to both products. By contrast, where the Court finds that a measure runs counter to the principle of non-discrimination because it imposes a financial burden on a product, rather than because it denies a financial benefit granted to another product, it will annul the measure even though it may subsequently be possible for the Council to restore equality by spreading the burden equally among all comparable products.[108]

An interesting question which arises in this context is, what are the duties and powers of national authorities responsible for implementing Community law where a Community measure is annulled? In R v. Ministry of Agriculture, Fisheries and Food, ex parte Ecroyd[109] the Court held that the conclusions which may be drawn in the national legal system from a ruling of invalidity delivered under Article 234[177] depend directly on Community law as it stands in the light of the ruling. In some cases, such consequences will be obvious or arise by necessary implication from the judgment.[110] In other cases, the consequences may not be so obvious. As already stated, the Court has no power to order the Community institutions to take the necessary measures and it is for the institutions to do so without undue delay in accordance with the principle of good administration.[111] In Ecroyd it was argued that the national authorities were required to grant a milk quota to the applicants, following the previous judgment in Wehrs.[112] In that case, the Court had annulled a Community regulation on the ground that it denied unlawfully a milk quota to a category of producers to which the applicants in Ecroyd belonged.

---

[107] Ruckdeschel, op.cit., paras. 11–13; Moulin Pont-a-Mouson, op.cit., paras. 24–9.

[108] See Joined Cases 103 and 145/77 Royal Scholten-Honig v. Intervention Board for Agricultural Produce [1978] ECR 2037, para. 86.

[109] Case C–127/94 [1996] ECR I–2731, para. 58.

[110] Thus, national authorities must revoke measures adopted on the basis of, or to give effect to, the act declared invalid: Ecroyd, op.cit., at I–2754 per Léger AG; see also Case 23/75 Rey Soda [1975] ECR 1279. On the powers of national authorities to reimburse sums unduly paid on the basis of Community acts declared invalid, see Case 130/79 Express Dairy Foods v. Intervention Board for Agricultural Trade [1980] ECR 1887; Case C–228/92 Roquette Frères [1994] ECR I–1445.

[111] An analogy may be drawn here with the duties of Member States following a judgment in enforcement proceedings finding an infringement of Community law. Under the case law, the necessary action to comply with the judgment must be commenced immediately and be completed as soon as possible: Joined Cases 227–30/85 Commission v. Belgium [1988] ECR 1.

[112] C–264/90 Wehrs v. Hauptzollamt Lüneburg [1992] ECR I–6285.

The claim of the applicants was that the national authorities should not have waited for the Council to adopt new rules to give effect to the judgment in *Wehrs* because the judgment annulled only a specific provision leaving intact the system governing the allocation of milk quotas. The Court rejected that claim. It held that the state of the law did not permit the allocation of a quota to a producer in the situation of the applicants before the adoption by the Council of measures to give effect to the ruling in *Wehrs*.[113] The Court was influenced by the particular complexity of the milk quota system. In other cases national authorities may find themselves in a precarious position. The consequences to be drawn from the illegality of a Community measure may be a matter for Community law but this is not to say that national authorities may not be required to draw them. This is a developing area of law where the case law has not yet laid down clear guidelines. It should be accepted that national authorities are under a duty, founded on Article 10[5] EC, to give as far as possible effect to a ruling of the Court declaring a Community act invalid, without prejudicing the powers of the Community institution which authored the act to take the necessary measures to comply with the ruling. Pursuant to that duty, they must uphold any legally complete rights which ensue from the Court's ruling. A more difficult issue is to what extent national authorities may intervene provisionally as trustees of the Community interest until the Community institution concerned takes the necessary measures.

An individual may attack, by way of incidental challenge, the validity of a Community measure before a national court on grounds of infringement of the general principles.[114] Under Article 234[177], the national court having jurisdiction may, and in certain circumstances must, make a reference for a preliminary ruling if it considers that such a ruling is necessary for it to give judgment. If the national court considers that the arguments put forward in support of invalidity are unfounded, it may reject them upholding the validity of the Community act. According to a well-established principle, however, a national court may not declare a Community act invalid.[115] If that were possible, divergencies would occur between courts in the Member States as to the validity of Community acts and those divergencies would be liable to jeopardize the unity and uniformity of Community law and detract from legal certainty.[116] A national court, however, may, under certain circumstances, order interim measures.[117]

1.5.3. Breach of general principles and liability in damages

The liability of the Community and the Member States is examined elsewhere in this book.[118] Suffice it to say here that breach of a general principle of law by a

---

[113] *Ecroyd*, op.cit., para. 59 and para. 65.

[114] See for a recent express declaration of this principle Case C–27/95 *Woodspring District Council* v. *Bakers of Nailsea Ltd*. [1997] ECR I–1847, para. 17.

[115] Case 314/85 *Foto-Frost* [1987] ECR 4199.

[116] Op.cit., para. 15.

[117] See below 8.6.2.

[118] See below Ch. 9.

Community institution may give rise to liability in damages on the part of the Community. This applies in particular to breach of equal treatment, legitimate expectations, proportionality, and fundamental rights. Also, although no case law exists in this area, it should be accepted that a Member State may be liable in damages for failing to observe those principles where it implements or acts within the scope of Community law, provided that the conditions for state liability are fulfilled.[119]

1.6. The scope of application of general principles

The general principles of law bind the Community institutions and the Member States.[120] The issue whether they also bind individuals is more controversial.[121] The application of general principles on Community measures does not pose particular problems. Suffice it to say that, as a rule, any Community act which is susceptible to judicial review can be challenged on grounds of breach of a general principle. It is less settled what types of national measures may be so challenged. The following categories may be distinguished:

- implementing measures;
- measures which restrict the fundamental freedoms but come within the ambit of an express derogation provided for in the Treaty;
- other measures falling within the scope of Community law.

1.6.1. Implementing measures

Where national authorities implement Community law, they act as agents of the Community and must observe the general principles of law. A national measure must respect general principles whether it was adopted specifically in order to implement a Community act or whether it pre-existed the Community act but gives effect to it upon its coming into force. The application of general principles to national implementing measures was recognized in passing in *Eridania* in 1979,[122] but was expressly declared by the Court some years later in cases concerning the milk quota regime. In *Klensch*,[123] decided in 1986, Community

---

[119] See Cases C–46 and C–48/93 *Brasserie du Pechêur* v. *Germany and the Queen* v. *Secretary of State for Transport, ex parte Factortame* [1996] ECR I–1029; Case C–5/94 *The Queen* v. *Ministry of Agriculture, Fisheries and Food ex parte Hedley Lomas (Ireland) Ltd.* [1996] ECR I–2553.

[120] See also below, 6.3.   [121] See below 1.6.6.

[122] Case 230/78 *Eridania* v. *Minister for Agriculture and Forestry* [1979] ECR 2749, para. 31. See also Case 77/81 *Zuckerfabrik Franken* v. *Germany* [1982] ECR 681; Joined Cases 205–215/82 *Deutsche Milchkontor* v. *Germany* [1983] ECR 2633.

[123] Joined Cases 201 and 202/85 *Klensch* v. *Secrétaire d'État à l'Agriculture et à la Viticulture* [1986] ECR 3477.

regulations provided for the imposition of a levy on quantities of milk produced beyond quotas allocated to producers. Regulation No. 857/84[124] provided that the quota was to be calculated on the basis of milk production in the calendar year 1981 but granted Member States the option to calculate it instead on the basis of production in the year 1982 or 1983. Luxembourg opted for the 1981 calendar year. The applicants argued that the adoption of that year favoured the largest dairy in Luxembourg which had links with the State to the detriment of other producers. The Court held that, where Community rules leave Member States free to choose among various methods of implementation, the Member States must comply with the principle of equal treatment. A Member State may not choose an option whose implementation in its territory would be liable to create, directly or indirectly, discrimination between producers, having regard to the specific conditions in its market and, in particular, the structure of agricultural activities.[125] Subsequently, in *Wachauf* the Court declared that, in implementing Community law, Member States must respect fundamental rights.[126]

The overwhelming majority of cases relating to the application of general principles on national implementing measures concern the principles of equality, respect for fundamental rights, and respect for legitimate expectations.[127] In one case,[128] the Court reiterated that implementing legislation must respect the principle of equality and held that the national authorities may treat differently different forms of associations formed by milk producers without infringing that principle where such different treatment is in accordance with the objectives of the milk quota regime. Also, the Court has accepted that the Member States may differentiate among milk producers using social criteria, for example, in order to accord some priority to small producers.[129]

Whether national implementing legislation leads to a breach of a general principle is a matter for the national court to decide on the basis of guidance given by the

---

[124] OJ 1984 L 90/13.

[125] *Klensch*, op.cit., paras. 10–11. The Court held that Article 40(3) (now 34(2)) covers all measures relating to the common organization of the market, irrespective of the authority which lays them down, and is therefore binding on Member States. Previous case law was not clear as to whether Article 40(3) itself bound national authorities: see e.g. Case 51/74 *Van der Hulst* [1975] ECR 79, Case 52/76 *Benedetti* v. *Munari* [1977] ECR 163 at 187 per Reischl AG; Case 139/77 *Denkavit* v. *Finanzamt Warendorf* [1978] ECR 1317, at 1342 per Reischl AG. In *Klensch* Slynn AG took the view that Article 40(3) was directed to the law-making function of the Community institutions and not to implementing measures taken by Member States. He considered, however, that Member States were required to observe the general principle of non-discrimination: op.cit., 3500.

[126] Case 5/88 *Wachauf* v. *Bundesamt für Ernahrung und Forstwirtschaft* [1989] ECR 2609. See also Case C–2/92 *Bostock* [1994] ECR I–955.

[127] For cases concerning the protection of legitimate expectations, see e.g. Joined Cases 196–8/88 *Cornée and Others* v. *Copall and Others* [1989] ECR 2309, Case C–16/89 *Sponk* [1990] ECR I–3185, and, earlier, Case 77/81 *Zuckerfabrik Franken* v. *Germany* [1982] ECR 681.

[128] Case C–15/95 *EARL de Kerlast* v. *Unicopa* [1997] ECR I–1961. See further Case C–351/92 *Graff* [1994] ECR I–3361.

[129] Joined Cases 196–8/88 *Cornée and Others* v. *Copall and Others* [1989] ECR 2309, para. 16. See also Case C–16/89 *Sponk* [1990] ECR I–3185.

Court of Justice under Article 234[177] proceedings. Depending on the circumstances of the case, such guidance may be very specific, leaving effectively no discretion to the national court, or more general.

1.6.2. Measures adopted under an express Treaty derogation

In its seminal judgment in *ERT*[130] the Court held that national measures which are adopted on the basis of an express derogation provided for in the Treaty must respect fundamental rights. The justification and ramifications of the judgment are examined elsewhere in this book.[131] For the purposes of the present discussion, it suffices to point out that the Court's finding applies not only to fundamental rights but, more widely, to all general principles of law.

In *ERT* the Greek Government sought to justify a State television monopoly by recourse to Articles 46[56] and 55[66] EC which permit derogations from the freedom to provide services on grounds of public policy, public security, and public health. The issue was raised whether the monopoly, by prohibiting other broadcasters from entering the field, might contravene freedom of expression. The Court held that, where a Member State relies on Articles 46[56] and 55[66] EC in order to justify rules which are likely to obstruct the exercise of freedom to provide services, such justification must be interpreted in the light of the general principles of law and the fundamental rights. Thus the national rules in issue could fall within Articles 46[56] and 55[66] only if they were compatible with the fundamental rights the observance of which is guaranteed by the Court.[132] The Court held that it was for the national court, and if necessary for the Court itself, to appraise the application of Articles 46[56] and 55[66] having regard to the general principle of freedom of expression embodied in Article 10 of the European Convention of Human Rights.[133]

1.6.3. Measures which fall within the scope of Community law

Although on the facts *ERT* concerned a measure which a Member State sought to justify under an express derogation of the Treaty, the language used by the Court was broader. It held that it has jurisdiction to determine the compatibility of national rules with fundamental rights where such rules 'fall within the scope of Community law'.[134] That begs the question what other national measures may be covered. So far, the case law has not positively ascertained any other category of such measures. The following comments may be made.

---

[130] Case C–260/89 [1991] ECR I–2925.   [131] See below 6.3.2.
[132] Op.cit., para. 43.   [133] Op.cit., paras. 44–5.
[134] *ERT*, op.cit., para. 42. See also Case 12/86 *Demirel* v. *Stadt Schwäbisch Gmünd* [1987] ECR 3719, para. 28; Case C–159/90 *Society for the Protection of Unborn Children Ireland Ltd.* v. *Grogan* [1991] ECR I–4685.

A purely hypothetical prospect of exercising the right to free movement does not establish a sufficient connection with Community law so as to trigger the application of the general principles.[135]

In the few areas where the Community enjoys exclusive competence by virtue of a Treaty provision, it is accepted that, in principle, Member States may not enact legislation on their own initiative even in the absence of Community measures. Community law occupies the field and pre-empts Member State action.[136] Member States may only intervene as trustees of the Community interest subject to strict conditions.[137] It is reasonable to assume that national measures in such an area, where permitted, are subject to review on the grounds of breach of a general principle. This is, however, a fairly exceptional case which affects only a limited range of national measures.

The binding effect of general principles does not extend to national measures in areas which fall within the potential non-exclusive competence of the Community, i.e. areas where the Community has competence but has not exercised it. For example, the fact that the Community has competence to adopt measures relating to the environment does not mean that a national measure in that field, which does not affect Community legislation, must comply with the principle of proportionality. The application of general principles in such a case is not warranted by the authorities. In *Maurin*,[138] a trader who was charged with selling food products after the expiry of their use-by date contrary to French law, sought the assistance of Community law with a view to overturning the conviction on the ground that his rights of defence had been infringed. The Court referred to Directive 79/112 on the approximation of the laws of the Member States relating to the labelling, presentation, and advertising of foodstuffs for sale to the ultimate consumer,[139] which was the applicable measure of Community law at the time. The Directive provides that the use-by date of a product must be indicated on the labelling and requires Member States to prohibit trade in products which do not comply with its provisions. The Court pointed out that the Directive does not regulate the sale of products complying with labelling requirements and concluded that it does not impose any obligation on Member States where there is a sale of products which comply with its provisions but whose use-by date has expired. It followed that the offence with which the accused was charged involved national legislation falling outside the scope of Community law. *Maurin* is correctly decided since the objective of Directive 79/112 is not to regulate the sale of foodstuffs correctly labelled.[140]

---

[135] Case 180/83 *Moser* [1984] ECR 2539, para. 18; Case C–299/95 *Kremzow* v. *Republik Österreich* [1997] ECR I–2629, para. 16.

[136] For the areas where the Community enjoys exclusive competence, see Tridimas and Eeckhout, 'The External Competence of the Community and the Case-Law of the Court of Justice: Principle versus Pragmatism' (1994) 14 YEL 143.

[137] Case 804/79 *Commission* v. *United Kingdom* [1981] ECR 1045.

[138] Case C–144/95 [1996] ECR I–2909.

[139] OJ 1979 L 33/1 as amended by Council Directive 89/395, OJ 1989 L 186, p. 17.

[140] See also Case C–299/95 *Kremzow*, op.cit., para. 16; C–177/94 *Perfili* [1996] ECR I–161.

Penalties adopted by Member States for failure to respect requirements of Community law must respect the general principles even if the adoption of such penalties is not expressly required by the Community measures in issue. This is because Member States are under a general obligation to provide for sufficient penalties for breach of Community law and therefore such penalties can be said to fall within the scope of its application.[141]

Where Community legislation confers an option on Member States to introduce special provisions in order to take into account the specific interests of a certain class of persons, and a Member State chooses to exercise that option, it must do so in accordance with the general principles of Community law. Is it, however, possible that those principles will require a Member State to exercise the option given to it by the Community rules, i.e. remove its discretion by imposing an obligation to act? In cases arising from the Community milk quota regime there are dicta to the effect that general principles bind the institutions and the Member States in exactly the same manner. Thus, where those principles do not impose an obligation on the Community legislature to allocate special quotas to producers who have implemented a development plan, they may not be relied upon to impose such an obligation on Member States.[142] Those dicta, however, must be read in the context in which they were made. They do not exclude the possibility that, in appropriate circumstances, the general principles may be relied upon not only to review the manner in which Member States exercise their discretion but also to review the failure to exercise that discretion.

1.6.4. The judgment in *First City Trading*

The issue which national measures fall within the scope of Community law has given rise to litigation also at national level. In *R* v. *Ministry of Agriculture, Fisheries and Food, ex parte First City Trading Limited*[143] the High Court was confronted with a question pertaining to the application of the principle of equal treatment. Following the BSE crisis and the imposition of a worldwide ban on the export of British beef by the Commission, the United Kingdom Government adopted the Beef Stock Transfer Scheme granting emergency aid to undertakings operating slaughterhouses and cutting premises. The applicants were exporters of beef who did not have their own slaughtering and cutting facilities and were therefore not entitled to aid. They argued that the aid scheme infringed the general principle of equal treatment as recognized in Community law. Laws J held that the aid scheme was not reviewable on grounds of compatibility with the general principle of

---

[141] See Case 77/81 *Zuckerfabrik Franken* v. *Germany* [1982] ECR 681.

[142] See Case C–63/93 *Duff and Others* v. *Minister for Agriculture and Food, Ireland, and the Attorney General* [1996] ECR I–569, per Cosmas AG at 583. See also Joined Cases 196–8/88 *Corneé and Others* v. *Copall and Others* [1989] ECR 2309; Case C–16/89 *Spronk* v. *Ministervan Landbouw en Visserij* [1990] ECR I–3185.

[143] [1997] 1 CMLR 250.

equality. He drew a distinction between, on the one hand, national measures adopted pursuant to Community law and, on the other hand, national measures adopted solely by virtue of domestic law. Although the first type of measure must comply with the general principles recognized by the case law of the Court of Justice, the second type of measure need comply only with the Treaty and written Community law. Laws J took the view that the contextual scope of the principle of equal treatment as an unwritten principle developed by the Court of Justice is narrower than the principle of non-discrimination enshrined in Article 12[6] of the Treaty. The first binds Member States only where they act pursuant to Community law. The second binds Member States more widely in that, even where Member States act solely by virtue of domestic law, they are constrained by Article 12[6].[144]

At first sight, the distinction drawn in *First City Trading* seems to run counter to the case law of the Court of Justice. If the prohibition of discrimination on grounds of nationality provided for in Article 12[6] is merely a specific illustration of the general principle of equal treatment, as the Court has declared,[145] how can it be said that the scope of application of the latter is narrower than that of Article 12[6]? But on closer examination, the distinction drawn by Laws J is correct. Perhaps, a better way of putting it is to say that the general principles of Community law form an integral part of the Community legal system, but are not by themselves capable of bringing a certain field of activity within the scope of Community law if that field is not otherwise so covered.[146]

According to the test enunciated by Laws J, a national measure is not subject to the general principles of Community law unless either (a) it has been adopted in order to implement a Community provision or (b) in enacting it, the Member State must rely on a permission or derogation granted by Community legislation.[147] On that basis, Laws J held that the Beef Regulations were not reviewable on grounds of compatibility with the principle of equality. The applicants in *First City Trading* proposed a different, more extensive, test. They argued that the Beef Regulations fell within the scope of Community law because their *fons et origo* was a Community act. They were enacted by the Government as a direct consequence of the Commission Decision banning the export of British beef. That test was rejected by Laws J. In his view, the fact that a national measure would not have been promulgated but for the adoption of a Community act is not sufficient to bring it within the scope of Community law.[148]

---

[144] Op.cit., at 267.

[145] Case 147/89 *Hochstrass* v. *Court of Justice* [1980] ECR 3005, para. 7; Case 810/79 *Überschär* v. *Bundesversicherungsanstalt für Angestellte* [1980] ECR 2747, para. 16.

[146] Note also Case C–249/96 *Grant* v. *South-West Trains Ltd.*, [1998] ECR I-621. The Court declared at para. 45 that, although respect for fundamental rights is a condition for the legality of Community acts, those rights cannot in themselves have the effect of extending the scope of Treaty provisions beyond the competences of the Community.

[147] Op.cit., at 271.

[148] This view finds support in the Opinion of Gulmann AG in Case C–2/92 *Bostock* [1994] ECR I–955 at 971.

The test proposed by Laws J seems correct.[149] Care should be taken, however, not to interpret it too restrictively. Where Member States are required to give effect to a Community act, all national measures which are necessary for the application of that act fall within the scope of Community law even if they are not expressly required by it. Also, any national measure which is capable of undermining or affecting the objectives of the Community act in issue falls within the scope of Community law and is reviewable on grounds of compatibility with the general principles.[150] Similarly, national legislation which affects interests whose protection falls within the ambit of Community legislation comes within the scope of Community law. Further, it is submitted that a national measure falls within the scope of application of Community law if its legal basis is a Community measure. If that is correct, a national act may need to observe the general principles even though its adoption is not required by Community law. That will be the case, for example, where a Member State chooses to implement by measures capable of producing legal effects a Community recommendation which in itself, under Article 249[189] EC, has no binding force. The duty of the national authorities to observe the general principles in such a case flows from Article 10[5] of the Treaty.

1.6.5. Public authorities bound by the general principles

The general principles bind, first and foremost, public authorities. The issues which arise in this context are the following. First, which public authorities are so bound and, secondly, whether under any circumstances general principles may be said to bind also private individuals.

Authorities which are considered as emanations of the State for the purposes of direct effect are bound to respect the general principles where they act within the scope of application of Community law. In *Foster*,[151] it was held that unconditional and sufficiently precise provisions of directives may be relied on against organizations or bodies which are subject to the authority or control of the State or have special powers beyond those which result from the normal rules applicable to relations between individuals.[152] It follows that the notion of State includes central government, local and regional authorities, and other constitutionally independent

---

[149] None of the cases decided hitherto by the Court of Justice settles conclusively the issue raised in *First City Trading*. Laws J decided not to make a reference since, in any event, he took the view that the scheme did not infringe the principle of equal treatment as provided for in Article 34(2)[40(3)] of the Treaty. His reasoning was that aid to undertakings operating their own slaughterhouses and premises was vital to maintain supply of fresh meat to the domestic market and meet consumer demand. Those aims did not justify granting aid to exporters.

[150] See Joined Cases C–286/94, C–340/95, C–401/95 and C–47/96 *Garage Molenheide BVBA and Others* v. *Belgian State*, [1997] ECR I-7281.

[151] Case C–188/89 *Foster and Others* [1990] ECR I–3313, para. 18. For a recent confirmation, see Joined Cases C–253 to C–256/96 *Kampelmann and Others* v. *Landschaftsverbanb Westfalen-Lippe and Others*, judgment of 4 Dec. 1997.

[152] *Foster* has given rise to some uncertainty. For a discussion, see Weatherill and Beaumont, *EC Law*, pp. 350–1; A. Clapham, *Human Rights in the Private Sphere*, pp. 264 *et seq.*

public authorities.[153] Although in *Foster* the House of Lords applied the ruling of the Court of Justice restrictively, recent cases suggest that English courts are prepared to accept a functional definition of the State. In *Griffin* v. *South West Water Services Ltd.*,[154] the High Court held that a privatized water company is a State authority against which directives can be enforced directly. Blackburn J stated that the material criterion for the purposes of direct effect is not whether the body in question is under the control of the State but whether the public service which it performs is under State control. In *NUT & Others* v. *Governing Body of St Mary's Church of England (Aided) Junior School*,[155] the Court of Appeal held that the governing body of a voluntary-aided school was an emanation of the State and therefore subject to the provisions of the Acquired Rights Directive which at the material time was incorrectly transposed in the United Kingdom. The judgment is important for two reasons: Schiemann LJ adopted a functional approach to State control; he also acknowledged that the criteria laid down by the Court of Justice in paragraph 22 of *Foster*, and applied literally by the House of Lords in that case, did not lay down an exclusive formula for the definition of the State.

The definition given by the Court of Justice in *Foster* seems sufficiently wide to encompass private bodies which have been entrusted with the performance of functions traditionally reserved to the State and over which the State retains residual control. It should also be accepted that self-regulatory bodies, namely authorities which exercise public power without being based on a statutory footing, are bound by the general principles in so far as such bodies implement Community law[156] or their actions affect fundamental freedoms. The issue is of importance in sports[157] but also in other sectors where self-regulation plays a significant role, for example, the financial services industry in the United Kingdom.[158]

---

[153] See e.g. Case 103/88 *Fratelli Constanzo* v. *Comune di Milano* [1989] ECR 1839, Case 222/84 *Johnston* v. *Chief Constable of the Royal Ulster Constabulary* [1986] ECR 1651.

[154] [1995] IRLR 15.

[155] [1997] IRLR 242. Cf *Rolls-Royce* v. *Doughty* [1987] IRLR 447; *Turpie* v. *University of Glasgow*, decision of the Scottish Industrial Tribunal of 23 Sept. 1986, unreported (university not a public authority for the purposes of applying the Equal Treatment Directive). Following *NUT*, the decision is an unreliable authority.

[156] The possibility of self-regulatory bodies being responsible for the implementation of Community law was left open by the judgment in Case 29/84 *Commission* v. *Germany* [1985] ECR 1661. In any event, self-regulatory bodies may be delegated powers by official bodies which are designated by national law as the competent authorities to implement Community obligations.

[157] See e.g. *Wilander and Novacek* v. *Tobin and Jude*, judgment of Lightman J (Chancery Division), 13 June 1996 (absence of a right of appeal against disciplinary decisions of the international tennis federation may render restriction on the freedom to provide services disproportionate). See also Case C–415/93 *Bosman* [1995] ECR I–4921.

[158] The Commission Proposal for a Thirteenth Company Law Directive on Takeovers, COM(95) 655 (1996) OJ C 162/5, requires Member States to appoint competent authorities but safeguards the position of the Panel on Take-Overs and Mergers in the United Kingdom, which is a self-regulatory body. It provides that the competent authorities designated by the Member States may include 'associations or private bodies'. See Article 4(1) and Article 4(5) of the Draft Directive.

1.6.6. The application of general principles against individuals

So far the case law has not pronounced on the issue whether the general principles of law may give rise to obligations against private parties. The issue acquires particular importance in relation to fundamental rights.[159] It may be argued that the historical origins and purpose of general principles, which is to protect the individual against public authorities, suggests a negative reply. But, that argument is hardly conclusive. In the modern pluralist State, the traditional public–private dichotomy is no longer valid and, in any event, it may be said that in certain cases fundamental rights deserve to be protected as much against private entities as against public authorities.

The case law accepts that certain provisions of the EC Treaty may produce horizontal effect. In *Defrenne* v. *Sabena*[160] it was held that Article 141[119], which provides for the principle of equal pay between men and women for equal work, establishes a right to equal pay which can be relied on in national courts against both public and private employees. In *Walrave and Koch* v. *Association Union Cycliste Internationale*[161] it was held that the prohibition of discrimination on grounds of nationality, as incorporated in Articles 12[6], 34[48] and 49[59] of the Treaty, does not apply only to the actions of public authorities but extends also to rules of private organizations which aim at regulating in a collective manner gainful employment and the provision of services. By contrast, the Court does not accept that directives may produce horizontal direct effect.[162]

Issues pertaining to the application of fundamental rights may arise in litigation between individuals.[163] This is not to say, however, that fundamental rights are horizontally applicable. It can be said that a fundamental right produces horizontal effect only if it is accepted that it can be breached by the conduct of a private party. A provision of Community law which imposes obligations on individuals may be interpreted in the light of fundamental rights. In that way, fundamental rights and general principles may have an indirect effect on relations between individuals. Beyond that, it is difficult to draw conclusions. It appears that, where the case law establishes obligations going beyond the text of the founding Treaties, it does so against the State. In the absence of written provisions, the case law seems reluctant to impose obligations on individuals. An interesting case in this context is *Bostock*.[164] Under the

---

[159] See in general A. Clapham, *Human Rights in the Private Sphere* (OUP, 1993); D. Spielmann, *L'effet potentiel de la Convention européenne des droits de l'homme entre personnes privées* (Bruylant, 1995).

[160] Case 43/75 [1976] ECR 455.

[161] Case 36/74 [1974] ECR 1405. See also *Doná* v. *Mantero* [1976] ECR 1333 and see further *Bosman*, op.cit.

[162] See Case 152/84 *Marshall* v. *Southampton and South-West Hampshire Area Health Authority* [1986] ECR 723; Case C–91/92 *Faccini Dori* v. *Recreb* [1994] ECR I–3325. Directives, however, may produce obligations against individuals indirectly, see *Marleasing*, op.cit. Cf. Case C–168/95 *Arcaro* [1996] ECR I–4705.

[163] See e.g. *Society for the Protection of Unborn Children Ireland Ltd.* v. *Grogan* [1991] ECR I–4685.

[164] Case C-2/92 [1994] ECR I–955.

Community milk quota regime, upon the termination of a farm tenancy, the milk quota is returned to the landlord.[165] In *Bostock*, it was argued that the general principles of Community law required Member States to introduce a scheme for payment of compensation by a landlord to the outgoing tenant or conferred directly on the tenant a right to compensation from the landlord. Earlier in *Wachauf*[166] the Court had accepted that the protection of fundamental rights may require that the departing lessee must be entitled to compensation where that is justified by the extent of his contribution to the building up of the milk production on the holding. But in *Bostock* the Court was not willing to disrupt relations between private parties by giving a right to the tenant against the landlord. The applicant argued that he was treated unequally *vis-à-vis* tenants whose leases had expired after a subsequent date in relation to which the UK had introduced a compensation scheme. After pointing out that the principle of equal treatment is a general principle of Community law, the Court held:[167]

> However, the principle of equality of treatment cannot bring about retroactive modification of the relations between the parties to a lease to the detriment of the lessor by imposing on him an obligation to compensate the outgoing lessee, whether under national provisions which the Member State in question might be required to adopt, or by means of direct effect.

The applicant also argued that, since his labour and his investments had contributed to the acquisition or the increase of the quota which reverted to his landlord on the expiry of the lease, the landlord was under an obligation to pay compensation in respect of his unjust enrichment. The Court, however, rejected that argument stating that legal relations between lessees and lessors, in particular on the expiry of a lease, are, as Community law now stands, still governed by the law of the Member State in question. Any consequences of unjust enrichment of the lessor on the expiry of a lease are therefore not a matter for Community law.

The judgment in *Bostock* must be read in the light of the peculiarities of the milk quota regime and it is difficult to draw general conclusions. The existing authorities do suggest, however, that the Court is reluctant to accept that the general principles may by themselves impose obligations on individuals.[168]

1.7. The general principles of law and the EC Treaty

1.7.1. The general principles in the hierarchy of Community rules

The Community legal order is based on a system of hierarchy of rules under which rules of a lower tier derive their validity from, and are bound to respect,

---

[165] The milk quota regime is discussed in more detail below 5.4.2. and 6.3.1.
[166] Case 5/88 *Wachauf* [1989] ECR I–2609.   [167] *Bostock*, op.cit., para. 14.
[168] See also Case C–60/92 *Otto* v. *Postbank NV* [1993] ECR I–5683.

the rules of the higher tiers. What is the position of the general principles of law in that order of hierarchy? It is clear that those principles which are accorded constitutional status are superior to secondary legislation since acts adopted by the institutions are subject to review on grounds of compatibility with them. By contrast, the position of such principles vis-à-vis primary Community law is not entirely clear. Since their origins lie in the EC Treaty, it is submitted that they have equivalent status with the founding Treaties. Their equal ranking with the Treaties derives from their character as constitutional principles emanating from the rule of law. This applies in particular to the principles of respect for fundamental rights, equality, proportionality, and legal certainty. One of the consequences which flow from this is that those principles bind the Community in the exercise of its treaty-making power. They form part of the rules of law compliance with which the Court ensures in the exercise of its jurisdiction under Article 300(6)[228(6)]. It follows that a proposed international agreement which the Court has found to infringe a general principle of law may not enter into force unless the procedure for the amendment of the Union Treaties provided for in Article 48 of the Treaty on European Union is followed. Also, it is arguable that where an international treaty which has already entered into force is found to infringe a general principle, the Court may annul the act by which the Community approved that treaty.[169] In practice, it is unlikely that the general principles will apply as self-standing rules in this context. It is more likely that the Court will use them as rules of interpretation. The Court may find, for example, that an international agreement runs counter to the EC Treaty, as interpreted in the light of the general principles of law.[170]

1.7.2. The general principles as rules of Treaty interpretation

The relationship between the general principles and primary Community law requires further analysis. Since the founding and the amending treaties are at the top of the Community law edifice, they are *ex hypothesi* valid. No provision in the founding treaties grants to the Court jurisdiction to rule on their validity. The Court, however, has jurisdiction to interpret Treaty provisions and may do so in the light of the general principles of law. The interpretative function of general principles acquires particular importance in this context precisely because it is the only function which they may fulfil. Where courts are called upon to interpret rules which they have no jurisdiction to annul, interpretation becomes the primary means by which they can influence the effectiveness of such rules. Interpretation in that context becomes particularly instructive as the expression of judicial policy:

---

[169] See Case C–327/91 *France* v. *Commission* [1994] ECR I–3641.

[170] See Opinion 1/91 *on the Draft Agreement relating to the creation of the European Economic Area* [1991] ECR I–6079, paras. 61–4. In its ruling, the Court found that the judicial system set up by the draft agreement was incompatible with the Treaty, *inter alia*, on grounds of incompatibility with the principle of legal certainty.

it tells us what the court perceives to be its function, what it considers to be the underpinnings of the legal system, and how it prioritizes the rules of primary law of that system. Needless to say, interpretation is a creative exercise. Even where a court gives to the words of a statute what appears to be their literal or natural meaning, it does not apply the statute mechanically. What appears to be the natural meaning of a rule to one judge may not appear to be the natural meaning to another.[171] Also, the very fact that a court follows a literal interpretation as opposed to a more liberal one is in itself significant as an indication of what the court perceives to be the limits of judicial province.

The case law suggests that, in the light of the general principles, the Court of Justice has interpreted Treaty provisions more liberally than acts of the institutions. In particular, it has understood its own jurisdiction widely in order to ensure respect for the fundamental right to judicial protection, which has a defining character in the Community legal order.[172] This approach is illustrated by the judgments in *les Verts* and *Chernobyl*.

In *les Verts*,[173] decided in 1986, the Court held that, although at that time the Parliament was not mentioned as a possible defendant in Article 173 (now 230), binding measures adopted by it were subject to judicial review.[174] The rationale of the judgment was as follows. First, the Court made a general declaration of the principle of legality. In the Court's peremptory language:[175]

> It must be emphasised . . . that the European Economic Community is a Community based on the rule of law, inasmuch as neither its Member States nor its institutions can avoid a review of the question whether the measures adopted by them are in conformity with the basic constitutional charter, the Treaty.

Then, the Court stated that by Articles 173, 184 and 177 (now 230, 241 and 234 respectively) the Treaty intended to establish a complete system of legal remedies. The Court justified the absence of an express reference to the Parliament as a possible defendant in Article 173 (now 230) on the ground that, under the original version of the Treaty, the Parliament only had powers of consultation and political control and no power to adopt acts intended to have legal effects vis-à-vis third parties. It referred to Article 38 of the ECSC Treaty, which expressly states that the Court may declare an act of the Parliament void, as evidence that where the Parliament was given power to adopt binding measures *ab initio* by one of the founding Treaties,[176] such measures were subject to annulment. *Les Verts* is a prime example of dynamic interpretation, an approach typical of the interpretation of a constitutional text, by which the Court sought to fulfil the requirements of the rule of law.

---

[171] See for a classic example in the House of Lords, *Liversidge* v. *Anderson* [1942] AC 206.
[172] See further A. Arnull, 'Does the Court of Justice have inherent jurisdiction?' (1990) 27 CMLRev. 683.
[173] Case 294/83 *Les Verts* v. *Parliament* [1986] ECR 1339.
[174] See now, Article 230(1)[173(1)] as amended by the TEU.   [175] Op.cit., para. 23.
[176] The Parliament has power to adopt binding acts under Article 95 ECSC.

In *Chernobyl*,[177] decided in 1990, the Court went one step further. It held that the Parliament may bring an action for annulment against acts of the Council or of the Commission in order to safeguard its prerogatives, although at that time Article 173 (now 230) did not mention the Parliament as a possible plaintiff.[178] The Court's reasoning stands on two pillars: the need to ensure that the provisions of the Treaty concerning the institutional balance are fully applied; and the need to ensure that the Parliament's prerogatives, as those of the other institutions, cannot be breached without it having available a legal remedy which may be exercised in a certain and effective manner.[179] The Court stated that the absence in the Treaties of any provision giving the Parliament the right to bring an action constitutes a procedural gap which cannot prevail 'over the fundamental interest in the maintenance and observance of the institutional balance laid down in the Treaties establishing the European Communities'.[180]

Those cases illustrate that, although unwritten general principles of law do not technically take priority over the Treaty, they may influence decisively its interpretation.[181] This is particularly evident in the judgment in *Chernobyl* where the Court adopted what was in effect a *contra legem* interpretation of Article 173 (now 230). It is important to point out that *les Verts* and *Chernobyl* concerned essentially the fundamental right to judicial protection. Both cases raised issues relating to the admissibility of the action and therefore pertaining to procedure. One may take the view that judicial activism can easier be justified in procedural matters, which fall *par excellence* in the judicial province, than in issues of substance. But that appears to be a false distinction. The boundaries between substance and procedure are not clear-cut and, in any event, procedural requirements may be as influential in forming political processes as substantive ones. There can be little doubt that in *Chernobyl* the Court intervened as a political actor. The judgments in *les Verts* and *Chernobyl* are based on the premise that access to judicial remedies is an integral part of the rule of law. Their rationale seems to be that the Community is by its nature a dynamic organization. As the Community develops, the ensuing increase in the powers of the institutions has to be accompanied by adequate control mechanisms, if the rule of law is to be observed.

The above cases can be contrasted with *Laisa* v. *Council*.[182] Spanish producers sought the annulment of certain provisions of the Act of Accession of Spain and

---

[177] Case C–70/88 *Parliament* v. *Council* [1990] ECR I–2041, para. 26. Cf. Case 302/87 *Parliament* v. *Council* [1988] ECR 5615 (*Comitology* case).

[178] See now Article 230(4)[173(3)] as amended by the TEU.

[179] Case C–70/88, op.cit., para. 25.   [180] Op.cit., para. 26.

[181] It has been argued that certain human rights may take priority even over primary Community legislation. See M. Dauses, 'The Protection of Human Rights in the Community Legal Order' (1985) ELRev. 398 at 412. The author draws a distinction between 'the substratum of supra-positive principles of law' incorporated in the ECHR and 'their substantive legal form'. The former are sources of law independent of the Treaties and take precedence even over primary Community law. The latter, by contrast, are superior to secondary Community law but take second place to the Treaties.

[182] Joined Cases 31 and 35/86 *Laisa* v. *Council* [1988] ECR 2285. See also Case 40/64 *Sgarlata and Others* v. *Commission* [1965] ECR 215 and note, more recently, Case C–321/95 *Greenpeace and Others* v. *Commission*, [1998] ECR I–1651 Cf. Case C–309/89 *Codorniu* v. *Council* [1994] ECR I–1853.

Portugal which amended a previous agricultural regulation of the Council. They argued that the contested provisions were acts of the Council subject to review under Article 230[173]. They relied on Article 8 of the Act of Accession which states that provisions of the Act the purpose or effect of which is to repeal or amend acts adopted by the Community institutions 'shall have the same status in law as the provisions which they repeal or amend and shall be subject to the same rules as those provisions'. The Court did not accept the submissions of the applicants. It held that provisions of the Act of Accession which amend existing Community measures are nonetheless rules of primary law, and cannot therefore be the subject of annulment proceedings under Article 230[173]. The Court pointed out that Article 8 fulfils a different purpose. It enables the Community institutions to amend provisions of the Act of Accession amending acts of secondary Community legislation without the need to follow the procedure for the amendment of the Treaties which, under Article 6, is normally applicable for the amendment of provisions of the Act of Accession.

The judgment establishes that adaptations to secondary Community legislation deriving directly from the Act of Accession enjoy entrenched value in that they are not subject to review of legality. This results in a gap in judicial protection but the Court accepted it as an inevitable consequence of the status of the contested rules as primary law. The Court was guided by the intention of the authors of the Act of Accession who, by dealing with certain issues in the Act itself rather than leaving them to be dealt with by consequential Community acts, intended those issues not to be justiciable. The Act of Accession incorporated the outcome of political negotiations and as such it expressed a certain balance of powers which the Court was keen not to disturb. In the words of the judgment, the interpretation of the Act of Accession given by the Court 'is rendered all the more compelling by the fact that the provisions of the Act of Accession affirm the results of Accession negotiations which constitute a totality intended to resolve difficulties which accession entails either for the Community or for the applicant State'.[183]

A final issue which arises in this context is the following. Are all the provisions of the founding Treaties of equal rank in law? Can it be said that some of them take priority over others and, if so, what does such priority mean?[184] As a general rule, it is not unreasonable to consider that, in the light of the objectives of the Community, certain rules of the Treaty are more fundamental than others. If that is so, the higher value of the more fundamental rules may express itself in two ways: a rule which is considered to be more fundamental will be important for the interpretation of other rules which are not perceived to be as fundamental; also, the more fundamental a rule is, the clearer the expression the Court may require before accepting that that rule is amended. The Court therefore may have difficulty in accepting that a fundamental rule is repealed or amended impliedly as a result of the

---

[183] Op.cit., para. 15. Cf. the Opinion of Lenz AG who held that the action was admissible.

[184] In his Opinion in *Laisa* v. *Council* Lenz AG suggested that not all rules of primary Community law may be of the same rank: op.cit., 2307.

express amendment of another, less important, rule. The ruling in Opinion 1/91 on the *Draft Agreement relating to the creation of the European Economic Area*[185] may provide some guidance as to the Court's views on the hierarchy of the provisions of the EC Treaty. In 1990 the Community entered into formal negotiations with the countries of the European Free Trade Area (EFTA) with a view to concluding an agreement on the establishment of a European Economic Area (EEA). The aim was to replace existing bilateral free trade agreements with the EEA agreement and to establish a homogeneous economic area subject to a legal framework substantially identical to that laid down by Community law. The Commission requested the opinion of the Court with regard to the compatibility of the judicial system provided for by the draft EEA Agreement with the Treaty under the procedure of Article 300(6)[228(6)] EC. In Opinion 1/91 the Court held that the judicial system of the draft EEA Agreement was not compatible with the Treaty.[186] In its request for an Opinion, the Commission also asked the Court whether Article 310[238] of the Treaty, which deals with the conclusion by the Community of association agreements, authorized the establishment of a system of courts such as that provided in the draft EEA Agreement and if not whether Article 310[238] could be amended so as to permit such a system to be set up. The Court held as follows:[187]

... Article 238 of the EEC Treaty does not provide any basis for setting up a system of courts which conflicts with Article 164 of the EEC Treaty and, more generally, with the very foundations of the Community.

For the same reasons, an amendment of Article 238 in the way indicated by the Commission could not cure the incompatibility with Community law of the system of courts to be set up by the agreement.

The brevity of the Court's reasoning has given rise to difficulties as to the exact meaning of the above statements. Some commentators have interpreted those dicta as meaning that the Community's judicial system may not be altered by an amendment of the Treaty and have criticized the Court for taking that view.[188] It is submitted that such interpretation is not correct. The true meaning of the Court's statements must be ascertained in the light of the ruling as a whole. The Court took

---

[185] *Draft Agreement relating to the creation of the European Economic Area* [1991] ECR I–6079.

[186] The Court gave the following reasons: (a) the jurisdiction of the EEA Court established under the draft Agreement affected adversely the autonomy of Community law (paras. 35–6); (b) the judicial system established by the draft Agreement would condition the future interpretation of the Community rules on free movement and competition (paras. 45–6); (c) the draft Agreement enabled courts of EFTA States to seek rulings from the Court of Justice on the interpretation of the draft Agreement but such rulings would be advisory and have no binding effect. That would change the nature of the Court's function (paras. 61–4); (d) the Court expressed doubts regarding the compatibility with the Treaty of the composition of the EEA Court (paras. 52–3).

[187] Paras. 71–2.

[188] See Sir Patrick Neil QC, 'The European Court of Justice: a Case Study in Judicial Activism', Evidence submitted to the House of Lords Select Committee on the European Communities, Sub-committee on the 1996 Inter-Governmental Conference, *1996 Inter-Governmental Conference, Minutes of Evidence, House of Lords, Session 1994–95, 18th Report*, p. 218 at 238. See also Hartley, 'The European Court and the EEA' (1992) 41 ICLQ 841 at 846 who states that the Court's view is 'plainly wrong'.

the view that the judicial system of the draft EEA Agreement would alter fundamentally the judicial system of the Community itself, which in turn would have far-reaching repercussions for the nature of the Community legal order. There can be no doubt that Member States remain free to make such fundamental changes to the nature of the Community by entering into an international agreement with third States but their intention to that effect must be expressed clearly and unequivocally. In declaring that an amendment of Article 310[238] of the Treaty could not cure the incompatibility of the draft Agreement with the Treaty, the Court employed, in effect, a presumption of legislative intention: a fundamental constitutional change will not be recognized by the Court unless it is supported by the clearest of expressions.[189] The Opinion on the draft EEA Agreement illustrates the importance that the Court attaches to Article 220[164] and the judicial structure of the Community.[190]

1.8. The general principles as a source of international law

Article 38(1)(c) of the Statute of the International Court of Justice lists among the rules which that court applies 'the general principles of law recognized by civilized nations'. The reference to general principles has been associated with concepts of natural law,[191] but objections have been expressed regarding the term 'civilised nations'.[192] It has been suggested that in terms of methodology, the mandate given to the International Court is similar to that of the European Court of Justice. It requires a synthesis of principles found in domestic legal systems rather than the mechanical application of the statistically predominant rules. As Professor Brownlie notes: 'An international tribunal chooses, edits and adapts elements from better developed systems: the result is a new element of international law the content of which is influenced historically and logically by domestic law.'[193] There are, however, significant differences in the application of general principles by the

---

[189] Hartley, op.cit., at 846 states an adverse opinion by the Court under Article 300(6)[228(6)] can be overridden by an amendment to the Treaty and that 'it makes little difference which precise Article of the EEC Treaty is amended'. It should be recognized, however, that the provisions of the Treaty which the draft Agreement was found to infringe occupy a cardinal position in the Community legal order and their amendment cannot be the incidental result of amending Article 310[238]. It is a different matter whether in Opinion 1/91 the Court was correct in concluding that the judicial system of the proposed EEA Agreement posed such a fundamental threat to the Community legal order. Arguably, the Court exaggerated the adverse repercussions of concluding the draft Agreement.

[190] As a result of the ruling the draft EEA agreement was amended and subsequently in Opinion 1/92 [1992] ECR I–2821 the Court held that, subject to certain conditions, the amended version was compatible with the Treaty.

[191] e.g. by Judge Tanaka in the *South West Africa* cases, ICJ Reports (1966) 6 at 294–9.

[192] See the Opinion of Judge Ammoun in the *North Sea Continental Shelf* cases, ICJ Reports (1969) 132–3.

[193] I. Brownlie, *Principles of Public International Law* (Fourth edn. 1990) p. 15.

International Court and by the European Court. Although general principles are referred to by individual judges, it is notable that so far no majority decision of the International Court has been based expressly upon a general principle of law.[194] Such principles are rarely cited by the parties and, when they are, it is by way of supplementary argument.[195] A second difference is that in international law the general principles perform a gap filling function, whereas in Community law their function goes further. They are, as already stated, an integral part of judicial methodology. A consequential difference is that the process of discovering general principles in European law is more eclectic: as shown in the *Staff Salaries* case the European Court may apply a principle creatively going significantly further than national laws. By contrast, a principle will not be recognized as a general principle of international law within the meaning of Article 38(1)(c) of the Statute unless it is adopted consistently as the solution to a specific legal problem by the various systems of municipal law.[196] It has to be specific and ubiquitous or near ubiquitous in municipal legal systems.[197] Those differences are accounted for by the different functions which the two courts perform in their respective legal orders. The International Court does not act as a constitutional court. It seems that the intention of the committee of jurists which prepared the Statute was to authorize the International Court of Justice to apply the general principles of law found in national, especially private, laws in so far as they could be transposed to relations between States.[198] This contrasts with the European Court of Justice which in its case law has developed primarily principles of public law.

The International Court of Justice has drawn on municipal systems of law, in particular, on issues of procedure. It has referred, for example, to the rules of *lis pendens*[199] and *res judicata*,[200] the rule that no one should be judge of his own cause,[201] and to rules pertaining to the admission of evidence.[202] Among the principles relied on one also finds the principle of acquiescence,[203] the principle that breach of an engagement involves an obligation to make reparation,[204] abuse of right and good faith,[205] and the principle of equality of States. Certain principles, such as the principle of non-discrimination on grounds of race, religion and sex, are recognized as part of *jus cogens* and could, as a result, override the effect of ordinary rules.[206]

---

[194] See H. Thirlway, 'The Law and Procedure of the International Court of Justice 1960–1989' (1990) 61 BYIL 1 at 110.

[195] Op.cit., 111.   [196] Op.cit., 114, 119.   [197] Op.cit., 119.

[198] Brownlie, op.cit., p. 16 where further references are made.

[199] *German Interests in Polish Upper Silesia* case, PICJ, Series A, no. 6, 1925, p. 20.

[200] *Administrative Tribunal* cases, ICJ Reports, 1954, p. 53.

[201] *Mosul Boundary* case, PICJ, Series B, no.12, 1925, pp. 31–2.

[202] See the *Corfu Channel* case, ICJ Reports, 1949, pp. 4, 18.

[203] *Temple* case, ICJ Reports, 1962, pp. 6, 23, 31–2.

[204] *Chorzow Factory* case, PICJ, Series a, no.17, 1928, p. 29.

[205] *German Interests in Polish Upper Silesia* case, PICJ, Series a, no. 7, 1926, p. 30; *The Free Zones* case, PICJ, Series a, no. 30, 1930, p. 12 and no. 46, 1932, p. 167.

[206] See McKean, *Equality and Discrimination under International law* (1983), p. 283; Brownlie, op.cit., p. 513.

2

The Principle of Equality

2.1. The principle of equality as a general principle of Community law

The notion of equality is closely linked to the idea of justice[1] and has perhaps greater resonance than any other legal concept.[2] A basic distinction is drawn between formal and substantive equality. The first refers to enforcement and requires equality before the law. Public authorities must apply the law consistently and treat equally citizens who are in the same position.[3] The second refers to the content of laws. It requires that laws must not discriminate between citizens on arbitrary grounds. Community law protects not only formal but also substantive equality.[4] Although certain provisions of the Treaty provide for the principle of equal treatment with regard to specific matters,[5] the Court has held that the principle of equality is a general principle of law 'to be observed by any court'[6] of which those provisions are merely specific expressions. As a general principle, it precludes comparable situations from being treated differently unless the difference

---

[1] Aristotle, who provided the first elaborate analysis of the notion, considered that equality and justice were synonymous: *Ethica Nicomachea* V.3. 1131a–b.

[2] For bibliography, see among others: Schwarze, op.cit., Ch. 4; A. Dashwood and S. O'Leary (eds.), *The Principle of Equal Treatment in E.C. Law* (Sweet & Maxwell, 1997); K. Lenaerts, 'L'Egalité de Traitement en Droit Communautaire' (1991) 27 CDE 3; J. Jowell, 'Is Equality a Constitutional Principle?' (1994) 47 CLP 1; R. Plender, 'Equality and Non-discrimination in the Law of the European Union' (1995) 7 Pace Internl. LR 57; P. Westen, 'The Empty Idea of Equality' (1982) 95 HLR 537. For the principle of equality as a principle of international law, see Plender, op.cit., and further McKean, *Equality and Discrimination under International Law* (1983).

[3] According to Dicey, formal equality is a constituent part of the rule of law primarily because it ensures legal certainty and predictability. See A. V. Dicey, *The Law of the Constitution* (Tenth edn., 1959), p. 193. See further J. Jowell, 'Is Equality a Constitutional Principle?' (1994) 47 CLP 1, at 4 *et seq.*

[4] An aspect of formal equality distinct to Community law is the judicially elaborated rule that the enforcement of Community rights in national courts must be subject to national rules which are not less favourable than those applicable to comparable claims based on national law. See below Ch. 8.

[5] See e.g. Article 12[6] (prohibition of discrimination on the grounds of nationality), Article 34(2)[40(3)] (prohibition of discrimination between producers and between consumers in the common agricultural policy), Article 86(1)[90(1)] (equal treatment between public and private undertakings), Article 141[119] (equal pay for equal work for men and women). For a comprehensive list of the Treaty provisions which prohibit discrimination, see K. Lenaerts, 'L'Egalite de Traitement en Droit Communautaire' (1991) 27 CDE 3, at 39–40.

[6] Case 8/78 *Milac* [1978] ECR 1721, para. 8.

in treatment is objectively justified.[7] It also precludes different situations from being treated in the same way unless such treatment is objectively justified.[8]

The question arises why the Court has established a general principle of substantive equality transcending the specific provisions of the Treaty. It may be that those provisions do not guarantee equal treatment in all cases so that the development of a general principle is necessary to cover the lacunae left in written law. The main reason for the development of a general principle, however, seems to be one of principle rather than one of practical necessity. In the light of the constitutions of the Member States, substantive equality is viewed as 'a constitutive of democracy',[9] an integral part of the rule of law which underlies the political systems and the legal traditions of the Member States. The historical and ideological origins of the principle determine in turn its limits. In declaring equal treatment as a general principle of law the Court does not endorse any particular theory of equality.[10] It does not seek to advance a particular idea of the social good.[11] Rather, the principle is seen as a democratic guarantee which prevents Community and national authorities from imposing differential treatment without good reason. It requires, in other words, that 'distinctions between individuals or groups must be reasonably related to government's legitimate purposes'.[12] Viewed in that perspective, the function of equality can be defined better in negative rather than in affirmative terms: it does not seek to resolve the issues but rather to act as a check on the decision makers.[13] It can be said that, as a general principle of Community law, equality performs two functions: it requires Community institutions to justify their policies; and it prohibits them from engaging in arbitrary conduct. What is arbitrary conduct, however, requires an evaluation which in turn is based on certain ideas which are not politically neutral. In its barest minimum, the principle of equal treatment as applied by the Court is based on models of egalitarianism and distributive justice and it is imbued by ideas of classical liberalism. In the sphere of economic law, the Court favours what can be termed a traditional, pluralistic, conception of equality which accepts State intervention as necessary for the fair redistribution of resources rather than a market-oriented idea of equal treatment which subordinates State action to market forces and gives primacy to property

[7] This is the standard formula used by the Court since 1977. See e.g. Joined Cases 117/76 and 16/77 *Ruckdeschel* v. *Hauptzollamt Hamburg-St.Annen* [1977] ECR 1753, para. 7; Case 810/79 *Überschär* v. *Bundesversicherungsanstalt für Angestellte* [1980] ECR 2747, para. 16; Joined Cases 201 and 202/85 *Klensch* v. *Secrétaire d' État à l'Agriculture et à la Viticulture* [1986] ECR 3477, para. 9; Case 84/87 *Erpelding* v. *Secrétaire d' État à l'Agriculture et à la Viticulture* [1988] ECR 2647, para. 29; Case C–56/94 *SCAC* v. *Associazione dei Produttori Ortofrutticoli* [1995] ECR I–1769, para. 27.

[8] Case 106/83 *Sermide* v. *Cassa Conguaglio Zucchero* [1984] ECR 4209, para. 28.

[9] Jowell, op.cit., 7.

[10] For such theories see Jowell, op.cit., 5; see further R. Dworkin, *Taking Rights Seriously* (London, Duckworth, 1978), Ch. 9; J. Rawls, *A Theory of Justice* (Clarendon Press, 1972); R. A. Posner, *The Problems of Jurisprudence* (Harvard University Press, 1990), Ch. 11. See also T. R. S. Allan, *Law, Liberty and Justice* (Oxford, 1993) Ch. 7.

[11] Jowell, op.cit., 7.   [12] Jowell, op.cit., 7.

[13] See Sir Robin Cooke, 'The Struggle for Simplicity in Administrative Law', in M. Taggart (ed.), *Judicial Review of Administrative Action in the 1980s* (Oxford , 1986) pp. 16–17.

rights.[14] In the sphere of social law, the Court has followed a proactive approach, going sometimes beyond the concept of equality as accepted in national law and seeking to form rather than follow an underlying societal consensus.[15]

The principle of substantive equality endorsed by the Court of Justice entails a stricter degree of judicial scrutiny than the concept of *Wednesbury*[16] unreasonableness. English law too seems to accept in various contexts that equal treatment is a principle of lawful administration[17] and in some cases *Wednesbury* unreasonableness has been interpreted to include 'partial and unequal' treatment.[18] A prime difference between Community law and English law, however, lies in that the former requires the decision maker to demonstrate a substantive justification or, in other words, to 'provide a fully reasoned case'.[19] The authority is not constrained merely by the requirement that the decision must be one which a reasonable authority might take.[20] It is submitted that the approach of the Court of Justice is better. If it is accepted that the purpose of the supervisory jurisdiction of the courts is to prohibit arbitrary conduct and control abuses by the administration, the principle of substantive equality is an appropriate and necessary ground of review. By contrast, the greater deference to the decision-making authority inherent in the *Wednesbury* test finds its historical explanation in the Diceyan concept of unitary democracy and can be justified only within the confines of that model. Adoption of substantive equality as a ground of review is advantageous also from the practical point of view. Increasing the burden of the administration to justify its actions is likely to lead to a more diligent assessment of the interests involved and, ultimately, to better decision making.

A distinction is sometimes drawn between non-discrimination and equality. It is said that the former requires abstention from discriminatory treatment whereas the second signifies more the notion of positive obligations.[21] Such a distinction is not drawn in the case law of the Community judicature which seems to use the terms equality and non-discrimination as interchangeable.[22]

---

[14] See the discussion by Craig, *Administrative Law*, pp. 36–7 and C. Harlow, 'Back to Basics: Reinventing Administrative Law' (1997) PL 245.

[15] See Case C–13/91 *P* v. *S and Cornwall County Council* [1996] ECR I–2143 discussed below.

[16] *Associated Provincial Picture Houses Limited* v. *Wednesbury Corporation* [1948] 1 KB 223.

[17] See De Smith, Woolf and Jowell, *Judicial Review of Administrative Action*, at p. 578 *et seq.*

[18] See *Kruse* v. *Johnson* (1889) 2 QB 291; *R* v. *Immigration Appeal Tribunal, ex parte Manshoora Bugum* [1986] Imm.AR 385. Judicial authorities in England, however, are not consistent and in the absence of procedural unfairness an applicant may have difficulties in establishing a substantive right to equal treatment. See e.g. *R* v. *Special Adjudicator, ex parte Kandasamy, The Times* 11 Mar. 1994 in relation to unequal treatment of asylum applications.

[19] *R* v. *Ministry of Agriculture, Fisheries and Food, ex parte First City Trading Limited* [1997] 1 CMLR 250 at 279 per Laws J.

[20] Ibid.

[21] Harris, O'Boyle and Warbrick, *Law of the European Convention on Human Rights* (Butterworths, 1995), p. 463.

[22] See e.g. *Überschär*, op.cit., at p. 2764.

2.2. The principle of equality in the European Convention on Human Rights

The principle of equal treatment is also provided for in the European Convention for the Protection of Human Rights and Fundamental Freedoms, Article 14 of which states as follows:

> The enjoyment of the rights and freedoms set forth in this Convention shall be secured without discrimination on any ground such as sex, race, colour, language, religion, political or other opinion, national or social origin, association with a national minority, property, birth or other status.

There are two differences between the general right to equal treatment recognized in Community law and Article 14 of the European Convention. Article 14 does not confer an independent, substantive, right to equal treatment. Rather, it complements the rights established in the other provisions of the Convention by providing for the equal enjoyment of those rights.[23] The second difference emanates from the first. Where a right falls outside the scope of the Convention, a Contracting State is not required to observe the principle of non-discrimination. It follows that the principle does not apply to social and economic rights which are not covered by the Convention. It has been observed that this is a substantial restriction since, in practice, anti-discrimination law acquires particular importance precisely in those areas.[24] By contrast, a number of economic and social rights which fall outside the scope of the Convention are protected by Community law and are subject to the principle of non-discrimination, such as the right to equal pay for equal work.[25]

Article 14 provides for an open-ended list of grounds on which discrimination is prohibited. 'Other status' within the meaning of Article 14 has been interpreted to include, among others, marital status, illegitimacy, military status, professional status, and conscientious objection.[26] There is no discrimination where there is objective and reasonable justification for the difference in treatment. Such justification is established where the provision in issue pursues a legitimate aim and, in addition, there is a reasonable relationship of proportionality between the means employed and the aim sought to be realized.[27] As the European Court of Human Rights has stated, the differences in treatment must 'strike a fair balance between

---

[23] Note, however, that Article 14 does not require breach of another article of the Convention in order to come into operation. Provided that the applicant's claim falls within the ambit of one of the rights guaranteed by the Convention, the applicant may establish violation of Article 14 even though he does not establish violation of another article. See e.g. *Inze* v. *Austria*, Series A, No. 126 (1987); *Belgian Linguistic (No. 1)* case, judgment of 9 Feb. 1967, Series A, No. 5 (1979–80) 1 EHRR 241; *Abdulaziz, Cabales and Balkandali* v. *UK*, judgment of 28 May 1985, Series A, No. 94 (1985) 7 EHRR 471.

[24] See Harris, O'Boyle and Warbrick, op.cit., p. 464.   [25] See Article 141[119] EC.

[26] Harris, O'Boyle and Warbrick, op.cit., p. 470.   [27] See the *Belgian Linguistic* case, op.cit.

the protection of the interests of the community and respect for the rights and freedoms safeguarded by the Convention'.[28] In a vein similar to that of the Court of Justice, the Court of Human Rights seeks to maintain a supervisory role rather than to substitute its own views for the views of the national authorities, although sometimes the distinction is difficult to draw. The European Court of Human Rights has acknowledged a margin of appreciation to States in deciding what means are reasonable to pursue a legitimate objective. The margin of appreciation differs depending on the ground on the basis of which the difference in treatment is practised. Thus, difference in treatment on grounds of race, sex or illegitimacy has been treated by the Court of Human Rights as particularly serious imposing a heavy burden on the State to provide justification.[29]

2.3. The application of equality in Community law: General observations

The principle of equality is applied in a number of diverse areas. Although the scope of the principle is wide, its precise content and effects depend on a series of factors, including the factual and legislative context in which it is applied, the objectives of the legislation in issue, the interests represented in the litigation, and economic, social and other considerations of policy which may influence the decision of the Court in the specific circumstances of the case. In short, far from being a mechanical process, the application of the principle entails an evaluation and involves striking a balance between conflicting interests. The following general points may be made.

The principle of equality binds the Community institutions and also the Member States, where they implement, or act within the scope of, Community law.[30] In certain circumstances, it may bind natural and legal persons. This occurs in particular in three areas: prohibition of discrimination on grounds of nationality,[31] prohibition of sex discrimination,[32] and prohibition of anti-competitive conduct.[33]

Equality of Member States is a general, unwritten, principle of Community law.[34] It has been referred to by the Court especially in enforcement actions under Article 226[169] EC. In one case, the Court stated:[35]

---

[28] See the *Belgian Linguistic* case, op.cit. [29] Harris, O'Boyle and Warbrick, op.cit., pp. 481–3.

[30] See *Klensch*, op.cit., and above 1.6.

[31] See e.g. Case 36/74 *Walgrave* v. *Union Cycliste Internationale* [1974] ECR 1405; Case 13/76 *Donà* v. *Mantero* [1976] ECR 1333; and see also Joined Cases C–92 and C–326/92 *Phil Collins* [1993] ECR I–5145, esp. at 5170 per Jacobs AG.

[32] See below 2.7. [33] See, in particular, Article 81(1)(d)[85(1)(d)] and Article 82(c)[86(c)] EC.

[34] By contrast, the Treaty does not incorporate any general principle enforceable by individuals which requires the Community to accord in its external relations equal treatment to third states: Case 245/81 *Edeka* v. *Germany* [1982] ECR 2745, para. 19.

[35] Case 39/72 *Commission* v. *Italy* [1973] ECR 101, para. 24.

In permitting Member States to profit from the advantages of the Community, the Treaty imposes on them also the obligation to respect its rules.

For a State unilaterally to break, according to its own conception of national interest, the equilibrium between advantages and obligations flowing from its adherence to the Community brings into question the equality of Member States before Community law and creates discriminations at the expense of their nationals . . .

A Member State, however, may not plead the principle of equality in order to justify its failure to comply with Community law. Thus, where the Commission institutes proceedings against a Member State, it is not a good defence to argue that the same breach has been committed by other Member States.[36] Nor may a State delay the coming into force of measures implementing a directive until other Member States adopt such measures, even though the prompt implementation of the directive in the first State may lead to discrimination against undertakings operating in its territory because they have to comply with the higher regulatory burdens imposed by the directive.[37] In such a case, the means of redressing any discrimination arising is by insisting on the timely implementation of Community law by all Member States and imposing penalties against the Member State in default.[38]

The principle of equality acquires particular importance in the field of economic law. The distinct function of the principle in that context was expressed by Tesauro AG as follows:[39]

. . . the principle of equal treatment is fundamental not only because it is a cornerstone of contemporary legal systems but also for a more specific reason: Community legislation chiefly concerns economic situations and activities. If, in this field, different rules are laid down for similar situations, the result is not merely inequality before the law, but also, and inevitably, distortions of competition which are absolutely irreconcilable with the fundamental philosophy of the common market.

Equality, therefore, is not only a constitutional necessity but also a keystone of integration. The notion of distortions of competition is central to understanding its function in Community economic law. Article 3(g) of the Treaty provides as one of the activities of the Community the establishment of 'a system ensuring that competition in the internal market is not distorted'. The notion of distortions of

[36] Case 52/75 *Commission* v. *Italy* [1976] ECR 277, para. 11; Case 78/76 *Steinike und Weinlig* v. *Germany* [1977] ECR 595. By the same token, when an undertaking has infringed Article 81[85] EC it cannot escape without penalty on the ground that another undertaking has not been fined, when the conduct of the latter undertaking is not even the subject of proceedings before the Community judicature: Joined Cases C–89, C–104, C–114, C–116, C–117 and C–125 to C–129/85 *Ahlström Osakeyhtiö and Others* v. *Commission* (*Woodpulp* cases) [1993] ECR I–1307, para. 197; Case T–77/92 *Parker Pen* v. *Commission* [1994] ECR I–549, para. 86.

[37] See Case C–38/89 *Blanguernon* [1990] ECR I–83.

[38] See Article 228[171] EC, as amended by the Treaty on European Union. Note also that Member States may be held liable in damages for breach of Community law to persons who have suffered loss as result. It is doubtful, however, whether State liability in damages may compensate adequately for loss arising out of inequalities in the national regulatory regimes.

[39] Case C–63/89 *Assurances du Credit* v. *Council and Commission* [1991] ECR I–1799, at 1829.

competition was examined by the Court in *SNUPAT* v. *High Authority*,[40] an early case arising from the scrap equalization scheme imposed under the ECSC Treaty. In an attempt to discourage the use of ferrous scrap, supplies of which had become scarce, and to maintain its supply at reasonable prices, purchases of that material were made subject to a levy. The High Authority exempted from the levy 'own arisings', namely scrap which an undertaking generated itself in its own plants. It also approved two exemptions from the levy in favour of an Italian and a Dutch undertaking on the ground that those undertakings were spatially linked with scrap-producing plants which did not belong to them to such an extent that they formed a single industrial complex. SNUPAT argued that the principle of non-discrimination required that scrap arising within the same corporate group must also be exempted. The Court did not accept that submission. It held that a measure is discriminatory where it is calculated 'by substantially increasing differences in production costs otherwise than through changes in productivity, to give rise to an appreciable disequilibrium in the competitive position of the undertakings concerned'.[41] It then continued:[42]

In other words, any intervention attempting to distort or actually distorting competition artificially and significantly must be regarded as discriminatory and incompatible with the Treaty, whilst measures which take into account the internal organization of an undertaking and the use by it of its own resources cannot be regarded as discriminatory.

The Court considered that the exemption of 'own arisings' from the levy was compatible with Community law. The use of its own arisings by a single undertaking producing steel and using ferrous scrap amounted to a production recycling of one of its by-products. The use of own arisings led to an increase in the quantity of steel obtained from the same quantity of ferrous scrap, which had already been subjected to the equalization levy, and thus represented an increase in productivity. By contrast, corporate group scrap was not in the same position. If such scrap were exempted, the High Authority would not reward a change in productivity which was the result of the efforts of the individual undertaking but would rather give a fortuitous advantage to undertakings belonging to a corporate group over other undertakings which also produced steel from ferrous scrap but were not linked to an undertaking that produced that raw material.[43]

It will be noted, however, that the objective of eliminating distortions of competition is subject to inherent limitations. First, in the absence of full harmonization of national laws, such distortions are bound to arise. The principle of non-discrimination does not go as far as to prohibit inequalities which arise from the fact that comparable legal relations are subject to different legal systems.[44] Secondly, the aim of ensuring equal conditions of competition is severely com-

---

[40] Joined Cases 32–3/58 [1959] ECR 127. For a detailed discussion of cases arising under the equalization scheme, see Schwarze, op.cit., pp. 574 *et seq.*

[41] Op.cit., 143.   [42] Ibid.   [43] Op.cit., 143–4.

[44] See below 2.5 and 2.8.1.

promised in sectors where the Treaty itself substitutes public intervention for market forces as the primary mechanism of resource allocation. That is particularly the case in agricultural law.[45] Thirdly, whether a competitive disadvantage exists such as to create an unacceptable distortion of competition between two products or two undertakings is in itself sometimes difficult to determine.[46] In short, the objective of eliminating distortions in competition has to be seen in context. At least in the field of economic law, as one author has put it, the function of equality is 'not to ensure fairness but to protect comparative advantage'.[47]

Although the principle of equality requires that traders who are in the same situation must be treated in the same manner, it is logically and practically impossible to take into account every difference which may exist among the various groups of economic operators. In an early case, the Court stated:[48]

By reason of the varied and changing nature of economic life, clear and objective criteria of general application and presenting certain common fundamental characteristics must be used in the establishment and functioning of the financial arrangements for safeguarding the stability of the Common Market. It is thus impossible to take account of every difference that may exist in the organization of economic units subject to the action of the High Authority for fear of fettering that action and rendering it ineffective.

The same point was made by Jacobs AG in a later case:[49]

The principle of equality cannot preclude the legislature from adopting a criterion of general application—indeed that is inherent in the nature of legislation. It may affect different persons in different ways, but beyond certain limits any attempt to tailor the legislation to different circumstances is likely only to lead to new claims of unequal treatment.

The same observations apply also to the principle of proportionality.[50] They acquire particular importance in certain areas, for example, agro–monetary legislation, where in view of the objectives of the measures in that field any search for objective criteria becomes virtually impossible.[51]

It will be noted that there are fundamental differences in the application of the principle of equality as a ground of review of Community measures and as a ground of review of national measures affecting the fundamental freedoms. In the first case, the application of the principle is qualified by the discretion of the Community legislature and the Court focuses more on the objectives of the measure in issue.[52] In

---

[45] See below. 2.4.

[46] See e.g. the disagreements between the Court and the Advocate General in Joined Cases C–267 and C–268/91 *Keck* [1993] ECR I–6097; Case C–387/93 *Banchero* [1995] ECR I–4663; Case C–320/93 *Ortscheit* [1994] ECR I–5243.

[47] D. Chalmers, 'The Single Market: From Prima Donna to Journeyman', in J. Shaw and G. More (eds.), *New Legal Dynamics of the European Union*, p. 55 at 65.

[48] Joined Cases 17 and 20/61 *Klockner* v. *High Authority* [1962] ECR 325 at 340.

[49] Joined Cases C–13 to C–16/92 *Driessen and Others* [1993] ECR I–4751 at 4780. See also Case 147/79 *Hochstraas* v. *Court of Justice* [1980] ECR 3005, para. 14.

[50] See e.g. Case 5/73 *Balkan-Import-Export* v. *Hauptzollamt Berlin-Packhof* [1973] ECR 1091, para. 22.

[51] See below 2.4.3.1.

[52] See esp. below 2.4. in relation to the common agricultural policy.

the second case, the Court applies the principle of equality as an instrument of integration, and focuses more on the effects of the measure.[53]

Historically, as a ground of review of Community measures, the principle of equality was first applied by the Court in the 1950s to measures adopted under the European Coal and Steel Community Treaty.[54] It has since been applied primarily in the following areas: agricultural law; harmonization measures; and disputes between the Community and its employees. The application of the principle will be examined primarily by reference to the first two categories of cases. A brief reference will also be made to staff cases. The final sections of this chapter will examine the prohibition of discrimination on grounds of sex as a general principle of Community law, and the prohibition of discrimination on grounds of nationality under Article 12[6] EC.

2.4. Agricultural law

Article 34(2)[40(3)] of the Treaty provides that the common organization of agricultural markets shall exclude any discrimination between producers or consumers within the Community. As a general principle of law, the prohibition of discrimination applies not only to producers and consumers but also to other categories of economic operators who are subject to a common organization of the market, including *inter alios*, importers, exporters, and the processing industry.[55] There is abundant case law concerning the application of the principle of equality.[56] As already stated, the principle requires that comparable situations must be treated in the same manner unless there are objective grounds which justify a difference in treatment. The constituent parts of the principle therefore are two: comparability and objective justification. In some cases the Court does not distinguish clearly between the two and treats them both as parts of the same inquiry.[57] Before examining those notions in more detail, it is necessary to investigate the function of equality in the specific context of the common agricultural policy.[58] As stated above, in the sphere of economic law, the concept of equality is inextricably linked with the notion of competition. The requirement to treat comparable products

---

[53] See further the discussion in Ch.4.

[54] For more recent cases where the principle of equality was examined in the context of ECSC measures, see e.g. Case 250/83 *Findsider* [1985] ECR 131; Case C–99/92 *Terni SpA and Italsider SpA* v. *Cassa Conguaglio per il Settore Elettrico* [1994] ECR I–541.

[55] Case C–280/93 *Germany* v. *Council* [1994] ECR I–4973, para. 68. See also *Ruckdeschel*, op.cit., para. 7; Case 8/78 *Milac* [1978] ECR 1721, para. 18.

[56] See R. Barents, *The Agricultural Law of the EC* (Kluwer, 1994), Ch. 17.

[57] See e.g. Case 8/82 *Wagner* v. *BALM* [1983] ECR 371, paras. 20–2; Joined Cases C–248 and C–249/95 *Sam Schiffahrt and Stapf* v. *Germany* [1997] ECR I–4475, paras. 55–6. In *Royal Scholten-Honig*, discussed below, the real issue was not whether there was objective justification but whether there was a difference in treatment between sugar and isoglucose, despite the fact that the Court used language which suggests otherwise.

[58] See further Barents, op.cit., p. 335.

alike is to ensure as far as possible neutrality, avoid distortions of competition, and enable market forces to allocate resources accordingly. This conception of equality, however, which under Article 3(g) of the Treaty is the cornerstone of the internal market, is incompatible with the special treatment reserved by the Treaty to the agricultural sector. Article 33[39] mandates the Community institutions to intervene to the extent necessary to attain the objectives provided therein and the Chapter on agriculture subordinates the application of the provisions on free movement and competition to the provisions on agriculture.[59] The formidable task assigned to the Community institutions is encapsulated in the case law according to which, in working out the common agricultural policy, the institutions must seek constantly to reconcile any possible conflict between those objectives when considered individually and must, from time to time, give one or other of those objectives such priority as appears necessary.[60] In short, the principle of equality cannot perform its function as a safeguard against distortions of competition since the very purpose of intervention is to modify the natural play of economic forces. The heavier the intervention, the less the margin for the application of equality. As Lagrange AG noted in an early case, the scope of the principle is necessarily narrower where intervention measures exist, in which case the principle is to be respected only within the sphere of the ends pursued.[61] This is of profound importance in determining the Court's supervisory function, for it means that in determining whether there is lack of objective justification particular importance must be attached to the objectives of the contested measure.

The discussion below is structured as follows. First the judgment in *Royal Scholten-Honig* will be examined. The case provides a prime example of how the Court applies the notion of substantive equality in economic law. Then, the notions of comparability and objective justification will be discussed with reference to examples from the case law.

2.4.1. The Royal Scholten-Honig *case*[62]

Isoglucose is a sweetener which can be used as a substitute for liquid sugar. Following its introduction in the Community market in 1976, the Council by Regulation No. 1111/77[63] imposed a production levy on its manufacture. The aim of the levy was to offset the economic advantage which isoglucose enjoyed over sugar which, in view of excessive surpluses, had been made subject to a quota system by previous Community regulations. In *Royal Scholten-Honig* it was argued that

---

[59] See Article 32(2)[38(2)] and Article 36[42].

[60] See e.g. Case 203/86 *Spain* v. *Council* [1988] ECR 4563, para. 10; Joined Cases 197 etc./80 *Ludwigshafener Walzmuhle* v. *Council and Commission* [1981] ECR 3211, para. 41.

[61] Case 13/63 *Commission* v. *Italy* [1963] ECR 165 at 190.

[62] Joined Cases 103 and 145/77 *Royal Scholten-Honig* v. *Intervention Board for Agricultural Produce* [1978] ECR 2037.

[63] OJ 1977 L 134/4.

Regulation No. 1111/77 put manufacturers of isoglucose in a disadvantageous position *vis-à-vis* sugar producers. The Court first established that isoglucose and liquid sugar were in competition with each other and therefore in a comparable situation. It then pointed out that the two products were treated differently. Whereas in the case of isoglucose the levy was applied to the whole of production, in the case of sugar a production levy was imposed only to quantities produced above a basic quota. The Court held that although the amount of levy was lower in the case of isoglucose than in the case of sugar, a difference in treatment nonetheless existed because isoglucose manufacturers did not enjoy the marketing guarantees given to sugar manufacturers by the quota system. The Court then turned to examine whether the difference in treatment was objectively justified. The most important argument submitted by the Council and the Commission was that the production levy on isoglucose was comparable to the charges borne by sugar. The Court dismissed that argument on the ground that 60 per cent of the charges imposed on sugar were borne not by sugar manufacturers but by sugar beet growers. Manufacturers of isoglucose therefore were discriminated against vis-à-vis manufacturers of sugar. The Court also identified the following difference in treatment: whereas sugar manufacturers were in a position to reduce production charges by limiting production, isoglucose manufacturers were unable to do so since a reduction in production had no effect on the amount of the production levy. In an attempt to justify the contested regulation, the Council and the Commission also argued that alternative solutions to ensure the sharing by isoglucose producers of the losses of the sugar industry encountered practical difficulties. The Court, however, rebutted that argument by stating that 'inconveniences of the type alleged cannot justify the imposition of a charge which is manifestly unequal'.[64]

Royal Scholten-Honig is one of the few cases where a measure of economic policy has been found to infringe the principle of equal treatment. What conclusions can be drawn from the judgment? The first conclusion concerns the relationship between an existing product and a new product entering the market. Manufacturers of an existing product do not enjoy an unfettered right to be protected from competition from a new product even where the relevant market suffers seriously from oversupply.[65] As the Advocate General pointed out:[66]

According to the basic system of the Treaty, which is liberal, access to the market must . . . be guaranteed on the same terms even if in certain circumstances this involves additional sacrifices for the general public.

The second conclusion relates to the objectives of production control measures. The underlying objective of the contested regulation was to provide for a fair allocation of burdens by requiring isoglucose producers to share the costs incurred by

---

[64] *Royal Scholten-Honig*, op.cit., para. 82.

[65] The sugar surpluses were by all accounts not inconsiderable. For example, the 1976–7 marketing year produced sugar surpluses of 1.7 million tonnes.

[66] Op.cit., at 2027 per Reischl AG.

the sugar sector. That was clearly a legitimate objective. The judgment indicates, however, that the allocation of burdens among producers of competing products must be based on rational criteria and a coherent regulatory system which, in the Court's view, was not the case in the circumstances. The third conclusion is closely linked to the second. In order to determine whether a measure complies with the principle of substantive equality, the Court scrutinizes closely the justification asserted by the institutions and assesses the effects of the measure on the groups of persons under comparison.

It is notable that the Advocate General took a different view.[67] He started from the assumption that isoglucose manufacturers operated large modern factories which had lower labour costs than sugar factories and that they should be compared with similar sugar manufacturers. In contrast to the Court, he accepted the argument of the Community institutions that the production levy on isoglucose manufacturers corresponded to the average charges borne by sugar manufacturers and concluded that there was no discrimination.

2.4.2. Comparability

In order to determine whether products or undertakings are in a comparable situation, the Court will normally have recourse to the criterion of competition.[68] In the case of products, the Court will consider whether the products in question fulfil the same function and therefore can be substituted for one another. Where products are interchangeable, they are in a comparable competitive position and should, in principle, be treated in the same manner. In the case of undertakings, the Court may have regard to their production[69] or to their legal structure[70] with a view to determining whether their competitive positions are comparable. The criterion of substitutability or competitiveness is used by the Court as the principal criterion throughout the field of economic law, for example, in relation to Article 28[30],[71] or Article 82[86].[72] For two products or two undertakings to be in a comparable situation it is sufficient, in principle, that they are potentially in competition.[73]

An example of the application of the criterion of comparability in agricultural law is provided by the quellmehl cases.[74] Community regulations granted a production refund for quellmehl, a product derived from maize, on the basis that that

---

[67] Op.cit., esp. 2028–30.
[68] *Royal Scholten-Honig*, op.cit., paras. 28–9. See also Toth, *The Oxford Encyclopaedia of European Community Law* (1990), Vol. I, pp. 191 *et seq.*
[69] Case 14/59 *Pont-à-Mousson* v. *High Authority* [1959] ECR 215 at 232.
[70] Joined Cases 17 and 20/61 *Klöchner* v. *High Authority* [1962] ECR 325 at 345.
[71] See e.g. Case C–391/92 *Commission* v. *Greece* [1995] ECR I–1621.
[72] See e.g. Case 27/76 *United Brands* v. *Commission* [1978] ECR 207. Cf. the difference between Article 90(1)[95(1)] and 90(2)[95(2)] EC.
[73] See e.g. Case 319/81 *Commission* v. *Italy*, op.cit., para. 16.
[74] Joined Cases 117/76 and 16/77 *Ruckdeschel* v. *Hauptzollamt Hamburg-St.Annen* [1977] ECR 1753. See also the 'gritz' cases: Joined Cases 124/76 and 20/77 *Moulins Pont-à-Mousson* v. *Office Interprofessionnel des Céréales* [1977] ECR 1795.

product was interchangeable with starch which benefited from such a refund. A subsequent regulation abolished the refund for quellmehl on the ground that experience had shown that the opportunity for substituting the two products was slight. The Court held that the Council and the Commission had not produced any new technical or economic data to establish that the two products were no longer in comparable situations.[75] The difference in their treatment amounted therefore to discrimination. The case establishes that two products are in a comparable situation where one can be substituted for the other in the traditional or usual use to which the latter is put.[76] By contrast, where a product is diverted from its normal use, it may cease to be in a comparable situation.[77] Similarly, products which have different applications are not in a comparable competitive situation and a difference in their treatment will not normally amount to discrimination.[78] The Court has held that, in order to determine whether products can be substituted for one another, reference may not normally be made exclusively to the customs of a specific region or even of a single Member State.[79]

A producer who benefits from the services of an organization the aim of which is to promote national production is not in a comparable situation with a producer who does not so benefit and therefore the first producer may be made subject to a charge to finance the activities of that organization.[80] Categories of producers which are not exposed to the same risks may not be in a comparable situation. In *Denkavit*,[81] a Council regulation enabled Germany to grant aid to German producers to compensate for the losses suffered as a result of the revaluation of the German mark. The German law adopted to give effect to the regulation differentiated between agricultural livestock breeders and industrial breeders. The Court held that the first category used their own farm produce and were subject to the risks inherent in working the soil whereas the second category purchased produce in the national and international market and were not exposed to such risks. By contrast, where the national currency was revalued they were able to obtain produce abroad at advantageous prices. The two groups of breeders therefore were not in a comparable situation.

In *Accrington*,[82] Community regulations provided for a tariff quota for the importation of beef from third countries and divided it between traditional importers and

---

[75] *Ruckdeschel*, op.cit., para. 8. By contrast, given the aims of the common agricultural policy, intra-Community trade is not comparable to trade with third countries so that different refunds may be applicable in the two cases: Case 6/71 *Rheinmuhlen* v. *Einfuhr- und Vorratsstelle Getreide* [1971] ECR 823.

[76] *Ruckdeschel*, op.cit., para. 8.

[77] Case 90/78 *Granaria* v. *Council* [1979] ECR 1081, paras. 9–10.

[78] See e.g. Case 125/77 *Koninklijke Scholten-Honig* v. *Hoofdproduktschap voor Akkerbouwprodukten* [1978] ECR 1991, paras. 30–1; Case C–18/89 *Maizena* [1990] ECR I–2587.

[79] Case 77/86 *The Queen* v. *Customs and Excise, ex parte National Dried Fruit Trade Association* [1988] ECR 757, para. 14.

[80] Joined Cases C–332, C–333 and C–335/92 *Eurico Italia and Others* [1994] ECR I–711. See also Case 2/73 *Ente Nazionale Risi* [1973] ECR 865.

[81] Case 139/77 *Denkavit* v. *Finanzamt Warendorf* [1978] ECR 1317.

[82] Case C–241/95 *The Queen* v. *Intervention Board for Agricultural Produce, ex parte Accrington Beef and Others* [1996] ECR I–6699.

new importers. Companies arising from mergers of traditional importers could cumulate their rights to individual quotas whereas companies arising from mergers and wishing to obtain a share of the new importers' quota could not combine their past trading performance to meet the eligibility criteria for the allocation of a quota. The Court held that the two categories of importers were not in a comparable situation. Traditional importers were allocated quotas in proportion to their imports in previous years. Newcomers were allocated quotas in proportion to the quantities applied for. If they could obtain a quota by merging, that would enable merger to be used as a ploy to obtain maximum allocation of quotas. Commercial groups would be able to spread their activities artificially over a large number of separate companies in the knowledge that if the thresholds for eligibility to the quota were unexpectedly raised they could continue, by making the necessary mergers, to make multiple applications for a share of the newcomers' quota.

In *Sam Schiffahrt and Stapf* v. *Germany*[83] it was argued that the imposition of a levy on owners of inland waterway vessels with a view to reducing overcapacity discriminated against inland waterway carriers in favour of road and rail carriers. The claim was rejected on the ground that the transport sectors were not in a comparable situation. Rail and road transport did not experience overcapacity comparable to that in the inland waterways and the Council was entitled to decide that responsibility for structural improvements in a given sector of the economy lay with operators in that sector.

2.4.3. Objective justification

Difference in treatment between comparable situations is not prohibited where it is objectively justified. The notion of objective justification is not easy to define in the abstract. Whether such justification exists depends on the particular circumstances of each case, account being taken of the objectives of the measure in issue. On the basis of the case law, Toth lists the cases where different treatment of comparable products or undertakings is justified as follows:[84]

1) where it is justified by the aims which Community institutions lawfully pursue as part of Community policy;
2) where its purpose is to obviate special difficulties in a sector of industry;
3) where it is not arbitrary in the sense that it does not exceed the broad discretion of the Community institutions;
4) where it is based on objective differences arising from the economic circumstances underlying the common organization of the market in the relevant products.

---

[83] Joined Cases C–248 and C–249/95 [1997] ECR I–4475, paras. 55–6.
[84] Toth, op.cit., p. 193.

The guiding principle seems to be that the difference in treatment must not be arbitrary,[85] i.e. it must be based on rational and objective considerations.[86] It should be emphasized, however, that the Community institutions are conceded wide discretionary powers.

A difference in treatment will no longer be justified where the objective justification ceases to exist. In such a case, the measure will become unlawful not *ab initio* but as from the time when objective justification lapses. A person affected may then challenge the validity of the measure incidentally in the course of proceedings against individual acts adopted on its basis under Article 241[184] of the Treaty or in proceedings under Article 234[177].[87] In *Altmann and Casson* v. *Commission* the CFI stated:[88]

Since any difference in treatment is . . . in the nature of an exception, derogating from a fundamental principle of Community law, it is self-evident that it can no longer be regarded as remaining valid, even if the rule establishing it does not explicitly limit its duration, once the circumstances constituting the objective justification for its existence have ceased to obtain.

In such a case it will be for the Court of Justice, or the CFI, to establish the specific time as from which the measure becomes illegal.

2.4.3.1. Discretion of the Community institutions

The Court has held that, in matters concerning the common agricultural policy, the Community legislature has a broad discretion which corresponds to the political responsibilities imposed upon it by Articles 34[40] and 37[43] of the Treaty and which qualifies judicial review.[89]

The Community institutions have been allowed a wide margin of discretion in the field of monetary compensatory amounts. In *Merkur*,[90] it was argued that by not fixing compensatory amounts for the export of products processed from barley, the Commission discriminated against German exporters vis-à-vis two other categories of traders: exporters from other Member States, and German exporters of other products in relation to which compensatory amounts had been fixed. With regard to exporters from other Member States, the Court stated that the system of compensatory amounts had been introduced because certain Member States, including Germany, had widened the margins of fluctuation for the exchange rates of their

---

[85] See e.g. Case 139/77 *Denkavit* v. *Finanzamt Warendorf* [1978] ECR 1317, para. 15; Case 106/81 *Kind* v. *EEC* [1982] ECR 2885, para. 22.

[86] Note, however, that the term 'arbitrary' has been used also with a more specific meaning, namely to characterize action which is not merely illegal but also unlawful and gives rise to liability in damages. See the second generation of isoglucose cases, where the Court held that the Community was not liable in damages on the ground that the conduct of the defendant institutions was not 'verging on the arbitrary': Joined Cases 116 and 124/77 *Amylum* v. *Council and Commission* [1979] ECR 3497, para. 19; Case 143/77 *Koninklijke Scholten-Honig* v. *Council and Commission* [1979] ECR 3583, para. 16.

[87] Joined Cases T–177 and T–377/94 *Altmann and Others* v. *Commission* [1996] ECR II–2041, para. 119. See also Case 36/83 *Mabanaft* v. *Hauptzollamt Emmerich* [1984] ECR 2497, para. 34.

[88] *Altmann and Casson* v. *Commission*, op.cit., para. 119.

[89] See e.g. Case 179/84 *Bozzetti* v. *Invernizzi* [1985] ECR 2301, para. 30.

[90] Case 43/72 *Merkur* v. *Commission* [1973] ECR 1055.

currencies. Although the Community institutions had the power to mitigate the effects of such national measures, they enjoyed wide powers of appraisal and they were not bound to compensate for all disadvantageous effects to traders in the Member States concerned. With regard to traders of other products, the Court held:[91]

As regards the comparison made with German exporters of goods which had the benefit of this compensatory system from the start, the different treatment of which the applicant complains would not be a violation of the principle of non-discrimination unless it appeared to be arbitrary.

. . . in applying the last sentence of Article 1(2) of Regulation No 974/71, the Commission has wide powers of appraisal in judging whether the monetary measures contemplated by the said regulation could lead to disturbances in trade in agricultural products.

After pointing out that the contested measures were emergency provisions, which had to be drawn within a short period of time and in relation to which the Commission had to assess whether disturbances in trade would occur in relation to specific products, the Court continued:[92]

Since the assessment which the Commission had to make was perforce an overall one, the possibility that some of the decisions it made might subsequently appear to be debatable on economic grounds or subject to modification would not in itself be sufficient to prove the existence of a violation of the principle of non-discrimination, once it was established that the considerations adopted by it for guidance were not manifestly erroneous.

As a rule of thumb it may be said that, in the field of agro-monetary measures, a claim that the principle of non-discrimination has been violated is virtually impossible to succeed,[93] save in the case of misuse of powers or a particularly blatant disregard of discretionary powers.[94] In the context of divergent national monetary policies, it is not easy to neutralize fully currency fluctuations. Measures of general application taken in order to stabilize the market may give rise to difference in treatment among producers but the Court is prepared to give the Community institutions the benefit of the doubt in order to discourage litigation and facilitate their speedy intervention to a highly technical area. In some cases, however, the reasoning of the Court does not appear satisfactory.[95]

The *Bananas* case[96] illustrates vividly the situation where the Court is called upon to apply the principle of non-discrimination in circumstances where the Community legislature seeks to balance diametrically opposed national interests.

---

[91] Op.cit., paras. 22–3.   [92] Op.cit., para. 24.

[93] See e.g. Case 138/78 *Stölting* [1979] ECR 713; Case 49/79 *Pool* v. *Council* [1980] ECR 569; Case 281/82 *Unifrex* v. *Commission and Council* [1984] ECR 1969; Case 244/83 *Meggle* [1986] ECR 1101; Case 195/87 *Cehave* v. *Hoofdproduktschap voor Akkerbouwprodukten* [1989] ECR 2199; Case C–244/95 *Moskof* v. *EOK*, [1997] ECR I–6441 and see Barents, op.cit., p. 170.

[94] See Case 29/77 *Roquette* v. *France* [1977] ECR 1835, paras. 20–1.

[95] See e.g. *Cehave*, op.cit. and contrast the judgment with the more persuasive Opinion of Tesauro AG.

[96] Case C–280/93 *Germany* v. *Council* [1994] ECR I–4973.

By Regulation No. 404/93,[97] the Council introduced a common organization of the market in bananas replacing the existing diverse national markets. Before the introduction of that regulation, there existed essentially two tendencies. Producer Member States imposed quantitative restrictions on imports from third countries with a view to ensuring an outlet for domestic production. Non-producer Member States favoured liberal importation rules. The Regulation granted preferential treatment to bananas produced in the Community and, in compliance with the provisions of the Fourth Lomé Convention, to those produced in the ACP States. An annual tariff quota was opened for imports of bananas from third countries other than ACP States. It was argued that the division of the tariff quota discriminated against traders traditionally trading in third country bananas because it reduced their existing market share. The Court stated that, before the introduction of Regulation No. 404/93, the traders among whom the tariff quota was subdivided were subject to different national regimes and not in comparable situations. Since the regulation came into force, traders were affected differently. Those who were traditionally supplied by third country bananas suffered, as a result of the regulation, restrictions in their imports. Those formerly required to market Community and ACP bananas could, as a result of the regulation, import specified quantities of third country bananas. The Court continued:[98]

However, such a difference in treatment appears to be inherent in the objective of integrating previously compartmentalized markets, bearing in mind the different situations of the various categories of economic operators before the establishment of the common organization of the market. The Regulation is intended to ensure the disposal of Community production and traditional ACP production, which entails the striking of a balance between the two categories of economic operators in question.

The circumstances of the *Bananas* case were distinct because of the strongly opposing national interests and the need to draw a balance between two competing forces, namely, protectionism and free market.[99] The Court came to the conclusion that there was no breach of the principle of equal treatment because the common organization of the market provided for a reasonable allocation of risks and benefits among the various categories of traders. The case illustrates that, in the sphere of economic law, the principle of equality prohibits only measures imposing on traders risks beyond those which they can reasonably be expected to bear in the light of the underlying economic circumstances.[100]

A further example of how the discretion of the Council conditions the application of the principle of equality is provided by the judgment in *Wuidart*.[101]

---

[97] OJ 1993 L 47/1. [98] Op.cit., para. 74.

[99] The Bananas Regulation has given rise to extensive litigation. See e.g. for another unsuccessful challenge on different grounds: Case C–466/93 *Atlanta Fruchthandelsgesellschaft* v. *Bundesamt für Ernährung und Forstwirtschaft* [1995] ECR I–3799.

[100] A claim that the introduction of a common organization to previously disparate markets led to discrimination has also been rejected in other cases, see e.g. Case 106/81 *Kind* v. *EEC* [1982] ECR 2885.

[101] Joined Cases C–267 to C–285/88 *Wuidart and Others* [1990] ECR I–435.

Community regulations imposed a levy on milk production in excess of the producer's quota and provided for two alternative formulas on the basis of which, at the option of the Member States, the levy was to be calculated. It was argued that producers subject to the first formula were subject to higher financial burdens than producers subject to the second formula. The Court held that where the Community legislature is required, in adopting rules, to assess their future effects and those effects cannot be accurately foreseen, its assessment is open to criticism only if it appears 'manifestly incorrect' in the light of the information available to it at the time of the adoption of the rules in question.[102] The Court found that the principle of non-discrimination had not been breached because, at the time when the Council introduced the rules, it could reasonably take the view that the higher rate of levy provided for under the second formula would neutralize the advantage which producers subject to that formula would derive.[103]

The above cases clearly illustrate that although the principle of equal treatment enables the Court to exercise more intense review than the test of *Wednesbury* unreasonableness, a range of option does remain available to the Community decision makers. As Laws J put it, it is highly unlikely that only one of the choices available to the legislature will pass the test of objective justification.[104] Of particular interest in this context is the Court's finding that, in taking policy decisions which require the assessment of a complex economic situation, the Community legislature enjoys wide discretion in the sense that the Court will only engage in marginal review. The Court cannot substitute its own assessment for that of the Community legislature but must confine itself to examining whether the assessment made contains a manifest error or constitutes a misuse of powers or exceeds clearly the bounds of the legislature's discretion. In such cases, the discretion of the institution which authored the act extends also 'to a certain extent, to the findings as to the basic facts, especially in the sense that it is free to base its assessment, if necessary, on findings of a general nature'.[105]

2.4.3.2. Different treatment of products of different Member States

Sometimes agricultural regulations provide for special provisions in relation to producers or goods in certain Member States. On a number of occasions the Court has been confronted with the question whether such provisions are compatible with the principle of non-discrimination. The Court has held that differences in

---

[102] Op.cit., para. 14; See also Case 59/83 *Biovilac* v. *EEC* [1984] ECR 4057, para. 17. But note that in Joined Cases C–248 and C–249/95 *Sam Schiffahrt and Stapf* v. *Germany* [1997] ECR I–4475, paras. 32, 46, 47, the Court left open the possibility that in some cases the validity of a Community measure may need to be assessed *ex posto facto*. See also the Opinion of Jacobs AG at 4489. See further *Altmann*, op.cit.

[103] See also Joined Cases C–133/93, C–300/93 and C–362/93 *Crispoltoni* [1994] ECR I–4863, discussed below 3.4.2.2.

[104] *R* v. *Ministry of Agriculture, Fisheries and Food, ex parte First City Trading Limited*, op.cit., 279.

[105] Joined Cases C–248 and C–249/95 *Sam Schiffahrt and Stapf* v. *Germany* [1997] ECR I–4475, paras. 24–5.

treatment which are based on objective differences arising from the underlying economic situations of Member States cannot be considered discriminatory.[106] In one case, it was held that the fact that economic structures in Italy were unusually fragmented into small production units created considerable difficulties for the implementation of the Community milk quota system and therefore justified the temporary postponement of certain aspects of that system.[107] It has also been accepted that differential treatment among economic operators established in different Member States may be the inevitable consequence of the fact that Community harmonization measures provide only for minimum requirements.[108]

Breach of the principle of non-discrimination was found in *Codorniu* v. *Council*.[109] A Council regulation adopted in 1989 reserved the term 'crémant' to certain quality sparkling wines traditionally produced in France and Luxembourg. The applicant was a Spanish company which was the holder of the Spanish graphic trademark 'Gran Cremant de Codorniu'. It alleged that the regulation was discriminatory. The Court observed that, whereas the first national measures providing in France and Luxembourg for the use of the term 'crémant' as a traditional description were adopted in 1975, the applicant company had been using that term since 1924. The reservation of the term for wines produced in France and Luxembourg could not therefore be justified on the basis of traditional use. The Court also held that the term 'crémant' referred to the method of manufacture of the product rather than to its geographical origin. It followed that there was no objective reason justifying the difference in treatment and the regulation was void. The case provides an example of what constitutes arbitrary conduct. The contested regulation can be seen as a blatant disregard of acquired rights, indeed, as verging on expropriation. *Codorniu* is also important from the point of view of procedure. It is the first case where the Court expressly acknowledged, outside the limited field of anti-dumping, that an individual may challenge a true legislative measure under Article 230(4)[173(4)]. The judgment shows that, where an applicant has a very strong case on the merits, the Court may be prepared to grant him *locus standi* to challenge a legislative measure despite the restrictive requirements of that provision.[110]

In a subsequent case, the Court held that producers who were entitled to use the registered designation 'champagne' were able to use the terms 'methode champenoise' for the description of their products to the exclusion of other producers who traditionally used those terms, the restricted use of the terms being justified in

---

[106] See *Eridania* v. *Minister for Agriculture and Forestry* [1979] ECR 2749, para. 19, Joined Cases C–181, C–182 and C–218/88 *Deschamps and Others* v. *Ofival* [1989] ECR 4381.

[107] Joined Cases C–267 to C–285/88 *Wuidart and Others* [1990] ECR I–435, paras. 28–30.

[108] Case C–128/94 *Hönig* v. *Stadt Stockach* [1995] ECR I–3389.

[109] Case C–309/89 [1994] ECR I–1853.

[110] The Court conceded that the contested provision was a legislative measure because it applied to traders in general. It held, however, that that did not prevent it from being of individual concern to some traders. The applicant was able to establish individual concern because the contested regulation prevented it from using a graphic trademark which it used traditionally, by reserving that trademark to other traders.

the interests of protecting registered indications of the geographical origin of wines.[111]

2.4.3.3. Similar treatment of dissimilar situations

As stated above, the principle of equal treatment prohibits not only comparable situations from being treated differently but also different situations from being treated in the same way unless such treatment is objectively justified.[112] In a number of cases, Community measures have been challenged on the ground that they fail to recognize material differences between products or producers.

2.4.3.3.1. Individual circumstances of producers

Clearly, it is not possible to tailor legislation so as take into account the individual circumstances of all traders.[113] In general, the Court's approach is to require the application of similar rules to groups of traders who are in similar situations notwithstanding that such rules may produce different effects. It has held that the introduction of general rules under the common organization of the market may affect producers in different ways depending on the nature of their production or on local conditions but that such differences cannot be regarded as discrimination, provided that the rules are based on objective criteria.[114] Thus in *Hierl*[115] it was argued that the temporary withdrawal of a uniform proportion of milk quota from all producers placed a heavier burden on small holdings than on large holdings, which operated on an industrial scale and were able to compensate for the withdrawal either by reducing purchases or by intensifying other production. The Court rejected that argument on the ground that the withdrawal was determined on the basis of objective criteria formulated to meet the needs of the general common organization of the market.

The principle of equal treatment has also been invoked together with the principle of proportionality to challenge measures which impose flat-rate reductions to all producers. In *SITPA*,[116] with a view to limiting production of tomato products, a Council regulation provided for a specified quantity as a guaranteed threshold for each marketing year. If the guaranteed threshold were exceeded, the aid payable to producers would be reduced for the following marketing year depending on the extent of the excess production. It was argued that the reduction in aid made by the Commission following a finding that the guaranteed threshold had been exceeded infringed the prohibition of discrimination. It applied uniformly throughout the Community so that French traders who were not responsible for

---

[111] Case C–306/93 *SMW Winzersekt* [1994] ECR I–5555.

[112] Case 106/83 *Sermide* v. *Cassa Conguaglio Zucchero* [1984] ECR 4209; Case 13/63 *Italy* v. *Commission* [1963] ECR 165, at 178; Case 8/82 *Wagner Bundesanstalt fur landwirtschaftliche Marktordnung* [1983] ECR 371.

[113] See above 2.3.

[114] Case 179/84 *Bozzetti* v. *Invernizzi* [1985] ECR 2301, para. 34; Case C–56/94 *SCAC* v. *Associazione dei Produttori Ortofrutticoli* [1995] ECR I–1769, para. 28.

[115] Case C–311/90 *Hierl* v. *Hauptzollamt Regensburg* [1992] ECR I–2061.

[116] Case C–27/90 *SITPA* [1991] ECR I–133.

the excess production were treated in the same way as traders in other Member States who were so responsible. Dismissing that argument, the Court held:[117]

In a common organization of markets with no system of national quotas all Community producers, regardless of the Member State in which they are based, must together, in an egalitarian manner, bear the consequences of the decisions which the Community institutions are led to adopt, in the exercise of their powers, in order to respond to the risk of an imbalance which may arise in the market between production and market outlets.

The Court has taken a similar view in other cases.[118] The possibility cannot be excluded that measures which require producers to bear the adverse consequences of an excess in production on a flat-rate basis may lead to unfair results in individual cases. The Court's approach is justified, however, because alternative policies, such as the introduction of individual quotas, are by their nature more restrictive of commercial freedom. Also, it is not practically possible to identify the producers who are responsible for excess production. By contrast, it is submitted that, where it is feasible for the Community administration to link excess production to a specific class of producers, the principles of equality and proportionality would require that class to bear commensurately the consequences of excessive production and a generally applicable measure penalizing all producers may be challenged on those grounds.

2.4.3.3.2. Similar treatment of products of different Member States

In general, agricultural regulations lay down uniform rules which are applicable to all Member States. The above discussion shows that, in reviewing the choices of the Community legislature in areas where it exercises wide discretion, the Court is content to accept similarity of rules and does not look for similarity of effects. It has been held that the various elements in the common organization of the market, such as protective measures or subsidies, may not be differentiated according to region or according to other factors affecting production or consumption except by reference to objective criteria which ensure a proportionate division of the advantages and disadvantages for those concerned without distinction between the territories of Member States.[119] In *Sermide*[120] it was argued that the method of calculating the production levy on sugar affected adversely Italian producers vis-à-vis producers from northern Member States owing to the differences in the crop cycle for sugar beet in southern and northern Europe. The Court rejected that argument by stating that,[121]

---

[117] Op.cit., para. 20.

[118] Joined Cases C–133, C–300 and C–362/93 *Crispoltoni* [1994] ECR I–4863; Case 250/84 *Eridania v. Cassa Conguaglio Zucchero* [1986] ECR 117, para. 32; Joined Cases C–248 and C–249/95 *Sam Schiffahrt and Stapf* v. *Germany* [1997] ECR I–4475, paras. 32 *et seq.*

[119] Case 106/83 *Sermide* v. *Cassa Conguaglio Zucchero* [1984] ECR 4209, para. 28; Case C–309/89 *Codorniu* v. *Council* [1994] ECR I–1853, para. 26. See also *Sam Schiffahrt and Stapf* v. *Germany*, op.cit., para. 64.

[120] Case 106/83 *Sermide* v. *Cassa Conguaglio Zucchero* [1984] ECR 4209.

[121] Para. 31. Cf. the Opinion of Verloren Van Themaat AG who found that the contested measure infringed the principle of proportionality.

That line of reasoning calls in question the Council's choice of dates for the commencement of the sugar marketing year and for the entry into force of the new intervention price, a choice which may be challenged only by contending that it constitutes a misuse of powers.

In some cases Community regulations make the granting of benefits conditional on the fulfilment of certain conditions by a specified date. It is possible that the setting of a uniform date throughout the Community may affect producers differently depending on soil and climatic conditions. In such cases the Court seems to focus on the following considerations: whether the fixing of a date is necessary for the common organization of the market; whether the specified date affects producers in a certain Member State disproportionately; and whether exceptions from the specified date are provided for deserving cases.[122]

2.4.3.4. *Other considerations*

The Court has accepted that, among others, the following considerations provide objective grounds justifying a difference in treatment between comparable situations:

- *Costs and burdens on the administration*. The obligation on the administration to ensure as much as possible equal competitive conditions to all market participants is conditioned by the need to implement structural objectives by means which are 'achievable and verifiable in practice'[123] and which do not give rise to undue administrative and supervisory difficulties. Thus the method of calculating a levy may work to the disadvantage of certain traders but, provided that it is based on objective criteria, it does not breach the principle of equal treatment.[124] Also, it has been held that the difference which arises from the fact that a regulation grants aid for a product in transit between warehouses situated in a single Member State but refuses such aid for the same product in transit between warehouses situated in different Member States is objectively justified on the ground that the supervisory measures which would be necessary if the aid were to be granted in the case of international transport would involve disproportionate administrative costs.[125]
- *Prevention of fraud*. The existence of a higher risk of fraud in relation to a category of products may justify the imposition of different rules to that category from those applicable to comparable products.[126] Similarly, the need to prevent speculative transactions may be an objective differentiating factor.[127]

---

[122] See e.g. Case C–353/92 *Greece* v. *Council* [1994] ECR I–3411. See further Case 224/82 *Meiko-Konservenfabrik* v. *Germany* [1983] ECR 2539.

[123] Joined Cases C–248 and C–249/95 *Sam Schiffahrt and Stapf* v. *Germany* [1997] ECR I–4475, para. 60.

[124] Ibid.   [125] Case 2/82 *Wagner* v. *BALM* [1983] ECR 371.

[126] *Wagner* v. *BALM*, op.cit.; See also Case C–256/90 *Mignini* [1992] ECR I–2651, at 2674 per Jacobs AG.

[127] Case C–241/95 *The Queen* v. *Intervention Board for Agricultural Produce, ex parte Accrington Beef and Others* [1996] ECR I–6699.

- *Legal certainty.* The Court has held that where a producer's milk production has been significantly reduced by an exceptional event throughout the years which, according to Community law, may be taken as reference years and, as a result, that producer has been unable to obtain an individual quota based on a representative production, the Community rules treat him adversely in comparison with other producers who are able to rely on a representative production, but that such an effect is justified by the need to limit the number of years which may be taken as reference years in the interests of both legal certainty and the effectiveness of the quota system.[128]
- *Economic differences in the markets of different products.* Different treatment of comparable products is justified where it is based on objective differences arising from the economic circumstances underlying the common organization of the market in the products in issue. In *Biovilac*[129] it was argued that by subsidizing skimmed-milk powder the Commission discriminated against competing products made from whey which were not subsidized. The Court held that the granting of subsidies to skimmed-milk powder was justified owing to the nature of the product and the market-supporting role it played in the common organization of the market in milk products. By contrast, whey did not present similar characteristics being a waste produce obtained in the making of cheese.

2.5. Equal treatment and harmonization of national laws

As a general principle of law, the principle of equal treatment binds the Community institutions in the exercise of their powers to co-ordinate national laws. In this context, as in the context of the common agricultural policy, the Court understands the principle of equal treatment as requiring primarily the application of similar rules irrespective of the fact that they may produce different effects. It has been held that a harmonization measure which is intended to standardize previously disparate national rules may produce different effects depending on the prior state of the national laws but that does not amount to discrimination, provided that the measure applies equally to all Member States.[130]

An interesting issue is to what extent the principle of equality imposes limitations on the Community legislature with regard to the choice of harmonization

---

[128] *Erpelding*, op.cit., para. 30; See also Case C–177/90 *Kühn* v. *Landwirtschaftskammer Weser-Ems* [1992] ECR I–35, para. 18 and Case C–85/90 *Dowling* [1992] ECR I–5305. For another case concerning the milk quota regime where the principle of equal treatment was held not to have been breached, see Case C–63/93 *Fintan Duff* v. *Minister for Agriculture and Food* [1996] ECR I–569. Cf. Case 120/86 *Mulder I* [1988] ECR 2321 and Case C–189/89 *Spagl* [1990] ECR I–4539.

[129] Case 59/83 *Biovilac* v. *EEC* [1984] ECR 4057, para. 19. See also Joined Cases 279, 280, 285 and 286/84 *Rau* v. *Commission* [1987] ECR 1069.

[130] Case C–331/88 *Fedesa and Others* [1991] ECR I–4023, para. 20; see also *Germany* v. *Council* (*Bananas* case), op.cit.

areas. The application of the principle in this context encounters certain fundamental obstacles. In co-ordinating national laws, partial, step-by-step, harmonization is the preferred, indeed the only feasible, Community policy. Incremental
harmonization may lead to differences in treatment since certain legal relations may
be subject to Community rules whereas other comparable relations remain subject
to national laws. Such difference in treatment may be provisional, where the
Community has not yet harmonized a certain area of law, or more permanent,
where the Community does not intend or, for one reason or another, is unable to
harmonize an area of law. The harmonization process is by its nature a complex
exercise surrounded by legal and political difficulties which are determinative both
of the order in time in which harmonization measures are adopted and the specific
contents of those measures. The issue arises whether such obstacles, which are
inherent in the harmonization process, can be considered as objective grounds justifying difference in treatment emanating from partial harmonization. In *Assurances
du Crédit* v. *Council and Commission*[131] the Court was concerned with the First
Insurance Directive[132] as amended by Directive 87/343.[133] The amending
Directive imposed additional financial requirements on private insurance companies but maintained the exclusion of public undertakings providing export credit
insurance from the burdens of the First Directive. In an action for damages against
the Community, the applicants argued that the Directive imposed discriminatory
burdens on the private sector. The Court held that export credit insurance operations transacted for the account of the State were in an objectively different situation from other such operations. In relation to the former, the protection of insured
persons was provided by the State itself so that the application of the financial guarantees provided by the directive was not justified. In the light of the arguments submitted by the Advocate General, who took the opposite view, the laconic
reasoning of the Court seems unpersuasive.[134] The Advocate General found that
in the field of export credit insurance private and public undertakings competed
with each other and should be subject to equal burdens. In his view, the fact that
public undertakings were supported by the financial backing of the State was not a
good reason to exclude them from the financial guarantees provided for in the
Directive. By contrast, he considered that financial intervention by the State was
in itself discriminatory and questioned its legality under Articles 86[90] and 88[93]
of the Treaty. The Advocate General also dismissed the argument that the difficulties surrounding harmonization in the area of export credit insurance justified the
exclusion of public operations from the scope of the Directive.

Francovich II[135] concerned Directive 80/987 on the approximation of the laws
of the Member States relating to the protection of employees in the event of the

---

[131] Case C–63/89 [1991] ECR I–1799.

[132] Directive 73/239 on the coordination of laws, regulations and administrative provisions relating
to the taking up and pursuit of the business of direct insurance other than life assurance, OJ 1973 L
228/3.

[133] OJ 1987 L 185/72.   [134] See *Assurances du Crédit*, op.cit, esp. 1832 *et seq*. per Tesauro AG.

[135] Case C–479/93 *Francovich* v. *Italian Republic* [1995] ECR I–3843.

insolvency of their employer,[136] which was adopted by the Council on the basis of Article 94[100] of the Treaty. The Court interpreted the Directive as applying only to employees whose employers may, under national law, be made subject to insolvency proceedings for the collective satisfaction of the creditors. It was argued that the Directive infringed the general principle of equality to the extent that it protected only those employees. In its judgment, the Court did not deny that the Directive resulted in a difference in treatment between two categories of employees.[137] Rather, it focused on whether the difference in treatment was objectively justified. It held that, in the exercise of the powers conferred upon them by Article 94[100], the institutions have a discretion in particular with regard to the possibility of pursuing harmonization in stages.[138] It also noted the difficulties surrounding the harmonization process given the complexity and divergence of national laws and the need to obtain unanimity in the Council under the procedure provided for in Article 94[100]. The Court held that, given the difficulties in finding a concept of insolvency capable of unambiguous application in the divergent laws of the Member States, the distinction between employees according to whether their employer may be subject to proceedings to satisfy collectively the claims of creditors derived from a concept of insolvency which was objective and justified. The Directive therefore did not infringe the principle of equal treatment.

It follows from *Assurances du Crédit* and *Francovich II* that difficulties surrounding harmonization may be objective reasons justifying a difference in treatment. That seems to be the case whether such difficulties result from divergencies in national laws or from policy disagreements which restrict the scope of application of a measure *ratione materiae*. A difference in treatment, however, will not be justified if it runs counter to the objectives of the Treaty provision on the basis of which the harmonization measure has been adopted. The judgments recognize that harmonization of national laws remains *par excellence* a political exercise. If in *Francovich II* the Court had reached the opposite result, it would have elevated the principle of non-discrimination to an autonomous source of harmonization. It is notable that in *Assurances du Crédit*, the Advocate General was not prepared to recognize a margin of discretion to the Community legislature as wide as that recognized by the Court. He stated:[139]

It is true . . . that different situations exist in the Member States. However, it is precisely such diversity which a harmonizing directive serves to eliminate and it cannot therefore in itself be regarded as an insuperable obstacle. The Council, when it decided to restrict harmonization to a single category of operators ought therefore to have justified that limitation—which

---

[136] OJ 1983 L 283/23.

[137] In his Opinion, Cosmas AG expressly rejected the argument that employees whose employers are subject to a collective procedure for the satisfaction of creditors deserve more protection than employees whose employers are not: see para. 31 of the Opinion.

[138] See also on the same point Case 37/83 *Rewe-Zentrale* v. *Landwirtschaftskammer Rheinland* [1984] ECR 1229, para. 20; C–193/94 *Skanavi and Chryssanthakopoulos* [1996] ECR I–929, para. 27.

[139] [1991] I–1837 (emphasis in the original).

. . . distorts competition—by adducing *additional, specific* difficulties other than those which normally exist when differing national rules are harmonized.

A final point may be made in relation to *Francovich II*. There, the difference in treatment resulted from the fact that the Directive pursued partial harmonization: one category of employees was subject to Community rules whereas another category of employees remained subject to the laws of the Member States. It would have been a different issue if the Directive applied *ratione materiae* to all categories of employees but introduced different standards of protection depending on the type of insolvency procedure to which their employer was subject. In such a case, the claim that the difference in treatment amounted to discrimination would be stronger. Legal relations which are covered by the same legal system must in principle be subject to the same rules and it is interesting to note that, in a different context, the Court has accepted in exceptional circumstances the analogical application of Community measures in the interests of ensuring equal treatment.[140]

2.6. Staff cases

The principle of equality is a fundamental principle of the Community civil service. It requires that Community officials who are in identical situations must be governed by the same rules.[141] In *Prais*[142] the Court recognized the principle of religious equality in Community law by stating that, in setting the date for a competition to fill a vacant post, the appointing authority is obliged to take reasonable steps to avoid dates which a candidate has informed it are unsuitable for religious reasons. In *Weiser*[143] the Court annulled a provision of the Staff Regulations which enabled a person upon joining the Community service to transfer pension rights from a national scheme to the Community scheme if he had acquired such rights as an employed person but not if he had acquired them as a self-employed person. But the refusal to grant to the ex-spouse of a Community official cover under the Community sickness insurance scheme where she is not covered by the insurance scheme in her country of origin was held not to infringe equality even though such cover is provided to members of the institutions. The differentiating factor is that members of the institutions, unlike officials, serve for a limited time. The purpose

---

[140] Case 165/84 *Krohn* v. *BALM* [1985] ECR 3997.

[141] Joined Cases 152, 158, 162, 166, 170, 173, 175, 177–9, 182 and 186/81 *Ferrario* v. *Commission* [1983] ECR 2357, para. 7.

[142] Case 130/75 *Prais* v. *Council* [1976] ECR 1589. For the principle of sex equality in staff cases, see e.g. Case 246/83 *De Angelis* v. *Commission* [1985] ECR 1253 and the cases mentioned below n. 155.

[143] Case C–37/89 [1990] ECR I–2395. The case is one in a series of cases concerning the transfer of pension rights where the Court followed an approach favourable to Community officials: see further Case 130/87 *Retter* v. *Caisse de Pension de Employes Prives* [1989] ECR 865, Case C–137/88 *Schneemann and Others* v. *Commission* [1990] ECR I–369. Cf. Joined Cases 81, 82 and 146/79 *Sorasio* v. *Commission* [1980] ECR 3557, where it was held that the principle of equality does not require account to be taken of possible inequalities which may ensue because the Community and national tax systems overlap.

of the benefit is to ensure that they have sickness cover in the event that, at the end of their term of office, they do not engage in gainful employment enabling them to be covered by a public sickness insurance scheme.[144]

In *Scaramuzza*,[145] it was held that a Community official who serves in a third country is in an objectively different position from an official who performs his duties within the Community inasmuch as the accommodation and medical costs of the former are covered by the Community. Thus, it is not contrary to the principle of equal treatment to pay to an official serving in a third country only 80 per cent of his remuneration in local currency whereas in the case of officials serving within the Community the entire remuneration is paid in the currency of the place of employment.

The conditions of recruitment, appointment and promotion in the Community civil service are subject to the principle of equal treatment.[146] An interesting example in relation to recruitment is provided by *Noonan*.[147] The Commission introduced the policy of restricting admission to certain secretarial posts to candidates who did not possess a university degree. The applicant was refused admission to a competition for such a post on the ground that she was a university graduate. The Court of First Instance held that the Commission's policy ran counter to the principle of equal treatment in conjunction with Article 27 of the Staff Regulations which provides that recruitment should seek to recruit for the institution the services of officials of the highest standard of ability, efficiency and integrity.

A prime example of the application of the principle of equal treatment in staff affairs is provided by the *JET* cases. In 1978 the Council set up the Joint European Torus (JET) Joint Undertaking to carry on research as part of the Community fusion programme. JET was based in Culham at the headquarters of UK Atomic Energy Authority (UKAEA), its constituent members being Euratom, the UKAEA, and the atomic agencies of the other Member States and of Switzerland. Under the Statutes of JET, staff made available to it by the UKAEA continued to be employed by that authority. By contrast, staff made available from the other national organizations had the status of temporary Community servants and received significantly higher remuneration. In *Ainsworth*[148] the Court held that the difference in treatment was objectively justified, reasoning as follows. The JET Joint Undertaking was devoted entirely to research and its duration was limited in time. An undertaking of such a nature could work effectively only in close association with a national organization already in existence. Hence, its close links with

---

[144] Case T–66/95 *Kuchlenz-Winter* v. *Commission* [1997] ECR II–637.

[145] Case C–76/93 P *Scaramuzza* v. *Commission* [1994] ECR I–5173.

[146] For a case where the CFI annulled a decision concerning the classification in grade of the applicant, see T–93/94 *Becker* v. *Court of Auditors* [1996] ECR II–141.

[147] Case T–60/92 *Noonan* v. *Commission* [1996] ECR II–215. See further on recruitment, Case T–132/89 *Gallone* v. *Council* [1990] ECR II–549 and Case C–100/88 *Oyowe and Traore* v. *Commission* [1989] ECR 4285.

[148] Joined Cases 271/83 and 15, 36, 113, 158 and 203/84 and 13/85 *Ainsworth* v. *Commission and Council* [1987] ECR 167.

UKAEA. The latter, being the host organization, was in a special position which distinguished it from the other national agencies. Its personnel were divided between staff working on its own projects and staff working on the JET project. The Court accepted that UKAEA was entitled to require that staff working on the JET project were subject to its own conditions of service so as to ensure equality of treatment among the two classes of its own staff. The reasoning of the Court is flawed in two respects. First, it is surprising that the Court found no discrimination on grounds of nationality. Although each national organization member of JET was free to make available to it employees of any nationality, the Statutes of JET were clearly indirectly discriminatory against British nationals since they were much less likely to be employed by the national organizations of other Member States. Secondly, although it was inevitable that differential treatment between some groups of employees would arise in any event, it is arguable that the appropriate comparator of UKAEA staff working for JET is staff of other organizations working on the same project rather than UKAEA staff working on other projects. The Court was clearly influenced by the fact that the UKAEA, which provided installations and technical support to JET and bore a much higher contribution to the expenses of the project than the other national authorities, was anxious not to disturb relations among its employees and the functioning of its own organization.

Subsequently, in *Altmann and Casson* v. *Commission*[149] the CFI made history by reversing the judgment of the Court of Justice in *Ainsworth*. The applicants were British nationals employed in the JET project as members of staff of the UKAEA. They challenged the Commission's refusal to appoint them as temporary Community servants on the grounds that it infringed the principle of equal treatment and the prohibition of discrimination on grounds of nationality. The CFI started by noting that all JET staff were in a comparable situation, irrespective of the national organization which made them available to the JET project. It found that staff made available by the UKAEA were treated less favourably in two respects: first, with regard to the conditions of employment, since they received lower salary than their colleagues employed by other national organizations, and secondly, with regard to security of employment, because staff employed as temporary Community servants had a much better opportunity of obtaining permanent posts in the Community civil service. The CFI considered that, owing to factual developments since the judgment in *Ainsworth* was delivered, the justification for the difference in treatment had ceased to exist. The CFI took into account the following factors: the extension of the duration of JET, the lesser role played by the UKAEA in the organization and functioning of the Joint Undertaking, the fact that the UKAEA no longer objected to staff employed by it in the JET project leaving its employment for that of the Commission, the disruption of the

---

[149] Joined Cases T–177 and T–377/94 *Altmann and Others* v. *Commission* [1996] ECR II–2041.

functioning of the Joint Undertaking as a result of industrial relations conflict, and the inability of the JET recruitment system to achieve the aims for which it was designed.

Having established that objective justification for the difference in treatment no longer existed, the CFI proceeded to determine the legal consequences thereof. In *Altmann and Casson*, as earlier in *Ainsworth*, the applicants challenged the validity of the JET Statutes incidentally under the plea of illegality,[150] the main challenge being against the Commission's refusal to recruit them. The CFI held that since the legality of the contested individual decisions must be assessed on the basis of the elements of fact and law existing at the time when the measure was adopted, the legality of the legislative measure which forms its legal basis must also be assessed at that time rather than the time of its own adoption.[151] The CFI held that its finding did not conflict with the principle of legality. The latter required the Commission to continue applying the JET Statutes even after they had, in the applicants' view, become illegal as a result of the supervening change in the circumstances. However, the applicants should not be denied the right to bring a challenge before the Community judicature seeking a declaration that they are inapplicable, not *ab initio* but as from the date of a specific change in circumstances.[152] The CFI declared the JET Statutes inapplicable in the cases of the applicants to the extent that they conflicted with the principle of equal treatment. It rejected, however, their claim for compensation on the ground that the breach of the principle of equal treatment did not amount to a manifest and grave disregard of discretionary powers by the Council and the Commission.

Altmann and Casson is a well-argued judgment on a delicate and complex issue. The CFI was walking on a tightrope having to balance, on the one hand, respect for the authority of the Court of Justice and, on the other, the requirements of equal treatment It succeeded in undoing injustice whilst carefully distinguishing precedent.

2.7. Prohibition of discrimination on grounds of sex and sexual orientation

2.7.1. Sex equality as a fundamental right

The Court regards sex equality as a fundamental human right whose observance it has a duty to ensure and which transcends Article 141[119] and the provisions of secondary Community law. The purpose of this section is not to examine in detail

---

[150] See Article 241[184] EC, Article 241[156] EAEC.   [151] *Altmann and Casson*, op.cit., para. 119.
[152] Para. 123.

the Community law on sex discrimination but rather to trace the development of the case law and assess judicial policy by reference to key decisions.[153]

In the *Third Defrenne* case[154] the Court refused to widen the scope of Article 119 (now 141) so as to require, apart from equality in pay, equality in respect of other working conditions. It declared, however, that the elimination of sex discrimination forms part of the fundamental rights recognized and enforced by the Court. On the facts, that declaration proved of little assistance to Ms Defrenne. The Court stated that, as regards employment relationships governed by national law, the Community had not, at the time of the events giving rise to the litigation, assumed any responsibility for securing the observance of equal treatment in working conditions other than remuneration. The dispute therefore was governed by the provisions of national law. The implication of the judgment was that Articles 117 and 118 (now 136 and 137), on the one hand, and Article 119 (now 141), on the other hand, were mutually exclusive.

The Court was more forthcoming in cases involving employment relationships governed by Community law. In *Razzouk and Beydoun* v. *Commission*[155] the Staff Regulations discriminated against widowers of Community officials in relation to pension rights.[156] Referring to *Defrenne* v. *Sabena*, the Court pointed out that sex equality is a fundamental right which must be ensured within the framework of the Staff Regulations. In relations between the institutions and their employees, therefore, the requirements of the principle of equal treatment 'are in no way limited to those resulting from Article 119 (now 141) of the EEC Treaty or from the Community directives adopted in this field'.[157] On that basis, the Court annulled the Commission's decision refusing a pension to the applicants since it was based on provisions of the Staff Regulations violating the right to sex equality.

2.7.2. Beyond discrimination on grounds of sex

The Court went further in *P* v. *S and Cornwall County Council*.[158] The applicant in the main proceedings was dismissed from his employment following his decision

---

[153] See among others: E. Ellis, *European Community Sex Equality Law* (Clarendon Press, Second edn., 1998); S. Prechal and N. Burrows, *Gender Discrimination Law of The European Community* (Dartmouth, 1990); C. McCrudden (ed.) *Women, Employment and European Equality Law* (Eclipse, 1987); C. Barnard, *EC Employment Law* (Wiley, 1995); B. Bercusson, *European Labour Law* (Butterworths, 1996), Part IV.

[154] Case 149/77 *Defrenne* v. *Sabena* [1978] ECR 1365.

[155] Joined Cases 75 and 117/82 [1984] ECR 1509. See also Case 20/71 *Sabbatini* v. *European Parliament* [1972] ECR 345; Case 21/74 *Airola* v. *Commission* [1975] ECR 221; and more recently Case T–45/90 *Speybrouck* v. *Parliament* [1992] ECR II–33.

[156] The regulations discriminated in more ways than one. The widow of an official or former official was entitled to a survivor's pension equal to 60% of the pension paid to her husband and her right to the pension was independent of her own resources. The husband of a deceased female official, by contrast, could only receive a pension if he had no income of his own and was unable for reasons of health to engage in gainful employment. The pension was paid to him at the lower rate of 50%. Also, although entitlement to pension ceased upon remarriage, the widow of an official could claim a capital sum to twice the annual amount of her survivor's pension. No such right was extended to a widower.

[157] Op.cit., para. 17. [158] Case C–13/94 [1996] ECR I–2143.

to undergo gender reassignment by surgical operation. The question referred was whether the Equal Treatment Directive[159] precludes dismissal of a transsexual for reasons related to gender reassignment. The Court held that, in view of sex equality as a fundamental human right, the scope of the Directive cannot be confined to discrimination based on the fact that a person is of one or other sex.[160] It stated that discrimination arising from gender reassignment is based essentially, if not exclusively, on the sex of the person concerned. Where a person is dismissed on the ground that he or she has undergone gender reassignment, he or she is treated unfavourably by comparison with persons of the sex to which he or she was deemed to belong before undergoing gender reassignment.[161] The Court concluded:[162]

To tolerate such discrimination would be tantamount, as regards such a person, to a failure to respect the dignity and freedom to which he or she is entitled, and which the Court has a duty to safeguard.

The case provides a prime example of the way the Court views the principle of equality as a general principle of Community law transcending the provisions of Community legislation. In effect, the Court applied a general principle of unwritten human rights law, according to which discrimination on arbitrary criteria is prohibited, rather than the provisions of the Equal Treatment Directive, a literal interpretation of which does not support the Court's finding.

The importance of *P* v. *S* can hardly be overstated. It is a sign that the Court takes rights seriously, endorses a substantive conception of equality, and, at least in some contexts, accords as much importance to social justice as to market integration.[163] One of the most crucial issues for establishing whether discrimination against transsexuals is sex discrimination is the identification of the appropriate comparator. The United Kingdom submitted that no discrimination was involved because a female to male transsexual would have been treated in exactly the same way as the applicant. The Court, however, had little sympathy for this argument, adopting instead as the appropriate comparator the transsexual's previous persona. It was led by the highly influential Opinion of Tesauro AG who submitted that it was necessary to go beyond the traditional man/woman dichotomy and accept that

[159] Council Directive 76/207 on the implementation of the principle of equal treatment for men and women as regards access to employment, vocational training and promotion, and working conditions, OJ 1976 L 39/40.

[160] *P* v. *S*, op.cit., para. 20. The Court (at para. 16) adopted the following definition of transsexual given by the European Court of Human Rights in its judgment of 17 Oct. 1986 *Rees* v. *United Kingdom*, Series A, No. 106: 'the term "transsexual" is usually applied to those who, whilst belonging physically to one sex, feel convinced that they belong to the other; they often seek to achieve a more integrated, unambiguous identity by undergoing medical treatment and surgical operations to adapt their physical characteristics to their psychological nature. Transsexuals who have been operated upon thus form a fairly well-defined and identifiable group.'

[161] Op.cit., para. 21.   [162] Op.cit., para. 22.

[163] See C. Barnard, '*P* v. *S*: Kite Flying or a New Constitutional Approach?', in A. Dashwood and S. O'Leary, *The Principle of Equal Treatment in E.C. Law*, pp. 59–79.

there is a range of other characteristics, behaviour and roles shared by men and women 'so that sex *itself* ought rather to be thought of as a continuum'.[164] The Advocate General emphasized that, for the purposes of the case, sex was important as a convention, a social parameter. He pointed out that the reason why women are frequently the victims of sex discrimination is their social role, the image traditionally ascribed to them in societal terms. In the same way, the unfavourable treatment suffered by transsexuals is most often linked to a negative image, a moral judgment which has nothing to do with their abilities in the sphere of employment.[165]

One of the issues which is left open by the judgment is whether differential treatment on grounds of gender reassignment necessarily amounts to discrimination or whether it may be justified on grounds of objective justification. On the facts, the applicant was working as a manager in an educational establishment operated by the County Council and there was no suggestion that her suitability for the employment in issue was affected by her change of sex. One suspects that different considerations will apply, for example, to a person who is employed as attendant of public lavatories and wishes to undergo a sex change operation. *P* v. *S* does not state clearly whether discrimination against a transsexual is direct or indirect discrimination. It has been observed that, if the appropriate comparator is the person's previous persona, discrimination against a transsexual should always be classified as direct discrimination.[166] It remains to be seen whether the Court will accept that differential treatment against transsexuals may be justified in employment relationships where sex discrimination strictly understood is not.

P v. *S* opened Pandora's box. An important issue is whether the Equal Treatment Directive is broad enough to encompass discrimination against other groups, in particular, homosexuals. In *Grant* v. *South West Trains Ltd.*[167] the applicant, a female employee, argued that she was the victim of sex discrimination because she was refused by her employer certain travel concessions, which had been made available to her predecessor for his cohabitee of the opposite sex, on the grounds that her cohabitee was of the same sex. The material contractual provision was Clause 8 of the British Railways Board Ticket Regulations which states that a member of staff is entitled to privilege tickets for his or her 'common law opposite sex spouse' subject to a statutory declaration being made that a 'meaningful relationship' has existed for a minimum period of two years. Elmer AG referred to *P* v. *S* and pointed out that the decisive criterion for the application of the Equal Treatment Directive is that the discrimination complained of is based essentially on gender. The same should therefore also apply to the interpretation of Article 141[119]. Then, the Advocate General stated that Clause 8 made no mention of the sexual orientation of the employee or the cohabitee and thus the question of sexual orientation was, under the objective content of the clause, irrelevant as far

---

[164] *P* v. *S*, op.cit., 2153 (emphasis in original).   [165] Op.cit., 2155.
[166] Barnard, op.cit., p. 61, n. 10.   [167] Case C–249/96, [1998] ECR I–621

as entitlement to the concessions was concerned. Clause 8 made the concessions conditional on the cohabitee being of the opposite sex to the employee and therefore, in the view of the Advocate General, discriminated exclusively on grounds of gender. This reasoning is not convincing. First, it is not correct to say that sexual orientation is irrelevant for the application of Clause 8. Clearly, the effect of the clause is to favour heterosexual vis-à-vis homosexual relations. Its effect therefore is to discriminate against the manifestation of sexual orientation. The crucial issue in the case was whether discrimination against a homosexual relationship can be classified as sex discrimination. Secondly, the Advocate General distinguished cohabitation from marriage stating that, if travel concessions were made conditional on the employee being married, that would not be contrary to Community law because, in such a case, the criterion would be defined by reference to a family law concept, the content of which is laid down by the laws of the Member States.[168] If, however, discrimination against homosexual cohabitation is discrimination on grounds of sex, the use of marriage as the decisive criterion is clearly indirect discrimination against homosexual couples. It would then be a matter of whether objective justification could be found.

In its judgment the Court did not follow the Opinion of Elmer AG. The Court started by examining whether Clause 8 gave rise to direct discrimination on grounds of sex and gave a negative reply. The condition that the worker must live in a meaningful relationship with a person of the opposite sex in order to benefit from the travel concessions is applied regardless of the sex of the worker concerned. Travel concessions are refused to a male worker if he is living with a person of the same sex just as they are refused to a female worker if she is living with a person of the same sex.[169] Then the Court turned to examine whether persons who have a stable relationship with a partner of the opposite sex are in the same situation as persons who have such a relationship with a partner of the same sex. After referring to the laws of Member States, the European Convention of Human Rights, and the fact that the Community has not yet adopted rules providing for such equivalence, it concluded that, in the present state of the law within the Community, stable relations between two persons of the same sex are not regarded as equivalent to marriages, or stable relationships outside marriage, between persons of opposite sex. In those circumstances, it was for the legislature to adopt, if appropriate, relevant measures.

Finally, the Court held that differences in treatment based on sexual orientation are not discrimination based on sex within the meaning of Article 141[119]. It stated that its reasoning in *P* v. *S* is confined to a worker's gender reassignment and cannot be extended to differences in treatment on grounds of sexual orientation. It is submitted that this distinction is correct. Discrimination on grounds of sex reassignment is effectively discrimination on grounds of sex. This becomes obvious if we view the difference in treatment from the point of view of the discriminator: an employer who discriminates against an employee on the ground that he has

---

[168] Para. 28 of the Opinion.   [169] *Grant*, op.cit., para. 27.

undergone a sex change operation draws a comparison between the sex of the employee before the operation and the sex following it. It practices discrimination between the sexes, albeit not the sexes of different persons but the different sexes of the same person existing sequentially at different points in time. Discrimination on grounds of sexual orientation, unacceptable as it may be, is a different concept.[170]

Issues such as those raised in *P* v. *S* and *Grant* are increasingly litigated in the national courts. Two English cases decided before *Grant* provide examples. In *R* v. *Secretary of State for Defence, ex parte Smith*,[171] the Court of Appeal held that discrimination on grounds of sexual orientation was not prohibited by the Sex Equality Directive and refused to make a reference to the Court of Justice on the interpretation of the Directive. In *R* v. *Secretary of State for Defence, ex parte Perkins*,[172] however, on facts similar to those in *Smith*, Lightman J decided to refer the question whether the Equal Treatment Directive prohibits discrimination on grounds of sexual orientation. In deciding to make a reference, Lightman J took into account in particular the judgment of the Court of Justice in *P* v. *S* and considered that, in the circumstances of the case, little importance should be attached to the fact that in *Smith* the House of Lords had refused leave to appeal. The difference between *Grant* and *Perkins* is that, in the first, the applicant was engaged in a lesbian relationship whereas, in the second, the only relevant factor was the existence of a state of mind, namely orientation, and not a manifestation of it. Following the judgment of the Court of Justice in *Grant*, it is difficult to see how the claim in *Perkins* can succeed.[172a]

Despite the Court's veritable efforts in *P* v. *S* to follow an evolutionary interpretation of the Equal Treatment Directive on the basis of the general principle of equality, it must be admitted that, as a matter of legislative policy, it is unsatisfactory to seek to resolve complex issues pertaining to discrimination on grounds of sexual preference on the basis of Article 119 (now 141) and the Equal Treatment Directive, the *raison d'être* of which is distinctly different. The judgment in *Grant* shows the limitations of general principles as unwritten sources of Community law. In some cases, judicial interpretation is simply no substitute for law reform.

2.7.3. Positive discrimination

Although the Court has interpreted the Equal Treatment Directive liberally, it has taken a cautious approach in relation to positive discrimination. The issue arose for the first time in *Kalanke* v. *Freie Hansestadt Bremen*.[173] The Law of the State of

[170] It will be noted that Article 13 EC, added by the Treaty of Amsterdam, refers separately to discrimination based on sex and discrimination based on sexual orientation. From this, a textual argument may be derived that, in Community law, the former does not include the latter. Article 6a, however, in itself is not conclusive since the objective of this provision is not to establish the scope of sex discrimination but rather to reiterate the Union's commitment to respect for equality and human rights.

[171] [1996] 1 All ER 257.   [172] [1997] IRLR 297.

[172a] Indeed, in the light of *Grant* the reference in Perkins was withdrawn: The Times, 16 July 1998.

[173] Case C–450/93 [1995] ECR I–3051.

Bremen governing sex equality in the public service provided that, in the case of appointment or promotion, women who had the same qualifications as men applying for the same post were to be given priority in sectors where women were under-represented. Under-representation was defined as existing in cases where women did not make up at least half of the staff in a salary bracket in a personnel group within a department. Mr Kalanke was refused promotion on the ground that a female candidate was equally qualified with him and should therefore be given priority. The Bundesarbeitsgericht (Federal Labour Court) sought a preliminary ruling regarding the compatibility of the Bremen law with Article 2(4) of the Equal Treatment Directive, which states that the Directive 'shall be without prejudice to measures to promote equal opportunity for men and women, in particular by removing existing inequalities which affect women's opportunities'. The Court started from the premise that national measures which automatically give priority to women involve discrimination contrary to Article 2(1) of the Directive. It proceeded to examine whether such measures were covered by the exception of Article 2(4). It held that Article 2(4) is exclusively designed to allow measures which, although discriminatory in appearance, are in fact intended to eliminate or reduce actual instances of inequality which may exist in social life. It thus permits national measures relating to access to employment, including promotion, which give a specific advantage to women with a view to improving their ability to compete on the labour market and to pursue a career on an equal footing with men. The Court pointed out that, as a derogation from an individual right provided for in the Directive, Article 2(4) must be interpreted strictly. It continued:[174]

National rules which guarantee women absolute and unconditional priority for appointment or promotion go beyond promoting equal opportunities and overstep the limits of the exception in Article 2(4) of the Directive.

The Court also held that, in so far as it seeks to achieve equal representation of men and women in all grades and levels within a department, such a system substitutes for equality of opportunity as envisaged in Article 2(4) the result which is only to be arrived at by providing such equality of opportunity.

The judgment draws a distinction between equality of opportunity and equality of result and identifies the first as the underlying rationale of the Equal Treatment Directive. The Advocate General took a similar view. Starting from the text of Article 2(4), Tesauro AG stated that the provision authorizes measures which seek to guarantee equality of opportunity, that is to say place men and women in a position of equality as regards starting points. By contrast, the Bremen Law in issue sought to achieve equality of results in the form of an equal distribution of posts in numerical terms. In the view of the Advocate General, that is not justified by the scope or the rationale of Article 2(4).[175] He considered that, since the objective of the Directive is to achieve equality of opportunity, the only derogations from the principle of equal treatment which are permissible, and which are not genuine

---

[174] *Kalanke*, op.cit., paras. 22–3.   [175] Op.cit., 3060.

derogations, are those which seek to give women effective equality of opportunity by eliminating the obstacles which result from social structures. He stated:[176]

Positive action must therefore be directed at removing the obstacles preventing women from having equal opportunities by tackling, for example, educational guidance and vocational training. In contrast, positive action may not be directed towards guaranteeing women equal results from occupying a job, that is to say, at points of arrival, by way of compensation for historical discrimination. In sum, positive action may not be regarded, even less employed, as a means of remedying, through discriminatory measures, a situation of impaired inequality in the past.

The model of equal treatment which emerged from *Kalanke* seems to be as follows. It is permissible to assist women preferentially so as to give them equality of opportunity but it is not permissible to place them in a similar position with men by granting them unequal treatment. The Court considered that, in the absence of clear legislative intention, it would not be appropriate to endorse a derogation from the principle of equal treatment. In other words, historical discrimination in fact cannot be undone by judicial interpretation.[177]

Kalanke is limited to national provisions 'which guarantee women *absolute and unconditional* priority'.[178] According to the Bremen Law in issue, where candidates were equally qualified, priority was to be given automatically to women.[179] The issue of affirmative action arose again in *Marschall* v. *Land Nordrhein-Westfalen*,[180] this time in relation to the Law on Civil Servants of the Land of North Rhine-Westphalia. That law gave priority to women among equally qualified candidates in relation to promotion but provided for a 'saving clause': the female candidate was to be given priority 'unless reasons specific to an individual [male] candidate tilt the balance in his favour'. The Court pointed out that, even where male and female candidates are equally qualified, male candidates tend to be promoted in preference to female ones. That is so particularly because of prejudices and stereotypes concerning the role and capacities of women in working life and the fear, for example, that women will interrupt their careers more frequently, that owing to household and family duties they will be less flexible in their working hours, or that they will be absent from work more frequently because of pregnancy, child birth and breastfeeding.[181] For those reasons, the mere fact that a male candidate and a female candidate are equally qualified does not mean that they have the same chances.[182] On that basis, the Court held that a national rule in terms of which,

---

[176] Op.cit., 3063.

[177] The judgment has been criticized, see S. Moore, 'Nothing Positive from the Court of Justice' (1996) 21 ELRev. 156.

[178] *Kalanke*, op.cit., para. 22, emphasis added.

[179] Notably, the referring court considered that the Bremen Law was compatible with the German Constitution. In particular, it held that Article 4 of the Law should be interpreted in accordance with the Basic Law to the effect that, even if priority for promotion was to be given in principle to women, exceptions should be made in appropriate cases.

[180] Case C–409/95, [1997] ECR I–6363. [181] Op.cit., para. 29.

[182] Op.cit., para. 30.

subject to the application of a saving clause, female candidates for promotion who are equally qualified as the male candidates are to be treated preferentially in sectors where they are under-represented may fall within the scope of Article 2(4) of the Directive if such a rule may counteract the prejudicial effects on female candidates of social attitudes and thus reduce actual instances of inadequacy which may exist in the real world.[183] The Court concluded that, unlike the rules in issue in *Kalanke*, a national rule which contains a saving clause comes within the exception of Article 2(4) if, in each individual case, it provides for male candidates who are equally as qualified as the female candidates a guarantee that the candidatures will be the subject of an objective assessment which will take account of all the criteria specific to the individual candidates and will override the priority accorded to female candidates where one or more of those criteria tilts the balance in favour of the male candidate. The Court pointed out that those criteria must not be such as to discriminate against female candidates.[184] It left it up to the national court to determine whether those conditions were fulfilled in the case of the Law of North Rhine-Westphalia.

Marschall suggests a shift of emphasis from *Kalanke*. Despite the saving clause, the national law in issue in *Marschall* provided for equality of result rather than equality of opportunity at the starting points since it established a presumption in favour of female candidates. The Court therefore seems to expand the scope of application of the derogation of Article 2(4) to authorize some forms of equality of result. *Marschall* starts from the factually correct premise that women are presumed to be disadvantaged in terms of employment prospects and puts the onus on the male candidates. The judgment evinces a pragmatic perception of justice but it is striking that it throws the ball back to the national laws whilst providing limited guidance to the national court that made the reference. In that respect, it contrasts with the judgments in *P* v. *S* and *Grant* where the Court felt able to provide leadership. Needless to say, a number of issues remain unresolved. What kind of circumstances may a male candidate plead to override the priority given to a female candidate? Would he be able to plead only circumstances personal to him or characteristics peculiar to a class of male candidates which dictate that the rule of priority is reversed? Could it be argued that the female candidate in issue belongs to a class in relation to which the rule of priority should not apply?

Finally, it should be noted that the judgments in *Kalanke* and *Marschall* contrast with the earlier judgment in *Commission* v. *France*.[185] There, the Court held that a French law which provided for the preservation of special rights for women in collective agreements was incompatible with the Equal Treatment Directive. The Court held that some of the special rights in issue related to the protection of women in their capacity as older workers or parents, categories to which both men and women may belong, so that the generalized preservation of special rights for women could not *en bloc* benefit from the exception of Article 2(4). In his Opinion

---

[183] Op.cit., para. 31.   [184] Op.cit., para. 33.   [185] Case 312/86 [1988] ECR 6315.

in *Kalanke* Tesauro AG considered that the judgment in *Commission* v. *France* was excessively severe in rejecting the special rights of women provided for by French law.[186] Nevertheless, the negative stance of the Court in *Commission* v. *France* may be explained by the fact that in that case the French Government made no attempt to justify specific derogations by recourse to Article 2(4) but rather invoked that provision to maintain by way of general derogation preferential treatment of women for an indefinite period.

2.8. Article 12[6] EC: The prohibition of discrimination on grounds of nationality

2.8.1. The content of the prohibition

The first paragraph of Article 12[6] EC states as follows:[187]

Within the scope of application of this Treaty, and without prejudice to any special provisions contained therein, any discrimination on grounds of nationality shall be prohibited.

Viewed in historical perspective, the right to equal treatment irrespective of nationality is the most important right conferred by substantive Community law. Traditionally, the laws of the Member States imposed restrictions on foreign citizens in most aspects of economic and social life. The prohibition of discrimination on grounds of nationality, and the cognate right to national treatment, was the first essential step to promote integration. The function of Article 12[6] was explained by Jacobs AG in *Phil Collins* as follows:[188]

. . . The fundamental purpose of the Treaty is to achieve an integrated economy in which the factors of production, as well as the fruits of production, may move freely and without distortion, thus bringing about a more efficient allocation of resources and a more perfect division of labour. The greatest obstacle to the realization of that objective was the host of discriminatory rules and practices whereby the national governments traditionally protected their own producers and workers from foreign competition. Although the abolition of discriminatory rules and practices may not be sufficient in itself to achieve the high level of economic integration envisaged by the Treaty, it is clearly an essential prerequisite.

The prohibition of discrimination on grounds of nationality is also of great symbolic importance, inasmuch as it demonstrates that the Community is not just a commercial arrangement between the governments of the Member States but is a common enterprise in which all the citizens of Europe are able to participate as individuals . . . No other aspect of Community law touches the individual more directly or does more to foster that sense of

---

[186] *Kalanke*, op.cit., 3063.
[187] In the original Treaty of Rome the prohibition of discrimination on grounds of nationality was provided for in Article 7. Article 7 was renumbered Article 6 by the TEU.
[188] Joined Cases C–92 and C–326/92 [1993] ECR I–5145 at 5163.

common identity and shared destiny without which the 'ever closer union among the peoples of Europe', proclaimed by the preamble to the Treaty, would be an empty slogan.

Article 12[6] has direct effect.[189] According to the case law it produces both vertical and horizontal direct effect so that national courts must enforce rights deriving from that provision not only against public authorities but also against individuals.[190] The prohibition of discrimination on grounds of nationality is implemented in specific spheres of Community law by a number of Treaty provisions, for example Article 39[48] (free movement of workers), Article 43[52] (right of establishment), Article 49[59] (free movement of services), and Article 294[221] (participation of non-nationals to the capital of companies). Article 12[6] has a residual character. It is of autonomous application only in situations governed by Community law in relation to which the Treaty does not lay down a specific prohibition of discrimination.[191] It performs therefore a 'gap-filling' function. The Court has held that, since Article 12[6] is implemented in specific domains by separate provisions of the Treaty, where national rules are compatible with the specific articles of the Treaty prohibiting discrimination, they are also compatible with Article 12[6].[192] Strictly speaking, that statement is inaccurate.[193] It is correct to say that where a specific article of the Treaty permits derogations from the principle of non-discrimination, such derogations are also permitted by Article 12[6].[194] It is wrong to say, however, that a national provision which discriminates against nationals of other Member States cannot be contrary to Article 12[6] simply because it is not caught by the specific provisions of the Treaty. If that were the case, Article 12[6] would lose its independent character.[195] As we shall see, the case law has understood Article 12[6] as being an autonomous source of rights and obligations outside the sphere of free movement.

The Court has interpreted the provisions of the Treaty on free movement as prohibiting not only discrimination on grounds of nationality but also discrimination against free movers irrespective of nationality.[196] Furthermore, it is now accepted that non-discriminatory restrictions are also prohibited by the provisions of the Treaty on free movement, of persons, i.e. Articles 39[48], 43[52] and 49[59].[197] In parallel, the

---

[189] See e.g. Case 24/86 *Blaizot v. University of Liège* [1988] ECR 379, para. 35; *Phil Collins*, op.cit., para. 35.

[190] Case 36/74 *Walrave v. Union Cycliste Internationale* [1974] ECR 1405, paras. 15–18, Case 13/76 *Donà v. Mantero* [1976] ECR 1333, paras. 17–19.

[191] See e.g. Case 9/73 *Schlüter* [1973] ECR 1135; Case 305/87 *Commission v. Greece* [1989] ECR 1461, para. 13; Case C–10/90 *Masgio v. Bundesknappschaft* [1991] ECR I–1119, para. 12; Case C–20/92 *Hubbard* [1993] ECR I–3777.

[192] See e.g. Case 305/87 *Commission v. Greece* [1989] ECR 1461, para. 12; Case C–41/90 *Hofner and Elser v. Macrotron* [1991] ECR I–1979, para. 36.

[193] *Phil Collins*, op.cit., per Jacobs AG, 5163–4.   [194] See below, *Rutili*.   [195] Op. cit. n. 193.

[196] See e.g. Case C–419/92 *Scholz* [1994] ECR I–505; C–18/93 *Corsica Ferries* [1994] ECR I–1783.

[197] See e.g. C–76/90 *Säger* [1991] ECR I–4221; Case C–384/93 *Alpine Investments BV* [1995] ECR I–1141; Case C–415/93 *Union Royale Belge des sociétés de Football Association and Others v. Bosman and Others* [1995] ECR I–4921. See further L. Daniele, 'Non-Discriminatory Restrictions to the Free Movement of Persons' (1997) 22 ELRev. 191; N. Bernard, 'Discrimination and Free Movement in EC Law' (1996) 45 ICLQ 82. For Article 28[30] see below, Ch. 4.2.

case law has, in the last two decades, increasingly broadened the scope of application of Article 12[6]. As the influence of discrimination on grounds of nationality has decreased in the context of free movement, the importance of Article 12[6] as an independent provision has increased.

Article 12[6] requires a Member State to provide 'perfect' or 'absolute'[198] equality of treatment between its own nationals and those of other Member States. The Court has stated that Article 12[6] requires 'perfect equality of treatment in Member States of persons in a situation governed by Community law and nationals of the Member State in question'.[199] It must be applied 'in every respect and in all circumstances governed by Community law to any person established in a Member State'.[200] The prohibition of discrimination on grounds of nationality binds also the Community institutions[201] and prohibits not only direct but also indirect discrimination, namely, discrimination which although based on a criterion other than nationality leads effectively to the same results, for example residence in the national territory.[202]

It is not clear what derogations are permitted from the principle of non-discrimination enshrined in Article 12[6]. As already stated, derogations from specific Treaty articles implementing the principle of non-discrimination on grounds of nationality are also derogations from Article 12[6].[203] The question arises whether exceptions exist where it applies outside the sphere of free movement and no specific derogations are provided for in the Treaty. If no exceptions were permitted in that context, it would follow that the residual content of Article 12[6] would be wider than the specific provisions of the Treaty prohibiting discrimination on grounds of nationality. Such a difference is not justified by the intrinsic importance of the rights protected. To give an example, it would be incongruous if the right of a Community national to take up employment in the host Member State provided for in Article 39[48] was subject to derogations on the grounds of public policy or public health whereas the right to access to education in the host State, which has been based by the Court on Article 12[6], was not. The very notion of discrimination in Article 12[6] suggests difference in treatment without good justification. Consequently, it should be accepted that derogations exist from Article 12[6] where it applies autonomously. Such derogations are as a general rule, analogous to those specified in the provisions of the Treaty on free movement, for example Articles 39(3)[48(3)] or 39(4)[48(4)]. Indirect difference in treatment against nationals of other Member States will be compatible with Article 12[6] if there is objective justification. In many cases the Court has examined, although it has invariably rejected, arguments of the defendant government that the less

---

[198] Case C–323/95 *Hayes* v. *Kronenberger* [1997] ECR I–1711, para. 18.
[199] Case C–43/95 *Data Delecta and Forsberg* [1996] ECR I–4661, para. 16.
[200] Case 137/84 *Ministère Public* v. *Mutsch* [1985] ECR 2681, para. 12.
[201] Case 147/79 *Hochstraas* v. *Court of Justice* [1980] ECR 3005.
[202] Case C–29/95 *Pastoors and Trans-Cap* [1997] ECR I–285.
[203] See e.g. Case 36/75 *Rutili* v. *Minister for the Interior* [1975] ECR 1219, paras. 12–13.

favourable treatment of nationals from other Member States is objectively justified. An interesting example is provided by *Pastoors and Trans-Cap*.[204] There, the Court accepted that difference in treatment between Belgian nationals and nationals of other Member States with regard to penalties for breach of Community transport legislation was objectively justified although on the facts it found the Belgian measures disproportionate.

The Court has held that the rule of non-discrimination applies to all legal relationships in so far as these relationships, by reason either of the place where they are entered into or of the place where they take effect, can be located within the territory of the Community.[205] Thus, the fact that an artistic performance takes place outside the Community does not prevent the artist from invoking Article 12[6] with a view to prohibiting the unauthorized marketing of a reproduction of the performance in a Member State.[206]

Where national law discriminates in general against nationals of other Member States, the fact that it treats certain categories of nationals of those States equally with its own nationals does not deny the existence of discrimination. Thus, in *Gravier*, where Belgian law required from foreign but not from Belgian citizens a registration fee in relation to vocational training courses, it was no defence that Luxembourg nationals and foreign nationals paying taxes in Belgium were exempted from payment of the fee.[207]

In *Costa* v. *ENEL*[208] the Court referred to Article 12[6] as an argument to support the primacy of Community law. The reasoning of the judgment was that, if national law adopted after the Treaty came into force was capable of taking precedence over Community law, that would prejudice the uniform application of Community law and give rise to discrimination on grounds of nationality. In other words, the Court viewed Article 12[6] as an instrument contributing to the elimination of distortions of competition in the common market. However, distortions of competition which ensue from the fact that citizens are subject to the laws of different Member States cannot be undone by Article 12[6]. The Court has held that Article 12[6] does not cover disparities in treatment or distortions which may result from divergencies existing between the laws of the various Member States, so long as the latter affect all persons subject to them, in accordance with objective criteria and without regard to their nationality.[209] Similarly, in the absence of harmonization measures, the fact that the rules applied by one Member State are stricter than those applied by other Member States does not constitute a breach of

---

[204] See also *Hayes* v. *Kronenberger GmbH* op.cit.; Case C–29/95 *Pastoors and Trans-Cap* [1997] ECR I–285, discussed below 2.8.2. Case 24/86 *Blaizot* v. *University of Liège and Others* [1988] ECR 379, paras. 22–3; and in the context of staff cases: Case 147/79 *Hochstraas* v. *Court of Justice* [1980] ECR 3005, para. 7.

[205] *Walrave* v. *Union Cycliste Internationale*, op.cit., para. 28.   [206] *Phil Collins*, op.cit.

[207] Case 293/89 *Gravier* v. *City of Liège* [1985] ECR 593, para. 14.

[208] Case 6/64 [1964] ECR 585, at 594.

[209] Case 14/68 *Wilhelm* v. *Bundeskartellamt* [1969] ECR 1.

Article 12[6], as long as those rules are applied equally to every person under the jurisdiction of that State.[210] Nor does Article 12[6] prohibit differences in treatment on the basis of the place where traders are established. In *Oebel*,[211] the Court found that German rules which prohibited night work in bakeries did not infringe Article 12[6] since it applied to all persons subject to them irrespective of nationality. It held that national rules which make no distinction, directly or indirectly, on the ground of nationality do not infringe Article 12[6], even if they affect the competitiveness of the traders subject to them.[212] Similarly, in another case, the Court held that Luxembourg rules which prohibited exporters from obtaining payment for their exports in banknotes and required foreign currency payable to them to be paid through a bank and to be exchanged on the regulated foreign exchange market were not in breach of Article 12[6] even though they might place exporters subject to them in a disadvantage *vis-à-vis* their competitors established in other Member States where different rules applied.[213] Also, Article 12[6] does not apply where the legislation of a Member State favours certain national undertakings in relation to other national undertakings,[214] unless that difference in treatment amounts to indirect discrimination on grounds of nationality.

2.8.2. Scope of application

Article 12[6] prohibits discrimination only 'within the scope of application of this Treaty'. The case law has interpreted those terms particularly broadly and, according to one view, the scope of application of Article 12[6] is wider than the scope of application of the general principle of equality as an unwritten principle of law.[215] In areas which fall outside the scope of application of the Treaty for the purposes of Article 12[6], a Member State may discriminate against nationals of other Member States. It may also discriminate between nationals from other Member States, i.e. grant more favourable treatment to citizens from Member State A than to citizens from Member State B.

The Court has had the opportunity to examine the scope of application of Article 12[6] in a number of cases concerning access of Community nationals to

---

[210] Case 223/86 *Pesca Valentia* v. *Minister for Fisheries and Forestry* [1988] ECR 83, para. 18; Joined Cases 185–204/78 *Van Dam* [1979] ECR 2345, para. 10. See also Case C–379/92 *Criminal proceedings against Peralta* [1994] ECR I–3453, para. 48. The absence of harmonization of national laws in a certain area, however, does not necessarily remove that area from the scope of application of the Treaty for the purposes of Article 12[6]. As the Advocate General stated in *Phil Collins*, op.cit., p. 5166 it is precisely where no harmonization has been achieved that the principle of national treatment assumes special importance.

[211] Case 155/80 [1981] ECR 1993. See also Case 31/78 *Bussone* v. *Italian Ministry for Agriculture and Forestry* [1978] ECR 2429, para. 38.

[212] *Oebel*, op.cit., para. 8.

[213] Case 308/86 *Criminal proceedings against Lambert* [1988] ECR 4369.

[214] *Pesca Valentia*, op.cit., para. 20.

[215] See *R* v. *Ministry of Agriculture, Fisheries and Food, ex parte First City Trading Limited* [1997] 1 CMLR 250 per Laws J and the discussion above in Ch. 1. 6.4.

education in the host State. In *Gravier* v. *City of Liège*,[216] Belgian law required students who did not possess Belgian nationality to pay a registration fee ('minerval') as a condition of attending vocational training courses. The Court held that, although educational organization and training was a matter for the Member States, access to vocational training fell within the scope of the Treaty. Consequently, the imposition on students who are nationals of other Member States of a registration fee as a condition of access to vocational training, where the same fee is not imposed on students who are nationals of the host Member State, constitutes discrimination prohibited by Article 12[6]. The judgment is important because it extended the application of the principle of non-discrimination to education, a sensitive area which until then was thought not to be affected directly by Community law. Indeed, various governments argued in their submissions to the Court that Member States have special responsibilities towards their own nationals in the field of education which may justify more favourable treatment. The judgment has had considerable financial repercussions as it forced Member States to rethink the educational budget.[217]

Subsequently, in *Blaizot*,[218] the Court took a broad view of what constitutes vocational training, holding that it includes university studies. In view of the serious economic implications of its ruling, however, and the fact that until then it had generally been assumed that vocational training did not include university studies, the Court limited the retroactive effect of its judgment.[219]

In *Lair* v. *Universitat Hannover*,[220] the Court drew a distinction between tuition fees and maintenance grants. In accordance with the judgment in *Gravier*, assistance granted by the host State to cover tuition fees falls within the scope of Article 12[6]. By contrast, assistance granted to students for maintenance falls in principle outside the scope of the Treaty for the purposes of Article 12[6]. That is so because such assistance is a matter of educational policy, which as such is not included in the spheres entrusted to the Community institutions, and also a matter of social policy, which falls within the competence of the Member States in so far as it is not covered by specific provisions of the Treaty.[221]

---

[216] Case 293/89 [1985] ECR 593. See also now Articles 149[126] and 150[127] EC.

[217] For the aftermath of *Gravier*, see Case 309/85 *Barra* v. *Belgium and another* [1988] ECR 355.

[218] Case 24/86 *Blaizot* v. *University of Liège and Others* [1988] ECR 379.

[219] In *Blaizot* the Court held that vocational training includes university studies whether such studies lead directly to a professional qualification or provide the academic knowledge for the pursuit of a profession. It excluded only courses of study which, because of their particular nature, were intended for persons wishing to improve their general knowledge rather than prepare themselves for an occupation. See also Case 263/86 *Belgian State* v. *Humbel* [1988] ECR 5365; cf. the notion of 'vocational school' in Article 7(3) of Regulation No. 1612/68 which was held not to cover universities: see Case 39/86 *Lair* v. *Universitat Hannover* [1988] ECR 3161, para. 26. See further Case 242/87 *Commission* v. *Council* [1989] ECR 1425.

[220] [1988] ECR 3161. See also Case 197/86 *Brown* v. *Secretary of State for Scotland* [1988] ECR 3205.

[221] *Lair*, op.cit., para. 15. Where a Member State provides a general student grant, it is for the national court to determine what proportion of the grant is intended to cover the cost of access to vocational training: Case C–357/89 *Raulin* [1992] ECR I–1027, para. 28.

The distinction between tuition fees and maintenance grants can be justified on the ground that the first are more closely related to access to vocational training and less closely related to social policy than the second.[222] The distinction draws a balance between, on the one hand, the desire to broaden the scope of Article 12[6] with a view to extending the protection afforded to non-nationals and, on the other hand, the concern to provide workable solutions which do not cause major upheaval to the educational policies of Member States. Since maintenance grants fall outside the scope of the Treaty for the purposes of Article 12[6],[223] it follows that a Community national may claim a maintenance grant for university training in the host State only in his capacity as a worker or as a member of the family of a worker. Those rights are provided for in Article 7(2) and Article 12 of Regulation No. 1612/68[224] respectively, which have been interpreted generously by the Court.[225] In *Brown*, however, the Court held that a person who has acquired the status of a worker in the host State exclusively as a result of his being admitted to university to undertake studies may not rely on his status as worker in order to claim a maintenance grant. That would be an abusive exercise of rights guaranteed by Community law since his employment relationship is merely ancillary to the studies to be financed by the grant.[226]

The judgments in the above cases leave open a number of issues. An interesting question is whether, and if so under what circumstances, a Member State may provide financial assistance for the payment of tuition fees to non-resident nationals without extending it to nationals of other Member States. The issue also arises what obligations Article 12[6] imposes on the Member State of origin. The cases discussed so far concern obligations imposed on the State of destination. Since financial assistance to cover tuition fees falls within the scope of Article 12[6], could it be said that a Community national has a right to receive such assistance from his Member State of origin to study in another Member State where such assistance is available to him to study in the State of origin? The answer seems to be in the negative. Where a Member State refuses financial assistance to one of its nationals in order to enable him to study in another Member State, it does not discriminate against him on grounds of nationality. It would be otherwise if the national intended to pursue studies in a private institution in another Member State, namely one which is not financed mainly by public funds. In such a case, the prospective

---

[222] In *Brown*, op.cit., at 3230, Slynn AG explained the distinction on the ground that allowances covering maintenance costs do not have a sufficiently direct link with access to the course of study itself.

[223] In *Lair* the Court expressly stated that maintenance grants fell outside the scope of the Treaty for the purposes of Article 6 'at the present stage of development of Community law': para. 15. See in this context Articles 126 and 127 as amended by TEU.

[224] OJ English Spec.Ed., 1968 II, p. 475.

[225] On Article 7(2), see *Lair*, op.cit.; on Article 12, see Joined Cases 389 and 390/87 *Echternach and Moritz* v. *Netherlands Minister for Education and Science* [1989] ECR 723; Case C–308/89 *Di Leo* v. *Land Berlin* [1990] ECR I–4185; Case C–7/94 *Gaal* [1995] ECR I–1031.

[226] *Brown*, op.cit., para. 27.

student would be a recipient of services and would be entitled to take advantage of Article 49[59], at least as regards financial assistance to cover tuition fees.[227]

The trend towards a wide interpretation of Article 12[6] was confirmed in *Cowan*.[228] In that case, it was held that a Community national who travels to another Member State as a tourist may benefit in his capacity as a recipient of services from a scheme to grant compensation to the victims of violent crime. The Court stated as follows:[229]

When Community law guarantees a natural person the freedom to go to another Member State the protection of that person from harm in the Member State in question, on the same basis as that of nationals and persons residing there, is a corollary of the freedom of movement. It follows that the prohibition of discrimination is applicable to recipients of services within the meaning of the Treaty as regards protection against the risk of assault and the right to obtain financial compensation provided for by national law when that risk materializes. The fact that the compensation at issue is financed by the Public Treasury cannot alter the rules regarding the protection of the rights guaranteed by the Treaty.

The rationale which underlies *Cowan* is the same with that of the education cases, namely, that the prohibition of discrimination on grounds of nationality extends to situations which are not related to the exercise of economic rights strictly understood.[230]

Subsequently, in *Phil Collins*[231] the Court held that copyright and related rights fall within the scope of application of the Treaty for the purposes of Article 12[6]. German law enabled German nationals to oppose the unauthorized reproduction of their musical performances irrespective of the territory where the performance took place but limited such protection of foreign artists to performances given in Germany. Referring to its previous case law, the Court held that exclusive rights conferred by literary and artistic property affect trade in goods and services as well as competition in the Community. It followed that, such rights, although governed by national law, are subject to the requirements of the Treaty and fall within the scope of its application. The Court held that, giving effect to the principle of non-discrimination, German courts must enable performing artists of other Member States to prohibit the marketing in the national territory of unauthorized performances given outside German soil. The Court held that the principle of non-discrimination can be relied on by an artist of a Member State or his successor in title. As the Advocate General pointed out, even in the case of an outright assignment without any provision for the payment of royalties, it would be wrong to discriminate on the basis of the nationality of the performer, who is the original right holder, since the indirect victim of discrimination remains the performer

---

[227] See Case C–109/92 *Wirth* [1993] ECR I–6447, esp. at 6460–3 per Darmon AG.

[228] Case 186/87 *Cowan* v. *Tresor Public* [1989] ECR 195.   [229] Para. 17.

[230] It may be said that that accords with the general approach of the Court to the interpretation of Treaty provisions on the free movement of workers. See e.g. Case 44/65 *Hessische Knappschaft* v. *Maison Singer* [1966] ECR 965.

[231] Joined Cases C–92 and C–326/92 [1993] ECR I–5145.

himself.[232] Although *Phil Collins* referred only to copyright and related rights, there can be no doubt that intellectual property rights in general fall within the scope of application of the Treaty and, where they are not covered by any specific provision, are subject to Article 12[6].

In a number of recent cases the Court has had the opportunity to examine the compatibility with Article 12[6] of national rules pertaining to judicial proceedings. In *Data Delecta and Forsberg*[233] in issue was a rule of Swedish law which required a foreign plaintiff not resident in Sweden to furnish security to guarantee payment of the costs of the judicial proceedings which the plaintiff might be ordered to pay. The Court held that the Swedish rule was liable to affect the economic activities of traders from other Member States. Although it was not, as such, intended to regulate an activity of commercial nature, its effect was to place such traders in a less advantageous position than Swedish nationals as regards access to domestic courts. The Court pointed out that a corollary of the free movement of goods and services is that traders from other Member States must be able, in order to resolve any disputes arising from their economic activities, to bring actions in the courts of a Member State in the same way as nationals of that State. It held that Article 12[6] prohibits a Member State from requiring a person established in another Member State, who has brought before one of its own courts an action against one of its own nationals, to lodge security for the costs of those proceedings where no such requirement is imposed on persons established in the first Member State and where the action is concerned with the exercise of fundamental freedoms guaranteed by Community law.

It follows from *Data Delecta* that any rule of national law, whether substantive or procedural, which bears even an indirect effect on trade in goods and services between Member States falls within the scope of Community law for the purposes of the application of Article 12[6].[234] *Data Delecta* goes further than the previous judgment in *Mund & Fester*[235] where the Court had found incompatible with Community law a German rule which authorized the seizure of assets of a foreign plaintiff as a precautionary measure. In that case the German provision was held to be incompatible with Articles 12[6] and 293[220] of the Treaty in combination with the Brussels Convention. In *Data Delecta* the Court held, following *Cowan* and *Phil Collins*, that the right to equal treatment cannot be made subject to the existence of international agreements concluded by the Member States.

Subsequently, however, in *Hayes* v. *Kronenberger GmbH*[236] the Court hinted that the Brussels and the Lugano Conventions may be relevant in this respect. Germany

---

[232] Op.cit., at p. 5170.

[233] Case C–43/95 [1996] ECR I–4661. For previous cases, see Case C–20/92 *Hubbard* [1993] ECR I–3777; Case C–398/92 *Mund & Fester* [1994] ECR I–467.

[234] *Data Delecta*, op.cit., para. 15.

[235] Case C–398/92 *Mund & Fester* [1994] ECR I–467; see also Case C–20/92 *Hubbard* [1993] ECR I–3777.

[236] Case C–323/95 [1997] ECR I–1711.

argued that the requirement that the plaintiff must lodge security for judicial costs is justified where an order for judicial costs cannot be enforced in the country of the plaintiff's domicile. In such a case, the requirement to lodge security is designed to avoid a foreign plaintiff being able to bring proceedings without running any financial risk should he lose his case. The Court pointed out that not all Member States are parties to the Brussels and to the Lugano Conventions and that, as a result, as between some Member States, it will be more difficult to enforce an order for costs made in a Member State against non-residents. It held, however, that it was not necessary for the purposes of the proceedings in issue to consider whether that situation might warrant the imposition of security for costs on non-residents where such risk existed. It focused on the German rule of procedure in question which applied to foreign nationals. It held that, in so far as that rule imposed different treatment depending on the plaintiff's nationality, it ran counter to the principle of proportionality. On the one hand, it could not secure payment of judicial costs in every trans-frontier case since security could not be required from a German plaintiff not residing in Germany and having no assets there. On the other hand, it was excessive because a non-German plaintiff who resided and had assets in Germany could also be required to furnish security. Notably, in *Chequepoint SARL* v. *McClelland and another*,[237] the English Court of Appeal held that a court order requiring an impecunious foreign company ordinarily resident in another Member State to provide security for costs was not discriminatory contrary to Community law since an English company in a similar position would be treated in the same manner and might be required to provide security for costs under the Companies Act 1985.

The application of Article 12[6] to criminal proceedings was examined in *Pastoors and Trans-Cap*.[238] Belgian law provided for criminal penalties for breach of Community social regulations in the field of road transport. Under the Belgian rules, a person found in breach of Regulation No. 3820/85 or 3821/85 had the option to pay immediately a fine of 10,000 francs per breach or face criminal proceedings. A person who did not have a permanent residence in Belgium however could not choose the second option unless he lodged a deposit of 15,000 per breach to cover the amount of any fine that might eventually be imposed and the legal costs of the proceedings. Failure to do so led to the impounding of his vehicle at his risk and expense. The Court started by pointing out that, although Belgian law established differential treatment on the basis of residence and not on nationality, it was liable to operate mainly to the detriment of foreign nationals and was therefore indirectly discriminatory. The Court accepted that it was objectively justified to require non-resident offenders to lodge a security. That requirement would prevent them from avoiding an effective penalty simply by declaring that they do not consent to the immediate levying of the fine and opting for criminal proceedings. It found the Belgian rules, however, contrary to the principle of proportionality. It

237 [1997] 2 All ER 384.
238 Case C–29/95 *Pastoors and Trans-Cap* [1997] ECR I–285.

pointed out that the sum of the deposit was 50 per cent higher than the fine payable immediately to extinguish prosecution. Also, a deposit was demanded separately in relation to each infringement with which the offender was charged. However, where various infringements are simultaneously found to exist, they give rise to a single set of proceedings. The Court concluded that a national measure which requires the payment of such sums, in default of which the vehicle is impounded, was excessive.

More recently, in *Bickel and Franz*,[239] the Advocate General opined that Article 12[6] requires a Member State which grants residents in part of its territory the right to use a language other than its official language in criminal proceedings against them to extend that right to nationals of other Member States visiting that territory, if they have that other language as their mother tongue.

The conclusion to be drawn from the above cases is that by creative case law the Court of Justice has transformed Article 12[6] from a general, programmatic, provision to an autonomous source of rights and obligations beyond the sphere of the internal market strictly understood which encompasses a diverse range of situations and whose outer limits remain elusive. In some areas, such as education, the normative prohibition of discrimination on grounds of nationality has been used as a vehicle to extend the scope of Community law to areas traditionally considered immune from Community obligations and has acted as the precursor to future Community legislation. In other cases, such as *Phil Collins* and the cases on judicial costs, Article 12[6] has become an instrument for promoting equal standards of judicial protection in the host State.

2.8.3. Article 12[6], second paragraph

The second paragraph of Article 12[6] mandates the Council, to adopt rules designed to prohibit discrimination on grounds of nationality. Article 12[6], paragraph 2, was considered by the Court in the *Students' right of residence Directive* case.[240] The Parliament sought annulment of Directive 90/366 on the right of residence for students,[241] which had been adopted by the Council on the basis of Article 308[235], on the ground that it should have been adopted on the basis of the second paragraph of Article 12[6]. The Directive sought to provide students from other Member States with a right of residence in the host Member State for the duration of their studies. The Council argued that because the Directive extended the right of residence to the student's spouse and dependent children it

---

[239] Case C–274/96 *Criminal Proceedings against Bickel and Franz*, Opinion of 19 Mar. 1998 (Jacobs AG). The Opinion was followed by the Court: judgment of 24 Nov 1998.

[240] Case C–295/90 *Parliament* v. *Council* [1992] ECR I–4193.

[241] OJ 1990 L 180/30. Until that Directive was adopted, the second paragraph of Article 6 had never been used as the only legal basis for a Community act although it had occasionally been used in combination with other provisions. See e.g. Regulation No. 2001/76 laying down a common structural policy for the fishing industry, OJ 1976 L 20/19.

conferred upon students a freedom of movement which was similar to that of migrant workers and went beyond a right of residence for the purposes of vocational training. Consequently, the Council claimed that Article 12[6] provided an insufficient basis for the adoption of the Directive. The Court held that measures adopted under the second paragraph of Article 12[6] need not be limited to the implementation of the right of non-discrimination strictly understood but may also cover aspects which are necessary for the effective exercise of that right. It pointed out that the right of residence conferred upon the spouse and dependent children was an essential element for the genuine exercise of the student's right to residence. On that basis, the Court held that the Council should have adopted the Directive on the basis of Article 12[6]. In compliance with the ruling, the Council subsequently adopted another Directive containing identical provisions on the correct legal basis.[242]

Finally, it should be noted that the Treaty of Amsterdam has amended the procedure in accordance with which measures under Article 12[6] may be adopted. Whereas previously the co-operation procedure was applicable, the second paragraph of Article 12 now refers to the co-decision procedure which gives to the Parliament's an enhanced role in the decision-making process.

---

[242] Directive 93/96, OJ 1993 L317/59.

3

The Principle of Proportionality: Review of Community Measures

3.1. The principle of proportionality and its function in Community law

In its most abstract level, the principle of proportionality requires that action undertaken must be proportionate to its objectives. The notion of proportionality goes back to ancient times[1] but as a general principle of law in modern legal systems it is inspired by ideas underpinning liberal democracy, in particular, the concern to protect the individual vis-à-vis the State and the premise that regulatory intervention must be suitable to achieve its aims.[2] The principle was developed in continental legal systems, especially in Germany and France, in the twentieth century. Its development as a ground of review can be seen as the judiciary's response to the growth of administrative powers and the augmentation of administrative discretion.[3] The principle found only limited expression in the Treaty of Rome[4] but has been developed by the Court as a fundamental principle deriving from the rule of law[5] and requiring in particular that 'the individual should not have his freedom of action limited beyond the degree necessary in the public interest'.[6] Although the principle is particularly important in the field of economic law, in its case law the

---

[1] The spirit of the principle is encapsulated in the ancient Greek dictum 'pan metron ariston'.

[2] Schwarze, op.cit., p. 679.

[3] In German law it is known as *Verhaltnismassigkeit* and, according to the case law of the Federal Constitutional Court, it underlies certain provisions of the Basic Law. For a review of the principle in Community law and the laws of the Member States, see N. Emiliou, *The Principle of Proportionality in European Law* (Kluwer, 1996); Schwarze pp. 680 *et seq.* See further Tridimas, 'The Principle of Proportionality in Community Law: From the Rule of Law to Market Integration' (1996) 31 *The Irish Jurist*, 83; G. de Bùrca, 'The Principle of Proportionality and its Application in EC Law' (1993) 13 YEL 105. For the application of the principle in the European Convention of Human Rights, see, *inter alia,* Schwarze, op.cit., pp. 704 *et seq.*; C. Picheral and A. D. Olinga, 'La théorie de la marge d'appréciation dans la jurisprudence récente de la Cour européenne des droits de l'homme' (1995) R Trim. Dr.Homme 567; L. Adamovich, 'Marge d'appréciation du législateur et principe de proportionnalité dans l'appréciation des "restrictions prévues par la loi" au regard de la Convention européenne des droits de l'homme' (1991) R Trim.Dr. Homme, 291.

[4] See now Article 5(3)[3b(3)]. Among the provisions which have been held in the case law to incorporate the principle are Articles 34(2)[40(3)], 134[115], 284[213], and those providing for derogations to the fundamental freedoms, i.e. Articles 30[36], 39(4)[48(3)], 46[56], 66[55].

[5] Case 4/73 *Nold* v. *Commission* [1974] ECR 491, at 513–14 per Trabbucchi AG.

[6] Case 11/70 *Internationale Handelsgesellschaft* v. *Einfuhr- und Vorratsstelle Getreide* [1970] ECR 1125 at 1147 per de Lamothe AG.

Court has applied it in diverse areas including, for example, remedies and interim measures,[7] and external trade,[8] so that it now permeates the whole of the Community legal system. As Jacobs AG stated 'there are few areas of Community law, if any at all, where [the principle of proportionality] is not relevant'.[9] The only cases where the Court appears reluctant to apply the principle is where it is invoked in an attempt to justify a failure to comply with Community law.[10] The principle is invoked by litigants more often than any other general principle of Community law.

The principle of proportionality applies both to Community and to national measures and covers both legislative and administrative action. It can be said that in Community law, it fulfils three primary functions:

- It is used as a ground of review of Community measures;
- It is used as a ground of review of national measures affecting one of the fundamental freedoms;
- By virtue of Article 5(3)[3b(3)] of the Treaty, it governs the exercise by the Community of its legislative competence.

It should be emphasized that the underlying interests which proportionality seeks to protect in each of the above cases are different. As a result, the intensity of review exercised by the Court varies considerably. Where proportionality is invoked as a ground of review of Community policy measures, the Court is called upon to balance a private *vis-à-vis* a public interest. The underlying interest which the principle seeks to protect is the rights of the individual but, given the discretion of the legislature, review of policy measures is based on the so-called 'manifestly inappropriate test'. The Court will not strike down a measure unless it considers that it is manifestly inappropriate to achieve its objectives. By contrast, where proportionality is invoked in order to challenge the compatibility with Community law of national measures affecting one of the fundamental freedoms, the Court is called upon to balance a Community vis-à-vis a national interest. The principle is applied as a market integration mechanism and the intensity of review is much stronger. It is based, at least in most cases, on the notion of 'necessity'exemplified by the 'less restrictive alternative' test. A national measure which affects the fundamental freedoms of the Treaty will be found incompatible with Community law unless it is

---

[7] See e.g. Case C–12/95 P *Transactiones Maritimas and Others* v. *Commission* [1995] ECR I–467; C–149/95 P(R) *Commission* v. *Atlantic Container Line and Others* [1995] ECR I–2165.

[8] See e.g. Case C–367/89 *Aime Richardt* [1991] ECR I–4621; Case C–111/92 *Lange* [1993] I–4677; Case C–26/90 *Wunsche* [1991] ECR I–4961; Case 112/80 *Durbeck* v. *Hauptzollamt Frankfurt am Main-Flughafen* [1981] ECR 1095.

[9] Case C–120/94 *Commission* v. *Greece* (*FYROM case*) [1996] I–ECR 1513, 1533.

[10] Thus, in relation to State aids, the Court has held that the obligation to recover unlawful State aid with interest cannot in principle be regarded as disproportionate to the objectives of the provisions of the EC Treaty: Case 142/87 *Belgium* v. *Commission* (*Tubemeuse* case) [1990] ECR I–959, para. 66; Case C–305/89 *Italy* v. *Commission* (*Alfa Romeo* case) [1991] ECR I–1603, para. 41; Case C–169/95 *Spain* v. *Commission* [1997] ECR I–135, para. 47.

necessary to achieve a legitimate aim and provided that that aim cannot be achieved by other measures which less restrict intra–Community trade.[11]

By virtue of Article 5(3)[3b(3)] of the EC Treaty, added by the Treaty on European Union, proportionality has been elevated to a fundamental principle underpinning the constitutional order of the Community. Although it is doubtful whether that provision has added anything to the existing case law, it was included in the Treaty with a view to protecting the interests of Member States rather than the interests of the individual. It seems, however, that the intensity of review is, in general, no different from when the principle is applied as a ground of review of Community measures for the protection of the individual.[12]

As a ground of review of Community measures, proportionality has been applied in the case law mainly in the following areas: agricultural law, measures concerning the external trade of the Community, and measures imposing charges, penalties and sanctions. The present chapter discusses the application of the principle to Community measures. Its application to national measures is examined in the next chapter. There is no attempt to deal exhaustively with the case law. The application of the principle in diverse areas is illustrated selectively.

3.2. What does proportionality entail?

The principle of proportionality requires that a measure must be appropriate and necessary to achieve its objectives. According to the standard formula used by the Court, in order to establish whether a provision of Community law is consonant with the principle of proportionality, it is necessary to establish whether the means it employs to achieve the aim correspond to the importance of the aim and whether they are necessary for its achievement.[13] Thus, the principle comprises two tests: a test of suitability and a test of necessity. The first refers to the relationship between the means and the end. The means employed by the measure must be suitable, namely reasonably likely, to achieve its objectives. The second is one of weighing competing interests. The Court assesses the adverse consequences that the measure has on an interest worthy of legal protection and determines whether those consequences are justified in view of the importance of the objective pursued. It has been said that the application of the principle of proportionality entails in effect a three-part test.[14] First, it must be established whether the measure is suitable to achieve a

---

[11] See below, Ch. 4.　　　　　　　　　　　　　　　　　　　　[12] See below p. 118

[13] See e.g. Case 66/82 *Fromançais* v. *Forma* [1983] ECR 395, para. 8; Case 15/83 *Denkavit Nederland* v. *Hoofdproduktschap voor Akkerbouwprodukten* [1984] ECR 2171, para. 25; Case 47/86 *Roquette Frères* v. *ONIC* [1987] ECR 2889, para. 19; Case 56/86 *Société pour l' exportation des sucres* [1987] ECR 1423, para. 28; Case 281/84 *Zuckerfabrik Bedburg* v. *Council* [1987] ECR 49, para. 36; Case C–358/88 *Oberhausener Kraftfutterwerk Wilhelm Hopermann GmbH* v. *Bundesanstalt für landwirtschaftliche Marktordnung* [1990] ECR I–1687, para. 13.

[14] G. De Bùrca, op.cit., at 113. See also C. Tomuschat, 'Le principe de proportionnalite: Quis iudicabit?' (1977) 13 CDE 97.

legitimate aim (test of suitability). Secondly, it must be established whether the measure is necessary to achieve that aim, namely, whether there are other less restrictive means capable of producing the same result (the least restrictive alternative test). Thirdly, even if there are no less restrictive means, it must be established that the measure does not have an excessive effect on the applicant's interests (proportionality *stricto sensu*). The tripartite test has received some judicial support[15] but in practice the Court does not distinguish in its analysis between the second and the third test. Also, as it will be shown, in some cases the Court finds that a measure is compatible with proportionality without searching for less restrictive alternatives or even where such alternatives seem to exist. The essential characteristic of the principle is that the Court performs a balancing exercise between the objectives pursued by the measure in issue and its adverse effects on individual freedom.

The principle of proportionality requires that the burdens imposed on an individual must not exceed what is necessary to achieve the objectives pursued. In assessing what is necessary, account must be taken of the specific circumstances of the case. Capotorti AG has stated that whether a measure exceeds what is necessary must be appraised in the light of the economic and social conditions, having regard to the means available.[16] Clearly, however, that does not prevent the Community legislature from adopting rules of general application. The Court has held that although, in exercising their powers, the Community institutions must ensure that the amounts which commercial operators are charged are no greater than is required to achieve the desired objective, it does not necessarily follow that that obligation must be measured in relation to the individual situation of any one particular group of operators. Given the multiplicity and complexity of economic circumstances, such an evaluation would not only be impossible to achieve but would also create perpetual uncertainty in the law.[17]

Proportionality as a ground of review differs from misuse of powers in that it involves an objective rather than a subjective test. In applying proportionality, the Court performs a balancing exercise guided by the tests of suitability and necessity. By contrast, in order to establish that an act is vitiated by misuse of powers the applicant must prove that the institution which adopted the act did so in order to pursue a purpose other than that which it is lawfully entitled to pursue. The allegation of misuse of powers therefore, unlike proportionality, involves an enquiry as to the motives of the author of the act.[18]

---

[15] See the Opinion of Van Gerven AG in Case C–159/90 *SPUG* v. *Grogan* [1991] ECR I–4685 and the Opinion of Mischo AG in Case C–331/88 *Fedesa and Others* [1990] ECR I–4023, at 4051—see below p. 102.

[16] Case 114/76 *Bela-Muhle* v. *Grows-Farm* [1977] ECR 1211, at 1232 per Capotorti AG.

[17] See e.g. Case 5/73 *Balkan-Import-Export* v. *Hauptzollamt Berlin-Packhof* [1973] ECR 1091, para. 22; Case 9/73 *Schlüter* v. *Hauptzollamt Lorrach* [1973] ECR 1135, para. 22; Joined Cases 154/78 etc. *Valsabbia* v. *Commission* [1980] ECR 907, para. 118. For similar limitations on the principle of equal treatment, see above, p. 47.

[18] See Hartley, *The Foundations of European Community Law* (4th edn.) p. 417. Hartley's view received judicial endorsement in Joined Cases C–133, C–300 and C–362/93 *Crispoltoni* [1994] ECR I–4863, by Jacobs AG at 4874, and implicitly by the Court at paras. 23–9 of the judgment.

The application of the tests of suitability and necessity enable the Court to review not only the legality but also, to some extent, the merits of legislative and administrative measures. Because of that distinct characteristic, proportionality is often perceived to be the most far-reaching ground of review, the most potent weapon in the arsenal of the public law judge. It will be noted, however, that much depends on how strictly a court applies the tests of suitability and necessity and how far it is prepared to defer to the choices of the authority which has adopted the measure in issue. As already stated, in Community law, far from dictating a uniform test, proportionality is a flexible principle which is used in different contexts to protect different interests and entails varying degrees of judicial scrutiny. Subject to this caveat, it is correct to say that in general the principle of proportionality goes further than *Wednesbury* unreasonableness and facilitates the application of higher standards of judicial scrutiny than those traditionally followed by English courts.[19]

3.3. The development of the principle in Community law

As a ground of review, the principle of proportionality was first developed by the Court to counterbalance the effects of market-regulation measures restricting economic freedom adopted under the ECSC Treaty. In *Fédéchar v. High Authority*,[20] decided in 1956, the Court referred to 'a generally-accepted rule of law' according to which the 'reaction by the High Authority to illegal action must be in proportion to the scale of that action'. An indirect reference to the principle was made in *Mannesmann*, where the Court held that:[21]

the High Authority, in working out and applying the financial arrangements which it has established to safeguard the stability of the market, has . . . a duty to take account of the actual economic circumstances in which these arrangements have to be applied, so that the aims pursued may be attained under the most favourable conditions and with the smallest possible sacrifices by the undertakings affected.

The principle was applied in early years also in staff cases.[22] It was not until 1971, however, that proportionality was expressly relied on by the Court. The

---

[19] In *R v. Home Secretary, ex parte Brind* [1991] 1 AC 696, the House of Lords declined to accept the principle of proportionality as a ground of judicial review. Note, however, that decisions of local authorities as opposed to those of central government may be subject to a requirement of proportionality: *R v. Secretary of State for the Environment, ex parte NALGO* (1992) 5 Admin.LR 785, at 799–801. For a discussion of the principle in English law, see de Smith, Woolf and Jowell, *Judicial Review of Administrative Action*, pp. 593 *et seq.*; Craig, *Administrative Law*, pp. 411 *et seq.* See also Jowell and Lester, 'Proportionality: neither novel nor dangerous', in (1988) CLP Special Issue, *New Directions in Judicial Review*, 51; S. Boyron, 'Proportionality in English Administrative Law: A Faulty Translation?' (1992) 12 OJLS 237.

[20] Case 8/55 *Fédération Charbonnière Belgique v. High Authority* [1954–6] ECR 292 at 299.

[21] Case 19/61 *Mannesmann AG v. High Authority* [1962] ECR 357 at 370–1. See also Case 15/57 *Hauts Fourneaux de Chasse v. High Authority* [1957–8] ECR 211 at 228.

[22] See e.g. Case 18/63 *Wollast v. EEC* [1964] ECR 97 at 99.

opportunity became available in the field of agriculture. In *Internationale Handelsgesellschaft*,[23] it was argued that the system of deposits accompanying import and export licences[24] infringed the principle of proportionality. Although on the facts the Court found that no breach had occurred, the judgment firmly established the principle as a ground of review. Dutheillet de Lamothe AG stated that 'citizens may only have imposed on them, for the purposes of the public interest, obligations which are strictly necessary for those purposes to be attained'.[25] He took the view that the principle forms part of Community law in the field of agriculture by virtue of Article 40(3) (now 34(2)) of the EC Treaty and more widely by virtue of the general principles of Community law which derive from the national legal systems.[26] The distinctive characteristics of proportionality, which the Court elaborated in subsequent cases, were laid down in the judgment in that case. After *Internationale Handelsgesellschaft*, the application of the principle as a ground of review gradually expanded beyond administrative and executive discretion to cover policy measures of general application.

The development of the principle as a ground of review of national measures followed a somewhat different pattern. Already at an early stage, the case law made it clear that a national measure could not take advantage of a derogation from the fundamental freedoms unless it was strictly necessary to achieve the objectives in view.[27] Proportionality, however, began to acquire particular importance in the early 1980s. Two reasons account for that development. The first relates to the increase in litigation. As national jurisdictions became more familiar with Community law, litigation before the Court of Justice increased and so did correspondingly reliance on proportionality as a ground of challenging national measures. The second reason relates to a fundamental shift in judicial policy. The extension of Article 28[30] to encompass non-discriminatory national measures, firmly established in the seminal *Cassis de Dijon*,[28] brought a vast range of national provisions within the scope of that provision, which hitherto were considered 'safe' from the point of view of Community law. The emancipation of Article 28[30] from the notion of discrimination elevated proportionality to the determining criterion of compatibility with Community law. Similar developments followed in the context of the free movement of services and persons.[29]

---

[23] Case 11/70 *Internationale Handelsgesellschaft* v. *Einfuhr- und Vorratsstelle Getreide* [1970] ECR 1125. See also Case 25/70 *Einfuhr- und Vorratsstelle* v. *Koster* [1970] ECR 1161; Case 26/70 *Einfuhr- und Vorratsstelle* v. *Henck* [1970] ECR 1183.

[24] For the system of deposits, see below p. 104.

[25] *Internationale Handelsgesellschaft*, op.cit., 1146.   [26] Op.cit., 1147.

[27] See e.g. Case 41/74 *Van Duyn* v. *Home Office* [1974] ECR 1337.

[28] Case 120/78 *Rewe-Zentrale AG* v. *Bundesmonopolverwaltung für Branntwein* [1979] ECR 649.

[29] See e.g. Case C–76/90 *Säger* v. *Société Dennemeyer & Co. Ltd*. [1991] ECR I–4221, Case C–415/93 *Union Royale Belge des Sociétés de Football Association and Others* v. *Bosman and Others* [1995] ECR I–4921.

3.4. Agricultural law[30]

The reason why proportionality has exerted particular influence in the field of agricultural law is not difficult to establish. The common organization of the market consists typically of market-regulation measures which inevitably entail restrictions on economic freedom. The principle of proportionality has been developed by the Court in order to counterbalance the restrictive effects of such measures. In effect, the fundamental difficulty which the Community's political institutions, and reflectively the Court, have encountered in the sphere of the common agricultural policy is how to allocate burdens in declining and oversupplied markets. Proportionality has been applied primarily to the following types of measures:

- market regulation measures involving choices of economic policy;
- the Community deposit system;
- measures imposing charges, sanctions and penalties.

Selected cases in those areas will now be examined.

3.4.1. Market-regulation measures: The 'manifestly inappropriate' test

Although the Court is prepared to assess whether a measure is appropriate and necessary in view of all relevant circumstances and to scrutinize the way the institution concerned has exercised its discretion, where it comes to the adoption of legislative measures involving economic policy choices, it will defer to the expertise and the responsibility of the adopting institution exercising only 'marginal review'.[31] In *Fedesa*,[32] it held that the lawfulness of the prohibition of an economic activity is subject to the condition that the prohibitory measures are appropriate and necessary in order to achieve the objectives legitimately pursued by the legislation. Where there is a choice between several appropriate measures, recourse must be had to the least onerous and the disadvantages caused must not be disproportionate to the aims pursued. The Court qualified that principle, however, by stating:[33]

with regard to judicial review of compliance with those conditions it must be stated that in matters concerning the common agricultural policy the Community legislature has a discretionary power which corresponds to the political responsibilities given to it by Articles 40 and 43 of the Treaty. Consequently, the legality of a measure adopted in that sphere can be

---

[30] See further R. Barents, *The Agricultural Law of the EC*, Ch. 18; Emiliou, op.cit., Ch. 6 ; S. Neri, 'Le principe de proportionnalité dans la jurisprudence de la Court relative au droit communautaire agricole' (1981) 17 RTDE 652.

[31] See Schermers and Waelbroeck, *Judicial Protection in the European Communities* (Fifth edn.), paras. 310–13.

[32] Case C–331/88 *Fedesa and Others* [1990] ECR I–4023, para. 13.

[33] Op.cit., para. 14. See also Case 265/87 *Schräder* v. *Hauptzollamt Gronau* [1989] ECR 2237, paras. 21–2; Case 179/84 *Bozetti* v. *Invernizzi* [1985] ECR 2301, para. 30.

affected only if the measure is manifestly inappropriate having regard to the objective which the competent institution is seeking to pursue . . .

The expression 'manifestly inappropriate'[34] delineates what the Court perceives to be the limits of judicial function with regard to review of measures involving choices of economic policy.[35] In fact, the test is rather reminiscent of that which the Court is directed to follow under Article 33(1) of the ECSC Treaty.[36] The test grants to the Community institutions ample discretion and applies to both aspects of proportionality, i.e. suitability and necessity. Although in a number of cases the suitability and effectiveness of a measure has been contested,[37] argument concentrates usually on the requirement of necessity. Necessity is more important because, in applying the principle of proportionality, the Court does not act as an appellate body exercising review of the merits but is concerned primarily with the restrictive effects of the measure on the freedom of the individual. The inquiry whether such restrictive effects are justified centres on their necessity to achieve the objective in view. In practice, review of suitability is closely linked to review of necessity and a measure which is clearly unsuitable to achieve its objectives cannot be justified and will be struck down by the Court.[38] In assessing whether a measure is suitable to achieve its objectives, it is relevant to consider the actual effects of the measure. But the fact that a measure has failed to attain its objectives in practice does not mean that it is manifestly inappropriate. The Court has held that the legality of a Community act cannot depend on retrospective considerations of its efficacy.[39]

In order to determine whether a measure is necessary, the Court is receptive to argument that the same objective may be attained by less restrictive means. The

[34] In other cases the Court has stated that the measure must not be 'patently' or 'manifestly unsuitable' to achieve its objectives. See Case 138/78 *Stölting* v. *Hauptzollamt Hamburg-Jonas* [1979] ECR 713, para. 7; Case 59/83 *Biovilac* v. *EEC* [1984] ECR 4057, para. 17.

[35] The test applies not only in relation to agricultural measures but in any area involving decisions of economic policy. See e.g. Joined Cases C–248 and C–249/95 *Sam Schiffahrt and Stapf* v. *Germany* [1997] ECR I–4475.

[36] Article 33(1) defines the jurisdiction of the Court in actions for judicial review against acts of the High Authority. It provides that 'the Court may not . . . examine the evaluation of the situation, resulting from economic facts or circumstances, in the light of which the High Authority took its decision or made its recommendations, save where the High Authority is alleged to have misused its powers or to have manifestly failed to observe the provisions of this Treaty or any rule of law relating to its application'. For the historical background to this provision, see Schermers and Waelbroeck, op.cit., para. 310. In Case 6/54 *Netherlands* v. *High Authority* [1954–6] ECR 103, at 115, the Court held that 'the term "manifest" within the meaning of Article 33 presupposes that a certain degree is reached in the failure to observe legal provisions so that the failure to observe the ECSC Treaty appears to derive from an obvious error in the evaluation . . . of the situation in respect of which the decision was taken'.

[37] See e.g. *Stölting*, op.cit.; *Schräder*, op.cit.; Joined Cases C–133/93, C–300/93 and C–362/93 *Crispoltoni* [1994] ECR I–4863.

[38] See e.g. Case C–368/89 *Crispoltoni I* [1991] ECR I–3695. In that case the Court held that a measure which retroactively fixed maximum quantities was incapable of achieving its objective of limiting production since production decisions had already been taken by the producers before its adoption.

[39] Case 40/72 *Schroeder* v. *Germany* [1973] ECR 125, para. 14. See also Joined Cases C–133/93, C–300/93 and C–362/93 *Crispoltoni* [1994] ECR I–4863, discussed below p. 98; Joined Cases C–267 to C–285/88 *Wuidart and Others* [1990] ECR I–435, para. 14.

case law suggests, however, that, in relation to policy measures, the Court does not apply the less restrictive alternative test scrupulously relying instead on some notion of reasonableness or arbitrary conduct. In *Fedesa*[40] it was claimed that the prohibition of certain hormones on health protection grounds was not necessary. The Court did not examine whether there were any less restrictive alternatives. It held that since the Council enjoyed discretion and had made no manifest error in considering that the prohibition was appropriate, it was also entitled to take the view that the objectives pursued could not be achieved by less onerous means. The less restrictive alternative argument has been unsuccessfully submitted in a number of other cases.[41]

The manifestly inappropriate test has been applied in particular to the following types of measures:

- measures seeking to control production;
- measures setting up a common organization of the market;
- measures prohibiting or restricting the use of certain products or substances;
- monetary compensatory amounts.

Some examples of the way the Court has used the manifestly inappropriate test and the solutions to which it has led will now be given.

3.4.2. Production control measures

Article 33[39] provides that one of the objectives of the common agricultural policy is to increase agricultural productivity. As a result of technological and legal factors, the Community moved into surplus production at a relatively early stage in the development of the common agricultural policy. Excessive growth had adverse consequences for everyone concerned, in particular, the producers, the agricultural markets, the economies of the Member States, and, not least, the Community budget. Faced with such difficulties, the Council and the Commission took measures with a view to controlling production. Since the mid-1970s various means have been employed, among which the introduction of a co-responsibility levy, maximum guaranteed quantities, and individual quotas allocated to producers.[42] Such measures have been challenged, mostly unsuccessfully, on grounds of proportionality.

---

[40] Op.cit.

[41] See e.g. the cases referred to above in n. 39 and also Case C–280/93 *Germany* v. *Council* (*Bananas* case) [1994] ECR I–4973; Case C–8/89 *Zardi* [1990] ECR I–2515; Case 138/79 *Roquette Frères* v. *Council* [1980] ECR 3333, per Reischl AG at 3380 *et seq.*

[42] Note in this context the redirection of the common agricultural policy since the 1990s and see the outline of new policy objectives by the Commission in 'The Development and Future of the Common Agricultural Policy', EC Bulletin, Suppl. 5/91.

3.4.2.1. Co-responsibility levy

A so-called co-responsibility levy was introduced by various Community regulations in an attempt to reduce surpluses in agricultural produce. Between 1975 and
1977 there was a considerable increase in surpluses of milk and milk products in the
Community. With a view to reducing those surpluses, the Council adopted
Regulation No. 1079/77[43] introducing a co-responsibility levy payable by producers. The amount of the levy was calculated by reference to the target price for
milk. In *Stölting* v. *Hauptzollamt Hamburg-Jonas*[44] it was argued that the levy was
inadequate to remedy the difficulties of disposal and to achieve a structural balance
in the market. After examining the characteristics of the levy, the Advocate General
stated that the adoption of Regulation No. 1079/77 indicated 'a choice of economic policy which [was] in certain respects regrettable', adding that his criticism
concerned only the expediency of the measure and did not affect its validity.[45] The
Court stated that the regulation was directed towards restraining production and
therefore, given the surpluses, it contributed to the attainment of the objective of
stabilizing the market. It added that the rate of the levy did not appear to be disproportionate. In *Schräder* v. *Hauptzollamt Gronau*,[46] it was argued that the co-
responsibility levy on cereals imposed by Council Regulation No. 1579/86[47] and
Commission Regulation No. 2040/86[48] was neither appropriate nor necessary to
stabilize the market on the ground that it affected less than half of the agricultural
produce concerned and that it caused a rise in the price of processed cereals, which
did not encourage reduction of surpluses. In dismissing those arguments, the Court
held:[49]

When the Community legislature introduced the levy . . . and fixed the rules for its application, it selected from the various possibilities open to it the one which seemed most appropriate for reducing the structural surpluses on the cereals market by exerting direct but
moderate pressure on the prices paid to cereals producers. Such a measure, which seeks to
limit supply by reducing prices for producers, must in principle be regarded as appropriate
to the objective of stabilizing agricultural markets, referred to in Article 39(1)(c) of the
Treaty, even if, because of certain exemptions, the measure does not affect all the products
in question.

On that basis, the Court concluded that the contested measure did not infringe the
principle of proportionality.

3.4.2.2. Maximum guaranteed quantities

The legality of the maximum guaranteed quantities system was put in issue in
Crispoltoni II[50] which concerned the Community regime governing the common
organization of the market in tobacco. With a view to controlling the increase in

---

[43] OJ 1977 L 131/6.   [44] Op.cit., n. 34.   [45] Op.cit., at 728 per Mayras AG.
[46] Op.cit., n. 33.   [47] OJ 1986 L 139/9.   [48] OJ 1986 L 173/65.
[49] Op.cit., para. 23.
[50] Joined Cases C–133/93, C–300/93 and C–362/93 *Crispoltoni* [1994] ECR I–4863.

Community production, Council Regulation No. 1114/88[51] provided for the annual fixing of a maximum guaranteed quantity for each variety of tobacco. For each percentage by which the maximum guaranteed quantity was exceeded, there would be a corresponding reduction in the intervention prices and the premiums up to a maximum reduction of 15 per cent. Some years after the regulation came into force, it was argued that the system of maximum guaranteed quantities was unsuitable to achieve its objectives since it had not in reality ensured compliance with the maximum guaranteed quantities. Italian producers argued that, in order to ensure that the guaranteed quantities were not exceeded, a system of individual quotas should have been instituted similar to that which was subsequently introduced by Council Regulation No. 2075/92.[52] The Court held that the mere fact that the system had proved ineffective was not sufficient to invalidate the regulation. When the Council adopted the regulation, it was entitled to consider, without making any manifest error of assessment, that a system based on maximum guaranteed quantities was less onerous for tobacco growers than a system based on individual quotas. Under the former, the production of growers was not limited since they could always sell their products to the intervention agencies, albeit at a reduced price or premium. Under the latter system, growers received no support for that part of their production which exceeded their individual quota.

An unsuccessful claim was also made in *Zardi*.[53] Community law provided for the collection of a levy from cereal producers as a condition for the placing of cereals on the market. The levy would be reimbursed in full only if production in the marketing year did not exceed the maximum guaranteed quantity. It was argued that it was not necessary to require payment of the levy as soon as the products were placed on the market since less restrictive means existed. The Court held, however, that collection of the levy in advance was likely, by reducing the price paid to producers, to persuade them not to increase production during the marketing year and that the Community legislature had not committed any manifest error of assessment in rejecting other options.

3.4.2.3. Individual quotas

The system of quotas imposed on the production of isoglucose was challenged in the second generation of the isoglucose cases.[54] It will be remembered that in the first isoglucose case, the Court annulled the production levy on isoglucose on the ground that it ran counter to the principle of equal treatment.[55] Following the annulment of the levy, the Council introduced a system of individual quotas. In

---

[51] OJ 1988 L 110/35.   [52] OJ 1992 L 215/70.
[53] Case C–8/89 [1990] ECR I–2515.
[54] For unsuccessful challenges on export quotas, see e.g. Case C–280/93 *Germany* v. *Council* [1994] ECR I–4973. Case C–241/95 *The Queen* v. *Intervention Board for Agricultural Produce ex parte Accrington Beef and Others* [1996] ECR I–6699.
[55] Joined Cases 103 and 145/77 *Royal Scholten Honig (Holdings) Ltd.* v. *Intervention Board for Agricultural Produce* [1978] ECR 2037, discussed above p. 49.

Roquette Frères v. *Council*[56] it was unsuccessfully argued that the system of quotas infringed the principle of proportionality in that it was excessively onerous. In a concisely reasoned judgment, the Court relied mainly on three arguments. First, it held that the introduction of a quota system was a usual procedure in Community law appropriate when necessary to control production. Secondly, in adopting measures of general interest, the Council could not have regard to the commercial choices and the internal policy of individual undertakings. Thirdly, the applicant had not used the quota allocated to it for the marketing year and was therefore unable to show that the introduction of the quota system had limited its production.[57]

3.4.2.4. The skimmed-milk cases

The principle of proportionality was successfully invoked to challenge production control measures in the skimmed-milk powder cases.[58] In an attempt to reduce stocks of skimmed-milk powder, accumulated as a result of overproduction of milk, Council Regulation No. 563/76[59] provided for the compulsory purchase of skimmed-milk powder by producers for use in feeding-stuffs. The compulsory purchase of powder was imposed at a price equal to about three times its value as animal feed. The Court annulled the regulation on two grounds. It stated that the obligation to purchase at such a disproportionate price was discriminatory. It also held that such an obligation was not necessary in order to attain the disposal of stocks of skimmed-milk powder.[60] The cases illustrate that the Court is prepared to engage in a cost-benefit analysis even in areas where the Community institutions enjoy a wide discretion. It is also instructive as regards the test of necessity. The Council argued that Regulation No. 563/76 was essential in order to reduce the accumulated 'mountain' of skimmed-milk powder since, if it had not been for the obligation to purchase, it would have been impossible for the surplus to be absorbed. The Court rejected that argument. Although it did not refer to any less restrictive alternatives, it came to the conclusion that the obligation to purchase at such disproportionate price was not necessary. The judgment implies that the imposition of an obligation to purchase at a lower price might have met the test of proportionality.[61]

Although the skimmed-milk powder cases can be taken as an indication that the Court is prepared to review the merits of economic policy decisions taken by the Community legislature, it should be acknowledged that the facts were exceptional,

---

[56] Case 138/79 [1980] ECR 3333. See also Case 139/79 *Maizena* v. *Council* [1980] ECR 3393. Note that in those cases, although the Court rejected the substantive grounds of review, it annulled the contested regulation on procedural grounds, namely, failure by the Council to consult the Parliament.

[57] *Roquette Frères*, op.cit., paras. 29–31. In *Maizena*, op.cit., para. 26, the Court relied more directly on the discretionary powers of the Council to reject the arguments for annulment.

[58] Case 114/76 *Bela-Mühle* v. *Grows-Farm* [1977] ECR 1211, Case 116/76 *Granaria* [1977] ECR 1247, Joined Cases 119 and 120/76 *Ölmühle and Becher* [1977] ECR 1269.

[59] OJ 1976 L 67/18.   [60] See *Bela-Mühle*, op.cit., para. 7.

[61] De Bùrca, op.cit., 121.

the contested regulation being an example of a legislative conundrum.[62] The cases are not an exception to the manifestly inappropriate test but rather an illustration of its application. As stated above, under the contested regulation, the purchase price of the powder was three times higher than that of the substances which it replaced. Furthermore, the breach of the principle of proportionality was closely linked to the breach of the principle of equality. The aim of the scheme being to sustain milk prices, its beneficiaries were milk producers who, in effect, were given preferential treatment at the expense of feeding-stuff producers and livestock owners. The Court did not balance only the Community interest in reducing stocks vis-à-vis the interest of feeding-stuff producers to use cheaper substances. It also balanced the interests of two separate categories of economic traders. It held that, in imposing on feeding-stuff producers the obligation to purchase skimmed-milk powder, the Council treated unfairly those producers vis-à-vis milk producers, stating that the 'obligation to purchase at such a disproportionate price constituted a discriminatory distribution of the burden of costs between the various agricultural sectors'.[63]

3.4.3. Establishment of a common organization of the market

Review is limited where, in establishing a common organization of the market, the Council has to reconcile divergent interests and thus select options 'within the context of the policy choices which are its own responsibility'.[64] Thus in *Germany* v. *Council*,[65] where the German Government sought the annulment of Council Regulation No. 404/93[66] setting up a common organization of the market in bananas, the Court refuted the argument that the regulation imposed a disproportionate burden on traders who traditionally marketed third country bananas by reducing their share of the market. It held that in adopting the regulation the Council had to reconcile the conflicting interests of those Member States which produced bananas and those which did not do so. The first category of States were concerned to ensure that their agricultural populations living in economically less-favoured areas were able to dispose of produce at acceptable prices and thus avoid social problems. The second category were primarily concerned to ensure that their consumers were supplied with produce at the best possible price.[67] In response to the argument that less onerous measures could achieve the desired result, the Court stated that it could not 'substitute its assessment for that of the Council as to the appropriateness or otherwise of the measures adopted by the Community legislature if those measures have not been proved to be manifestly inappropriate for

[62] *Quare* whether the milk powder purchase scheme would satisfy the *Wednesbury* test in English law.
[63] *Bela-Mühle*, op.cit., para. 7.
[64] C–280/93 *Germany* v. *Council (Bananas* case) [1994] ECR I–4973, para. 91.
[65] Op.cit. The case is also discussed above, p. 55. See also Case C–466/93 *Atlanta Fruchthandelsgesellschaft (II)* v. *Bundesamt Für Ernahrung und Forstwirtschaft* [1995] ECR I–3799.
[66] OJ 1993 L 47/1.
[67] C–280/93 *Germany* v. *Council* [1994] ECR I–4973, para. 92.

achieving the objective pursued'.[68] Where the adoption of a measure involves striking a balance between strongly conflicting national interests, the Court is prepared to defer to the choices made by the Council especially if, as in that case, the choice made expresses a hard-fought compromise between considerations of free market and considerations of protectionism.

3.4.4. Measures prohibiting or restricting the use of products or substances

In *Fedesa*[69] the Court was called upon to balance the financial interests of the traders concerned *vis-à-vis* considerations of health protection. The case concerned the validity of a Council directive which prohibited the use of certain hormones in livestock farming in the interests of public health. It was argued that the directive infringed the principle of proportionality in three respects. First, the outright prohibition of the hormones in question was inappropriate in order to attain the objectives of the directive, since it was impossible to apply in practice and led to the creation of a black market. Secondly, the prohibition was not necessary since consumer anxieties could be allayed by less restrictive measures such as information campaigns and labelling requirements. Thirdly, the prohibition entailed excessive disadvantages, in particular considerable financial losses on the part of the traders concerned. After emphasizing that in the sphere of agricultural policy the legality of a measure can be affected only if it is manifestly inappropriate, the Court came to the conclusion that the prohibition satisfied the test of proportionality. In response to the argument that it was not possible to apply the prohibition in practice, because the presence of natural hormones in all meat prevented the detection of the presence of the hormones prohibited by the directive, the Court held that adequate control methods existed to detect the presence of the prohibited hormones. Also, it was not obvious that the authorization of only one type of hormones, as suggested by the applicants, would be likely to prevent the emergence of a black market for dangerous but less expensive substances. Moreover, the Court stated that any system of partial authorization would require costly control measures whose effectiveness would not be guaranteed. With regard to the claim that the prohibition was not necessary, the Court attached particular importance to health protection, stating that 'the importance of the objectives pursued is such as to justify even substantial negative financial consequences for certain traders'.[70] It is clear that in *Fedesa* the Court attributed particular importance to the fact that the objective of the directive in issue was to protect public health. That also influenced Mischo AG who stated:[71]

As regards proportionality in the narrow sense, that is to say the weighing of damage caused to individual rights against the benefits accruing to the general interest, it should be stated

---

[68] Op.cit., para. 94.   [69] Op.cit. See also de Bùrca, op.cit., 117–20.
[70] At para. 16.   [71] [1990] ECR I–4051.

that the maintenance of public health must take precedence over any other consideration. Once the Council had taken the view, in the context of its discretionary power, that it could not ignore the doubts felt by many Member States, and a large proportion of public opinion, as to the harmlessness of these substances, it was entitled to impose financial sacrifices on the persons concerned.

Fedesa indicates that where issues of public health are involved, the Court concedes ample discretion to the Community institutions and applies the principle of proportionality laxly.[72] This contrasts with its strict approach in cases under Article 36 where claims of public health are made.[73] The reason for this variation in standards is to be found in the different functions that judicial review serves in either case. In reviewing policy measures adopted by the Community institutions, the Court seeks to safeguard the economic freedom of the individual but within the confines of the broad discretionary powers of the institutions inherent in the exercise of legislative power. The Community institutions have the benefit of the doubt. That is not the case with national measures restricting freedom of movement which, by the very reason of their effects on market integration, are viewed as suspect.

3.4.5. Monetary compensatory amounts

One of the earlier cases where the Court applied the manifestly inappropriate test concerned monetary compensatory amounts, the system of which was introduced by Council Regulation No. 974/71[74] to counterbalance the collapse of fixed exchange rates. In order to avoid inflationary effects caused by an abnormal influx of short-term speculative capital in early 1971, Germany and The Netherlands widened the margins of fluctuation for the exchange rates of their currencies in relation to their official parities. The *de facto* revaluation of those currencies was bound to create disturbances in agricultural trade which is based on a system of uniform prices. The prices of agricultural products continued to be determined by reference to the official parity of currencies but, following revaluation, transactions could take place according to the actual rate of exchange below the fixed prices laid down by Community regulations. To avoid distortion of prices, Regulation No. 974/71 authorized Member States to charge compensatory amounts on imports. In *Balkan Import-Export*,[75] amounts were charged on the importation into Germany of cheese from Bulgaria. It was argued that Regulation No. 974/71 ran counter to the principle of proportionality because the compensatory amounts were not based

[72] The same approach was subsequently followed in the politically sensitive *BSE* case, where the Court upheld emergency measures taken by the Community on health grounds giving priority to the protection of public health vis-à-vis economic and social interests. See Case C–180/96 R *United Kingdom* v. *Commission* [1996] ECR I–3903, esp. paras. 89–94. See also Case T–76/96 R *National Farmers' Union and Others* v. *Commission* [1996] ECR II–815.

[73] See e.g. Case 104/75 *De Peijper* [1976] ECR 613; Case 124/81 *Commission* v. *United Kingdom* (*UHT milk*) [1983] ECR 203, discussed below, pp. 134, 145.

[74] OJ 1971 L 106/1.

[75] Case 5/73 *Balkan Import-Export* v. *Hauptzollamt Berlin-Packhof* [1973] ECR 1091.

on any profit made by the importer on the rate of exchange but on the relationship between the official parity of the deutschmark and the dollar and its true parity, independently of the country of origin of the products. The Court accepted that since a general criterion was selected, it was possible that imports into Germany from countries whose currencies were fluctuating in relation to the deutschmark to an extent different from that of the dollar might be affected adversely by the compensatory amounts. However, it rejected the alternative methods of calculation of the compensatory amounts put forward by the applicant and came to the conclusion that, in opting for the system which was adopted by Regulation No. 974/71, the Council did not impose on traders burdens which were manifestly out of proportion to the object in view. The same reasoning was followed by the Court in other cases concerning monetary compensatory amounts decided at that time.[76]

It is interesting that in *Balkan Import-Export*, the Court applied the test of proportionality loosely. The preamble to Regulation No. 974/71 expressly stated that the compensatory amounts adopted should be limited to those strictly necessary to compensate the incidence of the monetary measures, namely the freeing of currencies from fixed exchange rates. However, the compensatory amounts imposed were based solely on the relationship between the official parity and the true parity of the deutschmark to the dollar. The result was that imports into Germany from countries the rate of exchange of whose currencies remained stable *vis-à-vis* the deutschmark were subjected to higher compensatory rates which could not be said to be 'strictly necessary'. Nonetheless, the Court refused to annul the regulation.[77] It seems that three considerations led the Court to that conclusion. The impracticality of the alternative methods of calculation suggested by the applicants; the pressing need to adopt corrective measures within a short period; and the assessment, implicit in the judgment of the Court, that although the system adopted could have adverse financial consequences on certain traders, those consequences were not beyond the sphere of commercial risks that economic operators could reasonably be expected to bear.

3.4.6. Administrative measures: Forfeiture of deposits and securities

In the case of administrative measures, the intensity of review is determined by criteria more exacting than the 'manifestly inappropriate' test. This is because, understandably, the Court is more willing to review the discretion of the administration than to question the policy choices made by the Community legislature. As

---

[76] See e.g. Case 9/73 *Schlüter* v. *Hauptzollampt Lörrach* [1973] ECR 1135; Case 10/73 *Rewe-Zentral* v. *Hauptzollamt Kehl* [1973] ECR 1175.

[77] In a different respect, the Court saw the system of monetary compensatory amounts as the least restrictive. It accepted that compensatory amounts constituted a partitioning of the market but held that, in the light of the aims of the common agricultural policy, diversions of trade which would be otherwise be caused by the freeing of exchange rates could be considered more damaging: *Balkan Import-Export*, op.cit., para. 29.

a principle of administrative law, proportionality requires that, where entitlement to a benefit is conditional upon the fulfilment of certain administrative requirements, failure to abide strictly by those requirements does not necessarily lead to the loss of benefit. Much depends on the specific circumstances of the case and the objectives of the requirements in issue. In one case where the granting of an export subsidy was conditional on the exportation of the total quantities of produce placed under supervision, it was held that, in the absence of bad faith, the fact that a negligible part of that quantity was missing was not material.[78] In other cases, however, the Court has taken a stricter view especially in relation to time limits.[79]

In the field of administrative law, the system of deposits has provided a fruitful area for the application of proportionality.[80] The purpose of a deposit is to ensure that a trader who gives an undertaking to the Commission in order to secure a benefit complies with that undertaking. Agricultural regulations typically make the issue of import and export licences subject to the lodging of a deposit, the purpose of which is to ensure that the export or import transaction will be fulfilled within the period of validity of the licence. Save in cases of *force majeure*, failure to carry out the transaction leads to forfeiture of the deposit.[81] *Internationale Handelsgesell-schaft*[82] put in issue the compatibility of the deposits system with the principle of proportionality. After explaining the objectives of the deposit system, the Court held that it was both necessary and appropriate to achieve its objectives and compared favourably with alternative systems. The Court stated that a system of fines imposed *a posteriori*, as suggested by the applicant, would involve considerable administrative and legal complications both at the stage of decision and execution, which were aggravated by the fact that the traders concerned may be beyond the reach of the national competent authorities by reason of their residence in another Member State.[83]

The Community administration is under a duty to take into account the specific circumstances of the persons affected by its decisions, and the indiscriminate character of a measure may infringe proportionality. In *Atalanta*,[84] Commission Regulation No. 1889/76,[85] laying down detailed rules for granting storage aid for pig meat, provided that the security would be wholly forfeit if the obligations imposed by the storage contract were not fulfilled. The Court held that the absolute nature of that provision ran counter to the principle of proportionality because it did not enable the penalty to be made commensurate with the degree of

---

[78] Case C–101/88 *Gausepohl* [1990] ECR I–23.

[79] See below p. 107.

[80] On the application of the principle to deposits and securities, see Schartze, pp. 727 *et seq.*; Emiliou, op.cit., pp. 206–23; W. Alexander, 'Perte de la caution en droit agricole communautaire' (1988) CDE 384.

[81] The notion of *force majeure* incorporates an element of proportionality; see Case 4/68 *Schwarzwaldmilch* v. *Einfuhr- und Vorratsstelle* [1968] ECR 377 at 385–6.

[82] Case 11/70 *Internationale Handelsgesellschaft* v. *Einfuhr- und Vorratsstelle Getreide* [1971] ECR 1125.

[83] Op.cit., para. 11, and see the analysis of the Advocate General, at 1147–52.

[84] Case 240/78 *Atalanta* v. *Produktschap voor Vee en Vlees* [1979] ECR 2137.

[85] OJ 1976, L 206, p. 82.

failure to implement the contractual obligations or with the seriousness of the breach of those obligations. *Maas*[86] concerned the validity of Article 20(1) of Commission Regulation (EEC) No. 1974/80,[87] laying down implementing rules in respect of certain food aid operations involving cereals and rice. Maas, a Belgian undertaking, had been declared successful tenderer for the supply of food aid to Ethiopia. It transported the goods to the intended destination but the intervention agency declared the security furnished forfeit, recording two violations. The undertaking had not shipped the goods within the period laid down by Community law and, contrary to Community rules, it had used vessels which were more than 15 years old. The Court held that forfeiture of the security was not justified since the shipment period had been exceeded by only a short time. It also held that Article 20(1) infringed the principle of proportionality in so far as it required that the security had to be wholly forfeit where the goods were transported in vessels which were more than 15 years old. The Court considered that that requirement was not of such importance as to justify total forfeiture.[88]

By contrast, the Court required strict compliance with the applicable requirements in *Beste Boter and Hoche*.[89] In issue was a Commission regulation which provided for the sale by tender of butter at reduced prices to processing undertakings. To ensure performance of the obligation to process, the regulation imposed the obligation to provide a deposit. The deposit would be forfeit even where the failure of the successful tenderer to fulfil his undertakings was not due to his own fault but to the fault of a subsequent purchaser of the product. The Court held that forfeiture was not a penalty. Its effect rather was to make the successful tenderer pay a total amount equivalent to the market price of the butter in accordance with the contractual obligation freely entered into, where the obligation to process was not fulfilled. On that basis, it concluded that forfeiture did not infringe the principle of proportionality.

Where Community rules impose a primary and a secondary obligation, the penalty for failing to fulfil the latter should in principle be less onerous than the penalty for failure to fulfil the former. In *Buitoni*,[90] Commission Regulation No. 193/75 made the issue of import and export licences for agricultural products conditional upon the giving of a security, release of which was subject to production of proof of completion of the customs formalities. The security would be released in proportion to the quantities of products in respect of which the requisite proof

---

[86] Case 21/85 *Maas v. Bundesanstalt für Landwirtschaftliche Marktordnung* [1986] ECR 3537.

[87] OJ 1980, L 192, p. 11.

[88] But where a trader receives advance payment of export aid and owing to *force majeure* he is unable to export the goods to the agreed destination and exports them instead to different destinations which qualify for a lower export aid or none at all, it is not contrary to the principle of proportionality to require that the security forfeited must be equal to the difference between the amount of the aid paid in advance and the amount actually due: Case C–299/94 *Anglo-Irish Beef Processors International v. MAFF* [1996] ECR I–1925.

[89] Joined Cases 99 and 100/76 *Beste Boter and Hoche v. Bundesanstalt für Landwirtschaftliche Marktordnung* [1977] ECR 861.

[90] Case 122/78 *Buitoni v. Forma* [1979] ECR 677.

was furnished. Regulation No. 499/76 provided for the total forfeiture of the security where the requisite proof had not been furnished within the six months following the expiry of the licence. That provision was said to be prompted by 'administrative reasons'. The Court held that it was invalid. It pointed out the inequality of treatment between the failure to fulfil the obligation to import or export imposed by the licence, which was the primary obligation and whose fulfilment the security was intended to guarantee, and the failure to furnish proof within the specified period, which was an ancillary obligation. Failure to perform the first carried a proportionate penalty. By contrast, failure to perform the second carried a fixed penalty, even though the obligation was considerably less serious. On that ground, the Court held that the fixed penalty was excessively severe in relation to the objectives of administrative efficiency. The Court held that the Commission should have sanctioned failure to furnish proof within the specified period with a penalty considerably less onerous and more closely allied to the practical effects of that failure.[91]

In assessing what is a primary obligation regard must be had to the objectives of the measure in issue. Particular importance attaches to the need to prevent fraud. In *Cereol Italia* v. *Azienda Agricola Castello*[92] the Court found that penalties which went as far as forfeiture of entitlement to aid for two marketing years, where a producer deliberately or by reason of serious negligence failed to notify the Commission of changes in the area sown, were proportionate in view of the importance of the obligation of notification for the operation of the aid system. It rejected the submission that the obligation of notification was merely a secondary obligation, breach of which could only have limited consequences.

In a number of cases, breach of the principle of proportionality has been pleaded against penalties imposed as a result of failure to observe time limits. We saw above that in *Buitoni* the failure to submit proof within the specified time limit was judged not to justify total forfeiture of the security lodged.[93] Similarly, in *Man (Sugar)* v. *IBAP*,[94] where the security was declared wholly forfeit although an application for export licence was made only a few hours after the expiry of the requisite time limit, the Court held that forfeiture infringed proportionality. Much depends on the objectives that the time limit is designed to serve. Where Community law requires a transaction to take place within a specified time limit, failure to observe it may justify forfeiture where its strict observance is to prevent speculative transactions. In *Fromançais* v. *Forma*,[95] Commission regulations provided for the sale of butter by tender for processing. The purpose of the tenders was to sell at reduced prices excess butter held by intervention agencies which could not be sold under

---

[91] See also *Atalanta*, op.cit. In *Man (Sugar)* v. *IBAP*, op.cit., the Court held that the obligation of the successful tenderer to obtain an export licence performs a useful administrative function but it is not as important as the obligation to export and, consequently, the automatic forfeiture of the entire security for failure to obtain an export licence within the specified period was too drastic a penalty.
[92] Case C–104/94 *Cereol Italia* v. *Azienda Agricola Castello* [1995] ECR I–2983.
[93] See also above, *Maas*, op.cit.   [94] Case 181/84 *Man (Sugar)* v. *IBAP* [1985] ECR 2889.
[95] Case 66/82 [1983] ECR 395.

market conditions. The regulations in issue provided for the lodging of a security and excluded its release if processing took place after the expiry of a specified period. In was argued that by totally excluding the release of the security in the event of processing after the expiry of the prescribed period, the provisions infringed the principle of proportionality. The essence of the argument was that failure to carry out the processing in time should not be penalized with the same penalty as failure to carry out the processing at all. The Court held that forfeiture of the security was proportionate in order to avoid speculative transactions. It pointed out that if no processing period was imposed, or if the processing period could be extended for long periods, the successful tenderer might be tempted to accumulate stocks by buying large quantities of butter with a view to avoiding the effect of a subsequent increase in the purchase price. Such speculation would conflict with the purposes of the regulations which was to remove surplus quantities from the market by promoting its use as a substitute for other fats. It would also encourage the accumulation of stocks at reduced prices to the detriment of the Community budget. Less convincingly, Reischl AG considered that the regulations were invalid inasmuch as they imposed the same penalty for a complete failure to carry out the processing of butter and for the carrying out of the processing after the expiry of the prescribed period.

The Court took a strict view of time limits also in *Denkavit* v. *Forma*.[96] A Commission regulation provided for a time limit of six months within which a claim for the payment of monetary compensatory amounts should be made. The Court held that according to current practice the necessary documents were submitted within a short period, and that the time limit of six months was not out of proportion to the aim of ensuring sound administration. Nor could the applicant claim that the loss of the relevant documents was due to *force majeure* since it had not availed itself of other opportunities provided by Community law to prove the completion of customs formalities. Notably, relying on *Buitoni*, Lenz AG took a different view holding that complete forfeiture of monetary compensatory amounts was unreasonable.[97] It is not without interest that in both *Fromançais* v. *Forma* and *Denkavit* v. *Forma* the Court disagreed with the Advocate General. Such disagreements are inevitable given that the application of the principle of proportionality involves in effect subjective judgments.

The strict approach of the Court is evident also in recent cases, especially where the purpose of the time limit is to avoid speculation. In *Hopermann*,[98] the Court was concerned with the Community system of aid for certain agricultural products. Council Regulation No. 1431/82 provided for the granting of aid to operators who purchased peas and field beans produced in the Community to use them for

[96] Case 266/84 *Denkavit France* v. *Forma* [1986] ECR 149.

[97] See *Denkavit France* v. *Forma*, op.cit., 161.

[98] Case C–358/88 *Oberhausener Kraftfutterwerk Wilhelm Hopermann GmbH* v. *Bundesanstalt für landwirtschaftliche Marktordnung* [1990] ECR I–1687. See also Case C–357/88 *Hopermann* [1990] ECR I–1669.

the manufacture of animal feed. A Commission implementing regulation provided, as a condition for the granting of the aid, that the operator must lodge an application not later than one working day after the application for placing the products under supervision.[99] The Court held that strict adherence with the time limit was essential to the proper functioning of the aid system. Under the applicable Community rules, the amount of the aid to be granted was that in force on the date on which the application for aid was lodged. If the period laid down for the submission of the application was not mandatory, operators might wait for a more favourable moment for doing so, thereby obtaining an unjustified advantage.

3.5. Protective measures in trade with third States

Regulations setting up a common organization of the market often contain provisions which enable the Community institutions to introduce appropriate measures in the event that imports from, or exports to, third States threaten to cause serious disturbances to the Community market.[100] The power to take protective measures is entrusted to the Commission which, in general, enjoys wide discretion. It is for the Commission to assess whether there is a risk of serious disturbance of the market and the Court will intervene only if the Commission has committed a manifest error of assessment.[101] In practice, a challenge to the Commission's evaluation of the market conditions is extremely difficult to succeed. Also, it is for the Commission to choose the appropriate protective measures. Such measures may include the temporary suspension of imports, the imposition of levies, or the imposition of countervailing charges.[102] Such measures inevitably impose restrictions on the economic freedom of traders and are subject to the principle of

---

[99] Placing the products under supervision signifies the operation whereby the competent authority determines in the premises of the operator the quantity and quality of the products to be used.

[100] See e.g. Council Regulation No. 1035/72 on the common organization of the market in fruit and vegetables (OJ , English Spec.Ed., 1972 (II) p. 437) and its implementing Council Regulation No. 2707/72 (OJ, English Spec.Ed., 1972 (28–30 Dec.), p. 3); Council Regulation No. 516/77 on the common organization of the market in products processed from fruit and vegetables (OJ 1977 L 73/1) and its implementing Council Regulation No. 521/77 (OJ 1977 L 73/28). Regulation No. 516/77 was replaced by Council Regulation No. 426/86 (OJ 1986 L 49/1). Regulation 521/77 was repealed, with effect from 1 July 1995, by Council Regulation No. 3290/94 on the adjustments and transitional arrangements required in the agriculture sector in order to implement the agreements concluded during the Uruguay Round of multilateral trade negotiations (OJ 1994 L 349/105).

[101] See e.g. Case C–205/94 *Binder* v. *Hauptzollamt Stuttgart-West* [1996] ECR I–2871, para. 17.

[102] In Case 345/82 *Wünsche* v. *Germany* [1984] ECR 1995 it was argued that the Commission regulation imposing a levy on the importation of preserved mushrooms was invalid on the ground that the enabling regulation of the Council provided for an exhaustive list of protective measures which did not include the imposition of an additional levy. The Court rejected that argument stating that, since the enabling regulation authorized the Commission to take protective measures leading to a complete suspension of imports, the Commission was, *a fortiori*, entitled to adopt less restrictive rules. This has been confirmed in subsequent cases: see e.g. Case 291/86 *Central-Import Münster* v. *Hauptzillamt Münster* [1988] ECR 3679; Case C–64/95 *Lubella* v. *Hauptzollamt Cottbus* [1996] ECR I–5105.

proportionality.[103] The Court has held that a countervailing charge is not unlawful merely because it is set at a fixed rate, its legality being dependent on a whole range factors, such as the prices charged for imports and the requirement of achieving the desired aim effectively.[104] The general principle, however, is that a charge may not be levied at a higher level than is necessary to achieve its objectives, and in a number of cases fixed-rate charges have been annulled. In *National Dried Fruit Trade Association*,[105] Commission Regulation No. 2742/82[106] introduced a minimum import price for dried grapes from third countries together with a fixed-rate countervailing charge applicable if the minimum price was exceeded. The Court stated that the aim of the countervailing charge was to enforce the minimum price so as to ensure Community preference in the market for dried grapes and not to inflict an economic penalty on traders who had imported below the minimum price. It followed that the introduction of a single, fixed-rate countervailing charge, imposed even where the difference between the import price and the minimum price was very small, amounted to an economic penalty and infringed the principle of proportionality.[107]

The Court's approach towards fixed-rate charges is best illustrated by reference to the mushroom cases. In 1980 the Community market in mushrooms was threatened by imports from third countries at prices well below the cost prices prevailing in the Community. In order to protect the Community industry, Commission Regulation No. 3429/80 made the importation of preserved mushrooms above certain quantities subject to a levy referred to as additional amount. The levy was imposed initially for a period of three months and had a fixed rate. It was set at approximately 150 per cent of the cost price of top quality mushrooms. In *Werner Faust*[108] and *Wünsche I*[109] the Court held that the regulation infringed the principle of proportionality on two counts. First, it penalized particularly imported mushrooms of lower quality, since it was calculated on the basis of the price of top quality mushrooms.[110] Secondly, it did not enable the levy to be set at different

---

[103] Examples are given in the text. See further Case 52/81 *Faust* v. *Commission* [1982] ECR 3745, where the Court held that suspension of imports of mushrooms from certain third States was proportionate to achieve the dual objectives of stabilization of the market and the implementation of a Community policy relating to external trade. Cf. Case 62/70 *Bock* v. *Commission* [1971] ECR 897. In *Lubella* v. *Hauptzollampt Cottbus*, op.cit., the Court found compatible with the principle of proportionality protective measures consisting in the introduction of a minimum import price and a countervailing duty on the import of sour cherries.

[104] Case 77/86 *The Queen* v. *Customs and Excise, ex parte National Dried Fruit Trade Association* [1988] ECR 757, para. 29.

[105] Op.cit.   [106] OJ 1982 L 290/28.

[107] Op.cit., para. 32 and see also the reasoning of Slynn AG at 775. For the calculation of the countervailing duty following the partial annulment of the regulation by the Court see Joined Cases C–351, 352 and 353/93 *Van der Linde and Tracotex* [1995] ECR I–85.

[108] Case C–24/90 [1991] ECR I–4905.   [109] Case C–25/90 [1991] ECR I–4939.

[110] Cf. *Binder*, op.cit.; In that case, the Commission imposed a minimum price and a countervailing charge on the importation of strawberries from Poland. It was argued that the protective measures breached the principle of proportionality because the minimum price was the same irrespective of the quality of the imported strawberries. The Court held that there was no breach of proportionality because, before the entry into force of the protective measures, the Polish authorities had agreed to

levels according to the quality of the products and the circumstances in which they were imported. The Court pointed out that the objective of the regulation was not to penalize imports without a licence but to protect the Community market from serious disturbance. It came to the conclusion that the levy was set at such a high level as to constitute a considerable financial charge for importers and was therefore disproportionate in relation to the objective of the regulation.[111]

Werner Faust and *Wünsche* illustrate a strict application of the principle of proportionality. They establish that, in applying protective measures, the Commission must choose the alternative which is least restrictive of commercial freedom. Whereas in *National Dried Fruit Trade Association* the fixed-rate charge was annulled because it was excessive in relation to its objectives, in *Werner Faust* and *Wünsche* the levy was annulled because it imposed an excessive burden on the traders concerned. An interesting argument submitted by the Commission was that the levy satisfied the test of proportionality because it was less restrictive of trade than a complete prohibition of imports which the Commission was authorized to impose under the enabling Council regulations. The Court dismissed that argument stating that the contested regulation was not intended to prohibit imports in excess of certain quantities. Rather, it left open the possibility of issuing import licences against payment of a levy even where those quantities were exceeded. Having opted for that solution, the Commission was required to comply with the principle of proportionality.[112] This reasoning evinces that whether a charge is proportionate is to be determined within the confines of the policy option chosen by the Commission. A charge imposed on the individual may not go beyond what is necessary to achieve the specific, avowed, objectives of the measure in issue. The fact that the institution which authored the measure might have chosen a different measure, more restrictive of commercial freedom, does not justify the charge. As Jacobs AG vividly put it:'The use of a cannonball to kill a fly cannot be defended on the ground that a nuclear missile might have been used instead.'[113] The mushrooms judgments also highlight a second function performed by the principle of proportionality. Not only does it protect the individual but it also requires the Community administration to ensure consistency between the objectives sought

---

ensure that their exporters would comply with a mean export price applicable to all products irrespective of quality. Also, the Polish authorities were not able to ensure that the quality of exported strawberries was checked and therefore Community customs authorities were unable to monitor that minimum prices linked to the quality of imported strawberries were respected.

[111] The Court followed identical reasoning in the third mushroom case: Case C–26/90 *Wünsche II* [1991] ECR I–4961. See also Case 95/75 *Effem* v. *Hauptzollamt Luneburg* [1976] ECR 361 where the Court held that the fixing of a standard export levy applicable irrespective of the quantity, whether negligible or substantial, of cereals in certain products used for animal feed infringed Community law. Although the judgment made no reference to the principle of proportionality, Reischl AG expressly referred to the principle: see [1976] ECR at 373.

[112] *Werner Faust*, para. 21. See also Case C–295/94 *Hüpeden* v. *Hauptzollamt Hamburg-Jonas* [1996] ECR I–3375, para. 30.

[113] *Werner Faust*, op.cit., at 4926.

and the means chosen. It thus contributes to the rationalization and coherence of the policy-making process.

It may be thought that in *Werner Faust and Wünsche* the Court applied the principle of proportionality strictly because the enabling Council regulation on the basis of which the Commission imposed the levy expressly provided that the Commission could take protective measures only to such extent and for such length of time as was strictly necessary. That, however, was not of paramount importance. Subsequently, in *Hüpeden* v. *Hauptzollamt Hamburg-Jonas*[114] the Court applied the same reasoning and annulled a fixed charge on imports of mushrooms applying the general principle of proportionality even though the enabling regulation did not incorporate a specific proportionality requirement.

Following the judgments in the mushrooms cases, the Commission reduced with retroactive effect the levy but maintained it at a fixed-rate. Under the new rules, the levy was calculated no longer on the basis of top quality mushrooms but on the basis of grade 3 mushrooms which were of lower quality. The levy was reduced from 150% to 90% of the value of the mushrooms. But the new regulation had no better fortune. In *Pietsch* v. *Hauptzollamt Hamburg-Waltershof*[115] it was annulled as being contrary to the principle of proportionality. The starting point of the Court's reasoning was that the aim of the regulation was not to prohibit all imports beyond the quantities specified but to protect the Community market from disruption owing to excessive imports. Even though the level of the levy was reduced, it still amounted to two-thirds of the cost price of top quality Community mushrooms. The levy substantially increased the cost of imported mushrooms and was thus equivalent to a substantive prohibition of imports. It exceeded clearly what was necessary to attain its objective and was therefore contrary to the principle of proportionality.

In the above cases the Court exercised review of high intensity scrutinizing closely the Commission's means and objectives. An interesting aspect of *Pietsch* and *Hüpeden* is that they were decided by a three-member chamber. This is noteworthy for the following reason. In January 1995, when Austria, Finland and Sweden acceded to the Community, the number of judges was increased to fifteen. Since then, cases which involve issues of some difficulty are heard by a five-member chamber. It is rare for a three-member chamber to annul a Community measure and it is arguable that the cases deserved a higher court formation.

A final point is that in cases where the Court annulled protective measures against imports from third States, it was motivated primarily by the concern to ensure the protection of the traders involved rather than the concern to liberalize free trade with third States. Given the protectionist objectives of Community measures in the field of agriculture, it could hardly be otherwise. It is notable, however, that in one case the Court held that preference for Community products was not a legal requirement breach of which would result in the invalidity of a Community

---

[114] Case C–295/94 [1996] ECR I–3375.   [115] Case C–296/94 [1996] ECR I–3409.

measure despite the fact that earlier authorities suggested that such a principle exists.[116]

3.6. Flat-rate reductions

It was seen in the previous sections that in a number of cases the Court has annulled measures which impose a fixed-rate charge.[117] The imposition of a fixed-rate charge, however, is not necessarily incompatible with the principle of proportionality. Much depends on the objectives of the measure. Cases like *Werner Faust* and *Wünsche* contrast with the Court's approach to economic policy measures of general application imposing flat-rate reductions with a view to controlling production. An example is provided by *Crispoltoni*.[118] We saw above[119] that in issue in *Crispoltoni* was the system of maximum guaranteed quantities introduced by the Council in order to curtail production of tobacco. For each percentage by which the maximum guaranteed quantity was exceeded, there was to be a corresponding reduction in the intervention prices and the premiums up to a maximum reduction of 15 per cent. It was argued that the regulation was contrary to the principle of proportionality and the principle of equal treatment because it penalized indiscriminately all producers for the excess production irrespective of whether, and if so the degree by which, they contributed to the maximum guaranteed quantities being exceeded. The Court held that in a common organization of the markets where no national quotas have been introduced, all Community producers, regardless of the Member State in which they are based, must together in an egalitarian manner bear the consequences of the decisions which the Community institutions are led to adopt in order to respond to the risk of imbalance which may arise in the market between production and market outlets.[120] The approach of the Court is not incompatible with its rulings in *Werner Faust* and *Wünsche*. As the Advocate General noted in *Crispoltoni* there is a clear difference between the imposition of a flat-rate economic penalty on traders and a sharing in the reduction of subsidies once the maximum guaranteed quantity is exceeded.[121]

---

[116] C–353/92 *Greece* v. *Council* [1994] ECR I–3411, para. 50. The Court stated that the institutions may take Community preference into account as an element in the common agricultural policy but it cannot affect their decision until all the economic factors influencing world trade have been taken into account. Cf. Case 5/67 *Beus* v. *Hauptzollamt München* [1968] ECR 83 at 89.

[117] See above, sections 3.4 and 3.5.

[118] Joined Cases C–133/93, C–300/93 and C–362/93 [1994] ECR I–4863. See also Case 179/84 *Bozzetti* v. *Invernizzi* [1985] ECR 2301; Case C–27/90 *SITPA* [1994] ECR I–133, *Wuidart* discussed above, Ch. 2.

[119] p. 98 above.   [120] *Crispoltoni*, op.cit., para. 52.   [121] Op.cit., 4880 per Jacobs AG.

3.7. Sanctions

Given that the primary objective of the principle of proportionality is to protect the citizen vis-à-vis public power, an area where its application is of particular importance is that of sanctions. The term 'sanction' may be understood broadly, as encompassing both compensatory and punitive penalties, whether or not of a criminal character. Lenaerts[122] defines as compensatory sanctions those imposed in order to remove the injury illegally caused by an individual or undertaking to competitors or the Community finances. Such sanctions include orders of restitution[123] or the levy of duties.[124] Punitive penalties are imposed because an individual or undertaking has engaged in conduct wrongful under Community law. Punitive sanctions may include the temporary exclusion from future benefits[125] or the imposition of pecuniary penalties. As a general principle of Community law, proportionality applies both to compensatory[126] and punitive sanctions but acquires particular importance in relation to the latter. The Community has limited competence to impose sanctions for breach of Community law so that in this context Community law has to rely on national law. Traditionally the emphasis has been on ensuring that penalties imposed by national law are not excessive. According to standard case law, penalties imposed by national law must not go beyond what is strictly necessary for the objectives pursued and the control procedures must not be accompanied by a penalty which is so disproportionate to the gravity of the infringement that it becomes an obstacle to the freedoms enshrined in the Treaty.[127] In recent years, however, emphasis has been placed also on the need to ensure that the sanctions provided by national law for breach of Community obligations are adequate. This has been, at least partly, the result of greater awareness of fraud against the Community budget.[128] When pronounced judicially, the need to ensure the adequacy of penalties has not been based on the principle of proportionality but on the need to provide for the effective protection of Community interests and the principle of equal treatment: Member States must pursue viola-

---

[122] See K. Lenaerts, General Report, in 'Procedures and Sanctions in Economic Administrative Law' 17 *FIDE Congress*, Vol. III (Berlin, 1996), p. 506 at p. 533.

[123] e.g. repayment of unduly paid or misused aid: see Joined Cases T–231/94 R, T–232/94 R and T–234/94 R *Transacciones Maritimas* v. *Commission* [1994] ECR II–885 and on appeal: C–12/95 P [1995] ECR I–467.

[124] e.g, anti-dumping or countervailing duties. For countervailing duties, see e.g. *The Queen* v. *Customs and Excise, ex parte National Dried Fruit Trade Association*, op.cit. For anti-dumping, see below.

[125] See e.g. Case C–135/92 *Fiskano* v. *Commission* [1994] ECR I–2885 (temporary exclusion from fishing rights).

[126] As Lenaerts observes, although a compensatory sanction must in principle correspond to the injury to be eliminated, the extent of the sanction may often depend on assessing the importance of that injury. Such assessment entails a discretionary power of appraisal which is subject to the requirements of proportionality: op.cit., p. 536, n. 150.

[127] See e.g. Case C–210/91 *Commission* v. *Greece* [1992] ECR I–6735, para. 19 and below, p. 157.

[128] It is estimated that 10–20% of the Community budget is abused for fraudulent purposes every year. See Lenaerts, op.cit., p. 534, n. 140, where further references are given.

tions against Community law with the same diligence as violations against national law.[129] In one case, where the Commission brought enforcement proceedings against Greece, the Court went as far as to say that Greece breached Community law by failing to institute criminal or disciplinary proceedings against civil servants responsible for fraud against the Community.[130]

An interesting illustration of the application of the principle of proportionality on punitive sanctions is provided by *Advanced Nuclear Fuels* v. *Commission*.[131] The case raised for the first time the question of sanctions for breach of the provisions of the Euratom Treaty on safeguards (Articles 77 to 85) the purpose of which is to ensure the security of nuclear materials. Under Article 83(1) of the Euratom Treaty, in case of infringement of the requirements imposed by the provisions on safeguards, the Commission may impose the following sanctions in order of severity: a warning; the withdrawal of special benefits such as financial or technical assistance; the placing of the undertaking responsible for the infringement for a period not exceeding four months under administration; total or partial withdrawal of source materials or special fissile materials. In *Advanced Nuclear Fuels*, radioactive material was exported inadvertently from Germany to the United States, as a result of a mistake in transportation. The Commission placed the applicant company under administration for a period of four months. The company alleged that the penalty was disproportionate, the appropriate one being a warning. The Court held that failure to observe the provisions of the Euratom Treaty, which seek to ensure that nuclear materials are not diverted to purposes other than those for which they are intended, is in itself a serious violation. It came to the conclusion that the sanction of administration was necessary in order to ensure that a similar incident would not occur in the future. The Court considered that the less severe option open to the Commission of appointing inspectors was not adequate because, unlike administrators, inspectors did not have the power to instruct the company to issue or modify its internal operating instructions. It is not surprising that in the area of nuclear safety, as in the area of external security,[132] the Court follows a loose application of the principle of proportionality, being prepared to err on the side of the adopting institution. That does not mean, however, that the Court considers those areas as non-justiciable. By contrast, it assesses carefully all the arguments submitted and is prepared to scrutinize the conduct of the adopting institution.

Anti-dumping duties and fines imposed by the Commission are also subject to the principle of proportionality. In the area of anti-dumping the Court is, in general, reluctant to intervene on the ground that the finding of dumping and the

---

[129] Case 68/88 *Commission* v. *Greece* [1989] ECR 2965, para. 25. Article 280(2)[209(a)(1)] EC, inserted by the Treaty on European Union, states that 'Member States shall take the same measures to counter fraud affecting the financial interests of the Community as they take to counter fraud affecting their own financial interests.' See also Council Regulation No. 2988/95 on the protection of the European Communities' financial interests, OJ 1995 L 312/1.

[130] *Commission* v. *Greece*, op.cit.; see also the comments of the Advocate General in Case C–56/91 *Greece* v. *Commission* [1993] ECR I–3433, at 3453.

[131] Case C–308/90 [1993] ECR I–309.   [132] For public security, see below, p. 149.

determination of injury involve the appraisal of complex economic and technical issues. The Court's reluctance to intervene has been criticized.[133]

In the area of penalties and fines imposed under competition law, the Community judicature exercises unlimited jurisdiction.[134] This differs fundamentally from judicial review on grounds of proportionality in that the Court of Justice and now the CFI act as appellate bodies 'rewriting' the decision of the Commission. Thus, the CFI may reduce a fine even when it appears that the Commission's decision finding an infringement of Articles 81[85] and 82[86] or of the Merger Regulation is not vitiated by any illegality.[135] The same applies where the Court exercises its jurisdiction under Article 36 ECSC which provides that the Court has unlimited jurisdiction in appeals against pecuniary sanctions and periodic penalty payments imposed under the ECSC Treaty. In a number of cases under the ECSC Treaty the Court has refused to annul decisions imposing fines on the ground that they infringe general principles of law but, acting as an appellate body, it has reduced the fine imposed by the Commission primarily on the ground that the Commission's conduct was such as to leave the undertaking concerned in a state of uncertainty. In one case,[136] the Court reduced the standard fine imposed on the ground that the undertaking by its own initiative took steps to minimize the excess production whereas the Commission had acted in breach of the rules of good administration leaving the applicant in doubt as to its intentions. In another case,[137] the Court reduced the fine imposed on the ground that the Commission did not notify the applicant in good time of the quota to which it was entitled and it was therefore unable to produce the quantity which it was entitled to produce. In *Estel*,[138] the Court found that the Commission had not informed the undertaking concerned of the method which it intended to apply for the calculation of the quota and that, as a result, the Commission erred as to the gravity of the infringement. In *Bertoli*,[139] the fine was reduced *inter alia* on the ground that in previous cases where it had uncovered infringements, the Commission had not imposed any

---

[133] See Egger, 'The Principle of Proportionality in Community Anti-Dumping Law' (1993) 18 ELRev. 367. Note, however, that in Joined Cases T–163 and T–165/94 *Koyo Seiko* v. *Council* [1995] ECR II–1381 the CFI annulled an anti-dumping regulation of the Council. Affirmed on appeal: Case C–245/95 P, [1998] [1998] ECR I–401.

[134] See Article 229[172] EC and, for specific provisions, Regulation 17, Article 17, and Regulation No. 4064/89 on mergers, Article 16.

[135] See Lenaerts, op.cit., p. 577 and see e.g. Case T–13/89 *ICI* v. *Commission* [1992] ECR II–1021, Case T–77/92 *Parker Pen* v. *Commission* [1994] ECR II–549; Case T–142/89 *Böel* v. *Commission* [1995] ECR II–867. Cf. T–83/91 *Tetra-Pak* v. *Commission* [1994] ECR II–755. By contrast, the Court of Justice adjudicating on appeal from the CFI may not reduce the fine imposed by the CFI on grounds of fairness since the appeal is on points of law only: Case C–310/93 P *BPB Industries and British Gypsum* v. *Commission* [1994] ECR I–865.

[136] Case 179/82 *Lucchini* v. *Commission* [1983] ECR 3083.

[137] Case 188/82 *Thyssen* v. *Commission* [1983] ECR 3721.

[138] Case 270/82 *Estel* v. *Commission* [1983] ECR 1195, para. 12.

[139] Case 8/83 *Bertoli* v. *Commission* [1984] ECR 1649. See further Case 9/83 *Eisen und Metall Aktiengesellschaft* v. *Commission* [1983] ECR 2071.

fines. The Court and the CFI, however, have not been particularly receptive to the same argument in relation to fines in the field of competition law.[140]

3.8. Harmonization of laws

The case law on the application of proportionality on measures of economic policy makes it obvious that the principle is an unreliable ground on the basis of which to question the choices of the Community legislature in the field of harmonization. Indeed since proportionality is, at least primarily, a concept of suitability rather than a concept of participation, it is less appropriate than equality as a means of challenging economic policy choices. In *Germany* v. *Parliament and Council*,[141] the German Government challenged the 'export prohibition' contained in Directive 94/19 on deposit-guarantee schemes[142] *inter alia* on the ground that it went beyond what was necessary to achieve its objectives. The Directive provides that branches of credit institutions located in other Member States are covered by the deposit guarantee scheme of the State where the credit institution has its registered office. Article 4(1), however, states that, until the end of 1999, the cover provided for depositors in branches located in other Member States may not exceed the cover offered by the corresponding guarantee scheme of the host Member State. The rationale of this provision is to avoid disturbances which may be caused if branches of foreign banks offer higher levels of cover than that offered by domestic banks in Member States with less developed financial markets. The German Government took issue on the ground that the underlying objective could be met with less restrictive measures, for example, a system authorizing intervention only where a disturbance in the market of a Member State was imminent. The Court rejected the claim holding that it was not its task to substitute its own assessment for that of the legislature. It can, at most, find fault with the legislative choice of the institutions 'only if it appears manifestly incorrect or if the resultant disadvantages for certain economic operators were wholly disproportionate to the advantages otherwise offered'.[143] The finding is hardly surprising. The German Government invoked proportionality to procure a solution which it had supported unsuccessfully in the Council negotiations leading to the adoption of the Directive. Its submissions, however sensible, were alternative legislative choices rather than grounds of illegality. The dispute encapsulates the complexities of the harmonization process in areas where wide variations exists in the economic sector in question. The Directive spelt a compromise. On the one hand, it brought about some degree of

---

[140] See e.g. Joined Cases 100–3/80 *Musique diffusion Française* v. *Commission* [1983] ECR 1825; *ICI* v. *Commission* , op.cit.

[141] Case C–233/94 [1997] ECR I–2405.   [142] OJ 1994 L 135/5.

[143] *Germany* v. *Parliament and Council*, op.cit., para. 56. The German Government also challenged unsuccessfully on grounds of proportionality the provisions of the Directive on supplementary cover. See paras. 66–74.

coordination of national laws thus facilitating the right of establishment. On the other hand, it sought to avoid, at least for an initial period, the level of guarantee cover becoming an instrument of competition. The net effect of the Directive was that credit institutions established in Member States providing for a high degree of consumer protection lost out in that they were unable to exploit commercially the advantages of consumer protection legislation. But the solution of the Community legislature seems compatible with the underlying perception of regulation as a public good.

3.9. Proportionality as a principle governing the exercise of Community competence

Article 5(3)[3b(3)] EC states that 'Any action by the Community shall not go beyond what is necessary to achieve the objectives of this Treaty.' According to the prevailing view, Article 5(3)[3b(3)] does not add to the existing case law. It merely reiterates the importance of the principle of proportionality and grants to it constitutional status.[144] The only difference seems to be one of emphasis. As a general principle of law, proportionality has been developed by the Court primarily with a view to protecting the individual from action by the Community institutions and by the Member States. By contrast, Article 5(3)[3b(3)] forms part of a system of provisions whose aim is to control the expansion of the Community legislative action and seeks to limit burdens on Member States rather than burdens on individuals. This is not to say that the protection of rights of the individual is excluded from the scope of Article 5(3)[3b(3)]. The provision is understood to mean that 'any burdens, whether financial or administrative, falling upon the Community, national governments, local authorities, economic operators and citizens, should be minimized and should be proportionate to the objectives to be achieved'.[145]

Proportionality is also incorporated by implication in the principle of subsidiarity. Article 5(3)[3b(2)] requires that the Community may take action 'only if and in so far as' the objectives of the proposed action cannot be sufficiently achieved by the Member States. There are, however, differences between the two. First, the principle of subsidiarity comes into play at an earlier stage than the principle of proportionality.[146] It defines whether or not action must be taken at Community level.

[144] See K. Lenaerts and P. Van Ypersele, 'Le principe de subsidiarité et son contexte: Étude de l'article 3B du traité CE' (1994) 30 CDE 3, at 61; T. C. Hartley, *The Foundations of European Community Law* (4th edn., Oxford, 1998) p. 148; Emiliou, op.cit. at p. 401. But see V. Constantinesco, R. Kovar, D. Simon, *Traité sur l'Union Européenne* (Economica), p. 113.

[145] European Council of Edinburgh, 11–12 Dec. 1992, Presidency Conclusions, Annex 1 to Part I A, Agence Europe, Special edn., No. 5878BIS , 13/14.12.1992.

[146] See K. Lenaerts and P. Van Ypersele, op.cit., para. 100; G. Strozzi, 'Le principe de subsidiarité dans la perspective de l'intégration européenne: une énigme et beaucoup d'attentes' (1994) 30 RTDE 373, at 379. Those texts received judicial recognition by Léger AG in Case C–84/94 *United Kingdom* v. *Council* [1996] ECR I–5755 at 5783.

Proportionality, by contrast, comes into play only once it is decided that Community action is necessary and seeks to define its scope. The second difference is this. Article 5(3)[3b(2)], which defines the principle of subsidiarity, applies only in cases where the competence of the Community is not exclusive whereas Article 5(3)[3b(3)] applies also where the Community enjoys exclusive competence. Indeed, it seems that the reason why Article 5(3)[3b(3)] was added by the Treaty of European Union was to ensure that the Community respects the interests of Member States not only where it exercises concurrent competence but also where it exercises its exclusive competence, which falls outside the scope of Article 5(3)[3b(2)].[147]

Article 5(3)[3b(3)] refers both to the extent and to the intensity of Community action. It requires Community action not to exceed what is necessary to achieve the objectives of the Treaty but does not itself limit those objectives nor does it require their restrictive interpretation. It lays down a principle which, like the principle of subsidiarity, is directed primarily, although not exclusively, at the political institutions of the Community and is designed to influence the legislative process *ex ante*, i.e. at the stage of preparation of legislation. The Conclusions of the Presidency of the European Council held in Edinburgh in December 1992 laid down guidelines for the adoption of Community legislation in the light of Article 5(3)[3b(3)].[148] The guidelines state *inter alia* that Community measures should leave as much scope for national decision as possible and that, while respecting Community law, care should be taken to respect well-established national arrangements and the organization and working of Member States' legal systems. Where appropriate and subject to the need for proper enforcement, Community measures should provide Member States with alternative ways to achieve the objectives of the measures.[149] Where it is necessary to set standards at Community level, consideration should be given to setting minimum standards, with freedom for Member States to set higher national standards, not only in the areas where the Treaty so requires (for example, Articles 176[130t]) but also in other areas where this would not conflict with the objectives of the proposed measure or with the Treaty.[150] The Community should legislate only to the extent necessary. Other things being equal, directives should be preferred to regulations and framework directives to detailed measures. Non-binding measures such as recommendations should be preferred where appropriate. Consideration should also be given where appropriate to the use of voluntary codes of conduct.[151] Where difficulties are localized and only certain Member States are affected, any necessary Community action should not be extended to other Member States unless this is necessary to achieve an objective of the Treaty.[152] The last point is important because it brings

---

[147] Lenaerts and Van Ypersele, op.cit., 62.

[148] See also now the Protocol on the application of the principles of subsidiarity and proportionality annexed to the EC Treaty by the Treaty of Amsterdam.

[149] See Conclusions, op.cit., para. (iii).   [150] Op.cit., para. (iv).   [151] Op.cit., para. (v).

[152] Op.cit., para. (vii).

into surface the relationship between the principle of proportionality and the principle of equality of Member States. In its case law the Court has accepted that it is compatible with the principle of equal treatment for the Community to adopt rules which apply only to certain Member States, where that is objectively justified.[153] The European Council conclusions recognize that differences in infrastructure or the underlying conditions of Member States in specific sectors where Community action is envisaged may make intervention by the Community proportionate in relation to some Member States but disproportionate in relation to others.[154]

Before the Treaty on European Union came into force, the case law accepted that the principle of proportionality can be invoked by Member States as well as by individuals.[155] In one case, the Court rejected the argument that the principle of proportionality amounted to a 'principle of minimum intervention' according to which, in interpreting Community measures, preference should be given to the interpretation which restricted Community intervention on Member States' sovereignty to the minimum.[156] Proportionality as a principle governing the exercise of Community competence came to the fore in *Germany* v. *Council*.[157] By Regulation No. 2186/93,[158] adopted under Article 284[213] EC, the Council required Member States to establish registers for statistical purposes containing information on commercial enterprises. The purpose of registers was to provide the Commission with reliable information so as to enable it to perform its various tasks. The German Government argued that the regulation infringed the principle of proportionality in two respects. First, it required the registration of certain data which were not necessary to achieve the objectives of the regulation. Secondly, the financial and administrative costs in establishing and periodically updating the national registers were disproportionate by comparison to the potential benefits. The Court rejected both arguments. With regard to the first, it held that the information required to be included was statistically relevant. With regard to the second, it stated that the German Government had not shown that the costs were 'manifestly disproportionate' to the advantages resulting for the Community from the availability of reliable data regarding the structure of the economy throughout the Community.

The case was introduced before the Treaty on European Union came into force so that Article 5(3)[3b(3)] was not directly relevant. But there is no reason to suppose that the solution would be different. It seems then that the Court will be reluctant to intervene unless it is shown that a measure manifestly goes beyond the objectives of the Treaty. The intensity of review is no different from when pro-

---

[153] See e.g. Case 13/63 *Italy* v. *Commission* [1963] ECR 338; Joined Cases C–181, 182 and 218/88 *Deschamps* v. *Ofival* [1989] ECR I–4381 and see further above p. 57.

[154] Lenaerts and can Ypersele, op.cit., 67.

[155] See e.g. Case 116/82 *Commission* v. *Germany* [1986] ECR 2519; see also Case 37/83 *Rewe-Zentrale* v. *Landwirtschaftskammer Rheinland* [1984] ECR 1229.

[156] Case 28/84 *Commission* v. *Germany* [1985] ECR 3097.

[157] Case C–426/93 [1995] ECR I–3723.

[158] Regulation No. 2186/93 on Community coordination in drawing up business registers for statistical purposes, OJ 1993 L 196/1.

portionality is applied for the protection of the individual to control the legality of policy measures.[159] This is confirmed by the *Organisation of the Working Time Directive* case[160] where the Court rejected the challenge of the United Kingdom against Council Directive 93/104[161] on grounds of breach of the principle of proportionality. The Court stated that, in making social policy choices, the Community legislature is required to make complex assessments and must be allowed wide discretion. Consequently, review is limited to examining whether the exercise of discretion has been vitiated by manifest error or misuse of powers or whether the institution concerned has manifestly exceeded the limits of its discretion.[162]

In the *Organisation of Working Time Directive* case, the United Kingdom objected to what it saw as the introduction of broad social policy measures by the back door, namely on the basis of Article 118a (now 138) which deals with health and safety at work and authorizes the adoption of directives by qualified majority as opposed to unanimity in the Council of Ministers. One of the arguments submitted by the Government was that the measures for the organization of working time provided in Directive 93/104, including minimum rest periods and maximum weekly working time, were disproportionate. The desired level of protection could have been achieved by less restrictive measures such as the use of risk assessments where working hours exceeded particular norms. The Court held that the measures of the Directive contributed directly to the improvement of health and safety of workers within the meaning of Article 118a and were therefore suitable to attain their objectives. With regard to the test of necessity, the Court held that the Council had not committed a manifest error in considering that the objectives of Article 118a could not be achieved by less restrictive measures. In reaching that conclusion, the Court placed particular emphasis on the flexibility of the Directive. Its provisions were subject to several derogations thus leaving scope for adjustments at national level.

It is submitted that the Court's approach to exercise only marginal review in cases such as the *Organisation of Working Time Directive* case is correct. Proportionality seems a less suitable criterion for assessing whether Community action interferes unduly with Member State sovereignty than for assessing undue restrictions on individual freedom. Whether Community action is necessary or not is primarily a question of policy not a question of law. It is likely that in most cases there will be a dearth of objective criteria on the basis of which the choices of the Community legislature may be assessed by a judicial body. Review therefore must necessarily be restricted to determining whether there is manifest error. By contrast, in such cases there is more scope for judicial intervention in determining whether the measure in issue is adequately reasoned and whether it has been adopted on the correct legal basis.

[159] See also Case C–206/94 *Brennet* v. *Paletta* [1996] ECR I–2357.

[160] Case C–84/94 *United Kingdom* v. *Council* [1996] ECR I–5755.

[161] Directive 93/104/EC of 23 Nov. 1993 concerning certain aspects of the organization of working time, OJ 1993 L 307/18.

[162] *United Kingdom* v. *Council*, op.cit., para. 58.

3. 10. Overview of factors to be taken into account

It has become clear from the above analysis that, far from dictating a uniform test, proportionality is a flexible principle which is used in different contexts to protect different interests and entails varying degrees of judicial scrutiny. It is by its nature flexible and open-textured. The Court applies the test of suitability and the test of necessity with varying degrees of strictness depending on a number of factors. It may be helpful here to recapitulate by listing some of those factors They include:

- *Power of appraisal*. The nature of the contested act and, in particular, the degree of discretion required is of decisive importance. The broader the power of appraisal that the adopting institution has, the less comprehensive the review exercised by the Court. In general, it can be said that the Court undertakes only marginal review in relation to legislative measures of economic policy and measures the adoption of which requires complex economic and technical evaluations.

- *The restrictive effect of the measure and the type of interest adversely affected*. The more severely a measure affects private interests, the more difficult it is to establish its necessity. For example, a charge or a penalty entails a greater restriction on commercial freedom than the refusal of a subsidy or a benefit and imposes a higher burden on the authorities to justify it. By contrast, it seems that limited importance is attributed on whether the provision under which the contested measure was adopted incorporates a test of necessity, for example requires action only where it is strictly necessary.[163]

- *The objective of the measure and the type of interest which the measure seeks to protect*. Thus, public health considerations may be accorded priority over the economic interests[164] as may nuclear safety[165] and public security considerations.[166]

- *Whether the same objective can be achieved by less restrictive measures*. The Court is open to argument that the same objective can be achieved by less restrictive means. But where policy measures are involved, the less restrictive alternative test gives way to the manifestly inappropriate test.

- *The treatment of comparable products or producers*. With a view to determining whether a measure is necessary, regard may be had to the way comparable situations are treated.[167] The principle of proportionality is closely linked to the principle of equal treatment and incorporates an element of participation.[168]

- *Whether the individual has suffered actual hardship as a result of the measure*.[169]

---

[163] See *Hüpeden* v. *Hauptzollamt Hamburg-Jonas*, op.cit. p. 112; *Balkan Import-Export*, op.cit.
[164] *Fedesa*, op.cit.   [165] *Advanced Nuclear Fuels*, op.cit.
[166] Case C–120/94 *Commission* v. *Greece* (*FYROM* case) [1996] ECR 1513, per Jacobs AG.
[167] See e.g. Case C–256/90 *Mignini* [1992] ECR I–2651.
[168] See e.g. *Bela Muhle*, op.cit. *Mignini* and see below p. 351.
[169] Case 138/79 *Roquette Freres* v. *Council* [1980] ECR 3333, paras. 29, 31. Case 106/83 *Sermide* v. *Cassa Conguaglio Zucchero* [1984] ECR 4209.

- *The temporary effect of the measure.* Measures restricting economic freedom may be easier to justify if they are only of limited temporal application.[170]
- *The urgency of the situation.* A pressing need to regulate the market may give wider discretion to the institution which authors the act. The same applies to transitional measures urgently drawn to deal with an emergency.[171]
- *The technicality of the subject matter and the degree of expertise required.* The Court is more reluctant to intervene in areas where legislative intervention requires a degree of technical expertise such as anti-dumping.

---

[170] But see *Bela Muhle*.

[171] *Balkan Import-Export*; Case 138/79 *Roquette Freres* v. *Council* [1980] ECR 3333, para. 27.

4

The Principle of Proportionality: Review of National Measures

4.1. From the rule of law to economic integration

We saw in the previous chapter that, where proportionality is applied as a ground of review of Community acts, the Court balances a private vis-à-vis a public interest. In that context, the principle operates in the traditional sphere of public law seeking to provide a check on public power and to protect the individual. In Community law, the principle performs another, distinct, but related, function. It is applied to determine the compatibility with the Treaty of national measures which interfere with the fundamental freedoms. The function of the principle in this context is to promote market integration. For that reason, the degree of scrutiny employed by the Court is much stricter and the 'manifestly inappropriate' test gives way to a test of necessity.[1] To state the obvious, the standard of deference to national policy choices is not determined by the principle itself but by the underlying objectives of the Community provisions whose interpretation it is recruited to assist. In the law of free movement, proportionality can be seen as the normative expression of negative integration and of the principle of free access to the market of the importing State. The importance of proportionality as an instrument of market integration is illustrated by contrasting the approach of the Court to restrictions on free movement imposed by national measures and such restrictions imposed by Community measures. Where Community measures restrict fundamental freedoms, the Court is more readily prepared to defer to the discretion of the Community institutions.[2] Also, provisions of agreements between the Community and third States which employ identical language with provisions of the EC Treaty are subject to a less stringent test of proportionality, the reason being that their underlying objective is merely to facilitate free trade rather than to promote an economic constitutional order.[3]

---

[1] See above, Ch. 3. This distinction in the use of proportionality is not always made by national courts. See e.g. *R* v. *Chief Constable of Sussex, ex parte International Trader's Ferry Ltd*. [1997] 2 All ER 65 per Kennedy LJ at 80–1.

[2] See Case C–51/93 *Meyhui* v. *Schott Zwiesel Glaswerke* [1994] ECR I–3879; cf. Case 27/80 *Fietje* [1980] ECR 3839 and Case C–369/89 *Piageme* v. *Peeters* [1991] ECR I–2971, and below p. 195.

[3] See Case 299/86 *Drexl* v. *Italian Republic* [1988] ECR 1213, Case C–312/91 *Metalsa* v. *Italian Republic* [1993] ECR I–3751; and see also Opinion 1/91 *Draft Agreement relating to the creation of the*

The distinction drawn above between proportionality as the guardian of individual rights and proportionality as an instrument for economic integration does not mean that the two concepts are unrelated. In fact, the second incorporates the first. In *Kraus*,[4] as earlier in the *Beer* case,[5] the Court was adamant that, to be proportionate, a restriction on the exercise of a fundamental freedom must comply with essential procedural guarantees enabling the person concerned to assert his Community rights. In other words, freedom to trade and the rule of law are closely intertwined aspects of the same constitutional order.[6] In particular, the case law provides that, in order to meet the requirements of proportionality, a restriction on a fundamental freedom must be adequately reasoned and be subject to judicial review.[7]

This chapter will illustrate the application of proportionality primarily by reference to the free movement of goods. Before embarking on that discussion, it may be helpful to recount briefly the most important types of national measures to which the principle applies.

1) *Escape clauses*. The Treaty provides for a number of express derogations from the principles established therein, the so-called 'exception' or 'escape' clauses.[8] Some of those clauses enable Member States to take action on well-defined, non-economic grounds.[9] Others include economic grounds.[10] In certain cases, Member States may act only after authorization by a Community institution[11] whereas in others they may act alone. Whatever their substantive or procedural requirements, escape clauses are governed by the following fundamental principles. First, they are exclusive in character. Member States have no power to derogate from the provisions of the Treaty except by virtue of express derogation.[12] Secondly, escape clauses must be

European Economic Area [1991] ECR I–6079. In those cases, the Court acknowledged that the internal market is not an end in itself but a means to achieving the ultimate objectives of the Community.

    [4] Case 19/92 *Kraus* v. *Land Baden-Württemberg* [1993] ECR I–1663.

    [5] Case 178/84 *Commission* v. *Germany* [1987] ECR 1227.

    [6] On the Treaty as an economic constitution, see W. Sauter, *Competition Law and Industrial Policy in the EU* (OUP), p. 26; Miguel Poiares Maduro, *We, the Court: The European Court of Justice and the European Economic Constitution* (Hart Publishing, 1998); and see by the same author, 'Reforming the Market or the State? Article 30 and the European Constitution: Economic Freedom and Political Rights' (1997) 3 ELJ 55.

    [7] See Case 222/86 *UNECTEF* v. *Heylens* [1987] ECR 4097; Case C–340/89 *Vlassopoulou* [1991] ECR I–2357; Case C–104/91 *Borrell and Others* [1992] ECR I–3003; Joined Cases C–65/95 and C–111/95 *The Queen* v. *Secretary of State for the Home Department, ex parte Mann Singh Shingara and Abbas Radiom*, [1997] ECR I–3343; See also Case C–189/95 *Franzén* [1997] ECR I–5909, paras. 50–1 and in relation to the 6th VAT Directive, Joined Cases C–286/94, C–340/95, C–401/95 and C–47/96 *Molenheide and Others* v. *Belgian State*, [1997] ECR I–7281.

    [8] For a discussion of escape clauses, see P. Oliver, *Free Movement of Goods in the European Community*, Ch. IX.

    [9] See e.g. Articles 30[36], 46[56], 55[66].

    [10] See e.g. Articles 119[109h] and 119[109i] which authorize a Member State to take measures to overcome difficulties relating to its balance of payments.

    [11] See e.g. Article 134[115]. See also Articles 224 and 225.

    [12] Case 222/84 *Johnston* v. *Chief Constable of the Royal Ulster Constabulary* [1986] ECR 1651, para. 26; Joined Cases C–19 and C–20/90 *Karella and Karellas* [1991] ECR I–2691 para. 31.

interpreted strictly.[13] Thirdly, measures taken pursuant to them may not be more restrictive than is necessary to realize the legitimate objective in view. The principle of proportionality is often incorporated in the text of escape clauses which use expressions such as that the measure in issue must be 'justified',[14] or be 'strictly necessary'[15] or 'cause the least disturbance of the functioning of the common market'.[16]

2) *Proportionality and indirect discrimination.* Community law prohibits both direct and indirect discrimination. Where difference in treatment is indirect, namely based on a criterion other than the prohibited one, such difference does not amount to discrimination if it is objectively justified. The notion of objective justification incorporates that of proportionality in that a difference in treatment will not be objectively justified unless it is necessary to achieve its objectives. The issue acquires particular importance in relation to indirect discrimination on grounds of nationality[17] and also in relation to indirect sex discrimination.[18] In both areas the Court applies proportionality as a stringent test of necessity.

3) *Measures falling within the scope of Community law.* As a general principle of law, proportionality applies more widely to all national measures which implement or otherwise fall within the scope of Community law.[19] In particular, where Member States act as agents of the Community implementing Community policies, they must respect proportionality. In this context, the principle operates in the sphere of public law rather than as an instrument of market integration.

4.2. Equality and proportionality: Complementary or alternative patterns of integration?

The notions of non-discrimination and proportionality have been used by the Court as conceptual tools for drawing the demarcation line between lawful and

---

[13] See e.g. in relation to Article 134[115], Case 41/76 *Donckerwolcke* v. *Procureur de la Republique* [1976] ECR 1921, para. 29; Case 62/70 *Bock* v. *Commission* [1971] ECR 897, para. 14.

[14] See e.g. Article 30[36].   [15] Article 120[109i].   [16] Article 134[115], third para.

[17] See e.g. Case C–330/90 *R* v. *Inland Revenue Commissioners, ex parte Commerzbank* [1993] ECR I–4017; Case C–237/94 *O'Flynn* v. *Adjudication Officer* [1996] ECR I–2617; and above, the discussion of Article 12[6].

[18] See e.g. Case C–328/91 *Secretary of State for Social Security* v. *Thomas and Others* [1993] ECR I–1247; Case C–457/93 *Kuratorium für Dialyse und Nierentransplanation* v. *Lewark* [1996] ECR I–243; Case C–278/93 *Freers and Speckmann* v. *Deutsche Bundespost* [1996] ECR I–1165; cf. Case C–317/93 *Nolte* v. *Landesversicherungsanstalt Hannover* [1995] ECR I–4625 and Case *Megner and Scheffel* v. *Innungskrankenkasse Rheinhessen-Pfalz* [1995] ECR I–4743 where the Court found that the exclusion of persons working less than 15 hours a week from the statutory sickness and old age insurance schemes did not amount to indirect discrimination on grounds of sex as it was necessary to achieve social policy aims. See also C–400/93 *Royal Copenhagen* [1995] ECR I–1275.

[19] See above p. 23.

unlawful impediments to free movement. In that respect, the two notions complement each other and can be seen as centripetal forces to the establishment of the internal market. There is, however, an underlying tension between the two as they evince alternative patterns of integration. If it is accepted that free movement is exhausted in the obligation of Member States to treat imported products or services on an equal footing with domestic ones, discrimination is the touchstone of integration. But if it is accepted that free movement goes beyond equal treatment and requires freedom of access to the market, then any obstacle to free access becomes an unlawful impediment unless objectively justified. Under the second model, proportionality is elevated to the principal criterion for determining the dividing line between lawful and unlawful barriers to trade. It may be said then that equality and proportionality are in an inverse relationship: the less one relies on the first, the more it has to rely on the latter in order to determine what is a permissible restriction on trade. As an instrument for determining the legality of restrictions on trade, proportionality is the most flexible instrument that the European judicature possesses. It certainly broadens the scope of the judicial inquiry and increases the power of the Court. But in economic terms it is not necessarily the most efficient. It inserts a degree of uncertainty, encourages litigation, and, in that respect, it is liable to increase transaction costs. Indeed, the judgment in *Keck and Mithouard*[20] may be seen as an effort by the Court to infuse a higher degree of certainty in the interpretation of Article 28[30] and stop unmeritorious claims at an earlier stage.

It may be interesting to examine at this juncture the correlation between equality and proportionality in the context of the free movement of goods by reference to the judgment in *Keck* and its aftermath.[21]

In *Keck* the Court redefined the scope of Article 28[30] by drawing a distinction between rules concerning the physical characteristics of goods and those concerning selling arrangements. With regard to the former, the principle enunciated in *Cassis de Dijon*[22] continues to apply. With regard to selling arrangements, the Court elevated discrimination to the determining criterion. At paragraph 16 of the judgment, it held that rules of the importing State pertaining to selling arrangements do not fall within the scope of Article 28[30] provided that they apply to all affected traders operating in the national territory and that they affect in the same manner, in law and in fact, the marketing of domestic products and those from other Member States. The judgment in *Keck* represents one of the most spectacular departures from precedent in the Court's history. To justify it, the Court referred to 'the increasing tendency of traders to invoke Article 28[30] of the Treaty as a means of challenging any rule whose effect is to limit their commercial freedom even where such rules are not aimed at products from other Member States'.[23]

---

[20] Joined Cases C–267 and C–268/91 [1993] ECR I–6097.

[21] There is no intention here to examine in detail Article 28[30], for a discussion of which the reader is referred to the general works of EC law. See e.g. Weatherill and Beaumont, *EC Law*, Ch. 17.

[22] Case 120/78 *Rewe* v. *Bundesmonopolverwaltung für Branntwein* [1979] ECR 649.

[23] Op.cit., para. 15.

But what are the specific reasons which necessitated such a change in judicial policy? *Keck* can only be understood in historical perspective. In previous case law, the Court had interpreted the notion of measures having equivalent effect to quantitative restrictions very broadly. In *Dassonville* it was held that all national trading rules which are capable of hindering, directly or indirectly, actually or potentially, intra-Community trade come within the scope of Article 28[30].[24] Subsequently, the seminal *Cassis de Dijon*[25] effectively introduced the 'home country control' principle to the free movement of goods and expanded the scope of Article 30 firmly beyond the notion of discrimination. As a result of *Cassis de Dijon*, the importing State was no longer able to impose restrictions applicable on goods produced in its territory to goods lawfully produced in other Member States unless that was justified. The concept of mandatory requirements was invented to counterbalance the expansion of Article 28[30]. The emphasis shifted from the criterion of equal treatment between national and imported products to the criterion of justification on grounds of mandatory requirements bringing with it a corresponding increase in the powers of the Court. The *Dassonville* formula, as applied in *Cassis de Dijon*, brought within the ambit of Article 28[30] a host of national market-regulation measures many of which were by no means designed to affect imports, were dictated by non-economic considerations, and had evolved over the ages crystallizing local preferences. Regulation of market transactions is a form of regulatory intervention going back to ancient times and influenced heavily by religious, cultural, social, local and other geopolitical factors serving a wide diversity of interests.[26] Such measures were suddenly put under scrutiny in the light of a new pan-european economic constitutional order exemplified by the broad scope of Article 28[30]. As *Dassonville* and *Cassis de Dijon* liberated Article 28[30] from the notion of discrimination, the Court had no option but to rely on the principle of proportionality in order to draw the demarcation line between lawful and unlawful impediments to trade. That, in effect, led the Court to make choices of a broadly political nature which many of its members thought exceeded the judicial province. Whence could the Court derive legitimacy to give priority to the liberal view of undistorted competition favoured by German law as opposed to the more protectionist view favoured by the French tradition?[27] As the late Judge Joliet vividly put it: 'Pouvions-nous, à nous treize, prétendre détenir plus de sagesse et d'intelligence que tous les gouvernements et les parlements nationaux de la Communauté?'[28]

There is a second reason which led the Court to revise the interpretation of Article 28[30]. The previous case law was not devoid of inconsistencies. The uncertain state of the law combined with the broad scope attributed to Article

---

[24] Case 8/74 *Procureur du Roi* v. *Dassonville* [1974] ECR 837, para. 5.
[25] Case 120/78 *Rewe* v. *Bundesmonopolverwaltung für Branntwein* [1979] ECR 649.
[26] Weatherill, *Law and Integration in the European Union*, Ch. 7.
[27] R. Joliet, 'La Libre Circulation des Merchandises: L'arrêt *Keck et Mithouard* et les nouvelles orientations de la jurisprudence (1994) *Journal des tribunaux, Droit Européen*, 145 at 149.
[28] Ibid.

28[30] encouraged unmeritorious claims and led to an increase in litigation. In short, following *Dassonville* and *Cassis de Dijon* the scope of Article 28[30] seemed to become overambitious: questionable in conceptual terms and counterproductive in its practical application. In the light of those problems, *Keck* sought to increase legal certainty by offering a more predictable filtering mechanism. Whether it has succeeded in doing so is a different matter although subsequent case law shows that, at least from the point of view of legal certainty, the *Keck* formula should be given more credit than has been suggested by commentators.[29]

The *Keck* formula became a contentious point but, despite repeated efforts by Advocates General, the Court proved impervious to calls to restrict or refine it. In *Leclerc-Siplec*,[30] Jacobs AG expressed misgivings about the distinction between physical characteristics and selling arrangements. He considered that a measure which restricts selling arrangements may create extremely serious obstacles to inter-State trade. That could be the case in particular with rules restricting advertising.[31] But his objection was more fundamental. He considered that the notion of discrimination, adopted by *Keck* in relation to selling arrangements, is not an appropriate criterion on which to base the establishment of the internal market. In his view, all undertakings which engage in a legitimate economic activity in a Member State should have unfettered access to the whole of the Community market, unless there is a valid reason for denying them full access to a part of that market. The appropriate test therefore is whether the rules of the importing State constitute is a substantial restriction on access. This amounts in effect to introducing a *de minimis* test into Article 28[30], contrary to previous case law.[32] But the Advocate General considered that a *de minimis* test was the best to achieve the desired objective, namely to limit the scope of Article 28[30] in order to prevent excessive interference in the regulatory powers of the Member States.[33]

Although in *Leclerc* Jacobs AG seemed in effect to favour proportionality over non-discrimination as the determining criterion of lawful impediments to trade, his test is not as different from *Keck* as it appears on first reading. In *Keck* the Court removed from the ambit of Article 28[30] non-discriminatory selling arrangements on the ground that the application of such rules to the sale of products from other Member States 'is not by nature such as to prevent their access to the market or to impede access any more than it impedes the access of domestic products'.[34]

---

[29] See e.g. N. Reich, 'The "November Revolution" of the European Court of Justice' (1994) 31 CMLRev. 459.

[30] C–412/93 *Leclerc-Siplec* v. *TFI Publicité and M6 Publicité* [1995] ECR I–179. See also, more recently, Joined Cases C–34 to C–36/95 *KO* v. *De Agostini and TV-Shop* [1997] ECR I–3843.

[31] Op.cit., 194.

[32] See Joined Cases 177/82 and 178/82 *Van de Haar and Kaveka de Meern* [1984] ECR 1797.

[33] In the view of the Advocate General, a *de minimis* test should apply only to non-discriminatory restrictions and would perform a particularly useful function in relation to selling arrangements which, contrary to rules prohibiting the marketing of products, cannot be presumed to have a substantial impact on access to the market. Op.cit., 196–7.

[34] *Keck*, op.cit., para. 16.

A negative approach towards *Keck* was adopted by Lenz AG in *Commission* v. *Greece*.[35] There the Commission challenged the compatibility with Article 28[30] of a Greek law which prohibited the sale of formula milk for infants outside pharmacies. The Advocate General opined that *Keck* did not intend to exclude a priori all selling arrangements from the scope of application of Article 28[30].[36] He pointed out that rules governing the marketing of products are generally more intensive in their effects than rules governing general conditions of sale. In his view, the judgment in *Keck* did not apply to monopolies at the marketing level. This is because a sales monopoly established by law, although a selling arrangement, is capable of guiding and channelling sales. It excludes perforce other sales channels and therefore makes imports more difficult. Although Lenz AG attempted to restrict *Keck's* scope of application rather than to criticize it openly, his views are hardly compatible with the judgment in that case. As might have been expected, the Court did not follow the Opinion and, on the basis of *Keck*, dismissed the Commission's action.

The Advocate General failed to persuade the Court also in *Banchero*.[37] The case concerned the Italian state monopoly on tobacco products. One of the issues raised was whether the distribution system provided for by Italian law, which reserved the retail sale of tobacco products to outlets authorized by the State, was compatible with Article 28[30]. The Commission had argued that, by channelling tobacco sales, the Italian distribution system was liable to affect marketing possibilities for imported products. The Court rejected that argument stating that the monopoly had been reorganized in such a way that the State no longer managed directly tobacco outlets and authorized retailers were guaranteed direct access to wholesalers. The Court found no evidence of discriminatory treatment against Community producers. Elmer AG reached the opposite conclusion. He drew a distinction between the Italian legislation in issue and the kind of provisions examined by the Court in *Keck* and in subsequent cases where the judgment had been applied.[38] He considered that the latter concerned provisions limiting specific forms of marketing in such a general and non-restrictive way that it could not be presumed that they had a serious effect on the marketing of imported goods.[39] By contrast, he found that the Italian rules governing the sale of tobacco did more than merely to restrict certain selling arrangements: they were, as a whole, liable to affect marketing opportunities for imported goods and should therefore be regarded as constituting a measure having equivalent effect within the meaning of Article 28[30] of the Treaty.[40]

It seems then that in *Banchero* the Advocate General did not question the *Keck* formula but considered that the selling arrangements of the importing State were discriminatory in fact because they affected adversely marketing opportunities.

[35] C–391/92 [1995] ECR I–1621.   [36] Op.cit., 1628 *et seq.*

[37] C–387/93 [1995] ECR I–4663.

[38] It is surprising that no reference to *Commission* v. *Greece* appears in the Opinion of the Advocate General.

[39] *Banchero*, op.cit., 4677.   [40] Op.cit., 4677–8.

Banchero may be contrasted with *Franzén*.[41] The latter case put in issue the compatibility with Article 28[30] of the Swedish monopoly on the retail sale of alcohol. Swedish law made the production and the wholesale trade in alcoholic beverages subject to the holding of a licence and granted to a company owned by the State the monopoly for the retail sale of such products. The Court held that the monopoly was compatible with Article 31[37] because it did not discriminate against products from other Member States. It held, however, that the requirement to possess a production licence or a wholesale licence in order to be able to import alcoholic drinks infringed Article 28[30]. It constituted an obstacle to imports from other Member States in that it imposed additional costs on imported products, such as intermediary costs, payment of charges and fees for the grant of a licence, and costs arising from the obligation to maintain storage capacity in Sweden.[42] The Court did not refer to *Keck* nor did it explain whether the licensing requirements were selling arrangements. But in the circumstances it was not necessary to do so since it found the licensing system discriminatory. Both in *Banchero* and in *Franzén* the Court engaged in an analysis of market structure, even though in the first case the analysis does not seem wholly convincing in the light of the Opinion of the Advocate General.

In *De Agostini*[43] the Court conceded that an outright ban, applying in one Member State, of a method of promotion of a product which is lawfully sold there might have a greater impact on products from other Member States and might therefore fall foul of the second condition specified in paragraph 16 of *Keck*.[44] The case concerned the compatibility with Community law of Swedish legislation which prohibited the broadcasting of television advertisements directed at children. *De Agostini* restricts the scope of the ruling in *Leclerc-Siplec* and acknowledges, for the first time, that the prohibition of television advertising, although a selling arrangement, may be caught by Article 28[30]. The difference between *Leclerc-Siplec* and *De Agostini* seems to be that in *Leclerc-Siplec* the French law in issue prohibited a particular form of advertising (television advertising) of a particular form of marketing of products (i.e. distribution) whereas in *De Agostini* Swedish law prohibited television advertising of the product itself.[45]

In post *Keck* case law on the free movement of persons and services the Court appeared to give contradictory signs as it suggested that freedom of access rather than merely non-discrimination is the principle which permeates Articles 39[48], 43[52] and 49[59]. In *Alpine Investments*[46] it was held that the prohibition of cold-calling imposed by Dutch law to providers of financial services established in The Netherlands 'directly affected access' to the market in services in other Member

---

[41] Case C–189/95, op.cit.   [42] Op.cit., para. 71.
[43] C–34 to C–36/95 *KO* v. *De Agostini and TV-Shop* [1997] ECR I–3843.
[44] Op.cit., para. 42.
[45] See also C–368/95 *Vereinigte Familiapress* v. *Bauer Verlag* [1997] ECR I–3689; C–120/95 *Decker* judgment of 28 April 1998; and more recently, Case C-67/97 *Ditler Bluhme*, judgment of 3 December 1998.
[46] Case C–348/93 [1995] ECR I–1141.

States and was thus capable of hindering inter-State trade in services. In *Bosman*[47] the Court took the view that the FIFA transfer rules applicable to footballers, although they applied both to transfers between clubs within the same Member State and in different Member States, affected directly players' access to the employment market in other Member States and were thus capable of impeding freedom of movement for workers.

What conclusions may be drawn from the case law? The language used by the Court seems to be one of free access rather than one of discrimination, and that includes even *Keck*.[48] In *Alpine Investments* and in *Bosman* the Court distinguished the rules in issue from that in *Keck* on the ground that they affected access to inter-State trade. This suggests that in *Keck* the Court took the view that the prohibition of sale at a loss imposed by French law was liable neither to prevent access to the market nor to give an advantage to domestic products.[49] *De Agostini* also suggests that, although the Court has retreated from using proportionality as the determining criterion in the case of selling arrangements, freedom of access rather than discrimination remains the underlying force of Article 28[30]: the latter concept is but a means for determining the former. All in all, it is difficult to see why Article 28[30] should be restricted to discriminatory restrictions when Articles 49[59] and 39[48] are given wider scope by post-*Keck* case law.[50]

Despite the uncertainties in the case law, there is no denying that proportionality plays a cardinal role in the context of the free movement of goods. The pattern which emerges from the case law is as follows. National laws which obstruct trade are permissible only if they are shown to be justified. The means of justification differ depending on the discriminatory or non-discriminatory character of the measure. Measures which are discriminatory can be justified only by the grounds of derogation expressly stated in Article 30[36]. Measures which are non-discriminatory may also be justified by recourse to mandatory requirements, the list of which is open.[51] It includes, *inter alia*, the prevention of tax evasion, consumer protection, and unfair trading;[52] the protection of the environment,[53] the improvement of working conditions,[54] and the promotion of national and regional culture.[55] It

---

[47] Case C–415/93 *Bosman* [1995] ECR I–4921.   [48] See para. 17 of the judgment.

[49] See C. Barnard in (1997) 22 ELRev. at 451. That finding, however, appears incorrect in the light of the well-argued Opinion of the Advocate General. See *Keck*, op.cit., per Van Gerven AG.

[50] See also Barnard, op.cit.

[51] In *De Agostini* the Court accepted that a selling arrangement which disadvantages the marketing of products from other Member States and therefore falls foul of para. 16 of *Keck*, may be justified not only by reference to Article 30[36] but also by reference to overriding requirements of general public importance. See: paras. 45–7 of the judgment.

[52] Those three mandatory requirements were mentioned in *Cassis de Dijon*.

[53] Case 302/86 *Commission* v. *Denmark* [1988] ECR 4607.

[54] Case 155/80 *Oebel* [1981] ECR 1993.

[55] Joined Cases 60 and 61/84 *Cinetheque* v. *Federation Nationale des Cinemas Français* [1985] ECR 2605. And see also in the area of services the *tourist guides* cases, e.g. Case C–154/89 *Commission* v. *France* [1991] ECR I–649; Case C–288/89 *Collectieve Anntenevoorziening Gouda* v. *Commissariaat voor de Media* [1991] ECR I–1709; Case C–353/89 *Commission* v. *Netherlands* [1991] ECR I–4069; Case C–17/92 *Federacion de Distribuidores Cinematograficos* v. *Spain* [1993] ECR I–2239.

should be emphasized that it is open to Member States to plead new mandatory requirements provided that the interests whose protection is sought are of a non-economic nature.[56]

An obstacle to trade cannot be justified, whether under the grounds of derogation provided for in Article 30[36] or under mandatory requirements, unless it is proportionate. In determining the compatibility with Community law of national rules imposing obstacles to inter-State trade, the Court performs a balancing exercise.[57] In *Stoke-on-Trent* it held:[58]

Appraising the proportionality of national rules which pursue a legitimate aim under Community law involves weighing the national interest in attaining that aim against the Community interest in ensuring the free movement of goods. In that regard, in order to verify that the restrictive effects on intra-Community trade of the rules at issue do not exceed what is necessary to achieve the aim in view, it must be considered whether those effects are direct, indirect or purely speculative and whether those effects do not impede the marketing of imported products more than the marketing of national products.

Although *Stoke-on-Trent* has been overtaken by *Keck* in that the prohibition of Sunday trading now falls outside the scope of Article 28[30] as a non-discriminatory selling arrangement, the above quote still captures the essence of the proportionality test where the principle applies.

4.3. The 'less restrictive alternative' test

In the context of Article 30[36] as in the context of mandatory requirements, the Court has interpreted the principle of proportionality as meaning that national measures will be justified only if the national interest which they seek to protect cannot be protected as effectively by measures which less restrict intra-Community trade. A Member State must therefore choose the least restrictive alternative available on the circumstances. The less restrictive alternative test will now be examined in more detail.

4.3.1. Article 30[36]

The free movement of goods is subject to the derogation of Article 30[36] which states as follows:

---

[56] See Case 7/61 *Commission* v. *Italy* [1961] ECR 317 at 329 and Oliver, *Free Movement of Goods in the European Community*, p. 247. Oliver takes the view that in Case C–18/88 *RTT* v. *GB-Inno* [1991] ECR I–5941, which concerned standards for telephone equipment to be connected to the public network, the Court intended to create a new mandatory requirement, namely, 'the protection of the public network and its proper functioning'.

[57] Part of that exercise is sometimes performed by national courts, see below p. 160.

[58] Case C–169/91 *Council of the City of Stoke-on-Trent and Another* v. *B & Q* [1992] ECR I–6635, para. 15.

The provisions of Articles 28 and 29 shall not preclude prohibitions or restrictions on imports, exports or goods in transit justified on grounds of public morality, public policy or public security; the protection of health and life of humans, animals or plants; the protection of national treasures possessing artistic, historic or archaeological value; or the protection of industrial and commercial property. Such prohibitions or restrictions shall not, however, constitute a means of arbitrary discrimination or a disguised restriction on trade between Member States.

As an exception to a fundamental freedom, Article 30[36] must be interpreted strictly.[59] According to consistent case law, the purpose of Article 30[36] is not to reserve certain matters to the exclusive jurisdiction of Member States, but merely to allow national legislation to derogate from the free movement of goods to the extent to which that is justified in order to achieve the objectives provided for in that Article.[60] A measure adopted on the basis of Article 30[36] can be justified only if it does not restrict intra-Community trade more than is absolutely necessary.[61] The Article has a 'provisional character' in that it applies only in so far as the Community has not adopted harmonization measures protecting the interest in issue.[62] Similar principles govern the express derogations from the right of establishment and the freedom to provide services which enable Member States to derogate on grounds of public security, public policy and public health.[63]

The application of the less restrictive alternative test in the context of Article 30[36] is vividly illustrated by the judgment in *de Peijper*.[64] Netherlands law made the importation of medicinal products conditional upon the production of certain documents which could be obtained only from the manufacturer. The effect of that requirement was to favour imports by importers associated with the manufacturer to the detriment of parallel importers. It was claimed that the requirement to produce the documents, which concerned the composition and method of preparation of the medicinal products, was justified on public health grounds. The Court held that, within the limits imposed by the Treaty, it is for the Member States to decide what degree of protection to grant to the protection of health and life of humans. National provisions do not fall within the exception of Article 30[36], however, if the health and life of humans can be protected as effectively by mea-

---

[59] Case 124/81 *Commission* v. *United Kingdom* [1983] ECR 203, para. 13.

[60] Case 153/78 *Commission* v. *Germany* [1979] ECR 2555, para. 5; Case 72/83 *Campus Oil Limited* v. *Minister for Industry and Energy* [1984] ECR 2727, para. 32; Case C–367/89 *Richardt and 'Les Accessoires Scientifiques'* [1991] ECR I–4621, para. 19.

[61] Case 72/83 *Campus Oil Limited* v. *Minister for Industry and Energy* [1984] ECR 2727, para. 37; Case C–367/89 *Richardt and 'Les Accessoires Scientifiques'* [1991] ECR I–4621, para. 20. See also Case 12/78 *Eggers* [1978] ECR 1935; Case 42/82 *Commission* v. *France* [1983] ECR 1013.

[62] See e.g. Case 5 /77 *Tedeschi* v. *Denkavit* [1977] ECR 1555; Case 251/78 *Denkavit Futtermittel* v. *Minister für Ernährung, Landwirtschaft und Forsten* [1979] ECR 3369; Case 73/84 *Denkavit Futtermittel* v. *Land Nordrhein-Westfalen* [1985] ECR 1013; Case 190/87 *Oberkreisdirektor des Kreises Borken and Another* v. *Moormann* [1988] ECR 4689. Adoption of a harmonization measure may preclude reliance on Article 36 even if the measure is not exhaustive: Case C–5/94 *The Queen* v. *Ministry of Agriculture, Fisheries and Food, ex parte Hedley Lomas (Ireland) Ltd.* [1996] ECR I–2553. Cf. Case C–347/89 *Eurim-Pharm* [1991] ECR I–1747, para. 26.

[63] See Articles 56 and 66.   [64] Case 104/75 [1976] ECR 613.

sures which less restrict intra-Community trade. In particular, the Court held that Article 30[36] cannot be relied on to justify rules or practices which, even though they are beneficial, contain restrictions which are explained primarily by a concern to lighten the administration's burden or reduce public expenditure, unless, in the absence of the said rules or practices, that burden or expenditure would clearly exceed the limits of what can reasonably be required.[65] On the basis of those considerations, the Court drew a distinction between, on the one hand, documents relating to a medicinal product in general and, on the other hand, documents relating to a specific batch of that product. With regard to the former, where the authorities of the importing Member State had in their possession, as a result of a previous importation, all the particulars relating to the product in order to be able to ascertain whether it was harmful to health, it was unnecessary to require a subsequent importer to produce the same particulars. With regard to documents relating to a specific batch, the Court accepted that the national authorities must be in a position to satisfy themselves that the batch imported complies with the particulars of the product. It continued:[66]

Nevertheless, having regard to the nature of the market for the pharmaceutical product in question, it is necessary to ask whether this objective cannot be equally well achieved if the national administrations, instead of waiting passively for the desired evidence to be produced to them—and in a form calculated to give the manufacturer of the product and his duly appointed representatives an advantage—were to admit, where appropriate similar evidence and, in particular, to adopt a more active policy which could enable every trader to obtain the necessary evidence.

This question is all the more important because parallel importers are very often in a position to offer the goods at a price lower than the one applied by the duly appointed importer for the same product, a fact which, where medicinal preparations are concerned, should, where appropriate, encourage the public health authorities not to place parallel imports at a disadvantage, since the effective protection of health and life of humans also demands that medicinal preparations should be sold at reasonable prices.

The Court pointed out two less restrictive alternatives. First, national authorities possessed the powers necessary to compel the manufacturer or his duly appointed representatives to supply particulars making it possible to ascertain the qualities of the medicinal product imported by the parallel importer. Secondly, co-operation between the authorities of the Member States would enable them to obtain on a reciprocal basis the documents necessary for checking largely standardized and widely distributed products. The Court concluded that, taking into account the possible ways of obtaining information, national authorities must consider whether the effective protection of health justifies a presumption of the non-conformity of an imported batch with the description of the medicinal preparation, or whether on the contrary it is sufficient to lay down a presumption of conformity placing on

---

[65] Op.cit., paras. 17–18.   [66] Op.cit., paras. 24–5.

the administration the onus of rebutting it.[67] *De Peijper* indicates that in applying the principle of proportionality, the Court is prepared to scrutinize closely restrictions on free movement and assess the legality of such restrictions taking into account all interests involved.

The less restrictive alternative test was also applied in *Commission* v. *United Kingdom* (*UHT milk* case).[68] UK legislation made the importation of UHT milk subject to an import licence on the ground that such licences were necessary to enable the competent authorities to identify consignments of imported milk and, upon receiving information from the exporting country, to trace infected consignments and destroy them before reaching the market. The Court had little sympathy for this argument, dismissing it as follows:[69]

. . . the issue of an administrative authorization . . . results in an impediment to intra-Community trade which, in the present case, could be eliminated without prejudice to the effectiveness of the protection of animal health and without increasing the administrative or financial burden imposed by the pursuit of that objective. That result could be achieved if the United Kingdom authorities abandoned the practice of issuing licences and confined themselves to obtaining the information which is of use to them, for example, by means of declarations signed by the importers, accompanied if necessary by the appropriate certificates.

In addition to the requirement of import licences, UK legislation required that imported UHT milk was packed on premises within the United Kingdom. That requirement was said to be indispensable in order to ensure that the milk was not infected. The Court held, however, that health protection could be ensured by requiring importers to produce certificates issued by the competent authorities of the exporting Member State.[70] Where co-operation between national authorities makes it possible to facilitate and simplify frontier checks, the authorities responsible for health inspection must ascertain whether the substantiating documents issued within the framework of that co-operation raise a presumption that the imported goods comply with the requirements of domestic health legislation thus enabling the checks carried out upon importation to be simplified. The Court came to the conclusion that in the case of the UHT milk the conditions were satisfied for there to be a presumption of accuracy in favour of the statements contained in such documents. It added that the necessary co-operation did not preclude the authorities of the importing Member State from carrying out controls by means of samples to ensure observance of the requisite standards.[71]

---

[67] Op.cit., paras. 26–8. In any event, the Court held that a parallel importer could not be compelled to prove the conformity of his products with the requisite standards on the basis of documents to which he had no access, where proof of such conformity can be provided by alternative means. Cf. Case 188/84 *Commission* v. *France* (*Woodworking machines* case) [1986] ECR 419, para. 39.

[68] Case 124/81 *Commission* v. *United Kingdom* [1983] ECR 203. See further Case C–62/90 *Commission* v. *Germany* [1992] ECR I–2575, below p. 146.

[69] Op.cit., para. 18.   [70] Op.cit., para. 29.   [71] Paras. 30–1.

4.3.2. Mandatory requirements

The case law suggests that, as a general rule, the degree of scrutiny exercised by the Court does not differ depending on whether a restriction is imposed in the interests of one of the express derogations provided in the Treaty or of a mandatory requirement. In relation to the latter, the Court has expressly stated that where a Member State has a choice between various measures to attain the same objective it is under an obligation to choose the means which least restrict the free movement of goods.[72]

In application of the less restrictive alternative test, the Court has laid down the principle that the sale of a product must not be prohibited where consumers may sufficiently be protected by adequate labelling requirements.[73] In *Commission* v. *Italy*[74] Italian law restricted the designation 'aceto' to vinegar produced from wine and prohibited the marketing of vinegar produced from other agricultural products under that designation. The Italian Government argued that the purpose of the prohibition was to protect the Italian consumer who was accustomed to treat all vinegars as wine vinegars and would otherwise run the risk of being misled as to the essential characteristics of the product. The Court held that the need for consumer protection could be satisfied by the 'compulsory affixing of suitable labels' indicating the nature of the product. Such a course would enable the consumer to make his choice in full knowledge of the facts and would guarantee transparency.[75] In the *German Beer* case,[76] German law provided that beer may be manufactured only from certain ingredients and prohibited the marketing as beer of drinks made by other methods. The German Government sought to justify the prohibition arguing that in the minds of German consumers the designation 'bier' was inseparably linked to the beverage manufactured solely from the ingredients specified in German laws. The Court rejected that argument. It held that it is legitimate for national law to enable consumers who attribute specific qualities to beers manufactured from particular ingredients to make their choice on the basis of that consideration. That, however, could be ensured by a less restrictive means, namely by indicating the raw materials used in the manufacture of beer. The Court added that such a system of consumer information could operate in practice even in relation to products, like beer, which are not necessarily supplied in bottles or cans. Where beer is sold on draught, the requisite information may appear on casks or the beer

[72] Case 261/81 *Rau* v. *De Smedt* [1982] ECR 3961, para. 12; Case 25/88 *Criminal Proceedings against Wurmser and Others* [1989] ECR 1105, para. 13; Case 407/85 *Gloken and Kritzinger* v. *USL Centro-Sud and Provincia autonoma di Bolzano* [1988] ECR 4233, para. 10.

[73] This is referred to by Oliver as the 'golden rule'. See, op.cit., p. 227.

[74] Case 193/80 *Commission* v. *Italy* [1981] ECR 3019. See also Case 788/79 *Gilli and Adres* [1980] ECR 2071.

[75] Op.cit., para. 27. Cf. the Opinion of Slynn AG.

[76] Case 178/84 *Commission* v. *Germany* [1987] ECR 1227.

taps.[77] Labelling requirements have been considered as sufficient alternatives in other cases. In *Rau*[78] the requirement that margarine can only be sold in cube-shaped packs so as to enable the consumer to distinguish it from butter was struck down on the ground that consumers could be protected by labelling requirements. Notably, in the *German Beer* case the Court stated that a system of mandatory consumer information must not entail negative assessments for products not complying with the requirements of national law.[79] It is arguable then that, depending on the circumstances, a requirement to indicate on the label of a product that it is produced by methods banned in the Member State of marketing may not meet the test of proportionality.

It is clear that, in assessing the compatibility with Community law of national measures which pursue a legitimate aim but restrict inter-State trade, the Court performs a weighing exercise. It juxtaposes the national interest in attaining that aim against the Community interest in ensuring the free movement of goods.[80] In performing that exercise, the Court follows a proactive rather than a reactive approach. Thus in examining restrictions allegedly justified for the protection of consumers the Court has seen the internal market as one of the factors set to influence consumer choices and has held that the legislation of a Member State must not 'crystallize given consumer habits so as to consolidate an advantage acquired by national industries concerned to comply with them'.[81] The case law evinces a tendency towards interpreting the fundamental freedoms not merely as exponents of free trade but as the normative expressions of a European economic constitution.

4.3.3. The limits of the less restrictive alternative test

The less restrictive alternative test entails a strict application of proportionality but by no means a mechanical one. The principle is by its nature open-textured and the degree of scrutiny remains far from uniform. Thus, the less restrictive alternative test does not necessarily mean that a restriction imposed by a Member State will fail if another Member State imposes a less restrictive requirement. In *Alpine Investments*,[82] the Dutch authorities prohibited financial intermediaries operating in the commodities futures market from making unsolicited contact with prospective clients by telephone (cold-calling). The Court held that the objectives of the pro-

---

[77] Op.cit., paras. 35–6. A similar reasoning was followed in Case 407/85 *Gloken and Kritzinger* v. *USL Centro-Sud and Provincia autonoma di Bolzano* [1988] ECR 4233. The Court found the prohibition of Italian law on the sale of pasta made from common wheat incompatible with Article 28[30] in so far as it applied to imported products. It considered labelling requirements as a sufficient alternative and indicated that Italian law could also require information to be given to the consumer as to the composition of pasta in restaurants.

[78] Case 261/81 *Rau* v. *de Smedt* [1982] ECR 3961.   [79] Para. 35.

[80] *Council of the City of Stoke-on-Trent* v. *B & Q*, op.cit.

[81] Case 170/78 *Commission* v. *United Kingdom* [1980] ECR 417; Case 178/84 *Commission* v. *Germany* [1987] ECR 1227, para. 32.

[82] C–384/93 [1995] ECR I–1141.

hibition, which were to protect investors and to safeguard the integrity of the Dutch financial services industry, were imperative reasons of public interest capable of justifying a restriction on the freedom to provide services. It was argued, however, that the total ban on cold-calling infringed proportionality. Alpine Investments referred to less stringent requirements applicable in the United Kingdom where financial intermediaries were under the obligation to keep records of telephone conversations. The Advocate General, whose view on this point was fully endorsed by the Court, stated that harmonization directives in the field of consumer protection usually permit Member States to impose additional or more stringent requirements. *A fortiori*, where no harmonization measures have been introduced, the rules of a Member State cannot be held disproportionate merely because another Member State applies less restrictive rules. If that were so, Member States would need to align their legislation with the Member State which imposed the least onerous requirements.[83] The obvious concern was to avoid a 'race to the bottom'.

Alpine Investments shows that whether a restriction on a marketing technique passes the test of proportionality should be assessed *inter alia* by reference to the conditions prevailing in the national market and the reasons which led to its adoption. Although in that case there was clearly a less restrictive alternative operative in another Member State, the Court focused on the effects of the restriction rather than on a comparison between the laws of different Member States. A similar approach has been followed in other cases. Thus, the Court has held that, in assessing the proportionality of measures taken on grounds of public health, account may be taken of 'national consumption habits'.[84]

In *Oosthoek*,[85] Netherlands law prohibited the giving of free gifts as a means of sales promotion unless the consumption or use of the free gift was related to the product in respect of the purchase of which it was given. The Court found that, although the requirement of related consumption or use had not been incorporated in the laws of other Member States, it did not exceed what was necessary for the attainment of the objectives pursued. In *Aragonesa de Publicidad*,[86] it was held that national legislation which prohibited the advertising in certain places of beverages having an alcoholic strength of more than 23 degrees was proportionate on the ground that it was not manifestly unreasonable as part of a campaign against alcoholism.[87] The Court concentrated on the notion of reasonableness rather than on

[83] Op.cit., at 1165 per Jacobs AG and para. 51 of the judgment. The point was confirmed in Case C–3/95 *Reisebüro Broede* v. *Gerd Sandker* [1996] ECR I–6511, para. 42. Cf. Case 40/82 *Commission* v. *United Kingdom* [1982] ECR 2793.

[84] Case 97/83 *Melkunie* [1984] ECR 2367, para. 19.

[85] Case 286/81 *Oosthoek's Uitgeversmaatschappij* [1982] ECR 4575.

[86] Joined Cases C–1/90 and C–176/90 *Aragonesa de Publicidad Exterior and Publivía* [1991] ECR I–4151. Cf. Case C–362/88 *GB-INNO-MB* [1990] ECR I–667.

[87] As Weatherill remarks, the approach of the Court in *Aragonesa* is compatible with that in *Cassis de Dijon* where the Court rejected the argument of the German Government that controlling the supply of *weak* alcoholic drinks was part of a policy for the protection of public health. See Weatherill, *Law and Integration in the European Union*, p. 238.

the existence of less stringent alternatives. In that case, however, the national measure in issue restricted freedom of trade only to a limited extent as it applied to a limited range of products. The more tenuous the restriction on free movement, the more lax the standard of proportionality.[88] In *Buet*,[89] French law prohibited canvassing for the purpose of selling educational material. The Court confirmed that rules seeking to protect the consumer must be proportionate and that Member States must make use of the least restrictive means at their disposal capable of attaining the objective pursued. It then stated that canvassing at private dwellings exposed potential customers to the risk of making an ill-considered purchase. Although, to guard against that risk, it was normally sufficient to ensure that purchasers had the right to cancel a contract, special considerations applied where the canvassing related to educational causes. That was because the potential purchaser often belonged to a group of people who were behind with their education and were seeking to catch up, which made them particularly vulnerable to salesmen. Also, the Court took into account the fact that the prohibition of canvassing had been introduced as a result of numerous complaints caused by abuses. Finally, it noted that the consequences of an ill-considered purchase were not only financial since the purchase of unsuitable material could compromise the consumer's chances of obtaining further training and thus consolidating his position in the labour market. In conclusion, it held that a Member State could legitimately consider that giving consumers a right of cancellation was not sufficient protection and that it was necessary to ban canvassing at private dwellings.[90]

The above cases illustrate that, inevitably, the notion of proportionality has a close affinity to that of reasonableness. In effect, the underlying judicial policy is to invite Member States to a dialogue. Member States are called upon to justify measures which cause obstacles to trade and to search for less restrictive solutions, but the application of the principle does not remove all discretion from national authorities. The model which emerges from the case law is one of selective judicial deference to the choices of national administrations. *Cinéthèque* and, more recently, *Alpine Investments* show that the wider the Court understands the scope of fundamental freedoms the less vigorously it is prepared to apply proportionality. Viewed in that light, a soft proportionality test is the quid pro quo for extending the scope of free movement.[91]

In some cases, it may be difficult, or even impossible, to ascertain on the basis of objective factors that a less restrictive rule is sufficiently effective to pursue the objective in view. The procedure before the Court of Justice does not lend itself to fact-finding missions and, inevitably, heavy reliance is placed on the submissions of the parties. In references for preliminary rulings, this is compensated by leaving the precise determination of the issue on the national court although that raises

---

[88] Joined Cases 60 and 61/84 *Cinéthèque* v. *Fédération Nationale des Cinémas Français* [1985] ECR 2605.
[89] Case 382/87 *Buet and another* v. *Ministère public* [1989] ECR 1235.
[90] Op.cit., paras. 12–15.   [91] This view is countenanced also by *De Agostini*.

other concerns.[92] Overall, the Court pursues only a limited economic analysis of market conditions. The subjective evaluations required in applying the principle of proportionality explain why disagreements between the Court and Advocates General are not infrequent in this area.

The difficulties in applying the less restrictive alternative test are illustrated by *Meyhui* v. *Schott Zwiesel Glaswerke*.[93] The case concerned the compatibility with Article 28[30] of a Directive 69/493 on the approximation of the laws of the Member States on crystal glass.[94] The Directive classifies crystal glass products into four categories. In relation to high quality products belonging to categories 1 and 2, the descriptions specified in the directive may be used freely whatever the country of destination. By contrast, in relation to lower quality products belonging in categories 3 and 4, the Directive provides that only the description in the language or languages of the country in which the goods are marketed may be used. Litigation arose as a result of the refusal of a German glass producer to affix to products belonging to categories 3 and 4 their description in Belgium's official languages. The Court pointed out that the purpose of the requirement pertaining to description is to protect both the consumer against fraud and the manufacturer who complies with the standards laid down in the Directive. It then held:[95]

It may . . . be considered that, in the case of the first two categories, consumers are adequately protected by the fact that in all the descriptions adopted by the directive (cristal supérieur 30%, cristallo superiore 30%, hochbleikristall 30%, volloodkristal 30%, full lead crystal 30%, krystal 30% . . .) the word 'crystal' is easily recognizable and, moreover, is always accompanied by an indication of the percentage of lead.

In the case of the lower two categories, on the other hand (crystallin, vetro sonoro superiore, kristallglass, kristallynglas, sonoorglas, crystal glass, crystallin, vidrio sonoro superior, vidro sonoro superior, verre sonore, vetro sonoro, vidrio sonoro, vidro sonoro . . .) the difference in the quality of the glass used is not easily discernible to the average consumer for whom the purchase of crystal glass products is not a frequent occurrence. It is therefore necessary for him to be given the clearest information possible as to what he is buying so that he does not confuse a product in categories 3 and 4 with a product in the higher categories and consequently that he does not pay too much.

The fact that consumers in a Member State in which the products are marketed are to be informed in the language or languages of that country is therefore an appropriate means of protection. In this regard it should be held that the hypothesis referred to by the national court that another language may be easily comprehensible to the purchaser is of only marginal importance.

Finally, the measure chosen by the Community legislature in order to protect consumers does not appear disproportionate to the goal pursued. There is nothing in the file to suggest that there might conceivably be some different measure which could achieve the same goal while being less constrictive for producers.

---

[92] See below p. 160.
[93] Case C–51/93 [1994] ECR I–3879.   [94] OJ, English Spec. ed., 1969 (II), p. 599.
[95] Op.cit., paras. 17–20.

The Court's reasoning contrasts with the approach of the Advocate General, who identified two limbs of the description requirement: the requirement to use the language of the country of marketing; and the prohibition against using any other languages in addition. The Advocate General found that the first requirement was justified in some cases but not in others. For example, it is reasonable to require that French products belonging to category 3 (crystallin) must be marketed in The Netherlands under the description applying in that country (sonooorglas). However, it may be unnecessarily restrictive to require a French producer of category 4 products (verre sonore) to use, when marketing them in Italy, Spain or Portugal, the descriptions applicable in those countries (vetro sonoro, vidrio sonoro and vidro sonoro). The Advocate General found the prohibition of using additional languages particularly onerous on traders. On balance, he came to the conclusion that both aspects of the requirement were invalid. He stated that corresponding requirements laid down by national law would be in breach of Article 28[30] and concluded that it was possible for the Community legislature to find an alternative rule which would take better account of the requirements inherent in the establishment of the internal market.[96] The case illustrates how difficult it is to apply the principle of proportionality which, in some cases, entails in effect a subjective test. The difference between the Opinion of the Advocate General and the Court is striking, but the answer may lie somewhere between the two. The Court seem to have authorized the most restrictive measure, that is to say, a prohibition on the use of other languages in addition to that of the State of marketing without good reason.[97] On the other hand, the Advocate General gave no concrete examples of measures less restrictive than the compulsory use of the language of the State of destination which would guarantee effective protection of consumers in all cases. The judgment contrasts sharply with other cases concerning the compulsory use of certain languages where the Court took a more critical view of such requirements,[98] but the distinction may lie on the fact that in *Meyhui* in issue was the validity of a Community measure and not of a national one. Article 28[30] binds not only Member States but also the Community institutions but the Court tends to allow the latter more latitude with regard to justification for restrictions on trade[99] and implied as much in *Meyhui*.[100]

4.3.4. Equivalence and duplication

The Court has derived from the principle of proportionality two specific, interrelated, requirements: the requirement of equivalence and the requirement of co-

---

[96] Op.cit., 3891–2.   [97] See the criticism by Oliver, op.cit., pp. 231–2.

[98] See e.g. Case 27/80 *Fietje* [1980] ECR 3839; Case C–369/89 *Piageme* v. *Peeters* [1991] ECR I–2971.

[99] See Oliver, op.cit., pp. 45 *et seq.*, p. 232.

[100] At para. 21 of the judgment the Court stated that by adopting the contested requirement the Council has not exceeded the limits of its discretion, implying a more lax application of the proportionality test. However, as Oliver notes, op.cit., p. 232, there is nothing to suggest that the ruling does not apply equally to national measures.

operation between national authorities. Regulatory restrictions imposed on goods or services by the host State must not duplicate requirements imposed by the State of origin. In the context of the free movement of goods[101] this applies in particular to health inspections. The Court has held that health inspections carried out by Member States in accordance with Article 30[36] are justified provided that the measures adopted are in reasonable proportion to the aim pursued and that the protection of health cannot be achieved as effectively by measures which restrict intra-Community trade to a lesser extent. According to the same line of cases, the free movement of goods is served by the carrying out of health inspections in the country of production and the health authorities of the Member States concerned should co-operate in order to avoid the repetition, in the importing country, of checks which have already been carried out in the country of production.[102] In *Frans-Nederlandse Maatschappij voor Biologische Producten*[103] the Court held, in relation to plant protection products containing toxic substances, that the national authorities are not entitled to require without good reason laboratory tests which have already been carried out in another Member State and their results are available to those authorities or may at their request be placed at their disposal. The principle of co-operation, however, does not impair the right of each Member State to apply its own legislation to protect public health, provided that the requirements of Article 30[36] are fulfilled.[104]

The principle of equivalence is a powerful tool of negative integration but its application is restricted where Member States espouse conflicting regulatory philosophies. In the *French Woodworking machines* case,[105] the Commission took issue with the safety standards imposed by French law on woodworking machines which severely inhibited imports by requiring prior technical inspection and, in the case of more dangerous equipment, approval by the Ministry of Labour. The safety requirements were the expression of the risk prevention philosophy underlying the French system. The legislation was based on the idea that users of machines must be protected from their own mistakes and that the machines must be designed so that the user's intervention is limited to the minimum. In other Member States, in particular Germany, the underlying idea was that the worker should receive thorough and continuing training. The Court held that a Member State is not entitled to prevent the marketing of a product originating in another Member State which provides a level of protection of the health and life of humans equivalent to that which the national rules are intended to ensure. It is therefore contrary to proportionality for national rules to require that such imported products must comply

---

[101] For services, see e.g. Case C–76/90 *Säger* [1991] ECR I–4221, para. 15.

[102] See Case 73/84 *Denkavit Futtermittel* v. *Land Nordrhein-Westfalen* [1985] ECR 1013, para. 14 and also Case 35/76 *Simmenthal* v. *Italian Minister for Finance* [1976] ECR 1871, Case 46/76 *Bauhuis* v. *The Netherlands State* [1977] ECR 5; Case 251/78 *Denkavit Futtermittel* v. *Minister für Ernährung, Landwirtschaft und Forsten* [1979] ECR 3369; *Commission* v. *United Kingdom* (*UHT milk*), op.cit.

[103] Case 272/80 [1981] ECR 3277, paras. 14–15.

[104] Case 97/83 *Melkunie* [1984] ECR 2367, para. 14.

[105] Case 188/84 *Commission* v. *France* [1986] ECR 419.

strictly and exactly with the provisions or technical requirements laid down for products manufactured in the Member State in question when the imported products afford users the same level of protection. The Court, however, dismissed the Commission's claim on the ground that it had not been proved that machines in free circulation in other Member States provided the same level of protection as French machines. The requirement of equivalence is effectively a requirement of non-discrimination and fundamental differences in the philosophy of control existing in the various Member States may make it impossible to carry out a meaningful comparison of the national requirements with a view to establishing comparability.

The principle of the less restrictive alternative applies in relation to the other fundamental freedoms. According to the case law, requirements imposed on providers of services must be such as to guarantee the achievement of the intended objective and must not go beyond what is necessary in order to achieve that objective. In other words, it must not be possible to obtain the same result by less restrictive rules.[106] The Court has accepted that Article 49[59] covers also non-discriminatory restrictions on the freedom to provide services.[107] Such restrictions, however, may be justified not only by reference to the express derogation of Article 56 but also by imperative reasons of public interest in so far as that interest is not protected by the rules to which the person providing the services is subject in the Member State in which he is established. In particular, those requirements must be objectively necessary in order to ensure compliance with the professional rules and to guarantee the protection of the recipient of services and they must not exceed what is necessary to attain those objectives.[108] Thus in *Säger*, the Court accepted that the requirement to possess a professional qualification in order to be entitled to give legal advice was necessary to protect the public. However, it came to the conclusion that the requirement to possess a professional qualification in order to offer patent renewal services of the type in issue in that case was not necessary for the protection of the public. The services in issue where of a straightforward nature and did not require any specific professional aptitudes. The provider of the patent renewal services did not advise his clients. He simply alerted them when renewal fees had to be paid and paid the fees on their behalf. Also, failure to renew the patent had only limited consequences for the patent holder.[109]

An example in relation to the right of establishment is provided by *Kraus v. Land Baden-Württemberg*.[110] The question raised was whether a German national could use in Germany a postgraduate law degree obtained in Scotland without prior authorization from the German authorities. The Court held that the requirement

---

[106] See e.g. Case C–288/89 *Collectieve Antennevoorziening Gouda* [1991] ECR I–4007; Case C–154/89 *Commission* v. *France* [1991] ECR I–659, para. 15; Case C–198/89 *Commission* v. *Greece* [1991] ECR I–727, para. 19.

[107] See Case C–76/90 *Säger* [1991] ECR I–4221 at 4234 per Jacobs AG.

[108] Op.cit., para. 15 and see cases referred to therein.

[109] See further Case C–55/94 *Gebhard* [1995] ECR I–4165.

[110] Case 19/92 [1993] ECR I–1663.

of authorization was not in itself incompatible with Community law. However, the Court derived from the principle of proportionality the following requirements: the procedure for authorization must have as its sole purpose to verify that the degree has been correctly awarded, the procedure must be readily available and not dependent on payment of excessive charges, any refusal of authorization must be subject to judicial review, the person concerned must be able to find out the reasons for a refusal, and the sanctions provided for disregard of the authorization procedure must not be disproportionate to the seriousness of the offence.

4.4. Specific grounds

We turn now to examine in more detail the application of the principle of proportionality on measures taken in the interests of public health, consumer protection and public security. Public security and public health are among the grounds of derogation expressly stated in the articles of the Treaty which provide for exceptions to the free movement of goods, persons and services.[111] The principle of proportionality will be examined here by reference especially to Article 30[36]. Consumer protection is one of the mandatory requirements recognized by the Court under the *Cassis de Dijon* formula and also one of the imperative reasons of public interest which may justify national measures restricting the free movement of services.

4.4.1. Public health

The Court has held that human health and life rank first among the interests protected by Article 30[36] and that, in the absence of Community legislation, it is in principle for the Member States to decide on the degree to which they wish to protect human health and life and how that degree of protection is to be achieved.[112] Nevertheless, measures taken to protect public health may not go beyond what is necessary to protect the objective in view. We saw above that in *de Peijper* and in the *UHT* case the Court was prepared to apply the test of proportionality strictly.[113] Clearly, measures taken on grounds of health protection must not constitute a disguised restriction on imports.[114] In *Commission* v. *United Kingdom*,[115] the Court held that the imposition of an import ban on poultry products from other Member States constituted a quantitative restriction on imports, which was

---

[111] See Articles 30[36], 39(3)[48(3)], 46[56] and 55[66].

[112] Joined Cases 266 & 267/87 R v. *Royal Pharmaceutical Society of Great Britain, ex parte Association of Pharmaceutical Importers* [1989] ECR 1295, para. 21.

[113] Above, p. 134.

[114] On restrictions on exports on grounds of public health, see e.g. Case 118/86 *Openbaar Ministerie* v. *Nertsvoederfabriek Nederland* [1987] ECR 3883.

[115] Case 40/82 [1982] ECR 2793.

not justified on the ground of preventing the spreading of the Newcastle disease, since there were other less stringent measures for attaining the same result. The Court found that on the facts the real aim of the ban was to protect the British producers and 'did not form part of a seriously considered health policy'.[116]

In *Commission* v. *Germany*,[117] German law prohibited the importation for personal use of medicinal products lawfully prescribed by a doctor and purchased in another Member State where such products were available in Germany only on prescription. The German Government argued that the foreign language on the label and the fact that the doctor who prescribed the product and the pharmacist who dispensed it were far away posed the danger that the imported product might be incorrectly used. The Court held that the purchase of a medicinal product in a pharmacy in another Member State provides a guarantee equivalent to that which would be provided if the product was purchased in the importing State. That finding was all the more compelling given that the provisions for access to, and the exercise of, the profession of pharmacist and the profession of doctor had been made subject to harmonization directives. It added that the fact that the doctor who prescribed the medicinal product or the pharmacist who sold it are established in another Member State does not prevent them from supervising the use of the product, if necessary, with the aid of a colleague established in the importing State. Also the doctor or the pharmacist supplying the product could make up for any problems arising from the foreign language of the label by giving oral instructions.

In *Freistaat Bayern* v. *Eurim-Pharm*[118] it was held that a requirement on a parallel importer to repackage medicinal products lawfully marketed in another Member State before they enter the national territory so as to comply with the packaging requirements of the importing State was not necessary for the protection of public health. The products were subject to a marketing authorization in the importing State and the importer held a permit for the purpose of labelling and packaging them in accordance with the legislation of that State. It was therefore disproportionate to require that the products must be repackaged before they entered the national territory. The contested measure clearly prevented the importer from operating an integrated sales strategy. If the measure were upheld, parallel importers would be required to move their packaging process to each of the States to which they import proprietary medicinal products.

In assessing whether a national measure meets the test of proportionality, the degree to which it restricts freedom of movement is obviously of crucial importance. A general ban is more likely to infringe the principle than one which is targeted to a certain category of products chosen on the basis of objective criteria. The intensity of risk is also of importance. In the *Newcastle disease* case the Court considered that, taking into account the situation prevailing in the UK and in the

---

[116] Op.cit, para. 38.

[117] Case C–62/90 *Commission* v. *Germany* [1992] ECR I–2575. See also Case 215/87 *Schumacher* v. *Hauptzollamt Frankfurt am Main-Ost* [1989] ECR 617.

[118] Case C–347/89 *Freistaat Bayern* v. *Eurim-Pharm* [1991] ECR I–1747.

Community as a whole, 'the possibility of infection by imported poultry products would be so much due to sheer hazard that it cannot justify a complete prohibition of imports from Member States which admit the use of vaccine'.[119] Similarly, the costs which importers have to meet in order to comply with the requirements imposed will be taken into account. In *Franzén*[120] it was held that the requirement to possess a licence in order to carry out wholesale trade in alcoholic beverages in Sweden was not justified on grounds of public health because the conditions for obtaining the licence were too onerous. The Court singled out in particular two such conditions: the requirement to provide storage capacity within Sweden and the imposition of high fees and charges on licence holders.

It is submitted that in none of the cases discussed above did the Court jeopardize health protection as in all of them it could objectively be said that there existed less restrictive alternatives which were equally effective to attain the objective in view. By contrast, the Court erred on the side of safety in *R* v. *Royal Pharmaceutical Society of Great Britain, ex parte Association of Pharmaceutical Importers.*[121] Professional rules prohibited a pharmacist from substituting, except in an emergency, a product specifically named in the prescription with another product even if the therapeutic effect and quality of the two products were identical. The prohibition affected severely parallel imports but was upheld as proportionate. The Court stated that the prohibition did not go beyond what was necessary to achieve its objective which was to leave the entire responsibility for the treatment of patients in the hands of the doctor responsible for treatment. The Court found itself unable to discount reasons based on 'psychosomatic phenomena', for which a specific proprietary medicinal product might be prescribed rather than another product having the same therapeutic effect.[122] The judgment has been criticized on the ground that it is based more on psychological than objective considerations[123] and sits uncomfortably with the German medicinal products case.[124]

A common regulatory tool used to pursue health protection policies is the requirement to approve or inspect products before they can be marketed. The Court has held that health inspections carried out by Member States in accordance with Article 30[36] are justified provided that the measures adopted are proportionate and that the protection of health cannot be achieved as effectively by measures which restrict intra-Community trade to a lesser extent.[125] The discretion of the importing State is restricted by the requirement of non-duplication.[126] But a lot depends on the circumstances in issue and in *Melkunie*[127] the Court upheld national legislation the purpose of which was to ensure that milk products did not contain micro-organisms in a quantity which may constitute a risk 'merely to the health of some, particularly sensitive consumers'.[128]

[119] Op.cit., para. 44.
[120] Case C–189/95, [1997] ECR I–5909. Cf. *Aragonesa*, op.cit.
[121] [1989] ECR I–1295.
[122] Op.cit., para. 22.
[123] See Oliver, op.cit., p. 215.
[124] See above *Commission* v. *Germany*, op.cit.
[125] See the cases referred to above in n. 102.
[126] See above p. 142.
[127] Case 97/83 [1984] ECR 2367.
[128] Op.cit., para. 18.

In a number of cases, issues pertaining to public health have arisen in connection with restrictions placed on food additives. According to standard case law, where there are scientific uncertainties, it is for the Member States to decide what degree of protection is needed on health grounds subject to the requirements of the free movement of goods.[129] A Member State may in principle make the importation of products containing additives lawfully marketed in the Member State of production subject to the requirement of authorization on grounds of public health. Proportionality, however, provides a number of substantive and procedural guarantees. In *Sandoz*,[130] Dutch law made the importation of products to which vitamins had been added subject to prior authorization. The Court held that, in view of the difficulty in assessing the harmful consequences of excessive intake of vitamins and the lack of harmonization, Member States enjoyed wide discretion. According to the principle of proportionality, however, Member States must authorize vitamins lawfully marketed in the Member State of production where the addition of vitamins to foodstuffs 'meets a real need, especially a technical or nutritional one'.[131] In *Motte*,[132] it was held that, in deciding whether to permit the importation of products containing additives, the national authorities must take into consideration the results of international scientific research and must grant authorization where there is a real need taking into account the eating habits in the State of importation. In the *German Beer* case, the Court found the ban on the use of additives applicable to beer disproportionate in view of its generality as it excluded all additives authorized in other Member States.[133] But the *German Beer* case does not provide authority for the proposition that a potential risk to public health is in itself insufficient to justify the prohibition of an additive. The Court stated that mere references to the potential risks of the ingestion of additives did not suffice to justify the imposition of *stricter* rules in the case of beer than those applicable to other beverages.[134] A Member State, nonetheless, must be in a position to defend the prohibition of an additive and a general ban on all products of a certain category on the ground that they may contain an additive harmful to health will be struck down.[135]

The onus of proving that a substance is harmful to health rests with the national authorities. They may require the importer to produce information regarding the product but it is for them to assess whether authorization must be granted in accordance with Community law.[136] Member States must make available to traders an

---

[129] See e.g. *de Peijper*, Case 272/80 *Frans-Nederlandse Maatschappij voor Biologische Producten* [1981] ECR 3277, para. 12; Case 174/82 *Sandoz BV* [1983] ECR 2445, para. 16.

[130] Case 174/82 *Sandoz BV* [1983] ECR 2445.   [131] Para. 19.

[132] Case 247/84 [1985] ECR 3887. See also Case 304/84 *Ministère Public* v. *Muller* [1986] ECR 1511; Case 53/80 *Officier van Justitie* v. *Kaasfabriek Eyssen* [1981] ECR I–409; Case 94/83 *Heijn* [1984] ECR 3263.

[133] Case 178/84 *Commission* v. *Germany* [1987] ECR 1227, para. 47.

[134] Para. 49.

[135] See Case 407/85 *3 Glocken and Another* v. *USL Centro-Sud and Another* [1988] ECR 4233, para. 13. Unless, one assumes, detection of the existence of the additive is impossible.

[136] *Sandoz*, paras. 22–4.

effective procedure by which they can apply for the authorization to use a specific additive. It must also be open to traders to challenge before the courts an unjustified failure to grant authorization.[137]

The conclusion to be drawn from the above cases is that, although, understandably, in matters of public health the Court has followed a cautious approach, the application of the principle of proportionality remains strict.

4.4.2. Public security

Article 30[36] does not provide for an order of priority among the grounds of derogation provided therein. All of them are equivalent in law in that they can justify a restriction on free movement. Public security, nonetheless, presents certain distinct characteristics. It is closely linked to State sovereignty. It is also more difficult to define objectively, and therefore less susceptible to judicial determination. It is reasonable to suggest that, once a genuine risk to public security is established, a Member State can exercise more discretion with regard to the measures which are appropriate to safeguard public security than with regard to the measures which are necessary to safeguard other interests. This is not to say of course that each case should not be judged on its merits.

In *Campus Oil*,[138] Irish law required importers of petroleum products to purchase a certain proportion of their requirements from a State refinery at fixed prices. It was argued that the operation of the State refinery, which was the only one in the national territory, was essential in order to guarantee the supply of petroleum products in Ireland and that, in turn, the purchasing obligation was necessary to guarantee that the refinery could dispose of its products. The Court pointed out that, because of the fundamental importance of petroleum products as an energy source in a modern economy, the aim of ensuring a minimum supply transcended purely economic considerations and was covered by the objective of public policy. It then examined whether the Irish rules could be justified on the basis of Article 30[36]. It accepted that the installation of a refinery in the national territory contributed to improving the security of supply of petroleum products. It was argued, however, that the purchasing obligation was disproportionate. The Court held that that obligation would be justified only if the major distributors refused to purchase from the State refinery despite the fact that it charged market prices. In addition, it specified, *inter alia*, the condition that the quantities of petroleum products which may be covered by the purchasing obligations must not exceed the minimum supply requirements of the State concerned 'without which the operation of essential public services and the survival of its inhabitants would be affected'. The application of the principle of proportionality in *Campus Oil* appears to be relatively strict.

---

[137] Case 304/84 *Ministère Public* v. *Muller* [1986] ECR 1511, para. 26; *Commission* v. *Germany*, op.cit., paras. 45–7. In that case German law did not provide for a procedure by virtue of which traders could obtain authorization of a specific additive.

[138] Case 72/83 *Campus Oil Limited* v. *Minister for Industry and Energy* [1984] ECR 2727.

In a carefully balanced judgment, the Court gave detailed guidelines to be applied by the national court. It is clear from the judgment that the purchasing obligation was considered compatible with Community law only in so far as it satisfied non-economic interests.[139] The Opinion of the Advocate General differs from the judgment in two respects. Slynn AG expressed doubts as to whether the purchasing obligation was necessary in view of Community measures which required Member States to maintain minimum stocks. By contrast, the Court took the view that the existing Community legislation fell short of providing 'an unconditional assurance' that sufficient supplies could be maintained. Also, applying the principle of the less restrictive alternative, Slynn AG considered that the holding of stocks of petroleum products may be a sufficient safeguard in the eventuality of shortages.[140]

Subsequently, in *Commission* v. *Greece*,[141] the Court found that special rights reserved to the Greek State with regard to the importation and marketing of petroleum products were not justified on grounds of public security. One of the requirements imposed by Greek law was that distribution companies had to submit annually to the Greek authorities a procurement programme setting out their projected sales and their sources of supply for the following year. The procurement programme was subject to approval by the Greek authorities. The Court held that the requirement of approval was not essential in order to ensure a minimum supply of petroleum products for the country at all times. It pointed out that Greece had two public sector refineries whose production capacity exceeded the country's minimum requirements in a period of crisis. It was therefore sufficient to require distribution companies merely to notify the authorities in due time of their procurement programmes and any significant amendments thereto.

In *Cullet* v. *Leclerc*,[142] the French Government sought to justify the imposition of minimum prices for the retail sale of petrol on grounds of public policy and public security. It argued that an unrestricted price war for the sale of fuel would result in social unrest, even violence, by disaffected retailers. This far-fetched submission was rejected by the Court on the ground that the Government had failed to show that it would be unable to deal with any public disorder using the powers at its disposal. Verloren van Themaat AG took a more stern view and was reluctant to accept that civil disorder could provide justification for restrictions on the free movement of goods.[143]

Issues concerning public security have arisen in relation to dual-use goods, i.e. goods that can be used for both military and civil purposes. In *Richardt*,[144] the Court held that the concept of public security within the meaning of Article 30[36] covers both the internal and the external security of a State.[145] It also held that the importation, exportation and transit of goods capable of being used for strategic purposes

---

[139] See *Campus Oil*, op.cit., para. 35.   [140] Op.cit., 2765.
[141] Case C–347/88 [1990] ECR I–4747.   [142] Case 231/83 [1985] ECR 305.
[143] Op.cit., at 312–13.
[144] Case C–367/89 *Richardt and 'Les Accessoires Scientifiques'* [1991] ECR I–4621.
[145] Para. 22.

may affect the public security of a State, and therefore that Member States are entitled to make the transit of such goods subject to the grant of a special authorization. The judgment in *Richardt* was followed in *Werner*[146] and in *Leifer*,[147] both of which arose from preliminary references from German courts. In *Werner*, the applicant in the main proceedings was refused licence to export a vacuum-induction oven to Libya on the ground that it was capable of being used for military purposes. In *Leifer*, the German authorities instituted criminal proceedings against traders on the ground that they had delivered certain chemical products to Iraq without export licences. In both cases, a broad interpretation of the common commercial policy was followed by an equally broad interpretation of the notion of public security and, in *Leifer*, by a relatively lax application of the principle of proportionality.[148] The Court held that a national measure whose effect is to restrict the export of certain products to third countries cannot be treated as falling outside the scope of the common commercial policy on the ground that it pursues foreign and security policy objectives. If that were so, a Member State could unilaterally restrict the scope of the common commercial policy in the light of its own foreign policy requirements.[149] The Court also made clear that dual-use goods fall within the scope of the common commercial policy.[150]

With regard to public security, the Court held that that notion comprises national measures seeking to avoid the risk of a serious disturbance to foreign relations or to peaceful coexistence of nations. It held that the notion of public security cannot be interpreted more restrictively in Article 11 of the Export Regulation[151] than in Article 30[36] of the Treaty for that would be tantamount to authorizing Member States to restrict the movement of goods within the internal market more than movement between themselves and third countries. In *Leifer*, the Court held that the exportation of goods capable of being used for military purposes to a country at war with another country may affect the public security of a Member State and that, in such cases, the national authorities have a certain degree of discretion when adopting measures which they consider to be necessary in order to guarantee their public security. Thus, where the export of dual-use goods involves a threat to public security, a Member State may require an applicant for an export licence to show that the goods are for civil use. Also, having regard to specific circumstances, such as the political situation in the country of destination, it is proportionate for a Member State to provide that the export licence shall be refused if the goods are objectively suitable for military use.[152]

---

[146] Case C–70/94 *Werner Industrie-Ausrushungen* v. *Germany* [1995] ECR I–3189.

[147] Case C–83/94 *Leifer* [1995] ECR I–3231.

[148] The issue of proportionality did not arise in *Werner*.   [149] *Werner*, paras. 10–11.

[150] *Leifer*, para. 11.

[151] Council Regulation No. 2603/69 establishing common rules for exports (OJ, English Spec. Ed. 1969 (II), p. 590), as amended by Council Regulation No. 3918/91 (OJ L 372). Article 11 authorizes Member States to impose quantitative restrictions on exports to third countries on grounds similar to those specified in Article 30[36].

[152] *Leifer*, paras. 35–6.

Leifer can be contrasted with cases such as *UHT* and *de Peijper*. In the former, the application of proportionality is more lax in that a greater margin of discretion is left to the Member States and more power is delegated to the national courts to make the final determination whether the national provision is compatible with proportionality.[153] A distinction could be drawn, however, between measures restricting exports of strategic goods on grounds of public security and criminal penalties imposed for breach of such restrictions. With regard to the former, as the Advocate General stated in *Leifer*, the scope for judicial review is necessarily limited as it is not easy for a court to assess the threat posed to the security of a State by the exportation of strategic goods.[154] By contrast, the Court may feel able to give more specific guidance with regard to the proportionality of penalties imposed for breaches of restrictions since the severity of criminal sanctions is a matter susceptible to judicial determination.

Although the standard of scrutiny is less rigorous, it is notable that even where issues of national security are at stake the Court is prepared to hold an inquiry on grounds of proportionality. That is to be contrasted with the approach of the English courts which are singularly reluctant to review executive decisions, for example a deportation order against an alien, certified by the Minister to have been taken in the interests of national security.[155] The need for judicial vigilance where public security is invoked in the context of Article 36 was underlined by Slynn AG in *Campus Oil* where he stated that if the standards adopted are not sufficiently vigorous, the derogations of public security and public policy may be used in such a way as to diminish the basic concept of the common market.[156]

Issues pertaining to public security arose also in cases concerning the imposition of sanctions against Serbia and Montenegro following the Yugoslav conflict. In *The Queen, ex parte Centro-Com v. HM Treasury and Bank of England*[157] the United Kingdom decided not to permit the release of funds from Yugoslav accounts held in British banks in order to pay for medical products sent to Serbia or Montenegro unless the export of the products concerned was authorized by the United Kingdom competent authorities. The decision was taken in the light of suspected abuses of the authorization procedure established by the UN Sanctions Committee and was aimed at ensuring that no funds were released for payments unconnected with medical or humanitarian purposes. As a result of that policy, Barclays Bank was refused authorization to transfer from a Yugoslav account sums needed to pay for medical products exported from Italy to Montenegro despite the fact that the exportation had been approved by the UN Sanctions Committee and authorized by the Italian authorities. The United Kingdom argued that the measures were justified on grounds of public security and were therefore covered by Article 11 of the Export Regulation which permits derogations from the freedom of export on the grounds referred to in Article 30[36]. The Court held that measures intended to

---

[153] Op.cit., paras. 34–6.   [154] Op.cit., per Jacobs AG, para. 42.
[155] See e.g. *R v. Secretary of State for the Home Department, ex parte Cheblak* [1991] 2 All ER 319.
[156] *Campus Oil*, op.cit., 2767.   [157] Case C–124/95 [1997] ECR I–81.

apply sanctions imposed by the United Nations fell within the scope of public security but that recourse to Article 11 could not be made if Community rules provided for the necessary measures to ensure protection of the interests enumerated therein. That was so in the circumstances, as the Sanctions Regulation[158] laid down the conditions on which exports of medical products to Serbia and Montenegro were to be authorized. The effective application of the sanctions could be ensured by the authorization procedures of the other Member States, as provided for in the Sanctions Regulation. A Member State could secure the effectiveness of such sanctions by less restrictive measures than those adopted by the UK. Thus, where it had particular doubts about the accuracy of descriptions of goods appearing in the export authorization issued by another Member State, it could before releasing funds from accounts held in its territory have resort to the collaboration established by Council Regulation No. 1468/81.[159] That measure contains provisions to facilitate mutual assistance between the administrative authorities of the Member States and co-operation between the latter and the Commission in order to ensure the correct application of the law on customs and agricultural matters.

Centro-Com contrasts with *Bosphorus Airways*[160] and *Ebony Maritime*,[161] where the Court upheld measures very restrictive of commercial freedom in order to ensure the effectiveness of sanctions against Serbia and Montenegro. The difference is that in the latter cases the measures in issue had been adopted by the Community whereas in *Centro-Com* they had been adopted by a Member State and the Court was concerned to safeguard the exclusive nature of commercial policy.

The protection of national security interests is also provided for in Articles 297[224] and 298[225] of the Treaty. Article 297[224] states that Member States must consult each other with a view to taking together the steps needed to prevent the functioning of the common market being affected by measures which a Member State may be called upon to take in the event of serious internal disturbances affecting the maintenance of law and order, in the event of war, serious international tension constituting a threat of war, or in order to carry out obligations it has accepted for the purpose of maintaining peace and international security. Article 298[225] provides for an expedited procedure, in derogation of Articles 226[169] and 227[170], by virtue of which the Commission or a Member State may bring enforcement proceedings directly before the Court if it considers that another Member State is making improper use of the powers provided for in Articles 296[223] and 297[224]. Article 297[224] concerns 'a wholly exceptional situation'.[162] It is distinct in that it enables a Member State to derogate not only

---

[158] Council Regulation (EEC) No. 1432/92 of 1 June 1992 prohibiting trade between the European Economic Community and the Republic of Serbia and Montenegro, OJ 1992 L 151/4.

[159] OJ 1981 L 144/1.

[160] Case C–84/95 *Bosphorus Hava Yollari Turizm ve Ticaret AS* v. *Minister for Transport and the Attorney General* [1996] ECR I–3953.

[161] Case C–177/95 *Ebony Maritime and Loten Navigation* v. *Prefetto della Provincia di Brindisi and Others* [1997] ECR I–1111.

[162] Case 222/84 *Johnston* v. *Chief Constable of the Royal Ulster Constabulary* [1986] ECR 1651, para. 27.

from a specific freedom but from the rules of the common market in general. In *Commission* v. *Greece* (*FYROM* case)[163] Jacobs AG held that the issue whether there is international tension constituting a threat of war within the meaning of Article 297[224] is justiciable. He accepted, however, that the scope and intensity of judicial review is severely limited on account of the nature of the issues raised. He pointed out the paucity of judicially applicable criteria on the basis of which an objective determination may be made as to whether there is a threat of war and held that issues of national security are primarily a matter for the appraisal of the State concerned. Similarly, the Advocate General accepted that the intensity of review under Article 298[225] is extremely limited. He considered that a Member State would be making improper use of its powers under Article 297[224] if the real purpose of the measures adopted was to protect its own economy, thus drawing a parallel between 'improper use' within the meaning of Article 298[225] and the concept of misuse of powers. Beyond that, the Advocate General stated, it was difficult to see how a Member State would be making improper use of its powers by imposing economic sanctions on a third State. But the Advocate General did not refuse to review the embargo imposed by Greece on the Former Yugoslav Republic of Macedonia on grounds of proportionality. He held that in determining whether the measures taken by a Member State under Article 297[224] were excessive, one would have to assess the damage caused by the measures taken on the Community interest in the functioning of the common market and the maintenance of undistorted competition. In the circumstances, the damage caused to those interests by the embargo was only slight since the embargo affected only a tiny percentage of the total volume of Community trade and was unlikely to have any perceptible impact on the competitive situation in the Community. Greece therefore could not be said to have breached Article 297[224] on grounds of proportionality.[164]

4.4.3. Consumer protection

Consumer protection is a mandatory requirement under the *Cassis de Dijon* formula and an imperative requirement of public interest which may justify restrictions to the free movement of services. As such, it may justify only non-discriminatory restrictions.[165] It is the most oft-invoked mandatory requirement and in many cases it is pleaded in combination with the protection public health or the defence of fair trading or both of those defences.[166] For example, in *Clinique*,[167] proceedings were

---

[163] Case C–120/94 [1996] ECR I–1513.   [164] Op.cit., 1533.

[165] The Court has expressly held that consumer protection as such is not covered by the derogations of Article 36: Case 177/83 *Kohl* v. *Ringelhan & Rennett* [1984] ECR 3651, para. 19; Case 25/88 *Criminal Proceedings against Wurmser and Others* [1989] ECR 1105, para. 10.

[166] See e.g. *Commission* v. *Germany* (*Beer* case), op.cit.; *Criminal Proceedings against Wurmser*, op.cit. In Case 12/74 *Commission* v. *Germany* [1975] ECR 181, the Court appeared to take the view that a measure may be justified only if it is necessary *both* on grounds of consumer protection and unfair trading. Following *Cassis de Dijon* that view is no longer valid. See also Oliver, op.cit., p. 226.

[167] C–315/92 *Verband Sozialer Wettbewerb* v. *Clinique Laboratories and Estée Lauder* [1994] ECR I–317.

brought against European subsidiaries of Estée Lauder to stop the marketing in Germany of cosmetic products under the name 'Clinique' on the ground that the name could mislead consumers into believing that the products in question had medicinal properties. The Court held that the prohibition was not justified either on grounds of consumer protection and prevention of unfair competition or on grounds of public health. The products in question were not available on pharmacies but were sold exclusively in perfumeries and department stores, they were not presented as medicinal products, and were ordinarily marketed in other countries under the name 'Clinique' without that name misleading consumers. The degree of protection which must be afforded to consumers depends on the products and the market in issue. In *Alpine Investments* the Court recognized that investors in financial investments require particular protection due to the intangible nature of securities and the inability of investors to exercise control over their value.[168] The defence of consumer protection is often relied upon to justify controls of marketing techniques and selling arrangements. A number of cases where the principle of proportionality has been applied to such measures have already been examined in the context of the less restrictive alternative test.[169] It may be interesting to examine here some cases concerning language requirements.[170] This is a particularly sensitive area since the Court has to balance commercial freedom and inter-State trade on the one hand with national concerns pertaining to cultural and regional identity on the other.

In *Piageme I*[171] a company marketed in Flanders bottled water labelled in French or in German in contravention of a Belgian law which required that food products marketed in the Flemish speaking region of Belgium must be labelled in Dutch. The issue arose whether the law was compatible with Article 28[30] and Directive 79/112 on the approximation of national laws relating to the labelling, presentation and advertising of foodstuffs for sale to the ultimate consumer.[172] Article 14 of the Directive provides that particulars must be in a language easily understood by purchasers, unless other measures have been taken to ensure that the purchaser is informed. The Court held that the purpose of the Directive is to prohibit the sale of products whose labelling is not easily understood by the purchaser rather than to require the use of a specific language. On that basis, it found that the obligation to use exclusively the language of the linguistic region where the goods are sold exceeded the requirements of the Directive. It also held that the requirement of exclusive use constituted a measure having equivalent effect to a quantitative restriction on imports prohibited by Article 28[30]. Surprisingly, the Court did not give guidance on whether a non-exclusive language requirement would infringe Article 28[30] although in fact the Belgian law in issue imposed a non-exclusive

---

[168] *Alpine Investments*, op.cit., paras. 42, 46 and per Jacobs AG at 1161.
[169] See above, p. 133.
[170] For a detailed examination, see Oliver, op.cit., pp. 226 *et seq.*
[171] Case C–369/89 *Piageme* [1991] ECR I–2971.   [172] OJ 1979 L 33/1.

requirement.[173] On appeal by the plaintiffs, the Court of Appeal of Brussels made a second reference and in *Piageme II*[174] the Court held that the obligation to use a specific language for the labelling of food products, even if the use of additional languages is not precluded, also exceeds the requirements of Directive 79/112. Since incompatibility with the Directive was established, the Court did not examine whether the non-exclusive language requirement would be incompatible also with Article 28[30].[175]

In *Piageme II* the Court held that it is for the national court to determine in each case whether labelling given in a language other than the language mainly used in the Member State or region concerned can easily be understood by consumers in that region. Various factors may be relevant in that respect, for example, the possible similarity of words in different languages, the widespread knowledge among the population concerned of more than one language, or the existence of special circumstances such as a wide-ranging advertising campaign or widespread distribution of the product.[176] The Belgian Court of Appeal also referred the question whether, in order to determine if the labelling is in a language easily understood by consumers, regard must be had only to the information provided on the packaging or account may also be taken of other circumstances which indicate that the consumer is familiar with the product, for example, its widespread distribution or a wide-ranging advertising campaign. The Court held that in order to provide adequate consumer protection, it is necessary for consumers to have access to the compulsory particulars specified in the Directive not only at the time of purchase but also at the time of consumption. That is particularly so as regards the date of minimum durability and any special storage conditions or conditions of the use of the product. The Court also pointed out that the ultimate consumer is not necessarily the person who purchased the products. It concluded that consumer protection is not ensured by measures other than labelling such as information supplied at the sales point or as part of a wide-ranging advertising campaign. All the compulsory particulars specified in the Directive must appear on the labelling in a language easily understood by purchasers or by means of other measures such as designs, symbols or pictograms. The approach of the Court in *Piageme II* contrasts sharply with its approach in the *German Medicinal products* case.[177] If one where to transpose to the latter the reasoning of *Piageme II*, the inevitable conclusion would be that the German law did not infringe the principle of proportionality.

---

[173] Belgian law required that the labelling must appear at least in the language or languages of the linguistic region where the products are offered for sale. See Article 10 of the Royal Decree of 2 Oct. 1980, replaced by Article 11 of the Royal Decree of 13 Nov. 1986.

[174] Case C–85/94 *Piageme and Others* v. *Peeters* [1995] ECR I–2955.

[175] Oliver (op.cit., p. 230) takes the view that such a requirement would also fall foul of Article 28[30], on the basis of the judgment in Case 27/80 *Fietje* [1980] ECR 3839. In *Piageme II*, Cosmas AG also came to the view that Article 28[30] precludes a non-exclusive language requirement but the Opinion does not discuss how that view can be compromised with *Meyhui* discussed above.

[176] *Piageme II*, op.cit., para. 30.

[177] Discussed above p. 146.

4.5. Criminal penalties

Penalties of whatever nature provided for breach of national provisions restricting the fundamental freedoms are subject to a strict test of proportionality. In *Casati* the Court stated:[178]

In principle, criminal legislation and the rules of criminal procedure are matters for which the Member States are still responsible. However, it is clear from a consistent line of cases decided by the Court, that Community law also sets certain limits in that area as regards the control measures which it permits the Member States to maintain in connection with the free movement of goods and persons. The administrative measures or penalties must not go beyond what is strictly necessary, the control procedures must not be conceived in such a way as to restrict the freedom required by the Treaty and they must not be accompanied by a penalty *which is so disproportionate to the gravity of the infringement that it becomes an obstacle to the exercise of that freedom*.

In a number of cases the Court has examined the proportionality of penalties imposed by the host State on Community nationals exercising their freedom of movement for failure to comply with formalities provided for by national law. The Court approaches the legality of such penalties in two stages. First, it considers the nature of the requirement for breach of which the penalty is imposed and then it assesses the penalty itself. Clearly, a penalty is incompatible with Community law where it is imposed for failure to comply with a provision which is itself so incompatible. In *Messner*[179] Italian law required nationals of other Member States who entered Italy as employed persons or as persons supplying or receiving services to make a declaration of residence within a period of three days of their arrival. Failure to make a declaration was punishable by imprisonment of up to three months or a fine. The Court held that the period of three days was not 'absolutely necessary' in order to protect the host State's interest in obtaining exact knowledge of population movements. That was confirmed by the fact that the majority of Member States imposing a similar obligation allowed appreciably longer periods.[180] The Court indicated that, in any event, imprisonment would be an excessive penalty for the offence in issue.[181] In *Pieck*[182] it was held that national authorities may impose penalties for failure to comply with requirements relating to residence permits but, given that residence permits issued to Community nationals only have a declaratory effect, such penalties must be comparable to those attaching to minor offences committed by nationals. Imprisonment would be a disproportionate penalty. In *Sagulo*[183] the Court held that a Community national who fails to obtain

---

[178] Case 203/80 [1981] ECR 2595, para. 27, emphasis added.
[179] Case C–265/88 *Criminal Proceedings against Messner* [1989] ECR I–4209. See also Case 118/75 *Watson and Belmann* [1976] ECR 1185; *Sagulo*, op.cit., paras. 6–7.
[180] *Messner*, op.cit., para. 11.
[181] *A fortiori*, deportation is also a disproportionate penalty: *Watson and Belmann*, op.cit., para. 20.
[182] Case 157/79 *Regina* v. *Pieck* [1980] ECR 2171.
[183] Case 8/77 *Sagulo, Brenca and Bakhouche* [1977] ECR 1495.

in the host Member State the identity documents required according to Community law may be made subject to reasonable penalties although such penalties are not imposed on nationals of the host State for comparable offences. It may not be permissible, however, to equate a Community national with an alien in that regard and, where national law does not provide penalties appropriate to the requirements of Community law, it is the task of the national court by using its judicial discretion to impose a penalty appropriate to the character and objectives of the Community provisions in issue. In any event, penalties imposed on nationals of other Member States resident in the national territory for failure to hold the necessary identification documents must not be disproportionately different from those imposed on the nationals of the host state for comparable offences.[184]

The strictness with which the Court applies the principle of proportionality in this context is illustrated by the judgment in *Scanavi*.[185] The German authorities fined two Greek nationals who had failed to exchange their driving licences within a year from taking up residence in Germany as required by German law pursuant to Directive 80/1263.[186] The Court held that the issue of a driving licence by the host State in exchange for a licence issued by another Member State does not constitute the basis of the right to drive a vehicle in the territory of the host State but evidence of the existence of such right. The obligation to exchange driving licences fulfils administrative requirements and a Community national who has failed to exchange his driving licence should not be assimilated to a person driving without a licence. The Court concluded that criminal penalties even of a financial nature for failure to exchange a licence are disproportionate since a criminal conviction may have adverse consequences for the exercise of a trade or profession, in particular as regards access to certain offices or activities.[187]

In relation to the free movement of goods, the Court has held that any penalties imposed must be restricted to what is strictly necessary. Confiscation of goods or pecuniary penalties calculated on the basis of the value of goods have been held to be excessive where imposed for administrative offences, such as failure by an importer to disclose the origin of goods in free circulation in the Community.[188] Where under Community law an importer does not need to disclose the origin of goods, a false declaration of origin may not be punished by the indiscriminate application of penalties provided against false declarations made in order to effect prohibited imports.[189] The Court has also held that seizure or confiscation of a product

---

[184] Case C–24/97 *Commission* v. *Germany*, [1998] ECR I-2133.

[185] Case C–193/94 *Skanavi and Chryssanthakopoulos* [1996] ECR I–929. See also Case C–29/95 *Pastoors and Trans-Cap* [1997] ECR I–285.

[186] Council Directive 80/1263 on the introduction of a Community driving licence (OJ 1980 L 375/1).

[187] As a result of Directive 91/439 on driving licences (OJ 1991 L 237/1), which became effective on 1 July 1996, Member States may no longer require the exchange of driving licences. The impending liberalization of the law may have influenced the Court in taking such a strict view in *Skanavi*.

[188] Case 41/76 *Donckerwolcke* v. *Procureur de la République* [1976] ECR 1921; Case 52/77 *Cayrol* v. *Rivoira* [1977] ECR 2261.

[189] Case 179/78 *Procureur de la République* v. *Rivoira* [1979] ECR 1147.

imported illegally could be considered disproportionate, and therefore incompatible with Article 30[36], to the extent to which the return of the product to the Member State of origin would be sufficient.[190]

Proportionality has also been applied in relation to tax offences. In *Drexl*[191] the Court held that national legislation which penalizes offences concerning the payment of value added tax on importation from another Member State more severely than those concerning the payment of value added tax on domestic transactions is incompatible with Article 90[95] of the Treaty in so far as the difference is disproportionate to the dissimilarity between the two categories of offences.[192] The Court found that such disproportion exists where the penalty provided for in the case of importation involves imprisonment and the confiscation of goods whereas comparable penalties are not imposed in the case of offences concerning the payment of value added tax on domestic transactions. In a subsequent case, the Court found that such disproportion also exists where failure to pay value added tax upon importation gives rise to the penalty of confiscation and in addition to the imposition of a fine up to twice the value of the goods whereas failure to pay value added tax on a domestic transaction gives rise only to a fine which is calculated by reference to a percentage of the tax due.[193] In *Metalsa*,[194] however, the Court refused to apply a similar rule of equivalence of penalties in relation to offences concerning the importation of goods from Austria, although Article 18 of the Agreement on Free Trade between the Community and Austria contained a provision similar to that of Article 90[95] EC. It held that Article 18 should be interpreted in the light of the Agreement, the objectives of which were more limited than those of the Treaty, and came to the conclusion that Article 18 did not require any comparison to be made between penalties imposed by Member States for tax offences on imports from Austria and penalties imposed for tax offences on domestic transactions or on imports from other Member States. The Advocate General, by contrast, went further, stating that, although the ruling in *Drexl* could not be transposed to the Agreement on Free Trade with Austria, Member States were nonetheless bound by the principle of proportionality in imposing penalties in relation to offences arising from imports from third countries with which the Community has concluded free trade agreements.

The above line of tax cases illustrate that, with a view to assessing whether a penalty infringes proportionality, regard may be had to the penalties imposed on comparable offences.[195] It is submitted that the argument of equivalent treatment of comparable offences carries less force where a penalty is imposed for breach of

---

[190] Case C–367/89 *Aimé Richardt* [1991] ECR I–4621, para. 24.

[191] Case 299/86 [1988] ECR 1213.

[192] The Court held that the two categories of offence were distinguishable both with regard to their constituent elements and with regard to their enforcement, and therefore Member States were not required to have the same system of rules for the two. Cf. the Opinion of Darmon AG.

[193] Case C–276/91 *Commission* v. *France* [1993] ECR I–4413.

[194] Case C–312/91 [1993] ECR I–3751.

[195] Cf. *Metalsa*, op.cit., per Jacobs AG at 3763.

national measures restricting freedom of movement, in particular freedom of movement of persons. In such cases, the material test is whether the penalty is so grave as to become an obstacle to the exercise of free movement. If so, it is likely to infringe the principle of proportionality even though similar penalties are imposed for comparable offences of a purely domestic nature.

4.6. The role of national courts

Where the principle of proportionality is invoked to challenge the validity of a Community act, it is for the Court of Justice to apply the principle and determine whether it is infringed by the contested act. But where the principle is invoked in preliminary reference proceedings to assess the compatibility with Community law of a national measure, the final determination of the issue may be left to the national courts.[196] More specifically, where proportionality is an issue in proceedings under Article 234[177], the Court has three options:

- It may decide that the national measure does not interfere excessively with a fundamental freedom;[197]
- It may decide that the national measure interferes excessively with a fundamental freedom and is therefore in breach of the principle of proportionality;[198]
- It may give guidelines as to what the principle of proportionality requires leaving it to the national court to apply the principle on the circumstances of the case. Such guidelines may vary in specificity.

Whether the principle of proportionality should be left to the national court to apply depends on the nature of the issue involved and the specific circumstances of the case. In some cases, because of the nature of the dispute, it will simply not be possible for the Court of Justice to apply the principle conclusively. That will be the case, for example, where in issue is the severity of criminal penalties. Whether a penalty is proportionate may depend on factors, such as the good faith of the accused, which the Court of Justice, because of the limits of its jurisdiction, is not in a position to determine.[199] One area where the Court has left considerable discretion to national courts is measures restricting free trade in the interests of national security.[200] In other cases, the issue may not be straightforward and opin-

---

[196] In enforcement proceedings, it will be for the Court of Justice to determine conclusively whether the national law or practice in issue infringes Community law in the light of proportionality. See e.g. *UHT milk* case; Case 193/80 *Commission* v. *Italy* (*Italian Vinegar* case) [1981] ECR 3019; Case 178/84 *Commission* v. *Germany* (*Beer* case) [1987] ECR 1227.

[197] See e.g. *Alpine Investments*, op.cit.; *R* v. *Royal Pharmaceutical Society of Great Britain, ex parte Association of Pharmaceutical Importers*, op.cit.

[198] See e.g. Case 215/87 *Schumacher* v. *Hauptzollamt Frankfurt am Main-Ost* [1989] ECR 617; Case C–347/89 *Freistaat Bayern* v. *Eurim-Pharm* [1991] ECR I–1747.

[199] See, e.g. *Richardt*, op.cit., para. 25.   [200] See , e.g. *Richardt*, op.cit.; *Leifer*, op.cit.

ions may differ. In *Clinique*,[201] the Court found that the prohibition imposed by German law on the marketing of products under the name 'Clinique' was not justified on grounds of consumer protection, leaving no discretion to the national court. Gulmann AG, however, took the view that such a conclusive answer by the Court would overstep the limits of its jurisdiction under Article 234[177] and urged the Court to leave the issue to the national court to decide giving only general guidelines.[202] The specificity of guidance given by the Court may also be influenced by the amount of information given by the national court in the order for reference and the way it has phrased the questions referred. The better the quality of reference the more helpful that the reply given by the Court is likely to be.

In some cases, because of the discretion left to it, the national court will have a creative role to play in applying the principle. In *Piageme II*,[203] the Court held that it is for the national court to determine in each individual case whether labelling given in other than the language mainly used in the Member State or region where the goods are marketed can easily be understood by consumers. Considerable discretion was also left to the national court in *De Peijper*,[204] where the Court held that the national rule in issue, which had the effect of impeding parallel imports, could not be maintained unless it was clearly proved that any other rule or practice less restrictive of trade between Member States would be beyond the means which could reasonably be expected of the national administration. Similarly, in *Wurmser* the Court stated that, where a Member State requires an importer to ensure that the composition of imported products complies with health and safety regulations, the importer may discharge that obligation by producing a certificate concerning composition issued by the authorities of the Member State of production or by a laboratory approved by those authorities. Where the Member State of production does not require official certificates concerning composition of the product to be supplied, the importer must be entitled to supply other attestations providing a similar degree of assurance. The Court concluded that it is for the national court to determine whether, having regard to all the circumstances of the case, the attestations provided by the importer are sufficient to establish that the latter has fulfilled his obligation to verify.[205] In some cases, leaving ample discretion to the national court may be seen as deference to local social or cultural preferences. In *De Agostini*,[206] the Court left the issue whether Swedish rules restricting television advertising satisfied the test of proportionality entirely to the national court, making little effort to develop a Community standard. Arguably, the Court should have gone further.

The approach of leaving considerable discretion to the national courts is not without drawbacks. The national court which made the reference may not get an answer to the question referred. Lengthy and costly litigation before the Court of

---

[201] Op.cit.   [202] [1994] ECR I–317 at 326–8 per Gulmann AG.
[203] Op.cit. See also Case 27/80 *Fitjie* [1980] ECR 3839; Case 220/81 *Robertson* [1982] ECR 2349.
[204] *De Peijper*, op.cit.   [205] *Wurmster*, op.cit., para. 19.
[206] Op.cit., paras. 46, 52.

Justice may prove inconclusive or even of little help for the solution of the dispute. This was clearly illustrated in the protracted Sunday trading litigation.[207] Also, leaving the application of proportionality to the national court inevitably gives rise to differences in the application of Community law in the various Member States. Despite those problems, entrusting, where appropriate, national courts with the application of the principle is the correct policy. In determining the demarcation line between lawful and unlawful impediments to fundamental freedoms, national jurisdictions cannot be denied a role and this is so for two reasons. The first is a practical one. As already stated, in some cases, national courts are better placed to perform the balancing exercise which is the essence of proportionality. The second reason is one of principle. The underlying objective of the case law is to achieve a balance between the need for uniform application of Community law and the need to respect the autonomy of Member States in areas where there is no Community harmonization. That is best served by leaving, within certain limits, discretion to the national jurisdictions. Drawing the appropriate balance is not an easy exercise. It is submitted that overall the Court of Justice has not followed an inconsistent approach, leaving the issue on national courts to decide only where the latter are by virtue of objective criteria better placed to do so.[208] It will be noted that, even where the Court of Justice does not give to the referring court a conclusive answer for the solution of the dispute, its reference to the principle of proportionality by no means lacks relevance. However large the discretion left to the national court in a specific case, it is under an overriding obligation to perform a balancing exercise paying due regard to the requirements of the fundamental freedoms. It is with this consideration in mind that the case law should be assessed. In effect, the Court infuses certain standards of judicial control and cultivates a propensity on the part of the national courts to 'think federal'. That is particularly important for legal systems like English law, where proportionality is not traditionally recognized as a ground of review.

---

[207] See especially *Stoke-on-Trent CC and Norwich CC* v. *B & Q* [1991] Ch. 48.

[208] There are, however, exceptions. See e.g. *De Agostini*, op.cit. A case in the area of sex discrimination where it is submitted the issue should have been left to the national court to decide as suggested by the Advocate General is *Lewark*, op.cit.

5

Legal Certainty and Protection of Legitimate Expectations

5.1. Legal certainty

The principle of legal certainty expresses the fundamental premise that those subject to the law must know what the law is so as to be able to plan their actions accordingly. The affinity of the principle with the rule of law is evident. In *Black Clawson Ltd.* v. *Papierwerke AG*, Lord Diplock stated that 'the acceptance of the rule of law as a constitutional principle requires that a citizen, before committing himself to any course of action, should be able to know in advance what are the legal consequences that will flow from it'.[1] In some ways, legal certainty is even more important than equality. A group of traders which knows that it will be discriminated against by public authorities can plan its actions accordingly so as to alleviate the adverse effects of such discrimination. The principle acquires particular importance in economic law. Economic and commercial life is based on advance planning so that clear and precise legal provisions reduce transaction costs and promote efficient business. Legal certainty may thus be seen as contributing to the production of economically consistent results.[2]

A specific expression of legal certainty is the protection of legitimate expectations. The Court of Justice does not always distinguish between the two.[3] Respect for legitimate expectations as a principle of law is particularly developed in French and German jurisprudence.[4] In English law, it has given rise to a thriving academic discussion[5] but English courts are reluctant to accept the protection of substantive

---

[1] [1975] AC 591 at 638.

[2] See the analysis of E. Sharpston, 'Legitimate Expectations and Economic Reality' (1990) 15 ELRev. 103.

[3] See e.g. Joined Cases 212–17/80 *Salumi* [1981] ECR 2735, para. 10; Case 120/86 *Mulder I* [1988] ECR 2321, discussed below 187 *et seq*.

[4] For a discussion of the principle in the laws of the Member States, see Schwarze, *European Administrative Law*, Ch. 6, Section 2.

[5] See De Smith, Woolf and Jowell, *Judicial Review of Administrative Action*, pp. 417 *et seq*.; C. Forsyth, '*Wednesbury*, Protection of Substantive Legitimate Expectations' [1997] PL 375. P. Craig, 'Substantive Legitimate Expectations in Domestic and Community Law' (1996) 55 CLJ 289; P. Craig, 'Legitimate Expectations: A Conceptual Analysis' (1992) 108 LQR 79; C. Forsyth, 'The Provenance and Protection of Legitimate Expectations' (1988) 47 CLJ 238; P. Elias, 'Legitimate Expectation and Judicial Review', in Jowell and Oliver (eds.), *New Directions on Judicial Review* (CLP Special Issue, 1988), pp. 37–50.

legitimate expectations as an independent ground of review.[6] In Community law, legal certainty and legitimate expectations, as all other general principles of law, bind not only the administration but also the legislature.

Legal certainty is by its nature diffuse, perhaps more so than any other general principle, and its precise content is difficult to pin down. The case law has used it with creativity, invoking it in diverse contexts to found a variety of propositions both in the substantive and the procedural plane. For example, in *Automec* the CFI invoked legal certainty to depart from the normal rule that the losing party must pay the costs of litigation.[7] Legal certainty has also been a consideration in determining the jurisdiction of national courts to apply Article 81[85] of the Treaty.[8] The cynic may argue that the principle is devoid of legal content because it can be used to support contradictory results. In the seminal *Van Duyn*, for example, the Court invoked legal certainty to support the direct effect of directives.[9] That principle, however, can also be invoked to support the opposite conclusion. It may be argued that, since Article 249[189] makes a clear distinction between regulations and directives, legal certainty prevents directives from producing direct effect. It is not submitted here that the reasoning of the Court in *Van Duyn* was unpersuasive. Rather, the case is used to show that legal certainty rarely dictates a specific result in itself. It is a conceptual tool which must not be viewed in isolation but in the context of judicial reasoning taken as a whole.

At least in some contexts, continental public lawyers seem more receptive to arguments based on legal certainty than English lawyers. This point may be illustrated by the divergent views expressed by Jacobs AG in *Vaneetveld*[10] and Lenz AG in *Faccini Dori*.[11] Both Advocates General argued in favour of horizontal effect of directives despite the earlier judgment in *Marshall I*[12] which appeared to have settled the issue.[13] Their views, however, differed on a crucial point. A classic argument against horizontal effect of directives was that, until the Treaty of European Union came into force, there was no obligation to publish directives.[14] Jacobs AG attributed little importance to that consideration. He pointed out that, according to established practice, all legislative directives were published in the Official Journal and was content to accept that, if a particular directive was not published,

---

[6] See in particular, the judgment of the Court of Appeal in *R* v. *Secretary of State for the Home Department, ex parte Hargreaves* [1997] 1 All ER 397. Cf. *R* v. *Ministry for Agriculture, Fisheries and Food, ex parte Hamble (Offshore) Fisheries Limited* [1995] 2 All ER 714 and *R* v. *Secretary of State for Transport, ex parte Richmond upon Thames London BC* [1994] 1 WLR 74.

[7] Case T–64/89 *Automec* v. *Commission* [1990] ECR II–367, para. 64.

[8] Case C–234/89 *Delimitis* v. *Henninger Bräu AG* [1991] ECR I–935, para. 47. See also in relation to the provisions of the Treaty on State aids, Case C–39/94 *SFEI and Others* [1996] ECR I–3547.

[9] Case 41/74 *Van Duyn* v. *Home Office* [1974] ECR 1337, para. 13.

[10] Case C–316/93 *Vaneetveld* v. *SA Le Foyer* [1994] ECR I–763.

[11] Case C–91/92 *Faccini Dori* v. *Recreb* [1994] ECR I–3325.

[12] Case 152/84 *Marshall* v. *Southampton and South-West Hampshire Area Health Authority* [1986] ECR 723.

[13] In *Faccini Dori* the Court confirmed that directives may not give rise to rights against individuals. See also Case C–192/94 *El Corte Inglés* v. *Blázquez Rivero* [1996] ECR I–1281.

[14] See now Article 254[191] EC, as amended by the Treaty on European Union.

the absence of publication might prevent it from producing legal effects.[15] Lenz AG by contrast, considered that the absence of a legal obligation to publish directives made horizontal effect extremely problematic on grounds of legal certainty.[16] He declared that the basic condition in order for a legislative measure to be capable of imposing burdens on the citizen is its 'constitutive publication' in an official organ. In his view, the consistent practice of publishing directives in the Official Journal had no effect since it was purely declaratory in character. He concluded that directives adopted on the basis of the EEC Treaty, before the Treaty on European Union came into force, were not capable of producing horizontal effect.[17]

Legal certainty is invoked more commonly as a rule of interpretation rather than as a ground of review. But a Community measure which breaches legal certainty will be held inapplicable by the Court. The case law suggests that the principle entails, in general, the following requirements.

Clarity of Community measures. Legal certainty requires that the effect of Community legislation must be clear and predictable.[18] The aim of the principle is 'to ensure that situations and legal relationships governed by Community law remain foreseeable'.[19] Obligations imposed on individuals must be clear and understandable and ambiguities arising from the language of the law should be resolved in favour of the individual.[20] The Court has held, in particular, that rules imposing charges on a taxpayer must be clear and precise so that he may be able to ascertain unequivocally his rights and obligations.[21] The principle has found fruitful ground for its application in customs law. In relation to the Common Customs Tariff, for example, it has consistently been held that, in the interests of legal certainty and ease of verification, the decisive criterion for the classification of goods for customs purposes is to be sought in their objective characteristics and properties, as defined in the Common Customs Tariff.[22]

An interesting example of the application of legal certainty in customs law is provided by *Van eS Douane Agenten*.[23] The issue arose whether a Commission regulation classifying goods under the old Common Customs Tariff Nomenclature lapsed

---

[15] *Vaneetveld*, op.cit., 772.   [16] *Faccini Dori*, op.cit., 3342.

[17] Op.cit., 3343.   [18] Joined Cases 212–17/80 *Salumi* [1981] ECR 2735, para. 10.

[19] Case C–63/93 *Duff and Others* v. *Minister for Agriculture and Food, Ireland, and the Attorney General* [1996] ECR I–569, para. 20.

[20] Case 169/80 *Administration des Douanes* v. *Gondrand Frères* [1981] ECR 1931, paras. 17–18.

[21] *Administration des Douanes* v. *Gondrand Frères*, op.cit. See also Case C–110/94 *Inzo* v. *Belgian State* [1996] ECR I–857, para. 21 (principle of legal certainty prevents the status of taxable person under the 6th VAT Directive from being withdrawn retroactively); Case 78/77 *Lührs* v. *Hauptzollamt Hamburg-Jonas* [1978] ECR 169 (in calculating tax on exports, the exchange rate which is less onerous for the taxpayer concerned should be applied). Not every difficulty in interpretation, however, leads to breach of legal certainty: Case C–354/95 *The Queen* v. *Minister for Agriculture, Fisheries and Food, ex parte National Farmers' Union and Others*, [1997] ECR I–4559.

[22] See e.g. Joined Cases C–59 and C–64/94 *Ministre des Finances* v. *Société Pardo & Fils and Camicas* [1995] ECR I–3159, para. 10.

[23] Case C–143/93 *Van Es Douane Agenten* v. *Inspecteur der Invoerrechten en Accijnzen* [1996] ECR I–431. Cf. Case C–103/96 *Directeur Général des Douanes et Droits Indirects* v. *Eridania Beghin-Say SA* [1997] ECR I–1453; Case C–315/96 *Lopex Export GmbH* v. *Hauptzollamt Hamburg-Jonas*, [1998] ECR I–317.

when the Council regulation which provided its legal basis was repealed and the new Nomenclature was adopted. The Court held that the Commission was under an obligation to amend classification regulations issued under the previous nomenclature so as to enable individuals to ascertain unequivocally their rights and obligations. Since there were significant differences between the sub-headings of the old and the new nomenclature, individuals were unable to determine the precise scope of the contested regulation. It followed that the regulation could not be applied to imports which took place after the new nomenclature came into force.

Full enforcement of Community law. Legal certainty has been used in order to reinforce the binding character of Community law and the obligations which ensue for Member States, in particular, in relation to directives. According to established case law, in areas covered by Community law, national rules should be worded unequivocally so as to give the persons concerned a clear and precise understanding of their rights and obligations and enable national courts to ensure that those rights and obligations are observed.[24]

The Court has accepted that it may not be necessary for a Member State to take implementing measures if existing legislation already fulfils the requirements of a directive.[25] But rights flowing from directives must be unequivocally stated so that citizens have a clear and precise understanding of them.[26] In *Commission* v. *Greece*,[27] the Commission brought enforcement proceedings claiming that Greece had failed to implement Directive 89/665[28] which requires Member States to ensure that decisions taken by contracting authorities as regards award procedures for public supply and public works contracts may be reviewed effectively. Greece conceded that it had not formally transposed the Directive but argued that existing provisions of administrative and civil law, as interpreted by the Greek *Conseil d'Etat*, afforded sufficient judicial protection. The Court considered that the provisions of national law were of a general character and insufficient in themselves to comply with the Directive. It acknowledged that the Greek *Conseil d'Etat* applied those provisions in conformity with the Directive but held that, having regard to the wording of the provisions which confined the capacity to bring proceedings only to certain categories of persons, the case law of the *Conseil d'Etat* could not satisfy the requirements of legal certainty. Greece therefore had failed to comply with the

---

[24] See e.g. Case 29/84 *Commission* v. *Germany* [1985] ECR 1661, Case 363/85 *Commission* v. *Italy* [1987] ECR 1733; Case C–120/88 *Commission* v. *Italy* [1991] ECR I–621; Case C–119/92 *Commission* v. *Italy* [1994] ECR I–393.

[25] Case 29/84 *Commission* v. *Germany* [1985] ECR 1673, para. 23.

[26] See the cases referred above in n. 24 and Case 143/83 *Commission* v. *Denmark* [1985] ECR 427. In Case C–96/95 *Commission* v. *Germany* [1997] ECR I–1653, it was held that the fact that a Member State informs the competent administrative authorities of the implications of directives does not in itself satisfy the requirements of publicity, clarity and certainty. Individuals must be able to ascertain clearly their rights under Community law.

[27] Case C–236/95 [1996] ECR I–4459. See also Case C–220/94 *Commission* v. *Luxembourg* [1995] ECR I–1589.

[28] Directive 89/665 on the coordination of laws relating to the application of review procedures to the award of public supply and public works contracts, OJ 1989 L 395/33.

Directive.[29] The requirement of legal certainty applies *a fortiori* in areas where it is particularly important to ensure that directives are transposed by binding measures as for example where non-implementation could endanger public health.[30]

Legal certainty not only reduces the implementation options available to Member States but may also render inapplicable time limits provided for by national law. In *Emmott*[31] it was held that, as long as a directive has not been properly transposed into national law, individuals are unable to ascertain the full extent of their rights and that, until proper transposition takes place, a Member State may not rely on an individual's delay in instituting proceedings to protect rights conferred upon him by the directive.

Unity and coherence of the Community legal order. Recourse to the principle of legal certainty has been made in order to safeguard the integrity of the Community legal order. In *Foto-Frost*, it was held that national courts do not have the power to declare Community acts invalid *inter alia* because divergencies between national courts as to the validity of a Community act would pose a threat to legal certainty.[32] In a different context, in the *First Opinion on the EEA Agreement*[33] it was held that the system of preliminary references by courts of the EFTA States to the Court of Justice, set up by the draft EEA Agreement, was incompatible with Community law. According to the draft Agreement, rulings delivered by the Court of Justice in reply to such references were to be purely advisory without any binding effect. The Court considered that that would be incompatible with its judicial function. It would have an adverse impact on legal certainty because it would give rise to doubt as to the legal value of such rulings for the courts of Member States.

Protection of Member States. Legal certainty may be invoked not only by individuals but also by Member States.[34] The principle is claimed in particular in the law relating to public finance. According to the system for the financing of the common agricultural policy, Member States effect the expenditure necessary to finance intervention and the Commission verifies on an annual basis the accounts of national authorities. Under established case law, a Member State has a legitimate expectation that expenditure will be charged to Community funds if it has been

---

[29] Note, however, that, for an enforcement action to succeed, the Commission must demonstrate that the general legal context of the implementing legislation fails to secure effectively full application of the directive: Case C–300/95 *Commission* v. *United Kingdom* [1997] ECR I–2649.

[30] Case C–298/95 *Commission* v. *Germany* [1996] ECR I–6747, para. 16; Case C–58/89 *Commission* v. *Germany* [1991] ECR I–4983, para. 14.

[31] Case C–208/90 *Emmott* [1991] ECR I–4269, paras. 21–3. For a discussion of the case, see below pp. 282 *et seq.*

[32] Case 314/85 *Foto-Frost* v. *Hauptzollamt Lübeck-Ost* [1987] ECR 4199, para. 15.

[33] Opinion 1/91 *Draft Agreement relating to the creation of a European Economic Area* [1991] ECR I–6079, paras. 61–4.

[34] See e.g. Case 44/81 *Germany* v. *Commission* [1982] ECR 1855. Case 26/69 *Commission* v. *France* [1970] ECR 565 suggests that the equivocal state of Community law may be a valid defence in enforcement proceedings brought by the Commission. The reasoning of the Court, however, is unclear. Cf. the Opinion of Roemer AG.

incurred as a result of an erroneous interpretation of Community law attributable to a Community institution but not if the incorrect application of the Community rules is attributable to national authorities.[35]

Procedural exclusivity. Rules providing for procedural exclusivity are often said to be justified on grounds of legal certainty. In *TWD*[36] the Court held that the recipient of State aid who has failed to challenge the Commission decision declaring the aid unlawful under Article 230[173] within the requisite time limit is time barred from challenging that decision under Article 234[177]. The Court stated that the time limit within which an action for annulment must be brought under Article 230[173] safeguards legal certainty by preventing Community measures from being called into question indefinitely. Once the time limit has passed, the Commission decision becomes definitive vis-à-vis the undertaking in receipt of the aid. Its definitive nature binds the national court by virtue of the principle of legal certainty and precludes it from questioning its validity in proceedings under Article 234[177].[37]

Since legal certainty is the underlying rationale of the judgment, it must also determine the scope of its application. It is submitted that *TWD* should be interpreted restrictively to the effect that proceedings under Article 234[177] are barred only where it is manifestly clear that a private individual has *locus standi* to bring proceedings under Article 230[173] and had the opportunity to do so within the requisite time limit. Two reasons countenance such a restrictive interpretation, the first being a reason of law, the other a reason of policy. If the *TWD* principle were extended to cases other than those where it is manifestly clear that an undertaking has *locus standi* under Article 230[173], it would lead to the following paradox. In order to prove that it is not precluded from challenging a measure under Article 234[177], an undertaking would have to establish that, according to the case law, it could reasonably take the view that it did not have *locus standi* under Article 230[173]. That would lead to argument being heard before the national court, and possibly the Court of Justice in proceedings under Article 234[177], on whether the undertaking had direct and individual concern. Far from serving the requirements of legal certainty, that would insert the ambiguity of Article 230(4)[173(4)] to Article 234[177]. Also an undertaking might find itself in a position where all procedural rules were closed. It may have decided not to bring a direct action under Article 230[173] on the understanding that it has no *locus standi* only to find that it is precluded from challenging the validity of the measure under Article 234[177] because in such proceedings the Court decides that it had *locus standi* under Article 230[173]. It is submitted therefore that the principles of effective judicial protection and access to justice require a restrictive application of *TWD*.

---

[35] See e.g. Case 820/79 *Belgium* v. *Commission* [1980] ECR 3537, para. 11; Case 1251/79 *Italy* v. *Commission* [1981] ECR 205; Case C–49/94 *Ireland* v. *Commission* [1995] ECR I–2683. For a successful claim, see C–56/91 *Greece* v. *Commission* [1993] ECR I–3433, paras. 33 *et seq.*

[36] Case C–188/92 *TWD Textilwerke Deggendorf* [1994] ECR I–833.

[37] Op.cit., paras. 16, 17 and 25.

The second reason is that rules of exclusivity tend to favour affluent litigants. They require by their nature swift action to take advantage of the only procedural route available and therefore expert legal advice. It should not, however, be taken for granted that small and medium sized undertakings in Europe whose economic operations are affected by Community law can afford such advice. In short, the *TWD* principle should be restricted only to those cases where it is patently clear that the undertaking concerned has *locus standi* under Article 230[173]. There are signs that the case law is favourably disposed towards such a view. In *The Queen* v. *Intervention Board for Agricultural Produce, ex parte Accrington Beef and Others*[38] the Court refused to apply the *TWD* principle in relation to a regulation and in *Eurotunnel SA* v. *SeaFrance* it refused to apply it in relation to a directive.[39]

5.2. Protection of legitimate expectations

Respect for legitimate expectations is one of the most oft-invoked general principles of Community law. It has found fertile ground for its application particularly in agriculture and staff cases. Although the overwhelming majority of claims based on breach of the principle have been rejected, in some cases such actions have succeeded leading to the annulment of the measure concerned[40] or liability in damages on the part of the Community.[41] The principle acquires particular importance in the context of retroactive application of laws. It may also be invoked in other contexts but only to the extent that the Community itself has previously created a situation which can give rise to a legitimate expectation.[42] Such expectations may arise out of previous legislation[43] or out of conduct of the Community institutions.[44] The principle may be invoked only where the legislation or conduct of the institution concerned is the proximate cause of the legitimate expectation. Also, breach of the principle may be pleaded only where the legitimate expectations in issue have been frustrated by the Community or its agents. In one case,[45] traders received advance payment of export aid to export goods to Iraq but, following the invasion of Kuwait, the goods were stopped in Turkey and never reached the agreed destination. The result was that the security lodged by the traders was

[38] Case C–241/95 *The Queen* v. *Intervention Board for Agricultural Produce, ex parte Accrington Beef and Others* [1996] ECR I–6699.
[39] Case C–408/95, 11 Nov. 1997. By contrast, *TWD* applies *a fortiori* where a Commission decision is addressed to the applicant: see Case 178/95 *Wiljo NV* v. *Belgian State* [1997] ECR I–585.
[40] See e.g. Case C–152/88 *Sofrimport* v. *Commission* [1990] ECR I–2477, Case C–368/89 *Crispoltoni* [1991] ECR I–3695 and the milk quota cases discussed below, p. 187.
[41] See e.g. *Mulder II*, below p. 191.
[42] Case C–177/90 *Kühn* v. *Landwirtschaftskammer Weser-Ems* [1992] ECR I–35, para. 14.
[43] See e.g. Case 74/74 *CNTA* [1975] ECR 533; Case C–152/88 *Sofrimport* v. *Commission* [1990] ECR I–2477, and the milk quota cases, below p. 187.
[44] See e.g. Case 127/80 *Grogan* v. *Commission* [1982] ECR 869; Case 289/81 *Mavridis* v. *Parliament* [1983] ECR 1731, para. 21.
[45] Case C–299/94 *Anglo-Irish Beef Processors International* v. *MAFF* [1996] ECR I–1925.

forfeited. It was argued that the security should be reimbursed because the goods failed to reach their destination as a result of a Community measure, namely Regulation No. 2340/90 preventing trade by the Community as regards Iraq and Kuwait. But the Court held that the Turkish authorities refused transit because of the trade embargo imposed by the UN and therefore the failure to perform the agreed transaction was not attributable to the Community.

Protection of legitimate expectations may be said to differ from legal certainty with regard to the time factor.[46] Legal certainty requires the rules which apply at a given time to be clear and precise for the benefit of the individual. Protection of legitimate expectations, on the other hand, requires public authorities to exercise their powers over a period of time in such a way as to ensure that 'situations and relationships lawfully created under Community law are not affected in a manner which could not have been foreseen by a diligent person'.[47] Legal certainty therefore has a static character whereas legitimate expectations are enjoyed for the future. This explains the different function of the principles. Legitimate expectations may be a source of substantive rights whereas legal certainty has a more general character and is usually invoked as a rule of interpretation. The various aspects of the principle of protection of legitimate expectations will now be examined.

5.3. Non-retroactivity

5.3.1. The principle against retroactive application of laws

The principle of respect for legitimate expectations imposes strict limitations on the retroactive application of Community law. With regard to criminal measures, the prohibition of retroactivity is absolute. In *R* v. *Kirk*, the Court referred to Article 7 of the ECHR, which prohibits the retroactive application of criminal laws, as incorporating a principle common to the laws of the Member States.[48] With regard to other measures, retroactivity is subject to strict conditions. According to established case law, a measure may exceptionally produce retroactive effect provided that two conditions are fulfilled:[49] (a) the purpose of the measure so requires; and (b) the legitimate expectations of those affected are duly respected. Those conditions must be satisfied whether retroactivity is expressly stated in the measure itself or it results from its contents.[50] Retroactive application is not subject to the above conditions where its purpose is to protect rather than to prejudice the interests of

---

[46] See Case C–63/93 *Duff and Others* v. *Minister for Agriculture and Food, Ireland, and the Attorney General* [1996] ECR I–569, per Cosmas AG at 582.

[47] Ibid.

[48] Case 63/83 *Regina* v. *Kirk* [1984] ECR 2689, paras. 21–2. See also Case C–331/88 *Fedesa* [1990] ECR I–4023, paras. 41–2.

[49] See e.g. Case 98/78 *Racke* v. *Hauptzollampt Mainz* [1979] ECR 69, para. 20; Case 99/78 *Decker* [1979] ECR 101, para. 8; Case C–331/88 *Fedesa* [1990] ECR I–4023, para. 45.

[50] Case C–368/89 *Crispoltoni I* [1991] ECR I–3695, para. 17.

the individual. In such a case retroactivity may be permitted,[51] and in certain cases it may even be required subject to any vested rights of third parties. Thus in one case the Court held that, where a measure infringes the principle of protection of legitimate expectations because it does not provide for adequate transitional arrangements, such arrangements must be introduced with retroactive effect.[52] Also it is arguable that, in accordance with principles common to the laws of Member States, Community law requires the retroactive effect of the most favourable criminal provision.[53] A measure whose retroactive effect is incompatible with Community law will normally be declared invalid, or where appropriate non-binding, in so far as it has retroactive effect.[54]

A measure which has retroactive effect must indicate in its statement of reasons why such effect is necessary.[55] In *Diversinte*,[56] the Court took a particularly strict view of the requirement of reasoning. A Commission Regulation imposing a levy on the exportation of milk powder from Spain to other Member States was published on 17 March 1987 and applied retroactively from 12 February 1987. The preamble to the regulation provided that it should be applied as a matter of urgency with a view to avoiding speculative transactions. The Court held that that statement did not provide adequate reasoning and annulled the regulation to the extent that it was retroactive.[57] The judgment shows that the statement of reasons must include specific justification for retroactivity. It also suggests that failure to provide adequate reasons is in itself a ground of annulment even if retroactive application can objectively be justified. If so, where a measure fails to provide adequate reasons, it is not open to the institution which authored the measure to defend retroactivity *ex posto facto* in a case where litigation arises. In this respect, however, the case law has not been wholly consistent. The procedural issue whether retroactivity is adequately reasoned is intertwined to the substantive issue whether retroactivity is objectively justified. More recently, in *Moskof*,[58] the Court held that

---

[51] Case C–345/88 *Butterabsatz Osnabruck-Emsland* [1990] ECR I–159. In that case, the Court attributed retroactive effect to a regulation so as to ensure that a previous regulation complied with the principle of proportionality.

[52] See Case 127/80 *Grogan* v. *Commission* [1982] ECR 869, para. 37, discussed below p. 195.

[53] For the retroactive application of the most favourable administrative penalty, see Case C–354/95 *The Queen* v. *Minister for Agriculture, Fisheries and Food, ex parte National Farmers' Union and Others*, [1997] ECR I–4559.

[54] See e.g. *Van Es Douane Agenten*, op.cit.; Case 158/78 *Biegi* v. *Hauptzollamt Bochum* [1979] ECR 1103.

[55] Case 1/84 R *Ilford* v. *Commission* [1984] ECR 423, para. 19.

[56] Joined Cases C–260 and C–261/91 *Diversinte and Iberlacta* [1993] ECR I–1885.

[57] Cf. the Opinion of Gulmann AG. The Advocate General favoured a different interpretation of the contested regulation according to which it applied to a well-defined category of products already subject to the levy under a previous regulation, its sole objective being to prevent traders from fraudulently avoiding payment of the levy. In his view the traders concerned could not invoke a 'legitimate' expectation as they abused the levy system. With regard to the requirement of reasoning, the Advocate General considered that those traders were in a position to understand the reasons which led the Commission to adopt the contested regulation on the basis of its preamble, their knowledge of the previous regulation, and the reasons which led to the adoption of the latter. Op.cit., 1906–7.

[58] Case C–244/95 *Moskof* v. *Ethnikos Organismos Kapnou*, [1997] ECR I–6441.

a Commission regulation which applied retroactively fulfilled the substantive conditions of retroactivity and refused to annul it despite the fact that its preamble provided scant reasoning to justify retroactivity.[59]

In determining whether a legislative measure has retroactive effect, account must be taken of the time of its publication rather than its adoption. Following continental legal doctrine, publication of a measure has a 'constitutive' character[60] so that failure to publish bars the measure from producing legal effects. Article 254[191] of the Treaty requires measures of general application to be published in the Official Journal. It provides that such measures enter into force on the date specified in them or, in the absence thereof, on the twentieth day following their publication. A regulation is regarded as published throughout the Community on the date borne by the issue of the Official Journal where it is published. Where it is proved, however, that the date when an issue was in fact available does not correspond to the date which appears on that issue, regard must be had to the date of actual publication.[61]

5.3.2. The conditions of retroactivity

As stated, retroactivity is subject to two conditions. Retroactive effect must be necessary to achieve the objectives of the measure, and the legitimate expectations of those affected must be respected.[62] The case law refers to those conditions as separate requirements which must be met cumulatively. If that is so, it means that even where the legitimate expectations of those affected are protected, a measure will not be valid if retroactive effect is not necessary to achieve its objectives. It is doubtful whether that is correct. There is no reason why a public authority should be deprived of a policy choice if the interests of those affected are duly protected, unless the measure is not necessary in the sense that it infringes the principle of

[59] In the context of competition law, the case law accepts that in principle the reasons for a Commission decision must appear in the actual body of the decision and explanations given *ex posto facto* cannot be taken into account: Case T–61/89 *Dansk Pelsdyravlerforening* v. *Commission* [1992] ECR II–1931; Case T–30/89 *Hilti* v. *Commission* [1991] ECR II–1439; but in exceptional circumstances it may be otherwise: Case T–352/94 *Mo och Domsjö AB* v. *Commission*, judgment 14 May 1998, paras. 276–9.

[60] Case C–91/92 *Faccini Dori* v. *Recreb* [1994] ECR I–3325, per Lenz AG at 3342. See above p. 164.

[61] Case 98/78 *Racke* v. *Hauptzollamt Mainz* [1979] ECR 69; Case 99/78 *Decker* v. *Hauptzollamt Landau* [1979] ECR 101; Case C–337/88 *SAFA* [1990] ECR I–1, para. 12.

[62] It is not correct to say that, in order for a measure to be retroactive, it is sufficient that retroactivity is justified by an overriding reason of public interest without need to take into account any legitimate expectations. *Contra*: F. Lamoureux, 'The Retroactivity of Community Acts in the Case Law of the Court of Justice' (1983) 20 CMLRev. 269, 292. In an early case, Case 37/70 *Rewe-Zentrale* v. *Hauptzollamt Emmerich* [1971] ECR 23, the Court considered a retroactive decision of the Commission to be compatible with Community law solely on the ground that retroactive effect was necessary to maintain the level of agricultural prices in Germany without examining the protection of legitimate expectations. That case is not a reliable authority as it has been superseded by subsequent judgments defining the conditions of retroactivity. See *Racke*, op.cit., and *Decker*, op.cit. See also the *milk quota cases*, discussed below p. 187.

proportionality. In reality, the two conditions laid down in the case law are inextricably linked and represent the conflicting interests which are involved. The Court weighs, on the one hand, the public interest which retroactivity is purported to serve and, on the other hand, the requirement that the legitimate expectations of those affected must be respected. Depending on the circumstances, it may decide that reasons of public interest override the legitimate expectations of the persons concerned or conversely that the legitimate expectations of those affected must take priority over the objective of the measure. In applying the principle, the Court performs *par excellence* a balancing exercise, in the context of which a variety of factors are taken into account. As Trabbuchi AG stated in *Deuka*:[63]

The existence of legitimate expectations worthy of protection can be established only on the merits of each case . . . By its very nature the principle does not lend itself to mechanical application, which might lead to unjustified generalizations and would accord neither with its specific equitable function nor with the day-to-day requirements of Community rules governing the economy.

In determining which interest takes priority the Court will consider the objective which retroactivity seeks to attain. Clearly, not every objective would be capable of taking priority over the legitimate expectations of those affected. In *Amylum* v. *Council*, Reischl AG considered that there must be an imperative reason of public interest and the Court referred to an objective to be achieved 'in the general interest'.[64] In general, a claim that a measure which has retroactive effect is incompatible with Community law is not easy to succeed. In the majority of cases, the Court has rejected such claims. Thus, to give but few examples from the case law, it has been held that the retroactive effect of transitional measures concerning the Accession of Greece was necessary to prevent speculative movements of agricultural products.[65] Also, the need to maintain the stability of prices of agricultural products, threatened as a result of the revaluation of the German mark, was held to justify retroactive imposition of countervailing duties.[66] In a more recent case, the Court accepted that the uniform application of the *acquis communautaire* throughout the Union may be a reason justifying the retroactive application of measures adapting existing Community acts following the accession of new Member States.[67] Also, it has been held that public health considerations may justify the immediate application of protective measures on products imported from third countries.[68]

---

[63] Case 5/75 *Deuka* v. *Einfuhr- und Vorratsstelle Getreide* [1975] ECR 759, at 777.
[64] Case 108/81 *Amylum* v. *Council* [1982] ECR 3107, paras. 6, 8 and per Reischl AG at 3144.
[65] Case C–337/88 *SAFA* [1990] ECR I–1.   [66] *Rewe-Zentrale*, op.cit.
[67] Case C–259/95 *Parliament* v. *Council*, [1997] ECR I–5303.
[68] Case C–183/95 *Affish BV* v. *Rijksdienst voor de Keuring van Vee en Vlees*, [1997] ECR I–4315.

5.3.3. Cases where the Court has annulled retroactive measures

A classic example of invalid retroactivity is provided by *Crispoltoni I*.[69] With a view to limiting production in tobacco, Council regulations fixed maximum guaranteed quantities excess of which would lead to a reduction in premiums and prices payable to producers and tobacco processors. The regulations were adopted and became applicable after producers had made their production decisions for the current year. The Court held that retroactive effect was not capable of limiting production as decisions regarding cultivation had already been taken and, indeed, the harvest had begun before the publication of the measures. It added that, although the measures were foreseeable, producers were entitled to expect that they would be notified in good time of any measures having effects on their investments. *Crispoltoni* was a clear case of a legislative conundrum, a policy hastily arranged and implemented in disregard of its consequences for the sector concerned. The introduction of maximum guaranteed quantities applicable in the current production year went beyond all economic predictions and entailed not only a quantitative but also a qualitative regulatory change.

In *Agricola Commerciale Olio*[70] and *Savma*[71] the Court struck down the retroactive revocation of certain measures. By a regulation adopted in January 1981, the Commission offered for sale by tender consignments of olive oil held by the Italian intervention agency. After the applicants were declared successful purchasers, the Commission by new regulations adopted on 3 August 1981 decided to cancel the sale and reopen the tender procedure. The Commission's rationale was that, during the period which elapsed between the adoption of the first regulation and the adoption of the subsequent ones, the conditions of the market had radically altered. The 1980/1 harvest was much below what had been predicted causing an unexpected increase in prices. In those circumstances, the conditions of sale under the initial regulation became unreasonably favourable and would have permitted a limited number of traders to make enormous profits at the expense of the taxpayer and to dominate the market in Italy. The Court found that the Commission's assessment was vitiated by factual errors. With the assistance of an independent witness, it was satisfied that no radical change in market conditions had taken place. The Commission's change of mind was not the result of supervening developments but of its own failure of appreciation. The Court pointed out that the means of observing market conditions at the disposal of the Commission should have permitted it to revise its forecasts regarding the 1980/1 harvest long before the contested regulations was adopted. The fact that the terms of the initial sale may have led to the

---

[69] Case C–368/89 [1991] ECR I–3695. Cf. C–324/96 *Odette and Simou*, [1998] ECR I–1333.
[70] Case 232/81 *Agricola Commerciale Olio* v. *Commission* [1984] ECR 3881.
[71] Case 264/81 *Savma* v. *Commission* [1984] ECR 3915.

successful tenderers deriving a windfall benefit was not sufficient to annul the sale retroactively:[72]

The mere fact that the conditions on which the Commission permitted the national agency to put the products up for sale proved to be favourable, and even extremely favourable, to the purchasers, does not entitle the Commission to prevent that agency from carrying out the contract which had been concluded in accordance with the said conditions.

It should be noted that the regulations were annulled as being vitiated by errors of fact. The Commission failed to show that a change in market conditions, or abuse by the successful purchasers, had taken place. The Court expressly left open the questions whether in other circumstances the Commission would have been entitled to cancel the initial sale retroactively and what would have been the consequences of such cancellation with regard to the right of successful purchasers to compensation.

Meiko-Konservenfabrik v. *Germany*[73] arose from the Community system of aid for processing fruit and vegetables. Under the applicable Community rules for the marketing year 1980/1, fruit processors were entitled to aid provided that two conditions were fulfilled. A processing contract had to be concluded by 31 July 1980 and a copy of the contract had to be forwarded to the competent national agency before the contract took effect, that is to say, before the first delivery of fruit for processing. Owing to weather conditions, the cherry harvest in 1980 was late. Processing contracts were concluded late and, since such contracts typically provide for prompt performance, processsors were unable to comply with the second condition. In recognition of those exceptional circumstances, the Commission by a regulation adopted in October 1980 provided that contracts concluded for cherries could be forwarded to agencies even after the date on which they took effect but not later than 31 July 1980. Meiko, an undertaking which had entered into processing contracts with producers of cherries, was refused aid as it notified the competent authority of the contracts after the time limit of 31 July. The Court found that the time limit ran counter to the principle of protection of legitimate expectations and the principle of equality. On the former, it stated:[74]

. . . by retroactively subjecting the payment of aid to the forwarding of the contracts by 31 July 1980 the Commission acted in breach of the legitimate expectations of the persons concerned, who, having regard to the provisions in force at the time the contracts were concluded, could not reasonably have anticipated the retroactive imposition of a time-limit for forwarding contracts which coincided with the time-limit for their conclusion.

It has been suggested that in *Meiko* the Court reached 'an eminently sound economic result'.[75] The reasoning of the judgment, however, is not entirely satisfactory. It is hard to see how there could be a breach of legitimate expectations since, when they entered into processing contracts, processors were not entitled to expect

---

[72] *Agricola Commerciale Olio*, op.cit., para. 18; *Savma*, op.cit., para. 18.
[73] Case 224/82 [1983] ECR 2539.   [74] Op.cit., para. 14.   [75] Sharpston, op.cit., 143.

that they would be granted aid if they failed to fulfil the second condition stated above. Indeed, the Court accepted that the Commission was under no obligation to alter the conditions applicable retroactively.[76] Although the judgment is couched in terms of breach of legitimate expectations, the main basis of the claim was breach of equal treatment.[77] The Court accepted that the date of 31 July gave rise to discrimination among processors. It stated that, once the Commission decided to take into account the processor's difficulties, it was under a duty, in adopting the appropriate measures 'to have regard to the legitimate expectations of the persons concerned and to ensure that they were accorded equal treatment'.[78] In the circumstances of the case, it is clear that the applicants did not suffer as a result of reposing their trust to the Commission, their 'legitimate expectation' being no more than that they would be treated equally with other processors.

5.3.4. Monetary compensatory amounts

The Court has had the opportunity to examine the conditions governing retroactivity in a number of cases involving monetary compensatory amounts. In *Racke*,[79] a regulation provided for the levying of monetary compensatory amounts on imports of wine from Yugoslavia from an earlier date than the date of its adoption. The Court found that the levying of the amounts was necessary and that the legitimate expectations of the traders concerned had been met. In view of the nature and the objectives of the system of monetary compensatory amounts, traders ought to expect that any appreciable change in the monetary situation may entail the extension of the system to new categories of products and the fixing of new amounts. The tenet of the judgment is that the nature of monetary compensatory amounts made the retroactive effect of the measures imposing them unavoidable.[80]

The balancing exercise performed by the Court in determining whether legitimate expectations have been respected is illustrated by *Staple Dairy Products*.[81] A Council regulation adopted in 1979 introduced a new system for the calculation of monetary compensatory amounts providing for a deduction ('franchise') at a set rate from the sum calculated. The regulation expired on 31 March 1980. On 26 April 1980 another Council regulation entered into force which extended retrospectively the application of the previous regulation 'without the individual rights acquired by operators being thereby affected'. The applicants, who exported dairy

---

[76] *Meiko*, op.cit., para. 16.

[77] Rozès AG considered that the contested regulation was invalid as being in breach of the principle of proportionality and, in the alternative, as being in breach of the principle of equal treatment.

[78] Op.cit., para. 17.

[79] Op.cit. See also *Decker*, op.cit.

[80] See also *IRCA*, op.cit. On the other hand, a trader may not have a legitimate expectation that the Commission will respond immediately to the devaluation of national currency since monetary compensatory amounts do not provide traders with absolute guarantees against risks of changes in the rates of exchange: Case 281/82 *Unifrex* v. *Commission and Council* [1984] ECR 1969.

[81] Case 84/81 *Staple Dairy Products* v. *Intervention Board for Agricultural Produce* [1982] ECR 1763.

products between 1 April and 26 April, argued that the monetary compensatory amounts applicable to them should be calculated without the deduction. This was because the first regulation had expired and the second regulation could not validly produce retroactive effect since it expressly protected acquired rights. The Court rejected their claim. It stated that the retroactive effect was necessary to prevent an interruption in the maintenance of agricultural prices. Also, the situation at the time when the applicants entered into the transactions in issue gave them no cause to expect that the deduction would be abolished. On the contrary:

the history of the rules in question, as well as their scope and purpose, were such as to lead traders to conclude that the franchise, which for years had constituted a well-established feature of the system of monetary compensatory amounts, would be maintained for some time.[82]

On the basis of the above considerations, the Court interpreted the protection of acquired rights in the second regulation narrowly, as referring only to rights definitely conferred on traders by individual decisions of the competent authorities. Neither the principle of legitimate expectations nor the express recognition of acquired rights excluded retroactive effect in the circumstances of the case.[83]

By contrast, in *CNTA* the Court considered that the withdrawal with immediate effect of monetary compensatory amounts without prior warning required the Commission to compensate traders who suffered loss as result since the withdrawal was not necessitated by any overriding reasons of public interest. The Court held that the Commission should have adopted transitional measures which would have enabled the traders concerned to avoid loss in the performance of export contracts.[84]

5.3.5. Reinstatement of effects of a measure declared void

Retroactive application of a measure may be permitted where its purpose is to reinstate the effects of a previous measure declared void on procedural grounds. This principle is illustrated by the last generation of the isoglucose cases.[85] By Regulation No. 1293/79,[86] the Council introduced a system of quotas and levies in relation to the production of isoglucose. In *Roquette* and *Maizena*,[87] the Court declared that regulation void because it was adopted without prior consultation of the

---

[82] Op.cit., para. 15.

[83] Cf. *Sofrimport*, discussed below p. 186.

[84] Case 74/74 *CNTA* v. *Commission* [1975] ECR 533. Cf. the Opinion of Trabucchi AG. The applicant's action for compensation failed in subsequent proceedings as it was unable to prove loss: [1976] ECR 797.

[85] Case 108/81 *Amylum* v. *Council* [1982] ECR 3107; Case 110/81 *Roquette Frères* v. *Council* [1982] ECR 3159; Case 114/81 *Tunnel Refineries* v. *Council* [1982] ECR 3189.

[86] OJ 1979 L 162/10.

[87] Case 138/79 *Roquette Frères SA* v. *Council* [1980] ECR 3333, Case 139/79 *Maizena GmbH* v. *Council* [1980] ECR 3393.

Parliament. Subsequently, after duly following the consultation procedure, the Council adopted Regulation No. 387/81,[88] which reintroduced with retroactive effect the same provisions. In *Amylum*[89] it was held that the retroactive application of Regulation No. 387/81 did not infringe Community law. Such application was necessary to ensure the stabilization of the sugar market. Also, the traders affected were limited in number and well aware of the need to restrict isoglucose production and of the intention of the Community institutions to take measures to that effect. Retroactivity was therefore foreseeable.

In *Amylum* the Court upheld for the first time a long period of retroactivity.[90] Although the judgment has been criticized,[91] retroactivity in that case can hardly be said to be in breach of legal certainty. Whilst in *Roquette* and *Maizena* the Court annulled Regulation No. 1293/79 on procedural grounds, it rejected the substantive grounds of review submitted by the applicants and expressly stated that nullity was without prejudice to the Council's power to take all appropriate measures pursuant to Article 233(1)[176(1)] of the Treaty. The effect of Regulation No. 387/81 was to comply with, rather than to nullify, the effects of the judgments in *Roquette* and *Maizena*. In that respect, Regulation No. 387/81 is to be distinguished from the War Damage Act 1965 which nullified the effect of the earlier judgment of the House of Lords in *Burmah Oil Co. Ltd.* v. *Lord Advocate*.[92] In that case, the House of Lords upheld the claim of the applicant company to receive compensation for the wartime destruction of its installations which had been ordered by the British authorities to prevent their falling into the hands of the advancing Japanese army. The difference is that, by the War Damage Act, the Westminster Parliament retroactively nullified rights recognized by a judicial decision. Arguably this runs counter to the separation of powers and raises questions of constitutionality. By contrast, the judgments in *Roquette* and *Maizena* did not create any rights in favour of isoglucose producers. The equivalent situation in Community law would be if, by amending the Treaties or adopting an act of primary Community law, the Member States undid substantive rights recognized by a judgment of the Court of Justice.[93]

Amylum was confirmed in *Fedesa*.[94] In that case the applicants challenged the validity of a directive by which the Council introduced with retroactive effect the provisions of a previous directive which had been annulled on procedural grounds. The Court pointed out that the period between the annulment of the first directive and the publication of the second was short, being less than a month, and that

---

[88] OJ 1981 L 44/1. [89] Op.cit., n. 85.

[90] See per Reischl AG, op.cit., 3144, and Lamoureux, op.cit., p. 283.

[91] Hartley, *The Foundations of European Community Law* (Fourth edn.), p. 145, n. 60.

[92] [1965] AC 75.

[93] See in this context, the Protocol concerning Article 119 annexed to the EC Treaty by the Treaty on European Union. The Protocol was introduced following the judgment in Case C–262/88 *Barber* [1990] ECR I–1889 with a view to limiting claims arising under it. In subsequent cases, the Court interpreted its unclear judgment in *Barber* in such a way as to comply with the Protocol: see Case C–109/91 *Ten Oever* [1993] ECR I–4879; Case C–200/91 *Coloroll* [1994] ECR I–4389.

[94] Case C–331/88 *Fedesa and Others* [1990] ECR I–4023, para. 47.

the first directive had been annulled on procedural grounds. In those circumstances, the persons concerned could not expect the Council to change its attitude on the issues involved.

5.3.6. The criterion of foreseeability

It has become clear from the above analysis that, in assessing whether a measure frustrates legitimate expectations, the Court places reliance on the criterion of foreseeability. If it is reasonably foreseeable that a forthcoming measure is likely to have retroactive or immediate application, affected traders may not be able to claim breach of a legitimate expectation.[95] The requisite degree of foreseeability is far from fixed. Depending on the circumstances, the advance warning given to traders must be express, sufficiently specific, and given in good time,[96] or general and even presumed.[97] Thus a qualitative, as opposed to merely a quantitative, change in the regulatory system requires specific advance warning to the economic operators affected.[98] In assessing whether the advance warning given is sufficient, account must also be taken of how easy it would be for the traders concerned to protect themselves against the possibility of a change in the law.

In applying the test of foreseeability, the Court pursues the inquiry whether a prudent and well-informed trader would have been able to foresee the change in the law.[99] In *Accrington*,[100] it was held that in a system which provides for the allocation of import quotas on an annual basis, a prudent and diligent trader must know that the conditions of eligibility may be subject to a quantitative change whenever a new annual quota is adopted. Articles in specialized press, or widely publicized correspondence between professional bodies and the Community authorities, may be taken into account in assessing whether impending changes in the law were foreseeable.[101] Proposals for legislation submitted by the Commission or communications published by the Commission in the Official Journal may also be relevant.[102] The participation of the undertaking concerned in Community committees and even the size and 'substantial economic importance' of the undertaking may be relevant factors.[103] The framework of applicable rules seen in

---

[95] *Amylum*, op.cit., para. 21.

[96] *Sofrimport* v. *Commission*, op.cit., para. 18; Joined Cases C–133, C–300 and C–362/93 *Crispoltoni II* [1994] ECR I–4863.

[97] See e.g. *Decker*, op.cit.; *IRCA*, op.cit. [98] *Crispoltoni I*, op.cit.

[99] Case C–350/88 *Delacre and Others* v. *Commission* [1990] ECR I–395, para. 37; Case 78/77 *Lührs* v. *Hauptzollamt Hamburg-Jonas* [1978] ECR 169, para. 6; Case 265/85 *Van den Bergh en Jurgen* v. *Commission* [1987] ECR 1155, para. 44.

[100] Op.cit.

[101] Joined Cases C–13 to C–16/92 *Driessen* [1993] ECR I–4751.

[102] See e.g. *Staple Dairy Products*, op.cit., para. 15; *Driessen*, op.cit.; Case C–22/94 *Irish Farmers Association and Others* v. *Ministry for Agriculture, Food and forestry, Ireland, and the Attorney General* [1997] ECR I–1809, para. 23.

[103] See the *ECSC Steel Aid* cases: Case T–243/94 *British Steel* v. *Commission*, [1997] ECR I–1887, para. 78.; Case T–244/94 *Wirtschaftsvereiningung Stahl and Others* v. *Commission*, [1997] ECR II–1963, para. 60.

historical perspective may alert traders to impending changes.[104] Another consideration to be taken into account is whether the transaction in issue falls within an area where changes in the law occur frequently.[105] In order for legitimate expectations to be honoured it is not necessary that a discerning trader must be able to predict every detail of the new rules.[106] It is sufficient that the likely possibility of a change in the law is foreseeable. Even where retroactive effect cannot be said to be foreseeable, a trader cannot have a legitimate expectation to derive a benefit which runs counter to the objectives of the legislation applicable at the time when he entered into the material act or transaction.[107]

5.3.7. Immediate Application of the Law

A distinction is sometimes drawn between retroactivity and immediate application of the law.[108] The first occurs where a rule applies to acts or transactions already completed at the time of its adoption. The second occurs where a rule applies to an act or transaction in progress.[109] It seems that the immediate application of the law is subject to less stringent rules than those applicable to true retroactivity. However, no hard and fast rules can be drawn. Sometimes, it may be difficult to establish whether there is immediate application or true retroactivity and the Court does not necessarily distinguish between the two. In any event, the case law makes it clear that any legitimate expectation of those affected must be protected also in case of immediate application.[110] Lamoureux argues that it is not a specific condition of validity that immediate application must be justified by overriding considerations.[111] But the case law seems to suggest that, in general, an overriding consideration must exist although the Community judicature does not always search for such a justification. In *Campo Ebro and Others* v. *Council*, the CFI held that there is a breach of legitimate expectations in the sphere of economic law where 'in the absence of an overriding matter of public interest, a Community institution abolishes with immediate effect and without warning a specific advantage, worthy of protection, for the undertaking concerned without adopting appropriate transitional measures'.[112] In reality, in determining whether legitimate expectations have been infringed, the Court performs a balancing exercise, part of which is an assessment of the importance of the objectives which immediate application seeks to achieve. The existence of legitimate expectations, however, may be

---

[104] *Staple Dairy Products*, op.cit.
[105] Case T–489/93 *Unifruit Hellas* v. *Commission* [1994] ECR II–1201.
[106] Joined Cases C–13 to C–16/92 *Driessen* [1993] ECR I–4751, per Jacobs AG, 4775.
[107] See e.g. Case C–337/88 *SAFA* [1990] ECR I–1; *Moskof*, op.cit.
[108] See e.g. Case 37/70 *Rewe-Zentrale* v. *Hauptzollamt Emmerich* [1971] ECR 23 at 45 per de Lamothe AG; Case 1/73 *Westzucker* v. *Einfuhr- und Vorratsstelle für Zucker* [1973] ECR 723 at 739 per Roemer AG. See also Case 74/74 *CNTA* v. *Commission* [1975] ECR 533, paras. 32–3.
[109] Immediate application is also referred to as 'material' or 'quasi-retroactivity'.
[110] *Driessen*, op.cit. at 4773 per Jacobs AG.   [111] Op.cit., 290.
[112] Case T–472/93 [1995] ECR II–421, para. 52.

more difficult to establish in the case of immediate application than in the case of true retroactivity.

The majority of cases concerning immediate application have arisen in the sphere of agricultural law.[113] In *Westzucker*,[114] a change in the law took place after export licences had been issued but before the actual exports had taken place, as a result of which exporters could no longer benefit from an increase in the intervention price. The Court held that, according to a generally accepted principle, the laws amending a legislative provision apply in principle to the future effects of situations which arose under the former law. It added that the former law did not confer on the persons concerned the certainty of profiting from an increase in the intervention price.[115] In *Tomadini*,[116] the issue was whether a regulation introducing monetary compensatory amounts was applicable to exports made pursuant to contracts concluded before its adoption. It was argued that the failure to provide for transitional measures ran counter to the principle of protection of legitimate expectations. The Court held that that principle cannot be extended to the point of generally preventing new rules from applying to the future effects of situations which arose under earlier rules. It added that the position is different where the Community institutions have laid down specific rules enabling traders to protect themselves with regard to transactions definitely undertaken from the effects of the frequent variations in the detailed agricultural measures in return for entering into specific obligations with the public authorities. Such rules cannot be amended without laying down transitional arrangements unless the adoption of transitional measures is contrary to an overriding public interest.[117] In *Delacre*,[118] the applicants were manufacturers of pastry products who applied to receive aid for butter in response to an invitation to tender. Their application was rejected on the ground that the amount of aid for which they applied was higher than the maximum amount of aid fixed by the Commission after their application was submitted. The reason for reducing the maximum amount in comparison with previous invitations to tender was the fall in the Community butter stock, the disposal of which the aid system was designed to achieve. The Court held that the adjustment of the amount of aid to the state of the market was inherent in the system set up to promote the disposal of surplus butter. The applicants could not claim a vested right to the maintenance of advantages which they had derived over a certain period from that system. The Court also held that the applicants, as prudent and well-informed traders, ought to have foreseen the progressive increase in the selling price of butter and the concomitant reduction of the amount of aid, which was the inevitable consequence of a fall in stock levels.

---

[113] See further R. Barents, *The Agricultural Law of the EC* (Kluwer, 1994), Ch. 16.

[114] Case 1/73 *Westzucker* v. *Einfuhr- und Vorratsstelle Zucker* [1973] ECR 723.

[115] Cf. Roemer AG, op.cit., 741.   [116] Case 84/78 *Tomadini* [1979] ECR 1801.

[117] Op.cit., para. 20. The judgment in *Tomadini* has been followed in subsequent cases. See e.g. Case 278/84 *Germany* v. *Commission* [1987] ECR 1, paras. 35 *et seq.*; Case 203/86 *Spain* v. *Council* [1988] ECR 4563.

[118] Case C–350/88 *Delacre and Others* v. *Commission* [1990] ECR I–395.

The theme underlying the above case law is that, in agricultural law, the possibility of changes in the rules governing pending transactions forms an integral part of the commercial risks to which economic operators are subject. They may not therefore have a legitimate expectation that a given system of market regulation will be maintained in force. Since changes in the applicable rules fall within the sphere of ordinary commercial risk, the issue of foreseeability becomes less important and it may not be necessary to examine whether the change in the law could have been foreseen in the specific circumstances of the case.[119]

An interesting example of immediate application is provided by *Driessen*.[120] A regulation aiming at reducing the structural overcapacity in the fleets operating in the Community inland waterways introduced a premium for scrapping existing vessels. It also provided that a new vessel could be brought into service only if the owner scrapped a tonnage equivalent to the new vessel without receiving a scrapping premium or paid a special contribution. The applicants had entered into shipbuilding contracts before the regulation came into force. They claimed that they concluded the shipbuilding contracts after the Commission had published a proposal for a regulation and that on the basis of that proposal they expected to be able to bring new vessels into service without being subject to conditions which made the exploitation of the new vessels uneconomic. The Court rejected their claim on two grounds. It held that a legitimate expectation could not be founded on a Commission proposal. It also held that the applicants ought to have known that the provisions of the proposal were not perceived as adequate to reduce overcapacity, given the view taken by the professional associations concerned and articles published in specialized professional press.

A different outcome was reached in *Bock*,[121] where the Commission, acting under Article 134[115], authorized Germany to prohibit the importation of Chinese mushrooms, including those in respect of which applications for import licences were pending at the time of the authorization. The Court held that the authorization was invalid in so far as it extended to products in respect of which applications for import licences were pending. Those products represented an insignificant percentage of the annual quantity of mushrooms imported into Germany and therefore the importation of that quantity would not affect the effectiveness of the protective measure. The Commission had therefore exceeded what was necessary within the meaning of Article 134[115]. The case shows that the principle of non-retroactivity incorporates an element of proportionality. The immediate application of the law, and *a fortiori* its retroactive application, may only be permitted to the extent that it is necessary.[122]

---

[119] See e.g. *Tomadini*, op.cit., where the Court did not examine the issue of foreseeability.
[120] Joined Cases C–13 to C–16/92 *Driessen* [1993] ECR I–4751.
[121] Case 62/70 *Bock* v. *Commission* [1971] ECR 897.
[122] See the Opinion of Dutheillet de Lamothe AG [1971] ECR at 915–16.

5.3.8. Maintenance of existing advantages and benefits

It is clear that producers and traders have no vested right that the existing common organization of the market or the current regulatory system will be maintained unchanged. It could hardly be otherwise since the Community institutions must be able to respond to changes in the underlying economic situations. According to the established case law, traders cannot have a legitimate expectation that an existing situation which is capable of being altered by the Community institutions in the exercise of their discretionary power will be maintained. That is particularly so in an area such as the common organization of the markets whose purpose involves constant adjustments to meet changes in the economic situation. Traders therefore cannot claim a vested right to the maintenance of an advantage which they derive from the establishment of the common organization of the markets and which they enjoyed at a given time.[123] In *Eridania*,[124] the applicants challenged the validity of a Council regulation on the basis of which the Italian authorities reduced their production quota for sugar. They claimed that undertakings had the right to produce the quantities of sugar corresponding to the basic quotas granted to them by Community legislation and that that right was inherent in the carrying on of economic activity. In rejecting the challenge, the Court pointed out that the basic quotas laid down by Community rules aimed at protecting and assisting the production of sugar in the Community. An essential feature of the common organization of the market in sugar was that:[125]

it is variable in terms of the economic factors which affect the development of the market and in terms of the general direction of the common agricultural policy. It follows that an undertaking cannot claim a vested right to the maintenance of an advantage which it obtained from the establishment of the common organization of the market and which it enjoyed at a given time.

In subsequent cases the Court has confirmed that, where a quota system is in force, the Commission is under no obligation to consult or notify the traders concerned before changing for the future the criteria of eligibility for the allocation of a quota.[126] In *Crispoltoni II*,[127] it was argued that the introduction of maximum

---

[123] See Case C–350/88 *Delacre and Others* v. *Commission* [1990] ECR I–395, paras. 34–5; Case 245/81 *Edeka* v. *Germany* [1982] ECR 2745, para. 27; Case 84/78 *Tomadini* v. *Amministrazione delle Finanze dello Stato* [1979] ECR 1801, para. 22; Case 230/78 *Eridania* v. *Minister of Agriculture and Forestry* [1979] ECR 2749; Case 52/81 *Offene Handelsgesellschaft in Firma Werner Faust* v. *Commission* [1982] ECR 3745; Joined Cases 424 and 425/85 *Frico* [1987] ECR 2755; Case 112/80 *Firma Anton Dürbeck* v. *Hauptzollamt Frankfurt am Main-Flughafen* [1981] ECR 1095; Joined Cases 133–6/85 *Walter Rau Lebensmittelwerke* v. *Bundesanstalt für Landwirtschaftliche Marktordnung* [1987] ECR 2289.

[124] Case 230/78 *Eridania* v. *Minister of Agriculture and Forestry* [1979] ECR 2749.

[125] Op.cit., paras. 21–2.

[126] Case C–241/95 *R* v. *Intervention Board for Agricultural Produce, ex parte Accrington Beef Co. and Others* [1996] ECR I–6699.

[127] Joined Cases C–133, C–300 and C–362/93 *Crispoltoni II* [1994] ECR I–4863, para. 61. See also Case C–280/93 *Germany* v. *Council (Bananas case)* [1994] ECR I–4973.

guaranteed quantities in relation to the production of tobacco, excess of which would result in a reduction in the prices and premiums, frustrated the legitimate expectations of producers. The Court held that producers could not claim a vested right in the maintenance of a certain market system. A possible reduction in their earnings could not be contrary to the principle of legitimate expectations. The contested regulation respected that principle since the maximum guaranteed quantities were known in advance.

A similar approach has been taken by the Court in the external trade of the Community. A trader has no legitimate expectation that an established pattern of trade with a non-member country will be maintained. In *Edeka*[128] and *Faust*,[129] importers challenged the imposition by the Commission of protective measures which virtually prohibited the importation of preserved mushrooms from Taiwan. The protective measures were the result of a reorientation in the Community's trade policy which favoured trade with China. In rejecting the applicants' claim that their legitimate expectations had been breached, the Court emphasized the wide margin of discretion enjoyed by the Community institutions:[130]

In the present case, there can be no question of a breach of the principle of the protection of legitimate expectation, particularly since the commercial agreement entered into on 3 April 1978 between the Community and the People's Republic of China . . . was of such a nature as to alert traders to an imminent change of direction in the Community's commercial policy and, in the absence of an obligation on the part of the Community to accord equal treatment to non-member countries, no informed trader was entitled to expect that patterns of trade existing when the protective measures were adopted would be respected.

The protective measures in issue in those cases were exceptional in that a total prohibition of imports from Taiwan was imposed within an unusually short period.[131] Yet it is difficult to see how, in the absence of retroactivity, the claim of the applicants could have succeeded.[132] Although, as stated in *Faust* and *Edeka*, the existence of a commercial agreement may be sufficient to impute knowledge on traders that a change of direction in the Community's trade policy is imminent, the existence of an international agreement does not necessarily establish a legitimate expectation that the Community will not take unilateral measures. In *Unifruit Hellas* v. *Commission*,[133] it was argued that the conclusion of a Framework Cooperation Agreement established a climate of confidence between the Community and Chile such as to preclude the introduction of a countervailing charge on imports from Chile. The Court held, however, that the Agreement did not intend to amend the

---

[128] Case 245/81 *Edeka Zentrale AG* v. *Germany* [1982] ECR 2745.

[129] Case 52/81 *Faust* v. *Commission* [1982] ECR 3745.

[130] *Faust*, op.cit., para. 27; *Edeka*, op.cit., para. 27.

[131] The Agreement with China was entered into on 3 Apr. 1978 and was published in the Official Journal on 11 May 1978. The protective measures against Taiwan came into effect in late May and June 1978.

[132] See further on protective measures, Case 112/80 *Firma Anton Dürbeck* v. *HZA Frankfurt am Main-Flughafen* [1981] ECR 1095; *Sofrimport*, discussed below, p. 186.

[133] Case C–51/95, [1997] ECR I–727. CFI, Case T–489/93 [1994] ECR II–1201.

provisions of a previous Council Regulation pursuant to which countervailing charges were adopted after the conclusion of the Agreement.

5.3.9. The presumption against retroactivity

The principle of non-retroactivity is not only a rule of substantive law but also a rule of interpretation according to which, in the absence of a clear indication to the contrary, a Community measure is presumed not to be retroactive.[134] In *Salumi*,[135] the Court held that rules of substantive law, as opposed to rules of procedure, apply to situations existing before their entry into force only if that clearly follows from their terms, objectives, or general scheme. Thus, in one case[136] where a regulation was published in the issue of the Official Journal dated 1 July 1976 and expressly stated that it would come into force on 1 July, but because of a strike the issue appeared on 2 July, the Court interpreted the regulation as not being in force until the date of its actual publication.

As already stated, the presumption against retroactivity does not apply to immediate application. At least in the sphere of economic law, a legislative provision applies in principle to the future effects of situations which arose in the past.[137] Where respect for legitimate expectations so requires, however, a measure may be interpreted as not having immediate application. In *Deuka*,[138] two successive Commission regulations reduced and abolished respectively a denaturing premium payable to producers with a view to maintaining stability in the market in cereals. On grounds of legal certainty, the Court interpreted the regulations as not applying to denaturing operations irrevocably undertaken before the regulations came into force even if the actual denaturing was not to take place until after that date. The judgment is particularly laconic as to why in the specific circumstances of the case legal certainty required the protection of pending transactions. It is notable that the Advocate General took the opposite view, submitting persuasive arguments.

In general, the case law concerning retroactivity and immediate application does not offer the consistency one may have wished for although that seems to be largely due to the distinct nature of agricultural policy measures which require frequent regulatory interventions to meet the demands of the market.

---

[134] Case 84/81 *Staple Dairy Products* v. *Intervention Board for Agricultural Produce* [1982] ECR 1763 at 1783 per Slynn AG. See also *IRCA*, op.cit., per Warner AG at 1237–9 for a comparative analysis of the laws of Member States.

[135] *Salumi*, op.cit., para. 9.

[136] Case 88/76 *Société pour l'exportation des sucres SA* v. *Commission* [1977] ECR 709. See also above, n. 61 and accompanying text.

[137] See *Westzucker*, op.cit; *Tomadini*, op.cit. p. 181.

[138] Case 5/75 *Deuka* v. *Einfuhr- und Vorratsstelle Getreide* [1975] ECR 759.

5.4. Legitimate expectations arising from legislation

5.4.1. Protection of specific interests

A legitimate expectation may be founded on previous[139] legislation where the legislation directs a Community institution to take into account a specific, well defined, interest. In *Sofrimport* v. *Commission*,[140] by two regulations adopted on 12 and 14 April 1988 respectively the Commission suspended, as a protective measure, the importation of dessert apples originating in Chile. On 31 March, Sofrimport had shipped a cargo of apples from Chile for import into the Community. While the goods were still in transit, it lodged an application for import licences which was refused by the French authorities pursuant to the regulations. Article 3(3) of Council Regulation No. 2702/72[141] required the Commission, in adopting protective measures, to take into account the 'special position of products in transit to the Community'. The Court held that Article 3(3) enabled an importer whose goods were in transit to rely on a legitimate expectation that no suspensory measures would be applied against him unless an overriding public interest required otherwise. The Commission argued that a reasonably careful trader should have envisaged the possibility that measures might be taken because in a previous regulation it had expressly reserved the power to do so. The Court held that simply informing traders of the possibility that protective measures might be taken was not sufficient. In order to meet the requirement of 'special protection', the Commission ought to have indicated the situations in which the public interest might justify the application of protective measures with regard to goods in transit. The Court added that the Commission had not demonstrated the existence of any overriding public interest.

Subsequently, in *Unifruit Hellas* v. *Commission*,[142] the CFI, and on appeal the Court of Justice, took a restrictive view of *Sofrimport* and refused to extend Article 3(3) of Regulation No. 2702/72 so as to protect goods in transit from the imposition of countervailing charges. The Court of Justice distinguished between countervailing charges and protective measures on the ground that the purpose of the first is to protect the level of Community prices whilst the second seek essentially to suspend imports where the Community market is threatened by serious disturbances. It stated that the effect of Article 3(3) is to allow traders to rely on a legitimate expectation that products already in transit will not be refused entry on arrival in the Community. It does not necessarily require the Commission to exempt goods in transit from other protective measures, such as countervailing charges,

---

[139] Clearly, a legitimate expectation may only be derived from an act or omission prior to the measure which is alleged to have infringed it: Joined Cases T–466, T–469, etc. *O'Dwyer and Others* v. *Council* [1995] ECR II–2071, para. 57.

[140] Case C–152/88 [1990] ECR I–2477.

[141] Council Regulation (EEC) No. 2707/72 of 19 Dec. 1972 laying down the conditions for applying protective measures for fruit and vegetables, OJ English Spec.Ed., 1972 (28 to 30 Dec.), p. 3.

[142] Case C–51/95 [1997] ECR I–727; CFI, Case T–489/93 [1994] ECR II–1201.

since such charges affect traders less severely. The Court added that, in any event, the system seeking to maintain the level of Community prices would be rendered completely ineffective if goods in transit were exempted from the levying of the countervailing charge in issue.[143]

A legitimate expectation may not arise out of proposed legislation. If a person were able to found a legitimate expectation on a proposal submitted by the Commission that would prejudice the powers of the other institutions in the decision-making process and the discretion of the Commission to amend its proposal.[144] Also, an expectation will not be protected unless it is reasonable.[145] A person may not rely on the principle to derive a speculative benefit which the legislation was not intended to confer.[146]

5.4.2. Milk quotas[147]

Perhaps the best illustration of the application of the principle of protection of legitimate expectations is provided by the milk quota cases. With a view to limiting surplus production in milk, Council Regulation No. 1078/77[148] offered to producers incentives to leave temporarily the market. A non-marketing premium was granted to producers who undertook not to market milk for a period of five years. A conversion premium was granted to producers who undertook to convert their dairy herds to meat production for a period of four years. It soon became clear that those measures were not sufficient and, in a further attempt to curb milk production, Council Regulation No. 856/84[149] introduced an additional levy payable on quantities of milk delivered beyond a guaranteed threshold, known as reference quantity (quota). The procedure for calculating the quota was provided for in Council Regulation No. 857/84.[150] According to that regulation, the Member States could provide that the quota was to be calculated on the basis of the quantity of milk delivered by the producer during 1981, 1982 or 1983. Regulation No. 857/84 did not provide for the allocation of a quota to returning producers, namely those who pursuant to a non-marketing or conversion undertaking did not deliver milk during the reference year adopted by the Member State concerned and who, upon the termination of their undertaking, were willing to restart milk production. In *Mulder* v. *Minister van Landbouw en Visserij (Mulder I)*,[151] the Court held that Regulation No. 857/84 was invalid in so far as it did not provide for the allocation of a reference quantity to returning producers on the ground that it infringed their legitimate expectations. The Court stated that a producer who has voluntarily ceased

---

[143] Case C–51/95 P, para. 27.

[144] Joined Cases C–13 to C–16/92 *Driessen* [1993] ECR I–4751, para. 33 and per Jacobs AG, 4774.

[145] Hartley, *The Foundations of European Community Law*, p. 145.

[146] See e.g. Case 2/75 *EVGF* v. *Mackprang* [1975] ECR 607.

[147] For a detailed discussion, see M. Cardwell, *Milk Quotas* (OUP, 1996).

[148] OJ 1977 L 131/1.   [149] OJ 1984 L 90/10.   [150] OJ 1984 L 90/13.

[151] Case 120/86 [1988] ECR 2321. See also Case 170/86 *Von Deetzen* v. *Hauptzollamt Hamburg-Jonas* [1988] ECR 2355.

production for a certain period cannot legitimately expect to be able to resume production under the same conditions as those which applied previously. Nor can he expect not to be subject to any rules of market or structural policy adopted in the meantime.[152] However, it continued:[153]

The fact remains that where such a producer, as in the present case, has been encouraged by a Community measure to suspend marketing for a limited period in the general interest and against payment of a premium he may legitimately expect not to be subject, upon the expiry of his undertaking, to restrictions which specifically affect him precisely because he availed himself of the possibilities offered by the Community provisions . . .

Contrary to the Commission's contention, total and continuous exclusion of that kind for the entire period of application of the regulations on the additional levy, preventing the producers concerned from resuming the marketing of milk at the end of the five-year period, was not an occurrence which those producers could have foreseen when they entered into an undertaking, for a limited period, not to deliver milk. There is nothing in the provisions of Regulation No. 1078/77 or in its preamble to show that the non-marketing undertaking entered into under that regulation might, upon its expiry, entail a bar to resumption of the activity in question. Such an effect therefore frustrates those producers' legitimate expectation that the effects of the system to which they had rendered themselves subject would be limited.

The reason, therefore, why the Court annulled the contested regulation was that returning producers had a legitimate expectation not to be excluded permanently from the market. They had agreed to suspend rather than to terminate production. As Slynn AG put it, to substitute a quota system for a non-marketing undertaking 'crosses the line between what is merely "hard luck" and what is unreasonable treatment'.[154]

In order to comply with the judgment in *Mulder I*, the Council provided for the allocation of a quota to returning producers. Article 3a, inserted to Regulation No. 857/84 by Regulation No. 764/89,[155] provided essentially that returning producers who, pursuant to their undertaking, had not delivered milk during the reference year adopted by the Member State concerned, were to receive a special reference quantity equal to 60 per cent of their milk production during the 12 months preceding the month in which the application for the non-marketing or conversion premium was made. Article 3a was also found to infringe the principle of protection of legitimate expectations. In *Spagl*,[156] the Court held that, in calculating the quota to be allocated to returning producers, the Community legislature was entitled to apply a reduction coefficient designed to ensure that returning producers were not accorded an undue advantage by comparison with continuing producers.[157] However, it added:[158]

---

[152] *Mulder I*, para. 23; *Von Deetzen*, para. 12.

[153] *Mulder I*, paras. 24, 26; *Von Deetzen*, paras. 13, 15.   [154] *Mulder I*, 2341.

[155] OJ 1989 L 84/2.   [156] Case C–189/89 [1990] ECR I–4539.

[157] Continuing producers were not entitled to 100 per cent of their production in the reference year but were subject to deductions imposed by the Community and to variable deductions imposed by Member States under Article 2(1) of Regulation No. 857/84.

[158] *Spagl*, para. 22; see also Case C–217/89 *Pastatter* [1990] ECR I–4585, para. 13.

the principle of the protection of legitimate expectations precludes the rate of reduction from being fixed at such a high level, by comparison with those applicable to [continuing producers], that its application amounts to a restriction which specifically affects them by very reason of the undertaking given by them under Regulation No. 1078/77.

The Court held that the reduction of 40 per cent specifically affected returning producers by reason of their undertaking since it was much higher than the rates of reduction applicable to continuing producers which did not exceed 17.5 per cent.

In *Spagl*, the Court saw legitimate expectations as a principle of participation, namely, as requiring proportionate allocation of burdens and benefits among comparable groups of producers.[159] In their attempt to justify the 60 per cent rule, the Council and the Commission argued that the allocation to returning producers of a quota based on more than 60 per cent of their production would entail an increase in the Community's overall quantities and would thus undermine the objective of the additional levy scheme which was to reduce structural surpluses. In response, the Court stated:[160]

Even if an increase larger than the Community reserve could not be contemplated without the risk of disturbing the balance of the milk market, the fact remains that it would have been sufficient to reduce the reference quantities of the other producers proportionately by a corresponding amount, so as to be able to allocate larger reference quantities to the producers who gave an undertaking under Regulation No. 1078/77.

The link between legitimate expectations and equal treatment is even more evident in the Opinion of Jacobs AG who reached a different conclusion. The Advocate General took the view that returning producers had no expectation to resume full production. Rather they had an expectation not to be treated less favourably than continuing producers. He considered that there was a difference in treatment but that it was objectively justified on the following grounds:[161]

* continuing producers were dependent for their livelihood on continuing production, whereas returning producers had been able to make use of their farms for other reasons;
* no exact comparison was possible between continuing and returning producers because the base figures on which their quotas were to be calculated were by their nature different;
* continuing producers would be adversely affected by any reduction in their existing production levels; that was not necessarily true about returning producers since they were returning to production from a nil base;
* unlike continuing producers who were a relatively homogeneous group, returning producers were not in a comparable position among themselves. Assessed by reference to all diverse cases, the 60 per cent rule was not discriminatory.

---

[159] This is also evident from the later judgment in Case C–63/93 *Duff and Others* v. *Minister for Agriculture and Food, Ireland, and the Attorney General* [1996] ECR I–569, para. 24.

[160] *Spagl*, para. 28; *Pastatter*, para. 19.   [161] *Spagl*, 4568–9.

It will be noted that, in view of the nature of the scheme and the Community's initial error, no solution would be wholly satisfactory. Both the Court and the Advocate General sought a fair solution attempting to remedy the most obvious shortcomings of a fundamentally flawed system.[162] The cases illustrate the Court's general approach in the field of the common agricultural policy: the case law can be seen as a search for fairness in declining markets, inspired primarily by considerations of participation, namely the fair allocation of burdens among different groups of producers.

In *Mulder I* and *Spagl*, the Court held that returning producers had a legitimate expectation as a class. The underlying rationale of the judgments is that those who repose faith on the authorities must not suffer as a result. This is the material criterion which distinguishes them from other cases where the Court refused to intervene to remedy hardship suffered by individual milk producers. In *Dowling*,[163] a returning producer was unable to resume milk production after the expiry of his non-marketing undertaking owing to ill health and made no deliveries during 1983, the year adopted as reference year by the Member State where he was established. The Court held that he had no legitimate expectation to receive a reference quantity as his failure to produce was unconnected with his undertaking. The applicant also argued that he was discriminated against vis-à-vis continuing producers on the following ground. Continuing producers whose milk production during the reference year chosen by the Member State concerned had been affected by exceptional events, such as occupational incapacity, had the right to obtain a reference quantity on the basis of their production in another year within the 1981 to 1983 period. He was unable to do so since, as a result of his undertaking, he had produced no milk in 1981 and 1982. He claimed therefore that he should obtain a reference quantity by reference to his production in another year. The Court held that the Community rules did no allow account to be taken of a reference year outside the period 1981 to 1983. The resulting difference in treatment between continuing and returning producers was objectively justified by the need to limit the number of years which may be taken as reference years in the interests of legal certainty and of the effectiveness of the additional levy system.

Clearly, the principle of legitimate expectations may not be relied upon to derive an advantage which the relevant legislation was not intended to grant. In *Von Deetzen II*,[164] the Court held that the legitimate expectations of returning producers were not frustrated by a Community provision which provided that if they sold or leased their holding the special quota allocated to them would be returned to the Community reserve and would not be passed on to the transferee. The Court's

---

[162] In order to comply with the judgment in *Spagl*, the Council adopted Regulation No. 1639/91 which provided for a new method for the calculation of reference quantities to returning producers. That method of calculation was also challenged but this time the challenge was unsuccessful: C–21/92 *Kamp* [1994] ECR I–1619.

[163] C–85/90 [1992] ECR I–5305.

[164] Case C–44/89 *Van Deetzen* [1991] ECR I–5119, para. 21.

rationale was that special reference quantities had been allocated to returning producers in order to enable them to resume their occupational activity and not to derive a profit by realizing the market value of the quota.

Overall, the cases on milk quotas indicate that the principle of protection of legitimate expectations imposes more severe restraints on the discretion of Community institutions than the principle of equal treatment, and a trader who is able to establish that somehow he has a legitimate expectation is more likely to succeed in his claim.[165]

Following *Mulder I* and *Spagl* the Community institutions were faced with claims for compensation. In *Mulder II*,[166] returning producers brought actions under Article 288[215(2)] EC with a view to recovering the loss which they had allegedly suffered as a result of the regulations which were annulled in *Mulder I* and *Spagl*. The Court recalled its established case law according to which in areas where the Community institutions enjoy wide discretion, the Community does not incur liability unless the institution concerned has manifestly and gravely disregarded the limits on the exercise of its powers. It then made a distinction. It found that the conditions of liability were fulfilled in relation to regulation No. 857/87, which totally excluded returning producers from the market, but that they were not fulfilled in relation to the 60 per cent rule. In relation to the total exclusion of returning producers, the Court held that the Community institutions failed completely to take into account their specific situation without invoking any higher public interest. It pointed out that returning producers constituted a clearly defined group of economic operators. Their total and permanent exclusion from the allocation of a quota could not be regarded as falling within the bounds of the normal economic risks inherent in the activities of a milk producer. The Community was therefore bound to make good the damage suffered by the applicants as a result of Regulation No. 857/84. By contrast, the 60 per cent rule was not a sufficiently serious violation. It represented a choice of economic policy made by the institutions which sought to draw a balance between the interests of returning producers and the interests of continuing producers in the light of the objectives of the milk quota scheme. The institutions took account of a higher public interest without gravely and manifestly disregarding the limits of their discretionary powers.[167] The material difference seems to be that, in the first case, the Community legislature totally failed to take into account the interests of returning producers whereas, in the second case, those interests featured in the balancing exercise performed by the legislature. The definitive effects of the regulation annulled in *Mulder I* were also

---

[165] For other cases on milk-quotas where claims based on breach of legitimate expectations were rejected see e.g. Case C–177/90 *Kühn* v. *Landwirtschaftskammer Weser-Ems* [1992] ECR I–35; Case C–63/93 *Duff and Others* v. *Minister for Agriculture and Food and Others* [1996] ECR I–569; Case C–22/94 *Irish Farmers Association and Others* v. *Minister for Agriculture, Food and Forestry, Ireland, and the Attorney General* [1997] ECR I–1809.

[166] Joined Cases C–104/89 and C–37/90 *Mulder* v. *Council and Commission* [1992] ECR I–3061.

[167] Op.cit., paras. 15–22.

crucial. The Court pointed out that producers were totally and permanently excluded from the market.

With regard to the extent of compensation, the Court held in *Mulder II* that it should cover the loss of earnings consisting in the difference between, on the one hand, the income which the applicants would have obtained in the normal course of events from the milk deliveries which they would have made if they had obtained a quota during the material period and, on the other hand, the income which they actually obtained from milk deliveries made during the same period in the absence of a quota plus any income which they obtained, or could have obtained, from any replacement activities. The Court laid down detailed guidelines in order to calculate the quota to which the applicants would have been entitled so as to ensure, as much as possible, equal treatment between them and continuing producers.[168]

5.5. Legitimate expectations arising from conduct of the Community institutions

A legitimate expectation may arise from the conduct of the Community administration but only as a result of precise assurances given by the administration.[169] Thus where an official requests confirmation of an entitlement and the Commission fails to answer, a legitimate expectation may not be founded on the Commission's silence.[170] Even where the Commission confirms the existence of an entitlement, such an undertaking cannot give rise to a legitimate expectation, since no official of a Community institution can give a valid undertaking not to apply Community law.[171] For the same reason, promises which do not take account of the provisions of the Staff Regulations cannot give rise to legitimate expectations on the part of those concerned.[172] The Court has also consistently held that the communication of an incorrect interpretation of Community rules cannot give rise to liability on the part of the Community administration, although there is an obligation to correct incorrect information previously circulated.[173]

---

[168] In a subsequent case it was held that the calculation of a hypothetical quota which a producer should have been granted in the past made by the Court in order to assess the quantum of damages is not binding on the Council where it calculates the quotas to be allocated to returning producers for the future. See Case C–21/92 *Kamp* [1994] ECR I–1619. For claims of compensation brought by individual producers following *Mulder II*, see Case T–554/93 *Saint and Murray* v. *Council and Commission* [1997] ECR II–563; Case T–541/93 *Connaughton and Others* v. *Council* [1997] ECR II–549; Case T–20/94 *Hartmann* v. *Council and Commission* [1997] ECR II–595.

[169] Case T–123/89 *Chomel* v. *Commission* [1990] ECR II–131, para. 26.   [170] Ibid.

[171] Case 188/82 *Thyssen AG* v. *Commission* [1983] ECR 3721, para. 11.

[172] Case 162/84 *Vlachou* v. *Court of Auditors* [1986] ECR 459, para. 6.

[173] Joined Cases 19, 20, 25 and 30/69 *Richez-Parise and Others* v. *Commission* [1970] ECR 325; Case 23/69 *Fiehn* v. *Commission* [1970] ECR 547; Case 137/79 *Kohll* v. *Commission* [1980] ECR 2601.

In applying the principle, the Court understands its jurisdiction equitably but in some cases its reasoning is not wholly convincing. In *Mavridis* v. *Parliament*,[174] the applicant's candidature for a post in the Community civil service was rejected on the ground that he had passed the requisite age limit. The age requirement had not been included in the vacancy notice published in the Official Journal but was introduced subsequently by the selection committee. Rozès AG opined that refusal to accept candidatures on the basis of a condition which did not appear in the vacancy notice disregarded the candidates' legitimate expectation that the information laid down in the notice was complete. In the circumstances of the case, she took the view that it was not necessary to annul the recruitment procedure since, even if the Parliament were to commence a new procedure following the correct form, the applicant would still be excluded. The Court considered that the submission based on the breach of legitimate expectations was unfounded but its reasoning is far from clear. It pointed out that an infringement of legitimate expectations would not automatically lead to the annulment of the contested measure but it might justify the award of damages, if the person concerned had suffered injury as a result. The applicant in the case had not submitted a claim in damages so the issue did not arise. The case suggests that, in certain circumstances, failure to disclose relevant information may infringe legitimate expectations.

An incorrect calculation of benefits by the Commission does not give rise to a legitimate expectation, at least not where the benefits are of a commercial nature and the Commission has discovered the error promptly. In *Töpfer* v. *Commission*,[175] a sugar exporter received lower compensation than in previous exports as a result of changes in the method of calculation. The compensation was provided to alleviate the adverse consequences of alterations in the unit of account. The Court stated that in previous transactions the Commission had calculated the compensation on bases which were more favourable but went beyond the objectives of the relevant regulations. The applicant had no right to the continuance of the incorrect calculations. On the contrary, as soon as the inaccuracy of these calculations was discovered the Commission was under a duty to correct it in the financial interest of the Community and in order to 'prevent privileged positions from becoming established'.[176]

An interesting example in the area of the European Social Fund is provided by *Interhotel*.[177] According to the applicable Community rules, applications for financial assistance from the Fund are submitted to the Commission by Member States on behalf of undertakings. The approval of an application is followed by the payment of an advance. Once the project is completed, the Commission pays the balance after receiving a report by the undertaking detailing the results and financial aspects of the project. In *Interhotel*, the CFI held that the Commission may not consider as ineligible certain expenditure on the ground that it does not fulfil the

---

[174] Case 289/81 *Mavridis* v. *Parliament* [1983] ECR 1731.
[175] Case 112/77 [1978] ECR 1019.		[176] Op.cit., para. 20.
[177] Case T–81/95 *Interhotel* v. *Commission*, [1997] ECR II–1265.

conditions laid down in the decision approving the granting of assistance, where those conditions were not communicated to the undertaking concerned.

Interhotel puts the onus firmly on the Commission and evinces a strict application of the principle of legitimate expectations. Two points may be made in relation to the judgment. The first concerns its reasoning, the second the scope of its application.

The Commission's decision approving the assistance had been communicated to the undertaking, albeit not by the Commission itself but by the national competent authority. But the CFI took the view that such communication was not sufficient. It stated that where the Commission does not take the necessary precautions to satisfy itself that the beneficiary of assistance is informed of the conditions imposed by the decision of approval, it cannot reasonably expect it to observe those conditions. That reasoning may be questioned. Where, according to the applicable procedure, the national authorities act as intermediaries between the Commission and the individual, the Commission's duty is to notify duly the details of the decision approving assistance to the national authority. Provided that the Commission has done so, the individual's inability to ascertain the conditions specified in the decision cannot be attributed to the Commission but only to the national authority. *Interhotel* seems to accept that, in dealing with disbursements from the European Social Fund, the Commission is 'vicariously' responsible for the conduct of the national authorities. The CFI may have taken that view because otherwise it would be difficult for the undertaking concerned to obtain a remedy against the national authority.

Secondly, it is noteworthy that the applicant undertaking did not seek clarification from the Commission regarding the expenditure declared ineligible by the decision approving the assistance. It is submitted, however, that the judgment must be read on its facts. In other cases, failure to seek clarification from the public authority may prevent a legitimate expectation from arising.

5.6. Revocation of beneficial administrative acts

The protection of legitimate expectations imposes limitations on the powers of the institutions to revoke retroactively favourable administrative acts. Revocation may take place where the beneficiary has procured the adoption of the act by means of false or incomplete information.[178] But where the beneficiary has acted in good faith, revocation is subject to strict conditions: it may take place only within a reasonable period and provided that the legitimate expectations of the beneficiary are respected.[179] There must also be a public policy interest which overrides the ben-

---

[178] Joined Cases 42/59 and 49/59 *SNUPAT* v. *High Authority* [1961] ECR 53.

[179] See e.g. Case 14/81 *Alpha Steel* v. *Commission* [1982] ECR 749; Case 15/85 *Consorzio Cooperative d'Abruzzo* v. *Commission* [1987] ECR 1005; Case C–24/89 *Cargill* v. *Commission* [1991] ECR I–2987; Case C–365/89 *Cargill* v. *Produktschap voor Margarine, Vetten en Oliën* [1991] ECR I–3045.

eficiary's interest in the maintenance of a situation which the beneficiary was entitled to regard as stable.[180] An interesting example is provided by *De Compte* v. *Parliament*.[181] The Parliament revoked with retroactive effect a decision recognizing that the appellant suffered from an occupational disease. The decision was revoked on the ground that the Parliament had erred in law. The justification put forward was that an illness may be justified as occupational only where it arises in connection with the lawful performance of an official's duties. In the circumstances, the appellant's illness was the result of stress brought about by disciplinary proceedings initiated against him because he had been found guilty of serious irregularities. The CFI considered the revocation lawful on the ground that it was made within a period of three months, which was reasonable, and the appellant had no legitimate expectations: after Parliament took the initial favourable decision, the appellant was informed that its implementation was in jeopardy because it might be vitiated by illegality. According to the CFI, therefore, reliance on the decision had been swiftly undermined in such a way that by the time the Parliament issued the revocation the appellant was no longer entitled to entertain any legitimate expectation as to the legality of the decision revoked. The Court of Justice overturned the decision of the CFI reasoning as follows. It pointed out that the appellant had not provoked the favourable decision by means of false or incomplete information. When the decision was notified to the appellant and he took cognizance of it, he was entitled to rely on its apparent legality. The Court held that legitimate expectations as to the legality of a favourable administrative act, once acquired, may not subsequently be undermined. In the circumstances, there was no overriding public policy interest which overrode the appellant's expectation.

5.7. Expectations of a non-commercial nature

In a number of staff cases, successful claims have been based on expectations of a non-commercial nature. We saw above that in the *Staff Salaries* case,[182] one of the first cases on legitimate expectations, the Council was held to be bound by its previous undertaking to use a certain formula for the revision of Community salaries. The Court was generous to the applicants in a series of cases decided in 1982 concerning the calculation of pension benefits payable to former Community employees.[183] In *Grogan* v. *Commission*,[184] the applicant, an Irish national, was a former official of the Commission. Upon retirement, he took up residence in his country of origin and chose, as he was entitled to do under the Staff Regulations, to have

---

[180] Case 14/61 *Hoogovens* v. *High Authority* [1962] ECR 253.
[181] Case C–90/95 P *De Compte* v. *Parliament* [1997] ECR I–1999.
[182] Case 81/72 *Commission* v. *Council* [1973] ECR 575. See above p. 12.
[183] Case 127/80 *Grogan* v. *Commission* [1982] ECR 869, Case 164/80 *De Pascale* v. *Commission* [1982] ECR 909, Case 167/80 *Curtis* v. *Parliament* [1982] ECR 931.
[184] Op.cit.

his pension paid in Belgian francs. The Community rules applicable at the time gave rise to unequal treatment among different categories of pensioners. Under the Staff Regulations, pensions paid in a currency other than Belgian francs were calculated on the basis of the exchange rates in force on 1 January 1965. Although in subsequent years the currencies of certain Member States devalued substantially, the Council continued to apply the fixed exchange rates of 1965 and, in order to maintain the purchasing power of pensions paid in weak currencies, it applied corrective weightings. Strictly speaking, the application of those weightings was unlawful since, under the Staff Regulations, they could be used only to alleviate the effects of differences in the costs of living rather than to compensate for currency fluctuations. In the case of pensioners residing in Ireland who had opted to have their pension paid in Irish pounds, the reduction in the purchasing power resulting from the application of fixed exchange rates was offset by the increase in the weighting applicable to Ireland. However, the weighting was of general application and benefited also those pensioners who had chosen to have their pension paid in Belgian francs and who therefore did not suffer a reduction in their purchasing power. In 1978 the Council adopted two regulations which introduced updated rates of exchange and reduced the weighting applicable to Ireland. The effect of those regulations was to reduce the amount of pension benefits payable to the applicant, who argued that the regulations infringed the principle of protection of legitimate expectations. The Court held that the new system was lawful since it was introduced in order to restore equality of treatment between various categories of pensioners residing in countries with weak currencies. However, the lack of adequate transitional measures infringed the principle of protection of legitimate expectations. The Court held that the inequality of treatment which occurred before the introduction of the new system was not in any way attributable to the conduct of pensioners but rather to the inaction of the Council which failed to rectify exchange rates which no longer bore any relation to economic reality. It stated that pensioners benefiting from that inaction were entitled to expect the Council to take account of the situation in which they had been placed by the prolonged application of the system temporarily used.[185]

The reasoning of the Court seems unpersuasive. It is not easy to see where the legitimate expectations of the applicants derived from. In principle, a class of persons which is treated preferentially without good reason cannot have a legitimate expectation to continue to be so treated in the future even if the preferential treatment has not been procured by that class and is wholly attributable to the legislature. That was particularly so in that case where the preferential treatment resulted from the use of the corrective weightings for a purpose different from that they were intended to fulfil. Nor, in the circumstances of the case, did the Community administration give any specific assurance to the applicants that the system relating

---

[185] *Grogan*, op.cit., para. 33. Capotorti AG considered that there was no infringement of legitimate expectations and advised the Court to dismiss the action.

to the payment of pensions would remain unalterable. In any event, it seems that the transitional arrangements introduced by the new system were adequate. The contested regulations were adopted in December 1978 and applied to the applicants from 1 October 1979, providing for a progressive reduction of benefits for a period of ten months. The Court held, however, that a period at least twice that length should have been envisaged.[186]

The pension cases should be treated as an aberration. The reasons which led the Court to find a breach of legitimate expectations seem to be the fact that the weighting system had been applied for many years, and the nature of the benefit involved. Understandably, the Court is more susceptible to a claim pertaining to pension benefits than to commercial claims.[187] In more recent years, it seems that the CFI has adopted a more sceptical approach to claims based on legitimate expectations in staff cases.[188]

5.8. Recovery of unduly paid charges

Legitimate expectations may arise against national authorities responsible for the enforcement of Community law. Their protection acquires particular importance in the recovery by national authorities of unduly paid out Community monies. According to the case law, to the extent that there are no Community rules, the recovery of such monies is governed by national law provided that two conditions are fulfilled: (a) the rules and procedures laid down by national law must not render the system for collecting Community charges less effective than that for collecting similar national charges; and (b) they must not render virtually impossible or excessively difficult the implementation of Community legislation.[189] In *Deutsche Milchkontor*,[190] the German authorities sought to recover aid granted in relation to a certain product on the ground that the product did not satisfy the conditions laid down by Community law. The applicants relied *inter alia* on rules of German law according to which an unlawful administrative act granting a pecuniary advantage cannot be revoked in so far as the beneficiary has relied upon the act and his expectation merits protection. The Court pointed out that, in principle, national authorities are under a strict obligation to demand repayment of Community sums unduly granted. The exercise of any discretion on whether to demand repayment would compromise the effectiveness of Community law. But it held that Community law did not prevent national law from having regard, in excluding the recovery of unduly paid aid, to the protection of legitimate

---

[186] Op.cit., para. 34.
[187] Compare the pension cases with Case 112/77 *Töpfer* v. *Commission* [1978] ECR 1019, above.
[188] See e.g. *Chomel*, op.cit.; cf. *De Compte* v. *Parliament*, op.cit.
[189] Case 265/78 *Ferwerda* v. *Produktschap voor Vee en Vlees* [1980] ECR 617.
[190] Joined Cases 205–15/82 *Deutsche Milchkontor* v. *Germany* [1983] ECR 2633. See also Joined Cases C–31 to C–44/91 *Lageder and Others* [1993] ECR I–1761.

expectations provided that the recovery of Community financial benefits was placed on an equal footing with the recovery of purely national ones and that the interests of the Community were taken fully into account.[191]

Where the recovery of sums due under Community law is governed by Community provisions, such provisions may specifically incorporate the protection of legitimate expectations. Regulation No. 1697/79[192] governs the post-clearance recovery of import or export duties where such duties have not been required of the person liable for payment. Article 5(2) authorizes the national authorities to waive post-clearance recovery where three conditions are cumulatively fulfilled: (a) the non-collection of the duties must have been due to an error by the authorities; (b) the person liable must have acted in good faith, in the sense that he must not have been reasonably able to detect the error of the authorities; and (c) he must have observed all the rules in force so far as his customs declarations are concerned. Where those conditions are satisfied, the person liable is entitled to waiver of recovery.[193] It is for the national courts to determine whether those conditions are satisfied on specific facts but the Court of Justice may give guidelines on a reference for a preliminary ruling. In *Faroe Seafood and Others*,[194] the Court suggested that the traders concerned were unable to detect the error committed by the competent authorities because the Community rules applicable were unclear and the traders had been issued on several occasions and over a relatively long period with certificates exempting the goods from customs duties.

With regard to the recovery of unlawful State aid, the case law draws a distinction between Member States and recipient undertakings. A Member State which has granted unlawful aid may not rely on the legitimate expectations of the recipient in order to justify its failure to comply with a Commission decision ordering recovery. If that were possible, national authorities would be able to rely on their own unlawful conduct in order to avoid their Community obligations.[195] Since the Member State concerned may not invoke the legitimate expectations of the recipient undertaking, it follows that the Commission itself may not decide to refrain from ordering recovery of unlawfully paid aid, relying on the submission of the national authorities that the legitimate expectations of the recipient undertakings would be infringed if recovery were ordered. If the Commission did so, its

---

[191] In a different context, the Court has held that a trader who has benefited from decisions of a national authority that do not comply with Community law is not entitled to expect that the same authority will adopt a further decision in breach of Community law: Case C–325/96 *Fábrica de Queijo Eru Portugesa Ltd.* v. *Subdirector-General das Alfândegas*, [1997] ECR I–7249, para. 22. See also below n. 207

[192] Council Regulation (EEC) No. 1697/79 on the post-clearance recovery of import duties or export duties which have not been required of the person liable for payment on goods entered for a customs procedure involving the obligation to pay such duties (OJ 1979 L 197/1).

[193] Case C–292/91 *Weis* v. *Hauptzollamt Würzburg* [1993] ECR I–2219; Case C–348/89 *Mecanarte* [1991] ECR I–3299.

[194] Joined Cases C–153 and C–204/94 *Faroe Seafood and Others* [1996] ECR I–2465.

[195] Case C–5/89 *Commission* v. *Germany* [1990] ECR I–3437, Case C–303/88 *Italy* v. *Commission* (*Lanerossi* case) [1991] ECR I–1433.

decision could be annulled at the instigation of an interested party, for example a competitor.[196]

The defence of legitimate expectations may be available to the undertaking which has received the unlawful aid. The case law suggests, however, that the circumstances where the recipient undertaking may avail itself of such a defence are restricted. An expectation may arise out of conduct of the Commission but only where such conduct is in accordance with the provisions of the Treaty. In *Deufil* v. *Commission*,[197] the Commission had issued guidelines stating that, in view of the conditions prevailing in the industry, aid in relation to certain synthetic fibres and yarns would not benefit from the exemption provided for in Article 87(3)(c) [93(2)(c)]. The Court held that the guidelines did not give rise to a legitimate expectation that aid in relation to a product not contained in the guidelines could be granted without first being notified in accordance with Article 88(3)[93(3)]. In *CIRFS* v. *Commission*,[198] the Court decided that a subsequent version of the same guidelines bound the Commission in a different way: the Commission was under an obligation to treat aid in relation to the products mentioned therein as new aid and require its notification. Enterprises competing with an undertaking to which such aid had been granted entertained a legitimate expectation that the Commission would open the procedure provided in Article 88(2)[93(2)].[199] The judgments in the two cases are fully compatible: a policy statement issued by the Commission may restrict its discretion for the future but may not derogate from the provisions of Articles 87[92] and 88[93].[200]

In *RSV* v. *Commission*, the Court accepted that the Commission's unreasonable delay in requiring the recovery of State aid gave rise to a legitimate expectation on the part of the recipient undertaking which prevented the Commission from requiring the national authorities to order recovery.[201] In that case, the Commission adopted the contested decision more than two years after opening the Article 88(2)[93(2)] procedure. The case should be treated as exceptional. The delay was unjustifiable and wholly due to the Commission;[202] and the aid in issue was intended to meet additional costs of an operation which had been in receipt of aid authorized by the Commission. The applicant therefore had reasonable grounds for believing that no objection would be raised.

[196] Case T–67/94 *Ladbroke Racing Ltd.* v. *Commission*, [1998] ECR II–1.

[197] See also Case 310/85 *Deufil* v. *Commission* [1987] ECR 901.

[198] Case C–313/90 [1993] ECR I–1125.

[199] But the adoption by the Commission of an Aid Code authorizing by way of exception certain categories of aid does not create a legitimate expectation that other categories will not be authorized: Case T–243/94 *British Steel* v. *Commission*, [1997] ECR II–1887, paras. 74 *et seq.*; Case T–244/94 *Wirtschaftsvereiningung Stahl and Others* v. *Commission*, [1997] ECR II–1963, paras. 56 *et seq.*

[200] According to standard case law, the Commission may lay down guidelines for the exercise of its discretionary powers in the field of State aid, provided that they contain directions on the approach to be followed by it and do not depart from Treaty rules: *CIRFS*, op.cit.; Case T–380/94 *AIUFFASS and AKT* v. *Commission* [1996] ECR II–2169, para. 57; Case T–149/95 *Établisssements Richard Ducros* v. *Commission*, [1997] ECR II–2031, para. 61.

[201] Case 223/85 *RSV* v. *Commission* [1987] ECR 4617.

[202] Cf. Case C–301/87 *France* v. *Commission* [1990] ECR I–307, para. 28 and 333 per Jacobs AG.

Notwithstanding *RSV* v. *Commission*, the rule remains that undertakings to which State aid has been granted may not entertain a legitimate expectation that the aid is lawful unless it has been granted in compliance with the procedure laid down in Article 88[93]. The Court attaches particular importance to this requirement as is evident from *Spain* v. *Commission*.[203] The Commission had adopted a decision finding that certain aid granted by Spain to a steel foundry in Aragon was compatible with the common market. Following an action by an English company, the Court annulled the Commission decision.[204] In compliance with the Court's judgment, the Commission initiated the procedure under Article 88(2)[93(2)] of the Treaty and, by a new decision, it declared the aid unlawful and ordered recovery. The Spanish Government argued that the decision ordering recovery frustrated the legitimate expectations of the recipient undertaking. The Court confirmed that undertakings to which aid has been granted cannot, in principle, entertain a legitimate expectation that the aid is lawful unless it has been granted in compliance with the procedure laid down in Article 88[93]. A diligent operator should normally be able to determine whether that procedure has been followed. In the case in issue the aid had been granted without first being notified. The fact that the Commission initially decided not to raise any objections could not be regarded as capable of having caused the recipient undertaking to entertain any legitimate expectation since that decision was challenged in due time before the Court which annulled it. However regrettable it might have been, the Commission's error could not erase the consequences of the unlawful conduct of the Spanish authorities.

The defence of legitimate expectations may be available to the recipient undertaking against the national authorities effecting recovery if it is provided by national law in relation to domestic claims of a similar nature. This follows from the general principle that recovery of State aid is subject to the national rules of procedure provided that such rules do not render recovery virtually impossible and do not treat Community claims less favourably than comparable domestic claims.[205] In this context, however, the Court gives priority to ensuring that national law does not override the effective enforcement of Community obligations and the defence is particularly difficult to succeed. The Court has held that a recipient of State aid unduly granted may rely, when the aid is to be repaid, only on exceptional circumstances on the basis of which it has legitimately assumed the aid to be lawful.[206] In *Land Rheinland-Pfalz* v. *Alcan Deutschland GmbH*,[207] the Court held that the competent national authority must revoke a decision granting unlawful aid even if the time limit laid down under national law for the revocation of unlawful admin-

---

[203] Case C–169/95 [1997] ECR I–135.

[204] Case C–198/91 *Cook* v. *Commission* [1993] ECR I–2487.

[205] Case C–142/87 *Belgium* v. *Commission* [1990] ECR I–959; Case T–459/93 *Siemens* v. *Commission* [1995] ECR II–1675.

[206] See e.g. Case C–5/89 *Commission* v. *Germany* [1990] ECR I–3437, paras. 13–16; *Siemens* v. *Commission*, op.cit., para. 104.

[207] Case C–24/95 [1997] ECR I–1591.

istrative acts has elapsed. Where aid is found to be incompatible with the common market by the Commission, the national authorities do not have any discretion, their role being merely to give effect to the Commission's decision. Since the national authorities have no discretion, the recipient of unlawfully granted State aid ceases to be in a state of uncertainty once the Commission has adopted a decision finding the aid incompatible with the common market and requiring recovery. The principle of legal certainty cannot therefore preclude repayment of the aid on the ground that the national authorities were late in complying with the decision requiring repayment.[208] The Court also held that the competent authority must revoke a decision granting unlawful aid even if the competent authority is responsible for the illegality of the decision to such a degree that revocation appears to be a breach of good faith towards the recipient.[209] The obligation to recover subsists where such recovery is excluded by national law because the gain no longer exists.[210]

---

[208] Op.cit., para. 37.   [209] Op.cit., para. 41.   [210] Op.cit., para. 50.

6

Fundamental Rights

6.1. Introduction

The protection of fundamental rights in the Community legal order has been almost entirely the product of case law.[1] The Court's creative jurisprudence has not been without its critics. Coppel and O'Neil have argued that the high rhetoric of human rights employed in the case law is not based on a genuine concern to take human rights seriously but on a desire to extend the scope and impact of Community law which lacks legitimacy.[2] A more balanced assessment suggests that the gradual elaboration of judicial standards has been well founded and that the impact of the Courts jurisprudence has been more positive.[3] As far as the case law is concerned, it may be said that the following topics merit particular attention. The first refers to the level of protection. In the absence of a Community catalogue, which human rights must be protected by the Community judicature? Should Community law adopt a minimalist approach seeking the lowest common denominator of the national constitutions or should it follow a maximalist approach? The second issue concerns the scope of human rights protection. What types of measures may be said to be subject to review on grounds of compatibility with human

[1] For extensive references, see the bibliography at the end of this book. A selective bibliography in English includes *inter alia*: N. Neuwahl and A. Rosas (eds.), *The European Union and Human Rights* (Kluwer, 1995); A. Cassese A. Clapham and J. Weiler (eds.), *Human Rights and the European Community*, Vols. II–III (1991); A. Clapham, 'A Human Rights Policy for the European Community' (1990) 10 YEL 309; D. Curtin and T. Heukels (eds.) *Institutional Dynamics of European Integration, Essays in Honour of H. G. Schermers*, Vols. I–III (Kluwer); F. G. Jacobs, 'Human Rights in Europe: New Dimensions' (1992) 3 King's College LJ 49; F. G. Jacobs (ed.), *European Law and the Individual* (1976); S. Hall, 'Loss of Union Citizenship in Breach of Fundamental Rights' (1996) 21 ELRev. 129; L. B. Krogsgaard, 'Fundamental Rights in the European Community after Maastricht' (1993) LIEI 99; K. Lenaerts, 'Fundamental Rights to be Included in a Community Catalogue' (1991) 16 ELRev. 367; M. H. Mendelson, 'The Impact of European Community Law on the Implementation of the European Convention on Human Rights' (1983) 3 YEL 99; M. H. Mendelson, 'The European Court of Justice and Human Rights' (1981) 1 YEL 125; H. G. Schermers, 'The Eleventh Protocol to the European Convention on Human Rights' (1994) 19 ELRev. 367; H. G. Schermers, 'The European Communities bound by Fundamental Human Rights' (1990) 27 CMLRev. 249; R. M. Dallen jun., 'An Overview of European Community Protection of Human Rights, with some special references to the UK' (1990) 27 CMLRev. 761; C. Duparc, *The European Community and Human Rights* (EC Commission, 1992); De Bùrca, 'Fundamental Human Rights and the Reach of European Law' (1992) 13 OJLS 283.

[2] J. Coppel and A. O'Neill, 'The European Court of Justice: Taking Rights Seriously' (1992), 29 CMLRev. 669.

[3] J. H. H. Weiler and N. J. S. Lockhart, ' "Taking Rights Seriously" Seriously: The European Court and its Fundamental Rights Jurisprudence' (1995) 32 CMLRev. 51 and 579.

rights? Does review apply only to Community measures or does it also extend to national measures, and if so, what types of measures are covered and why? This issue also raises questions pertaining to the standard of review. Where national measures are subject to review on grounds of compatibility with human rights, what standard of review is applicable? Is it the Community standard or that applicable in the Member State concerned? The question acquires practical importance where Community and national standards differ. The final issue refers to the relationship between Community law and the European Convention on Human Rights. That issue came to the fore with the Opinion of the Court on the *Accession of the Community to the ECHR*.[4] The present chapter examines those issues through a wider analysis of the case law. There is no attempt to give an exhaustive account of the issues involved but rather to outline developments, highlight trends, and assess the current state of the case law in selected areas.

The interrelationship between the case law and legislative developments in the area of human rights falls beyond the scope of this book. Suffice it to say that, encouraged by the Court's case law, the political institutions of the Community have increasingly employed a language of human rights. De Bùrca attributes that to two reasons:[5] fundamental rights are seen as a force of integration and also as a source of legitimacy for the Community legal order. Notably, the Treaty of Amsterdam provides for a new enforcement mechanism in the event that a Member State fails to observe fundamental rights. Article 6(1) of the Treaty on European Union, as amended by the Treaty of Amsterdam, declares that: 'The Union is founded on the principles of liberty, democracy, respect for human rights and fundamental freedoms, and the rule of law, principles which are common to the Member States.' Article 7 provides that, where a Member State is found responsible[6] for a 'serious and persistent' breach of one of the principles mentioned in Article 6(1), the Council, acting by a qualified majority, 'may decide to suspend certain of the rights deriving from the application of this Treaty to the State in question, including the voting rights of the representative of the Government of that Member State in the Council'. Although the new provision may be seen as a new qualitative change of approach, it seems almost too draconian to be of any practical use. It does suggest, however, that the Amsterdam Treaty seeks to provide for a clearer hierarchy of rules and attach particularly severe political and legal consequences to breach of the rules of the highest tier.

---

[4] Opinion 2/94 [1996] ECR I-1759.

[5] G. De Bùrca, 'The Language of Rights in European Integration', in J. Shaw and G. More (eds.), *New Legal Dynamics of European Union*, p. 29.

[6] The determination is made by the Council meeting in the composition of the Heads of State or Government and acting by unanimity (but without taking into account the vote of the representative of the Member State concerned) and after obtaining the assent of the European Parliament.

6.2. Review of Community measures

6.2.1. The early years

Apart from an oblique reference in the preamble,[7] the Treaty of Rome makes no reference to the protection of fundamental rights.[8] The reasons for this silence is to be found in the historical origins of the Community. In the aftermath of the Second World War, the protection of human rights at a pan-European level was the subject of a separate political structure. The Council of Europe was established in 1949 with the main task of drafting and implementing the European Convention for the Protection of Human Rights and Fundamental Freedoms (ECHR). The Convention was concluded on 4 November 1950 and came into force on 3 September 1953. The Draft Treaty for a European Political Community of 1953 provided for the application of Section I of the European Convention and its First Protocol as part of its provisions, but the Draft Treaty encountered insuperable political difficulties and its all-embracing, federalist, structure gave way to less ambitious, sectoral, economic integration. Although the EEC was perceived as a dynamic entity, bound to evolve in subsequent years, its goals were first and foremost economic. It was thought that the protection of human rights did not merit specific reference in a Treaty setting up a Community with enumerated competences mainly in the economic sphere. This applied *a fortiori* to the European Coal and Steel Community and Euratom.

In a series of early cases, the Court did not accept that the Community was bound by fundamental rights guaranteed by the constitutions of the Member States.[9] That early case law is not to be attributed to a lack of commitment on the part of the Community judicature to the protection of human rights. The reason was a more pragmatic one. The Court was fearful of subordinating the Treaty to the laws of Member States and thus prejudicing the effect of Community law. The first reluctant step was taken in *Stauder* v. *City of Ulm*.[10] A Commission decision provided for the sale of butter at reduced prices to citizens in receipt of social assistance. The German and the Dutch versions of the decision required as a condition of entitlement the presentation of a coupon indicating the name of the beneficiary. A German national argued that the requirement to reveal the identity of the beneficiary was an infringement of fundamental rights. The French and the Italian

---

[7] The eighth recital states that the Member States are resolved 'to preserve and strengthen peace and liberty'.

[8] 'Fundamental' rights and 'human' rights are used interchangeably in the text. See further, Clapham, 'A Human Rights Policy for the European Community' (1990) 10 YEL 309, at 310–11.

[9] See e.g. Case 1/58 *Stork* v. *High Authority* [1959] ECR 17 at 25–6; Joined Cases 36, 37, 38 and 40/59 *Geitling* v. *High Authority* [1960] ECR 423 at 438–9; Case 40/64 *Sgarlata* v. *Commission* [1965] ECR 215 at 227. As Mendelson points out, op.cit., 130, it is not an accident that the first cases came from Germany and Italy, the two Member States which, fearful of their troubled past, had entrenched fundamental rights constitutionally.

[10] Case 29/69 [1969] ECR 419.

versions of the decision employed more general language. On the basis of those versions, the Court held that the decision did not require the identification of beneficiaries by name but enabled Member States to employ other methods by which the coupons could refer to the person concerned. Interpreted in that way, the Court held, the provision 'contains nothing capable of prejudicing the fundamental human rights enshrined in the general principles of Community law and protected by the Court'.[11]

6.2.2. From Internationale Handelsgesellschaft to Hauer

The reference to fundamental rights in *Stauder* was incidental but paved the way for the seminal *Internationale Handelsgesellschaft*.[12] German traders challenged the system of deposits established by Community agricultural regulations on the ground that it ran counter to the fundamental rights protected by the German Constitution, in particular the principle of proportionality and the freedom to pursue trade and professional activities. Reasserting the primacy of Community law, the Court stated that it could not be overridden by rules of national law. It was not therefore possible to test the validity of Community acts vis-à-vis fundamental rights as protected by the constitutions of the Member States. The Court, however, continued:[13]

. . . respect for fundamental rights forms an integral part of the general principles of law protected by the Court of Justice. The protection of such rights, whilst inspired by the constitutional traditions common to the Member States, must be ensured within the framework of the structure and objectives of the Community.

In the constitutional development of the Community, *Internationale Handelsgesellschaft* marks a distinct development. The passage quoted above is testament to the Court's creative jurisprudence. On the one hand, the Court reiterates the supremacy of Community law and takes the principle of primacy to its outmost limits: Community law takes precedence even over the most precious provisions of the national constitutions. On the other hand, the Court reassures the Member States that the Treaty shares their constitutional values and ensures ideological continuity. At the same time, it takes care to safeguard the autonomy of Community law. The national constitutional traditions provide 'inspiration' for respect of human rights in the Community legal order. There their function ends. The balance to be struck where fundamental rights conflict with each other and the application of general principles borrowed from the national constitutions to specific cases is a matter for the Court, since the protection of human rights must be secured 'within the framework of the structure and the objectives of the Community'. To be sure, the Court arrogates to itself important functions as it is the concrete effects

[11] Op.cit., para. 7.
[12] Case 11/70 *Internationale Handelsgesellschaft* v. *Einfuhr- und Vorratsstelle Getreide* [1970] ECR 1125. See further above, chapter on proportionality p. 94.
[13] Op.cit., para. 4.

of human rights that matter. One, however, could hardly advocate a different view. *Internationale Handelsgesellschaft* is not a paradigm of unwarranted judicial activism. The assertion that the Community is bound by fundamental rights finds justification in the constitutional traditions of the Member States. As Mancini and Keeling note, it is hardly conceivable that 'the national parliaments would have ratified a Treaty which was capable of violating the fundamental tenets of their own constitutions'.[14] Once it is accepted that human rights form part of the Community legal order and bind the Community institutions, their protection must be ensured within the four corners of the Community polity. It would simply not be possible to apply mechanically human rights as recognized in one or another national legal system without taking into account the specific qualities of Community law.

If *Internationale Handelsgesellschaft* reconciled the primacy of Community law with respect for national constitutional traditions, *Nold*[15] made the first step towards the establishment of Community standards for the protection of human rights. The Commission authorized new terms of business in the coal sector, as a result of which the applicant undertaking lost its status as a direct wholesaler and with it entitlement to direct supplies from the producer. It argued that the new trading rules jeopardized its profitability to the extent of endangering its very existence and therefore infringed the right to property and the freedom to trade as protected by the German Constitution. The Court held that, in safeguarding human rights, it draws inspiration from the constitutional traditions common to the Member States and cannot therefore uphold measures which are incompatible with fundamental rights recognized and protected by the Constitutions of those States.[16] It then identified as a source of human rights international treaties for the protection of human rights on which the Member States have collaborated or of which they are signatories. Such treaties, the Court stated, 'can supply guidelines which would be followed within the framework of Community law'.[17] It also laid down the basic formula on the basis of which human rights would be protected by the Court. It held that the right to property and the right to practise freely a trade or profession do not constitute unfettered prerogatives but must be viewed in the light of their social function. They should, where necessary, be subject to certain limits justified by the overall objectives pursued by the Community, on condition that the substance of those rights is left untouched.[18] In reaching that conclusion, the Court drew inspiration from the constitutions of Member States where the right to property and the freedom to trade and practise a profession are made subject to limitations in the public interest.

The judgment in *Nold* was reiterated in *Hauer*.[19] In issue there was a Council regulation which, with a view to controlling wine surpluses, prohibited the new

[14] Mancini and Keeling, 'Democracy and the European Court of Justice' (1994) 57 MLR 175 at 187.
[15] Case 4/73 *Nold* [1974] ECR 491.　　　　　[16] Para. 13.　　　　　[17] Para. 13.
[18] Op.cit., para. 14. Cf. *Geitling* v. *High Authority*, op.cit., where the Court had refused to recognize the protection of the right of property in the Community legal order.
[19] Case 44/79 *Hauer* v. *Land Rheinland-Pfalz* [1979] ECR 3727. See also Joined Cases 154 etc./78 and 39 etc./79 *Valsabbia* v. *Commission* [1979] ECR 907.

planting of vines for a period of three years. It was argued that the prohibition infringed the right to property and the right to trade. With regard to the former, the Court stated that it is guaranteed in the Community legal order in accordance with the ideas common to the constitutions of the Member States. Referring to the First Protocol of the ECHR, the Court distinguished between a measure which deprives the owner of his right and a measure which restricts its exercise and held that the contested regulation belonged to the second category. It then referred to the constitutions of several Member States and came to the conclusion that the restriction on the planting of new vines was a type of restriction familiar to, and accepted as lawful by, the Member States. It proceeded to examine whether the contested regulation was justified in the circumstances and gave an affirmative answer. The contested measure was of a temporary nature. It was intended to deal immediately with the problem of surpluses whilst at the same time preparing the introduction of permanent structural measures. Also, in view of the underlying situation of the market, the cultivation of new vineyards would make no economic sense. It would worsen the underlying economic situation making more difficult the implementation of a structural policy and perhaps posing the risk that more restrictive measures would need to be introduced in the future.[20]

Nold and *Hauer* evince a firm but cautious approach. The determination to ensure that the Community institutions are bound by fundamental rights coexists with the eagerness to secure the autonomy of the Community polity. The Court appeared more accommodating to the national constitutions than in *Internationale Handelsgesellschaft* declaring that measures which are incompatible with fundamental rights recognized and protected by the constitutions of the Member States cannot be upheld.[21] This more conciliatory approach may have been the result of the defiant reaction of the German Constitutional Court following *Internationale Handelsgesellschaft*.[22] It is, however, doubtful whether there is much difference in substance. Respect for the same rights does not mean reaching the same outcome on the facts. It is clear from *Nold* and *Hauer* that the content of a right as recognized in the Community legal order may be different from its content as recognized in the constitutions of the Member States. This reflects the general position of the Court in deriving general principles of law from the national legal systems, according to which the Court does not seek to derive common denominators but makes a synthesis guided by the spirit of the Treaty and the requirements of Community polity. As Weiler points out, the Community is a new polity the constitutional ethos of which must give expression to a multiplicity of national traditions.[23] The frequent references to the constitutions of the Member States in *Nold* and *Hauer*, however, suggest that, in the field of human rights, concepts of national law are more influential than in relation to other general principles. The reason for this is that respect for rights recognized as fundamental by the laws of the Member States

[20] Op.cit., paras. 28–9.   [21] *Nold*, op.cit., para. 13; *Hauer*, op.cit., para. 15.
[22] See below p. 208.
[23] Weiler, in Newhaul and Rosas, op.cit., p. 66.

provides political legitimacy and ideological grounding for the Community legal order.

6.2.3. The National Reaction

Although in *Internationale Handelsgesellschaft* the Court went at lengths to address the concerns of the German judiciary relating to the protection of fundamental rights at Community level, the German Constitutional Court remained unconvinced. In a subsequent judgment arising from the same dispute,[24] it held that fundamental rights were insufficiently protected by Community law because the Community lacked a codified catalogue of fundamental rights and also (at that time) a directly elected Parliament. It considered that the case law of the Court of Justice did not provide adequate protection because it was subject to change and did not satisfy the requirements of legal certainty. It held that the German courts should not apply rules of Community law which infringed fundamental rights as guaranteed by the German Constitution as long as Community law did not itself provide sufficient protection and reserved itself jurisdiction to decide whether such infringement existed. Some years later, in the so-called *Second Solange* case,[25] the German Constitutional Court was prepared to reconsider its earlier ruling and accepted that supervening developments had rendered the protection of fundamental rights at Community level sufficient. It referred to *Nold* and subsequent case law, the 1977 Joint Declaration of the political institutions on human rights,[26] and the European Council Declaration on Democracy of 1978.[27] The Constitutional Court now accepted that it would not rule on whether secondary Community law was sufficiently in conformity with the German Constitution as long as the Community continued to protect human rights at the current level.

The Constitutional Court seemed to confirm that position in the *European Union Treaty* case[28] where Germany's ratification of the Treaty on European Union was challenged on the ground that it was unconstitutional. The Constitutional Court held that it guarantees the essential content of fundamental rights not only against German authorities but also against the sovereign powers of the Community but that it does so in a relationship of co-operation with the Court of Justice, under which the Court of Justice provides protection of fundamental rights in the Community legal order and the Constitutional Court restricts itself to a general guarantee of the constitutional standards that cannot be dispensed with. In the specific case, the Constitutional Court rejected the submission that the potential

---

[24] See Bundesverfassungsgericht, judgment of 29 May 1974 [1974] 2 CMLR 551.

[25] See Bundesverfassungsgericht, judgment of 22 Oct. 1986, 2 BvR 197/83, 73 BVerfGE 339, [1987] 3 CMLR 225.

[26] OJ 1977 No. C 103, 1.   [27] EC Bull. 3–1978, p. 5.

[28] See Bundesverfassungsgericht, judgment of 12 Oct. 1993, 2 BvR 2134/92 and 2159/92, 89 BverfGE 155 [1993] 1 CMLR 57. For a powerful critique, see Weiler, 'Does Europe Need a Constitution? Demos, Telos and the German Maastrich Decision' (1995) 1 ELJ 219.

replacement of the German mark by a common currency would infringe the right to property and the freedom to trade and carry out professional activities.

The above case law evinces the dialectical development of Community constitutional law. In *Internationale Handelsgesellschaft* the Constitutional Court 'asked', in *Nold* and *Hauer* the Court of Justice 'gave', and in the *Second Solange* case the Constitutional Court 'conceded'. But the provisional character of the Constitutional Court's deference to the jurisdiction of the Court of Justice is of particular importance. Firmly based on the idea that sovereignty derives from the nation State, the Constitutional Court sees itself as the guarantor of universal democratic values and is keen to retain residual authority.[29]

6.2.4. What is a fundamental right?

In *Nold* and in *Hauer* the Court made clear that the Community legal order is committed to protecting, subject to appropriate limitations set by the objectives and the scheme of the Treaty, the rights recognized in the European Convention of Human Rights and the national constitutions. Since the Treaty does not provide for a catalogue of fundamental rights, which rights are expressly recognized by the Court depends on the accidents of litigation. The rights which have been expressly recognized so far may be classified into three broad categories: economic and property rights, civil and political liberties, and rights of defence.[30]

Economic and property rights include the right to property,[31] the freedom to trade, and the right to choose and practise freely a trade or profession.[32] Civil and political liberties include human dignity,[33] religious equality,[34] freedom of expression,[35] prohibition of discrimination based on sex,[36] including gender reassignment,[37] the right to respect for privacy,[38] including family life[39] and medical confidentiality,[40] freedom

---

[29] But see Weiler, op.cit., esp. 222 *et seq.*   [30] For the rights of defence, see below Ch. 7.

[31] See e.g. Case 44/79 *Hauer* [1979] ECR 3727, and below p. 215.

[32] *Nold*, op.cit.; Hauer, op.cit.; Case 240/83 *Procureur de la République* v. *ADBHU* [1985] ECR 531.

[33] *Stauder*, op.cit.

[34] Case 130/75 *Prais* v. *Council* [1976] ECR 1589.

[35] Case C–100/88 *Oyowe and Traore* v. *Commission* [1989] ECR 4285; Case C–260/89 *ERT* [1991] ECR I–2925; Case C–159/90 *SPUC* v. *Grogan* [1991] ECR I–4685; Case C–219/91 *Ter Voort* [1992] ECR I–5485. See also for the freedom of the press, e.g. Case 246/83 *Binon* v. *AMP* [1985] ECR 2015, para. 46.

[36] Case 149/77 *Defrenne* v. *Sabena* [1978] ECR 1365.

[37] Case C–13/94 *P* v. *S and Cornwall County Council* [1996] ECR I–2143; but not sexual orientation, see Case C–249/96 *Grant* v. *South-West Trains Ltd.*, [1998] ECR I–621.

[38] Case 136/79 *National Panasonic* v. *Commission* [1980] ECR 2033; Case C–62/90 *Commission* v. *Germany* [1992] ECR I–2575; Case C–76/93 P *Scaramuza* v. *Commission* [1994] ECR I–5173. Reference has also been made to the duty of Community institutions to protect the personal integrity and honour of the Community employees: Case T–203/95 R *Connolly* v. *Commission* [1995] ECR II–2919.

[39] Case 249/86 *Commission* v. *Germany* [1989] ECR 1263.

[40] Case C–62/90 *Commission* v. *Germany* [1992] ECR I–2575; Joined Cases T–121/89 and T–13/90 *X* v. *Commission* [1992] ECR II–2195 and on appeal Case C–404/92 P [1994] ECR I–4780; Case T–10/93 *A* v. *Commission* [1994] ECR II–179.

of association and trade union activity,[41] and the right to an effective legal remedy.[42] More recently, the case law has pronounced on the right to public access to documents held by the Community institutions.[43] The Court has also expressly confirmed that the Community abides by the general principle of *nulla poena sine lege*,[44] and has declared as a general principle that any intervention by the Community authorities in the sphere of private activities of any person, whether natural or legal, must have a legal basis and be justified on grounds laid down by law.[45]

By contrast, it has been held that the principle of *nulla poena sine culpa* does not necessarily prohibit the imposition of strict criminal liability provided that such liability is proportionate and aims at the protection of important interests. This was first pronounced by the Court in *Hansen*[46] in relation to a measure concerning the liability of the employer for failure to respect worker-protection standards and was subsequently expressly confirmed in *Ebony Maritime and Loten Navigation* v. *Prefetto della Provincia di Brindisi and Others*.[47] That case arose from the imposition of sanctions against Yugoslavia. The Court held that Regulation No. 990/93 implementing UN sanctions against Yugoslavia[48] did not preclude an Italian law which provided for confiscation of the cargo where a vessel infringed the provisions of the regulation even though the penalty of confiscation was imposed without any proof of fault on the part of the owner of the cargo. The Court dismissed the argument that the Italian law violated the principle *nulla poena sine culpa* and that it was imposed to the principle of proportionality. It stated that a system of strict criminal liability is not in itself incompatible with Community law. Where it is for the Member States to provide sanctions for breach of Community measures, such sanctions must be analogous to those applicable to infringements of national law of a similar nature and also, in any event, they must be effective, proportionate and dissuasive. It is for the national court to determine whether the penalty of confiscation complies with those requirements. The Court, however, stated that, in making that determination, the national court had to take into account that the objective pursued by Regulation No. 990/93, which was to bring to an end the state of war

---

[41] C–415/93 *Union Royale Belge des Sociétés de Football Association and Others* v. *Bosman and Others* [1995] ECR I–4921, para. 79; Case 175/73 *Union Syndicale Massa and Kortner* v. *Council* [1974] ECR 917.

[42] *Rutili*, para. 21; Case 222/84 *Johnston* v. *Chief Constable of the Royal Ulster Constabulary* [1986] ECR 1651.

[43] See below p. 221.

[44] Case 63/83 *Regina* v. *Kirk* [1984] ECR 2689, paras. 21–2; Case C–331/88 *Fedesa* [1990] ECR I–4023, paras. 41–2. See also Case 85/76 *Hoffmann-La Roche* v. *Commission* [1979] ECR 461, at 510 and 553 *et seq.*

[45] Joined Cases 46/87 and 227/88 *Hoechst* v. *Commission* [1989] ECR 2859, para. 19.

[46] Case C–326/88 *Hansen* [1990] ECR I–2911; see esp. 2925 *et seq.* per Van Gerven AG.

[47] Case C–177/95 [1997] ECR I–1111. See also Case C–124/95 *The Queen, ex parte Centro-Com* v. *HM Treasury and Bank of England* [1987] ECR I–81.

[48] Regulation No. 990/93 concerning trade between the Community and the Federal Republic of Yugoslavia, OJ 1993 L 102/14.

in the region concerned and the massive violation of human rights, was one of fundamental general interest for the international Community.

An interesting example of the application of the right to medical confidentiality is provided by X v. *Commission*.[49] There, it was held that the right to medical confidentiality prohibits the Commission from subjecting a candidate for employment to a pre-recruitment medical test without his consent. The Court held that, if the person concerned, after being properly informed, withholds his consent to a test which the medical officer considers necessary in order to evaluate his suitability for recruitment, the institutions cannot be obliged to take the risk of recruiting him. The Court, however, understood the right to medical confidentiality more broadly than the CFI. The latter held that the Commission was under an obligation to respect the candidate's refusal to undergo an Aids test but could carry out without his consent other tests which might point to the presence of the Aids virus. Reversing the judgment of the CFI, the Court of Justice held that, 'the right to respect for private life requires that a person's refusal be respected in its entirety'. Since the appellant had expressly refused to undergo an Aids screening test, the administration was precluded from carrying out any test liable to point to, or establish, the existence of that illness, in respect of which he had refused disclosure.[50]

It is interesting that linguistic protection has not received recognition as a fundamental right in Community law. In *PIAGEME II*, for example, the Court appeared reluctant to give priority to the protection of regional languages over the free movement of goods.[51] The issue acquires particular importance in the domain of procedure. The first Council Regulation issued under the EEC Treaty provided for the citizen's right to send correspondence to the institutions in any of the official languages of the Community and to receive answers in that language.[52] The case law, however, has not gone further than upholding the guarantees provided by Community written law,[53] and there does not seem to be a general principle guaranteeing the conduct of administrative proceedings before Community bodies in the citizen's native language.[54]

---

[49] Op.cit.   [50] Op.cit., para. 23.

[51] Case C–85/94 *PIAGEME and Others* v. *Peeters* [1995] ECR I–2955.

[52] Council Regulation No. 1 of 15 Apr. 1958 determining the languages used by the European Economic Community, OJ English Spec.Ed., 1952–8, p. 59.

[53] See K. Lenaerts, 'General Report, Procedures and Sanctions in Economic Administrative Law', 17 *FIDE Congress*, at p. 530.

[54] See Article 115 of Regulation No. 40/94 on the Community Trademark, OJ 1994 L 11, p. 1. The Regulation permits persons to send applications for a Community trademark to the Office in any of the official Community languages but subsequent communications will normally be conducted in one of the five languages of the Office. See also Case T–77/92 *Parker Pen* v. *Commission* [1994] ECR II–549, where, in the context of competition proceedings, the Court dismissed the argument that statements made by German-speaking parties should have been translated in English. Lenaerts, op.cit., suggests that the case might have had a different outcome if protection of native language was recognized as a general principle. See also, in a different context, Case C–274/96 *Criminal Proceedings against Bickel and Franz*, judgment of 24 Nov 1998.

The recognition of a right as fundamental by the Court marks only the beginning of the inquiry. It does not tell us much about the level of protection afforded to that right nor of its legal value vis-à-vis other competing interests or rights which can be determined only by studying outcomes. Two general points may be made in this context. First, the classification of a right as fundamental indicates that the Community legal order grants to that right at least a minimum of weight and consequently increases the burden on public authorities to justify restrictions upon it.[55] The individual has, to use Dworkian terminology, 'a trump card' against public authorities given to him by Community law. Secondly, the case law evinces a marked difference between social rights, on the one hand, and economic rights, on the other. With regard to the former, the Court is prepared to take a proactive approach and pioneer solutions often stretching beyond written law. Thus, since the 1970s the Court has led the way in establishing the principle of sex equality and working out the specific consequences which flow from it, forcing effectively the national judiciaries to follow.[56] More recently, the Court took a step further holding that Community law prohibits discrimination on grounds of gender reassignment.[57] By contrast, the recognition of economic rights as rights protected by Community law, for example the right to property or the freedom to trade, seems to serve a prophylactic function. The Court recognizes in the abstract a core element of such rights upon which the Community authorities are not permitted to encroach but beyond that the freedom of the individual may be required to give way to the public interest. To put it in a different way, in the field of social law and sex equality, the case law establishes positive rights. In the field of economic rights, the case law prescribes limitations on public action. The balancing exercise performed by the Court in the field of economic rights will be illustrated below by reference to the right of property and the freedom to trade.

The Community's priorities have been questioned. In particular, the issue has been raised why Community law elevates certain rights to a fundamental status but refuses such status to others.[58] In the latter category belong, for example, immigration and asylum rights, rights for people with disabilities, environmental, language and cultural rights. This question refers mainly to the political institutions whose use of the language of rights in certain areas, in particular the social sphere, contrasts with the absence of such terminology in other areas. As far as the Community judicature is concerned, suffice it to say that there are no a priori excluded areas. The fact that certain rights but not others have been recognized as fundamental is

---

[55] The additional burden to justify restrictions applies also to the Community judicature itself. In Case C–76/93 P *Scaramuzza* v. *Commission* [1994] ECR I–5173, para. 30, the Court held that the CFI should have provided full reasoning in rejecting an unmeritorious plea based on the alleged breach of human rights.

[56] See e.g. *Defrenne* v. *Sabena*, op.cit.; Case C–262/88 *Barber* v. *Guardian Royal Exchange Assurance Group* [1990] ECR I–1889; Case C–32/93 *Webb* v. *Emo (Air Cargo) Ltd.* [1994] ECR I–3567.

[57] *P* v. *S and Cornwall County Council*, op.cit.

[58] See the thoughtful critique of G. De Bùrca, 'The Language of Rights in European Integration', in J. Shaw and G. More (eds.), *New Legal Dynamics of European Union*, p. 29, at p. 39.

explained by the historical origins and nature of the judicial protection of human rights in the Community legal order.

6.2.5. Searching for the appropriate standard of protection

A vexed issue is whether the Court should be bound to accept as fundamental any right which is safeguarded by the constitution of any one of the Member States. An affirmative answer was given by Warner AG in *IRCA*[59] and the same view has been supported also by Professor Schermers.[60] The reasoning goes as follows. Community law owes its existence to a partial transfer of sovereignty by the Member States. No Member State can be said to have included in that transfer power for the Community to legislate in infringement of rights protected by its own constitution. If that were so, ratification of the Treaty by a Member State would entail capacity to flout its own constitution which is not possible.[61] The problem with this reasoning is that what matters is not so much recognition of a right as fundamental but the consequences which flow from it, in particular, the weight attributed to it where it conflicts with another fundamental right. It is correct to say that, where a Member State considers a particular right so important as to incorporate it in its constitution, that right forms part of a European legal heritage.[62] The case remains that a right does not exist in a vacuum but incorporates the outcome of a balancing exercise between conflicting rights and interests within a certain polity. That balancing exercise is influenced by a number of factors which may be legal, economic, social, political or cultural in nature. The outcome reflects ultimately the values espoused by a society and may vary from State to State or even within the same State at different times. As far as the Community polity is concerned, it is for the Community judicature to draw that balance. No. doubt, as Warner AG remarked, in ratifying the Treaties the Member States did not give a *carte blanche* to the Community nor did they agree to forgo protection of their constitutionally entrenched rights. But membership is not a bilateral relationship. It is a multilateral one and no Member State has a right to expect that in a given conflict the Community, and through it the other Member States, will endorse *simpliciter* its own balance and the fundamental societal values which go with it. This in turn poses the issue what standards of protection must the Court of Justice adopt in reviewing the compatibility of measures with Community law. Should it adopt a maximalist approach searching for the highest standard provided in the national laws or a minimalist approach searching instead for the lowest common denominator? The answer is neither. The Court should aim for the most suitable

---

[59] Case 7/76 *IRCA* v. *Amministrazione delle Finanze dello Stato* [1966] ECR 1213, at 1237.

[60] H. Schermers, 'The European Community Bound by Fundamental Human Rights' (1990) 27 CMLRev. 249, at 252 *et seq.*

[61] *IRCA*, op.cit., 1237.   [62] Schermers, op.cit., 254

solution to the Community polity and, as *Hauer* made clear, that is precisely its approach:[63]

the question of a possible infringement of fundamental rights by a measure of the Community institutions can only be judged in the light of Community law itself. The introduction of special criteria for assessment stemming from the legislation or constitutional law of a particular Member State would, by damaging the substantive unity and efficacy of Community law, lead inevitably to the destruction of the unity of the Common Market and the jeopardizing of the cohesion of the Community.

The fallacy of the minimalist–maximalist dichotomy has aptly been exposed by Weiler.[64] To think in terms of low and high standards is to think in two dimensions. What is a maximum protection of one right can be seen as a minimum protection of another. As Weiler points out, to say that Member State A provides for the highest protection of the right to property means that that Member State imposes the largest restriction on the public authorities to act in the general interest and consequently provides for the lowest level of protection for the public at large.[65] Human rights are not empty, abstract ideas but express core societal choices as to the balance between the interests of the individual and interests of the society at large.[66] The maximalist approach would have two consequences. It would favour the Member State which happens to accord the highest protection to a certain right and transpose its values to Community law even if they are unrepresentative of the values of other Member States. Also, the aggregate of maximum protection of individual rights would result in maximum restrictions being imposed on the Community. As Weiler puts it, a maximalist approach to human rights would result in a minimalist approach to Community government[67] even though that might render unworkable a Community policy.

The issue remains whether it is possible for the Court to afford a lesser level protection to a fundamental right than that afforded by any Member State. In other words, could it be said that the national constitutions provide at least a minimum of protection below which the Court may not go? As we have seen the Court does not accept that view and the above discussion would suggest that the Court's approach is the correct one. In practice it is difficult to envisage circumstances where the Court would uphold a Community measure which would have been struck down by the national courts of all Member States as being contrary to fundamental rights. The reverse question may also be asked: is it possible for the Court to recognize a right which is not recognized by any of the Member States? An affirmative answer cannot be precluded. In *P* v. *S* the Court made no reference to the laws of the Member States, although it referred to the European Convention.

---

[63] *Hauer*, op.cit., para. 14.

[64] Weiler, 'Fundamental Rights and Fundamental Boundaries: On Standards and Values in the Protection of Human Rights', in N. Neuwahl and A. Rosas (eds.), *The European Union and Human Rights*, pp. 51–76.

[65] Op.cit., p. 60.   [66] Op.cit., pp. 54–6.   [67] Op.cit., p. 61.

[68] [1996] ECR I–2149 *et seq.*

Tesauro AG made extensive references to the position of transsexuals in the laws of Member States although the findings seemed inconclusive.[68] It seems that in order for a right to be recognized by the Court without the assistance of express Community legislation, it must be based either on 'a solid consensus of generally shared values'[69] in the Member States or belong in a broader area where the Community legislature has been active.[70]

The following two sections examine the case law relating to two specific areas. The first is the right to property and the freedom to trade. These are the most oft-invoked fundamental rights in actions for judicial review of Community measures. The second is the right of access to official documents held by the Community authorities. This can be viewed as part of a new generation of participatory rights inspired by democratic values and, although the Community judicature has stopped short of recognizing it as a fundamental right, in recent years it has given rise to interesting case law.

6.2.6. The right to property and the freedom to trade

The Court has held that the right to property[71] and the right to trade or choose freely a professional activity are not absolute but must be viewed in the light of their social function.[72] They may be restricted, particularly in the context of a common organization of the market, provided that two conditions are fulfilled: the restrictions imposed must correspond to objectives of general interest pursued by the Community; and they must not 'constitute a disproportionate and intolerable interference, impairing the very substance of the right'.[73] Although the language used by the Court seems to suggest that these are distinct requirements each of which must be satisfied separately, they are in fact different aspects of the same inquiry.

We saw above how in *Nold* and in particular in *Hauer* the Court scrutinized the contested regulations with a view to determining whether they infringed Community law. A more recent example is provided by *Germany* v. *Council* (*Bananas* case).[74] It will be remembered that Council Regulation No. 404/93,

---

[69] The expression is used by Jachtenfuchs, 'Theoretical Perspectives on European Governance' (1995) 1 ELJ 115 at 126.

[70] In this category belong, for example, the rights of transsexuals, see *P* v. *S*, op.cit.

[71] The Treaty is neutral as regards the system of ownership and property rights recognized by Member States: see Article 295[222]. On the right to property, see further F. Campbell-White, 'Property rights: A Forgotten Issue under the Union', in Neuwahl and Rosas, op.cit., pp. 249–63.

[72] *Nold*, op.cit.; *Hauer*, op.cit.; Case 240/83 *Procureur de la République* v. *ADBHU* [1985] ECR 531, para. 12. This is the general formula used by the Court in relation to all fundamental rights. See e.g. in relation to the freedom of expression: *Ter Voort*, op.cit., para. 38; and the right to private life: *X* v. *Commission* op.cit.

[73] Case C–280/93 *Germany* v. *Council* [1994] ECR I–4973, para. 78; Case 265/87 *Schräder* v. *Hauptzollamt Gronau* [1989] ECR 2237, para. 15, Case 5/88 *Wachauf* [1989] ECR 2609, para. 18; Case C–177/90 *Kühn* v. *Landwirtschaftskammer Weser-Ems* [1992] ECR I–35.

[74] Case C–280/93 op.cit.; for other aspects of the case see above, pp. 55 and 101.

setting up a common organization of the market in bananas, limited the volume of imports from third countries by introducing a tariff quota and subdividing it among various categories of traders. The Regulation affected severely the competitive position of German importers who, before its coming into force, were able to import third-country bananas free of tariff restrictions within a quota which was adjusted annually to take into account the needs of the market. The German Government objected to the introduction of the tariff quota, its subdivision among various categories of traders, and the principle of free transferability of import licences. It alleged that the loss of market share suffered by traders in third-country bananas was an infringement of their freedom to pursue their trade. The Court stated that the restriction of the right to import third-country bananas imposed on German traders was inherent in the establishment of the common organization of the market, which was designed to promote the realization of the objectives of the common agricultural policy and to ensure that the international obligations of the Community were complied with. Restrictions on the volume of imports from third countries were necessary in order to ensure that, after the introduction of the common organization of the market, Community and ACP bananas were not displaced from the common market following the disappearance of the protective barriers enabling them to be disposed of with protection from competition from third-country bananas. In response to the argument that the principle of free transferability of import licences had adverse consequences for German importers of third-country bananas,[75] the Court held that the transfer of import licences was an option which the Regulation allowed the various categories of economic operators to exercise according to their commercial interests. The financial advantage which such a transfer might in some cases give traders in Community and ACP bananas was a necessary consequence of the principle of transferability of licences and should be assessed in the more general framework of all the measures adopted by the Council to ensure the disposal of Community and traditional ACP products. In that context, it ought to be regarded as a means intended to contribute to the competitiveness of operators marketing Community and ACP bananas and to facilitate the integration of the Member States' markets.[76] The Court concluded that the restriction imposed by the Regulation on the freedom of traditional traders in third-country bananas to pursue their trade or business corresponded to objectives of general Community interest and did not impair the very substance of that freedom.

The case illustrates that the economic interests of a certain category of traders may be affected severely as a result of introducing a common organization of the market, without that constituting a breach of the right to exercise a trade or

---

[75] The argument of the German Government reflected economic reality in that the principle of free transferability of import licences resulted in transferring profit potential from traditional dealers in third country bananas to traditional dealers in Community and ACP bananas. See further the Opinion of Gulmann AG, op.cit., at 5004.

[76] Op.cit., paras. 81–6.

profession.[77] In the circumstances of the case the Court took the view that, although German importers suffered significant loss, that was within the normal economic risks which commercial operators could be expected to undertake. In that respect, the case is to be distinguished from the milk quota cases[78] where the producers concerned suffered specifically as a result of relying on Community legislation and were exposed to adverse financial consequences exceeding normal commercial risks. A factor which may have operated against the annulment of the Regulation in the *Bananas* case was that, before the introduction of the common organization of the market, German traders enjoyed an exceptional benefit in that imports from third countries were exempt from customs duties pursuant to the Banana Protocol.[79] The loss of market share suffered by them was perceived as the termination of an exceptional benefit rather than as the denial of a vested right. Crucially, although the judgment dealt extensively with the requirement that the restriction imposed on the right to trade must correspond to objectives of general Community interest, it did not address specifically the requirement that the very substance of the right must not be impaired. This indicates that, as already stated, the two requirements are in fact two sides of the same test.

Notably, in no case so far has the Court found a violation of the right to property or the freedom to trade. Where Community legislation seriously threatens such rights the Court prefers to address the claim on different grounds such as breach of the principle of equality, as for example in *Codorniu*,[80] or of the protection of legitimate expectations, as in the milk quota cases.[81] Leaving to one side cases of expropriation of property rights or the complete prohibition, without good reason, of the carrying on of a professional activity, it is not easy to imagine a violation of the former set of rights which does not also constitute a violation of one or another of the latter principles.[82]

---

[77] Note, however, that in a subsequent case which arose from the application of the Bananas Regulation, the Court held that the Community institutions have a duty to adopt transitional measures in order to alleviate difficulties encountered by traders in the transition from national arrangements to the common organization of the market, 'in particular when the transition to the common organization of the market infringes certain traders' fundamental rights protected by Community law, such as the right to property and the right to pursue a professional or trade activity': Case C–68/95 *T. Port v. Bundesanstalt für Landwirtschaft und Ernährung* [1996] ECR I–6065, para. 40.

[78] See above p. 187.

[79] See Protocol annexed to the Implementing Convention on the Association of the Overseas Countries and Territories with the Community, provided for in Article 136 EC.

[80] Case C–309/89 *Codorniu v. Council* [1994] ECR I–1853.

[81] See Case 120/86 *Mulder I* [1988] ECR 2321, Case C–189/89 *Spagl* [1990] ECR I–4539. In the latter case, Jacobs AG took the view that the 60% rule applicable to the calculation of the reference quantities of returning producers did not violate the right to property.

[82] For the combined examination of pleas based on breach of the principle of proportionality and the right to property see Joined Cases C–153 and C–205/94 *Faroe Seafood and Others* [1996] ECR I–2465 at 2549. In that case, the Court held that the post-clearance recovery of import duties in circumstances where the conditions of Article 5(2) of Regulation No. 1697/79 were not fulfilled did not breach the right to property and the principle of proportionality because it fell within the sphere of normal commercial risks of the traders concerned.

The affinity between the right to property and the principle of protection of legitimate expectations is illustrated in many other cases. In *SMW Winzersekt*,[83] a Council regulation restricted, subject to a transitional period, the use of the designation 'methode champenoise' to sparkling wines which were entitled to the registered designation 'Champagne'. Before the adoption of the regulation, the designation 'methode champenoise' could be used by all producers of sparkling wines. German wine growers challenged the regulation on the ground that it infringed the right to property and the freedom to pursue a trade or profession. The Court held that since, prior to the adoption of the regulation, all producers of sparkling wines were entitled to use the term 'methode champenoise', the prohibition of the use of that designation could not be regarded as an infringement of a property right 'vested in the applicants'. With regard to the freedom to pursue a trade or profession, the Court held that the regulation pursued an objective of general interest, namely, the protection of registered indications of the geographical origin of wines. In accordance with that objective, in the exercise of its discretionary powers, the Council considered that a wine producer should not be able to use, in descriptions relating to the method of production of his products, geographical indications which do not correspond to the actual provenance of the wine. The regulation took sufficient account of the interests of producers who, prior to the adoption of the regulation used the term 'methode champenoise', by adopting transitional provisions and by allowing them to use alternative expressions.

The freedom to pursue an economic activity confers the assurance that a trader may not be arbitrarily deprived of the right to pursue his professional activities but it does not guarantee him a particular volume of business or a specific share of the market.[84] A distinction may be drawn between access to a trade or profession and restrictions on its exercise. Restrictions on access may be more difficult to justify than restrictions on its exercise. Thus in *Hauer* the Court held that the contested regulation did not affect access to the occupation of wine growing or the freedom to pursue that occupation on land at present devoted to wine growing.[85] With regard to the prohibition on planting of new vines, the Court held that that was no more than a consequence of the restriction upon the exercise of the right of property which the Court had found to be compatible with Community law.

With regard to the right to property, there are dicta to the effect that the substance of the right may be impaired where the measure deprives a person of his property or of the freedom to use it,[86] but the Court has not given more specific guidelines. It is evident from the case law that a right may be deprived of much if its economic value without that amounting to a breach of the right to property. It seems that the purpose of that right is to prohibit expropriation. It has been sug-

---

[83] Case C–306/93 *SMW Winzersekt* [1994] ECR I–5555.
[84] See e.g. Case T–521/93 *Atlanta and Others* v. *European Community* [1996] ECR II–1707, para. 62.
[85] *Hauer*, op.cit., para. 32.
[86] See Case 59/83 *Biovilac* v. *EEC* [1984] ECR 4057, para. 22.

gested that the hallmarks of an expropriation measure are two, namely, the measure must result in the deprivation of all appreciable economic value in the (tangible or intangible) asset in issue and the deprivation must be permanent.[87] By contrast, a trader cannot claim a right to property in a market share which he held at a time before the establishment of a common organization of the market, since such a market share constitutes 'only a momentary economic position exposed to the risks of changing circumstances'.[88] In *Irish Farmers Association*,[89] it was held that the conversion of the temporary suspension of a percentage of the quota allocated to milk producers to permanent withdrawal without compensation did not affect the substance of the right to property inasmuch as the applicants were able to continue to pursue their trade as milk producers. Moreover, the Court noted, the reduction in milk production led to an increase in the price of milk, thus compensating partly the loss suffered.

Among the measures which have been found by the Court not to violate the right to property or the freedom to trade are the imposition of a co-responsibility levy on cereals with a view to stabilizing the market,[90] and the imposition on vessel owners of the obligation to finance a scrapping scheme with a view to reducing the structural overcapacity in the Community's inland waterway networks.[91] More generally, it has been held that restrictions on production owing to the economic situation cannot be regarded as being an infringement of the right to property on the ground that they may harm the profitability of an undertaking.[92] The Court has also held that the right to property does not include the right to dispose for profit of an advantage, such as a milk quota allocated in the context of the common organization of the market, which does not derive from the assets or occupational activity of the person concerned.[93] In *Wachauf*, by contrast, the Court declared that Community rules which had the effect of depriving a tenant farmer of the fruits of his labour would be incompatible with fundamental rights but did

[87] *Hauer*, op.cit., per Capotorti AG at 3759–62; Case 5/88 *Wachauf* [1989] ECR 2609 at 2629–30, per Jacobs AG.

[88] *Germany* v. *Council*, op.cit., para. 79.

[89] Case C–22/94 *Irish Farmers Association and Others* v. *Minister for Agriculture, Food and Forestry, Ireland, and the Attorney General* [1997] ECR I–1809, para. 29.

[90] Case 265/87 *Schräder* v. *Hauptzollamt Gronau* [1989] ECR 2237.

[91] Joined Cases C–248 and C–249/95 *SAM Schiffahrt GmbH and Heinz Stapf* v. *Germany* [1997] ECR I–4475.

[92] See e.g. Case 258/81 *Metallurgiki Halyps* v. *Commission* [1982] ECR 4261, para. 13; Joined Cases 172/83 and 226/83 *Hoogovens Groep* [1985] ECR 283, para. 29.

[93] This dictum, first made in Case C–44/89 *Von Deetzen II* [1991] ECR I–5119, para. 27, was confirmed in Case C–2/92 *Bostock* [1994] ECR I–955, para. 19. It will be noted, however, that the context of the two cases was different. In *Von Deetzen* the applicant sought to derive an advantage by transferring for profit the special quota allocated to him as a returning producer. The Court rightly held that the purpose of allocating special quotas to returning producers was in order to enable them to resume their occupational activity following their temporary exit from the market and not to realize their economic value. In *Bostock*, on the other hand, the applicant was not a returning producer but sought compensation upon surrendering his lease for increasing the production capacity of the holding during his tenancy. The claim in *Bostock* was more meritorious although it is not suggested here that the right to property was violated in that case.

not specify which rights would be infringed as a result. The context of the case suggests that the Court was referring to the right to property.[94]

An interesting case arose from the sanctions imposed by the Community on Yugoslavia. In *Bosphorus Hava Yollari Turizm ve Ticaret AS* v. *Minister for Transport and the Attorney General*,[95] in issue was Article 8 of Regulation No. 990/93[96] which required Member States to impound all vessels, freight vehicles and aircraft 'in which a majority or controlling interest is held by a person or undertaking in or operating from the Federal Republic of Yugoslavia'. Pursuant to that provision, the Irish authorities impounded an aircraft which Bosphorus Airways, a Turkish company, had leased from the Yugoslav national airline. The Court interpreted Article 8 as applying to an aircraft based in or operating from the Federal Republic of Yugoslavia even though the owner had leased it to another undertaking, which was neither based nor operating from there, and which was not controlled by Yugoslav interests. The Court dismissed the argument of the Turkish company that such a broad interpretation of Article 8 infringed its fundamental right to property and its freedom to pursue a commercial activity. It held that any measure imposing sanctions has, by definition, consequences which affect the right to property and commercial freedom, thereby causing loss to innocent third parties. The importance of the aims pursued by the regulation was such as to justify negative consequences, even of a substantial nature. This is clearly an exceptional case where private rights had to give way to overriding objectives pertaining to public security.

Although in practice it is difficult to establish a violation of the right to property, it may be noted that the case law has adopted a functional rather than formalistic approach of the notion of 'assets' upon which property rights may be recognized. The milk quota cases imply that the right to property encompasses in principle instruments of market control, such as milk quotas, which have a market value and can be disposed of for profit.[97]

The freedom to pursue a trade or profession seems to entail a higher level of judicial scrutiny in German law, from where it originates.[98] In one case, the Bundesverfassungsgericht held, applying the principle, that the administrative courts have jurisdiction to review whether the answers given by a candidate in the State examinations to obtain a legal qualification were incorrect and therefore whether the candidate could be refused admission to the legal profession on their basis.[99] This difference in the standard of scrutiny, however, should not be attributed to the intrinsic qualities of the freedom to pursue a trade or profession but rather to a more deeply rooted division between German and Community admin-

---

[94] See the Opinion of Jacobs AG, at 2630.   [95] Case C–84/95 [1996] ECR I–3953.
[96] Op.cit.

[97] This is borne out, for example, by the judgments in *Wachauf* and *Von Deetzen II*. For an express recognition, see Jacobs AG in *Wachauf*, op.cit., at 2630.

[98] See Article 12 of the Grundgesetz.

[99] (1991) 84 BverfGE 34. The case is referred to by G. Nolte, 'General Principles of German and European Administrative Law—a Comparison in Historical Perspective' (1994) 57 MLR 191, at 196.

istrative law. The former, unlike the latter, traditionally recognizes administrative discretion, in principle, only where it is expressly granted. Unless the law employs language which signifies that the administration has a margin of discretion, it is accepted, as a general rule, that there is only one correct way of resolving the issue. This, in turn, enables the courts to exercise a higher degree of scrutiny.[100]

6.2.7. Access to official documents[101]

The citizen's right of access to documents held by public authorities is not traditionally recognized as part of the core rights guaranteed by liberal constitutions. In Community law, it is not the product of case law but of Community legislation. Although it cannot be classified as fundamental in the sense of the rights discussed above, its constitutional status is gaining recognition. Its practical importance is reflected by the fact that, although it was only recently recognized, it has already given rise to some case law.

The right of access came to the fore in the early 1990s when, in line with developments in some Member States,[102] the Governments and the Commission took steps to promote transparency in the decision making of the Community institutions. Declaration 17 annexed to the Final Act of the Treaty on European Union pointed out that transparency in the decision-making process strengthens the democratic nature of the institutions and the public's confidence in the administration, and called upon the institutions to adopt the necessary measures to improve public access to information. After some preparatory work by the Commission,[103] in December 1993, the Council and the Commission adopted a Code of Conduct concerning public access to documents in their possession.[104] The Code was implemented by Decision 93/731 on public access to Council documents,[105] and Decision 94/90 on public access to Commission documents.[106] Those measures were designed to cultivate an ethos of transparency as, before their adoption,

---

[100] Nolte, op.cit. 196.

[101] See D. Curtin and H. Meijers, 'Access to European Union Information: An Element of Citizenship and a Neglected Constitutional Right', in N. Neuwahl and A. Rosas (eds.), *The European Union and Human Rights* (1995), pp. 77–104; D. Curtin and H. Meijers, 'The Principle of Open Government in Schengen and the European Union: Democratic Retrogression?' (1995) 32 CMLRev. 391. F. Lafay, 'l'accès aux documents du Conseil de l'Union: contribution à une problématique de la transparence en droit communautaire' (1997) 33 RTDE 37.

[102] See esp. the White Paper, *Open Government* (Cm. 2290, 1993), of the United Kingdom. The White Paper led to the publication of a Code of Practice on Access to Government Information which took effect on 4 Apr. 1994. For a brief discussion and further bibliography, see S. H. Bailey, D. J. Harris and B. L. Jones, *Civil Liberties, Cases and Materials* (4th edn., 1995), pp. 512–15. Among other countries, Denmark, Sweden and Norway recognize a statutory public right of access to information held by public authorities.

[103] See esp. EC Commission, 'Public Access to Information', COM(93)191, OJ 1993 C 156/5, and Communication 93/C 166/04 of 2 June 1993 'Openness in the Community', OJ 1993 C 166/4.

[104] 93/730/EC, OJ 1993 L 340/41.

[105] Decision 93/731/EC of 20 Dec. 1993, OJ 1993 L 340/43.

[106] Decision 94/90/ECSC, EC of 8 Feb. 1994, OJ 1994 L 46/58.

the internal workings of the institutions were based on the principle of confidentiality.

The way the Council gave effect to the principles set out in the Code of Conduct was challenged in *Netherlands* v. *Council*.[107] The Netherlands Government, supported by the European Parliament, contended that the Council wrongly used as the legal basis of Decision 93/731 Article 151(3) EC and its Rules of Procedure. Essentially, the argument was that those provisions are concerned solely with matters of internal organization and the Council was wrong to categorize as such matters the public's right of access to information which is a fundamental right. The Court dismissed the challenge against the Code of Conduct as inadmissible on the ground that the Code was not intended to produce legal effects in itself but merely to set general guidelines for future specific measures. The rest of the action was dismissed as unfounded. The Court pointed out that the public's right of access to documents held by public authorities has received 'progressive affirmation' in the laws of the Member States and at Community level,[108] and that the domestic legislation of most Member States now enshrines it in a general manner as a constitutional or legislative principle.[109] It held that, so long as the Community legislature has not adopted general rules on that right, it falls to the institutions themselves to take measures to enable them to respond to requests for access to documents held by them by virtue of their powers of internal organization. The Court also dismissed the argument that the legal basis used by the Council infringed the principle of institutional balance. Since the Council could adopt the measure under its powers of internal organization, such adoption did not detract from the prerogatives of the Parliament.[109a]

It is evident that access to documents cannot be an unlimited right. Restrictions must be imposed on it in order to ensure the protection of overriding public or private interests served by confidentiality. In recognition of this, Article 4 of Council Decision 93/731 lists the grounds on which access to a public document may not be granted. Article 4(1) provides that the Council shall refuse access to a document where disclosure would undermine the following interests:

(a) the protection of the public interest (public security, international relations, monetary stability, court proceedings, inspections and investigations);
(b) the protection of the individual and of privacy;
(c) the protection of commercial and industrial secrecy;
(d) the protection of the Community's financial interests;
(e) and the protection of confidentiality as requested by the person who supplied any of the information contained in the document or as required by the law of the Member State which supplied any of that information.

---

[107] Case C–58/94 [1996] ECR I–2169.

[108] *Netherlands* v. *Council*, op.cit., para. 36.

[109] However, both the Court and, especially, the Advocate General pointed out the affinity between the right to access and democracy. See para. 35 of the judgment and 2182 per Tesauro AG.

[109a] See now Articles 207(3) EC and 255(2) and (3) as amended by the Treaty of Amsterdam.

In addition, Article 4(2) enables the Council to refuse access to a document in order to protect the confidentiality of its proceedings.

An equivalent provision is contained in Article 4 of Commission Decision 94/90. Both provisions emanate from the Code of Conduct itself.

In *Carvel and Guardian Newspapers* v. *Council*,[110] the CFI held that it was unlawful for the Council to refuse disclosure of certain documents pursuant to Article 4(2). The applicants had unsuccessfully requested access to the preparatory reports, minutes, attendance and voting records of certain Council meetings pertaining to justice and home affairs and agriculture. The CFI drew a distinction between Article 4(1) and Article 4(2). The first provision contains mandatory exceptions. It requires the Council to refuse disclosure once the conditions prescribed therein are shown to be fulfilled. Under Article 4(2), the Council has discretion whether or not to refuse a request for access. The CFI held that, in exercising its discretion, the Council must genuinely balance the interests of citizens in gaining access to its documents against any interest of its own in maintaining the confidentiality of its deliberations.[111] It must make a 'specific assessment of the interests involved'.[112] In the circumstances, the Council had not done so. It refused access automatically without engaging in a balancing exercise, considering that it was obliged to refuse access merely because the documents referred to its deliberations.

In *World Wide Fund for Nature* v. *Commission*,[113] the CFI explained the distinction between the categories of exception contained in Articles 4(1) and 4(2) as follows. The first category protects the interests of third parties or of the general public in cases where disclosure of documents by the institution concerned would risk causing harm to persons who could legitimately refuse access to those documents if held in their own possession. By contrast, the second category comprises documents in relation to which the interest of the institution alone is at stake.[114] An institution may invoke jointly both categories of exception, since it is possible that disclosure of certain documents may cause damage both to the interests protected by Article 4(1) and the interest protected by Article 4(2).[115] It is not sufficient, however, for the institution simply to invoke in general both categories of exception jointly. It must indicate which exception or exceptions apply in relation to each of the documents or class of documents requested.

In *World Wide Fund for Nature* v. *Commission*, the CFI annulled the decision of the Commission refusing access to documents relating to an investigation into a possible breach of environmental law by Ireland. The CFI pointed out that the exceptions to the right of public access must be interpreted strictly. It accepted that the Commission may refuse access to documents relating to an investigation into a possible breach of Community law by a Member State on grounds of public interest as provided in Article 4(1). In the case of investigations which may lead to the initiation of an enforcement action, a Member State is entitled to expect

[110] Case T–194/94 [1995] ECR II–2765.
[111] Op.cit., para. 65.
[112] Op.cit., para. 75.
[113] Case T–105/95 [1997] ECR II–313.
[114] Op.cit., para. 60.
[115] Op.cit., para. 61.

confidentiality which bars disclosure 'even where a period of time has elapsed since the closure of the investigation'.[116] The CFI gave more specific guidelines. It stated that the Commission may not merely invoke the possible opening of an infringement procedure as justification for refusing access to all documents. It is required to indicate, at the very least by reference to categories of documents, the reasons for which it considers that the documents detailed in the request are related to a possible opening of an infringement procedure. It should indicate to which subject matter the documents relate and particularly whether they involve inspections or investigations relating to a possible procedure for infringement of Community law. It is not necessary, however, for the Commission to furnish, in respect of each document, imperative reasons to justify non-disclosure. The CFI pointed out that it would be impossible to give reasons justifying the need for confidentiality in respect of each individual document without disclosing the content of the document, thereby depriving the exception of its very purpose.[117]

In *Interporc Im- und Export GmbH* v. *Commission*[118] the CFI reiterated that in the cases specified in Article 4(1), where the relevant conditions are fulfilled, the Commission has no discretion and is bound to refuse disclosure. Refusal is not automatic, however, in that, before the Commission refuses access, it is under an obligation to consider, for each document requested, whether it is in fact likely to undermine one of the interests protected under Article 4(1) and to provide specific reasons justifying refusal.[118a]

Some provisional conclusions may be drawn from the above discussion. The Community judicature seems prepared to give teeth to the right of access to documents held by the Community institutions. Also, given that in most of the cases decided so far the decision of the institution concerned to refuse access was annulled, it seems that the Council and the Commission have not assimilated the obligations imposed by the newly established right. Clearly, as a participatory right, public access strengthens the position of pressure groups. It is notable that in *World Wide Fund for Nature* v. *Commission* the applicant sought to stop the allocation of structural funds to Ireland on the ground that the project in issue infringed environmental law. The citizen's right of access also brings into surface underlying tensions between Member States. In *Carvel and Guardian Newspapers* the success of the action was assisted by the submissions of certain Member States which in Council voted in the minority against refusing to the applicants access to the documents requested. The CFI attributed particular importance to their evidence that, in taking the decision to refuse access, the Council made no comparative evaluation of

---

[116] Op.cit., para. 63.   [117] Op.cit., paras. 64–5.

[118] Case T–124/96, [1998] ECR II–231.

[118a] In Case T-83/96 *Van der Wal* v. *Commission*, judgment of 19 March 1998, the CFI held that the Commission may refuse access to documents in order to protect the confidentiality of court proceedings under Article 4(1) even where the documents in question relate to proceedings in which the Commission itself is not a party. By contrast in Case T-174/95 *Svenska Journalistförbundet* v. *Council*, judgment of 17 June 1998, a Council decision refusing access to certain documents pertaining to Europol was annulled on the ground that the Council had not provided adequate reasons for its refusal.

the interests of the citizens seeking information, on the one hand, and the interests of the Council in preserving the secrecy of its deliberations, on the other. This suggests that the right of public access may be pursued more effectively against a supranational body, such as the Council, the constituent members of which represent a multiplicity of interests, rather than the national administration.

Now Article 255(1) EC, added by the Treaty of Amsterdam, elevates the right of access to a constitutional right. It provides as a general principle that any citizen of the Union, and any natural or legal person residing or having its registered office in a member State, has a right of access to Council, Commission and Parliament documents. Under Article 255(2), that right is made subject to limits on grounds of public or private interest to be determined by the Council acting in accordance with the co-decision procedure within two years of the entry into force of the Treaty of Amsterdam. In accordance with institutional practice, whose legality was upheld by the judgment in *Netherlands* v. *Council*, Article 255(3) mandates each institution to elaborate specific provisions concerning access to its documents in its rules of procedure.

6. 3. Review of national measures

The issue which types of national measures are subject to review on grounds of compatibility with the general principles of law was discussed in Chapter 1.[119] This section focuses in particular on the application of fundamental rights. It will be remembered that, according to the case law, the following types of national measures are subject to review on grounds of compatibility with fundamental rights: measures implementing Community acts; measures which interfere with the fundamental freedoms but come within the ambit of an express derogation provided for in the Treaty; other measures which fall within the scope of Community law. Each of those types of measure will now be examined in turn.

6.3.1. Implementing measures

The first case which expressly established that fundamental rights bind the Member States when implementing Community measures was *Wachauf*.[120] The case arose from the Community milk quota regime, the salient features of which have been explained elsewhere in this book.[121] Suffice it to recall here that, with a view to discouraging milk production, Community regulations provided for a system of milk quotas. A key feature of the scheme was that the quota followed the land on transfer so that in the case of farm tenancies, upon the expiry of the lease, the quota

---

[119] Above p. 23.
[120] Case 5/88 *Wachauf* v. *Bundesamt für Ernährung und Forstwirtschaft* [1989] ECR 2609. See also Joined Cases 201 and 202/85 *Klensch* v. *Secrétaire d'État à l'Agriculture et à la Viticulture* [1986] ECR 3477.
[121] Above p. 187.

reverted to the landlord. The rules also enabled Member States to grant compensation to producers who undertook to discontinue milk production definitively.
German law took advantage of that option and provided, as a condition of entitlement to compensation in the case of tenant farmers, that the authorization of the
landlord must be obtained. The rationale behind that condition was to protect the
interests of the landlord since, if the tenant obtained compensation for definitely
leaving the market, the quota allocated to him could not be returned to the landlord. In *Wachauf* the applicant argued that the milk quota regime infringed fundamental rights. If the Community rules were interpreted as meaning that, upon the
expiry of the lease, the lessee's milk quota must be returned to the lessor, they could
have the effect of precluding the lessee from benefiting from the system of compensation for discontinuance of milk production if the lessor were opposed to it. It
was argued that such a consequence would be unacceptable if, as it was in the circumstances, the lessor had never engaged in milk production since the lessee, who
would have acquired the milk quota by his own labour, would then be deprived
without compensation of the fruits of that labour. After recalling its judgment in
Hauer, the Court stated:[122]

. . . Community rules which, upon the expiry of the lease, had the effect of depriving the
lessee, without compensation, of the fruits of his labour and of his investments in the ten-
anted holding would be incompatible with the requirements of the protection of fundamental rights in the Community legal order. Since those requirements are also binding on
the Member States when they implement Community rules, the Member States must, as far
as possible, apply those rules in accordance with those requirements.

The rationale for the Court's finding is not difficult to understand. Since
Community legislation must respect fundamental rights, the national authorities, in
implementing such legislation, must also be so bound. As Weiler and Lockhart
argue, far from being an arbitrary extension of the Court's jurisdiction, *Wachauf* is
the natural progression of the Court's jurisprudence, its foundations resting on cases
such as *Nold* and *Hauer*.[123] In areas where the national authorities act as the agents
of the Community institutions, it would be inconsistent and contradictory not to
subject them to the requirement to observe fundamental rights. Why should the
Commission be so subject when implementing a Council regulation but not the
Member States?[124] The extension of the application of human rights in that context seems 'self-evident'.[125]

Although the justification of review in an agency situation is not difficult to
grasp, its implications are not inconsiderable. In effect, *Wachauf* increases the onus
on the national authorities and the national courts. National authorities must take
care to ensure that the way they implement Community rules does not infringe
fundamental rights. The role of national courts becomes critical. It falls upon them

---

[122] *Wachauf*, op.cit., para. 19.
[123] J. H. H. Weiler and N. J. S. Lockhart, ' "Taking Rights Seriously" Seriously: The European
Court and its Fundamental Rights Jurisprudence—Part I' (1995) 32 CMLRev. 51 at 73.
[124] Op.cit., 74.   [125] *Wachauf*, op.cit., at 2629 per Jacobs AG.

to review national measures on grounds of compatibility with fundamental rights, if necessary by making a reference to the Court of Justice. This way, they acquire a power which they may not possess under national law in relation to domestic measures unconnected with Community law. This is, for example, the case with English courts which hitherto have not had the power to review the compatibility of statutes and acts of the administration with human rights as enshrined in the European Convention.[126]

In assessing whether national implementing measures comply with human rights, the question arises which standard of protection should apply. Is it the standard provided by national law, which may vary from State to State, or the standard provided by Community law? Weiler correctly argues that it is the Community standard that should apply since, in implementing Community law, Member States act as agents of the Community.[127] In such a case, therefore, the implementing legislation should be struck down where it violates the Community standard for the protection of fundamental rights even if it does not violate the said standard set by national law. Weiler's proposed solution in the converse situation also seems persuasive. He argues that if the implementing measure clears the human rights protection standard set by Community law but fails to clear the higher standard set by national law, the national court is entitled to strike down the measure. Where the Community provision gives the Member States discretion for its implementation, provided that the provision is fully implemented one way or another, the requirements of Community law are satisfied. Community law does not require the national standards to be violated.[128] The higher standard of protection provided by national law, however, must in any event apply equally to domestic areas unconnected with Community law and must not prejudice the effective enforcement of the Community rules.[129]

The principle that national implementing measures must respect fundamental rights was reiterated in *Bostock*.[130] Whilst in *Wachauf* the applicant was seeking compensation for the definite discontinuance of milk production, in *Bostock* the applicant sought compensation from the landlord upon surrendering his lease. His argument was that if the quota was transferred to the landlord, he would be deprived of the fruits his labour, since he had made substantial improvements to the farm which had increased its milk production capacity. He claimed that the general principles required Member States to introduce a scheme for payment by a landlord to an outgoing tenant or conferred directly on the tenant a right to

---

[126] But see now, Human Rights Act 1998, s.4.

[127] See Weiler, in Neuwahl and Rosas, op.cit., at pp. 72–3.

[128] Ibid. Weiler's view seems to be supported by the Opinion of Cosmas AG in Case C–63/93 *Duff and Others* v. *Minister for Agriculture and Food, Ireland, and the Attorney General* [1996] ECR I–569, at 583.

[129] See Cosmas AG, ibid.

[130] Case C–2/92 [1994] ECR I–955. See also Case C–63/93 *Duff and Others* v. *Minister for Agriculture and Food, Ireland, and the Attorney General* [1996] ECR I–569; Joined Cases 196–8/88 *Cornée and Others* v. *Copall and Others* [1989] ECR 2309; Case C–16/89 *Spronk* v. *Ministervan Landbouw en Visserij* [1990] ECR I–3185; and more recently Case C–463/93 *St Martinus Elten* v. *Landwirtschaftskammer Rheinland* [1997] ECR I–255.

compensation from the landlord. The Court first pointed out that the Community regulations did not require Member States to introduce a scheme for the payment of compensation by landlords nor did they confer directly on tenants a right to such compensation. It then carried on to examine whether failure on the part of Member States to provide for such a scheme infringed the general principles of Community law and gave a negative reply. It seems that the Court was not willing to intervene because Community legislation left it to the Member States to provide for the protection of the economic interests of tenants and their rights vis-à-vis landlords. Any judicial intervention in the landlord-tenant relationship would entail direct regulation of disputes between private parties on the basis of unwritten Community law.[131]

6.3.2. Measures derogating from the fundamental freedoms

The second type of national measure which is reviewable on grounds of compatibility with fundamental rights is measures which a Member State seeks to justify on the basis of an express derogation from a fundamental freedom, for example Article 30[36]. The issue was settled in *ERT*[132] but, before discussing that case, it may be helpful to trace the development of the law.

Earlier case law suggested that exceptions to fundamental freedoms must be construed in the light of human rights. However, the scope of application of human rights was unclear and the judicial authorities equivocal. In *Rutili*,[133] the Court referred to the ECHR in order to support the finding that restrictions on the right to free movement on grounds of public policy cannot be justified unless they are limited to what is necessary in order to protect the objective in view. But Directive 64/221[134] with which the Court was concerned in that case actually required Member States to protect certain fundamental rights enshrined in the European Convention. In subsequent cases, there were dicta in Opinions of Advocates General to the effect that in assessing the compatibility with Community law of national measures derogating from the fundamental freedoms account must be taken of respect for fundamental rights.[135] An invitation to review national measures on grounds of breach of fundamental rights was rejected by the Court in

---

[131] See also above p. 31. In *Bostock*, op.cit., at 966, Gulmann AG identified three differences between the two cases. In *Wachauf* the applicant sought compensation for the definitive discontinuance of production whereas in *Bostock* the applicant sought compensation from the landlord; in the former, the lease was ended by the landlord whereas in the latter it was the tenant who terminated the agreement; and in *Wachauf* milk production on the holding was established in its entirety by the tenant whereas in *Bostock* the tenant increased milk production already in place.

[132] Case C–160/89 [1991] ECR I–2925.

[133] Case 36/75 *Rutili* v. *Minister for the Interior* [1975] ECR 1219.

[134] Directive 64/221 on the coordination of special measures concerning the movement and residence of foreign nationals which are justified on grounds of public policy, public security or public health (OJ English Spec.Ed., 1963–4, p. 117).

[135] Case 118/75 *Watson and Belmann* [1976] ECR 1185 at 1207 per Trabucchi AG; Case 34/79 *Regina* v. *Henn & Darby* [1979] ECR 3795 at 3821 per Warner AG.

Cinéthèque.[136] French law prohibited the release of films on video cassettes for a period of one year following their release on cinema. It was argued that the prohibition was in breach of the principle of freedom of expression recognized by Article 10 of the ECHR and was therefore incompatible with Community law. Having established that the French law was justified under Article 28[30] in the interests of encouraging the creation of cinematographic works, the Court dismissed the argument based on the Convention stating that it had no power to examine the compatibility with the Convention of national legislation which concerns an area falling within 'the jurisdiction of the national legislator'.[137] Slynn AG took a different view stating that the exceptions of Article 30[36] and the scope of mandatory requirements should be construed in the light of the European Convention.[138]

Two years later in *Demirel*,[139] the Court used a slightly different formula stating that it has no power to examine the compatibility with the European Convention of national legislation 'lying outside the scope of Community law'.[140] The case concerned the interpretation of the Association Agreement with Turkey. The wife of a Turkish national, who was lawfully employed in Germany, was refused leave to stay on the ground that she did not fulfil the conditions for family reunification applicable to nationals of third States under German law. The Court held that the provisions of the Association Agreement concerning free movement of workers were insufficiently precise and therefore incapable of producing direct effect. In response to the argument that the provisions of German law run counter to Article 8 of the European Convention, the Court held that, at that time, there was no provision of Community law defining the conditions in which Member States must permit the family reunification of Turkish workers lawfully settled in the Community. Since the issue fell outside the scope of Community law, the Court did not have jurisdiction to determine whether national rules specifying the conditions for family reunification of such workers were compatible with the Convention.

Six years after *Cinéthèque* the Court expanded the range of national measures which may be subject to review on grounds of human rights in *ERT*.[141] In that case, it held that a national measure may not take advantage of an express derogation from the fundamental freedoms unless it respects fundamental rights. A number of issues arise from the judgment. What is the justification for extending the application of human rights to such measures? Is the jurisdiction of the Court limited to measures based on an express derogation provided for in the Treaty or does it also extend to measures justified by judge-made exceptions, for example mandatory requirements? What is the applicable standard of review?

---

[136] Joined Cases 60 and 61/84 *Cinéthèque* v. *Fédération Nationale des Cinémas Français* [1985] ECR 2605.

[137] Op.cit., para. 26.   [138] Op.cit., at 2616.

[139] Case 12/86 *Demirel* v. *Stadt Schwabisch Gmund* [1987] ECR 3719.   [140] Op.cit., para. 28.

[141] Case C–260/89 [1991] ECR I–2925. See Slot (1991) 28 CMLRev. 978. For subsequent confirmation, see e.g. Case C–62/90 *Commission* v. *Germany* [1992] ECR I–2575.

At first sight, *ERT* appears striking. Where a Member State relies on a provision of the Treaty which provides expressly for a derogation, it acts within its sphere of competence. Why then should its actions be subject to review on grounds of compatibility with human rights? The underlying rationale of *ERT* is that, where a Member State takes advantage of an express derogation, its actions do not fall outside the scope of Community law. An escape clause needs to be relied on only where the national provisions in issue interfere with the fundamental freedoms. An express derogation is thus seen as a concession granted by the Community to the Member States rather than as defining the outer limits of Community competence.[142]

In *ERT* it was stated that review on human rights grounds must be exercised where national rules 'fall within the scope of Community law . . . *in particular* where a Member State relies on the combined provisions of Articles 56 and 66'.[143] It could be argued that the effect of mandatory requirements is to take a national measure outside the scope of Article 28[30] altogether rather than to permit a derogation from it. If that view were correct, it would follow that a restriction on the free movement of goods which is justified by mandatory requirements (or a restriction on the free movement of services which is justified by imperative reasons of public interest) falls outside the scope of Community law and therefore the Court has no jurisdiction to examine its compatibility with human rights. Support for that view could be derived from *ERT* itself. There, the Court cited *Cinéthèque* as authority for the proposition that it has no power to examine the compatibility with the ECHR of national rules which do not fall within the scope of Community law. *ERT* therefore gives the impression that *Cinéthèque*, which concerned a restriction justified by mandatory requirements, remains good law.

It is highly doubtful, however, whether the above view is correct. It would be incongruous if a national measure could take advantage of an express derogation only if it was compatible with human rights but could be justified under mandatory requirements even though it violated such rights. Whether the State invokes an express derogation or a mandatory requirement, it relies on a provision of the Treaty and no distinction should be drawn between the two cases.[144] The effect of *ERT* is that considerations of human rights are part of the inquiry which the Court performs in order to assess whether a national measure which interferes with one of the fundamental freedoms is permitted under Community law. As for *Cinéthèque*, the effects of the French measure in issue in that case on the free movement of goods

---

[142] See the discussion by J. Weiler, 'Fundamental Rights and Fundamental Boundaries: On Standards and Values in the Protection of Human Rights', in N. Neuwahl and A. Rosas, *The European Union and Human Rights* (Martinus Nijhoff, 1995), pp. 51–76 at pp. 69–71.

[143] See paras. 42–3 (emphasis added).

[144] This view is supported by the Opinion of Van Gerven AG in *Society for the Protection of Unborn Children Ireland Ltd.* v. *Grogan* [1991] ECR I–4685, at 4723 and also by J. Weiler, 'The European Court at a Crossroads: Community Human Rights and Member State Action', in F. Capotorti, C.-D. Ehlermann et al., *Du Droit international au droit de l'intégration*, Liber Amicorum Pierre Pescatore (Nomos, 1987), p. 821 at pp. 840–1.

were only tenuous and indirect. The reason why in the latter case the Court took such a restrictive view regarding the scope of application of human rights is probably because the facts of the case did not lend themselves to far-reaching pronouncements on such matters. The Court might have been reluctant to advance the case law along the lines suggested by the Advocate General in circumstances where the French legislation in issue was clearly compatible with Article 28[30].

The issue whether a national provision which falls within the scope of Community law infringes human rights is, in the first place, for the national courts to decide. On a reference for a preliminary ruling, the Court of Justice must provide the necessary criteria of interpretation in order to enable the national court to make that determination.[145] In *ERT* the Court left it, in the first place, up to the national court to decide whether the Greek television monopoly could be justified by Articles 46[56] and 55[66] of the Treaty having regard to the freedom of expression.[146] The issue which arises in this context is what standard of human rights protection must be applied. Weiler[147] argues that, in contrast to national legislation implementing Community measures, in this case it is the national standard of protection that should be applicable. That is so because in this case the Member State does not act as agent of the Community but implements a national policy. The Court should not seek to impose on Member States the Community's own standard but rather to prevent only the violation of core human rights as provided in the European Convention. If that view is correct, a national measure which fails to meet the standard of protection afforded by Community law but passes the lower hurdle imposed by national law need not be struck down by the national court.

ERT extends even further the powers of national courts to review national measures on grounds of human rights protection. As already stated, that is particularly significant for the United Kingdom where the ECHR has not been part of domestic law.[148]

6.3.3. Other measures falling within the scope of Community law

What other types of measures may be said to fall 'within the scope of Community law' for the purposes of the application of fundamental rights? Although the meaning of that expression is not entirely clear,[149] the following cases provide examples of instances where the Court, for one reason or another, rejected invitations to review national measures on grounds of fundamental rights.

The Court rejected the Advocate General's invitation to take the law one step further in *Konstantinidis*.[150] A Greek national established in Germany complained

---

[145] *ERT*, op.cit., paras. 42, 44.   [146] See *ERT*, para. 44.

[147] See Weiler in Neuwahl and Rosas, op.cit., p. 73.

[148] See above, n. 126. For a recent decision of the Value Added Tax and Duties Tribunal applying Article 6(1) of the ECHR in the context of Community rights, see *Hodgson* v. *Commissioners of Customs and Excise* [1997] Eu.LR 116, discussed below. See also in relation to Article 8 ECHR *U* v. *W* [1997] 2 CMLR 431.

[149] See above, p. 25.   [150] Case C–168/91 [1993] ECR I–1191.

that the transliteration of his name into Latin characters by the German authorities was wrong. The Court saw the dispute solely as one of economic rights. It relied on the criterion of discrimination and held that the German rules on the transliteration of foreign names would be caught by Article 44[52] only if they placed the applicant in a disadvantageous position in law or in fact vis-à-vis German nationals. That would be the case if a Greek national was obliged to use in his professional activities a spelling of his name which distorted its pronunciation so much as to create a risk of confusion among prospective clients. Jacobs AG examined the applicant's claim not only from the point of view of Article 43[52] but also from the point of view of the protection of human rights. The Advocate General criticized the absence in the European Convention of an express recognition of the individual's right to his name and personal identity. He found a common principle underpinning the constitutions of the Member States according to which the State is required to respect not only the physical well-being of the individual but also 'his dignity, moral integrity and sense of personal identity'.[151] He argued that Article 8 of the European Convention should be interpreted broadly so as to include protection of the right to one's name and that the applicant should be able to rely on the Convention in order to avoid the wrong transcription of his name. In his view, a Community national who goes to another Member State to work is entitled not only to pursue his trade or profession and to enjoy the same living and working conditions as nationals of the host State; he is in addition entitled to assume that, wherever he goes to earn his living in the European Community, he will be treated in accordance with a common code of fundamental values and moral rights protected by law, part of which is the *jus nominis*.[152]

Konstantinidis was an ambitious attempt by the Advocate General to provide a link between European citizenship and fundamental rights. The cardinal ideas emanating from the Opinion are two: that Community law protects the *jus nominis* as a fundamental right; and that a Community citizen who exercises his freedom of movement is entitled to a certain standard of protection of his fundamental rights set by Community law, even if the host state does not guarantee that standard to its own nationals. In contrast with other cases pertaining to fundamental rights decided by the Court, Jacobs AG sought a maximalist approach to their protection. The Opinion contrasts sharply with that of Van Gerven AG in *Grogan*,[153] where the Advocate General followed a minimalist approach. The issues raised in the two cases, however, were entirely different and the former did not involve a clash of values such as that raised in the latter.

Finally, an unsuccessful attempt to invoke Community law was made in *Kremzow* v. *Republic Österreich*.[154] The applicant had been sentenced by an Austrian court to life imprisonment for murder. In subsequent proceedings, the European Court of Human Rights held that Article 6 of the European Convention had been violated on the ground that the applicant had not been given the opportunity to

---

[151] Op.cit., at 1209.   [152] Op.cit., 1211–12.   [153] See below 6.3.4.
[154] Case C–299/95 [1997] ECR I–2629.

defend himself in person.[155] Following the judgment of the Strasbourg Court, the applicant brought proceedings in Austrian courts seeking a reduction in his sentence and damages for illegal detention pursuant to Article 5(5) of the Convention. In the course of those proceedings, the Oberster Gerichtshof referred a number of questions, seeking essentially to ascertain whether it was bound, as a matter of Community law, by the judgment of the Strasbourg Court and if so what were the legal consequences. The argument of the applicant was essentially that, as a citizen of the Union, he was entitled to protection by Community law. The Court of Justice declined jurisdiction on the ground that the dispute fell outside the scope of Community law. The applicant's situation was not connected in any way with the free movement of persons. Whilst detention may impede a person from exercising his right to free movement, a purely hypothetical prospect of exercising that right does not establish a sufficient connection with Community law to justify the application of Community rules.[156] The Court also pointed out that the applicant had been sentenced pursuant to provisions of national law which were not designed to secure compliance with rules of Community law.

Although in the light of previous cases, the judgment in *Kremzow* was wholly predictable, it does highlight the limits of the fundamental rights rhetoric as a force of integration. Citizenship of the Union does not carry with it the paramount feature of citizenship as understood in the context of the nation State, namely constitutional protection of core rights.[157]

6.3.4. The Grogan case: Deference or intervention?

The Court was confronted with the highly sensitive issue of abortion in *Society for the Protection of Unborn Children Ireland Ltd. v. Grogan*.[158] From all the cases concerning the application of fundamental rights on national measures *Grogan* stands out because it involved a conflict of fundamental values: on the one hand, the right to life of the unborn, as enshrined in the Constitution of a Member State, and on the other hand, the freedom of expression as a Community right. Irish law prohibits abortion as a criminal offence and entrenches the right to life of the unborn child as a constitutional right.[159] In *Attorney General v Open Door Counselling Limited*,[160] decided in 1988, the Irish Supreme Court held that to assist pregnant women to travel abroad to obtain abortions by providing information about specific clinics offering abortion services was contrary to the Constitution. In *Grogan*, students unions in Ireland circulated guidebooks giving details of clinics in the United Kingdom where medical termination of pregnancy was available. A pro-life organization brought proceedings in the Irish High Court seeking a declaration

---

[155] *Kremzow* v. *Austria*, Judgment of 21 Sept. 1993, Series A, No. 268-B.

[156] Op.cit., para. 16.

[157] See on citizenship, Weiler, 'Does Europe Need a Constitution: Demos, Telos and the German Maastricht' (1995) 1 ELJ 219.

[158] Case C–159/90 [1991] ECR I–4685.   [159] See Article 40.3.3 of the Irish Constitution.

[160] [1988] IR 593.

that the distribution of such information was unlawful and an injunction restraining distribution. The High Court considered that issues of Community law were involved and made a reference for a preliminary ruling to the Court of Justice. The Court pointed out that termination of pregnancy is lawfully practised in several Member States and is a medical activity which is normally provided for remuneration. On that basis, it found that the medical termination of pregnancy, performed in accordance with the law of the State where it is carried out, is a service within the meaning of Article 50[60] EC. But the Court did not address the substantive issue of the compatibility of the Irish prohibition with Community law on the ground that the link between the students unions which circulated the information and the clinics in other Member States was too tenuous. Since the students were not acting in co-operation with the clinics, the circulation of the information was not the marketing of a service but a manifestation of their freedom of expression. In the circumstances, the prohibition on the distribution of information could not be regarded as a restriction within the meaning of Article 49[59]. The students unions argued that the prohibition of Irish law infringed their freedom of expression as enshrined in Article 10 of the ECHR. But in view of the conclusion that the prohibition was not a restriction on services, that argument was bound to fail. Referring to *ERT*, the Court pointed out that it had no jurisdiction to examine the compatibility with Community law of national legislation lying outside the scope of Community law.

The Court's reluctance to address the issue of fundamental rights in *Grogan* has been attributed to many factors.[161] There was a risk that the national judiciary might not look favourably to intervention by the Court of Justice.[162] The political climate and public opinion did not seem receptive to the imposition of external standards on moral issues. Member States may have felt that national policies reflecting basic philosophical and moral choices were unjustifiably being questioned in the name of economic freedoms. Also, the Court might have been reluctant to adjudicate on such a highly sensitive matter at a time when proceedings were pending at the European Court of Human Rights.[163] Whatever the reasons which led the Court to avoid the issue of substance, it did so only at the expense of adopting a narrow interpretation of the freedom to provide services. The Advocate General's reasoning seems more convincing. Van Gerven AG pointed out that Article 49[59] covers not only the right to provide but also the right to receive services and assessed the existence of a restriction from the point of view of

---

[161] See S. O'Leary, 'Aspects of the Relationship between Community Law and National Law', in Neuwahl and Rosas, op.cit., p. 23 at pp. 28–9.

[162] The Irish Supreme Court was critical of the High Court judge's decision to make a reference in *Grogan* although it did not interfere with her decision to do so: see [1990] 1 CMLR 689 and O'Leary, op.cit., p. 27.

[163] Following the judgment of the Supreme Court in *Attorney General v Open Door Counselling Limited* the defendant clinics launched a complaint with the European Commission of Human Rights alleging that the injunctions prohibiting the dissemination of information infringed Articles 8, 10 and 14 ECHR. See further below n. 168.

the recipient. He stated that the right to receive services encompasses the right to obtain information about providers of services in other Member States regardless of whether the information came from a person who was not himself the provider and did not act on the latter's behalf. That approach seems correct. What matters is whether the prohibition of distributing information about providers restricts the recipient's right to receive services. That may be so, even where the prohibition relates to dissemination made by a third party for non-economic reasons. To put it differently, the fact that information about services is disseminated by a third party, acting independently of the provider on a non-commercial basis, does not preclude the prohibition of disseminating such information from being a restriction on the freedom to provide services. In fact, in the case of services, such as medical ones, which are not normally marketed by the usual means of promotion on a cross-border basis, dissemination by independent sources acquires particular significance since it is one of the relatively few means by which information about providers may be obtained by recipients.

Having established that the prohibition of Irish law constituted a restriction on the freedom to provide services, the Advocate General proceeded to examine whether it was justified. As a non-discriminatory restriction, it could be justified not only on the basis of Article 55[66] but also on grounds of imperative requirements of public interest. The Advocate General had no difficulty in accepting that the Irish prohibition promoted such an imperative requirement as it related to a policy choice of moral and philosophical nature which the Member State was entitled to make. He also accepted that the prohibition of disseminating information which was designed to assist abortion was proportionate.[164] In relation to fundamental rights, he pointed out that it was a question of balancing two competing interests: on the one hand, the right to life of the unborn enshrined constitutionally in the law of a Member State and, on the on the hand, the freedom of expression as guaranteed in Article 10 ECHR. The Advocate General considered that, in an area where a uniform moral standard is lacking among Member States, individual States should be allowed a fairly considerable margin of discretion.[165] He concluded that the restriction imposed by Irish law on the freedom of expression satisfied the test of proportionality.[166]

---

[164] By contrast, a ban on pregnant women going abroad to receive abortion services or a rule under which they would be subjected to unsolicited examinations upon their return from abroad would fail the test of proportionality: op.cit., at 4721, per Van Gerven AG.

[165] Op.cit., 4728.

[166] Following the *Grogan* decision, the Irish Government attached a Protocol in the Treaty on European Union which states as follows: 'Nothing in the Treaty on European Union, or in the Treaties establishing the European Communities . . . shall affect the application in Ireland of Article 40.3.3. of the Constitution of Ireland.' An addendum included in the Protocol stated that: 'This protocol shall not limit the freedom to travel between Member States or to obtain or make available in Ireland legislative information relating to services lawfully available in a Member State.' For the background to the Protocol, see O'Leary, op.cit., p. 32; D. Curtin, The Constitutional Structure of the Union: A Europe of Bits and Pieces' (1993) 30 CMLRev. 17, at 47.

[167] O'Leary, op.cit., p. 33.

One may venture to suggest that, had the Court found a restriction on the freedom to provide services to exist, it would have probably reasoned along the lines of the Advocate General.[167] In the circumstances, and at the time when the litigation arose, his Opinion seems entirely correct. Given that the legal and social orders of the Member States lack 'a uniform European conception of morals', it would have been wrong for the Court to overrule fundamental societal values espoused by a Member State in the name of economic freedoms. The problem was that, in the circumstances, Article 10 of the ECHR could only come into play indirectly, i.e. in order to establish whether the prohibition of disseminating information was an acceptable restriction on the freedom to provide services. In the absence of explicit political consensus, the Advocate General was wise to defer to the moral choices of Ireland. It is notable that subsequently, in its judgment in the *Open Door* case,[168] the European Court of Human Rights found that the injunctions restraining welfare clinics in Ireland from providing information about abortion services abroad were not 'necessary in a democratic society' and ran counter to Article 10(1) ECHR. The Strasbourg Court considered that the ban on counselling was too broad as it applied to all women regardless of their age, health, or reasons for seeking advice. It considered that there was no definite link between counselling and abortion as counselling advised women about options and did not direct them to have abortion. Also, the ban gave rise to health risk because, as a result of it, women sought abortions later and did not have the benefit of counselling services offered previously.

6.4. Community law and the European Convention on Human Rights[169]

6.4.1. The status of the Convention in Community law

We saw above that in *Nold* the Court identified the Convention as one of the primary sources of fundamental rights whose observance is guaranteed in the Community legal order.[170] Express reference to the Convention was made for the first time in *Rutili*.[171] As the case law evolved, the function of the Convention in judicial reasoning became more instrumental: general references gave way to

---

[168] *Open Door Counselling and Dublin Well Woman Centre Ltd.* v. *Ireland*, Judgment of 29 Oct. 1992, Series A, no. 246.

[169] Bibliography on this issue abounds. See the works quoted in subsequent footnotes and also, among others, F. G. Jacobs, 'European Community Law and the European Convention of Human Rights', in D. Curtin and T. Heukels (eds.), *Institutional Dynamics of European Integration, Essays in Honour of H.G. Schermers*, Vol. II (Kluwer), 561–72; Schermers, 'The European Community Bound by Fundamental Human Rights' (1990) 27 CMLRev. 249, Grief [1991] PL 555, J. McBride and L. N. Brown, 'The United Kingdom, The European Community and the European Convention of Human Rights' (1981) 1 YEL 167; A. Drzemczewski, 'The Domestic Application of the European Human Rights Convention as European Community Law' (1981) 30 ICLQ 118; H. G. Schermers, 'The Communities under the European Convention of Human Rights' (1978) 1 LIEI 1.

[170] See above p. 206.   [171] Op.cit.

detailed analysis of its provisions.[172] The case law acknowledged the 'special significance' of the Convention, the underlying principles of which 'must be taken into consideration in Community law'.[173] References to its provisions have been made in numerous cases. Among the most oft-quoted articles are Articles 6 and 13,[174] 8,[175] and 10.[176] References are also made in numerous Community documents[177] and measures of secondary law.[178] Given the special status of the Convention, it would be unthinkable for the Court not to recognize as fundamental a right enshrined in its provisions. Although the Community is not formally bound by it, leading commentators accept that 'the Convention has the same effect as if the Community was formally bound'.[179] This view is countenanced by Article 6(2) of the TEU which commits the Union to respect fundamental rights 'as guaranteed by the European Convention . . . and as they result from the constitutional traditions common to the Member States, as general principles of Community law'. It seems therefore that the Community is bound to respect, as a minimum, the standards of the Convention which forms an integral part of Community law.[180]

Since the Court of Justice has jurisdiction to apply the Convention in areas which fall within the scope of Community law, the possibility exists that conflicting rulings may be delivered by the Court of Justice and the Court of Human Rights on the interpretation of the Convention. This is illustrated by the case law of the two courts pertaining to the right of privacy. Article 8(1) of the Convention states that '[e]veryone has the right to respect for his private and family life, his home and his correspondence'. In *Hoechst* v. *Commission*,[181] the Court of Justice held in the context of Commission investigations in the field of competition law, that the right to the inviolability of the home applies only to the private dwellings of natural persons and does not extend to undertakings. The Court reasoned that

[172] See e.g. most recently, Case C–249/96 *Grant* v. *South-West Trains Ltd.*, [1998] ECR I–621.

[173] Case 222/84 *Johnston* v. *Chief Constable of the Royal Ulster Constabulary* [1986] ECR 1651, para. 18. Case C–260/89 *ERT* [1991] ECR I–2925, para. 41.

[174] See e.g. Case 98/79 *Pecastaing* v. *Belgium* [1980] ECR 691; Case 374/87 *Orkem* v. *Commission* [1989] ECR 3283; *Johnston* v. *Chief Constable of the Royal Ulster Constabulary*, op.cit.

[175] See e.g. Case 36/75 *Rutili* v. *Minister for the Interior* [1975] ECR 1219; Case 136/79 *National Panasonic* v. *Commission* [1980] ECR 2033; Case 249/86 *Commission* v. *France* [1989] ECR 1263; Joined Cases 46/87 and 227/88 *Hoechst* v. *Commission* [1989] ECR 2859; *Konstantinidis*, op.cit. (per Jacobs AG).

[176] See e.g. *ERT*, op.cit.; *Grogan*, op.cit. (per Van Gerven AG).

[177] See e.g. Joint Declaration on Fundamental Rights by the European Parliament, the Council and the Commission, 5 Apr. 1977; Declaration of Fundamental Rights and Freedoms, European Parliament, 12 Apr. 1989; Declaration on Racism and Xenophobia, Maastricht European Council, 9–10 Dec. 1991. For other measures, see Duparc, op.cit., n. 1.

[178] See e.g. the reference to Article 10(1) in the eighth recital of the Preamble to Council Directive 89/552/EEC on the co-ordination of national laws concerning the pursuit of television broadcasting activities, OJ 1989 L 298/23.

[179] Jacobs, op.cit., p. 563; see also P. Pescatore, 'La Cour de justice des Communautés européennes et la Convention européenne des droits de l'Homme', in Matscher and Petzold (eds.), *Protecting Human Rights and Freedoms: The European Dimension* (1988), p. 441.

[180] See Krogsgaard, op.cit., n. 1, 108.

[181] Joined Cases 46/87 and 227/88 [1989] ECR 2859. The ruling was confirmed in Case 85/87 *Dow Benelux* v. *Commission* [1989] ECR 3137 and Joined Cases 97–9/87 *Dow Chemical Ibérica* v. *Commission* [1989] ECR 3165.

the protective scope of Article 8(1) is concerned with 'the development of man's personal freedom and may not therefore be extended to business premises'.[182] Subsequently, in *Niemietz* v. *Germany*,[183] the European Court of Human Rights held that the protection of Article 8(1) extends to the professional offices of a lawyer. Rejecting the literal interpretation of the Court of Justice, it held that a restrictive construction of Article 8(1) posed the risk of unequal treatment because self-employed persons may carry on professional activities at home and, conversely, private activities in their place of work. The Court of Human Rights held that its broad interpretation of the right of privacy is more compatible with the underlying objective of Article 8 which is to protect the individual from arbitrary interference from the public authorities.

Conflicting rulings have also been delivered in relation to the right against self-incrimination. In *Orkem*,[184] the Court of Justice held that Article 6 of the Convention does not include the right not to give evidence against oneself. Subsequently, in *Funke* v. *France*,[185] the European Court of Human Rights held that, under Article 6, any person charged with a criminal offence has the right to remain silent and not to contribute towards self-incrimination. Toth[186] attributes those discrepancies to the different contexts in which the rulings have been delivered, in particular the distinct importance of competition law for the attainment of Community objectives and the need to ensure effective enforcement mechanisms for its implementation. Conflicting rulings may evince that the two courts have, at least in some issues, different priorities. It remains to be seen whether the Court of Justice will be prepared to depart from its precedent in order to align its case law with developments in the jurisprudence of the Strasbourg jurisdiction. If it is accepted that the Convention forms part of the corpus of Community law, it must also be accepted that, on issues of law, the Court of Justice is bound to follow the interpretation given to the Convention by the Court of Human Rights. The Convention occupies a special position in the Community legal order. It is not only a source of inspiration on human rights but much more: it is the expression of a fundamental core of moral, political and social values underlying the legal systems of the Contracting States and underpinning the Community legal order. The interpretation of the Convention should be left to the Court of Human Rights, that being the competent judicial body. The Court of Justice, on its part, has jurisdiction to apply the Convention within the confines of that interpretation in the light of the distinct requirements of the Community polity. Thus, to give an example, following the judgment in *Niemietz* v. *Germany*, the Court of Justice should give way by acknowledging that Article 8(1) of the Convention also extends to business premises. It will still be for the Court of Justice to draw the appropriate balance

---

[182] *Hoechst*, op.cit., para. 18.
[183] Judgment of 16 Dec. 1992, Series A, No. 251-B, 16 EHRR 97.
[184] Case 374/87 *Orkem* v. *Commission* [1989] ECR 3283, para. 30.
[185] Series A, No. 256-A, 16 EHRR 297.
[186] A. G. Toth, 'The European Union and Human Rights: The Way Forward' (1997) 34 CMLRev. 491, at 500.

between the right to privacy and the need to ensure the effective enforcement of Community competition law on concrete cases.

A case which also deserves reference in this context is *Vermeulen* v. *Belgium*.[187] The European Court of Human Rights found, by fifteen votes to four, that the participation of the *procureur général* of the Belgian Cour de Cassation in the adjudication of a civil case infringed Article 6(1) of the Convention.[188] The main duty of the *procureur général* is to assist the Cour de Cassation and to help in ensuring the consistency of its case law. The Court noted that the *procureur général* acts with the strictest objectivity but pointed out that his opinion, intended as it is to advise and to influence the Cour de Cassation, may rebound on the legal position of the person concerned. The Court found a violation of Article 6(1) on two counts. First, the fact that the person concerned does not have the right to reply to the submissions of the *procureur général* before the end of the hearing infringes his right to adversarial proceedings. Secondly, the participation of the *procureur général* in the deliberations of the Cour de Cassation, even though he takes part only in an advisory capacity, violates the right to a fair hearing. Such participation, the Court noted, offers him, if only in appearance, an additional opportunity to bolster his submissions in private without the fear of contradiction.

Vermeulen raises a question mark over the office of the Advocate General of the European Court of Justice. Clearly, the second infringement of Article 6(1) established in *Vermeulen* cannot be substantiated as the Advocate General does not take part in the deliberation of the Court of Justice. The reasoning of the Court of Human Rights regarding the first infringement, however, raises questions. The delivery of the Opinion of the Advocate General concludes the oral hearing and the litigants have no right of reply. Does the fact that the Advocate General has the last word infringe the right to judicial protection? It may be possible to distinguish *Vermeulen* on the ground that in Belgian law the *procureur général* acts under the title of 'ministère public', whereas under Community law the Advocate General does not represent any form of public authority separate from the Court.[189] It is not clear from the judgment how much importance the Court of Human Rights attributed to the fact that the *procureur général* derives its authority from the *ministère public*. It seems, however, that the Strasbourg Court saw the *procureur général* as part of a State authority rather than as an integral part of the Cour de Cassation. That must be so for, if it accepted that the *procureur général* is the court's *alter ego*, he cannot be considered as a party to the litigation in relation to whom the principle of equality must be respected.[190] In the light of the function of the Advocate General and the

---

[187] Case 58/1994/505/587, Judgment of 22 Jan. 1996.

[188] Earlier, a similar finding had been made in relation to the participation of the *procureur général* in criminal proceedings: *Borgers* v. *Belgium*, Judgment of 30 Oct. 1991, Series A, No. 214 (1993) 15 EHRR 92.

[189] See N. Fennelly, 'Reflections of an Irish Advocate General' (1996) Irish J Eur.L 5, at 13.

[190] Notably, Judges Gölcüklü, Matscher and Pettiti in their joint dissenting opinion, took the view that the judgment of the majority illustrated 'excessive formalism'. They stated: 'In our view, to see the *procureur général*, when he acts in civil proceedings, as an adversary of either of the parties is to

contribution of the office in the development of Community law, the suggestion that it may violate the right to legal protection appears odd.[191] There can be no doubt that the Advocate General is an integral part of the Community judicial system. He performs *par excellence* a judicial function being 'the embodied conscience' of the Court.[192] Arguably, the fact that the litigants may not submit observations on the Opinion is no more of a threat to the right to judicial protection than the fact that the litigants have no right of appeal against the judgment of the Court itself. By the nature of things, there must be a court which is the final arbiter of a dispute and against the decision of which there is no legal remedy. It is precisely as a member of such a court that the Advocate General can fulfil a most useful function.

Despite the potential problems arising from conflicting rulings, it should be emphasized that the two jurisdictions are in a relationship of co-operation and not one of confrontation. The organs charged with the implementation of the Convention respect the level of protection of human rights offered by the Community legal order. A case instructive of the relationship between the Convention and the Community legal order is *Melchers*.[193] There, the European Commission of Human Rights rejected as inadmissible an application by a German national alleging that the execution by the German authorities of a decision of the European Court of Justice in competition law violated Article 6 of the Convention. The Commission considered that it was not competent to examine the claim in view of the transfer of powers in the field in issue from Germany to the Community. It held that such transfer of powers was compatible with the Convention provided that an equivalent standard of protection was guaranteed to fundamental rights and referred to that effect to the case law of the Court of Justice.[194]

The Convention seems to have proved particularly influential in recent cases concerning the rights of transsexuals and homosexuals under Community law. In *P v. S* the Court referred to the definition of transsexual given by the Strasbourg Court pointing out that they are a 'well-defined and identifiable group'.[195]

---

misunderstand the nature of the institution, since his rôle—of what one might call an *amicus curiae*—is solely that of a neutral and objective guardian of the lawfulness of the proceedings and of the uniformity and consistency of the case law. To that extent, his participation in the hearing and—in an advisory capacity—in the deliberations in no way offends against the principle of equality of arms as he is placed above the parties.'

[191] See further Tridimas, 'The Role of the Advocate General in the Development of Community Law: Some Reflections' (1997) CMLRev 1349 at 1380.

[192] C. Hamson, *Executive Discretion and Judicial Control* (1954) p. 80.

[193] Decision of 9 Feb. 1990, Application No. 13258/87, Decisions and Reports, No. 64. See also C.F.D.T., Commission of Human Rights, Decisions and Reports, vol. 13, p. 231.

[194] It has been noted, however, that in *Melchers* the national authorities were merely acting as agents of the Community. Where the national authorities enjoy discretion in implementing Community law the question may arise whether an alleged breach of the Convention is attributable to the Community or the Member States and that in turn may pose delicate questions concerning the interpretation of the Community measure in issue. See F. G. Jacobs, 'European Community Law and the European Convention on Human Rights', in D. Curtin and T. Heukels, op.cit., n. 1, at 568.

Reliance on the Convention was placed in particular in *Grant* v. *South-West Trains Ltd.*,[196] where the Court refused to equate for the purposes of the application of Article 119 (now 141) a stable relationship between two persons of the same sex with cohabitation outside marriage of persons of opposite sex. The Court pointed out that stable homosexual relationships do not fall within the scope of the right to respect family life under Article 8 nor are they covered by Article 12 of the Convention. Also, national measures favouring heterosexual relationships over homosexual ones have been held by the Strasbourg Court not to contravene Article 14 of the Convention.[197] Such statements by the Court of Justice provide the clearest indication yet that Luxembourg looks to Strasbourg to provide leadership in the recognition of new rights.

6.4.2. Opinion on the accession of the Community to the European Convention on Human Rights

Although in the mid-70s the Commission had considered that formal accession of the Communities to the European Convention was not necessary,[198] in 1979 it floated the idea that the Communities should accede with a view to strengthening the protection of human rights.[199] That proposal re-emerged in 1990, and in 1993 the Commission published a working document entitled 'Accession of the Community to the European Convention of Human Rights and the Community Legal Order' where it considered, among others, issues pertaining to the legal basis of accession and the jurisdiction of the Court of Justice. In 1994 the Council sought the Opinion of the Court pursuant to Article 300(6)[228(6)] EC on whether accession would be compatible with the Treaty. In its Opinion[200] the Court distinguished between two issues, first, whether accession would be compatible with the Treaty and, secondly, whether the Community has competence to accede. It considered that the issue of compatibility was not admissible because, at the time when the Opinion was sought, no specific arrangements had been made concerning the way in which the Community would become subject to the machinery of judicial control established by the Convention. On the issue of competence, the Court gave a negative reply. It referred to Article 5(1)[3b(1)] which provides that the Community may act only within the limits of the powers conferred upon it by the Treaty and of the objectives assigned to it therein. It stated that no Treaty provision confers on the Community institutions any general power to enact rules on

---

[195] Case C–13/94 *P* v. *S and Cornwall County Council* [1996] ECR I–2143, para. 16, and see per Tesauro AG 2150–1.

[196] Case C–249/96, [1998] ECR I–621.   [197] Op.cit., paras. 33–4.

[198] See EC Commission Report, 'The Protection of Fundamental Rights as Community Law is Created and Developed, EC Bull. Suppl. 5/76 and, for a general discussion, see Mc Bride and Brown, op.cit., pp. 171 *et seq*.

[199] See 'Accession of the European Communities to the European Convention on Human Rights', EC Bull. Suppl. 2/79.

[200] Opinion 2/94 [1996] ECR I–1759.

human rights or to conclude international conventions in that field.[201] In the absence of express or implied powers for that purpose, the Court turned to examine whether the residual provision of Article 308[235] EC may constitute the legal basis for accession. It stated that Article 308[235] cannot serve as the basis for widening the scope of Community powers beyond the general framework created by the provisions of the Treaty as a whole and, in particular, by those which define the tasks and the activities of the Community.[202] It pointed out that, under the case law, respect for human rights is a condition of the lawfulness of Community acts. It stated, however, that accession to the Convention would entail a substantial change in the present Community system for the protection of human rights, as it would 'entail the entry of the Community into a distinct international institutional system as well as integration of all the provisions of the Convention into the Community legal order'.[203]

The reasoning of the Opinion is not wholly convincing. The core argument in favour of competence submitted by the Commission and by several Member States[204] was that respect for fundamental rights is a component of all Community policies or, as the Commission put it, a transverse objective forming an integral part of the Community's objectives. The Opinion contains virtually no discussion of that argument which, it is submitted, is not unmeritorious. The Opinion blurs the distinction between the competence of the Community and the powers of the institutions. Allott suggests that it would be more appropriate to say that Article 308[235] does not provide the Council with the power, rather than that the Community does not have the competence, to accede to the European Convention.[205] This view, however, is also problematic because the question of powers is subordinate to the question of competence. The Treaty, assisted by the case law, strives to ensure that in the fields where the Community enjoys competence the institutions have the necessary powers to act in order to pursue the objectives of the Treaty. Article 308[235] is designed to fulfil precisely that function. Clearly, Article 308[235] may not be used to grant the Community institutions powers in areas which fall beyond the competence of the Community. Thus, it is not possible for the Council to legislate on the basis of Article 308[235] on fundamental rights in fields which do not otherwise fall within the scope of the Treaty.[206] That does not mean, however, that the Community does not have com-

---

[201] Op.cit., para. 27.

[202] This point has subsequently been confirmed in Case C–249/96 *Grant* v. *South-West Trains Ltd.*, 17 Feb. 1998, para. 45.

[203] Op.cit., para. 34.

[204] The Commission, the Parliament, Austria, Belgium, Denmark, Finland, Germany, Greece, Italy and Sweden argued that the Community had competence to accede to the Convention. France, Portugal, Spain, Ireland and the United Kingdom argued against accession.

[205] P. Allot [1996] 55 CLJ 409, at 411.

[206] See A. Arnull, 'Opinion 2/94 and its Implications for the future Constitution of the Union' (CELS, in *The Human Rights Opinion of the ECJ and its Constitutional Implications* (CELS Occasional Paper No. 1, University of Cambridge, 1996), 7.

petence to accede to the Convention and be bound by it within the scope of application of Community law. Whether accession is compatible with Community law will depend on the specific arrangements concerning the relationship between the European Court of Human Rights and the European Court of Justice.[207] In previous opinions the Court had accepted that, in principle, it is possible for the Community to become part of a supranational structure with its own, separate, system of judicial control.[208] The issue of accession to the Convention therefore, it is submitted, is an issue of compatibility not an issue of competence.[209] It will be noted that the view advocated here would not prejudice the powers of Member States. This is because Article 308[235] requires the Council to act with unanimity. Also, given the case law of the Court, it can be said that the Community, although not formally bound by the Convention, is in effect subject to it and so are the Member States in so far as they act within the scope of Community law.

A further point may be made regarding the exact scope of the Court's ruling. The Opinion does not seem to stand as authority that the Community may not conclude measures in the field of human rights on the basis of Article 308[235].[210] The Court nowhere made such a broad pronouncement. It rather stated that recourse to Article 308[235] may not be made with a view to establishing a system for the protection of human rights which has fundamental institutional and constitutional implications. Such a system may be brought about only by way of Treaty amendment.[211]

---

[207] For further comments on Opinion 2/94, see Gaja (1996) 33 CMLRev. 973; *The Human Rights Opinion of the ECJ and its Constitutional Implications*, op.cit.

[208] Opinion 1/76; Opinion 1/91.

[209] Notably, Jacobs AG writing extrajudicially before the Court delivered its ruling took the view that it would be compatible with the EC Treaty for the Community to accept the jurisdiction of the European Court of Human Rights, basing his views on Opinion 1/91 *On the draft agreement relating to the creation of the EEA* [1991] ECR I–6079. See F. G. Jacobs, 'European Community Law and the European Convention on Human Rights', in D. Curtin and T. Heukels, op.cit., n. 1, at 568.

[210] That view is espoused by Arnull, op.cit., p. 7.   [211] Op.cit., para. 35.

7

The Rights of Defence

7.1. Introduction

The EC Treaty does not provide for a general right to a hearing in administrative proceedings.[1] Recognition of such a right in Community legislation seems to be coincidental rather than principled. A right to a hearing is recognized, for example, in competition, anti-dumping, and trademark proceedings[2] but not in proceedings for State aids[3] or the common customs tariff. Those differences are not based on any objective reasons but are rather due to historical happenstance. The gaps left by the Community legislature are covered by judge-made law. Already at an early stage, the Court of Justice elevated the rights of defence to a general principle of law. In *Alvis* v. *Council*,[4] a staff case, it declared:

According to a generally accepted principle of administrative law in force in the Member States . . . the administration of these States must allow their servants the opportunity of replying to allegations before any disciplinary decision is taken concerning them.

This rule, which meets the requirements of sound justice and good administration, must be followed by Community institutions.

The importance of the last statement lies in that it encapsulates the dual rationale of the right to a hearing. It is perceived by the Court as a functional requirement promoting the quality of administration: the information supplied and the views expressed by the persons affected are seen as contributing to better decision making. It is also perceived as a requirement of formal justice akin to a human right and deriving from the rule of law: the persons concerned must be given the opportu-

[1] See K. Lenaerts and J. Vanhamme, 'Procedural Rights of Private Parties in the Community Administrative Process' (1997) 34 CMLRev. 531, at 533. General contributions include K. Lenaerts, 'Procedures and Sanctions in Economic Administrative Law, General Report', 17 *FIDE Congress*, Vol. III (Berlin, 1996), pp. 506–77; O. Due, 'Le respect des droits de la défense dans le droit administratif communautaire' [1987] CDE 383; L. Goffin, 'La jurisprudence de la Cour de justice sur les droits de défense', 16 (1980) CDE 127; A. Braun, 'les droits de la défense devant la Commission et la Cour de justice des Communautés européennes', 141 (1980) IRCL 2; Schwarze, op.cit., 1243–371, esp. 1320 *et seq.*; see also the specialized bibliography given under the specific sections of this chapter.

[2] For competition and anti-dumping, see below 7.6 and 7.7. For trademarks, see Council Reg. No. 40/94 on the Community trademark, OJ 1994 L 11/1 and its implementing Commission Reg. No. 2868/95, OJ 1995 L 303/1.

[3] As Lenaerts and Vanhamme observe, op.cit., at 533 n. 4, Article 88(2)[93(2)] requires the Commission to give notice to the parties concerned to submit their comments but no secondary legislation exemplifies that requirement.

[4] Case 32/62 [1963] ECR 49, at 55.

nity to defend their rights and participate in the decision-making process. Those two justifications for the right to a hearing are referred to respectively as the instrumental and the non-instrumental rationale and underlie procedural rights in general.[5]

The right to a hearing is an area where Community law most resembles common law rather than the systems of continental Member States in that it does not provide by legislation for a comprehensive right to a hearing in all administrative proceedings.[6] In English administrative law, the requirements of natural justice traditionally occupy a distinct position.[7] This is not only because of their intrinsic importance as guarantors of objective and impartial decision making but also for reasons peculiar to the development of the law in England. Natural justice as a legal concept thrived in the nineteenth century, where extensive case law applied the principles derived from it to a wide variety of decision-making bodies.[8] Also, the traditional limitations on substantive grounds of review inherent in the Diceyan concept of unitary democracy and the *ultra vires* doctrine forced preoccupation with requirements of procedural fairness. Procedure, unlike substance, was an area which could undisputably be said to fall within the judicial province. In contrast to English and Irish law,[9] many of the laws of the continental Member States recognize by statute a general right to a fair hearing. For example, the German Act on Administrative Procedure requires that the persons concerned must be heard before decisions are taken that affect their legal positions. Provisions of general application are found *inter alia* in the laws of Austria, Netherlands, Luxembourg, Finland, Spain and Portugal.[10] Despite the fact that most Member States incorporate in their legislation a general right to a hearing in dealings with the administration, no enthusiasm has emerged from regulators or academics for the introduction of a similar right by Community legislation.[11] By contrast, preference seems to lie with reliance on the general concepts of fairness and due process borrowed from the common law.[12]

Natural justice was one of the first areas where, following the accession of the United Kingdom, the influence of common law on the jurisprudence of the Court of Justice was felt. Such influence was particularly evident in the *Transocean Marine*

[5] See e.g. the dicta by Lord Mustill in *R* v. *Secretary of State for the Home Department, ex parte Doody* [1993] 3 All ER 92 at 98 and see further, Craig, *Administrative Law*, p. 282.

[6] Lenaerts and Vanhamme, op.cit., n. 1, 534.

[7] For a discussion of English law, see De Smith, Woolf and Jowell, *Judicial Review of Administrative Action*, Chs. 7–12; Craig, *Administrative Law*, Chs. 8–9.

[8] The scope of its application was limited in the first half of the twentieth century but the House of Lords breathed new air into the doctrine in the seminal *Ridge* v. *Baldwin* [1964] AC 40. For the development of English law, see further Craig, op.cit.

[9] Irish law, as English law, does not provide by statute a general right to a hearing but parties affected by administrative decisions enjoy variable procedural rights under specific statutes or regulations. See 'The Irish Report' by P. Lee in *17 FIDE Congress*, Vol. III, op.cit., pp. 204–48

[10] For a detailed review see the national reports in *17 FIDE Congress*, Vol. III, op.cit., n. 1, and also Schwarze, op.cit.,

[11] Lenaerts and Vanhamme, op.cit., n. 1, 534.   [12] Ibid.

Paint case.[13] The Commission had exempted from the prohibition provided for in Article 85(1) (now 81(1)) of the Treaty an agreement concluded between the members of the Transocean Marine Paint Association. Subsequently, it renewed the exemption but made renewal subject to an onerous condition, in relation to which the Association considered that the Commission had not given to it the opportunity to make its views known in advance. The problem for the Association was that Community written law did not provide for a hearing in the circumstances. Regulation No. 99/63[14] required the Commission to inform undertakings of the objections raised against them but did not provide for a hearing in relation to the conditions which the Commission intended to attach to a decision granting exemption. The Court, however, held:[15]

It is clear . . . both from the nature and objective of the procedure for hearings, and from Articles 5, 6 and 7 of Regulation No. 99/63, that this Regulation . . . applies the general rule that a person whose interests are perceptibly affected by a decision taken by a public authority must be given the opportunity to make his point of view known. This rule requires that an undertaking be clearly informed, in good time, of the essence of conditions to which the Commission intends to subject an exemption and it must have the opportunity to submit its observations to the Commission. This is especially so in the case of conditions which, as in this case, impose considerable obligations having far reaching effects.

In *Transocean* the Court followed the lead of Warner AG who, after reviewing the scope of the *audi alteram partem* principle in the laws of the Member States, concluded that 'the right to be heard forms part of those rights which "the law" referred to in Article 164 of the Treaty upholds, and of which, accordingly, it is the duty of this Court to ensure the observance'.[16] The influence of common law concepts of procedural fairness was also evinced in *AM & S* v. *Commission*,[17] where, prompted by Warner AG and Slynn AG, the Court recognized the confidentiality of communications between lawyer and client (legal professional privilege) as a general principle of Community law, viewing it as an essential corollary to the rights of defence.[18]

In English law, the concept of natural justice connotes two ideas:[19] (a) the parties should be given adequate opportunity to be heard and, as a corollary, they should be given due notice of the hearing (*audi alteram partem*), and (b) the adjudicator should be disinterested and unbiased (*nemo judex in causa sua*). In Community law, reference is usually made to the rights of the defence (*droits de la défense*), the principal component of which is the first requirement of natural justice. By contrast, the second aspect of natural justice has received minimal reference in the case law. The reason seems to be that, at Community level, decisions are not taken by tribunals or quasi-judicial bodies but by the administration itself, typically the

---

[13] Case 17/74 *Transocean Marine Paint* v. *Commission* [1974] ECR 1063.
[14] See further for the provisions of this regulation, below 7.6.
[15] *Transocean Marine*, op.cit., para. 15.   [16] *Transocean Marine*, op.cit., at 1089.
[17] Case 155/79 [1982] ECR 1575.   [18] Op.cit., para. 23.
[19] De Smith, Woolf and Jowell, op.cit., p. 379.

Commission, whose decisions are reviewable by the Community judicature.[20] The principle of *nemo judex in causa sua* is, of course, guaranteed by the Statutes of the Court of Justice.[21]

Apart for the right to be heard, the rights of the defence include the following rights:

- the right to be assisted by a lawyer;[22]
- legal professional privilege; and,
- in a qualified form, the right against self-incrimination.

In *AM & S* the Court recognized legal professional privilege subject to two conditions: the communications between lawyer and client in relation to which privilege is claimed must be made for the purposes and in the interests of the client's rights of defence, and they must emanate from an independent lawyer, namely a lawyer who is not bound to the client by a relationship of employment.[23] By contrast, advice given by an in-house lawyer is not covered by privilege and the Commission may rely on such advice to prove an infringement of competition law.[24]

The right against self-incrimination was examined in *Orkem*.[25] The case concerned a request for information made by the Commission pursuant to Article 11 of Regulation 17,[26] which enables the Commission to ask undertakings to supply information in the course of its investigations to establish a possible breach of competition law. The regulation does not expressly provide for the right to remain silent. The issue raised was whether the general principles of Community law included the right of an undertaking not to supply information capable of being used in order to establish against it the existence of an infringement of Community competition law. The Court held that the Commission is entitled to compel an undertaking to provide all necessary information concerning such facts as may be known to it and to disclose to the Commission all relevant documents which are

---

[20] Lenaerts and Vanhamme, op.cit., n. 1, 555–6.

[21] See Protocol of the Statute of the Court of Justice of the EEC, Articles 2, 4, 16 and 44. For a manifestly unmeritorious claim against the impartiality of a member of the CFI, see Case T–47/92 *Lenz* v. *Commission* [1992] ECR II–2523 and Case C–277/95 P *Lenz* v. *Commission* [1996] ECR I–6109.

[22] See Case 115/80 *Demont* v. *Commission* [1981] ECR 3147; Joined Cases 46/87 and 227/88 *Hoechst* v. *Commission* [1989] ECR 2859, para. 16. By contrast, the rights of defence do not entitle a person to bring a direct action at the CFI without legal representation: C–174/96 P *Lopes* v. *Court of Justice* [1996] ECR I–6401; Case C–175/96 P *Lopes* v. *Court of Justice* [1996] ECR I–6409.

[23] *AM & S*, op.cit., para. 21; for the application of the privilege, see Case T–30/89 *Hilti* [1990] ECR II–163. See further Lasok, 'The Privilege Against Self-incrimination in Competition Cases' (1990) II ECLR 90; Guerrin and Kyriazis, 'Cartels: Proof and Procedural Issues, 16 Fordham Int.LJ 266; I. S. Forrester, 'Legal Professional Privilege: Limitations on the Commission's Powers of Inspection Following the AM & S Judgment' (1983) 20 CMLR 75; J. Faull, 'Legal Professional Privilege (AM & S): The Commission Proposes International Negotiations', 10 (1985) ELRev. 119.

[24] See *John Deere* [1985] 2 CMLR 554.

[25] Case 374/87 *Orkem* v. *Commission* [1989] ECR 3283. See also Case 27/88 *Solvay* v. *Commission* [1989] ECR 3355.

[26] OJ, English Spec.Ed., 1962, p. 87.

in its possession, even if the latter may be used to establish the existence of anti-competitive conduct. The Commission, however, may not, by means of a decision calling for information, undermine the rights of defence of the undertaking concerned. Thus, it may not compel an undertaking to provide it with answers which might involve an admission on its part of the existence of an infringement, which it is incumbent upon the Commission to prove.[27] On that basis, the Court found that the Commission was entitled to ask the undertaking concerned to supply factual information but not information pertaining to the objectives of its actions. Nor was it entitled to procure an acknowledgement by the undertaking concerned of its participation in anti-competitive conduct.

The judgment can be understood as endorsing a qualified privilege against self-incrimination. Kerse submits that the recognition of the privilege is narrow and that it does not restrict seriously the Commission's investigatory powers in practice.[28] Notably, the Court interpreted Article 6 of the European Convention of Human Rights as not including the right not to give evidence against oneself, an interpretation which was rejected in subsequent case law by the European Court of Human Rights.[29] *Orkem*, however, does not evoke an unduly restrictive approach and the balance drawn by the Court of Justice does not seem unfair. Its obvious concern was that a full endorsement of the right against self-incrimination might render Article 11 of Regulation 17 ineffective.[30] Nor was a wider recognition of the right to remain silent warranted by principles common to the laws of the Member States. The Court pointed out that the right against self-incrimination is recognized by national laws, as a general rule, only to natural persons and only in the context of criminal proceedings.

Does the principle established in *Orkem* apply also in national proceedings? In *Otto v. Postbank NV*,[31] on a reference by a Dutch court, it was held that a national court which examines a claim that Articles 81[85] and 82[86] have been breached in proceedings between private parties is not bound to recognize the privilege against self-incrimination where such privilege is not recognized by national law. The Court, however, made such deference to the national rules of procedure subject to an important proviso. If information thus disclosed comes to the possession of the Commission, the latter may not use it to initiate proceedings for the infringement of Articles 81[85] and 82[86]. The criticism may be raised that the rights of defence should not differ depending on whether proceedings for the violation of Community competition law are undertaken at Community or national level. The rationale of the judgment, however, is that the proceedings in issue were civil proceedings between private parties and not administrative ones initiated by the national authorities. The Court saw that as the material difference, pointing out that Community law does not require respect for the qualified right against self-

[27] Op.cit., paras. 34–5.   [28] C. Kerse, *EC Anti-Trust Procedure*, p. 135.
[29] See the judgment in *Funke* v. *France* [1993] 1 CMLR 897 and above, Ch. 6.4.1.
[30] The same concern was voiced by Warner AG in the earlier *AM & S*, op.cit., 1621.
[31] Case C–60/92 [1993] ECR I–5683.

incrimination as laid down in *Orkem* in national proceedings between private parties which may not lead directly or indirectly to the imposition of sanctions by public authorities.[32] Given that reasoning, it would appear that the qualified privilege against self-incrimination binds not only the Commission but also national competition authorities: they should also be prevented from using information obtained in civil actions for the initiation of proceedings against the undertaking concerned.

Otto brought into surface an underlying tension. On the one hand, the Commission's policy is to encourage the enforcement of Community competition law by private parties at the national level. On the other hand, the diversity of national rules of procedure is such that uniformity in its application may be severely compromised. Notably, a situation converse to that accepted by the Court in *Otto* prevails in English law. The privilege against self-incrimination recognized in the Civil Evidence Act 1968 may have the effect of preventing a party alleging infringement of Article 81[85] or 82[86] from gaining access to the information necessary to prove his case.[33] In *Rio Tinzo Zinc* v. *Westinghouse Electric*,[34] the House of Lords held that section 14 of the 1968 Act extends to the discovery of documents by companies which might expose them to the risk of a fine by the Commission under Article 15 of Regulation 17. In the light of *Otto*, however, such a risk has eclipsed and the issue may be raised whether such a wide recognition of the right against self-incrimination might be incompatible with Community law in that it makes enforcement of Articles 81[85] and 82[86] by private parties in the national legal order excessively difficult.

7.2. When does the right to a fair hearing apply?

The right to a hearing was first recognized in relation to disciplinary proceedings.[35] Subsequent case law extended it to administrative proceedings which led to the imposition of sanctions on economic operators, in particular fines or penalty payments.[36] It is now well established that it is 'an absolutely fundamental principle in the administrative law of the Community'[37] and applies to all proceedings 'initiated against a person which are liable to culminate in a measure adversely affecting that person'.[38] In certain cases it may also apply in proceedings which are not

---

[32] Op.cit., para. 16.   [33] See Kerse, op.cit., p. 380.

[34] [1978] 1 All ER 434. See also *British Leyland* v. *Wyatt Interpart* [1979] 3 CMLR 79.

[35] See above *Alvis*, op.cit., n. 4.

[36] Joined Cases 56 and 58/64 *Consten and Grundig* v. *Commission* [1966] ECR 299 at 338; Case 85/76 *Hoffmann-La Roche* v. *Commission* [1979] ECR 461, para. 9.

[37] Case T–1/89 *Rhône-Poulenc* v. *Commission* [1991] ECR II–867 at 883 per Vesterdorf AG.

[38] Case C–135/92 *Fiscano* v. *Commission* [1994] ECR I–2885, para. 39; Case 234/84 *Belgium* v. *Commission* [1986] ECR 2263, para. 27; Case C–301/87 *France* v. *Commission* [1990] ECR I–307, para. 29; Joined Cases C–48/90 and C–66/90 *Netherlands and Others* v. *Commission* [1992] ECR I–565, paras. 37, 44. Note also the broad formulation in *Transocean Marine Paint Association*, according to which the right to a hearing applies in every case where a person's interests 'are perceptibly affected by a decision'. Above, n. 15.

initiated against a person but may lead to a decision directly affecting his interests.[39] The specific requirements of the right, however, may differ depending on the type of proceedings in issue. As a general principle of Community law, the right to be heard takes priority over Community legislation and therefore 'cannot be excluded or restricted by any legislative provision'.[40] Respect for it must be ensured both where there is no specific legislation and also where legislation exists but does not in itself take account of the right.[41] In principle, it is for the party concerned to raise the plea that the rights of the defence have been violated. At least in relation to the limited rights of defence enjoyed by complainants in State aid and competition law proceedings, the CFI has held those rights do not enjoy entrenched procedural protection and a plea that they have been infringed must be raised by the applicant in his original application unless it is based on matters of law or fact which came to the light in the course of the procedure.[42]

The archetypal case where the principle of *audi alteram partem* must be guaranteed is where proceedings are initiated against a person. In *Fiscano* v. *Commission*,[43] the Commission prohibited temporarily a Swedish vessel from fishing in Community waters on the ground that it had allegedly infringed the Agreement on Fisheries between the Community and Sweden. The company which owned the vessel was not granted the opportunity to be heard before the prohibition was imposed as neither the Agreement on Fisheries nor the Council Regulation ratifying it provided for a right to a hearing. The Court annulled the Commission's decision on the ground that the right to a hearing must be respected as a general principle of Community law.

A procedure is 'initiated against' a person for the purposes of the right to a hearing where it is liable to lead to a decision which directly affects his legal position even if he is not the addressee of the decision. In *Netherlands* v. *Commission*,[44] the Commission adopted a decision finding that the Netherlands law regulating postal services infringed Article 86(1)[90(1)] EC because it gave an unfair advantage to PTT, a State undertaking, vis-à-vis private messenger services. The Court held that PTT and associated undertakings had the right to be heard because they were the direct beneficiaries of the State measure in issue, they were expressly named in the postal law, the contested decision related directly to them, and its economic consequences directly affected them.[45] Similarly, in *Air Inter SA* v. *Commission*,[46] the Commission adopted a decision pursuant to Article 8 of Regulation No. 2408/92

---

[39] See below p. 252.

[40] Case T–260/94 *Air Inter* v. *Commission* [1997] ECR II–997, para. 60.

[41] Case C–32/95 P *Commission* v. *Lisrestal and Others* [1996] ECR I–5373, para. 30.

[42] Case T–106/95 *Fédération Française des Sociétés d' Assurances (FFSA) and Others* v. *Commission* [1997] ECR II–229, paras. 48–9; Case T–16/91 *Rendo and Others* v. *Commission* [1992] ECR II–2417, para. 131. The existing authorities do not preclude the possibility that in appropriate circumstances the Community judicature may raise the plea of its own motion as a matter of public policy.

[43] Op.cit.

[44] Joined Cases C–48 and C–66/90 *Netherlands and Others* v. *Commission* [1992] ECR I–565.

[45] Op.cit., para. 50.   [46] Case T–260/94 [1997] ECR II–997.

on access for Community carriers to intra-Community air routes[47] by which it prohibited France from refusing Community air carriers traffic rights over certain internal air routes. The effect of the decision was that Air Inter SA, a company to which the French Government had granted exclusive rights over those routes, could no longer enjoy exclusivity. The CFI held that although Article 8(3) did not provide for the direct participation of air carriers in the administrative procedure, the rights of defence of the persons affected should be guaranteed. Air Inter had the right to be heard because it was the direct beneficiary of the State measure which guaranteed to it privileged position. It was expressly named in that measure, it would bear the economic consequences of the contested decision, and was repeatedly mentioned in it.

The case law takes a similar approach in relation to decisions regarding financial assistance programmes. In *Lisrestal* v. *Commission*,[48] the Commission addressed a decision to the Portuguese authorities requiring partial repayment of the financial assistance which had been granted to the applicant undertakings from the European Social Fund. The request for repayment was made following inspections which revealed financial irregularities in the management of the assistance. The CFI held that the decision to reduce the assistance was taken by the Commission and not by the national authorities which, under the applicable Community rules, had no power to make their own assessment. Although the contested decision was addressed only to the Portuguese authorities, it expressly referred to the undertakings in issue which were directly and individually concerned by the contested decision. Under Regulation No. 2950/83, the primary responsibility for repayment rested with the undertakings.[49] The CFI concluded that the Commission, which alone assumes legal liability to the undertakings concerned for the contested decision, was not entitled to adopt it without first giving them the opportunity of expressing their views on the proposed reduction in assistance. On appeal, the Court of Justice confirmed the decision of the CFI stating that, even though the Member State is the sole interlocutor of the Fund, there was a direct link between the Commission and the recipient of the assistance.[50]

A common feature of the above cases is that the person claiming the right to be heard was affected by Community decisions directly and in a manner which distinguished it from other persons. It is less certain whether a right to a hearing would be recognized in relation to administrative measures of general application. In *Air Inter SA* the CFI left open the question whether the rights of defence must be respected in a case where a procedure initiated under Article 8(3) of Regulation No. 2408/92 would affect an indeterminate number of undertakings. Needless to say that the right to a hearing does not apply in relation to the adoption of Community legislation, the only obligation incumbent on the Community

---

[47] OJ 1992 L 240/8.   [48] Case T–450/93 [1994] ECR II–1177.
[49] Council Regulation No. 2950/83 on the implementation of Decision 83/516 on the tasks of the European Social Fund, OJ 1983 L 289/1.
[50] Case C–32/95 P *Commission* v. *Lisrestal and Others* [1996] ECR I–5373.

institutions in that context being the obligation of consultation as provided for in the various articles of the Treaty.[51]

In certain circumstances, the case law has extended the right to a hearing further so as to apply even in cases where proceedings cannot be said to have been initiated against a person. An important decision in this context is *Technische Universität München*.[52] Community legislation exempted from customs duty scientific instruments imported from third countries for non-commercial purposes subject to the condition that no instruments of equivalent scientific value were manufactured in the Community. Under the applicable rules, in order to reach a decision, the Commission consulted a group of experts. In *Universität München* the Commission refused the importation free of customs duty of a scientific instrument imported by the applicant on the ground that equivalent apparatus was manufactured in the Community. The decision was annulled, *inter alia*, for breach of the right to a hearing. The Court held that the importer of the scientific apparatus had the right to a hearing although the applicable regulation did not expressly provide so. It stated that the person concerned should be able to put his own case before the Commission, properly make his views known on the relevant circumstances, and, where necessary, express his views on the documents taken into account by the Commission.[53] The judgment departs from previous case law which accepted that undertakings did not have the right to be heard in relation to decisions finding that scientific instruments are not eligible for duty-free importation.[54] The Advocate General considered that the Commission's decision was invalid for lack of reasoning but was content to accept that the principle of *audi alteram partem* did not apply on the ground that the applicant did not suffer a penalty but merely the refusal of a benefit applied for.[55]

Subsequently, in *France-Aviation* v. *Commission*,[56] the CFI extended the application of *Universität München*. It held that the right to a hearing applies not only where the Commission makes 'complex technical evaluations', as was the case in *Universität München*, but in any procedure where it has power of appraisal, for example in procedures for the repayment on equitable grounds of customs duty. By contrast, in *Windpark Groothusen* v. *Commission*,[57] the CFI held that an undertaking, whose application for financial assistance under Community legislation for the promotion of energy technology had been refused, did not have the right to be heard. The CFI held that it was in accordance with the procedure in financial support programmes for candidates not to be given a hearing during the selection procedure which is conducted on the basis of the documentation submitted by them.

---

[51] Case T–521/93 *Atlanta and Others* v. *European Community* [1996] ECR II–1707.

[52] Case C–269/90 [1991] ECR I–5469.   [53] Op.cit., para. 25.

[54] See Case 185/83 *University of Gronigen* v. *Inspecteur der Invoerrechten en Accijnzen* [1984] ECR 3623; Case 203/85 *Nicolet Instrument* v. *Hauptzollamt Frankfurt am Main-Flughafen* [1986] ECR 2049; Case 303/87 *Universität Stuttgart* v. *Hauptzollamt Stuttgart-Ost* [1989] ECR 715.

[55] *Universität München*, op.cit., 5492 per Jacobs AG.

[56] Case T–346/94 [1995] ECR II–2841, paras. 33–4.

[57] Case T–109/94 [1995] ECR II–3007; confirmed on appeal C–48/96P, judgment of 14 May 1998.

The CFI noted that such procedure is appropriate in situations where hundreds of applications must be evaluated and does not therefore constitute an infringement of the right to a hearing.[58]

The view has been expressed that, where no specific legislation exists granting the right to a hearing, the recognition of such a right in cases where a person applies for a benefit is the exception rather than the rule.[59] Such a right is recognized where 'the administration has gathered evidence against him or targets him with his own behaviour while handling his application'.[60] *Windpark Groothusen* is correctly decided since it cannot be accepted that the right to a hearing must be guaranteed to every applicant whose application for a benefit is unsuccessful. In such cases, the duties of the decision-making body are to assess individually the merits of each application and to give all applicants the opportunity to support their candidature. By contrast, a right to a hearing may be established if the applicant has peculiar attributes which distinguish him from other candidates.[61] One of the differences between *Windpark Groothusen* and *Universität München* is that whereas in the first the Commission enjoyed discretion as to the eligibility of projects, in the second Community legislation granted a right of free importation provided that certain conditions were fulfilled. Also, in the latter case, the contested decision suffered from other procedural irregularities which rendered the decision-making procedure unfair as a whole. Finally, it is highly doubtful whether the recognition of a right to a hearing in circumstances such as those of *Windpark Groothusen* would be economically justifiable. In cases where a high number of applications are submitted it becomes more difficult to argue that the recognition of process rights would be an efficient method for ensuring the substantive correctness of the decision in issue.[62]

The Community administration must respect the rights of defence not only in its dealings with natural and legal persons but also in administrative proceedings involving Member States. The Member States' right to a fair hearing acquires particular importance in practice in the following cases:

- in the administrative stage of enforcement proceedings under Article 226[169];[63]
- in State aid proceedings;[64]

---

[58] But note that in a different context, it has been held that reliance on practical grounds may not justify infringement of the rights of defence: Case C–32/95 *Lisrestal*, op.cit., para. 37. Cf. Case T–30/91 *Solvay* v. *Commission* [1995] ECR II–1775, para. 102.

[59] Lenaerts and Vanhamme, op.cit., 537.   [60] Ibid.

[61] In *Windpark Groothusen* the CFI identified a second reason why the right of defence had not been infringed. That was the fact that the applicant undertaking did not request further information from the Commission following its decision not to include it in the list of successful applicants and to place its project in a reserve list.

[62] See further for the economic analysis of procedural safeguards, Craig, *Administrative Law*, pp. 298 et seq.

[63] See e.g. for an interesting difference of view between the Court and the Advocate General as to whether the rights of defence were breached, Case C–274/93 *Commission* v. *Luxembourg* [1996] ECR I–2019.

[64] See e.g. Case 234/84 *Belgium* v. *Commission* [1986] ECR 2263.

- in proceedings for the clearance of accounts presented by Member States for expenditure to be charged to the European Guidance and Guarantee Fund (EAGGF);[65]
- in proceedings relating to financial assistance programmes under the European Social Fund.[66]

Where the legal position of an undertaking is affected adversely by a decision addressed by the Commission to a Member State, the undertaking may have an interest in claiming an infringement of the principle of *audi alteram partem* also as regards the Member State. That is the case where it is an essential procedural requirement for the adoption of the contested decision that the Commission must invite the Member State to submit its observations.[67]

7.3. Content of the right to a fair hearing

The right to a hearing requires that the persons adversely affected by a decision must be placed in a position where they may 'effectively'[68] or 'properly'[69] put their own case and make known their views. The precise requirements of the right depend on the type of procedure in issue and the particular circumstances of the case. It may be said that, in general, the right to a hearing requires the following:

- the party concerned must receive an exact and complete statement of the objections raised against it;[70]
- it must have the opportunity to make its views known on the information taken into account by the decision-making body to reach the contested decision, including observations submitted by interested third parties;[71]
- the decision-making body must not take into account information and documents which it may not disclose to the party concerned because they are covered by the obligation of professional secrecy.[72]

---

[65] For an example of a successful challenge, see Case C–61/95 *Greece* v. *Commission*, [1986] ECR I–207.

[66] See Council Regulation No. 2950/83 on the implementation of Decision 83/516 on the tasks of the European Social Fund, OJ 1983 L 289/1, Article 6(1). For an example of a successful challenge, see Case C–291/89 *Interhotel* v. *Commission* [1991] ECR I–2257.

[67] *Air Inter*, op.cit., para. 80; *Interhotel*, op.cit.; Case C–304/89 *Oliveira* v. *Commission* [1991] ECR I–2283, paras. 17, 21; Joined Cases T–432 to T–434/93 *Socurte and Others* v. *Commission* [1995] ECR II–503, para. 63.

[68] Case C–301/87 *France* v. *Commission* [1990] ECR I–307. *Fiscano*, para. 40; *Lisrestal*, op.cit., para. 21.

[69] *Technische Universität München*, op.cit., para. 25; *France-Aviation* v. *Commission*, op.cit., para. 32.

[70] *Netherlands* v. *Commission*, op.cit., para. 45. To state the obvious, the right to a hearing does not impose on the authorities the obligation to accept the arguments submitted by the person concerned: Case T–155/94 *Climax Paper Converteres* v. *Council* [1996] ECR II–873, para. 118.

[71] Case C–301/87 *France* v. *Commission* [1990] ECR I–307; *Netherlands* v. *Commission*, op.cit., para. 46.

[72] See further below 7.4.

According to standard case law, the right to a hearing requires that the undertaking concerned must be afforded the opportunity to make known its views on the truth and relevance of the facts, charges and circumstances relied on by the decision maker.[73] Where the Commission decides to initiate a procedure against an undertaking on its own initiative, such as a procedure for finding an infringement of competition law, it must give a full and precise statement explaining the reasons why it decided to do so.[74] Where it initiates a procedure following a complaint by a third party, it must communicate to the undertaking the complaint or an exact and complete summary thereof.[75] In *Netherlands* v. *Commission*,[76] the Court annulled the Commission decision finding that the Netherlands law regulating postal services infringed Article 86(1)[90(1)], on the ground that the rights of defence of The Netherlands and of PTT had not been respected. Before adopting the decision, the Commission had sent a telex to the Government informing it that, in its view, the postal law was incompatible with Article 86[90]. The Government responded to that telex but the Court found that the rights of defence had not been observed because in its telex the Commission had raised only in general terms the issue of incompatibility of the postal law without setting out the various features which constituted an infringement of Article 86(1)[90(1)] as they were subsequently set out in the contested decision. Also, the Commission should have given to the Government a further hearing after it had consultations with organizations representing private messenger services since those consultations had influenced the Commission in forming the view that the law infringed Article 86[90].

The burden of proving that the necessary information has been communicated to the undertaking concerned rests on the Commission. Thus even where the information in issue can be communicated orally, the Community authorities are still under an obligation to provide evidence that the information was actually communicated.[77] Also, the Commission has the onus of proving that notification of a decision has taken place and the addressee of an unregistered letter is not required to show the reasons for any delay in the delivery.[78]

Where the Commission addresses a decision which directly affects the interests of a person to a Member State and the national authorities act as interlocutor between the Commission and the party affected, it is sufficient if the rights of defence are respected directly in the person's dealings with the Commission, or indirectly through the national authorities, or through a combination of these two administrative channels.[79] It is not sufficient, however, for the national authorities simply to inform the undertaking concerned that the Commission has undertaken

---

[73] See e.g. *Hoffman La-Roche*, op.cit., paras. 9 and 11; Case T–30/91 *Solvay* [1995] ECR II–1775 para. 59.

[74] *Air Inter*, op.cit., para. 83.   [75] Op.cit., para. 84.

[76] Joined Cases C–48 and C–66/90 *Netherlands and Others* v. *Commission* [1992] ECR I–565.

[77] Case C–49/88 *Al Jubail Fertiliser* v. *Council* [1991] ECR I–3187, para. 20.

[78] Case 108/79 *Belfiore* v. *Commission* [1980] ECR 1769, para. 7; Case 195/80 *Michel* v. *Parliament* [1981] ECR 2861, para. 11. See also *Greece* v. *Commission*, op.cit.

[79] *Air Inter*, op.cit., para. 65.

an investigation into its conduct. They must inform it of the reservations and sus-
picions of the Commission.[80] Problems may arise where the procedure leading to
the contested decision is 'mixed', namely comprises two stages, one before the
national authorities and another before the Commission. Such problems arose in
France-Aviation v. *Commission*,[81] which concerned the procedure for repayment of
customs duties. Article 13 of Regulation No. 1430/79[82] provides that import duties
may be repaid or remitted in special situations 'which result from circumstances in
which no deception or obvious negligence may be attributed to the person concerned'. The French authorities transmitted the applicant's case to the Commission
taking the view that no negligence or deception could be imputed and proposing
the repayment of customs duty. The Commission decided that repayment was not
justified on the ground that the applicant had displayed obvious negligence. The
applicant sought the annulment of that decision on grounds of breach of the principle *audi alteram partem*. The Commission argued that the right to be heard was
observed because the applicant was able to put its arguments to the French authorities which, in turn, made them available to the Commission. The Court held that
in a procedure such as that in issue the right to be heard must be secured in the first
place in the relations between the person concerned and the national administration. It continued that, although Regulation No. 2454/93[83] does not provide for
direct contacts between the Commission and the person concerned, that does not
necessarily mean that the Commission may deem itself satisfied in every case with
the information transmitted to it by the national administration. The Court found
that the file transmitted to the Commission by the French authorities omitted
material information and therefore the Commission had taken the contested decision on the basis of an incomplete file. It held that, in so far as the Commission
contemplated diverging from the recommendation of the French authorities and
rejecting the application for repayment, it had a duty to arrange for the applicant
to be heard by the French authorities.[84]

In *France-Aviation* the purpose of the hearing was to remedy the insufficiency of
the information submitted by the national authority to the Commission. The CFI
took a unitary conception of public authorities making in effect the Commission
responsible for rectifying the defects in the national administrative proceedings.

---

[80] Case C–32/95 P *Commission* v. *Lisrestal*, op.cit., paras. 41–2.

[81] Case T–346/94 *France-Aviation* v. *Commission* [1995] ECR II–2841. Cf. Joined Cases C–121 and
C–122/91 *CT Control (Rotterdam) and JCT Benelux* v. *Commission* [1993] ECR I–3873. See also Case
294/81 *Control Data* v. *Commission* [1983] ECR 911; Joined Cases 98 and 230/83 *Van Gend en Loos* v.
Commission [1984] ECR 3763.

[82] See Council Regulation (EEC) No. 1430/79 on the repayment or remission of import or export
duties (OJ 1979 L 175/1) as amended by Council Regulation (EEC) No. 3069/86 (OJ 1986 L 286/1).

[83] Commission Regulation No. 2454/93 laying down rules for the implementation of the
Community Customs Code, OJ 1993 L 253/1.

[84] Op.cit., para. 36.

7.4. Fair hearing and confidentiality

As stated above, the right to a hearing requires the Commission to inform the undertaking concerned of the facts upon which the Commission's adverse decision is based. The requirement to disclose the necessary information, however, may come into conflict with the obligation of professional secrecy incumbent upon the institutions. Article 287[214] EC states that Community officials and other employees must not 'disclose information of the kind covered by the obligation of professional secrecy, in particular information about undertakings, their business relations or their costs components'.[85] How are the two principles to be compromised? The general answer given in the case law is that the Commission may not use to the detriment of an undertaking facts or documents which it is under an obligation not to disclose, where the failure to make such disclosure adversely affects the undertaking's opportunity to be heard.[86] Where a document has not been disclosed by the Commission, it is for the undertaking concerned to show that it has been deprived of evidence needed for its defence.[87]

In general, the case law accords confidential status to the following categories of documents:[88] (a) confidential documents belonging to third parties; (b) internal Commission documents;[89] (c) correspondence between the Commission and Member States or other international bodies. The first category encompasses business secrets, correspondence between undertakings and their lawyers,[90] and correspondence between the Commission and third parties, for example complainants or customers who collaborated with the Commission during the investigation and may fear that the undertaking will adopt retaliatory measures against them.[91] Business secrets are afforded 'very special protection' and third parties may under no circumstances be given access to documents containing business secrets.[92] Whether a document contains a business secret is for the Commission and, ultimately, the Court to decide. The Commission may not disclose a document which

---

[85] The obligation to respect business confidentiality receives mention also in specific Community measures, see e.g. Article 20(2) of Regulation No. 17.

[86] *Hoffman-La Roche*, op.cit., para. 14; C–62/86 *AKZO* v. *Commission* [1986] ECR I–3359, para. 21; Case 234/84 *Belgium* v. *Commission* [1986] ECR 2263, para. 29.

[87] Joined Cases 209–15 and 218/78 *Van Landewyck* v. *Commission* (*FEDETAB*) [1984] ECR 3125, para. 39, and see Case C–310/93 P *BPB Industries and British Gypsum* v. *Commission* [1995] ECR I–865, at 887 per Léger AG.

[88] Lenaerts and Vanhamme, op.cit., 541; Levitt, op.cit., p. 1424; and see *BPB Industries* op.cit., paras. 25 *et seq.*

[89] In competition law, internal Commission documents which are not accessible include the hearing officer's report: see Case T–2/89 *Petrofina* v. *Commission* [1991] ECR II–1087, para. 55; and the opinion of the Advisory Committee which, as provided in Article 10(6) of Regulation No. 17, is not made public: see *Musique Diffusion Française*, op.cit., para. 36.

[90] See Case T–30/89 *Hilti* [1990] ECR II–163.   [91] *BPB*, op.cit., para. 26.

[92] Case 53/85 *AKZO Chemie* v. *Commission* [1986] ECR 1965, para. 28; Joined Cases 142 and 156/84 *BAT and Reynolds* v. *Commission* [1987] ECR 4487, para. 21. But unauthorized disclosure does not necessarily lead to annulment of the Commission's decision finding an infringement: see below 7.5.

the undertaking subject to investigation claims to contain a business secret without first giving to that undertaking the opportunity to express its views and bring an action before the Court to prevent disclosure.[93] However, the obligation to protect business secrets must be balanced with two important countervailing principles: the rights of the defence and the public interest in the administration of justice.[94] The Commission's notice concerning access to the file in competition proceedings expressly provides for this balancing exercise.[95] It states as follows:

Where business secrets provide evidence of an infringement or tend to exonerate a firm, the Commission must reconcile the interest in the protection of sensitive information, the public interest in having the infringement of the competition rules terminated, and the rights of the defence. This calls for an assessment of:

(i) the relevance of the information to determining whether or not an infringement has been committed;
(ii) its probative value;
(iii) whether it is indispensable;
(iv) the degree of sensitivity involved (to what extent would disclosure of the information harm the interests of the firm?);
(v) the seriousness of the infringement. Each document must be assessed individually to determine whether the need to disclose is greater than the harm which might result from disclosure.

The Court has held that Article 287[214] EC must be interpreted is such a way that rights of defence are not deprived of their substance. A notable example is provided by *Timex* v. *Council and Commission*.[96] In that case, the Court annulled a Council regulation imposing anti-dumping duties on the ground that the Commission had wrongly failed to disclose certain information to the complainant because it considered that it was covered by the obligation of confidentiality. The Court held that the Commission ought to have made every effort, as far as was compatible with the obligation not to disclose business secrets, to supply the complainant with information relevant to the defence of its interest, choosing on its own initiative the appropriate means of providing such information. Thus a request by a party that information should not be disclosed for reasons of business secrets is not a trump card which compromises *simpliciter* the rights of defence. In the *Soda-Ash* cases[97] the CFI made it clear that the Commission must protect the business secrets of an undertaking in such a way as to cause the least possible interference with the right

---

[93] *AKZO*, op.cit., and see for anti-dumping proceedings Case 236/81 *Celanese* v. *Council and Commission* [1982] ECR 1183.

[94] For the protection of the administration of justice, see Case 110/84 *Municipality of Hillegom* v. *Hillenius* [1985] ECR 3947.

[95] Commission Notice 97/C23/03 on the internal rules of procedure for processing requests for access to the file in cases pursuant to Arts. 85 and 86 EC, Arts. 65 and 66 ECSC and Council Reg. (EEC) No. 406/89, OJ 1997 C 23/3.

[96] Case 264/82 [1985] ECR 849.

[97] Case T–30/91 *Solvay* v. *Commission* [1995] ECR I–1775, paras. 89 *et seq.*; Case T–36/91 *ICI* v. *Commission* [1995] ECR I–1847, paras. 99 *et seq.*

to a hearing. In particular, the CFI found that in the circumstances of the case the Commission had two options. It could either prepare non-confidential versions of the documents annexed to the statement of objections by deleting confidential passages, or if that was difficult, it could send a list of the documents annexed to the statement of objections giving the opportunity to the applicant to request specific documents. If the applicant requested documents which might contain business secrets, then the Commission should contact the undertaking concerned with a view to ascertaining which passages contained sensitive information and should therefore be kept secret from the applicant.

The Commission's refusal to disclose a document is a preparatory act which cannot be challenged under Article 230[173] during the course of the administrative procedure. The undertaking concerned may only challenge the final decision of the Commission. This is because, until a final decision has been adopted, the Commission may abandon or amend its objections or rectify procedural irregularities which may have occurred by granting access to the file.[98] By contrast, the decision of the Commission to disclose certain documents to a third party, for example, the complainant, may be challenged by the undertaking which considers that the documents contain business secrets and objects to disclosure. This is because the decision to disclose has irreversible consequences. The damage done by disclosure cannot be repaired whether the Commission's final decision is upheld or annulled.[99]

7.5. Consequences of failure to observe

The Community judicature views the right to a hearing as a functional rather than as an objective requirement. Infringement of the right leads to the annulment of the act in question only if it can be shown that the outcome of the procedure might have been different had the right to a hearing been respected.[100] In *Belgium* v. *Commission*,[101] the Belgian Government sought the annulment of a decision finding that State aid which had been granted to a company was unlawful on the ground that the Commission took into account representations made by other States and by competing undertakings without giving the opportunity to the Government to comment on those representations. The Court's response was to require the Commission to produce the observations made by third parties. After examining them, it found that they contained no information in addition to that which the Commission already possessed and of which the Belgian Government

---

[98] *Cimenteries CBR*, op.cit., para. 47.

[99] Case 53/85 *AKZO* v. *Commission* [1986] ECR 1965.

[100] Case T–7/89 *Hercules Chemicals* v. *Commission* [1991] ECR I–1711, para. 56; Case C–142/87 *Belgium* v. *Commission (Tubemeuse)* [1990] ECR I–959, para. 48; Case 234/84 *Belgium* v. *Commission* [1986] ECR 2263, para. 30; Case 30/78 *Distillers Company* v. *Commission* [1980] ECR 2229, para. 26.

[101] *Tubemeuse*, op.cit.

was already aware. Under those circumstances, the fact that the Belgian Government had no opportunity to comment on the observations was not of such a nature as to influence the result of the administrative procedure.[102]

It may be objected that the right to a hearing is a requirement of form, not one of substance, and that whether the hearing might have made a difference to the outcome should be irrelevant.[103] The courts should not attempt to step *ex posto facto* into the shoes of the administration. *Belgium* v. *Commission*, however, does not suggest that the Court attempts to second guess what would have been the outcome of the procedure had the right to a hearing been respected. It merely exercises a residual control based on the criterion of reasonableness. Is it conceivable that the outcome *might* have been different if a hearing had been given? Only if that question is answered in the affirmative, may breach of the rights of defence be sanctioned by annulment. The limits of this residual control were pinpointed by the CFI in *Solvay*.[104] The applicant's argument was that the Commission had taken into account documents which it had not disclosed to the applicant. The CFI held:[105]

. . . it is not for the Court of First Instance to rule definitively on the evidential value of all the evidence used by the Commission to support the contested decision. In order to find that the rights of the defence have been infringed, it is sufficient for it to be established that the non-disclosure of the documents in question might have influenced the course of the procedure and the content of the decision to the applicant's detriment. The possibility of such an influence can therefore be established if a provisional examination of some of the evidence shows that the documents not disclosed might—in the light of that evidence— have had a significance which ought not to have been disregarded. If it were proved that the rights of the defence were infringed, the administrative procedure and the appraisal of the facts in the decision would be defective.

The approach of the Community courts can best be described as pragmatic. It seeks to balance two conflicting principles: on the one hand, to uphold the rights of the defence as procedural safeguards for the protection of the individual and, on the other hand, to avoid undue formalism which might encourage abusive reliance on procedural principles. The undertaking concerned must prove that the results might be different if the documents in issue had been disclosed. It seems that, overall, the burden imposed on the undertaking is not a difficult one to discharge.[106]

---

[102] Op.cit., para. 48. A similar approach had been followed much earlier in *Alvis* v. *Council*, op.cit. There a Community official was dismissed for gross misconduct without first being given the opportunity to express his views on the allegations made against him. The Court held that the rights of the defence had been breached but took the view that the breach was not sufficient to annul the decision of dismissal as it was correct in substance. The judgment appears to fly in the face of process rights but could be defended on the ground that the Court was exercising 'unlimited' and not merely supervisory jurisdiction.

[103] See the discussion in Craig, op.cit., p. 301.

[104] Case T–30/91 *Solvay* v. *Commission* [1995] ECR II–1775.   [105] Op.cit., para. 68.

[106] Depending on the circumstances, the Court may not even examine the assertion of the defendant institution that even if a hearing had been given, the outcome would not have been different. See e.g. *Al-Jubail*, op.cit.; cf. Opinion of Darmon AG at 3226.

The consequences of failing to observe the right to a hearing will depend on the circumstances of the case. The Court seeks to establish whether the procedure, as a whole, has been fair. In a number of cases decisions of the Commission have been annulled wholly or in part.[107] But where the breach of the right to a hearing relates to matters of secondary importance, it may not affect the validity of the decision as a whole.[108] Thus where the Commission fails to communicate to the undertaking concerned documents which it has taken into account, that may result in those documents being excluded as evidence. It would not lead to the annulment of the entire decision unless the objection raised by the Commission could be proved only by reference to those documents.[109] In one case[110] the decision to disclose confidential information to a complainant was annulled even though disclosure had already taken place. But in another case[111] disclosure to the complainant of confidential information relating to the target undertaking was held not to vitiate the Commission's final decision because it did not affect its substance.

A related issue is whether irregularities during the administrative procedure may be remedied in the course of the proceedings before the Court. As a matter of principle, to admit such *ex posto facto* remedy would negate the value of process rights. The case law gives contradictory signs focusing in effect on whether the irregularity has been serious. In *Hoffmann-La Roche* v. *Commission*, it was held that breach of the rights of defence during the administrative procedure before the Commission may be remedied in the proceedings before the Court itself if such belated remedy does not prejudice the interests of the person concerned.[112] That finding was criticized in a subsequent Opinion.[113] In *Solvay*, the CFI followed a more orthodox approach, holding that the Commission's failure to disclose certain documents was not justified by the obligation to respect professional secrecy and that the ensuing breach of the rights of defence could not be regularized during the proceedings before the CFI.[114]

In practice, the right to a hearing acquires particular importance in the following areas: competition, anti-dumping, State aids,[115] staff cases, and proceedings relating to financial assistance programmes.[116] By way of illustration, it will be examined by reference to the areas where it is most oft-invoked, namely competition,

---

[107] See e.g. *Solvay*, op.cit., and Case T–36/91 *ICI* v. *Commission* (*Soda Ash* cases) [1995] ECR II–1847; Joined Cases C–89/85 etc. *Ahlström Osakeyhtiö and Others* v. *Commission* [1993] ECR 1307; *Al-Jubail*, op.cit.; *Fiscano*, op.cit.; *Netherlands* v. *Commission*, op.cit., *France-Aviation* v. *Commission*, op.cit.

[108] *Musique Diffusion Française* v. *Commission* [1983] ECR 1825, para. 30.

[109] Case 107/82 *AEG* v. *Commission* [1983] ECR 3151, para. 30; cf. *Solvay*, op.cit., paras. 58 and 97.

[110] Case 53/85 *AKZO Chemie* v. *Commission* [1986] ECR 1965, para. 28.

[111] Joined Cases 209–15 and 218/78 *Van Landewyck* v. *Commission* [1980] ECR 3125, paras. 46–7.

[112] Case 85/76 [1979] ECR 461, para. 15.

[113] *Distillers Company*, op.cit., at 2297–8 per Warner AG.

[114] *Solvay*, op.cit., para. 98; Case T–36/91 *ICI*, op.cit., para. 113.

[115] For examples on State aids, see Case 234/84 *Belgium* v. *Commission* [1986] ECR 2263; Case C–142/87 *Belgium* v. *Commission* [1990] ECR I–959; Case C–301/87 *France* v. *Commission* (*Boussac* case) [1990] ECR I–307.

[116] See e.g. *Lisrestal*, op.cit.; *Windpark Groothusen*, op.cit.

anti-dumping, and staff cases. There is no intention to be exhaustive but rather to show the approach of the Community judicature in selected areas.

7.6. Competition proceedings

The right to a hearing has given rise to extensive litigation in the context of competition proceedings.[117] Article 85[89] EC charges the Commission with the responsibility to enforce Community competition law and investigate suspected infringements of Articles 81[85] and 82[86]. The powers of the Commission are provided for in Regulation 17.[118] The procedure before the Commission is administrative and not judicial in character[119] but this does not affect the rights of the defence which, as already stated, must be respected in all proceedings liable to culminate in a decision having adverse consequences for the person concerned.[120]

Article 19 of Regulation 17 provides that before taking certain decisions the Commission must give the undertaking or associations of undertakings concerned the opportunity of being heard on the matters to which the Commission has taken objection. This applies, in particular, to decisions concerning negative clearances, the finding of an infringement, individual exemptions, and the imposition of fines or periodic penalty payments.[121] Matters regarding the hearing are regulated by Regulation No. 99/63.[122] Apart from the undertakings or associations of undertakings concerned, any other persons who are able to show a sufficient interest must be afforded the opportunity to make their views known.[123] Failure to hear third parties who are able to show sufficient interest may result in the annulment of the decision.[124]

[117] See, among others, C. S. Kerse, *EC Anti-Trust Procedure* (1994), Ch. 4; Bellamy and Child, *Common Market Law of Competition*, Ch. 12; 'Droits de la défense et droits de la Commission dans le droit communautaire de la concurrence', Proceedings of the Colloquium held on 24 and 25 Jan. 1994 by the Association européenne des avocats, Bruylant, 1994; V. Korah, 'The Rights of the Defence in Administrative Proceedings Under Community Law' (1980) 33 CLP 73.

[118] First Regulation implementing Articles 85 and 86 of the Treaty, OJ, English Spec.Ed., 1959–62, p. 87.

[119] According to the case law, the Commission is not a 'tribunal' within the meaning of Article 6(1) ECHR. See Joined Cases 100–3/80 *Musique Diffusion Française* v. *Commission* [1983] ECR 1825, para. 7; Case T–11/89 *Shell* v. *Commission* [1992] ECR II–757, para. 39. Note, however, that in Joined Cases T–213/95 and T–18/96 *SCK and FNK* v. *Commission* [1997] ECR II–1739, para. 56, the CFI left open the issue whether Article 6(1) applies to administrative proceedings before the Commission relating to competition law. The issue was whether the Commission had breached Article 6(1) by delaying the adoption of a decision finding an infringement for an unreasonable time. The CFI held that, in any event, it is a general principle of Community law that the Commission must act within a reasonable time in adopting decisions following administrative proceedings. It was therefore not necessary to examine whether Article 6(1) was applicable as such.

[120] See above n. 35 and Case 85/76 *Hoffmann-La Roche* v. *Commission* [1979] ECR 461, para. 9.

[121] This provision, however, does not prejudice the all-embracing character of the right to a hearing. See *Transocean Marine Paint Association case*, op.cit.

[122] OJ, English Spec.Ed., 1963–4, p. 47.

[123] Regulation 17, Article 19(2) ; Reg. 99/63, Articles 5, 7(1).

[124] Joined Cases 228 and 229/82 *Ford* v. *Commission* [1984] ECR 1129 at 1174–5 per Slynn AG. See also Joined Cases 209–15 and 218/79 *Van Landewyck* v. *Commission* [1980] ECR 3125, para. 17.

Where the Commission considers that there has been a violation, it must provide the undertakings concerned with a statement of objections.[125] The undertakings and persons able to show sufficient interest have the right to a hearing.[126] Regulation No. 99/63 distinguishes between the right to submit written comments and the right to be heard orally. The Commission must give to natural or legal persons who show a sufficient interest the opportunity to make their views known in writing within such time limit as it may fix.[127] The Commission must also afford to persons who have so requested in their written comments the opportunity to put forward their arguments orally, if those persons show a sufficient interest or if the Commission proposes to impose on them a fine or periodic penalty payment.[128] The Commission may likewise afford to any other person the opportunity to present oral observations.[129] Hearings are conducted by officers appointed by the Commission for this purpose. The hearing is not public but persons attending may be represented by their legal advisers.[130] In its decision, the Commission may deal only with those objections raised against undertakings which are contained in the statement of objections and in respect of which they have been afforded the opportunity of making known their views.[131]

Where a plea is raised that the rights of the defence have been breached, the claim is usually that the Commission failed to disclose to the party concerned information on which its decision was based.[132] A vexed question is whether undertakings investigated by the Commission in relation to a violation of Articles 81[85] or 82[86] have the right of access to the administrative file established by the Commission.[133] Regulations No. 17 and No. 99/63 are silent on the issue. By contrast, the Merger Regulation, adopted in 1989, provides for access to the complete file in relation to mergers.[134] The traditional stance of the Court of Justice has been

---

[125] Reg. 99/63, Article 2(1).

[126] The undertakings concerned may waive their right to a hearing: Joined Cases T–213/95 and T–18/96 *SCK and FNK* v. *Commission* [1997] ECR II–1739, para. 219. The Commission, however, may omit to communicate documents only where the undertaking concerned has declared its intention unambiguously: Case T–30/91 *Solvay* v. *Commission* [1995] ECR II–1775, para. 57.

[127] Reg. 99/63, Article 5.   [128] Op.cit., Article 7(1).

[129] Op.cit., para. 7(2). The Commission enjoys reasonable discretion in deciding which persons to hear: Joined Cases 43 and 63/82 *VBVB and VBBB* v. *Commission* [1984] ECR 19, para. 18; Case 43/85 *Ancides* v. *Commission* [1987] ECR 3131.

[130] Op.cit., Article 9.

[131] Op.cit., Article 4. See Joined Cases T–213/95 and T–18/96 *SCK and FNK* v. *Commission* [1997] ECR II–1739, para. 65. Note, however, that the Commission decision need not be a replica of the statement of objections: Joined Cases 209–15 and 218/78 *Van Landewyck* v. *Commission* [1980] ECR 3125, paras. 68–70; *Musique Diffusion Française*, op.cit., paras. 19–20. But the Commission must set out clearly and distinctly in the statement of objections each of the infringements which it claims to have taken place: Joined Cases C–89/85 etc. *Ahlström Osakeyhtiö and Others* v. *Commission* [1993] ECR 1307.

[132] See e.g. *Musique Diffusion Française*, op.cit., paras. 24 *et seq.*

[133] See for detailed discussions, M. Levitt, 'Access to the File: The Commission's Administrative Procedures in Cases under Articles 85 and 86' (1997) 34 CMLRev. 1413; Ehlermann and Drijber, 'Legal Protection of Enterprises: Administrative Procedure, in particular Access to File and Confidentiality' (1996) ECLR 375. See further Lenaerts in FIDE, op.cit., pp. 519 *et seq.*

[134] Council Regulation (EEC) No. 4064/89 on the control of concentrations between undertakings, OJ 1989, L 395/1. Article 18(3) states: 'Access to the file shall be open at least to the parties

that the rights of defence do not include the right to have access to the complete file. In *VBVB and VBBB* v. *Commission*, the Court held, confirming previous case law, that the Commission is under no obligation to divulge the contents of the complete file and, in order to respect the rights of defence, only those documents on which the Commission has based its decision must be made available.[135] An undertaking may complain that the Commission has failed to disclose a document only if it can adduce evidence that the Commission has based its decision on documents which were not made public.[136]

In fact, on its own accord, the Commission promised to adhere to higher standards. In its Twelfth Report on Competition Policy, it undertook to disclose to undertakings the documents in the file concerning them, whether incriminating or exculpatory, and to permit the undertakings involved in the procedure to inspect the file of the case.[137] The CFI has held that the Commission may not depart from the rules which it has imposed on itself. In *Hercules Chemicals* v. *Commission*,[138] it derived from the Twelfth Report an obligation incumbent on the Commission to make available to the undertakings involved in proceedings under Article 81(1)[85(1)] all documents, whether in their favour or otherwise, which it has obtained during the course of the investigation, save where the business secrets of other undertakings, the internal documents of the Commission, or other confidential information are involved.[139]

Subsequently, in *Solvay*[140] and *ICI*[141] (*Soda Ash* cases), the CFI saw the right of access to the file as an integral part of the rights of defence. It held that the purpose of providing access to the file is to allow the addressees of a statement of objections to examine the evidence in the Commission's file so that they are in a position effectively to express their views on the conclusions reached by the Commission on the basis of the evidence. Access to the file is thus one of the procedural guarantees intended to protect the rights of the defence and to ensure the exercise of the right to be heard.[142]

In *BPB Industries and British Gypsum* v. *Commission*,[143] Léger AG also took the view that the right of access to the file should be recognized as an integral part of

directly involved, subject to the legitimate interest of undertakings in the protection of their business secrets'.

[135] Joined Cases 43 and 63/82 [1984] ECR 19, para. 25. See also Joined Cases 56 and 58/64 *Consten and Grundig* v. *Commission* [1966] ECR 299, at 338; Case 42/69 *ACF Chemiefarma* v. *Commission* [1970] ECR 661, para. 42; Case C–62/86 *AKZO* v. *Commission* [1991] ECR I–3359, para. 16.

[136] Case 322/81 *Michelin* v. *Commission* [1983] ECR 3461, paras. 7 and 9; Case C–310/93 P *BPB Industries and British Gypsum* v. *Commission* [1995] ECR I–865, at 887 per Léger AG; *SCK and FNK*, op.cit., para. 220.

[137] Twelfth Report on Competition Policy, pp. 40–1

[138] T–7/89 [1991] ECR II–1711, para. 53.   [139] Op.cit., para. 54.

[140] Case T–30/91 *Solvay* v. *Commission* [1995] ECR II–1775.

[141] Case T–36/91 *ICI* v. *Commission* [1995] ECR II–1847.

[142] *Solvay* , op.cit., para. 59; *ICI*, op.cit., para. 69. See also Joined Cases T–10 to T–12, T–15/92 *Cimenteries CBR and Others* v. *Commission* [1992] ECR II–2667, para. 38; T–65/89 *BPB Industries and British Gypsum* v. *Commission* [1993] ECR II–389, paras. 30–1.

[143] Case C–310/93 P [1995] ECR I–865.

the rights of defence. He put forward three arguments.[144] First, a right of access to the file is recognized in relation to mergers.[145] Secondly, such a right is enshrined in the laws of a number of Member States. It would be incongruous if undertakings enjoyed a lower degree of protection in Community law given especially that a finding of infringement of Community competition law leads to more severe financial implications. Thirdly, in its Twelfth and subsequently in its Twenty Third Report on Competition Policy,[146] the Commission itself has shown willingness to raise the standard of protection. He concluded that an undertaking under investigation is entitled to have access to the whole file, save where the business secrets of other undertakings, the internal documents of the Commission, or other confidential information are involved.[147] In its judgment, the Court was more reticent. It did not expressly endorse the Opinion of the Advocate General and chose instead to repeat the standard formula that observance of the rights of the defence requires that the undertaking must have been enabled to express its views effectively on the documents used by the Commission to support its allegation for an infringement.[148]

Subsequent judgments of the CFI suggest that there is no absolute right of access to the file in the sense that the Community courts will not annul failure to disclose a document in the file unless it has affected adversely the exercise of the right to a hearing.[149] The party concerned must be communicated, and have the opportunity to express its views on, the documents on which the Commission based its decision. Whether the rights of defence require in addition complete access to the file will depend on the circumstances of the case. The undertaking concerned must adduce evidence to show that undisclosed documents belonging to the file might contain information material to its defence.[150] Overall it could be said that the law as it stands does not provide the parties concerned with the requisite degree of clarity.[151] The view expressed by Ole Due in 1987[152] that the case law has not as yet provided a clear and satisfactory answer to the parties' access to the administrative file remains to a good extent valid today.

It may be noted that providing access to the compete file, subject to confidentiality, is not without problems. It is particularly onerous where a large number of parties are involved and some of the documents may have only remote connection with the case in issue.[153] On the other hand, it must be accepted that giving access

---

[144] Op.cit., 890 *et seq.*

[145] See above n. 134.

[146] COM(94) 161, 5 May 1994, point 202.

[147] Op.cit., 892.

[148] Para. 21. The judgment could be interpreted as accepting by implication that the Commission may refuse disclosure of documents to the party concerned only if the document is confidential and not because the Commission did not rely on it in making its decision: see paras. 23–4. It is doubtful, however, whether that is the true meaning of the judgment.

[149] Case T–145/89 *Baustahlgewebe* v. *Commission* [1995] ECR II–987; *SCK and FNK*, op.cit.

[150] *SCK and FNK*, op.cit., para. 220.

[151] Note also that the term 'file' lacks an objective, generally agreed, meaning. See Levitt, op.cit. 1420.

[152] Due, op.cit., 396.

[153] See further Korah, *EC Competition Law and Practice*, p. 125, and J. M. Joshua, 'Balancing the Public Interests: Confidentiality, Trade Secrets and Disclosure of Evidence in EC Competition Procedures' (1994) 2 ECLR 68.

provides added guarantees for the undertakings under investigation. It acquires particular importance in cases where the Commission adopts composite statements of objections, i.e. statements which assert multiple violations by a number of undertakings. The main argument in favour of giving access to the complete file is to ensure that the Commission has assessed the documents correctly. Also, it should not be left to the Commission to decide which documents are useful for the defence. In the *Soda Ash* cases the CFI expressly pointed out that, where difficult and complex economic appraisals are to be made, the Commission must give the advisers of the undertakings concerned the opportunity to examine documents which may be relevant so that their probative value for the defence can be assessed.[154]

Complainants do not enjoy, strictly speaking, rights of defence but 'merely a right to defend their legitimate interests'.[155] Even in relation to complainants, however, the case law has recognized more extensive process rights than those provided by written law. Article 6 of Regulation No. 99/63 states that where the Commission, having received a complaint, considers that there are insufficient grounds for granting the application it must inform the complainants of its reasons and invite them to submit further comments in writing.[156] The regulation does not require the Commission to respond to any further submissions made. In *Automec II*,[157] the CFI held that although the Commission is not required to investigate alleged anti-competitive conduct following the submission of a complaint, it is under an obligation to examine with due care the factual and legal points raised by the complainant and, in a case where it decides to reject the complaint, provide a fully reasoned final decision. Suffice it to make two points in relation to the judgment. First, the Court saw the imposition of more extensive procedural requirements as counterbalancing the recognition of broad discretion to the Commission to prioritize its tasks in the light of what the Community interest requires.[158]

---

[154] *Solvay*, op.cit., para. 81; *ICI*, op.cit., para. 91.

[155] *BPB Industries*, op.cit., at 888 per Léger AG, and Joined Cases 142 and 156/84 *BAT and Reynolds* v. *Commission* [1987] ECR 4487, para. 20. In that case, the Court stated: 'the procedural rights of the complainants are not as far-reaching as the right to a fair hearing of the companies which are the object of the Commission's investigation. In any event, the limits of such rights are reached where they begin to interfere with those companies' right to a fair hearing.' For a detailed account, see Kerse, 'The Complainant in Competition Cases: A Progress Report' (1997) 34 CMLRev. 213; Vesterdof, 'Complaints concerning infringements of competition law within the context of European Community Law' (1994) 31 CMLRev. 77.

[156] In Case C–282/95 P *Guérin Automobiles* v. *Commission* [1997] ECR I–1503, the Court held that the notification to the complainant under Article 6 amounts to a definition of position for the purposes of Article 232[175] but is not a final act subject to challenge under Article 230[173]. Cf. the Opinion of Tesauro AG. For previous case law, see Case T–37/92 *BEUC and NCC* v. *Commission* [1994] ECR II–285, para. 30.

[157] Case T–24/90 *Automec* v. *Commission* [1992] ECR II–2223.

[158] For cases where the Court annulled the Commission decision rejecting a complaint on the ground that it was inadequately reasoned, see Case T–37/92 *BEUC* v. *Commission* [1994] ECR II–285 and Case T–7/92 *Asia Motor France and Others* v. *Commission* [1993] ECR II–669. Cf. Case T–114/92 *BEMIM* v. *Commission* [1995] ECR II–147; Case T–5/93 *Tremblay and Others* [1995] ECR II–185. See also for the same principle in State aids: Case T–95/94 *Sytraval and Brink's France* v. *Commission* [1995] ECR II–2651, para. 78.

Secondly, the process rights established in favour of complainants seem to derive less from the right to a hearing and more from the general principles of legality and good administration.[159]

7.7. Anti-dumping proceedings

Regulation No. 384/96[160] expressly provides for the rights of defence of interested parties. Anti-dumping proceedings are initiated at the behest of a complaint or, in special circumstances, by the Commission itself, through the publication of a notice in the Official Journal. Article 6(5) states that interested parties who have made themselves known must be heard provided that the following conditions are fulfilled: (a) they must make a written request to that effect within the period specified in the notice; (b) they must show that they are an interested party likely to be affected by the result of the proceedings, and that there are particular reasons why they should be heard. It has been noted that there are two major differences between the right to a hearing in anti-dumping proceedings and in competition proceedings.[161] Unlike Regulation No. 99/63, Regulation No. 384/96 does not require the Commission to invite complainants to submit further comments where it intends to dismiss the complaint. Also, the oral hearing acquires more importance in anti-dumping proceedings.[162] A third difference which may be added is that the need for confidentiality is exacerbated in anti-dumping proceedings because of their often politically sensitive nature and the involvement of governments of third States.[163]

Article 6(7) of Regulation No. 384/96 provides that interested parties[164] may, upon written request, inspect all information made available to any party in the investigation, as distinct from internal documents prepared by the authorities of the Community or the Member States, which is relevant to the presentation of their cases provided that it is not confidential and that it is used in the investigation. In *Al Jubail Fertiliser* v. *Council*,[165] it was held that the provisions of the basic

---

[159] See the cases referred in the previous footnote and *Guérin Automobiles* v. *Commission*, op.cit., para. 37.

[160] Council Regulation No. 384/96 on protection against dumped imports from countries not members of the European Community, OJ 1996 L 56/1, as amended.

[161] Lenaerts, in FIDE, op.cit., at p. 517. See further O. Due, 'Le respect des droits de la défense dans le droit administratif communautaire' (1987) CDE 383 at 387.

[162] To this effect, Article 6(6) provides for an adversarial procedure, where importers, exporters, representatives of the government of the exporting country, and complainants are given the opportunity to meet each other so that the opposing views may be presented.

[163] See further Von Heydebrand und der Lasa, 'Confidential Information in Anti-dumping Proceedings before United States Courts and the European Court' (1986) 11 ELRev. 331.

[164] This includes the complainants, importers and exporters and their representative associations, users, and consumer organisations which have made themselves known, as well as the representatives of the exporting country. See Article 6(7).

[165] Case C–49/88 [1991] ECR I–3187.

regulation[166] must be interpreted in the light of the right to a hearing as a fundamental right of general application. According to the judgment, the right must be
respected in anti-dumping proceedings despite the fact that anti-dumping measures
are imposed by means of general regulations rather than individual decisions. The
main consideration which led the Court to take that view was that anti-dumping
regulations, although of general scope, affect directly and individually the undertakings concerned and entail adverse consequences for them. In *Al Jubail* the
Commission had relied, *inter alia*, on internal documents drawn up by its officials,
the contents of which had not been placed at the disposal of the undertakings
against which the duty was imposed. It was held that those documents could not
be accorded any probative force. In reaching that conclusion, the Court was concerned to ensure that Community law did not provide a lesser standard of procedural protection than that which was recognized by national laws.[167] The Court
held that the institutions should seek with all due diligence,[168]

to provide the undertakings concerned, as far as is compatible with the obligation not to disclose business secrets, with information relevant to the defence of their interests, choosing,
if necessary on their own initiative, the appropriate means of providing such information. In
any event, the undertakings concerned should have been placed in a position during the
administrative procedure in which they could effectively make known their views on the
correctness and relevance of the facts and circumstances alleged and on the evidence presented by the Commission in support of its allegation concerning the existence of dumping
and the resultant injury.

The importance of *Al Jubail* lies in that the Court continued the trend towards a
broad application of the right to a hearing, developed first in relation to competition proceedings, despite the differences between the latter and anti-dumping
investigations. Following the judgment in *Al Jubail* it became increasingly common
for undertakings on which anti-dumping duties were imposed to challenge the
legality of the duty on grounds of breach of the rights of defence. In the overwhelming majority of those cases the challenge has proved unsuccessful.[169]

   Under the case law, the undertakings concerned must be informed during the
anti-dumping proceedings of the principal facts and considerations on which the
Community authorities based their decision. Not all aspects of the decision-
making process are subject to the right to a hearing. Thus, it is within the discretion of the Council to choose any one of the methods provided for by the
Community rules for the purposes of calculating the export price and therefore the
Council is under no obligation to give to the undertaking concerned the opportunity to present its observations in advance.[170] Also the CFI has held that failure to

---

[166] The basic regulation applicable at the time was Regulation No. 2176/84, OJ 1984 L 201/1.
[167] See para. 16 and per Darmon AG at 3224.   [168] Op.cit., para. 17.
[169] See e.g. Case C–69/89 *Nakajima* v. *Council* [1991] ECR I–2069; Case T–155/94 *Climax Paper
Converters* v. *Council* [1996] ECR II–873; cf. Case C–216/91 *Rima* [1993] ECR I–6303 where a Council
regulation imposing a definitive anti-dumping duty was annulled on procedural grounds.
[170] Case C–178/87 *Minolta* v. *Council* [1992] ECR I–1577; *Al Jubail*, op.cit., para. 24.

communicate information and considerations which did not form part of the statement of reasons of the contested decision, and which is simply confirmatory in
character, does not amount to a breach of the right to a hearing.[171]

Article 6(5) is supplemented by Article 20. Article 20(1) states that the complainants, importers and exporters and their representative associations, and representatives of the exporting country may request disclosure of the details underlying
the essential facts and considerations on the basis of which provisional measures
have been imposed. Under Article 20(2) those parties also have the right to request
final disclosure of the essential facts and considerations on the basis of which it is
intended to recommend the imposition of definitive duties. In *Ajinomoto Co. Inc.
and the NutraSweet Company* v. *Council*,[172] the CFI held that the extent to which
the Commission must disclose information to the undertakings subject to investigation may depend on the relative economic strength of those undertakings in the
market and the informational advantage that such strength might give them. Where
the undertakings under investigation are the principal actors in the field and as a
result possess a thorough knowledge of the market, their right to receive information from the Commission is conditioned by the obligation on the latter not to
reveal information which might enable the undertakings to work out confidential
data information regarding the complainant. The CFI also held that failure to
inform exporters of the essential facts and considerations on the basis of which it is
intended to impose provisional duties does not in itself vitiate the regulation imposing definitive duties. This is because the latter is distinct from the regulation imposing provisional duties and its validity must be assessed on the basis of the rules
applying at the time of its adoption. If in the course of the procedure leading to the
adoption of a regulation imposing a definitive duty, the institutions take steps to
remedy a defect vitiating the adoption of the corresponding regulation imposing a
provisional duty, the illegality of the latter does not render the former illegal.

7.8. Staff cases

As already stated, staff cases was the first area where the Court applied the rights of
defence. In *Alvis* v. *Council*,[173] the Court held that, although the defendant institution had disregarded its obligation to allow the applicant to submit his defence
before being dismissed, given the gravity of the irregularities committed by the
applicant breach of that obligation was not sufficient to annul the decision of
dismissal. In *Moli* the Court annulled the refusal of the Commission to engage a
candidate as an official on account of physical unfitness, on the ground that the
Commission had not given to the applicant the opportunity to express his views

---

[171] Case T–121/95 *European Fertiliser Manufacturers Association (EFMA)* v. *Council*, [1997] ECR
II–2391.
[172] Joined Cases T–159 and T–160/94, [1997] ECR II–2461.
[173] Op.cit. n. 102. See also Case 35/67 *Van Eick* v. *Commission* [1968] ECR 329.

despite the fact that the Commission had undertaken to do so.[174] The right to be heard acquires particular importance in disciplinary proceedings. It requires the appointing authority to inform the official concerned of the complaints against him and to grant him a reasonable time to prepare his defence.[175] In *Almini*,[176] the applicant applied for the annulment of the Commission's decision to retire him under Article 50 of the Staff Regulations which provides for the retirement of certain categories of officials in the interests of the service. The Court held that Article 50 gives to the appointing authority wide discretionary powers, the exercise of which requires that the official concerned must have the opportunity of effectively defending his interests. The Court annulled the contested decision on the ground that the Commission had only given four days to the applicant to make his views known. Also, the reasons which were stated in the contested decision as justifying his retirement were different from those stated in the minutes of the meeting of the Commission where that decision was taken. The applicant therefore had not been given the opportunity to comment on the factors which influenced the Commission in taking the contested decision.

The rights of defence include the right of an official to have access to his personal file. Article 26 of the Staff Regulations provides that the personal file of an official must contain all documents relating to his administrative status and his performance and safeguards the official's right to have access to the file. The purpose of this provision is to ensure that decisions taken by the appointing authority concerning the administrative status and career of the official are not based on matters concerning his conduct which are not included in his personal file and have not been communicated to him.[177] In *Ojha* v. *Commission*,[178] the Court of Justice held, reversing the decision of the CFI, that where an official is redeployed in the interests of the service, redeployment may not take place on the basis of documents which concern the official's conduct in the service and which are not communicated to him. That would be contrary to Article 26 because, although redeployment is not a disciplinary offence, it affects the official's administrative status and may affect his future career.

---

[174] Case 121/76 *Moli* v. *Commission* [1977] ECR 1971. See also *Case 2/87 Biedermann* v. *Court of Auditors* [1988] ECR 143, Case T–154/89 *Vidrányi* v. *Commission* [1990] ECR II–445; Case 35/67 *Van Eick* v. *Commission* [1968] ECR 329.

[175] Case 319/85 *Misset* v. *Council* [1988] ECR 1861.

[176] Case 19/70 *Almini* v. *Commission* [1971] ECR 623.

[177] For previous case law, see Case 233/85 *Bonino* v. *Commission* [1987] ECR 739; Case 140/86 *Strack* v. *Commission* [1987] ECR 3939.

[178] Case C–294/95 P [1996] ECR I–5863.

7.9. The relationship between the right to a hearing and other procedural rights

In *Technische Universität München*,[179] the Court saw the right to a hearing as part of a wider network of process rights which ensue from the principle of good administration and are essential to ensuring the protection of the individual. Those process rights encompass the duty of the competent institution to examine carefully and impartially all the relevant aspects of the individual case, the right of the person concerned to make his views known, and the right to a reasoned decision.[180] In the circumstances of the case, it found that all the three guarantees had been infringed. The judgment is of particular interest because the Court recognized more extensive procedural requirements than had been accepted in previous cases concerning Commission decisions on the duty-free importation of scientific apparatus.[181]

The case arose as a result of a reference by the Federal Finance Court of Germany and brought to the fore a clash of conflicting philosophies of administrative law.[182] The traditional stance of the Court of Justice had been that, in matters involving technical evaluations, the Community decision-making body enjoyed wide discretionary powers. Judicial review was limited to ascertaining whether there is manifest error of fact or law or whether there is misuse of power.[183] The starting point of German law is the opposite. It adheres to the principle of limited, as opposed to discretionary, administrative power which, in general, accepts that the administration has no discretion unless the measure under which it acts expressly provides so. Unless the enabling statute vests the administration with discretion, there is deemed to be only one correct solution to the issue involved, which the decision-maker is bound to follow. The principle seeks to control the discretion of the executive and is said to derive from the right of effective judicial review guaranteed by the Basic law.[184] In *Universität München*, the strengthening of process rights was the Court's response to calls by the referring German court for a thorough substantive review of the Commission's decision-making powers. It will be remembered that the Commission adopted a decision refusing the duty-free importation of an instrument on the ground that equivalent scientific apparatus was available in the Community. The Federal Finance Court found itself in a position of divided loyalties. On the one hand, German doctrine required the reviewing court to undertake full review of the substantive merits of the Commission's decision. On the other hand, the previous case law of the Court of Justice required

---

[179] Op.cit.   [180] Op.cit., para. 14.   [181] See above p. 252,
[182] The point is aptly illustrated by Nolte, 'General Principles of German and European Administrative law—A comparison in Historical Perspective' (1994) 57 MLR 191.
[183] See e.g. *Universität Stuttgart*, op.cit., para. 20.
[184] See Article 19(4) Grundgesetz and (1983) 64 BVerfGE 261, 179. See further Nolte, op.cit., 196, 200.

that the review of the Commission's discretion should be limited to determining whether there is manifest error, an approach foreign to German culture. In the words of the referring court: 'The more difficult the technical questions to be decided the more immune from challenge the Commission's decision would be. It is questionable whether such a restriction of the legal protection of Community citizens is compatible with the constitutional principle guaranteeing effective legal protection which is recognised by Community law.'[185] The response of the Court of Justice was to accommodate the concerns of the Finance Court by entrenching process rights rather than increasing the degree of substantive scrutiny. This is in a way ironic since under the influence of German law the Court increased procedural safeguards, to which German law traditionally attaches less weight. *Universität München* illustrates not only the role of the Court as the melting pot of national legal cultures but also the relative distinction in functional terms between process and substantive rights.[186] The case law now seems to accept that procedural and substantive scrutiny are in an inverse relationship. Where the Court exercises only marginal review on substantive grounds because the decision-making process involves complex technical evaluations and the Community institutions enjoy broad discretion, the need to ensure respect of process rights becomes all the more important.[187]

The question which arises in this context is what is the relationship between the right to a hearing and other procedural requirements. Is it for example possible to say that consultation in advance with representative professional organizations or pressure groups to which the person affected by the decision belongs alleviates the need to provide a right to a hearing? The answer must be in the negative since the two requirements essentially pursue different objectives. Consultation ensures indirect participation in the policy-making process whereas the right to a hearing goes beyond that: it is an individual right which is seen as an integral part of the adjudication process. The fact that Community legislation requires the Commission to consult certain bodies before taking a decision does not mean that the right to a hearing need not be observed. Article 6(1) of Regulation No. 2950/83 concerning the administration of the European Social Fund requires the Commission to consult the Member State concerned before it adopts a decision to suspend, reduce, or withdraw financial assistance which has been granted from the Fund. In *Lisrestal* the Court held that the requirement of consultation 'does not justify the conclusion that a principle of Community law as fundamental as that which guarantees every person the right to be heard before the adoption of a decision capable of adversely affecting him does not apply'.[188]

An issue of particular interest is how the right to a hearing interrelates with the requirement to give reasons. In general, a breach of the requirement of reasoning

---

[185] *Universität München*, op.cit., at 5483.   [186] See further Nolte, op.cit., 207–8.
[187] *Universität Munchen*, op.cit., para. 14; Case T–44/90 *La Cinq* v. *Commission* [1992] ECR II–1, para. 86; Case T–7/92 *Asia Motor France and Others* v. *Commission* [1993] ECR II–669, para. 34.
[188] Case C–32/95 P *Commission* v. *Lisrestal*, op.cit., para. 30.

exists where a decision does not contain an adequate statement of the reasons on which it is based. A breach of the right to be heard occurs where the party is denied the opportunity to express its views on the facts and considerations taken into account by the authority. The requirement of reasoning is broader in its scope of application since, under Article 253[190] of the Treaty, it applies not only to administrative acts but also to legislative measures. It is also perceived as serving not only the interests of the persons affected but also the public interest in the administration of justice. According to standard case law, one of the objectives of the requirement to give reasons is to enable the Court to exercise its power of review.[189] This explains why the Court is more willing to examine of its own motion the adequacy of reasoning of Community acts.[190]

The two requirements are closely interconnected but distinct and an administrative procedure may be in breach of one but not the other.[191] In *Bonino*, the Court found that the contested decision of the Commission was adequately reasoned but annulled it for breach of the right to a hearing.[192] In *Technische Universität München*, Jacobs AG reached the converse conclusion. In his view, the applicant university did not have the right to a hearing in relation to a decision refusing the duty-free importation of scientific apparatus but found that the decision was vitiated by defective reasoning. Notably the Advocate General took the view that the inadequacy of reasoning might have been compensated if the information on the basis of which the Commission reached its decision had been communicated to the applicant. If that happened, one of the essential functions of the requirement of reasoning would have been fulfilled, since the university would have been able to ascertain whether the decision was well founded or whether it was vitiated by an error that would allow its legality to be challenged.[193] In some cases the Court has excused paucity of reasons on the ground that the person affected by the decision had the opportunity to present his arguments and a form of dialogue took

[189] Its other objectives being to give an opportunity to the parties involved of defending their rights, and to third persons of ascertaining the circumstances in which the institution concerned applied the Treaty: see e.g. Case 24/62 *Germany* v. *Commission* [1963] ECR 63 at 69; Case 294/81 *Control Data* v. *Commission* [1983] ECR 911, para. 14; Joined Cases T–79/89 etc. *BASF AG and Others* v. *Commission* [1992] ECR II–315, para. 66.

[190] Case 18/57 *Nold* v. *High Authority* [1959] ECR 41; Case 185/85 *Usinor* v. *Commission* [1986] ECR 2079, para. 19; Case C–166/95 P *Commission* v. *Daffix* [1997] ECR I–983, para. 24; Case T–95/94 *Sytraval and Brink's France* v. *Commission* [1995] ECR II–2651, para. 75. The Community judicature, however, is not under a duty to raise the issue on its own motion in all cases and, depending on the circumstances, it may reject as inadmissible a plea that the contested act is insufficiently reasoned if it is not submitted in time: Case T–106/95 *Fédération Française des Sociétés d' Assurances (FFSA) and Others* v. *Commission* [1997] ECR II–229, para. 62.

[191] In a number of cases, Community acts have been found to breach both requirements. See e.g. *Lisrestal* v. *Commission*, op.cit.; *Technische Univesität München*, op.cit.

[192] *Bonino* v. *Commission*, op.cit. The Court held that the Commission is not required to give reasons for refusing to appoint an official in a new post but annulled the procedure because the rights of defence of the unsuccessful candidate had been violated. See also *Moli* v. *Commission*, op.cit.

[193] *Technische Universität München*, op.cit., 5493. See also Case C–216/91 *Rima Eletrometalurgia* v. *Council* [1993] ECR I–6303, esp. at 6345 per Lenz AG.

place between the Commission and the party, or at least the party concerned was given that opportunity.[194]

Insofar as a general conclusion can be drawn from the cases, the statement of reasons need not rebut all objections raised by the parties concerned in the hearing.[195] In other words, there is no obligation on the part of the Community decision maker to engage in a 'dialogue' with interested parties.[196] According to consistent case law, under Article 253[190] the Commission is required to mention the factual and legal elements which provide the legal basis of the decision concerned and the considerations which have led it to adopt its decision, but 'it is not required to discuss all the issues of fact and law raised by every party during the administrative process'.[197] Although this still remains in general the position in law, recent case law of the CFI suggests a shift in emphasis. In *Sytraval and Brink's France* v. *Commission*,[198] the CFI accepted that in certain circumstances the Commission's duty to state reasons may require an exchange of views and arguments with the complainant, since in order to justify to the requisite legal standard its assessment of the nature of a measure characterized by the complainant as State aid, the Commission must ascertain what view the complainant takes of the information gathered by it in the course of the inquiry.

7.10. The right to a hearing before national authorities

It should be accepted that a person may invoke the rights of defence not only against the Community institutions but also against national authorities where they act within the scope of Community law even in the absence of specific measures to that effect.[199] This view derives from the general pronouncement of the Court that fundamental rights bind the national authorities where they act within the scope of Community law. In some cases, Community legislation guarantees

---

[194] Case 238/86 *Netherlands* v. *Commission* [1988] ECR 1191; Case 240/84 *NTN Toyo Bearing Co. Ltd*. v. *Council* [1987] ECR 1809.

[195] See in this context the excellent analysis of M. Shapiro, 'The Giving Reasons Requirement', in *The University of Chicago Legal Forum: Europe and America in 1992 and Beyond: Common Problems . . . Common Solutions?* (1992), 179.

[196] This is clearly the case in relation to the requirement of consultation. The statement of reasons of a legislative measure must refer to any opinions which must be obtained but the Treaty does not require that it must refer, and *a fortiori* that it must try to refute, the divergent opinions expressed by the consultative bodies: Case 4/54 *ISA* v. *High Authority* [1954–6] ECR 91, at 100; C–62/88 *Greece* v. *Council* [1990] ECR I–1527, para. 29.

[197] Case T–114/92 *Bemim* v. *Commission* [1995] ECR II–147, para. 41; Joined Cases 240, 242, 261, 262, 268, 269/82 *Stichting Sigarettenindustrie* v. *Commission* [1985] ECR 3831 at 3882; Case 42/84 *Remia and Nutricia* v. *Commission* [1985] ECR 2545.

[198] Case T–95/94 [1995] ECR II–2651, para. 78.

[199] The issue was raised in Case C–144/95 *Maurin* [1996] ECR I–2909 but was not examined by the Court because the national legislation in issue fell outside the scope of Community law. See above 1.6.3.

specific procedural rights to the persons concerned.[200] More generally, the case law has derived, from the ·fundamental right to judicial protection, that decisions of national authorities which deny rights guaranteed by Community law must be reasoned and be subject to judicial remedies.[201] So far, however, the Court has not recognized a general right to a hearing in national administrative proceedings where Community rights are at stake. It is submitted that such a right should be recognized to exist although its precise requirements will depend on the circumstances of the case. In principle, the rights of the individual should not differ depending on whether he or she is dealing with the Community or national authorities. Thus the general approach must be that the principles applicable to the Community administration must apply *mutatis mutandis* to the national administration unless there is good reason which justifies the application of different standards.

---

[200] See e.g. Council Directive 64/221 on the coordination of special measures concerning the movement and residence of foreign nationals which are justified on grounds of public policy, public security or public health, OJ English Spec.Ed., 1964, p. 117, Articles 8 and 9. See further A. Arnull, *The General Principles of EC Law and the Individual*, Ch. 5.

[201] Below, 8.3.1.

8

The Principle of Effective Remedies in National Courts

8.1. The enforcement of Community rights in national courts[1]

The principle of effectiveness underlies a series of developments in the sphere of judicial protection and has been recognized as a general principle of Community law by the Court of Justice.[2] It requires the effective protection of Community rights and, more generally, the effective enforcement of Community law in national courts. Effectiveness differs from the general principles of law examined so far in that it is not based directly on the laws of the Member States but derives from the distinct characteristics of Community law, primacy and direct effect. The origins of the principle lie in the interpretative techniques of the Court. Already at an early stage, the Court favoured a liberal construction of Treaty provisions so as to ensure their *effet utile*. Such an approach was particularly evident in recognizing the direct effect of directives.[3] As a principle governing the exercise of Community

---

[1] Academic contributions include: C. Lewis, *Remedies and the Enforcement of European Community Law* (1996); C. Kakouris, 'Do the Member States possess judicial procedural autonomy?' (1997) 34 CMLRev. 1389; R. Caranta, 'Judicial Protection Against Member States: A New *Jus Commune* Takes Shape' (1997) 34 CMLRev. 703; M. Hoskins, 'Tilting the Balance: Supremacy and National Procedural Rules' (1996) 21 ELRev. 365; E. Szyszczak, 'Making Europe More Relevant To Its Citizens: Effective Judicial Process' (1996) 21 ELRev. 351; A. Ward, 'Effective Sanctions in EC Law: A Moving Boundary in the Division of Competence' (1995) 1 ELJ 205; C. Himsworth, 'Things Fall Apart: The Harmonization of Community Judicial Procedural Protection Revisited' (1997) 22 ELR 291; M. Ruffert, 'Rights and Remedies in European Community Law: A Comparative View' (1997) 34 CMLRev. 307; W. Van Gerven, 'Bridging the Gap Between Community and National Laws: Towards a Principle of Homogeneity in the Field of Legal Remedies?' (1995) 32 CMLRev. 679; D. Curtin, 'The Decentralised Enforcement of Community Law Rights. Judicial Snakes and Ladders', in D. Curtin and D. O'Keeffe, *Constitutional Adjudication in European Community and National Law* (1992), pp. 33–49. See further C. Harlow, 'Codification of EC Administrative Procedures? Fitting the Foot to the Shoe or the Shoe to the Foot' (1996) 2 ELJ 3; M. Shapiro, 'Codification of Administrative Law: The US and the Union' (1996) 2 ELJ 26.

[2] See e.g. Joined Cases C–46 and C–48/93 *Brasserie du Pêcheur* v. *Germany and the Queen* v. *Secretary of State for Transport, ex parte Factortame Ltd.* [1996] ECR I–1029, para. 95 and the Opinion of Léger AG in Case C–5/94 *The Queen* v. *Ministry of Agriculture, Fisheries and Food, ex parte Hedley Lomas (Ireland) Ltd.* [1996] ECR I–2553 at paras. 174–6. In earlier cases, the Court referred to the 'effectiveness of Community law' rather then the principle of effectiveness, see e.g. Case 106/77 *Amministrazione delle Finanze dello Stato* v. *Simmenthal* [1978] ECR 629, paras. 18, 20, 22–3; Case C–213/89 *Factortame and Others* [1990] ECR I–2433, para. 21.

[3] See e.g. Case 9/70 *Frans Grad* v. *Finanzamt Traunstein* [1971] ECR 825, Case 41/74 *Van Duyn* v. *the Home Office* [1974] ECR 1337.

rights, effectiveness has close affinity to the fundamental right of judicial protection which is guaranteed by Articles 6(1) and 13 of the ECHR.

The case law seeks to facilitate the effective enforcement of Community rights vis-à-vis both the Community and the national authorities. Such effective enforcement requires in turn the right of access to the courts and the availability of adequate remedies. The concern to uphold the rule of law and to provide effective judicial protection has led the Court to understand broadly its own jurisdiction under Articles 230[173] and 234[177]. The judgments in *les Verts*,[4] *Chernobyl*[5] and *Codorniu*[6] provide celebrated examples. In recent years, attention has increasingly focused on the national jurisdictions. This is understandable since the enforcement of Community law is not only a matter for the Community judicature but also for the national courts. Indeed, the system of judicial protection established by the Treaty[7] in combination with the principle of direct effect, makes national courts the primary venue for the assertion of Community rights by individuals. The importance of national courts for the enforcement of Community law can hardly be overstated even in areas, such as competition law and State aids, where the implementation of Community policy is not left to national authorities but is entrusted directly to the Commission.[8]

Where claims based on Community law fall to be applied by national courts they are in principle subject to the national rules of procedure and remedies. But the case law has evolved almost beyond recognition. In the absence of Community rules, the traditional approach of the Court has been to make the enforcement of Community rights subject to the rules of national law provided that those rules are not less favourable than those governing similar domestic actions and that they do not render the exercise of Community rights excessively difficult or virtually impossible.[9] Although those requirements still remain the starting point, the Court is now prepared to take a more assertive approach and require the removal of all obstacles posed by national law which prevent the full and effective enforcement of Community rights.[10] Notably, Article 10[5] EC has proved instrumental in this development. The Court has read in it a principle of co-operation between the national and the Community judicature, from which it has derived specific obligations on national courts regarding the enforcement of Community rights.[11] As we

---

[4] Case 294/83 *Les Verts* v. *Parliament* [1986] ECR 1339.

[5] Case C–70/88 *Parliament* v. *Council* [1991] ECR I–4529.

[6] Case C–309/89 *Codorniu* v. *Council* [1994] ECR I–1853.

[7] See the restrictive *locus standi* requirements provided for individuals by Article 230(4)[173(4)] EC. Cf. Article 234[177] EC.

[8] For the functions of national courts in relation to competition law and State aids see respectively, Case C–234/89 *Delimitis* [1991] ECR I–935 and Case C–39/94 *SFEI and Others* [1996] ECR I–3547.

[9] See below 8.2.1.

[10] See De Smith, Woolf and Jowell, *Judicial Review of Administrative Action*, p. 876.

[11] For references to Article 5 (now 10), see e.g. Case 33/76 *Rewe* v. *Landwirtschaftskammer für das Saarland* [1976] ECR 1989; Case 45/76 *Comet* v. *Productschap voor Siergewassen* [1976] ECR 2043; *Simmenthal*, op.cit.; Case C–213/89 *Factortame and Others* [1990] ECR I–2433; Joined Cases C–6 and C–9/90 *Francovich* [1991] ECR I–5357.

shall see, the incremental and fragmentary development of the case law has made
for an unsystematic body of rules. In particular, it is not clear which aspects of procedure and remedies are subject to Community law and which are left for the
national laws to decide for no objective criteria governing the demarcation of competences are readily identifiable in the case law. Depending on one's point of view,
such obscure demarcation of boundaries may be seen as inevitable, harmful, desir-
able or simply the lesser of two evils. It is important to emphasize, however, that
the Court sees the development of the law in this area as a dialectical one where
the co-operation of national courts is of paramount importance. The Court's
reliance on Article 10[5] has not been accidental. The development of no
other area of Community law depends as much on the Co-operation national
courts as the law of remedies.

Community measures do not usually specify the sanctions applicable and the
remedies available where the obligations contained therein are not complied
with.[12] It is therefore left to the Member States to cover the gap. In *Rewe* v.
Hauptzollamt Kiel,[13] the question was referred whether a person whose interests are
adversely affected either by national legislation incompatible with Community law
or by the application of an unlawful Community measure may take action before
the national courts in order to have measures contrary to Community law declared
inoperative. In response, the Court held:[14]

the Treaty . . . was not intended to create new remedies in the national courts to ensure the
observance of Community law other than those already laid down by national law. On the
other hand the system of legal protection established by the Treaty, as set out in Article 177
in particular, implies that it must be possible for every type of action provided for by national
law to be available for the purpose of ensuring observance of Community provisions having
direct effect, on the same conditions concerning the admissibility and procedure as would
apply were it a question of ensuring observance of national law.

More recent cases, however, show that the case law has made significant inroads in
the area of remedies so much so that the statement that the Treaty was not intended
to provide new remedies is no longer valid. Gradually, the case law has transformed
the principle of primacy from a general principle of constitutional law to a specific
obligation on national courts to provide full and effective protection of
Community rights. The seminal judgment in *Simmenthal* marked the first step in
that direction.[15] The question arose whether a national court could disregard a
national law which had been held by the Court to be incompatible with
Community law or whether it should follow the procedure provided for by the

---

[12] In some cases Community measures provide for remedies but even then the relevant provisions
tend to be general in character: see e.g. Directive 76/207 on Equal Treatment for men and women,
Article 6, below n. 77; Directive 89/592 on insider dealing, Article 13. See also Directive 89/665 on
review procedures to the award of public supply and public works contracts, on which see Case
C–236/95 *Commission* v. *Greece* [1996] ECR I–4459; and Directive 85/374 on the approximation of
national laws concerning liability for defective products, on which see Case C–300/95 *Commission* v.
United Kingdom, [1997] ECR I–2649.

[13] Case 158/80 [1981] ECR 1805.   [14] Op.cit., para. 44.   [15] *Simmenthal*, op.cit., n. 2.

Italian Constitution and refer that law to the Italian Constitutional Court which under the Constitution was the only competent body to rule on the validity of national law. The Court held:[16]

> . . . any provision of a national legal system and any legislative, administrative or judicial practice which might impair the effectiveness of Community law by withholding from the national court having jurisdiction to apply such law the power to do everything necessary at the moment of its application to set aside national legislative provisions which might prevent Community rules from having full force and effect are incompatible with those requirements which are the very essence of Community law.
>
> This would be the case in the event of a conflict between a provision of Community law and a subsequent national law if the solution of the conflict were to be reserved for an authority with a discretion of its own, other than the court called upon to apply Community law, even if such an impediment to the full effectiveness of Community law were only temporary.

Procedural protection was further extended in *Factortame*.[17] The culmination of this trend in the case law has been the establishment of Member State liability in damages.[18] The various aspects of the case law will now be examined in detail.

8.2. The conditions governing actions for the protection of Community rights

8.2.1. The dual requirements of equivalence and effectiveness

According to the *Rewe* and *Comet* case law,[19] in the absence of Community rules, it is for the domestic legal system of each Member State to designate the courts having jurisdiction and to lay down the rules governing actions intended to ensure the protection of rights conferred by Community law. Such national rules, however, must comply with two conditions:

(1) they must not be less favourable than those governing similar domestic actions (the requirement of equivalence or non-discrimination); and
(2) they must not render the exercise of Community rights virtually impossible or excessively difficult[20] (the requirement of minimum protection).

---

[16] Op. cit., paras. 22–3.   [17] See below p. 303.
[18] See below, Ch. 9.
[19] See Case 33/76 *Rewe* v. *Landwirtschaftskammer für das Saarland* [1976] ECR 1989, para. 5; Case 45/76 *Comet* v. *Productschap voor Siergewassen* [1976] ECR 2043, paras. 12–16. For subsequent confirmation, see *inter alia* Case 68/79 *Hans Just* v. *Danish Ministry of Fiscal Affairs* [1980] ECR 501, para. 25; Case 811/79 *Amministrazione delle Finanze dello Stato* v. *Ariete* [1980] ECR 2545; Case 826/79 *Amministrazione delle Finanze dello Stato* v. *MIRECO* [1980] ECR 2559; Case 199/82 *Amministrazione delle Fiannze dello Stato* v. *San Giorgio* [1983] ECR 3595, para. 14; Joined Cases 331, 376 and 378/85 *Bianco and Girard* v. *Directeur Général des Douanes des Droits Indirects* [1988] ECR 1099, para. 12; Case 104/86 *Commission* v. *Italy* [1988] ECR 1799, para. 7; Joined Cases 123 and 330/87 *Jeunehomme and EGI* v. *Belgian State* [1988] ECR 4517, para. 17; Case C–96/91 *Commission* v. *Spain* [1992] ECR

The application of those requirements to specific rules of substance and procedure will be examined in detail in the pages that follow. The following general observations may be made at this stage.

The requirement of minimum protection is separate from, and applies in addition to, the requirement of non–discrimination. A rule of evidence[21] or a time limit[22] which renders the protection of Community rights virtually impossible must be set aside by the national court even if it applies equally to similar claims arising from an infringement of national law. In *Peterbroeck*,[23] the Court held that, in order to determine whether a national procedural rule renders the application of Community law excessively difficult, the following inquiry should be pursued:

. . . a national procedural provision . . . must be analysed by reference to the role of that provision in the procedure, its progress and its special features, viewed as a whole before the various national instances. In the light of that analysis the basic principles of the domestic judicial system, such as protection of the rights of the defence, the principle of legal certainty and the proper conduct of procedure, must, where appropriate, be taken into consideration.[24]

In general, although the requirement is expressed in terms of minimum protection, the standard required by the case law is high and any national rule of procedure or substance which unduly restricts the protection of Community rights will be struck down.

The Court of Justice is prepared to grant national courts more latitude with regard to the requirement of equivalence than with regard to the requirement of minimum protection. This is understandable since the question whether the conditions governing the exercise of a Community claim offer the requisite degree of protection is a matter for the Court to decide. By contrast, the requirement of equivalence requires a comparison to be made with the rules applicable to similar domestic actions and national courts are better placed to determine whether such actions exist under national law. But what is a 'comparable' claim? As it stands, the case law offers limited clues. Clearly, the claims must not be wholly unrelated. Thus the fact that, under domestic law, a national court may exceptionally take into account certain pleas of its own motion even if they have not been raised by the parties, such as the issue that the dispute is *res judicata* or that the action is time-barred, does not mean that the national court may also raise of its own motion any plea based on Community law.[25] In some cases, it suffices that the actions are broadly similar and a detailed search for a comparable claim under national law

---

I–3789, para. 12; Joined Cases C–6 and C–9/90 *Francovich and Others* v. *Italian Republic* [1991] ECR I–5357, para. 43.

[20] The term 'excessively difficult' first appeared in *San Giorgio*, op.cit., para. 14. It has since been used in a number of cases. See e.g. *Francovich*, op.cit., para. 43; *Van Schijnder*, op.cit., para. 17.

[21] See e.g. *San Giorgio*, op.cit., discussed below p. 288.

[22] See e.g. Case C–312/93 *Peterbroeck* v. *Belgian State* [1995] ECR I–4599, discussed below p. 299.

[23] Op. cit.   [24] *Peterbroeck*, op.cit., para. 14.

[25] See *Peterbroeck*, discussed below, paras. 23–7 of the Advocate General's Opinion.

need not be undertaken. In *BP Supergas* v. *Greek State*,[26] a case concerning overpaid VAT contrary to the Sixth Directive, the Advocate General opined that, where a taxable person is entitled to a refund of tax in respect of a particular tax year on grounds recognized by national law, that possibility must extend to grounds based on Community law without need to find a comparable claim under national law. In particular, where national law provides for revision of a tax assessment on the ground that the taxpayer made an excusable error, it must be open to the taxpayer to claim revision on the ground that the national law in accordance with which he calculated the tax applicable to him is incompatible with Community law. This is because in dealing with the tax authorities, an individual is entitled to assume that the State has correctly implemented all Community directives and complied with Community obligations.[27]

Whether actions are comparable must be assessed by reference to the nature and objectives of the right which they seek to protect. In *Palmisani*,[28] it was held that an action to recover the loss suffered as a result of the belated implementation of a directive is comparable to a claim for the non-contractual liability of the State brought under ordinary national law and therefore the two claims may be subject to the same limitation period. By contrast, an action to recover the loss suffered as a result of the failure to implement a directive is not comparable with an action to claim benefits provided by the directive in issue and the two actions may be subject to different time-limits. In *Singhara and Radiom*,[29] it was held that the right of nationals from other Member States to enter the host Member State cannot be equated with the right of the host State's own nationals to enter the national territory and therefore the remedies for breach of the two need not be the same.[30]

It should be accepted that the requirement of equivalence prohibits not only direct but also indirect discrimination against claims based on Community law. Where a procedural rule applies to certain categories of claims most of which are claims based on Community law and a more favourable rule applies to other categories of claims most of which are claims based on national law, the first rule may run counter to the requirement of equivalence unless it is objectively justified.

8.2.2. Limitation periods

A classic example of national procedural rules which may qualify the enforcement of Community rights is rules on limitation periods. The issue first arose in *Rewe* v. *Landwirtschaftskammer für das Saarland*[31] and in *Comet* v. *Productschap voor Siergewassen*.[32] In *Rewe*, imports of French apples had been subjected to inspection

---

[26] Case C–62/93 [1995] ECR I–1883.   [27] Op.cit., p. 1904 per Jacobs AG.
[28] Case C–261/95 *Palmisani* v. *Istituto Nazionale della Previdenza Sociale (INPS)* [1997] ECR I–4025.
[29] Joined Cases C–65 and C–111/95 *The Queen* v. *Secretary of State for the Home Department, ex parte Mann Singh Shingara and Abbas Radiom* [1997] ECR I–3343.
[30] See further below p. 293.   [31] Op. cit.
[32] Op. cit.

charges which, subsequently, the Court found to be charges equivalent to customs duties.[33] The appellants sought to have the decisions imposing charges annulled and the amounts paid refunded but their claim was rejected on the ground that the time limit of 30 days laid down by German law had expired. The Court held that, in the absence of harmonization measures, the rights conferred by Community law must be exercised before national courts in accordance with the conditions laid down by national rules. The position would be different only if those conditions made it impossible in practice to exercise Community rights. The Court held that that is not the case where reasonable periods of limitation are fixed. The fixing of such time-limits is an application of the fundamental principle of legal certainty which protects both the public authorities and the person affected.[34]

The Court did not express a view as to whether the 30 day time limit provided for by German law was reasonable, leaving the issue to the national court. In subsequent cases it has been more forthcoming in ruling on the compatibility with Community law of specific time limits imposed by national law. Thus it has been held that a five year limitation period provided for the recovery of port duties levied in infringement of Article 90[95] is reasonable[35] as is a five-year period provided for the repayment of charges imposed in infringement of Directive 69/335 concerning indirect taxes on the raising of capital.[36] A one-year limitation period for bringing an action to recover loss arising from the failure to implement a directive has also been upheld.[37] It has been held, however, that the fact that a Member State has levied a charge in breach of Community law over a long period without either the public authorities or the persons liable to pay it having been aware of its unlawful nature does not constitute excusable error justifying the dismissal of claims for recovery. If the defence of excusable error were accepted, that would make it excessively difficult to obtain recovery of unduly paid charges and 'would encourage infringements of Community law which would have been committed over a long period'.[38]

A particularly important judgment concerning time limits is *Emmott*,[39] decided in 1991. The Court held that so long as a directive has not been properly transposed into national law, individuals are unable to ascertain the full extent of their rights. Consequently, until a directive has been properly transposed, a defaulting Member State may not rely on an individual's delay in initiating proceedings against it in order to protect rights conferred upon him by the directive, and a

---

[33] Case 39/73 *Rewe-Zentralfinanz* [1973] ECR 1039.

[34] *Rewe*, op.cit. para. 5; *Comet*, op.cit., para. 18.

[35] Case C–90/94 *Haahr Petroleum* v. *Åbenrå Havn and Others* [1997] ECR I–4085; Joined Cases C–114 and C–115/95 *Texaco and Olieselskabet Danmark* [1997] ECR I–4263.

[36] Case C–188/95 *Fantask A/S and Others* v. *Industriministeriet (Erhvervsministeriet)*, judgment of 2 Dec. 1997.

[37] *Palmisani*, op.cit.

[38] Case C–188/95 *Fantask A/S and Others* v. *Industriministeriet (Erhvervsministeriet)*, [1997] ECR I–6783.

[39] Case C–208/90 [1991] ECR 4269.

period laid down by national law within which proceedings must be initiated cannot begin to run before that time. *Emmott* concerned Directive 79/7 on the progressive implementation of the principle of equal treatment between men and women in matters of social security,[40] which Ireland had failed to implement within the specified period. Article 4(1) prohibits discrimination on grounds of sex, in particular as regards the calculation of benefits including increases due in respect of a spouse and for dependants. Mrs Emmott was married and had two dependent children. On the basis of an earlier judgment of the Court[41] which held that Article 4(1) was directly effective, she sought to obtain, as from the date when the Directive should have been transposed into national law, the same amount of benefits as that paid to a married man in a situation identical to hers. The defendants argued that her delay in initiating proceedings rendered her claim time barred under national law. The Court held that the time limit for bringing an action imposed by national law cannot be relied on before the directive is fully transposed into national law. That is the case even if the Court has delivered a judgment finding that the Member State in issue has failed to fulfil its obligations under the directive and even if the Court has held that a particular provision of the directive is sufficiently precise as to be relied upon before a national court.[42]

Emmott was hailed as introducing a new, more assertive, approach on the part of the Court. In subsequent cases, however, the scope of the ruling was restricted. In *Steenhorst-Neerings*,[43] it was held that the failure of a Member State to transpose properly Article 4(1) of Directive 7/79 did not preclude it from relying on a rule of national law according to which benefits for incapacity for work were payable not earlier than one year before the date when benefit was claimed. The Court held that the national rule in issue which restricted the retroactive effect of a claim for benefits applied equally to claims based on national law and claims based on Community law and did not make virtually impossible the exercise of rights conferred by Community law. *Emmott* was distinguished on the ground that the rule of Irish law in issue in that case fixed a time limit for bringing actions and made it impossible for the applicant to rely on Article 4(1). By contrast, the rule in issue in *Steenhorst-Neerings* did not affect the right of individuals to rely on Directive 79/7 but restricted the retroactive effect of claims for benefits. That restriction was justified by the need to ensure that the claimant satisfied the conditions for eligibility and the need to preserve the financial balance of the social security system.[44]

[40] OJ 1979 L 6/24.

[41] Case 286/85 *McDermott and Ann Cotter* v. *Minister for Social Welfare and Attorney General* [1987] ECR 1453.

[42] Micho AG took the view that a time-limit provided for by national law should begin to run from the time when the persons concerned should reasonably have been aware of their rights: *Emmott*, op.cit., 4289–91.

[43] Case C–338/91 *Steenhorst-Neerings* v. *Bestuur van de Bedrijfsvereniging voor Detailhandel, Ambachten en Huisvrouwen* [1993] ECR I–5475.

[44] Cf. the 'dissenting' opinion of Darmon AG, op.cit., 5492–3.

Steenhorst-Neerings was confirmed in *Johnson*.[45] Following a judgment in which the Court had found United Kingdom legislation incompatible with Article 4(1) of Directive 79/7,[46] the Social Security Commissioners granted to Mrs Johnson a severe disablement allowance with effect from 16 August 1986, that is to say 12 months prior to her claim, but refused to grant payments in respect of any period prior to such date. The refusal was based on section 165A(3) of the Social Security Act 1975 which restricted entitlement to benefit to a period of 12 months before the date on which the claim was made. The issue was whether Mrs Johnson was entitled to receive benefits as from 22 December 1984, the date when the period for transposing Directive 79/7 expired. The Court held that the legislation in issue did not constitute a bar to proceedings but merely limited the period prior to the bringing of the claim in respect of which arrears of benefit were payable. An attempt to distinguish the case form *Steenhorst-Neerings* failed. It was argued that the benefit in issue, unlike that in issue in *Steenhorst-Neerings*, was non-contributory and consequently that there was no need to preserve the financial balance of the system. The Court, however, stated that the issue in the two cases was identical in that the application of the applicable rules did not make it impossible to exercise rights based on the Directive.

Thus, in the above cases the Court distinguished between national rules which prescribe time limits within which proceedings must be brought and national rules which limit the period prior to the bringing of a claim in respect of which arrears of benefit may be claimed. The two types of rules, however, may lead in practice to the same result. In *Steenhorst-Neerings* and *Johnson* the Court focused on whether the national rules applicable made it impossible to exercise rights based on Community law rather than on whether an individual suffered as a result of late transposition. The judgments do not require that an individual should be put in the same position that he would have been if a Member State had transposed Directive 79/7 properly into national law within the requisite period of implementation. They leave open the possibility that a Member State may derive a benefit as a result of its failure to implement a directive in time.[47]

The trend towards a restrictive interpretation of *Emmott* reached is climax in *Fantask A/S and Others* v. *Industriministeriet (Erhvervsministeriet)*.[48] The case concerned charges on the registration of companies levied by the Danish authorities which were found to be contrary to Directive 69/335 concerning indirect taxes on the raising of capital. Danish law made the recovery of such claims subject to a limitation period of five years but the applicants argued pursuant to *Emmott* that a Member State could not rely on that limitation period as long as Directive 69/335

---

[45] Case C–410/92 [1994] ECR I–5483.

[46] Case C–31/90 *Johnson* v. *Chief Adjudication Officer* [1991] ECR I–3723.

[47] But see now Case C–66/95 *R* v. *Secretary of State for Social Security, ex parte Sutton* [1997] ECR I–2163, according to which the individual concerned may recover any loss suffered by bringing an action for damages against the State: see below p. 347.

[48] Case C–188/95, [1997] ECR I–6783.

had not been properly transposed into national law. Confirming *Johnson* and *Steenhorst-Neerings*, the Court stated that the solution adopted in *Emmott* was justified by the particular circumstances of that case where the time bar had 'the result of depriving the applicant of any opportunity whatever' to rely on her right arising from the Directive in issue. The five-year limitation period imposed by Danish law was reasonable and applied without distinction to domestic claims and those based on Community law and was therefore compatible with Community law.

Fantask gave a fatal blow to *Emmott* and it is now settled that the latter must be read on is facts. It applies only in relation to directives and only given the specific circumstances of that case.[49] It does not detract from the general rule that the limitation period imposed by national law starts from the date when the claim arises rather than the date when national legislation has complied with the Community obligation in issue.[50]

Steenhorst-Neerings and *Johnson* were distinguished in *Magorrian* v. *Eastern Health and Social Services Board*.[51] The applicants were women employed as mental health nurses. They were refused additional pension benefits payable under a voluntary contracted-out pension scheme on the ground that they did not have the status of full-time workers at the time of their retirement. The national court held that their exclusion from the additional benefits amounted to indirect sex discrimination. The question then arose from which date their periods of service as part-time workers should be taken into account for the purpose of calculating the additional benefits to which they were entitled. In response to a preliminary reference, the Court held that the appropriate date as from which periods of service of part-time workers who have suffered indirect sex discrimination must be taken into account is 8 April 1976, the date of the judgment in *Defrenne*.[52] The claim of the applicants, however, encountered an obstacle posed by national law. Regulation 12 of the Northern Ireland Occupational Regulations[53] provides that, in proceedings concerning access to membership of occupational schemes, the right to be admitted to the scheme is to have effect from a date no earlier than two years before the institution of proceedings. The Court held that Regulation 12 deprived the applicants of the additional benefits under the scheme to which they were entitled to be affiliated, since those benefits could be calculated only by reference to periods of service completed by them as from 1990, that is to say two years prior to their

---

[49] See Case C–90/94 *Haahr Petroleum* v. *Åbenrå Havn and Others* [1997] ECR I–4085, paras. 52–3; Joined Cases C–114 and C–115/95 *Texaco and Olieselskabet Danmark* [1997] ECR I–4263, paras. 48–9.

[50] In Case C–2/94 *Denkavit International and Others* v. *Kamer van Koophandel en Fabrieken voor Midden-Gelderrland and Others* [1996] ECR I–2827, at 2851 Jacobs AG held that *Emmott* applies only where 'a Member State is in default both in failing to implement a directive and in obstructing the exercise of a judicial remedy in reliance upon it, or perhaps the delay in exercising the remedy—and hence the failure to meet the time-limit—is in some other way due to the conduct of the national authorities'. The Advocate General pointed out that a further factor in *Emmott* was that the applicant was in the particularly unprotected position of an individual dependent on social welfare.

[51] Case C–246/96, [1997] ECR I–7153.   [52] Case 43/75 *Defrenne* [1976] ECR 455.

[53] Occupational Pension Schemes (Equal Access to Membership) Regulations (Northern Ireland) 1976 No. 238.

commencing proceedings. The Court distinguished *Steenhorst-Neerings* and *Johnson* on the following ground. The rules in issue in those cases limited the period, prior to commencement of proceedings, in respect of which backdated benefits could be obtained. By contrast, Regulation 12 prevented the entire record of service completed by those concerned after 8 April 1976 until 1990 from being taken into account for the purposes of calculating the additional benefits which would be payable even after the date of the claim. Consequently, Regulation 12 was such as to strike 'at the very essence of the rights conferred by the Community legal order'.[54] Also, the effect of the regulation was to limit in time the direct effect of Article 141[119] of the Treaty in cases where no such limitation has been laid down either in the Court's case law or in Protocol No. 2 annexed to the Treaty on European Union. The distinct feature of Regulation 12 was that it restricted claims for future benefits based on past service. Are all national rules which have such restrictive effects caught by the ruling in *Magorrian*? Given the generality of the ruling one may venture to suggest that that is so but it is to be noted that in a recent case where the same issue of principle has arisen the House of Lords has made a further reference to the Court of Justice.[55]

The Court takes a stringent view with regard to rules which are introduced by Member States after it has been established judicially that a specific charge is incompatible with Community law and which apply specifically to claims for the recovery of such charges. That was the situation in *Barra*.[56] Previously, in *Gravier* v. *City of Liège*,[57] the Court had found that the imposition by Belgian law of a registration fee called 'minerval' on nationals of other Member States as a condition for following vocational training in Belgian establishments was contrary to Article 12[6] EC. Following the judgment in *Gravier*, a Belgian law was passed which restricted the right of reimbursement of registration fees already paid only to those nationals of other Member States who had instituted proceedings for that purpose before 13 February 1985, the date when the judgment in *Gravier* was delivered. In *Barra*, the Court held that that restriction rendered the exercise of the rights conferred by Article 6 impossible for those Community nationals who had not brought proceedings before the specified date and was therefore incompatible with Community law.

A further example is provided by *Deville* v. *Administration des Impôts*.[58] France imposed a special fixed tax on cars rated at more that 16 CV. In *Humblot* v. *Directeur des services fiscaux*,[59] it was held that the special tax was prohibited by Article 90[95] EC. Following the judgment in *Humblot*, a French law was passed which abolished the tax and enabled taxpayers to obtain a refund. The French law provided that claims for refund had to be made within a certain period from the year in which

---

[54] *Magorrian*, op.cit., para. 44.
[55] *Preston* v. *Wolverhampton NHS Trust* [1998] 1 All ER 528.
[56] Case 309/85 *Barra* v. *Belgium and Another* [1988] ECR 355.
[57] Case 293/89 [1985] ECR 593. The judgment is discussed above p. 82.
[58] Case 240/87 [1988] ECR 3513.   [59] Case 112/84 [1985] ECR 1367.

the contested tax was paid. Mr Deville argued that that time limit was more restrictive than that which would have applied if the French law had not been adopted. In the latter case, a taxpayer could have made a claim within a certain period from the time when 'the event giving rise to the claim occurred'. Mr Deville argued that the judgment of the Court in *Humblot* was the event giving rise to his claim and therefore in the absence of the law the time limit would have started from the date the Court delivered its judgment. The Court held that a national legislature may not, subsequent to a judgment from which it follows that certain legislation is incompatible with the Treaty, adopt a procedural rule which specifically reduces the possibilities of bringing proceedings for recovery of taxes which were wrongly levied under that legislation.

8.2.3. Recovery of unduly paid charges: Other obstacles imposed by national law

The right to recover charges levied by a Member State in breach of Community law is a consequence of, and an adjunct to, the rights conferred on individuals by the Community provisions as interpreted by the Court.[60] In principle, therefore, a Member State is required to repay charges levied in breach of Community law. In the absence of Community rules governing the issue, however, the recovery of unduly paid charges is governed by national law subject to the dual requirement of non-discrimination and minimum protection. Thus, the recovery of unduly paid sums is subject not only to time limits but also to other rules of substance and procedure provided by national law. In *Pigs and Bacon Commission* v. *McCarren*,[61] it was held that it is for the national court to assess whether an unduly paid levy may be set off against sums paid to the trader by way of a wrongly paid export bonus. Also, whether a trader is entitled to the payment of interest, and if so the rate of interest and the date from which it must be calculated, is in principle a matter for the national law to decide.[62]

Issues of particular interest have arisen in relation to the defence of unjust enrichment. In *Just*,[63] an importer of spirits sought in a national court repayment of excise duties levied in breach of Article 95 by the Danish authorities. Under Danish law, a claim for recovery of unduly paid charges will not succeed if the charge may be presumed to have been passed on to the consumer. The Danish Government

---

[60] *San Giorgio*, op.cit., para. 12; Case 309/85 *Barra* v. *Belgium and Another* [1988] ECR 355, para. 17; Joined Cases C–192 to C–218/95 *Comateb and Others* v. *Directeur Général des Douanes et Droits Indirects* [1997] ECR I–165, para. 20.

[61] Case 177/78 [1979] ECR 2161.

[62] Case 130/79 *Express Dairy Foods* v. *Intervention Board for Agricultural Produce* [1980] ECR 1887; Case 54/81 *Fromme* v. *Balm* [1982] ECR 1449. The Court, however, has not followed an entirely consistent approach: see Case C–271/91 *Marshall* v. *Southampton and South-West Hampshire Area Authority* [1993] ECR I–4367, cf. Case C–66/95 *R* v. *Secretary of State for Social Security, ex parte Sutton*, op.cit. Discussed below p. 347. For an important recent case on set-off, see C–132/95 *Jensen*, judgment of 19 May 1998.

[63] Case 68/79 *Just* v. *Ministry for Fiscal Affairs* [1980] ECR 501.

argued that the plaintiff had recovered the unlawful taxes by passing them on to the consumer as part of the normal profit margin. After referring to the dual requirement of non-discrimination and minimum protection, the Court held that Community law does not require an order for the recovery of unduly paid charges to be granted in conditions which would involve the unjust enrichment of those entitled. National courts therefore can take into account in accordance with national law the fact that the unduly levied taxes have been incorporated in the price of goods and thus passed on to the consumer.[64] Although the principle enunciated by the Court is correct, it is highly doubtful whether the argument of the Danish Government was economically justifiable. Where the amount of an unduly paid levy has been recovered by the undertaking selling its products at the normal, as opposed to a higher, profit margin it cannot be said that the tax has been passed on to the consumer.[65] In *Just*, as earlier in *Rewe*, the Court followed a non-interventionist approach. It referred to the general requirements of Community law, leaving ample discretion to the national court.

The Court gave more specific directions in *San Giorgio*.[66] The plaintiff had been required to pay health inspection charges contrary to Community law upon importation to Italy of dairy products from other Member States. Italian law provided that a person was not entitled to the repayment of sums unduly paid where the charge had been passed on in any way to other persons. It also provided that the charge was presumed to have been passed on whenever the goods in respect of which the charge was paid had been transferred, 'in the absence of documentary proof to the contrary'. The Court repeated its finding in *Just* that national courts may take into account the fact that the unduly paid charges have been passed on to the purchasers. It stated, however, that any requirement of proof which made it virtually impossible or excessively difficult to obtain repayment was incompatible with Community law. It continued:[67]

That is so particularly in the case of presumptions or rules of evidence intended to place upon the taxpayer the burden of establishing that the charges unduly paid have not been passed on to other persons or of special limitations concerning the form of the evidence to be adduced, such as the exclusion of any kind of evidence other than documentary evidence. Once it is established that the levying of the charge is incompatible with Community law, the court must be free to decide whether or not the burden of the charge has been passed on, wholly or in part, to other persons.

Of particular interest is the presence in the judgment of elements of an economic analysis which was absent in *Just*:[68]

In a market economy based on freedom of competition, the question whether, and if so to what extent, a fiscal charge imposed on an importer has actually been passed on in

---

[64] Op. cit., para. 26.

[65] The judgment has been criticized by P. Oliver, 'Enforcing Community Rights in the English Courts' (1987) 50 MLR 881 at 889.

[66] Case 199/82 *Amministrazione delle Finanze dello Stato* v. *San Giorgio* [1983] ECR 3595.

[67] Op. cit., para. 14.   [68] Op. cit., para. 15.

subsequent transactions involves a degree of uncertainty for which the person obliged to pay a charge contrary to Community law cannot be systematically held responsible.

It will be noted that in *San Giorgio*, as in all cases in this area, the Court laid down negative rather than positive requirements. It struck down the requirement of documentary evidence as being incompatible with Community law but did not specify what type of evidence would be sufficient to protect Community rights. This is inevitable as, in contrast to legislative intervention in the form of harmonization measures, judicial intervention has a residual character.

It is noteworthy that the Court has been less willing to accept the defence of unjust enrichment in the field of social law than it has been in the field of economic law. In *Cotter and McDermott* v. *Minister for Social Welfare and AG*,[69] it held that Article 4(1) of Directive 79/7 had to be interpreted as meaning that married women were entitled to the same increases in benefits and compensatory payments as those awarded to married men in family situations identical to theirs even if that would result in double payments or infringe the prohibition of unjust enrichment laid down by Irish law.

The defence of passing on was re-examined in *Société Comateb and Others* v. *Directeur Général des Douanes et Droits Indirects*.[70] The dispute arose from the imposition by French law of dock dues (*octroi de mer*) on the importation of goods from other Member States to the French overseas departments. In *Administration des Douanes et Droits Indirects* v. *Legros and Others*,[71] the Court had found that dock dues were charges having equivalent effect to customs duties. The Court, however, limited the temporal effect of its judgment so that claims for refund could not be brought in relation to dock dues paid before the date of the judgment except by claimants who had initiated proceedings before that date. In *Comateb*, the applicants sought the recovery of dock dues paid on the importation of goods into Guadeloupe in the period between 17 July 1992, the day after the judgment in *Legros* was delivered, and 31 December 1992. Their claim, however, encountered an obstacle posed by national law. French law required a person liable to pay dock dues to incorporate them in the cost price of the goods sold. The applicants were unable to obtain recovery because, under the French Customs Code, a person may obtain reimbursement of unlawfully paid duties only where they have not been passed on to the purchaser. The Court first pointed out that, in principle, a Member State is required to reimburse charges levied in breach of Community law. Referring to *San Giorgio*, it stated that repayment is not required where it is established that the person required to pay the charges has actually passed them on to other persons. The fact, however, that there is an obligation under national law to

---

[69] Case C–377/89 [1991] ECR I–1155. See also the previous case law from which the issue of unjust enrichment arose: Case 286/85 *McDermott and Cotter* v. *Minister for Social Welfare and AG* [1987] ECR 1453; Case 71/85 *Netherlands* v. *federatie Nederlandse Vakbeweging* [1986] ECR 3855.

[70] Joined Cases C–192 to C–218/95 *Comateb and Others* v. *Directeur Général des Douanes et Droits Indirects* [1997] ECR I–165.

[71] Case C–163/90 [1992] ECR I–4625.

incorporate the charge in the cost price of goods does not mean there is a presumption that the entire charge has been passed on, even when failure to comply with that obligation carries a penalty. Accordingly, a Member State may resist repayment to the trader concerned only where it is established that the charge has been borne in its entirety by someone other than the trader and that reimbursement would constitute unjust enrichment. If the burden of the charge has been passed on only in part, the national authorities must repay the amount not passed on. The Court also held that, even where the charge has been passed on, repayment to the trader of the amount thus passed on does not necessarily entail his unjust enrichment. The trader may claim that, although the charge has been passed on to the purchaser, its inclusion in the cost price has, by increasing the price of goods and reducing sales, caused him damage which excludes, in whole or in part, any unjust enrichment. Where domestic law permits the trader to plead such damage in the main proceedings, it is for the national court to give such effect to the claim as may be appropriate. Furthermore, traders may not be prevented from applying to the courts having jurisdiction, in accordance with the conditions laid down in *Brasserie du Pêcheur and Factortame*,[72] for reparation of loss caused by the levying of charges not due, irrespective of whether those charges have been passed on.[73]

Comateb goes further than *San Giorgio* and signifies that the standards of protection expected of national law are much higher than previous case law suggested. Emphasis lies not so much on the requirement of equivalence as on the requirement that the protection of Community rights must be effective.

Provided that the dual requirements of minimum protection and equivalence are respected, it falls on the Member States to determine the entities from which unduly paid charges may be recovered. In one case it was held that, where the proceeds of a duty levied contrary to Community law have been allocated to independent operators subject to local authority control, national law may require that the action for repayment lies against such persons.[74]

8.3. Effective judicial review

8.3.1. Judicial review as a constitutional right

The right to judicial protection includes the right of access to the courts and, in particular, the right to obtain effective judicial review before the Court itself and before national courts. The need for effective judicial review before the Community judicature was highlighted by the Court itself in *Les Verts*.[75] National

---

[72] Joined Cases C–43 and C–48/93 [1996] ECR I–1029.
[73] On the relationship between claims for the recovery of unduly paid charges and State liability in damages, see below p. 347.
[74] Joined Cases C–114 and C–115/95 *Texaco and Olieselskabet Danmark*, 17 July 1997, paras. 42–3.
[75] Case 294/83 *Les Verts* v. *Parliament* [1986] ECR 1339, para. 23. See above p. 34.

courts are also under a duty to provide effective judicial review for the protection of Community rights. The leading case is *Johnston* v. *Chief Constable of the Royal Ulster Constabulary*.[76] Because of the high number of police officers assassinated in Northern Ireland, the Chief Constable decided that only male officers would carry firearms and that female officers would no longer be assigned to operations requiring the carrying of firearms. Pursuant to that policy, the Chief Constable decided not to offer or renew any more contracts for women in the RUC full-time reserve except when they had to perform duties assigned only to female officers. As a result of the new policy, Mrs Johnston, a member of the RUC full-time reserve, was refused renewal of her contract. She brought proceedings in the Industrial Tribunal challenging the refusal on grounds of sex discrimination. The measure applicable on the circumstances was the Sex Discrimination (Northern Ireland) Order 1976 which bans sex discrimination in relation to employment with the police. Article 53(1) of the Order stated that none of its provisions prohibiting discrimination rendered unlawful an act done for the purpose of safeguarding national security or of protecting public safety or public order. Article 53(2) provided that a certificate issued by the Secretary of State certifying that an act specified in the certificate was done for a purpose mentioned in Article 53(1) provided conclusive evidence to that effect. In the proceedings before the Industrial Tribunal, the Secretary of State produced such a certificate in relation to the decision to refuse the renewal of Mrs Johnston's contract. On a reference for a preliminary ruling, the Court referred to Article 6 of the Sex Discrimination Directive[77] and stated that the requirement of judicial control stipulated in that provision reflects 'a general principle of law which underlies the constitutional tradition common to the Member States' and which is laid down in Articles 6 and 13 of the ECHR. By virtue of Article 6 of the Directive, interpreted in the light of that principle, all persons have the right to obtain 'an effective remedy in a competent court against measures which they consider to be contrary to the principle of equal treatment for men and women laid down in the directive'. The Court concluded that a provision which requires a certificate to be treated as conclusive evidence that the conditions for derogating from the principle of equal treatment are fulfilled allows the competent authority to deprive an individual of judicial protection and is therefore contrary to the principle of effective judicial control laid down in Article 6 of the Directive.[78]

The case shows that Community law provides individuals not only with rights but also with remedies. It also signifies the affinity between the principle of effectiveness and the right of judicial protection as a fundamental right. The first is a

---

[76] Case 222/84 [1986] ECR 1651.

[77] Article 6 states as follows: 'Member States shall introduce into their national legal systems such measures as are necessary to enable all persons who consider themselves wronged by failure to apply to them the principle of equal treatment within the meaning of Articles 3, 4 and 5 to pursue their claims by judicial process possibly after recourse to other competent authorities.'

[78] *Johnston*, op.cit., paras. 18–20.

specific application of the second. On the basis of the Court's reasoning, it seems that, as a general rule, any provision of Community or national law which enables a certificate issued by the administration to exclude recourse to the courts in circumstances where the rights of the individual are adversely affected will be struck down as 'unconstitutional'. The judgment is particularly notable because in that case the clause excluding recourse to the courts pertained to matters of national security, an area not easily susceptible to judicial scrutiny.[79]

The importance of providing effective judicial review has been stressed in subsequent cases. In *UNECTEF* v. *Heylens*,[80] the Court held that, since free access to employment in the host Member State is a fundamental Community right, the existence of a judicial remedy against any decision of a national authority refusing the benefit of that right is essential in order to secure for the individual effective protection for his right. Thus, a refusal by the competent authorities of the host State to recognize as equivalent a diploma granted to a migrant worker by the Member State of which he is a national must be subject to judicial proceedings in which its legality under Community law can be reviewed. The Court has followed a similar approach in relation to the free movement of goods.[81] The case law regards the availability of judicial review against decisions of national authorities which restrict the fundamental freedoms as necessary in order to ensure that the restrictions imposed meet the requirement of proportionality.[82]

Notably, the case law has derived from the right to effective judicial review a requirement on national authorities to give reasons to justify decisions which affect adversely Community rights.[83] The right to a judicial remedy and the duty to state reasons are limited to final decisions and do not extent to preparatory decisions or opinions.[84] Also, the duty to state reasons applies only to individual decisions against which the person concerned may have some remedy of a judicial nature and not to national rules of general application.[85]

It is of particular interest that the case law has viewed the requirement of reasoning as a general principle incumbent on national authorities in all cases where

---

[79] The Court's approach in *Johnston* is consistent with its application of the principle of proportionality. As we saw in Ch. 4, acts done in the interests of national security do not escape control on grounds of proportionality although the degree of scrutiny exercised by the Court may be less strict than in other areas.

[80] Case 222/86 [1987] ECR 4097. The case concerned the refusal of French authorities to recognize a Belgian football trainer's diploma. See further C–340/89 *Vlassopoulou* [1991] ECR I–2357; Case C–104/91 *Colegio Oficial des Agentes de la Propiedad Immobiliaria* v. *Aguirre Borrell and Others* [1992] ECR I–3003; *Molenheide*, [1997] ECR I–7281.

[81] See Case 178/84 *Commission* v. *Germany* [1987] ECR 1227, para. 46. See also C–18/88 *GB-INNO-BM* [1991] ECR I–5941; Joined Cases C–46/90 and C–93/91 *Lagauche* [1993] ECR I–5267.

[82] See C–19/92 *Kraus* v. *Land Baden-Württemberg* [1993] ECR I–1663 and above Ch. 4.

[83] *UNECTEF* v. *Heylens*, op.cit., para. 15; *Vlassopoulou*, op.cit., para. 22; *Kraus*, op.cit., para. 40; Case C–249/88 *Commission* v. *Belgium* [1991] ECR I–1275, para. 25.

[84] *UNECTEF* v. *Heylens*, op.cit., para. 16.

[85] Case C–70/95 *Sodemare SA and Others* v. *Regione Lombardia* [1997] ECR I–3395, para. 19.

they take decisions which affect adversely Community rights.[86] As Fennelly AG stated in *Sodemare and Others* v. *Regione Lombardia.*[87]

The obligation to give reasons for national decisions affecting the exercise of Community-law rights does not arise from any extension of Article 190 of the Treaty, but from the general principle of Community law, flowing from the constitutional traditions of the Member States, that judicial remedies should be available to individuals in such cases.

The recognition of such a requirement of reasoning may have a salutary effect on English law in that it may contribute to the establishment of a general requirement to give reasons in relation to administrative decisions. Such a general requirement is currently lacking in English law.[88] As a result, developments in the case law of the Court have given rise to reverse discrimination against claims based entirely on domestic law.

In *The Queen* v. *Secretary of State for the Home Department, ex parte Mann Singh Shingara and Abbas Radiom,*[89] on a reference by the Queen's Bench Division, the Court had the opportunity to examine the legal remedies available to Community nationals who are refused entry in the territory of a Member State on grounds of public security. Mr Shingara, a French national, was refused leave to enter the United Kingdom on grounds of national security. Mr Radiom, who had both Iranian and Irish nationality, applied for a residence permit but his application was rejected on grounds of national security. Under section 13(5) of the Immigration Act 1971, where a foreign national is refused leave to enter on such grounds, he has no right of appeal although he may seek leave to apply for judicial review. One of the issues referred for a preliminary ruling was whether the applicants had as a matter of Community law a right to appeal to an immigration adjudicator against the decisions refusing them entry. Article 8 of Directive 64/221[90] provides that a Community national shall have the same remedies in respect of any decision concerning entry, or refusing the issue or renewal of a residence permit, or ordering expulsion from the territory, 'as are available to nationals of the State concerned in respect of acts of the administration'. The applicants and the Commission argued that where nationals of a Member State have a specific right of appeal against any refusal of recognition of their right to entry, nationals of other Member States must

---

[86] Cf. *R* v. *Secretary of State for the Environment, Transport and Regions, and Parceloforce, ex parte Marson*, judgment of 8 May 1998. In that case the Court of Appeal held that the Secretary of State was under no obligation to give reasons for refusing to carry out an environmental impact assessment under the Town and Country Planning (Assessment of Environmental Effects) Regulations 1988 implementing Directive 85/337 on the assessment of the effect of certain public and private projects on the environment, OJ 1985 L 175/40.

[87] *Sodemare*, op.cit., at 3405.

[88] See e.g. *R* v. *Home Secretary, ex parte Doody* [1994] 1 AC 531, 564 per Lord Mustill, and for a general discussion, De Smith, Woolf and Jowell, op.cit., pp. 457 *et seq.*

[89] Joined Cases C–65/95 and C–111/95 [1997] ECR I–3343.

[90] Council Directive 64/221 on the coordination of special measures concerning the movement and residence of foreign nationals which are justified on grounds of public policy, public security or public health (OJ, English Spec.Ed., 1963–4, p. 117).

have the same right of appeal in respect of a similar refusal even if the reasons for
the refusal differ. The fact that both their cases concern the right of entry into the
national territory provides a sufficient degree of similarity to require that judicial
remedies of appeal must be available. Dismissing that argument, the Court stated:[91]

> The two situations are . . . in no way comparable: whereas in the case of nationals the right
> of entry is a consequence of the status of national, so that there can be no margin of discre-
> tion for the State as regards the exercise of that right, the special circumstances which may
> justify reliance on the concept of public policy as against nationals of other Member States
> may vary over time and from one country to another, and it is therefore necessary to allow
> the competent national authorities a margin of discretion . . .
>
> Consequently, the reply to the . . . question is that on a proper construction of Article 8
> of the directive, where under the national legislation of a Member State remedies are avail-
> able in respect of acts of the administration generally and different remedies are available in
> respect of decisions concerning entry by nationals of that Member State, the obligation
> imposed on the Member State by that provision is satisfied if nationals of other Member
> States enjoy the same remedies as those available against acts of the administration generally
> in that Member State.

It follows that it is permissible for a Member State to treat nationals of other
Member States less favourably than its own nationals with regard to the remedies
available against decisions refusing entry or ordering expulsion from the national
territory. The obligation incumbent on the Member State is to make available to
nationals of other Member States the same remedies as those provided against acts
of the administration generally. The Court did not express a view as to what the
minimum content of such remedies must be. Two points must be made, however,
in this context. First, it follows from the case law that such remedies must provide
full and effective protection. Secondly, it will be remembered that Article 9 of
Directive 64/221 provides for minimum procedural guarantees for the persons
concerned. Colomer AG stated that a Community national is entitled to challenge
a decision refusing him leave to enter or ordering his expulsion on grounds of public security or public policy by means of an effective remedy which ensures that 'the
entire administrative decision, including its substantive grounds, is subjected to
judicial scrutiny'.[92] He took the view that, in English law, the requirements of
Article 8 are in principle satisfied by allowing the person concerned to apply for
judicial review. He added, however, the caveat that if judicial review of decisions
concerning the entry or expulsion of foreign nationals did not allow the courts to
undertake complete and effective examination of such decisions, including review
of their substance, Community law would require such restrictions to be set
aside.[93]

In *Shingara and Radiom* the Court also examined Article 9 of Directive 64/221.
It held that, under Article 9(2), a decision refusing the issue of a first residence permit or ordering expulsion of the person concerned before the issue of the permit

---

[91] Paras. 30–1.   [92] See the final paragraph of the Opinion.   [93] Para. 64 of the Opinion.

must be referred for consideration to an independent authority as provided by Article 9(1) only where there is no right of appeal to a court of law against that decision, or where such appeal may be only in respect of the legal validity of the decision, or where the appeal cannot have suspensory effect. Notably, the Advocate General took the view that the first two cases provided for by Article 9(1), namely, where there is no right of appeal to a court of law, or where such appeal may only be in respect of the legal validity of the decision, are contrary to the general principles of Community law which guarantees individuals full and effective judicial protection. The Court did not endorse that view. Referring to its previous case law, it stated that the purpose of Article 9 is to provide minimum procedural guarantees for the persons concerned. It pointed out that, where the right of appeal is restricted to the legality of the decision, the purpose of the intervention of the independent authority is to enable an exhaustive examination of all the facts and circumstances, including the expediency of the proposed measure, to be carried out before the decision is finally taken.

Finally, in *Shingara and Radiom* the Court held that a national of a Member State against whom an initial decision refusing entry into another Member State has been made on grounds of public order or public security has a right of appeal under Article 8 of the Directive and, if appropriate, a right to obtain the opinion of an independent competent authority in accordance with Article 9, with respect to a fresh decision taken by the administrative authorities on an application made by him after a reasonable period has elapsed since the last decision prohibiting him from entering the country.

The obligation to provide effective remedies has given rise to interesting case law also at national level. In *Hodgson* v. *Commissioners of Customs and Excise*,[94] the Value Added Tax and Duties Tribunal held that judicial review was not a sufficient remedy capable of securing the effective protection of Community rights in the case of a person required to pay a penalty for failure to pay excise duties. The case concerned Article 5(3) of the Excise Duties (Personal Reliefs) Order 1992 which establishes a presumption to the effect that where a person, upon entering the United Kingdom, imports from another Member State goods in excess of certain specified quantities, he is presumed to have done so for a commercial purpose and is subject to a penalty if he has failed to pay excise duties, unless he satisfies the Commissioners to the contrary. In an earlier case,[95] the Divisional Court had held that, according to Article 5(3), it was for the Commissioners to decide whether a person imported goods for a commercial purpose and that the magistrates were bound by that decision which was only subject to judicial review. In *Hodgson*, the Tribunal found that Article 5(3) did not properly implement Article 9(2) of Directive 92/12 on excise duties.[96] It held that Article 9(2) provides for certain criteria which Member States must take into account in order to establish whether

---

[94] [1997] Eu.LR 116.   [95] *Customs and Excise Commissioners* v. *Carrier* [1995] 4 All ER 38.
[96] Council Directive 92/12 on the general arrangements for products subject to excise duty and on the holding, movement and monitoring of such products (OJ 1991 L 76/1).

goods are imported for a commercial purpose but does not authorize Member States to adopt a provision such as that of Article 5(3) which, as interpreted by the Divisional Court, lays down an irrebuttable presumption. The Tribunal took the view that the restriction of the available remedies to judicial review did not satisfy the two limbs of the *Rewe* test, namely the requirement of non-discrimination and the requirement of minimum protection. It concluded that an individual's Community law rights include the procedural right to have any interference with his primary right (namely, in that case, the right to import tobacco for his personal use) effectively justiciable by the courts.[97]

8.3.2. Locus standi before national courts

So far, the Court has had little opportunity to pronounce on what are the minimum standards that should be guaranteed as regards *locus standi* before national courts to challenge national measures infringing Community law. The following observations may be made.[98] National law must provide *locus standi* to the addressee of an individual act. It must also provide *locus standi* to its 'direct victim'.[99] For example, the dependants of an employee claiming payment of a survivor's pension may rely on Article 119 to contest an occupational pension scheme involving sex discrimination.[100] In *Verholen*,[101] the Court declared that, although in principle it is for national law to determine an individual's standing and legal interest in bringing proceedings, national law must not undermine the right to effective judicial protection. On that basis, it held that an individual who did not come *ratione personae* within the scope of Directive 79/7 could rely on it if he had a direct interest in ensuring that the principle of non-discrimination was respected *vis-à-vis* persons who were protected by its provisions, for example, the plaintiff's spouse.

More problems arise in relation to the recognition of *locus standi* to challenge conduct of private parties infringing Community law. The issue arises for example whether national law must guarantee to a competitor *locus standi* to challenge unnotified State aid. Oliver answers the question in the affirmative.[102] Such an approach must be considered correct. It receives implicit support from the case law,[103] it is necessary to secure effective enforcement of the provisions on State aid, and it conforms with the tendency of the case law to encourage greater involvement of national jurisdictions in the resolution of such disputes.[104] The same may be said in

---

[97] See further *Wilander and Another* v. *Tobin and Another* [1997] 2 CMLR 346.

[98] See further Oliver, 'State Liability in Damages Following *Factortame III*: A Remedy Seen in Context, in Beatson and Tridimas (eds.), *New Directions in European Public Law*, p. 49 at pp. 54–6.

[99] Oliver, op.cit., p. 55.

[100] See Case C–200/91 *Coloroll Pension Trustees* v. *Russell* [1994] ECR I–4389.

[101] Joined Cases C–87 to C–89/90 *Verholen and Others* v. *Sociale Verzekeringsbank Amsterdam* [1991] ECR I–3757.

[102] Oliver, op.cit., p. 55.

[103] See Case C–254/90 *Fédération Nationale du Commerce Extérieur* v. *France* [1991] ECR I–5505.

[104] See *SFEI and Others*, op.cit.

relation to conduct violating Articles 81[85] and 82[86] of the Treaty. Beyond that, we enter unchartered territory. Where Community law imposes an obligation on a private party, it is uncertain to what extent other private parties may enforce that obligation. The issue acquires particular importance in the sphere of environmental law[105] and also in the sphere of commercial law and consumer protection.[106]

This is a developing area of law where little guidance has been offered by the Court. By way of provisional conclusion, it is difficult to disagree with Oliver[107] who argues that, in determining the standards that national laws governing *locus standi* must respect, Article 230[173] provides a misleading comparator. In other words, it cannot be argued that because Article 230(4)[173(4)] makes *locus standi* subject to establishing direct and individual concern, national laws should be permitted to impose equally restrictive requirements. On the contrary, liberal *locus standi* rules should be favoured precisely because Article 230(4)[173(4)] is so restrictive.[108]

8.4. Compensation

Issues pertaining to the duty of national courts to award compensation for breach of obligations prescribed by Community measures have arisen in connection with Article 6 of the Equal Treatment Directive.[109] In *Von Colson and Kamann*,[110] the applicants in the main proceedings were unsuccessful in their applications to obtain employment in a prison for reasons relating to their sex. The national court found that there had been discrimination on grounds of sex but held that, under the applicable German law, candidates who were victims of sex discrimination were entitled only to compensation for the loss that they suffered as a result of their expectation that they would not be refused employment in breach of the principle of sex equality. On that basis, the applicants in the main proceedings were entitled only to reimbursement of the travel expenses which they had incurred in relation to their applications for employment. The Court held that the objective of the Equal Treatment Directive is to provide equality of opportunity between men and women as regards access to employment and that it is not possible to provide real equality of opportunity without an appropriate system of sanctions. Although Article 6 does not require any specific form of sanction, it requires that sanctions must be such as to guarantee real and effective judicial protection and to have a real deterrent effect on the employer. Thus, where a Member State chooses to penalize the breach of the prohibition of discrimination by the award of compensation, that compensation must be adequate in relation to the damage sustained. It follows

---

[105] See Case T–585/93 *Stichting Greenpeace and Others* v. *Commission* [1995] ECR II–2205 and on appeal Case C–321/95 P, [1998] ECR I–1651.
[106] See e.g. in this context Case C–194/94 *CIA Security* v. *Signalson and Securitel* [1996] ECR I–2201.
[107] Op. cit., p. 56.   [108] Id.   [109] For the text of Article 6, see above n. 77.
[110] Case 14/83 *Von Colson and Kamann* v. *Land Nordrhein-Westfalen* [1984] ECR 1891. See also Case 79/83 *Harz* v. *Deutsche Tradax* [1984] ECR 1921.

that national legislation limiting the right to compensation of persons who have been discriminated against as regards access to employment to a purely nominal amount, such as the reimbursement of expenses incurred in connection with their application, cannot satisfy the requirements of an effective transposition of the Directive.

The judgment in *Von Colson* indicated for the first time that the sanctions available under national law may not be sufficient for the enforcement of Community measures even in areas where such measures do not provide for specific sanctions, and that it is primarily by reference to the objectives of Community measures that the appropriate sanctions should be determined. It thus laid the seeds for the development of a corpus of Community rules on remedies. In *Marshall II*[111] the Court went further. Miss Marshall was dismissed from her employment on the ground that she had passed the retirement age applied by her employer to women. In *Marshall I*,[112] the Court held that her dismissal constituted discrimination on grounds of sex contrary to the Equal Treatment Directive. Following that ruling, the Industrial Tribunal awarded Miss Marshall compensation, including a sum by way of interest, in excess of the statutory maximum provided for by section 65(2) of the Sex Discrimination Act 1975. In *Marshall II*, the House of Lords referred to the Court questions seeking primarily to determine (a) whether it is contrary to Article 6 of the Directive for national provisions to lay down an upper limit on the amount of compensation recoverable by a victim of discrimination; and (b) whether Article 6 requires that the compensation for the damage sustained as a result of the illegal discrimination should be full and that it should include an award of interest on the principal amount from the date of the unlawful discrimination to the date when compensation is paid. Referring to its judgment in *Von Colson*, the Court held that the objective of the Directive is to arrive at real equality of opportunity between men and women and that that objective cannot be attained unless there are measures appropriate to restore such equality when it has not been observed. Those measures must be 'such as to guarantee real and effective judicial protection and have a real deterrent effect on the employer'. The Court continued:[113]

Where financial compensation is the measure adopted in order to achieve the objective indicated above, it must be adequate, in that it must enable the loss and damage actually sustained as a result of the discriminatory dismissal to be made good in full in accordance with the applicable national rules.

. . . the fixing of an upper limit of the kind at issue in the main proceedings cannot, by definition, constitute proper implementation of Article 6 of the Directive, since it limits the amount of compensation a priori to a level which is not necessarily consistent with the

---

[111] Case C–271/91 *Marshall v. Southampton and South-West Hampshire Area Health Authority* [1993] ECR I–4367.

[112] Case 152/84 *Marshall v. Southampton and South-West Hampshire Area Health Authority* [1986] ECR 723.

[113] Paras. 26, 30 and 31.

requirement of ensuring real equality of opportunity through adequate reparation for the loss and damage sustained as a result of discriminatory dismissal.

With regard to . . . the award of interest, suffice it to say that full compensation for the loss and damage sustained as a result of discriminatory dismissal cannot leave out of account factors, such as the effluxion of time, which may in fact reduce its value. The award of interest, in accordance with the applicable national rules, must therefore be regarded as an essential component of compensation for the purposes of restoring real equality of treatment.

In *Marshall II* the Court also took a broad view of direct effect. In *Von Colson*, it had held that Article 6 required Member States to provide sufficiently effective remedies to achieve the objectives of the Equal Treatment Directive but left Member States free to choose between various solutions suitable for achieving those objectives. The Directive therefore did not contain unconditional and sufficiently precise obligations as regards sanctions. In *Marshall II*, by contrast, the Court held that the combined provisions of Articles 5 and 6 gave rise on the part of a person who has been injured as a result of discriminatory dismissal to rights which that person must be able to rely upon before the national courts as against the State. In other words, the Directive allows Member States discretion to determine the remedies available for breach of its provisions. But once the United Kingdom chose to provide the remedy of compensation, the requirement that compensation must be adequate meant that the national authorities had no degree of discretion in applying the chosen solution.[114]

8.5. Is a national court required to raise a point of Community law of its own motion?

Does the duty of national courts to provide effective protection of Community rights extend so far as to require them to raise a point of Community law of their own motion where the parties to the proceedings have failed to do so? That issue arose in *Peterbroeck*[115] and in *Van Schijndel*.[116] Both cases are of constitutional importance and were treated as such by the Court.[117]

Peterbroeck concerned the compatibility with Community law of certain provisions of the Belgian Income Tax Code. Under the Code, a taxable person may

[114] Cf. Case C–66/95 *R* v. *Secretary of State for Social Security, ex parte Sutton*, [1997] ECR I–2163 discussed below, p. 347. See further Case C–180/95 *Draehmpaehl* v. *Urania Immobilienservice OHG* [1997] ECR I–2195.

[115] Case C–312/93 *Peterbroeck* v. *Belgian State* [1995] ECR I–4599.

[116] Joined Cases C–430 and C–431/93 *Van Schijndel and Van Veen* v. *SPF* [1995] ECR I–4705. For a comment on both cases, see T. Heukels (1996) 33 CMLRev. 337.

[117] In *Peterbroeck* the Court decided to reopen the oral hearing and invited all Member States to submit argument on the power of a national court to raise on its own motion points based on Community law. A joined hearing was held for *Peterbroeck* and *Van Schijndel*. In the litigation as a whole, eight Member States submitted argument. Only two of them, Spain and Greece, suggested that a national court is required to consider of its own motion points of Community law notwithstanding any national procedural rules to the contrary.

contest the imposition of a tax before the Regional Director of direct contributions. If his complaint fails, he may appeal to the Court of Appeal where he may submit new arguments, namely arguments other than those examined by the Director, within a period of 60 days. Arguments presented after that period are rejected as inadmissible. In *Peterbroeck* the applicant raised arguments based on Community law for the first time in the Court of Appeal after the expiry of the 60-day time limit. The national court considered that the provisions of the Income Tax Code prevented it from examining of its own motion a point which a taxpayer could no longer raise before it, but referred to the Court of Justice the question whether those provisions were compatible with Community law. The Court gave a negative reply. After recalling its case law that a national procedural provision must not render the application of Community law excessively difficult, the Court held that although a 60-day time limit is not objectionable *per se*, the time limit provided by the Belgian Code was incompatible with Community law in the light of the special features of the procedure in issue. The Court relied on four arguments.[118] First, it pointed out that the Court of Appeal was the first authority capable of making a reference for a preliminary ruling since the Director of taxes was an administrative body and as such not a court or tribunal within the meaning of Article 234[177]. Secondly, it stated that the 60-day time limit started to run from the time when the Director lodged a certified copy of the contested decision. That meant that the period during which new pleas could be raised by the appellant had expired by the time the Court of Appeal held its hearing so that it was denied the possibility of considering the question of compatibility with Community law. Thirdly, no other national court in subsequent proceedings could consider of its own motion the question of compatibility. Fourthly, the Court held that the impossibility for national courts to raise points of Community law of their own motion does not appear to be reasonably justifiable by principles such as the requirement of legal certainty or the proper conduct of procedure.

The reasoning of the Court is not beyond criticism and the above arguments are not necessarily conclusive.[119] In relation to the first argument, it may be noted that the fact that the Court of Appeal is the first court capable of making a reference under Article 234[177] does not prohibit, nor indeed does it make it any more difficult for, the taxable person to raise a point of Community law either before the Director or before the Court of Appeal. Similarly, the fact that no other Belgian court consider issues of Community law *ex propriu motu* should not have any bearing in the 60 day time-limit. The second argument used by the Court is difficult to compromise with Article 42(2) of its own Rules of Procedure. That article provides that no new plea in law may be introduced in the course of proceedings unless it is based on matters of law or of fact which come to light in the course of the pro-

---

[118] Op.cit., paras. 17–20.

[119] In contrast to the Court, the Advocate General considered that the 60-day time limit was not unreasonably short and did not prevent a taxable person from claiming rights based on Community law.

cedure.[120] It will also be noted that Article 230(5)[173(5)] EC provides for a restrictive two-month time limit for actions for judicial review before the Community courts. Finally, the generality of the fourth argument appears to contradict statements made in the judgment in *Van Schijndel*.[121] It seems that the latter judgment lays down the general principle and *Peterbroeck* should be read on its facts.

In *Van Schijndel* the Court was asked to rule, on a preliminary reference by the Hoge Raad, on whether a national court is required to raise of its own motion a point of Community law in civil proceedings pending before it. Applying the *Rewe* case law, the Court held that where, by virtue of domestic law, national courts must raise of their own motion points of law based on binding domestic rules which have not been raised by the parties, such an obligation also exists in relation to binding rules of Community law. The Court went a step further holding that national courts must raise of their own motion points based on binding rules of Community law, where domestic law does not require but confers discretion on them to apply of their own motion binding rules of national law. That obligation is based on Article 10[5] EC and the duty to ensure the legal protection which persons derive from the direct effect of Community law.[122]

In *Van Schijndel*, however, the Court held that a national court is not required to raise of its own motion an issue concerning the breach of provisions of Community law where examination of that issue would oblige the national court to abandon the passive role assigned to it by going beyond the ambit of the dispute defined by the paries themselves and relying on facts other than those on which the party with an interest in application of those provisions bases his claim.[123] That limitation should be considered in principle as correct. As the Court pointed out, it is justified by the principle that, in a civil suit, it is for the parties to take the initiative, the court being able to act of its own motion only in exceptional cases where the public interest requires its intervention. That principle reflects conceptions prevailing in most of the Member States as to the relation between the State and the individual. It also safeguards the rights of defence and ensures proper conduct of the proceedings.[124]

The approach of the Court in *Van Schijndel* accords broadly with that of the Advocate General. In his Opinions in *Peterbroeck* and in *Van Schijndel*, Jacobs AG concluded that Community law does not require that a national court must be free to raise an issue of Community law of its own motion irrespective of any time limit

[120] See also Article 48(2) of the Rules of Procedure of the CFI.

[121] See paras. 21–2 of the judgment in *Van Schijndel*.

[122] *Van Schijndel*, op.cit., para. 14. Those findings were confirmed in Case C–72/95 *Kraaijeveld and Others* v. *Gedeputeerde Staten van Zuid-Holland* [1996] ECR I–5403. It is not clear whether the duty of national courts to raise of their own motion points of Community law applies only in relation to directly effective provisions. Para. 14 of the judgment in *Van Schijndel* suggests so but it is probably sufficient that the provision is binding and that it is intended to confer rights even if it is not directly effective. Contra: Heukels, op.cit., n. 116.

[123] *Van Schijndel*, op.cit., para. 22.

[124] Op.cit., para. 21. Cf.

imposed by national law. The Advocate General rejected the argument that such a requirement derives from *Simmenthal* and *Factortame*. Those judgments establish that it must always be possible for an individual to bring a claim before a national court and to require it to protect Community rights. They do not establish that it must in all circumstances be open to the national court, as a matter of Community law, to raise *ex propriu motu* issues which the parties have failed to raise. Nor does such a requirement derive from Article 234[177]. The Advocate General interpreted the Court's case law as meaning that where a question of Community law is raised before the national court, no rule of national law may preclude the national court from making a reference. However, Article 234[177] does not address the prior question in what circumstances a national court may itself raise of its own motion a point of Community law.[125] In the view of the Advocate General, the principle of effectiveness requires that individuals are given, by the national procedural rules, an effective opportunity of enforcing their rights.[126] He stated:[127]

. . . if the view were taken that national procedural rules must always yield to Community law, that would . . . unduly subvert established principles underlying the legal systems of the Member States. It would go further than is necessary for effective judicial protection. It could be regarded as infringing the principle of proportionality and, in a broad sense, the principle of subsidiarity, which reflects precisely the balance which the Court has sought to attain in this area for many years. It would also give rise to widespread anomalies, since the effect would be to afford greater protection to rights which are not, by virtue of being Community rights, inherently of greater importance than rights recognized by national law.

The judgments in *Peterbroeck* and *Van Schijndel* are finely balanced. On the one hand, the Court recognizes that in principle the protection of Community rights remains subject to national procedural rules. On the other hand, *Peterbroeck* illustrates that the Court is prepared to take a broad view of what constitutes a rule of national law which makes the protection of Community rights 'excessively difficult'. The judgments indicate that the Court prefers to follow a case-by-case approach rather than precipitate major changes in the national procedural systems. It is highly unlikely that *Van Schijndel* has provided the last word on the powers and duties of the national courts to raise point of Community law. A number of important issues still remain unresolved. It is notable, for example, that the Court did not address the issue whether, and if so what, pleas in law derived from Community law may be regarded as matters of public policy in the national jurisdictions.[128]

---

[125] Jacobs AG adopted a restrictive interpretation of Case 166/73 *Rheinmühlen* v. *Einfuhr- und Vorratsstelle Getreide* [1974] ECR 33 and Joined Cases C–87 to C–89/90 *Verholen and Others* v. *Sociale Verzekeringsbank Amsterdam* [1991] ECR I–3757. See *Peterbroeck*, op.cit., 4612.

[126] *Van Schijndel*, op.cit., 4715.   [127] Op.cit., 4715–16.

[128] See Heukels, op.cit., p. 351 and see also *Peterbroeck*, per Jacobs AG, 4609–10.

8.6. Interim measures

In direct actions, the Court of Justice and the Court of First Instance have wide powers to grant interim relief.[129] In proceedings before national courts, interim relief is a matter for the national court to decide even where a reference for a preliminary ruling is made. The matter, however, is not governed exclusively by national law. The Court has laid down certain principles regarding the availability of interim measures.

8.6.1. Interim relief in national courts to protect Community rights

In *Factortame I*,[130] it was held that national courts may be required to provide interim relief for the protection of Community rights even in cases where they would be unable to do so under national law. The litigation arose as a result of changes made by Part II of the Merchant Shipping Act 1988 and the Merchant Shipping (Registration of Fishing Vessels) Regulations 1988 to the system for the registration of British vessels. The Act tightened the conditions for the registration of vessels to the British register in order to stop the practice known as quota hopping whereby, according to the United Kingdom, its fishing quotas were plundered by vessels flying the British flag but having no genuine link with the United Kingdom. The applicants in the main proceedings were the owners or operators of ninety-five fishing vessels which were registered in the register of British vessels under the previous legislation but failed to satisfy the new conditions imposed by the Merchant Shipping Act 1988. The applicants challenged the compatibility of the Act with Community law by means of an application for judicial review and also applied for the grant of interim relief. The House of Lords[131] held that the grant of interim relief was precluded by the common law rule that an interim injunction may not be granted against the Crown and also by the presumption that an Act of Parliament is in conformity with Community law until such time as a decision on its compatibility with that law has been given. It referred, however, to the Court of Justice the question whether, notwithstanding the rules of national law, an English court has the power to grant an interim injunction against the Crown where it has sought a preliminary ruling. The Court replied in the affirmative relying on Article 10[5], Article 234[177], and the requirement to provide effective protection of Community rights. After referring to its judgment in *Simmenthal*, it held:[132]

---

[129] See Articles 242[185] and 243[186] EC. The CFI has similar powers, see Article 4 of Council Decision 88/591 of 24 Oct. 1988 establishing a Court of First Instance of the European Communities, OJ 1988 L 319/1, as amended.

[130] Case C–213/89 *Factortame and Others* [1990] ECR I–2433.

[131] [1989] 2 WLR 997.   [132] Paras. 21–2.

. . . the full effectiveness of Community law would be just as much impaired if a rule of national law could prevent a court seised of a dispute governed by Community law from granting interim relief in order to ensure the full effectiveness of the judgment to be given on the existence of the rights claimed under Community law. It follows that a court which in those circumstances would grant interim relief, if it were not for a rule of national law, is obliged to set aside that rule.

That interpretation is reinforced by the system established by Article 177 of the EEC Treaty whose effectiveness would be impaired if a national court, having stayed proceedings pending the reply by the Court of Justice to the question referred to it for a preliminary ruling, were not able to grant interim relief until it delivered its judgment following the reply given by the Court of Justice.

In *Factortame*, therefore, the Court established that, where a national court considers that it is necessary to grant interim relief for the protection of Community putative rights, it is under a duty to make such relief available, setting aside a rule of national law which prevents it from doing so.[133] The effect of the judgment was to lead to reverse discrimination in the procedural plane. With regard to claims based on Community law, English courts acquired a power which hitherto they did not possess, namely, the power to suspend the application of an Act of Parliament pending a preliminary reference to the Court regarding its compatibility with Community law. With regard to claims based on national law, the old common law rule which prevented the suspension of an Act of Parliament continued to apply. Such differential treatment is clearly unsatisfactory and was criticized by the Law Commission.[134] It has since partly been remedied as result of the House of Lords decision in *M* v. *Home Office*,[135] where it was established that an injunction can be obtained against a Minister of the Crown as a matter of English law. One of the reasons which led the House of Lords to recognize injunctive relief against Ministers was precisely the need to avoid reverse discrimination.[136]

8.6.2. Interim relief in national courts to suspend national measures implementing Community regulations

The *Factortame* litigation involved a conflict between national legislation and Article 43[52] of the Treaty and raised therefore the issue of interim relief in the

---

[133] In subsequent proceedings, the House of Lords granted interim relief to the applicants: see [1991] 1 All ER 70. For a critique of the *Factortame* litigation from the point of view of English law, see H. W. R. Wade (1991) 107 LQR 1 and 4. In Case C–393/96 P(R) *Antonissen* v. *Council and Commission* [1997] ECR I–441 it was held that the CFI may award provisional damages by way of interim measure in proceedings under Article 288(2)[215(2)] EC. It is arguable that national courts also have jurisdiction to grant interim damages. See Oliver, op.cit., p. 59.

[134] Law Commission Consultation Paper No. 126, para. 6.6.

[135] [1994]1 AC 377 [1993] 3 All ER 537.

[136] Note the dicta of Lord Woolf, op.cit., at 551. See also the dicta by Lord Donaldson MR in the Court of Appeal: *M* v. *Home Office* [1992] QB 270, 306H–307A. Note that the extension of the common law rule to cover injunctions against Ministers has been strongly criticized: see H. W. R. Wade, *New Law Journal*, 18 and 25 Sept. 1992.

context of primacy of Community law. The judgment, however, opened the way to developments in the sphere of interim measures extending beyond primacy. If interim relief is 'a fundamental and indispensable instrument of any judicial system', as Tesauro AG declared,[137] the requirement to provide such relief derives from the rule of law rather than the principle of primacy. The question therefore arises whether a national court may suspend by way of interim relief the application of national measures implementing Community rules. That question was examined in *Zuckerfabrik*.[138] A Council regulation required sugar manufacturers to pay a special levy. The applicant undertaking challenged the demand for payment in the Finance Court of Hamburg claiming that the regulation was void. They also sought suspension of enforcement of the demand pending the outcome of the proceedings concerning its validity. Earlier, in *Foto-Frost*,[139] the Court had held that national courts do not have the power to declare Community acts invalid but had expressly left open the possibility that a national court may be able to order the temporary suspension of a Community measure by way of interim relief. In *Zuckerfabrik* the Court saw the availability of interim protection as emanating from the right to judicial protection itself. It stated that the right of individuals to challenge the legality of regulations before national courts under Article 234[177] would be compromised if, pending delivery of the judgment of the Court in the preliminary reference proceedings, individuals did not have the right to obtain suspension of enforcement of the Community measure in issue. Referring to Article 242[185] EC, the Court held that the coherence of the system of interim legal protection requires that national courts should also be able to order suspension of enforcement of a national administrative measure based on a Community regulation, the legality of which is contested. The Court concluded as follows:[140]

The interim legal protection which Community law ensures for individuals before national courts must remain the same, irrespective of whether they contest the compatibility of national legal provisions with Community law or the validity of secondary Community law, in view of the fact that the dispute in both cases is based on Community law itself.

The Court's reasoning is instructive of its general approach in the area of remedies. It views national measures and measures adopted by the Community institutions as belonging to different tiers of the same legal order rather than as emanating from different legal orders. The principle of effective protection of Community rights is a constituent of the rule of law and binds not only the Member States but also the Community institutions. The task of national courts to uphold Community rights extends not only to protecting such rights against State action but also against Community action. However, the power of national courts to question Community action is made subject to limitations deriving from the principle of

---

[137] Case C–213/89 *Factortame*, op.cit., at 2457.
[138] Joined Cases 143/88 and C–92/89 [1991] ECR I–415.
[139] Case 314/85 *Foto-Frost* v. *Hauptzollamt Lübeck-Ost* [1987] ECR 4199.
[140] *Zuckerfabrik*, op.cit., para. 20.

primacy and the need to ensure, as much as possible, the uniform application of Community law.

In *Zuckerfabrik* the Court held that the following conditions must be satisfied in order for a national court to be able to suspend the application of national measures based on a Community regulation:[141]

(1) The national court must have serious doubts as to the validity of the Community regulation on which the contested administrative measure is based;

(2) The national court must refer the question of validity of the Community regulation in issue to the Court of Justice if the question is not already before it;

(3) The granting of relief must be subject to uniform conditions in all the Member States.

Drawing an analogy with Articles 242[185] and 243[186] EC, the Court held that suspension may only be granted if there is urgency, namely if it is necessary to do so in order to avoid serious and irreparable damage to the applicant, and if the national court takes due account of the Community's interests.

On the requirement of urgency, it was held that the damage invoked by the applicant must be liable to materialize before the Court has been able to rule on the validity of the contested Community measure. In accordance with the case law under Article 242[185] EC, the Court stated that purely financial damage cannot in principle be regarded as irreparable.[142] The Court pointed out , however, that it is for the national court to examine the circumstances before it. In particular, the national court must consider whether immediate enforcement of the measure would be likely to result in irreversible damage to the applicant which could not be made good if the Community act were to be declared invalid. On the requirement to take into account the interests of the Community, the Court emphasized that national courts are under an obligation to give full effect to Community law and consequently the application of regulations must not be suspended without proper guarantees. The national court must examine whether the regulation in issue would be deprived of all effectiveness if not immediately implemented.[143] The Court added that if suspension of enforcement is liable to involve a financial risk for the Community, the national court must be in a position to require the

---

[141] Op.cit., paras. 23 *et seq.*

[142] The case law, however, has held that, exceptionally, pecuniary damage may be regarded as irreparable where compensation cannot restore the injured person to the position prior to the occurrence of the damage: Case C–195/90 R *Commission* v. *Germany* [1990] ECR I–3351, para. 38.

[143] The balancing exercise which the national court is called upon to perform is analogous to that which the Community judicature carries out in the context of Article 242[185]. The Community court hearing the application for interim measures examines whether the possible annulment of the contested Community act in the main action would make it possible to reverse the situation that would have resulted from its immediate implementation and conversely whether suspension of the operation of the act would be such as to prevent it being fully effective in the event of the main application being dismissed. See e.g. Joined Cases 76, 77 and 91/89 R *RTE and Others* v. *Commission* [1989] ECR 1141; Case C–149/95 P (R) *Commission* v. *Atlantic Container Line and Others* [1995] ECR I–2165.

applicant to provide adequate guarantees, such as the deposit of money or other security.

The conditions for the granting of interim relief laid down in *Zuckerfabrik* are strict and may be seen as limiting the scope of interim protection available under some national laws. It is submitted, however, that the judgment is a successful attempt to strike a balance between competing principles namely, on the one hand, the principle of effective judicial protection which requires that interim protection must be made available and, on the other hand, the requirement to ensure that full effect is given to Community law and that Community law is applied uniformly throughout the Community. It need hardly be emphasized that the power of national courts to suspend the application of Community law must be exercized with caution. Otherwise, the uniform application of Community law would be jeopardized and distortions of competition may ensue.[144]

An important consideration is whether, in the absence of interim relief, the applicant is likely to suffer irreversible damage. An interesting issue is how much reliance can be placed on the possibility that the applicant may be able to obtain damages against the Community institution which authored the measure in the event that the measure is declared invalid. Suffice it to say here that this factor may not necessarily be decisive as the case law under Article 288(2)[215(2)] does not enable a national court to predict with a sufficient degree of certainty that liability of damages may ensue.

In *Foto-Frost*, Mancini AG had suggested as one of the requirements for the granting of interim relief by national courts that it must be impossible for the applicant to have recourse to other remedies, such as an action under Article 230[173], under which interim measures are available.[145] In *Zuckerfabrik* the Court did not refer to that condition. Failure of the applicant to have recourse to alternative remedies, however, may well be relevant to the national court in deciding whether to grant interim measures.

The requirement to make a reference for a preliminary ruling, if such a reference has not already been made, is a *sine qua non* condition for the granting of interim relief. The following points may be noted in this context. First, one presumes that the national court may still need to make a reference even where the validity of the regulation is already pending before the Court of Justice or the CFI as a result of another preliminary reference or a direct action, if the national court questions the validity of the regulation on grounds different from those already pending before one of the Community courts. Secondly, it seems that a reference must be made

---

[144] The danger of distortions in the conditions of competition being created was identified by the United Kingdom in its submissions in *Zuckerfabrik*. If national courts are able to release undertakings from the obligation to pay levies imposed by Community law, temporary exemption from the payment of a levy may give a competitive advantage to the undertakings so exempted. Whilst the possibility of such distortions cannot deny the power of national courts to provide interim measures, it does underline that national courts are entrusted with a high degree of responsibility and that they should exercise their power cautiously in accordance with the case law of the Court of Justice.

[145] See *Foto-Frost*, op.cit., at 4221.

by the court hearing the application for interim measures, even if that court is different from the one responsible for hearing the main action. This derives from paragraph 24 of the judgment in *Zuckerfabrik*. The final point concerns the issue of appeal. In *Krüger* v. *Hauptzollamt Hamburg-Jonas*,[146] it was held that the national court which has suspended the application of national measures based on a Community act and has made a reference for a preliminary ruling is not precluded from granting leave to appeal against its decision to grant interim relief. This is because the granting of leave does not compromise the application of Community law. If the interim order were to be reversed on appeal, the preliminary ruling procedure would have no further purpose and Community law would again be fully applicable. Nor does a successful appeal compromise the implementation of the preliminary ruling procedure. If the interim decision was set aside, that would not prevent the court of last instance from making a reference, as it is required to do under Article 234(3)[177(3)], if it has doubts regarding the validity of the Community act in question. It is submitted, however, that the decision to refer cannot be set aside on appeal by a superior national court without the interim suspension also being set aside. If the superior court quashes the decision to refer, the interim measures must also be withdrawn. The opposite solution would be tantamount to accepting that national courts may suspend the application of Community law without the safeguard of the preliminary reference and question the monopoly of the Court of Justice to determine the validity of Community acts.

The power of national courts to provide interim relief was extended in *Atlanta*.[147] The difference between *Zuckerfabrik* and *Atlanta* is that whereas in the first interim protection was sought to preserve the status quo, in the second it was sought to establish a new situation. The applicants were importers of bananas from third countries who challenged the validity of the Bananas Regulation[148] in proceedings before a German court, and by way of interim relief requested import licences in addition to those which they had been granted pursuant to that regulation. The Court held that the interim protection which national courts must afford to individuals must be the same whether they seek suspension of enforcement of a national measure adopted on the basis of a Community regulation or the grant of interim measures 'settling or regulating the disputed legal positions or relationships for their benefit'.[149] The Court dismissed the argument that the grant of such interim relief had more radical consequences for the Community legal order. It held that the consequences of the interim measure for the Community legal order, whatever they may be, must be assessed as part of the balancing exercise between

---

[146] Case C–334/95 [1997] ECR I–4517.

[147] Case C–465/93 *Atlanta Fruchthandelsgesellschaft I* v. *Bundesamt für Ernährung und Forstwirtschaft* [1995] ECR I–3761. For a recent English case concerning interim relief pending the outcome of a preliminary reference, see *R* v. *The Licensing Authority established by the Medicines Act 1968, ex parte Generics (UK) Limited and E. R. Squibb & Sons* [1997] 2 CMLR 201.

[148] Council Regulation No. 404/93, OJ 1993 L 47/1 examined by the Court in Case C–280/93 *Germany* v. *Council* [1994] ECR I–4973 discussed above pp. 55, 101.

[149] *Atlanta*, op.cit., para. 28.

the Community interest and the interests of the individual which the national court is required to perform. That approach is correct. The argument that national courts may only grant interim relief in order to preserve the status quo and not otherwise to settle provisionally the dispute runs counter to the fundamental objective of interim protection which requires that such measures as are necessary in the circumstances must be granted. On the other hand, it should be accepted that the balancing exercise performed by the national court may be affected by the type of relief sought and account may be taken of the fact that positive rather than negative action is requested by the individual.

In *Atlanta* the Court also clarified the conditions for granting interim relief laid down in *Zuckerfabrik*, providing the following guidelines:

- When making the interim order, the national court must set out the reasons for which it considers that the Court of Justice should find the regulation invalid in the preliminary reference proceedings.[150]
- In assessing whether the regulation may be declared invalid by the Court of Justice, the national court must take into account the discretion enjoyed by the Community institutions in the sector concerned.[151] Thus in the field of the common agricultural policy, regard must be had to the established case law according to which the Community institutions enjoy a wide margin of discretion which reflects their political responsibilities.
- In considering the damage which may be caused to the regime established by the regulation if interim measures are ordered, the national court must take into account, on the one hand, the cumulative effect which would arise if a large number of national courts were also to adopt interim measures for similar reasons and, on the other hand, the special features of the applicant's situation which distinguish him from all other operators concerned.[152]
- In accordance with Article 10[5] EC, the national court must respect the case law of the Community courts. Thus if the Court of Justice has dismissed on the merits an action for annulment of the regulation in issue, the national court can no longer order interim measures, or must revoke existing ones, unless the grounds of illegality submitted to it differ from those rejected by the Court in its judgment. The same applies if the CFI has dismissed on the merits an action for annulment of the regulation by a final judgment.[153]

In *Atlanta*, the Court left open the possibility that a national court may grant interim measures even in a case where the Court of Justice itself has refused to grant interim measures against the same regulation in previous proceedings before it brought by a Member State under Article 230[173]. This is understandable given that the type of damage which an interim order seeks to avoid differs in the two cases. Where a Member State brings annulment proceedings against a regulation

---

[150] *Atlanta*, op.cit., para. 36; *Zuckerfabrik*, op.cit., para. 24.
[151] *Atlanta*, op.cit., para. 37.   [152] Op.cit., para. 44.   [153] Op.cit., para. 46.

and seeks interim measures in the context of that action, it acts in the national public interest and is entitled to invoke damage suffered by a whole sector of the economy. By contrast, where an individual trader brings proceedings and seeks interim protection, he invokes damage suffered by him in his private capacity.

In *Atlanta*, the Court stressed that, in assessing whether interim relief should be granted, the national court hearing the application must take due account of the Community interest. But how is the Community represented in national proceedings? In *Krüger* v. *Hauptzollamt Hamburg-Jonas*,[154] the Commission argued that, where a national court is minded to grant interim relief, the Community institution which adopted the act whose validity is in issue should be given the opportunity to express its views. But the Court did not heed to that request, holding that it is for the national court to decide, in accordance with its own rules of procedure, which is the most appropriate way of obtaining all relevant information pertaining to the Community act in question. This, it is submitted, is the correct approach. If the Commission's view were followed, that would lead to the proceedings before the national court becoming unduly complicated. The intervention of the Community institutions concerned as of right would impose a heavy burden on national courts, especially on those at the lower tiers of the national judicial system. It would lead to undue formalism of the proceedings and be liable to lengthen what is by definition a summary procedure. All in all, it would be incompatible with the division of competence between the Court of Justice and the national court as envisaged in Article 234[177].

National courts do not have the power to order interim protection where, by virtue of a Community regulation, the existence and scope of individual rights must be established by another Community measure implementing the regulation and that measure has not yet been adopted. In *T. Port GmbH* v. *Bundesanstalt für Landwirtschaft und Ernährung*,[155] an undertaking importing bananas claimed that additional import licences should be allocated to it. On a reference for a preliminary ruling by the Higher Administrative Court of Hesse, the Court held that Article 30 of the Bananas Regulation enables and, depending on the circumstances, even requires the Commission to lay down transitional rules providing for the allocation of additional import licences in cases of hardship. The Court held, however, that the national court did not have power to grant additional import licences by way of interim measure. It distinguished the case in issue from *Zuckerfabrik* and *Atlanta* on the following basis. The case in issue concerned granting traders interim protection in a situation where, by virtue of a Community regulation, the existence and scope of traders' rights was to be established by a Commission measure which the Commission had not yet adopted.[156] The Treaty, however, makes no provision for a preliminary reference procedure by which a national court can ask the Court of Justice to rule that an institution has failed to act. Consequently, national

---

[154] Case C–334/95 [1997] ECR I–4517. See also the Opinion of Cosmas AG in Case C–183/95 *Affish* v. *Rijksdienst Keuring Vee en Vlees* [1997] ECR I–4315, at 4335– 6.

[155] Case C–68/95 [1996] ECR I–6065.   [156] Op. cit., para. 52.

courts have no jurisdiction to order interim measures pending action on the part of an institution. Judicial review of alleged failure to act can be exercised only by the Community courts.[157]

In *Port* the applicants were seeking to obtain by way of interim order a remedy which went beyond the scope of the main action. That is what distinguishes the case from *Atlanta*. The issue arises what are the alternative remedies available to a trader in the position of the applicants. The Court referred to the possibility of a trader bringing an action for failure to act against the Commission before the Court of First Instance. It held expressly that Article 232[175] entitles an individual to bring an action for failure to act against an institution which he claims has failed to adopt a measure which would concern him directly and individually.[158] It also stated that interim measures may be adopted in proceedings for failure to act. What is of particular interest is the implied suggestion in the judgment that a banana trader in the position of the applicant in *Port* would be able to establish direct and individual concern so as to require the Commission to adopt rules of general application catering for cases of hardship pursuant to Article 30 of the Banana Regulation. If that is correct, it means that in *Port* the Court was prepared to interpret the requirements of direct and individual concern particularly liberally.

By way of conclusion, it may be helpful to summarize the conditions which must be satisfied in order for a national court to be able to grant interim relief as stated by the Court in *Atlanta* and confirmed in subsequent cases.[159] Interim relief can be grant only if:

- the court entertains serious doubts as to the validity of the Community act and, if the validity of the contested act is not already in issue before the Court of Justice, itself refers the question to the Court of Justice;
- there is urgency, in that the interim relief is necessary to avoid serious and irreparable damage being caused to the party seeking such relief;
- the court takes due account of the Community interest; and
- in its assessment of all those conditions, it respects any decisions of the Court of Justice or the Court of First Instance ruling on the lawfulness of the regulation or on the application for interim measures seeking similar interim relief at Community level.

The Court of Justice entrusted national courts with wide powers to grant interim protection suspending the application of Community regulations. That development was inevitable given that the enforcement of Community law is a matter not only for the Community judicature but also for the national courts. As the Court observed, the interim protection available to individuals should be the same irrespective of whether they contest the legality of national measures or Community

---

[157] Op. cit., para. 53.

[158] In Case C–107/91 *ENU* v. *Commission* [1993] ECR I–599 the Court had made a similar finding in relation to Article 148 Euratom which is equivalent to Article 232[175].

[159] *Atlanta*, op.cit., para. 51; *Port*, op.cit., para. 48; *Krüger*, op.cit., para. 44.

measures since in both cases the challenge is based on Community law itself. There is no denying, however, that the power of national courts to suspend the application of Community law creates risks as it is liable to be applied diversely. If the coherence of the Community system of legal remedies and uniformity in the application of Community law are to be observed, that power must be exercised with caution.

9

Principles Governing Liability in Damages

There is no doubt that the most important aspect of the principle of effectiveness is the establishment by the Court of State liability in damages for breach of Community law and of the cognate right to reparation of injured parties. The development of the case law in this area, in particular the judgments in *Francovich*[1] and *Brasserie du Pêcheur*,[2] eminently illustrates the creative function of the Court. The subject has attracted vast bibliography[3] and will be examined in this chapter in some detail. By way of introductory comment, it may be said that the most controversial aspects of this area of law are the legal basis of liability, the conditions of liability, and the interaction between Community law and national law in defining the right to reparation. Before embarking on a discussion of State liability, however, it may be helpful to give an overview of the rules which govern Community liability under Article 288(2)[215(2)] EC. The development of the case law in this area is important for a number of reasons. It shows how the Court has understood its mandate to build up a common law on the liability of Community authorities. Also, it illustrates the role of general principles, such as equality, proportionality, etc., as rules of law, breach of which may give rise to liability. Finally, it has proved influential in developing State liability in damages for breach of Community law.

---

[1] Joined Cases C–6 and C–9/90 [1991] ECR I–5357.

[2] Joined Cases C–43 and C–48/93 *Brasserie du Pêcheur* v. *Germany and the Queen* v. *Secretary of State for Transport, ex parte Factortame Ltd.* [1996] ECR I–1029.

[3] See *inter alia*, the contributions in Beatson and Tridimas (eds.), *New Directions in European Public Law* (1998); T. Heukels and A. McDonell (eds.), *The Action for Damages in Community Law* (Kluwer, 1997); P. Craig, 'Once More unto the Breach: The Community, the State and Damages Liability' (1997) 113 LQR 67; M. Wathelet and S. Van Raepenbusch, 'La responsabilité des États Membres en cas de violation du droit Communautaire. Vers un alignement de la responsabilité de l'État sur celle de la Communauté ou l' inverse?' (1997) 33 CDE 13; W. Van Gerven, 'Bridging the Unbridgeable: Community and National Tort Laws after *Francovich* and *Brasserie*' (1996) 45 ICLQ 507; C. Harlow, 'Francovich and the Problem of the Disobedient State' (1996) 2 Eur.LJ 199; T. Downes, 'Trawling for a Remedy: State Liability under Community Law' (1997) 17 LS 286; N. Gravells (1996) PL 567; N. Emiliou (1996) 21 ELRev. 399; L. Neville Brown: 'State Liability to Individuals in Damages: An Emerging Doctrine of EU Law' (1996) 31 Ir.Jur. 7; Tridimas (1996) 55 CLJ 412. For earlier contributions, see W. Van Gerven, 'Non-Contractual Liability of Member States, Community Institutions and Individuals for Breaches of Community Law with a View to Common Law for Europe' (1994) 1 MJ 6; P. Craig, '*Francovich*, Remedies and the Scope of Damages Liability' (1993) 109 LQR 595; C. Lewis and S. Moore, 'Duties, Directives and Damages in European Community Law' (1993) PL 151.

9.1. Community liability: Article 288(2)[215(2)]

Article 288(2)[215(2)] provides that the Community must make good any damage caused by its institutions or by its servants in the performance of their duties, 'in accordance with the general principles common to the laws of the Member States'. The express reference to the laws of the Member States in Article 288(2)[215(2)] is less helpful than it appears. Save for very general principles which themselves offer little guidance to the judicial inquiry, there is in fact no common corpus of rules governing the non-contractual liability of public authorities in the national laws. The search for appropriate standards is perforce selective. According to the case law of the Court of Justice, in order for the Community to incur liability, the following conditions must be fulfilled: (a) there must be illegal conduct; (b) there must be damage, and (c) there must be a causal link between the unlawful conduct and the damage claimed.[4] In its seminal judgment in *Zuckerfabrik Schöppenstedt* the Court held that liability may arise not only as a result of an individual act but also as a result of legislation.[5] There is no intention here to discuss in detail the conditions of liability. This section seeks to give a short survey of the way the Court has approached the interpretation of Article 288(2)[215(2)] especially in relation to the concept of illegal conduct.[6]

9.1.1. Administrative action

In the field of administrative action, in principle, any infringement of law may constitute illegality which may give rise to extra-contractual liability. Thus the Commission may be liable for the improper application of protective measures suspending the issue of import licences,[7] for failing to keep secret the identity of an informant who provided information regarding the breach of competition law,[8] and for co-operating unlawfully with national authorities investigating the conduct of a Community official in the context of a criminal inquiry.[9] In one case it was held that, save in exceptional circumstances, the adoption of an incorrect interpretation of Community measures does not constitute illegality for the purposes of Article 288(2)[215(2)] and cannot give rise to liability on the part of the Commission. The Commission's delay in correcting that information, however, may give rise to liability.[10]

---

[4] See e.g. Case 4/69 *Lütticke* v. *Commission* [1971] ECR 325, para. 10; Case T–575/93 *Koelman* v. *Commission* [1996] ECR II–1, para. 89.

[5] Case 5/71 *Zuckerfabrik Schöppenstedt* v. *Council* [1971] ECR 975.

[6] This section examines only liability as a result of action attributable to the Community institutions (*faute de service*). Liability as a result of action attributable to the servants of the Community (*faute personelle*) falls beyond the scope of this book.

[7] Joined Cases 5, 7 and 13–24/66 *Kampffmeyer* v. *Commission* [1967] ECR 245.

[8] Case 145/83 *Adams* v. *Commission* [1985] ECR 3539.

[9] Case 108/87 *Hamill* v. *Commission* [1988] ECR 6141.

[10] Joined cases 19, 20, 25 and 30/69 *Richez-Parise* v. *Commission* [1970] ECR 325.

Liability may arise as a result of omission only where an institution has infringed a legal obligation to act under a provision of Community law. It follows that where the institutions enjoy discretion it would be extremely difficult for an action to succeed. In *KYDEP* v. *Council and Commission*,[11] a co-operative of Greek producers sought compensation arguing that the Council's failure to adopt special measures in favour of the cereals sector in Greece discriminated against Greek products which were affected much more than other Community products from the Chernobyl nuclear accident. The Court dismissed the claim on the facts holding that Greece was not the only region to have been affected seriously by the Chernobyl accident. The judgment leaves open the possibility that failure on the part of the institutions to redress inequality may give rise to liability. This, however, may be contemplated only in very exceptional circumstances.

9.1.2. Legislative measures

Liability of the Community arising as a result of legislative acts (normative injustice) is subject to more stringent conditions.[12] Clearly, a finding of invalidity is not in itself sufficient for the Community to incur liability.[13] In *Zuckerfabrik Schöppenstedt* the Court stated that, with regard to measures of economic policy, the Community does not incur liability for damage suffered by individuals 'unless a sufficiently flagrant violation of a superior rule of law for the protection of the individual has occurred'.[14] It follows that the conditions for liability in relation to measures of economic policy[15] are the following: (a) there must be violation of a superior rule of law for the protection of the individual, and (b) such violation must be sufficiently serious. The reason why liability is subject to such strict conditions is not difficult to understand. In making policy decisions, legislative and administrative authorities should be able to enjoy wide discretion and their decision making must not be inhibited by the threat of liability in case where a measure is subsequently found to be illegal. It is not the objective of liability in damages to be a sword of Damocles over the policy makers. Also, where an action in damages is successful, it is ultimately the taxpayer who is called upon to cover the costs. Viewed from that perspective, a public authority should incur liability as a result of legislative action only where the interest of compensating a group of persons who suffer loss as a result of that action is judged as more worthy of protection than the interest of the taxpayer. The *Schöppenstedt* formula is designed to meet the legitimate concern that liability in damages should not be a readily available remedy in relation to all invalid legislative acts.

[11] Case C–146/91 [1994] ECR I–4199, para. 58.

[12] Not only regulations but any act of general application is a legislative act. In the context of Article 288(2)[215(2)], the characterization of an act as legislative is important as the conditions of liability vary. See Case T–390/94 *Aloys Schröder, Jan Thamann and Karl-Julius Thamann* v. *Commission* [1997] ECR II–501, paras. 54 *et seq.*

[13] See e.g. Case C–282/90 *Vreugdenhil* v. *Commission* [1992] ECR I–1937, para. 19.

[14] Op.cit., para. 11.   [15] For other types of measures, see below p. 320.

9.1.2.1. Superior rule of law

In order for liability to arise, the superior rule of law whose violation is claimed must be for the protection of the individual.[16] It suffices that the rule is intended to protect interests of a general nature, for example the interests of producers in a certain sector. The test is therefore less stringent than the requirement of direct and individual concern applicable to establish *locus standi* in actions for judicial review under Article 230(4)[173(4)].[17] Certain principles are fundamental to the Community legal order but do not have as their purpose the protection of individual rights. This is for example the case with the principle of institutional balance. The objective of the rules governing the division of powers between the institutions is not to protect the individual but to maintain a balance between the institutions. Therefore, illegality of a measure which arises from failure to observe the institutional balance, as for example where the Commission exceeds its implementing powers, is not sufficient on its own to give rise to liability in damages.[18]

The principles of equality, proportionality, protection of legitimate expectations and fundamental rights are superior rules of law for the protection of the individual, breach of which may give rise to the extra-contractual liability of the Community, at least where they impose substantive obligations. It is less clear whether a breach of a procedural requirement can give rise to extra-contractual liability. The Court has held, for example, that breach of the requirement of reasoning may not give rise to liability in damages.[19] However, liability for breach of procedural requirements the purpose of which is to protect the individual may not be excluded as a matter of principle subject of course to the requirements of damage and causal effect. The case law has accepted that moral damage may also be compensated.[20] Such damages may be awarded, for example, in appropriate cases where fundamental rights have been infringed but the individual has not suffered any material loss.

It is notable that by far the greatest percentage of cases concerning the liability of the Community for normative injustice involve the alleged breach of a general principle of law deriving from the laws of Member States. In the overwhelming majority of those cases the action has been dismissed. The principle most usually

---

[16] So far, the case law has not addressed the issue whether a Member State may claim damages against the Community. There is no reason why such liability should be excluded a priori.

[17] See Joined Cases 5, 7 and 13–24/66 *Kampfmeyer* v. *Commission* [1967] ECR 245, at 263; See also *Schöppenstedt*, op.cit.; Joined Cases 9 and 12/60 *Vloeberghs* v. *High Authority* [1961] ECR 195; Case 9/56 *Meroni* v. *High Authority* [1958] ECR 133; Joined Cases 9 and 11/71 *Compagnie d'Approvisionnement* v. *Commission* [1972] ECR 391.

[18] Case C–282/90 *Vreugdenhil* v. *Commission* [1992] ECR I–1937.

[19] Case 106/81 *Kind* v. *EEC* [1982] ECR 2885, para. 14, and see more recently the CFI's case law: Case T–167/94 *Nölle* v. *Council and Commission* [1994] ECR II–2589, para. 57; *Aloys Schröder, Jan Thamann and Karl-Julius Thamann* v. *Commission*, op.cit., para. 66.

[20] See e.g. Case 110/63 *Williame* [1965] ECR 667 and see further Schermers and Waelbroeck, op.cit., p. 359.

pleaded is the principle of equal treatment[21] but breach of respect for legitimate expectations has also been asserted, in some cases successfully.[22] By contrast, so far there has been no successful action in damages for breach of fundamental rights[23] or the principle of proportionality.[24]

9.1.2.2. Seriousness of the violation

The violation of a superior rule of law does not *per se* give rise to liability in damages. In order for such liability to arise the violation must be sufficiently serious. But what is a sufficiently serious breach? The case law in this area appears to be evolving. Although few actions have been successful, recent cases evince a relaxation of the strict approach of earlier case law. In *HNL* v. *Council and Commission* the Court held that in legislative areas where the exercise of wide discretion is essential for the implementation of a Community policy, the Community may not incur liability 'unless the institution concerned has manifestly and gravely disregarded the limits on the exercise of powers'.[25] The case concerned the Community regime for the compulsory purchase of skimmed-milk powder. Owing to imbalance between supply and demand, the Community accumulated a skimmed-milk 'mountain'. With a view to disposing of the surpluses, Council Regulation No. 563/76[26] provided for the compulsory purchase of skimmed-milk powder by producers for use in feeding-stuffs. In a series of cases, the Court declared the regulation void as being contrary to the principles of equality and proportionality.[27] In *HNL* the applicants were animal producers who, following the annulment of the regulation, applied for compensation of the damage which they allegedly suffered

---

[21] For examples of unsuccessful actions see *Zuckerfabrik Schöppenstedt* v. *Council*, op.cit.; Case 49/79 *Pool* v. *Council* [1980] ECR 569 (alleging breach of the principle of non-discrimination as expressed in Article 34(2)[40(3)] EC as a result of the conversion rate fixed for the pound sterling); Case 20/88 *Roquette Frères* v. *Commission* [1989] ECR 1553 (breach of the principle of equal treatment resulting from the miscalculation of monetary compensatory amounts was an insufficiently serious technical error); *KYDEP* v. *Council and Commission*, op.cit. (alleged breach of Article 34(2)[40(3)] by the fixing of maximum permitted levels of radioactive contamination); *Aloys Schröder, Jan Thamann and Karl-Julius Thamann* v. *Commission*, op.cit. (alleged breach arising from measures seeking to contain the spreading of swine fever).

[22] For successful actions see Joined Cases C–104/89 and C–37/90 *Mulder* v. *Council and Commission* (*Mulder II*) [1992] ECR I–3061; Case C–152/88 *Sofrimport* v. *Commission* [1990] ECR I–2477. In Case 74/74 *CNTA* [1975] ECR 533, which concerned monetary compensatory amounts, the Court found violation of the principle of protection of legitimate expectations but, in subsequent proceedings, the applicant company failed to establish loss: [1976] ECR 797.

[23] In a number of cases, applicants have unsuccessfully sought to recover damages allegedly flowing from breach of the right to property or the freedom to trade. See e.g. Case 59/83 *Biovilac* v. *EEC* [1984] ECR 4057; *Aloys Schröder, Jan Thamann and Karl-Julius Thamann* v. *Commission*, op.cit.

[24] See e.g. Joined Cases 83 and 94/76, 4, 15 and 40/77 *HNL* v. *Council and Commission* [1978] ECR 1209, cf. Opinion of Capotorti AG; Joined Cases 63 to 69/72 *Werhahn* v. *Council* [1973] ECR 1229, cf. Opinion of Roemer AG.

[25] Joined Cases 83 and 94/76, 4, 15 and 40/77 *HNL* v. *Council and Commission* [1978] ECR 1209, para. 6.

[26] OJ 1976 L 67/18.

[27] Case 114/76 *Bela-Mühle* v. *Grows-Farm* [1977] ECR 1211, Case 116/76 *Granaria* [1977] ECR 1247, Joined Cases 119 and 120/76 *Ölmühle and Becher* [1977] ECR 1269.

as a result of the regulation. After explaining that liability in damages should be subject to strict conditions so as not to hinder the institutions in taking policy decisions, the Court stated that individuals may be required to accept within reasonable limits harmful effects on their economic interests as a result of a legislative measure without being able to obtain compensation from public funds even if that measure has been declared null and void. On the facts of the case, the Court found that there was no manifest and grave disregard by the institutions of the limits of their powers. It based its judgment on two considerations. First, the regulation in issue affected very wide categories of traders so that its effects on individual undertakings were considerably lessened. Secondly, the effects of the regulation on the production costs of those traders were only limited. The Court concluded that the effects of the regulation on the profit-earning capacity of the traders 'did not ultimately exceed the bounds of the economic risks inherent in the activities of the agricultural sectors concerned'.[28] It is interesting that in his Opinion Capotorti AG took a different view concluding that the Community was liable.[29]

Subsequently in the quellmehl and gritz cases,[30] which involved breach of the principle of equal treatment, the Court found that there was 'manifest and grave disregard'. The Court held that, in the circumstances, the violation of the principle of equality affected a limited and clearly defined group of commercial operators; the damage suffered by the applicants went beyond the bounds of the economic risks inherent in the sector concerned; and equality of treatment between the products in issue had been terminated without sufficient justification. The last ground indicates that discrimination in those cases was linked to a loose notion of vested rights: the discrimination was the result of terminating without good reason equality in treatment which existed under previous regulations. In the isoglucose cases,[31] however, the Court found that a breach of the principle of equality did not lead to liability in damages on the ground that the conduct of the defendant institutions was not 'verging on the arbitrary',[32] despite the fact that the group of traders involved was equally limited and clearly defined. One of the considerations which the Court took into account was that the regulation imposing a levy on isoglucose which had been found to infringe the principle of equal treatment in previous proceedings was an urgent measure adopted to deal with an

---

[28] Op.cit., para. 7.

[29] See *HNL*, op.cit., 1231–7.

[30] Case 238/78 *Ireks-Arkady* v. *Council and Commission* [1979] ECR 2955; Joined Cases 261 and 262/78 *Interquell Stärke-Chemie* v. *Council and Commission* [1979] ECR 3045; Joined Cases 241, 242 and 245–50/78 *DGV* v. *Council and Commission* [1979] ECR 3017; Joined Cases 64 and 113/76, 167 and 239/78, 27, 28 and 45/79 *Dumortier Frères* v. *Council* [1979] ECR 3091. Cf. Case 90/78 *Granaria* v. *Council and Commission* [1979] ECR 1081 where the action was unsuccessful since no breach of the principle of equality was established.

[31] Joined Cases 116 and 124/77 *Amylum* v. *Council and Commission* [1979] ECR 3497. Case 143/77 *Koninklijke Scholten-Honig* v. *Council and Commission* [1979] ECR 3583.

[32] See Case *Amylum* v. *Council and Commission*, op.cit., para. 19. Note, however, that it is not a separate requirement of liability that the conduct verges on the arbitrary: Case C–220/91 *Commission* v. *Stahlwerke Peine-Salzgitter* [1993] ECR I–2393, para. 51.

emergency situation. The isoglucose cases are not easy to reconcile with the quellmehl and gritz cases[33] and illustrate how difficult it is to quantify legally the existence of a sufficiently serious breach. That difficulty has led in some cases to divergence of views between the Advocates General and the Court.[34]

It follows from the above cases that, in determining whether there is a manifest and grave disregard of the limits on discretionary powers, the Court refers to two elements:[35] (a) the effect of the measure on individuals, in other words, the degree of harm suffered by them as a result of the measure; and (b) the extent to which the law has been violated. The first element refers to the nature of the damage suffered rather than to the infringement *per se*. Under the case law, however, it is a necessary condition for the establishment of unlawfulness.[36] In particular, a requirement which consistently appears in the case law is that, in order for liability to ensue, the damage alleged by the applicants must go beyond the bounds of the economic risks inherent in the activities in the sector concerned.[37]

The Court was more generous to the applicants in *Mulder II*,[38] a case which determines with greater accuracy than any other the dividing line between illegality and unlawfulness. The case concerned breach of legitimate expectations and arose from the Community milk quota regime. It is discussed elsewhere in this book.[39] Suffice to mention here certain conclusions which may be derived from the case with regard to the liability of Community institutions. In contrast to previous cases, in *Mulder II* liability was established although the measure in issue affected a wide category of traders. It is notable that, whereas in the quellmehl and gritz cases the Court referred to 'a *limited* and clearly defined group of commercial operators',[40] in *Mulder II* reference was made merely to 'a clearly defined group of economic agents'.[41] It follows that it is not a strict requirement of liability that the group of persons affected must be limited in number. It does not follow, however, that the limited number of the persons affected may never be a relevant issue. It is a consideration to be taken into account together with other considerations, in particular, the extent to which the law has been violated. *Mulder II* makes clear that liability is more likely to arise where, in exercising its discretion, the Community legislature totally fails to take into account relevant interests rather than where it

---

[33] See further, Hartley, *Foundations of European Community Law*, p. 471.

[34] See *HNL*, op.cit.; Case C–63/89 *Assurances du Crédit* v. *Council and Commission* [1991] ECR I–1799. Cf. Case C–152/88 *Sofrimport* v. *Commission* [1990] ECR I–2477.

[35] Hartley, op.cit., p. 471.

[36] See further, F. Grondman, 'La Notion de violation suffisamment charactérisée en matière de responsabilité non contractuelle' (1979) CDE, No. 1, p. 86; E-W. Fuss, 'La responsabilité des Communautés européennes pour le comportement illégal de leur organes' (1981) RTDE 1.

[37] See e.g. Joined Cases C–104/89 and C–37/90 *Mulder* v. *Council and Commission* [1992] ECR I–3061, para. 13.

[38] Joined Cases C–104/89 and C–37/90 *Mulder* v. *Council and Commission* [1992] ECR I–3061.

[39] See above, p. 191.

[40] *Ireks-Arcady* v. *Council and Commission*, op.cit., para. 11 (emphasis added).

[41] *Mulder II*, op.cit., para. 16.

does take such interests into account but fails to grant them due consideration. The Community institutions were found liable to the extent that they totally excluded returning producers from the allocation of a quota but were not found liable for allocating to them a quota reduced to 60 per cent of their production.

The action succeeded also in *Sofrimport* v. *Commission*.[42] The applicant was refused an import licence for goods in transit as a result of Commission protective measures suspending import licences. The Court found that the suspensory measures ran counter to the principle of protection of legitimate expectations in so far as they applied to goods in transit and that the Community was liable to make good the damage suffered by the applicant. In that case the legitimate expectation of the applicant was based on a Council Regulation which specifically intended to protect goods in transit from the unfavourable consequences of protective measures. Overall, the cases decided in the 1990s evince a more liberal attitude towards establishing liability of Community institutions than the cases decided in the 1970s.[43] The number of cases decided, however, is relatively small and it is difficult to draw reliable conclusions.[44] Indeed, one of the general observations which may be made is that this area of law does not lend itself to certainty. The existing authorities make it difficult to predict whether in a given case the requirements of liability are likely to be fulfilled.

9.1.3. Measures other than measures of economic policy

The requirement of 'manifest and grave disregard' applies not only in relation to measures of economic policy but also in relation to all measures where the institution concerned enjoys wide discretion. In *Assurances du Crédit* v. *Council and Commission*,[45] the Court applied the same test to determine whether the Community was liable for the alleged breach of the principle of non-discrimination by a harmonization directive. In any event, the concept of a measure of economic policy for the purposes of Article 288(2)[215(2)] is a broad one. It seems to cover all decisions adopted in the exercise of a discretion and intended to organize a sector, in particular a common organization of the market.[46] Where, however, the Commission does not enjoy wide discretionary powers, the requirement that the violation must be sufficiently serious is not exemplified by the condition that it must have manifestly and gravely disregarded the limits of its powers.[47]

---

[42] Case C–152/88 [1990] ECR I–2477.   [43] Hartley, op.cit., p. 494.

[44] Note also Case C–220/91 P *Commission* v. *Stahlwerke Peine-Salzgitter* [1993] ECR I–2393, where the Court upheld on appeal a judgment of the CFI finding the Commission liable in damages in an action under Articles 34 and 40 of the ECSC Treaty.

[45] Case C–63/89 *Assurances du Crédit* v. *Council and Commission* [1991] ECR I–1799.

[46] See e.g. *Aloys Schröder, Jan Thamann and Karl-Julius Thamann* v. *Commission*, op.cit.; T–472/93 *Campo Ebro Industrial and Others* v. *Council* [1995] ECR II–421.

[47] See e.g. *Sofrimport*, op.cit. The measure in issue in that case was not a policy measure. Indeed, its truly legislative character may be questioned since the Court found that it was of direct and individual concern to the applicant.

9.1.4. Liability for valid acts

Illegality of a measure, although in itself not sufficient, seems to be a necessary condition of liability.[48] Could there be liability for valid acts? In *Biovilac*,[49] relying on the notion of 'special sacrifice' developed in German and French law,[50] the applicant argued that the Community is liable to make good loss which a trader suffers as a result of lawful measures taken in the public interest if he is harmed by them in a distinct way and much more severely than other traders. In the circumstances of the case, the Court rejected the claim on the ground that the damage allegedly suffered did not exceed the limits of the economic risks inherent in the sector concerned. The Court, however, expressly left open the possibility of liability arising without illegality on the basis of the theory of special sacrifice.[51] Following the Advocate General, it stated that, even if that theory were accepted in Community law, it could not cover loss from a measure which was or should have been foreseeable.

9.2. The legal basis of State liability

The EC Treaty is silent on the issue whether Member States may be liable in damages to injured parties for breach of Community law. Traditionally, it was accepted that the matter was governed by national law. In its case law under Article 226[169], the Court had repeatedly pointed out that a judgment finding an infringement of Community law may serve as the basis of liability that a Member State may incur under national law against private parties.[52] In *Russo* v. *AIMA*,[53] decided in 1976, an Italian producer claimed that he had suffered loss as a result of action by the Italian intervention agency which made available in the market products at prices lower than those guaranteed to producers by Community agricultural regulations. The Court held that under Community law, a producer may claim that

---

[48] This is not to say that the measure must have already been declared illegal in proceedings for annulment in order for an action for damages to succeed. The action for damages is an autonomous form of action: see *Zuckerfabrik Schöppenstedt*, op.cit.

[49] Case 59/83 *Biovilac* v. *EEC* [1984] ECR 4057.

[50] In German law the notion is known as 'sonderopfer' and in French law it is referred to as 'rupture de l'egalité devant les charges publiques'.

[51] *Biovilac*, op.cit., para. 28. Note that the issue had been left open by the Court also in previous cases: Joined Cases 9 and 11/71 *Compagnie d'Approvisionnement* v. *Commission* [1972] ECR 391 and Case 169/73 *Compagnie Continentale* v. *Commission* [1975] ECR 117. Even in *Zuckerfabrik Schöppenstedt* v. *Council* [1971] ECR 975 at para. 11, the Court stated (emphasis added): 'In the *present* case the non-contractual liability of the Community presupposes at the very least the unlawful nature of the act alleged to be the cause of the damage.' In *Biovilac*, op.cit., at 4091, Slynn AG drew parallels between the requirement to pay compensation for the expropriation of property and the notion of special sacrifice.

[52] See e.g. Case 39/72 *Commission* v. *Italy* [1973] ECR 101, para. 11; Case 154/85 *Commission* v. *Italy* [1987] ECR 2717, para. 6.

[53] Case 60/75 *Russo* v. *AIMA* [1976] ECR 45.

he should not be prevented from obtaining a price approximating to the target price and in any event not lower than the intervention price. It then stated that it was for the national court to decide, on the basis of the facts of each case, whether an individual producer has suffered damage. If damage had been caused through an infringement of Community law, the State was liable to the injured party in accordance with the provisions of national law on the liability of public authorities.[54] The traditional approach of the Court towards remedies was encapsulated in a dictum, made in *Rewe* v. *Hauptzollamt Kiel* in 1981, that the EC Treaty 'was not intended to create new remedies'.[55]

The issue of liability for breach of Community law was not addressed again by the Court until 1991.[56] In its seminal judgment in *Francovich*,[57] the Court established that a Member State may be liable in damages to an injured party for breach of Community law. The case concerned loss arising as a result of failure by a Member State to implement a directive. The Court based liability on two grounds: the principle of effectiveness and Article 10[5] EC. Its reasoning is instructive of the way it interprets the Treaty and of the way it understands its function in developing Community law. It first recalled that Community law gives rise to rights for individuals which become part of their legal heritage and that such rights arise not only where they are expressly provided in the Treaty but also by virtue of obligations which the Treaty imposes in a clearly defined manner on Member States. It also stated that national courts must provide full protection to rights which Community law confers on individuals. It then continued:[58]

The full effectiveness of Community rules would be impaired and the protection of the rights which they grant would be weakened if individuals were unable to obtain redress when their rights are infringed by a breach of Community law for which a Member State can be held responsible.

The possibility of obtaining redress from a Member State is particularly indispensable where, as in this case, the full effectiveness of Community rules is subject to prior action on the part of the State and where, consequently, in the absence of such action, individuals cannot enforce before the national courts the rights conferred upon them by Community law.

It follows that the principle whereby a State must be liable for loss and damage caused to individuals as a result of breaches of Community law for which the State can be held responsible is inherent in the system of the Treaty.

The Court found a further basis of liability in Article 10[5], stating that among the measures which Member States must take to ensure fulfilment of their obligations,

---

[54] Op.cit., paras. 8–9. See also Case 181/82 *Roussel* [1983] ECR 3849 and the earlier dicta in Case 101/78 *Granaria* v. *Hoofdproductschap voor Akkerbouwprodukten* [1979] ECR 623, para. 14.

[55] Case 158/80 [1981] ECR 1805, para. 44. See above 8.1.

[56] The question whether liability in damages may arise for breach of Community law by national administrative measures was referred in Case 380/87 *Enichem Base and Others* v. *Comune di Cinisello Balsamo* [1989] ECR 2491. The Court did not examine that question as it was not necessary to do so in the light of its reply to the other questions referred. The issue of damages as a remedy for breach of the Equal Treatment Directive was discussed briefly by Van Gerven AG in Case C–188/89 *Foster and Others* v. *British Gas* [1990] ECR I–3301, at 3341.

[57] Op.cit., n. 1.   [58] Op.cit., paras. 33–5.

as required by Article 10[5], is the obligation to nullify the unlawful consequences of a breach of Community law.

The question may well be asked what changed between 1981, when the Court declared that the Treaty is not intended to create new remedies, and 1991, when the Court proclaimed that State liability in damages 'is inherent in the system of the Treaty'. Why did the Court take such a fundamentally different approach in *Francovich* than it had taken in previous years? The answer may be found only if one looks at the development of the case law on judicial remedies as a whole. In the early 1990s the case law moved from an approach based on rights to an approach based on remedies. Establishment of State liability in damages is the high point in the evolution of the principle of primacy from a general principle of constitutional law to a specific obligation on national courts to provide full and effective remedies for the protection of Community rights.[59] It has been noted that the principles of direct and indirect effect of directives were developed in the light of persistent failures by Member States to fulfil their obligations with a view to securing the enforcement of Community law.[60] *Francovich* could be seen as another such 'expedient'. This analysis is correct but does not give the whole picture. It is an implicit premise in every legal system that the courts which are entrusted with upholding its laws must avoid consequences which would undermine its fundamental presuppositions. Viewed in that perspective, direct effect and State liability in damages can be seen merely as the means to achieve results or, to put it in a different way, as the directed use of judicial power. Such an analysis, however, is one-sided and liable to give the impression that judicial developments occur in a theoretical vacuum. That is not the case. The Court's approach can be encapsulated in the principle *ubi jus, ibi remedium*. According to this approach, the value of a right is determined by the legal consequences which ensue from its violation, namely the remedies available from its enforcement. The common thread underlying the Court's case law on remedies is the concern to ensure the availability of effective judicial protection. Such reasoning is by no means unique to the Community judicature. In his dissenting judgment in *Bourgoin*,[61] Oliver LJ (as he then was) followed a similar approach. At the risk of becoming 'too metaphysical', he distinguished between a general right to have the provisions of the law observed, shared by everyone, and an individual right requiring protection. He then continued: 'It is only when the breach of the public duty inflicts loss or damage on the individual that he has, as an

---

[59] Traces of the Court's approach in *Francovich* can already be found in the Opinion of the Advocate General in *Russo* v. *AIMA*. Reischl AG stated that the issue of Member State liability was one for the national courts in accordance with the national legal system. He added, however, that, in order to avoid the risk of unequal treatment of individuals under the national legal system which applied to them, it was necessary to work out principles, as the Court had done in other cases, upon which a uniform and effective enforcement of Community rights could be established. *Russo* v. *AIMA*, op.cit. n. 53, 62.

[60] J. Steiner, 'From Direct effects to Francovich: shifting means of enforcement of Community law' (1993) 18 ELRev. 3, at 10. That view received judicial recognition by Léger AG in Case C–5/94 *The Queen* v. *Ministry of Agriculture, Fisheries and Food, ex parte Hedley Lomas (Ireland) Ltd.* [1996] ECR I–2553, at 2575.

[61] *Bourgoin SA* v. *Ministry of Agriculture* [1986] 3 All ER 585.

individual, a cause of complaint. *If the law gives him no remedy for that damage then he would not ordinarily be said to have any "individual right".*[62] In *Francovich* the Court viewed State liability as the natural consequence of the breach of individual rights granted by Community law. The question still remains, why did the Court feel able to do so in *Francovich* although it had been so reticent in previous cases? It seems that three factors precipitated a change of attitude. First, the Commission's internal market programme, heralded by the 1985 White Paper, provided a new impetus for the completion of the internal market and made all the more important the provision of adequate remedies for failure to implement directives. Secondly, previous case law, in particular the judgment in *Factortame*,[63] had prepared the ground for increasing judicial intervention in the area of remedies. Thirdly, the facts of *Francovich* lent themselves to the recognition of State liability in damages given the manifest and inexcusable breach of Community law in the circumstances of the case. In short, the legal and political climate was such as to enable the Court to make a quantum leap.

The next step came in *Brasserie du Pêcheur and Factortame*.[64] In *Brasserie du Pêcheur*, a French company was forced to discontinue exports of beer to Germany because the German authorities considered that the beer it produced did not satisfy the requirements of German law. Earlier, in the *Beer* case,[65] the Court had found in enforcement proceedings brought by the Commission that German law infringed Article 28[30] in two respects: (a) by prohibiting the marketing under the designation 'beer' of beers lawfully produced in other Member States by different methods (the designation prohibition) and (b) by prohibiting the importation of beers containing additives (the additives prohibition). The French company brought an action for reparation of the loss that it suffered as a result of the import restrictions. In *Factortame*, the applicants sought to recover the loss that they incurred as a result of the registration conditions imposed by the Merchant Shipping Act 1988, which in previous proceedings had been found by the Court to be incompatible with Article 43[52] of the Treaty.[66]

The difference between *Francovich* and *Brasserie du Pêcheur* is that, whereas the former concerned liability arising from inaction, the latter concerned liability arising from an act of the national legislature. The Court did not find that to be a material difference. It held that, since the principle of State liability is inherent in the system of the Treaty, it 'holds good for any case in which a Member State breaches Community law, whatever be the organ of the State whose act or omission was responsible for the breach'.[67] It follows that a Member State is liable irrespective of whether the breach which gave rise to the damage is attributable to the legislature,

---

[62] Op.cit., at 616, emphasis added.
[63] Case C–213/89 *Factortame and Others* [1990] ECR I–2433.   [64] Op.cit., n. 2.
[65] Case 178/84 *Commission* v. *Germany* [1987] ECR 1227.
[66] See Case C–221/89 *Factortame II* [1991] ECR I–3905, Case C–246/89 *Commission* v. *United Kingdom* [1991] ECR I–4585.
[67] *Brasserie du Pêcheur*, op.cit., n. 2, para. 32.

the judiciary or the executive. The Court rejected the argument submitted by some Member States that, where a provision is directly effective, it is unnecessary to provide individuals who are affected by its breach with a right to reparation. It pointed out that direct effect cannot secure for individuals in every case the benefit of the rights conferred upon them by Community law nor can it avoid their sustaining damage as a result of a breach of Community law attributable to a Member State. The right of reparation is 'the necessary corollary' rather than a substitute for direct effect.[68]

In *Brasserie*, the German government argued that a general right of reparation for individuals could be created only by legislation and that for such a right to be recognized by judicial decision would be incompatible with the allocation of powers between the Community institutions and Member States. Dismissing that argument, the Court held that the existence and extent of State liability for breach of Community law are questions of interpretation of the Treaty which fall within the jurisdiction of the Court. Referring to Article 220[164], it stated that since the Treaty contains no provision governing the consequences of breaches of Community law by Member States, it is for the Court to rule on such questions, in accordance with general principles of interpretation, by reference in particular to the fundamental principles of the Community legal system and, where necessary, legal principles common to the legal systems of the Member States.[69] That reasoning is indicative of the way the Court approaches Article 220[164] and understands its function in the development of Community law.[70]

The extension of State liability to cases where a breach of Community law is the result of action by the national legislature was to be expected. Once the principle of State liability in damages was established in *Francovich*, there was no longer any valid reason why such liability should be restricted only to cases where a Member State had failed to take implementing measures to transpose a directive into national law. However, the basis of State liability arising as a result of acts of the legislature is not identified with sufficient clarity in *Brasserie*. That basis is to be found in the distinct nature of Community law and in the principle of primacy. It is not based in principles common to the laws of the Member States as the Court implied. As Léger AG stated in *Hedley Lomas*, with regard to State liability arising from acts of the legislature, 'there are no general principles which are *truly common* to the Member States'.[71]

9.3. The conditions of State liability: An overview

The Court has repeatedly emphasized that the conditions which must be fulfilled in order for State liability to arise differ depending on the nature of the breach of

---

[68] Op.cit., para. 22.   [69] Op.cit., para. 27.   [70] See above, Ch. 1.
[71] *Hedley Lomas*, op.cit., n. 60, at 2579 (emphasis in the original).

Community law giving rise to the damage.[72] In *Dillenkofer*, however, an attempt was made to unify the conditions of liability and, as a general rule, the following conditions must be fulfilled:[73]

* the rule of law infringed must be intended to confer rights to individuals;
* the breach must be sufficiently serious;
* there must be a direct causal link between the breach of the obligation resting on the State and the damage sustained by the injured party.

So far, the Court has examined the following types of breach: failure to transpose a directive into national law; breach of a Treaty provision by the national legislature; breach of a Treaty provision by the national administration; and incorrect transposition of a directive into national law. These types of breach will be examined in turn in the sections that follow. It should be noted at this stage that the existence of a direct causal link[74] is a condition of liability common to all types of breach, on which the Court has not given specific guidelines. The Court has held that it is for the national court to determine whether there is a direct causal link between the breach of Community law and the damage sustained by the injured parties.[75] That reference is somewhat ambiguous. It must be accepted that it is for the national court to establish whether there is a causal link on the specific facts of the case but the rules governing causation should not be left entirely to national law. That would amount to a 'renationalization' of the conditions of liability. One would expect that subsequent case law will provide guidelines regarding the requirement of causation. In fact, as Professor Van Gerven has noted, it is surprising that the Court did not refer in the context of State liability to the principles governing causation laid down in its case law under Article 288(2)[215(2)].[76]

9.4. Failure to transpose a directive into national law

Where a Member State fails to take implementing measures in order to transpose a directive into national law, the conditions of liability are the following:

(1) the result prescribed by the directive must entail the grant of rights to individuals;

[72] See e.g. *Francovich*, op.cit., n. 1, para. 35; *Brasserie*, op.cit., n. 2, para. 31.

[73] Joined Cases C–178, C–179, C–188 to C–190/94 *Dillenkofer and Others* v. *Federal Republic of Germany* [1996] ECR I–4845, paras. 21–4; See also Joined Cases C–283, C–291 and C–292/94 *Denkavit Internationaal BV and Others* v. *Bundesamt für Finanzen* [1996] ECR I–5063, para. 48.

[74] The term 'direct' did not appear in *Francovich* where the Court referred to the 'existence of a causal link': op.cit., n. 1, para. 40. It was added in *Brasserie* and has appeared since in subsequent cases.

[75] *Brasserie*, op.cit., n. 2, para. 65; *Hedley Lomas*, op.cit., n. 60, para. 30.

[76] See W. Van Gerven, 'Taking Article 215(2) EC Seriously', in Beatson and Tridimas, *New Directions in European Public Law*, p. 35 at p. 38. For a recent case where liability was denied for lack of causation, see: C-319/96 *Brinkmann Tobakfabriken* v. *Skatteministeriet*, judgment of 24 Sept. 1998.

(2) it must be possible to identify the content of those rights on the basis of the provisions of the directive; and

(3) there must exist a causal link between the breach of the State's obligation and the harm suffered by the injured parties.

Those conditions were laid down in *Francovich*[77] and, subsequently, reiterated in *Dillenkofer*,[78] a case which arose from Germany's failure to implement Directive 90/314 on package travel.[79] Directive 90/314 seeks to protect the purchaser of package travel in the event of the insolvency of the travel operator and, to that effect, Article 7 provides that the organizer or retailer of package travel must provide the consumer with 'sufficient evidence of security for the refund of money paid over and for the repatriation of the consumer in the event of insolvency'. The Directive required implementation by 31 December 1992 but it was not implemented in Germany until 1994. The applicants were purchasers of package tours who, following the insolvency of their tour operators in 1993, either never left for their destination or incurred expenses to return home. Having failed to obtain reimbursement of the sums paid to the operators or the repatriation expenses, they sought compensation from the German State on the ground that, if Germany had implemented the Directive within the prescribed time limit, they would have been protected against the insolvency of the tour operators.

In *Dillenkofer* it was argued by several governments that a State may incur liability for late transposition of a directive only where there has been a serious breach of Community law. The Court declined to accept that argument. It stated that failure of a Member State to implement a directive within the prescribed period is *per se* a serious breach and, consequently, it gives rise to a right of reparation for individuals subject to the conditions of liability provided for in *Francovich*. No other condition need be taken into consideration.[80] In particular, liability does not depend on the circumstances which caused the period of transposition to be exceeded. Also, liability does not depend on the prior finding by the Court of an infringement of Community law attributable to the State nor on the existence of intentional fault or negligence on the part of the State.[81] The Court proceeded to examine whether the first two conditions of liability provided for in *Francovich* were

---

[77] In *Francovich* the Court drew a distinction between provisions which are sufficiently precise and unconditional so as to be able to produce direct effect and provisions which, although lacking sufficient precision for the purposes of direct effect, are nonetheless capable of giving rise to a right to reparation. The right to reparation is therefore a correlative right, separate in law from direct effect. The provisions of Directive 80/987 in issue in *Francovich* were sufficiently precise with regard to the identity of the right holder and the content of the right but not with regard to the persons on whom the corresponding obligation was imposed. The right granted by the Directive was therefore incomplete. The right to reparation, however, was complete since there can be no doubt about the identity of the person on whom the obligation to implement a directive is imposed. That obligation burdens *ex hypothesi* the State.

[78] Op.cit., n. 73.

[79] Council Directive 90/314/EEC on package travel, package holidays and package tours, OJ 1990 L 158/59.

[80] *Dillenkofer*, op.cit., n. 73, para. 27.   [81] Op.cit., para. 28.

fulfilled in relation to the Package Travel Directive and found that Article 7 of the Directive entailed the grant to package travellers of rights the content of which were sufficiently identifiable.

Despite the generality of the judgment in *Dillenkofer*, which appears to recognize no exceptions, the question may be asked whether there may be circumstances in which failure to transpose a directive within the prescribed period does not in itself constitute a serious breach. The following cases may be examined.

Transposition through existing legislation. Where a Member State does not transpose a directive on the assumption that existing national legislation already complies with its provisions,[82] and subsequently it transpires that the existing legislation does not satisfy the requirements of the directive because the State misinterpreted the directive, it is submitted that liability should not be automatic.[83] That case should be equated with the situation where a Member State implements a directive incorrectly and should be subject, *mutatis mutandis*, to the same conditions of liability. It will be necessary therefore to establish that the error of interpretation committed by the Member State constitutes a serious breach.[84]

Failure to implement attributable to a Community institution. Where the implementation of a Community measure (for example, an agricultural regulation) by the national authorities is subject to prior action by the Commission and the latter has failed to take the requisite action, it may be argued that the failure to implement is not attributable to the State but to the Commission. Any loss suffered therefore by an individual may not be causally linked to the State's but to the Commission's inaction. Whether such a defence may succeed will depend on the circumstances and on the obligations incumbent on the State in such a case.

Illegality of directive as defence. May a State plead as a defence that the unimplemented directive is vitiated by illegality? This question gives rise to intricate issues and, so far, has not been addressed by the Court. It should be noted that a Community measure is voidable and not void in that it can be annulled by the Court of Justice or the Court of First Instance only if it is challenged via certain procedural routes by an applicant having *locus standi* within the specified time limit. The case law on enforcement proceedings may here be instructive. It has been held that a Member State cannot plead the unlawfulness of a decision addressed to it as a defence in an action for a declaration that it has failed to fulfil its obligations arising out of its failure to implement that decision.[85] The rationale behind this approach is that enforce-

---

[82] The case law accepts that, subject to certain safeguards, where national law already complies with the requirements of a directive, a Member State need not take implementing measures. See e.g. Case 29/84 *Commission* v. *Germany* [1985] ECR 1661.

[83] For an example of unsuccessful transposition by existing legislation, see Case C–334/92 *Wagner Miret* [1993] ECR I–6911.

[84] See below, p. 337 the *BT* case and the guidelines given by the Court there.

[85] See e.g. Case 156/77 *Commission* v. *Belgium* [1978] ECR 1881, para. 24; Case 52/84 *Commission* v. *Belgium* [1986] ECR 89, para. 13; Case 226/87 *Commission* v. *Greece* [1988] ECR I–3611, para. 14.

ment actions under Articles 226[169] and 227[170] and actions for judicial review under Article 230[173] are different remedies, which pursue different objectives and are subject to different rules.[86] This general rule, however, is subject to two caveats. The case law seems to recognize an exception where the Community measure in issue 'would lack all legal basis in the Community legal system'[87] or infringe 'a principle of a constitutional nature'.[88] Secondly, the existing authorities refer to enforcement proceedings initiated by the Commission in relation to failure to comply with individual decisions addressed to a Member States.[89] It has been argued that the position would be different in relation to enforcement proceedings for failure to comply with regulations.[90] In such a case, the defendant State could challenge the applicability of the regulation by virtue of the plea of illegality. This view finds support in Article 241[184] which states that the inapplicability of regulations may be invoked 'in proceedings in which a regulation . . . is at issue', and therefore should be taken to include proceedings under Article 226[169]. Suffice it to say here that, if that view is correct, it should apply not only to regulations but to all legislative acts, including directives.

In the context of actions for liability in damages, the following points may be made. In some cases, the defendant Member State may not succeed in its attempt to plead invalidity. Thus, a Member State which considers that a directive has been adopted in violation of an essential procedural requirement but does not bring an action for its annulment within the time limit provided for in Article 230[173] and chooses instead not to implement it, may not necessarily succeed in pleading procedural impropriety as a defence in an action for damages. Since the directive was not annulled, it continues to produce legal effects. In any event, even if it had been annulled in proceedings under Article 230[173], the Court might have declared its effects definitive pursuant to Article 231[174], in which case there would still be an obligation on Member States to implement it. It does not seem correct that the individual's right to reparation should depend on whether the State was diligent enough to seek clarification of the status of the directive by bringing an action for annulment. On the other hand, where a directive is vitiated by a substantive defect such as to make the right which the directive is intended to grant to the individual incompatible with a higher rule of Community law,[91] it would be inappropriate to impose liability on the State. How can the individual be said to have a 'right' under Community law, if the legal measure which confers him that right infringes a superior rule of the Community legal order? Imposing liability in those circumstances

---

[86] *Commission* v. *Greece*, op.cit., para. 14.

[87] Joined Cases 6 and 11/69 *Commission* v. *France* [1969] ECR 523, para. 13.

[88] Case 226/87 *Commission* v. *Greece* [1988] ECR 3611, per Mancini AG at 3617.

[89] Most of the cases that have arisen so far concern proceedings under Article 88(2)[93(2)] in relation to unlawful State aids.

[90] Schermers and Waelbroeck, *Judicial Protection in the European Communities*, p. 301.

[91] e.g. where the directive in issue lies beyond the competence of the Community or exceeds the powers of the institution which adopted it. Cf. *Commission* v. *France*, op.cit.

would run counter to the principle of legality. It would also give rise to odd consequences. For example, an individual could bring proceedings to recover damages for failure to implement a directive in the courts of a Member State whereas, in another State which has implemented the directive, another individual, whose interests are affected adversely by the directive, could challenge its validity and obtain its annulment with the assistance of Article 234[177]. Clearly, that would be an oxymoron and breach 'the coherence of the system of judicial protection established by the Treaty'.[92]

9.5. Breach of Community law as a result of action by the national legislature

In *Brasserie* the Court modelled the liability of Member States for breach of Community law to the liability of the Community institutions. Such an approach had been advocated by Mischo AG in *Francovich* but the judgment did not follow his view. This is probably because the breach in issue, namely failure to implement a directive, was of such a nature that it was not necessary for the Court to draw an analogy with Article 288(2) [215(2)]. In *Brasserie* the Court stated that the conditions under which a State may incur liability to individuals for breach of Community law may not, in the absence of particular justification, differ from those governing the liability of the Community in like circumstances.[93] It then referred to its case law under Article 288(2 [215(2)] and stated that the strict approach which it has taken in relation to the liability of the Community institutions for legislative measures is justified by two considerations. The first reason is that the exercise of the legislative function must not be hindered by the prospect of actions for damages. The second reason follows from the first. It is in the public interest that, in taking policy decisions, the legislature must enjoy ample discretion. It follows that in a legislative context characterized by the exercise of a wide discretion, which is essential for implementing a Community policy, the Community may not incur liability unless the institution concerned has manifestly and gravely disregarded the limits on the exercise of its powers (*Schöppenstedt* test).[94] Turning to State liability, the Court held that where the breach emanates from the national legislature in circumstances where the legislature has wide discretion comparable to that of the Community institutions in implementing Community policies, Community law confers a right of reparation where three conditions are fulfilled:[95]

(1) the rule of law infringed must be intended to confer rights on individuals;
(2) the breach must be sufficiently serious;

---

[92] Case 314/85 *Foto-Frost* v. *Hauptzollamt Lübeck-Ost* [1987] ECR 4199, para. 16.
[93] *Brasserie*, op.cit., n. 2, para. 42.   [94] See above p. 315.
[95] *Brasserie*, op.cit., n. 2, para. 51.

(3) there must be a direct causal link between the breach of the obligation resting on the State and the damage sustained by the injured parties.

The Court stated that those conditions satisfy the need to ensure that Community provisions are fully effective and also that they correspond in substance to the conditions which must be satisfied in order for liability to arise on the part of the Community institutions as a result of legislative action.[96] In *Brasserie* the Court stated that the three conditions referred to above are necessary and sufficient to found State liability. It left open the possibility that liability may be incurred under less strict conditions on the basis of national law.[97] Presumably that possibility exists not only in relation to liability arising as a result of a breach by the national legislature but also in relation to liability arising from other types of breach.

For the first condition of liability to be satisfied, it suffices that a provision is intended to confer rights to individuals. The fact that it may be designed to protect general, as opposed to individual, interests does not prevent the provision from being for the protection of individuals for the purposes of the right to reparation.[98] The first condition laid down in *Brasserie* is similar to the first two conditions of liability laid down in *Francovich* despite the fact that the Court used different language.[99] There seems to be no reason why failure to implement a directive should be distinguished in this respect from breach of a Treaty provision by an act of the national legislature. The material requirement is the same, namely, that the rule of Community law in issue must be intended to confer rights on individuals. The reason why the Court used different language in its judgments seems to be that it sought to emphasize different points. In *Francovich* it was material to distinguish between the right to reparation and direct effect.[100] By contrast, it was not necessary to draw such a distinction in *Brasserie*. In practice, the distinction between provisions which are directly effective and those which fall short of direct effect but intend to give rights to individuals seems to be more important in the case of failure to implement directives than in the case of Treaty provisions.

The most important condition of liability is the second one laid down in *Brasserie*. The extent of State liability will depend mostly on the interpretation to be given to the term 'sufficiently serious'. Drawing a parallel with the liability of the Community institutions under Article 288(2)[215(2)], the Court stated that the decisive test for finding that a breach of Community law is sufficiently serious is whether the Member State concerned manifestly and gravely disregarded the

---

[96] Op.cit., paras. 52–3.   [97] Op.cit., para. 66.

[98] Op.cit., at 1107 per Tesauro AG. This applies not only to Treaty provisions but also to provisions of directives. See *Dillenkofer*, op.cit., n. 74, paras. 36–9.

[99] See above pp. 326–327.

[100] It was material to do so because Directive 80/987 did not fulfil the requisite conditions of direct effect. See above, n. 77.

limits of its discretion.[101] The Court listed the following factors as being material in determining whether the infringement passes the threshold of seriousness:[102]

- the clarity and precision of the rule breached;
- the measure of discretion left to the national authorities;
- whether the infringement and the damage caused was intentional or involuntary;
- whether any error of law was excusable or inexcusable;
- the fact that the position taken by a Community institution may have contributed towards the omission;
- the adoption or retention of national measures or practices contrary to Community law.

In any event, a breach of Community law will be sufficiently serious if it has persisted despite a judgment which establishes the infringement in question or a preliminary ruling or settled case law of the Court on the matter from which it is clear that the conduct in question constitutes an infringement.[103]

The notion of serious breach incorporates the notion of 'fault'. The Court stated that the obligation to make reparation cannot be made dependent on any notion of fault going beyond that of a sufficiently serious breach. Given that the notion of 'fault' does not have the same meaning in the laws of the Member States,[104] the Court was keen to avoid reliance on concepts of national law which might lead to the right of reparation being subject to different conditions in the national legal systems.

In its judgment, the Court proceeded to give more specific guidelines with regard to the cases in issue. In relation to *Brasserie*, it drew a distinction between the provisions of German law prohibiting the marketing as beer of beverages which did not conform to the purity laws and those prohibiting the import of beers containing additives. With regard to the first, the Court held that it would be difficult to regard the breach of Article 28[30] as an excusable error, since the incompatibility of the purity requirements with Article 28[30] was manifest in the light of earlier case law. By contrast, in the light of the existing case law, the criteria available to the national legislature to determine whether the prohibition of the use of additives was contrary to Community law was significantly less conclusive until the judgment in the *Beer* case.

The Court also gave guidelines with regard to the situation in *Factortame*. It stated that different considerations apply to the provisions of the Merchant Shipping Act 1988 making registration of fishing vessels subject to the requirement of nationality and those imposing residence and domicile requirements for vessel owners and operators. The requirement of nationality constitutes direct discrimination manifestly contrary to Community law. The breach committed therefore by imposing that requirement is sufficiently serious. In assessing whether the requirements imposing residence and domicile are sufficiently serious the national court may take

---

[101] *Brasserie*, op.cit., n. 2, para. 55.   [102] Op.cit., para. 56.   [103] Op.cit., para. 57.
[104] Op.cit., para. 76.

into account, *inter alia*, the particular features of the common fisheries policy, the attitude of the Commission, which made its position known to the United Kingdom in good time, and the assessments as to the state of certainty of Community law made by the national courts in the interim proceedings brought by individuals affected by the Merchant Shipping Act. A further consideration to be taken into account is whether the United Kingdom failed to adopt immediately the measures needed to comply with the Order of the President of the Court made in proceedings for interim measures requested by the Commission.[105]

9.6. A critique of the Court's reasoning

The notion of 'serious breach' provides a flexible tool for the development of State liability in damages. However, the comparison drawn between the liability of Member States and the liability of Community institutions for legislative acts is not necessarily accurate. The *Schöppenstedt* formula has been developed by the Court in its case law under Article 288(2)[215(2)] in relation to Community legislative measures in the field of economic policy and has been applied primarily to measures of agricultural policy. The discretion of Member States when they act within the sphere of Community law remains both in terms of its nature and in terms of its extent different from the discretion exercised by the Community institutions in the field of agricultural law. It is doubtful therefore whether the discretion of Member States can be referred to as 'comparable' to that of the Community institutions.

Also, it is not clear that the conditions of State liability for legislative acts correspond in substance to those defined by the case law in relation to the liability of the Community institutions for legislative acts as the Court stated in *Brasserie*. As stated above, in its case law under Article 288(2)[215(2)], the Court refers to two elements in determining whether there is a manifest and grave disregard of discretionary powers, namely, the effect of the measure on individuals and the extent to which the law has been violated. The damage alleged by the applicants must go beyond the bounds of the economic risks inherent in the activities in the sector concerned.[106] That requirement, however, was not mentioned in *Brasserie* as a prerequisite for the establishment of State liability in damages.

The case where Member State liability for breach of Community law may be most akin to the liability of the Community institutions is where a Member State exercises discretion conferred upon it by Community regulations in the field of the common agricultural policy in breach of one of the fundamental principles, for example equality or proportionality.[107] Even in such a case, however, considerable differences exist as the discretion of the national authorities is confined by the relevant Community measures.

[105] Case 246/89 R *Commission* v. *United Kingdom* [1989] ECR 3125.
[106] See above p. 319.
[107] Cf. 5/88 *Wachauf* v. *Bundesamt für Ernährung und Forstwirtschaft* [1989] ECR 2609.

The fundamental premise of the Court's rationale in *Brasserie* was that, unless specific reasons dictate otherwise, the liability of Member States and the liability of the Community institutions must be governed by the same principles. As a starting point, that is undoubtedly correct. As the Court pointed out, the protection of the rights which individuals derive from Community law cannot vary depending on whether a national authority or a Community authority is responsible for the breach.[108] There is, however, a fundamental difference between the liability of Community institutions arising from legislation and the liability of Member States for breach of Community law. That difference was identified by Léger AG in *Hedley Lomas*. The Community institutions act as a primary legislature. In the case of primary legislative action, liability must be imposed, if at all,[109] only in exceptional circumstances since, as the Court pointed out in *Brasserie*, the freedom of the legislature must not be obstructed by the prospect of action for damages. As Capotorti AG put it in an earlier case, the 'power to express the sovereignty of the people'[110] may justify immunity of the legislature from the general rules of liability. By contrast, within the scope of Community law, Member States do not act as primary legislatures. They are confined by the norms of Community law which, according to the principle of supremacy, are higher-ranking. As Léger AG stated, it is no longer possible to seek refuge behind the sovereign nature of legislation.[111] Reparation for damage is the corollary of the principle of primacy which requires not only that legislation contrary to Community law should be disapplied but also that reparation must be made for damages resulting from its past application.[112]

It is a pity that the Court did not expressly state the different legal foundation of State liability in damages for breach of Community law. As it stands, the reasoning of *Brasserie* is inconsistent. On the one hand, the Court declares that the liability of Member States for breach of Community law by acts of the legislature must be governed by the same rules which govern the liability of the Community institutions but, on the other hand, it specifies conditions of liability which are not fully comparable. The Court acknowledges the differences between the liability of Member States and the liability of Community institutions only indirectly by stating that the conditions must be the same 'in the absence of particular justification'[113] and that 'the national legislature . . . does not systematically have a wide discretion when it acts in a field governed by Community law'.[114] The judgment, however, does not emphasize sufficiently the differences between Community liability and State liability for breach of Community law.

---

[108] *Brasserie*, op.cit., n. 2, para. 42.

[109] The legal systems of many Member States do not recognize State liability for legislative action: this is the case, for example, in Italy, Germany, Belgium, Ireland, Luxembourg and the United Kingdom. See Léger AG in *Hedley Lomas*, op.cit., n. 60, at 2579.

[110] See *HNL* v. *Council and Commission*, op.cit., n. 25, at 1229.

[111] Léger AG, op.cit., n. 60, 2580.   [112] Ibid.

[113] *Brasserie*, op.cit., n. 2, para. 42.   [114] Op.cit., para. 46.

9.7. Breach of the Treaty by the national administration

Liability will be easier to establish where a Member State commits a breach of Community law in circumstances where it has limited discretion or no discretion at all. In *Hedley Lomas*,[115] the United Kingdom imposed a general ban on the export of animals to Spain for slaughter on the ground that their treatment in Spanish slaughterhouses was contrary to Directive 74/577 which requires the stunning of animals before slaughter.[116] In accordance with the general ban, Hedley Lomas was refused an export licence for a quantity of sheep intended for slaughter in a Spanish slaughterhouse. The licence was refused even though the authorities had no evidence to suggest that the slaughterhouse involved was not complying with the Directive. Hedley Lomas applied for a declaration that the refusal to issue an export licence ran counter to Article 29[34] and for damages. The United Kingdom authorities conceded that the refusal to issue an export licence was contrary to Article 29[34] but claimed that it was justified under Article 30[36]. The Court held that recourse to Article 30[36] is not possible where Community directives provide for harmonization of the measures necessary to achieve the specific objective which would be furthered by reliance upon that provision. The fact that Directive 74/755 did not lay down any Community procedure for monitoring compliance with its provisions made no difference. The Court added that a Member State may not unilaterally adopt, on its own authority, corrective or protective measures to obviate any breach by another Member State of Community rules.

On the issue of damages, the Court found that the conditions of liability laid down in *Brasserie* were fulfilled. With regard to the first condition, the Court recalled that Article 29[34] creates rights for individuals which national courts must protect. With regard to the seriousness of the breach, it held that where, at the time when it committed the infringement, the Member State was not called upon to make any legislative choices and had only considerably reduced discretion, or even no discretion, the mere infringement of Community law may be sufficient to establish the existence of a sufficiently serious breach. The Court noted that in the circumstances of the case, the United Kingdom authorities were not even in a position to produce any proof of non-compliance with the Directive by the slaughterhouse concerned.

---

[115] Case C–5/94 *The Queen v. Ministry of Agriculture, Fisheries and Food, ex parte Hedley Lomas (Ireland) Ltd.* [1996] ECR I–2553.
[116] Council Directive 74/577 on stunning of animals before slaughter, OJ 1974 L 316/10.

9.8. Incorrect transposition of a directive

In *The Queen* v. *HM Treasury, ex parte British Telecommunications*,[117] the Court held that the conditions provided for in *Brasserie* must also be fulfilled in order for liability to arise where a Member State incorrectly transposes a directive into national law. In such a case, therefore, liability does not ensue automatically and it must be established that the breach is sufficiently serious. The Court held that a strict approach to State liability in the case of incorrect transposition of directives is justified for the same reasons as those given in *Brasserie*, namely the concern to ensure that the exercise of legislative functions is not hindered by the prospect of actions for damages.

In issue in *British Telecommunications* was Article 8(1) of Directive 90/531 on the procurement procedures of entities operating in the water, energy, transport and telecommunications sectors.[118] The Court found that the United Kingdom had interpreted the Directive erroneously and, as a result, it had implemented it incorrectly, but held that the incorrect implementation did not amount to a serious breach. The Court stated that Article 8(1) was imprecisely worded and was reasonably capable of bearing the interpretation given to it by the United Kingdom in good faith. That interpretation was shared by other Member States and was not manifestly contrary to the wording of the Directive and the objectives pursued by it. Also, no guidance was available to the United Kingdom from the case law of the Court with regard to the interpretation of Article 8. Finally, the Commission did not raise the matter when the implementing legislation was adopted. It is submitted that the last consideration is of lesser importance. The fact that the Commission considers that the interpretation which a Member State has given to a directive is incorrect is not conclusive as the Commission has no power to give authentic interpretation to Community law. The most important factors seem to be the existence of case law which can offer guidance on the issue and whether the interpretation given by the Member State is reasonable.

In *Denkavit*,[119] the Court found that the incorrect transposition by Germany of a taxation directive[120] did not amount to a serious breach. The Court relied on the following considerations. First, it noted that the interpretation given to the Directive by Germany, which proved to be incorrect, had been adopted by almost all other Member States which had exercised the option to derogate given by Article 3(2) of the Directive. Secondly, those Member States had taken the view

---

[117] Case C–392/93 [1996] ECR I–1631.

[118] OJ 1990 L 297/1. That Directive has now been superseded by Directive 93/38 co-ordinating the procurement procedures of entities operating in the water, energy, transport and telecommunications sectors, OJ 1993 L 199/84.

[119] Joined Cases C–283, C–291 and C–292/94 *Denkavit Internationaal BV and Others* v. *Bundesamt für Finanzen* [1996] ECR I–5063.

[120] Council Directive 90/435 on the common system of taxation applicable in the case of parent companies and subsidiaries of different Member States, OJ 1990 L 225/6.

that they were entitled to adopt such an interpretation, following discussions within the Council. Thirdly, the incorrect interpretation furthered the objective of preventing tax fraud which was compatible with the Directive. Fourthly, the case law did not provide any indication as to how the contested provision was to be interpreted.

The second point mentioned above is of interest. In *Denkavit*, to support the interpretation of the Directive given by Germany, a number of Member States referred to discussions in the Council while the Directive was being adopted. Following its previous case law, the Court held that expressions of intent made by Member States in the Council have no legal status unless they are actually expressed in the legislation. It seems, therefore, that discussions in proceedings of the Council bear no consequences on the interpretation of Community measures but may be of relevance in establishing excusable error on the part of a Member State in an action for damages.

9.9. The right to reparation: The importance of national law

Although the conditions of liability are provided for by Community law, the remedy of reparation is subject to national law. In *Brasserie* the Court held that the State must make reparation for the consequences of the loss caused in accordance with the domestic rules on liability, provided that the dual requirement of non-discrimination and minimum protection laid down in the *Rewe* and *Comet* case law[121] are satisfied: the conditions for reparation laid down by national law must not be less favourable than those relating to similar domestic claims and they must not be such as in practice to make it impossible or excessively difficult to obtain reparation. The Court identified two such conditions which make the exercise of the right to reparation excessively difficult and are thus incompatible with Community law.[122] The first is a condition imposed by German law, and the second a condition imposed by English law. Under German law, where a legislative act is in breach of a higher-ranking national law, for example the Constitution, a right of reparation ensues only where the applicant can be regarded as the beneficiary of the obligation breached. The Court held that such a restriction would make it in practice impossible or extremely difficult to obtain effective reparation for loss or damage resulting from a breach of Community law, since the tasks falling to the national legislature relate in principle to the public at large and not to identifiable persons or classes of person. Referring to English law, the Court held that State liability for breach of Community law cannot be made subject to proof of

---

[121] Case 33/76 *Rewe* v. *Landwirtschaftskammer für das Saarland* [1976] ECR 1989; Case 45/76 *Comet* v. *Productschap voor Siergewassen* [1976] ECR 2043.
[122] *Brasserie*, op.cit., n. 2., paras. 71–3.

misfeasance in public office as such a condition would make it in practice impossible to obtain reparation for loss arising from breach by the national legislature.[123]

With regard to the extent of reparation, the Court held that reparation for loss or damage caused to individuals as a result of breaches of Community law must be commensurate with the loss or damage sustained so as to ensure the effective protection of their rights.[124] In the absence of Community provisions, it is for the domestic legal system of each Member State to set the criteria for determining the extent of reparation. The Court laid down the following guidelines:

- The national court may inquire whether the injured person showed reasonable diligence in order to avoid the loss or damage or limit its extent and whether, in particular, he availed himself in time of all the legal remedies available to him.[125]
- Total exclusion of loss of profit as a head of damage for which reparation may be awarded in the case of a breach of Community law is not acceptable. The Court pointed out that in the context of economic or commercial litigation, such a total exclusion of loss of profit would make reparation of damage practically impossible.[126]
- An award of exemplary damages pursuant to a claim or an action founded on Community law cannot be ruled out if such damages could be awarded pursuant to a similar claim or action founded on domestic law.[127]

Subject to those guidelines and the general conditions laid down in the *Rewe* and *Comet* case law, the remedy of reparation is governed by national law. Reliance on the laws of Member States is a source of divergence but lack of uniformity is inevitable given that the right to reparation is an entirely judge-made right. One would expect that, as the case law develops, Community law will gradually occupy some of the area currently left to national laws.

9.10. The aftermath of *Francovich*

It was inevitable that sooner or later the Court would be confronted with issues pertaining to the conditions imposed by national law on the right to reparation. Following the judgment in *Francovich*, by a Legislative Decree adopted on 27 January 1992, Italy took steps to implement Directive 80/987[128] and provide compensation to those who suffered loss as a result of its belated implementation. The Legislative Decree provided that actions for reparation must be brought within a

---

[123] *Brasserie* therefore put it beyond doubt that the judgment of the Court of Appeal in *Bourgoin* is no longer good law. After *Francovich*, doubt had already been expressed about the correctness of that decision by the House of Lords in *Kirklees MBC* v. *Wickes Building Supplies Ltd.* [1992] 3 WLR 170.

[124] *Brasserie*, op.cit., para. 82.   [125] Op.cit., n. 2, para. 84.

[126] Op.cit., para. 87.   [127] Op.cit., para. 89.

[128] Council Directive 80/987 on the approximation of the laws of the Member States relating to the protection of employees in the event of the insolvency of their employer, OJ 1908 L 283, p. 23. The Directive has been amended by Directive 87/164, OJ 1987 L 66, p. 11.

period of one year from the date of its entry into force. Also, it applied retroactively to claims for reparation the implementing measures and the limitations imposed therein on the liability of the guarantee institutions to meet outstanding wage claims of employees of insolvent employers. Both these aspects of the Legislative Decree were challenged on grounds of compatibility with Community law.

9.10.1. Time limit

The time limit of one year was challenged in *Palmisani* v. *INPS*.[129] It will be remembered that according to *Francovich* and *Brasserie du Pêcheur*, the conditions governing the right to reparation must not be less favourable than those relating to similar domestic claims (the requirement of non-discrimination or equivalence) and must not be such as to make it virtually impossible or excessively difficult to obtain reparation (the requirement of effective protection). In *Palmisani* the Court had no difficulty in finding that the one-year time limit satisfied the requirement of effective protection. It was a reasonable period within which persons harmed by the belated transposition could protect their rights. The requirement of equivalence was more contentious. The national court referred for the purposes of comparison to time limits applicable to other claims. Thus, in implementation of Directive 80/987, the Legislative Decree provided a limitation period of one year for benefits payable under the Directive, running from the date of submission of the application for the benefit to the Guarantee Fund. The Court held that applications for payments provided by the Directive and those made under the compensation scheme for its belated transposition differ as to their objective. The former aim to provide employees with specific guarantees of payment of unpaid remuneration in the event of the insolvency of their employer. The latter, by contrast, seek to make good the loss sustained by the beneficiaries of the Directive as a result of its belated transposition. The Court also noted that reparation cannot always be ensured by retroactive and proper application in full of the measures implementing the directive. Given the different nature of the claims, it was not necessary to undertake a comparison of the time limits applicable to them. For the same reason, the Court rejected a comparison with the time limit applicable under Italian law for obtaining social security benefits.[130]

The national court also referred to the limitation period applicable under ordinary law to claims for non-contractual liability. This is set by the Italian Civil Code to five years. The Court held that compensation for the belated implementation of a directive and the ordinary system of non-contractual liability pursued essentially the same objective, namely to effect reparation of the loss sustained as a result of unlawful conduct. They were therefore comparable. The Court did not possess all the information necessary to determine whether an action for damages brought by

---

[129] Case C–261/95 *Palmisani* v. *Istituto Nazionale della Previdenza Sociale* (*INPS*) [1997] ECR I–4025.
[130] *Palmisani*, op.cit., n. 129, paras. 33–7.

an individual pursuant to the Italian Civil Code could be directed against public authorities and left it to the national court to undertake that examination. The Court stated that if the ordinary system of non-contractual liability were to prove incapable of serving as a basis for an action against public authorities and the national court were unable to undertake any other relevant comparison between the time limit in issue and the conditions relating to similar claims of a domestic nature, the conclusion would have to be drawn that the one year time limit was not precluded by Community law.[131]

The judgment in *Palmisani* is somewhat inconclusive and leaves ample discretion to the national court. It illustrates, as mentioned in the previous chapter, that the Court is prepared to recognize more discretion to national courts with regard to the requirement of equivalence than with regard to the requirement of minimum protection.[132]

9.10.2. Retroactive application of implementing measures

Article 4(2) of Directive 80/987 allows Member States to limit the liability of the guarantee institutions to payment of outstanding claims for certain periods of the employment relationship and grants to Member States a number of options for determining those periods. In implementation of the Directive, the Legislative Decree took advantage of Article 4(2) and applied the same limitation of liability retrospectively to the compensation payable to employees who suffered loss from the belated transposition of the Directive. The Legislative Decree also provided for an upper limit on payments by guarantee institutions pursuant to Article 4(3) of the Directive[133] and applied the same limitation to reparation.

In *Maso* v. *INPS*[134] and *Bonifaci* v. *INPS*,[135] the question was referred whether a Member State is entitled to apply retroactively to claims of reparation belatedly adopted implementing measures, including the limitations provided for in Article 4(2). The Court held that retroactive application in full of the measures implementing the Directive to employees who have suffered loss as a result of belated transposition enables in principle the harmful consequences of the breach to be remedied, provided that the Directive has been transposed properly.[136] Such appli-

---

[131] Op.cit., paras. 38–9.   [132] See above 8.2.1.

[133] Article 4(3) allows Member States to set a ceiling on payments by guarantee institutions in order to avoid the payment of sums going beyond the social objective of the Directive.

[134] Case C–373/95 *Maso, Graziana and Others* v. *Istituto Nazionale della Previdenza Sociale (INPS) and Italian Republic* [1997] ECR I–4051.

[135] Joined Cases C–94 and C–95/95 *Bonifaci, Berto and Others* v. *Istituto Nazionale della Previdenza Sociale (INPS)* [1997] ECR I–3936.

[136] In *Maso* and *Bonifaci* the Court found that the Legislative Decree fell short of implementing the Directive properly. It calculated the period of employment for the outstanding wage claims of which guarantee institutions were responsible by reference to the date of declaration of insolvency rather than the date of the onset of insolvency, namely, the date when a request was made for the opening of insolvency proceedings. Given that the judgment declaring insolvency may be delivered long after the request to open proceedings, the effect of the Legislative Decree was that payment of outstanding wage

cation, should have the effect of guaranteeing to those employees the rights from which they would have benefited if the Directive had been transposed within the prescribed period. With regard to Directive 80/987, retroactive application of implementing measures necessarily implies that a limitation of the guarantee institution's liability may also be applied, in accordance with Article 4(2), where the Member State has in fact exercised that option when transposing the Directive into national law. The Court, however, added a caveat. It stated that it is for the national court to ensure that reparation for the loss sustained is adequate. Retroactive and proper application in full of the measures implementing the Directive will suffice unless the beneficiaries establish the existence of complementary loss sustained on account of the fact that they were unable to benefit at the appropriate time from the financial advantages guaranteed by the Directive. In such a case, the complementary loss must also be made good.[137]

In principle, therefore, retroactive application of implementing measures suffices to ensure reparation. It follows that, where a directive grants several options to Member States, a Member State is not estopped from exercizing the most favourable option under the directive *vis-à-vis* those who have suffered as a result of belated implementation. The Court, however, pointed out that reparation is not always wholly ensured by retroactive application of implementing measures even where such measures transpose the directive fully into national law. The purpose of reparation is to ensure that the person who has suffered loss as a result of non-implementation is put in the same position that he would have been had the directive been implemented fully in time. A number of questions remain unanswered. For example, it is not clear what complementary losses can be said to have been sustained 'on account of the fact'[138] that the employees were unable to benefit at the appropriate time from the financial advantages guaranteed by the Directive. Although the Court did not discuss further the issue of causation of consequential losses, it is not safe to conclude that it is governed solely by national law. It is not realistic to expect the Court to give detailed guidance on such issues in a general and abstract manner. The case law can be expected to develop incrementally in response to specific questions asked by national courts. Finally, it seems that a Member State may not apply to those who have suffered loss as a result of belated implementation a less favourable regime than that provided by the implementing measures. It is not permissible, for example, to provide a lower ceiling for

claims might not be guaranteed for any period of employment. That would contrary to the objectives of the Directive.

[137] *Maso*, op.cit., paras. 39–42; *Bonifaci*, op.cit., paras. 51–4. In *Maso* the Court also held that any rules against aggregation of claims contained in the implementing legislation may also be applied provided that they do not affect the rights conferred by the Directive. The Legislative Decree prohibited aggregation of outstanding wage claims and of claims to reparation with the *indennità di mobilità* (job seekers allowance) granted by Italian law in the three months following the termination of the employment relationship. The Court found that the prohibition of aggregation was incompatible with the Directive because the *indennità di mobilità* was provided in the three months following the termination of employment and did not arise from the employment relationship.

[138] See *Maso*, op.cit., para. 41; *Bonifaci*, op.cit., para. 53.

compensation than that provided for payments by the guarantee institutions to meet outstanding wage claims in the future. Those who suffered loss as a result of belated implementation must be brought into the same position that they would have been if the Member State had adopted the directive in time as it chose to adopt it belatedly.

9.11. The national reaction

Following the judgment in *Brasserie and Factortame*, it fell upon the national courts which made the references to the Court of Justice to determine whether the applicants' claim for damages could succeed on the facts. In its judgment of 24 October 1996, the Bundesgerichtshof rejected the claim of Brasserie du Pêcheur for damages against the State as unfounded.[139] By contrast, in its judgment of 31 July 1997 in *R v. Secretary of State, ex parte Factortame*, the Divisional Court held that the breach committed by the United Kingdom was serious.

9.11.1. The response of the Bundesgerichtshof

The Bundesgerichtshof referred to the judgment of the Court of Justice in *Brasserie* and held that the damage suffered by the applicant was the result of the additives prohibition imposed by German law, which was not a serious breach, and not the result of the designation prohibition which constituted a serious breach.[140] It could be argued that, since German law imposed the designation prohibition, the existence of a serious breach could not be negated by the fact that it also imposed another prohibition which was not sufficiently serious. The Bundesgerichtshof rejected that reasoning. It referred to the Opinion of Tesauro AG in *Brasserie* who stated that, if the damage suffered by the applicant was causally connected with the prohibition on additives rather than the designation prohibition, the failure of the claim 'could not be ruled out'.[141]

It should be accepted that, where there are separate breaches of Community law, only the damage which is actually causally connected with the serious breach must be compensated. In the case of overlapping breaches, one of which is serious and the other of which is not, identifying the damage which is connected with the serious breach may give rise to difficulties. It appears odd, however, that the Bundesgerichtshof was unable to establish causal connection between any of the damage suffered by the applicant and the designation prohibition, given that the latter was in itself sufficient to restrict the importation of its products.

The Bundesgerichtshof also rejected the claim of the applicant for the damage which it allegedly incurred after 12 March 1987, the date when the judgment in the *Beer* case was delivered. Brasserie argued that it had suffered loss of profits dur-

---

[139] See [1997] 1 CMLR 971.   [140] See above, p. 332.   [141] *Brasserie*, op.cit., n. 2, 1126.

ing the transitional period that it needed after the judgment in the *Beer* case in order to build a distribution network. The court accepted, however, that the German authorities took immediate steps to comply with the judgment and held that the loss suffered during the transitional period was the result of the previous additives prohibition which was not a serious breach.

9.11.2. The response of the Divisional Court

The Divisional Court delivered its long awaited judgment in *R* v. *Secretary of State for Transport, ex parte Factortame Ltd.* on 31 July 1997.[142] The issues before it were whether the breach of the United Kingdom was sufficiently serious and whether the applicants were entitled to exemplary damages.

With regard to the seriousness of the violation, the Divisional Court found that the United Kingdom had acted in good faith. At the time when the Merchant Shipping Act was implemented, the Government reasonably believed on the basis of the legal advice which it had obtained that the rules enacted to prevent quota hopping did not constitute a breach of Community law. It held, however, that each of the conditions of registration imposed by the Act, namely, nationality, domicile and residence, constituted a sufficiently serious breach of the Treaty. It reached that conclusion on the basis of the following factors:

- The intended effect of the domicile and residence conditions was to discriminate on grounds of nationality. On the facts, therefore, there was little to choose between direct and indirect discrimination.
- The Government was aware that the imposition of the conditions would necessarily injure the applicants since the conditions were intended to ensure that the applicants would no longer fish against the British quota.
- The effect of introducing the registration requirements by primary legislation was to make it impossible for the applicants to obtain interim relief without the intervention of the Court of Justice. The Divisional Court noted that the applicants were deprived of the opportunity to prevent damage being caused to them. The situation was aggravated because, at least arguably, the measures adopted infringed the principles of proportionality and legitimate expectations. Other methods could have been chosen which would have enabled applications for interim relief to be considered on their merits by the national court. Given that the applicants were forbidden from continuing business activities which they lawfully carried out until the implementation of the Act, they should have been afforded a reasonable opportunity to take measures to avoid serious damage to their interests.

---

[142] The Divisional Court was composed of Hobhouse LJ and Collins and Moses JJ. The account given in the text is based on an unrevised version of the judgment. The judgment of the Divisional Court was upheld by the Court of Appeal: *The Times*, 24 Apr. 1998.

- The attitude of the Commission before the Act was adopted, which it made known to the United Kingdom Government, was hostile to the proposed legislation.

The Divisional Court noted that those factors coupled with the fundamental importance of the principle breached, namely the prohibition of discrimination on grounds of nationality, amounted to a manifest and grave disregard of the limits of the UK's discretion and gave rise to liability in damages.

The following points may be made with regard to the reasoning of the Divisional Court. It is notable that each of the conditions of registration was found to be a serious breach.[143] The rationale of this finding was that all conditions were intended to pursue the same objective, namely to prohibit vessels controlled by Spanish interests to fish against British quotas. The Court noted that, even if registration of vessels had been made subject only to a residence requirement, although the discrimination would have been indirect, it would nevertheless be the intended rather than an incidental effect of the requirement.[144] In the circumstances, therefore, there was no difference between direct and indirect discrimination. The Court was particularly critical of the requirement of domicile. It pointed out that given the strict meaning of domicile in English law, that requirement would be particularly difficult for a foreign national to satisfy and was equally, if not more, discriminatory than the requirement of nationality. The Divisional Court criticized the Government for not making clear to the Commission and the Court of Justice the stringency of that requirement.

The Divisional Court rejected the thrust of the Government's defence which was that liability would arise only if it was shown that it acted without legitimate justification. The Government argued essentially that it committed an error of law which was excusable because it had acted in good faith on the basis of legal advice about the compatibility of the registration requirements with Community law. The Divisional Court rejected that contention stating that, under *Brasserie*, the fact that an error is excusable does not automatically relieve a State of liability. In the circumstances, reliance on legal advice could not carry any great weight since there was a substantial argument to the contrary and the Government could never have been sure that its view was correct.

Notably, the Divisional Court held that, in assessing whether a breach is serious, account may be taken of the importance of the principle infringed. It pointed out that the prohibition of discrimination on grounds of nationality was one of the fundamental principles of the Treaty. Although that importance of the rule breached was not referred to as a relevant factor by the Court of Justice in *Brasserie and Factortame*, the Divisional Court held that the enumeration of relevant factors in

---

[143] It will be remembered that in *Brasserie and Factortame* the Court of Justice held that the requirement of nationality was a serious breach but was more equivocal about the requirements of domicile and residence. Above pp. 332–333.

[144] That point was expressly upheld by the Court of Appeal.

Brasserie was not intended to be exhaustive. Two points may be made in relation to this finding. First, it must be borne in mind that the fact that the rule breached is a fundamental one does not necessarily mean that the infringement is manifest. It seems that the material factor was the Government's insistence to continue to apply the registration requirements even though it became progressively clear that they would be found incompatible with the Treaty.[145] Indeed, one may sympathize with the Government's initial position that any discrimination on grounds of nationality arising from the requirements of registration was a natural consequence of the system of national quotas. Secondly, the importance of the rule breached as a factor of the seriousness of the breach calls for a note of caution. If the basis of State liability in damages is the primacy of Community law, in principle, breach of any rule of Community law by the national legislature may give rise to liability provided that it is intended to confer rights on individuals. The *raison d'être* of liability is that the rule breached emanates from a hierarchically superior legal order rather than the intrinsic importance of the rule. Liability therefore may not be denied on the ground that the rule of Community law breached is not sufficiently 'important'.

It is of particular interest that in establishing the rules governing State liability for breach of Community law, the Divisional Court relied not only on *Brasserie and Factortame* but also on the case law of the Court of Justice under Article 288(2)[215(2)]. The factors influencing liability of Community institutions referred to by Van Gerven AG in *Mulder II* proved particularly influential.[146]

All in all, the Divisional Court found that the breach was serious for two reasons. Because of the manifest character of the breach, which was constituted by the importance of the rule breached and the circumstances in which the breach occurred, and also because its adverse effects on the applicants' interests were grave. In discussing the manifest and grave test, however, the Divisional Court considered that the term 'grave' did not refer exclusively to the consequences of the breach. It held that, where a breach is effected deliberately and with knowledge that what is being done is unlawful, such breach can properly be described as manifest and grave even if its consequences, taken overall, are not grave. The Divisional Court attributed particular importance to the views of the Commission as the guardian of

---

[145] See the judgments in Case C–3/87 *R* v. *Ministry of Agriculture, Fisheries and Food, ex parte Agegate* [1989] ECR 4459 and Case C–216/87 *R* v. *Ministry of Agriculture, Fisheries and Food, ex parte Jaderow* [1989] ECR 4509 and the interim order in Case C–246/89 R *Commission* v. *United Kingdom* [1989] ECR 3125. The Divisional Court held, in the light of *Brasserie and Factortame*, that the failure of the Government to comply with the Order of the President of the Court in that case by suspending immediately the nationality requirement amounted to a serious breach giving rise to a right to reparation.

[146] Joined Cases C–104/89 and C–37/90 *Mulder* v. *Council and Commission* [1992] ECR I–3061, at 3104. In his Opinion, Van Gerven AG referred to the following factors: the importance of the principle of Community law infringed; the fact that the disregard of the principle affected a limited and clearly defined group of commercial operators; the fact that the damage alleged by the applicant went beyond the bounds of economic risks inherent in the operators' activities in the sector concerned; and the fact that the principle in question was infringed without sufficient justification. The Divisional Court found that all those conditions were satisfied on the facts.

Community interest, stating that, where there is doubt about the legality of any proposed legislation, a failure by a Member State to seek the views of the Commission or, if it receives them, to follow them is likely to lead to any breach being regarded as inexcusable and so manifest. It is doubtful, however, whether the failure to follow the Commission's opinion should carry the grave consequences suggested by the Divisional Court.

The judgment of the Divisional Court suggests that a reasonable and bona fide interpretation on the part of a Member State of the limits of its discretionary powers may not suffice to avoid liability. There must be in addition sufficient objective grounds which justify the breach and which were lacking in the circumstances.

On the issue of exemplary damages, the Divisional Court rejected the arguments of the applicants. It will be remembered that in *Brasserie and Factortame* the Court held that exemplary damages could be awarded pursuant to a claim founded on Community law if they could be awarded for a similar claim founded on domestic law.[147] The Divisional Court took the view that the award of exemplary damages is an inappropriate remedy for the breach of Community law. It pointed out that such damages are punitive rather than compensatory in nature. Referring to *Rookes v. Barnard*[148] and *A.B. v. South West Water Services Ltd.*,[149] it held that exemplary damages may be awarded for oppressive, arbitrary or unconstitutional action by the servants of the government or where statute expressly provides so. The Divisional Court understood liability for breach of Community law as a breach of statutory duty.[150] It followed that exemplary damages could not be awarded since the European Communities Act 1972 did not provide so. The applicants argued that the breach of statutory duty was similar to the tort of misfeasance in public office for which exemplary damages could be awarded and that therefore the refusal to award such damages would be discriminatory. The Court, however, rejected the analogy pointing out that misfeasance was dependent on knowledge by the defendant that he is breaking the law or at least that he is reckless. By contrast, an action in damages for breach of Community law does not depend on subjective factors nor was there on the facts a case of misfeasance on the part of the United Kingdom.

There is no doubt that the Divisional Court was disposed unfavourably towards the award of exemplary damages for breach of Community law. One may sympathize with that view. The Court referred to a number of problems of the law of punitive damages, especially where a large number of individuals are affected by the unlawful conduct of the defendant. Pointing out that the concept of exemplary damages is peculiar to common law, it stated that to make available the remedy of such damages for breaches of Community law would decrease the move towards uniformity, it would involve distinctions between the practice of national courts and the liability of the United Kingdom and other Member States, and might give rise to inequalities.

---

[147] Brasserie, op.cit., n. 2, at n. 70.   [148] [1964] AC 1129.   [149] [1993] QB 507.
[150] For a different view, see Hoskins: Rebirth of the Innominate Tort? in Beatson and Tridimas, op. cit., 91–100.

9.12. Relationship with other remedies

State liability remains a new remedy the full ramifications of which are still to be determined. An important area which remains largely uninvestigated is the relationship between State liability and other remedies for breach of Community law. The judgment in *R* v. *Secretary of State for Social Security, ex parte Sutton*[151] appears to suggest that, at least for some purposes, the right to reparation is an independent remedy which may be sought in addition to other remedies available in national courts.[152] The case concerned Directive 79/7,[153] Article 7(1)(a) of which states that the Directive is without prejudice to the right of Member States to exclude from its scope the determination of pensionable age for the purposes of granting retirement pensions and 'the possible consequences thereof for other benefits'. In *Secretary of State for Social Security* v. *Thomas and Others*,[154] the Court gave a restrictive interpretation to that derogation holding that it was limited to the forms of discrimination existing under the other benefit schemes which are necessarily and objectively linked to the difference in retirement ages. *Sutton* came as the aftermath of *Thomas*. Mrs Sutton was refused invalid care allowance on the ground that she had reached retirement age. Following the judgment in *Thomas*, the Social Security Commissioner held that Article 7(1)(a) of Directive 79/7 could not be relied on to refuse to award an invalid care allowance to women over 60. He awarded to Mrs Sutton the allowance with effect from 19 February 1986, i.e. one year before her application. Mrs Sutton claimed interest on the arrears of benefit on the basis of Article 6 of Directive 79/7 or, alternatively, on the basis of the principle that a Member State is liable in damages for breach of Community law. Article 6 of the Directive requires Member States to introduce the necessary measures to enable persons who consider themselves wronged by failure to apply the principle of equal treatment to pursue their claims by judicial process. Despite the similarity between that provision and Article 6 of Directive 76/207 on Equal Treatment,[155] the Court refused to transpose the principle laid down in *Marshall II*[156] to the effect that full financial compensation must include the award of interest. It held that *Marshall II* concerned the award of interest on amounts payable by way of reparation for

[151] Case C–66/95 [1997] ECR I–2163.

[152] This view is confirmed also by other authorities. See Joined Cases C–192 to C–218/95 *Comateb and Others* v. *Directeur Général des Douanes et Droits Indirects* [1997] ECR I–165 and the Opinion of Jacobs AG in Case C–188/95 *Fantask a/S and Others* v. *Ministry of Trade and Industry* [1997] ECR I–6783. See further Eeckhout, 'Liability of Member States in Damages and the Community System of Remedies', in Beatson and Tridimas, op.cit., p. 63.

[153] Directive 79/7 on the progressive implementation of the principle of equal treatment for men and women in matters of social security, OJ 1979 L 6/24.

[154] Case C–328/91 [1993] ECR I–1247.

[155] Council Directive 76/207 on the implementation of the principle of equal treatment for men and women as regards access to employment, vocational training and promotion, and working conditions (OJ 1976 L 39/40).

[156] Case C–271/91 *Marshall* v. *Southampton and South-West Hampshire Area Health Authority* [1993] ECR I–4367, n. 67.

damage sustained as a result of discriminatory dismissal. By contrast, the case in issue concerned the right to receive interest on social security benefits. According to the judgment, payment in arrears of such benefits is not compensatory in nature and therefore interest on them cannot be regarded as an essential component of the right to equal treatment. The Court, prompted by the Advocate General, seems to have followed an unduly restrictive interpretation of *Marshall II* and Oliver correctly criticizes that part of the judgment[157] on the ground that it runs counter to the principle of effectiveness. The Court focused on the wrong criterion since what matters is not the compensatory or otherwise nature of the claim but the need to ensure that the effluxion of time does not deprive a pecuniary right from its substance.

Having established that Mrs Sutton was not entitled to interest on the basis of Article 6 of Directive 79/7, the Court turned to examine whether the right to payment of interest on arrears of social security benefit could be based on the principle of State liability for breach of Community law. It did not give an answer to that issue but merely repeated the conditions of liability laid down in the case law and held that it was for the national court to determine whether Mrs Sutton was entitled to reparation for the loss which she claimed to have suffered. It is significant that the Court did not exclude the possibility that interest could be obtained on the basis of State liability in damages although it was invited to do so by the United Kingdom Government. It follows that the possibility of obtaining interest on arrears of social security benefit by way of a claim in damages where the delay in payment of the benefit is the result of discrimination prohibited by Community law remains open.

---

[157] See Oliver, 'State Liability in Damages following Factortame III: A Remedy Seen in Context', in Beatson and Tridimas, op.cit., p. 49 at p. 60.

10

Conclusions

An attempt was made in the preceding chapters to show how the Community judicature uses the general principles of law as sources of rights and obligations. A number of descriptive and prescriptive conclusions may be drawn from the above analysis.

The study of the case law makes it clear that the use of the general principles is not exhausted in their gap-filling function. They form an integral part of the Court's methodology and express constitutional values. There can be no doubt that, as sources of rights and obligations, the general principles pose significant limitations on the policy-making power of the Community institutions. It is true that the cases where they have been successfully invoked leading to the annulment of Community acts are concentrated mainly in certain areas, such as agriculture and staff cases. Measures, however, have also been annulled in other fields, and no area of Community action remains immune from their application. This, all-embracing, character of the general principles should not hide their relative nature. Far from establishing a uniform standard, concepts such as proportionality and equality are used to protect diverse interests and entail varying degrees of judicial scrutiny depending on the context in which they are applied. It is appropriate to emphasize here once more the dual nature of judicial review exercized by the Community judicature. Where it exercizes judicial review of Community measures, it seeks to protect the individual vis-à-vis arbitrary conduct of the Community authorities and balances private vis-à-vis public interests. Where it exercises 'judicial review' of national measures, it controls State action vis-à-vis the Community objectives and uses the concepts of non-discrimination and proportionality as instruments of market integration. The standard of judicial scrutiny is much higher in the latter case than it is in the former.

The general principles derive from the laws of the Member States but in the Court's case law they acquire, by a process of 'creative appropriation', independent normative value and are applied subject to the exigencies of the Community polity. The Community judiciary ascribes to a substantive rather than a formal version of the rule of law. The Court perceives the general principles as expressing fundamental democratic values enshrined in the common cultural and political heritage of the Member States. In that sense, general principles can be seen as the expression of a 'shared political morality'.[1] This line of reasoning can be accepted only if

---

[1] See T. R. S. Allan, 'The Limits of Parliamentary Sovereignty' [1985] PL 614, 621.

it is read subject to an important proviso, namely, that the Court does not only reflect but also shapes political morality. Judicial intervention is not only negative but also positive in the sense that it not only seeks to protect the citizen vis-à-vis public authority but also to promote political and social values. The judgment in *Chernobyl*[2] and, in a different context, in P v. S[3] provide testament to the cultivation of positive judicial standards. In terms of their ideological foundations, the general principles make an odd hybrid. They incorporate standards deriving from the liberal constitutional tradition but also express social ideals apposite to the needs and aspirations of contemporary European society.

One may identify the following as the underlying objectives of the case law on general principles:

(1) to protect the individual vis-à-vis arbitrary public power;
(2) the promote European integration in accordance with the putative intentions of the authors of the founding treaties;
(3) to achieve a balance of powers among the political institutions of the Community inspired by ideas of participatory democracy;[4]
(4) to uphold the paramountcy of the principle of judicial protection;[5] and
(5) to preserve the autonomy of the Community judicial system.[6]

As grounds of review of Community action, the general principles seek to impose on the institutions a high burden to justify their actions, enhance the protection of the individual, and, ultimately, contribute to better decision making. The contribution of the Court of First Instance in this context should not be underestimated. Although, to paraphrase Dworkin, the judgments of the Court of Justice remain the most dramatic expression of judicial power, the CFI has made its own mark in the case law especially, but by no means exclusively, by the elaboration and application of procedural principles.

A specific comment may be appropriate here in relation to the principle of proportionality. It is submitted that the principle structures the judicial inquiry better than the concept of *Wednesbury* unreasonableness traditionally applicable under English law. This is because proportionality enables the court to identify better the various competing interests and to ascribe normative value to them. It will be noted that the intervention of the Court remains perforce negative rather than positive in that the Court may annul a measure but has no jurisdiction to give directions to its author as to the precise course of action which needs to be followed in order to redress illegality. The institution concerned must try again, attempting to second-guess the Court's standards. As the milk quota litigation and the mushrooms cases

---

    [2] Case C–70/88 *Parliament v. Council* [1990] ECR I–2041.
    [3] Case C–13/94 *P v. S and Cornwall County Council* [1996] ECR I–2143.
    [4] *Parliament* v. *Council*, op.cit.
    [5] See *Parliament* v. *Council*, op.cit.; Case 294/83 *Les Verts* v. *Parliament* [1986] ECR 1339; Case 222/84 *Johnston* v. *Chief Constable of the Royal Ulster Constabulary* [1986] ECR 1651.
    [6] See Opinion 1/91 *on the Draft Agreement relating to the creation of the European Economic Area* [1991] ECR I–6079; Opinion 2/94 *on the accession of the Community to the ECHR* [1996] ECR I–1759.

poignantly prove,[7] that may not be an easy task: successive measures dealing with the same issue may be annulled. It is true that the use of proportionality, in particular, encourages the Court to replicate the balancing process which the decision maker himself performs. It must be emphasized, however, that the Court does not act as an appellate body. Although the threshold of legality is higher than that applicable under English law, a range of options remain available to the Community legislature.

The general principles of law are closely interrelated. Proportionality, as a principle requiring that the means used must correspond to the objective sought, has a transverse character and forms part of all other principles. It is a component of fundamental rights since, although certain restrictions on such rights may be permitted, no restriction may be justified if it constrains the freedom of the individual more than is necessary to serve the public interest. Similarly, the principle of protection of legitimate expectations may need to give way to overriding public interests. That assessment entails a balancing exercise which involves considerations of proportionality.

The affinity between equality and proportionality requires closer examination. The starting point of the two principles is different. Equality is a principle of participation whereas proportionality is a principle of merits. But the link between them is evident in a number of respects. A test of proportionality is inherent in the concept of 'objective justification', which negates breach of the principle of equal treatment. Also, proportionality incorporates an element of participation. In order to assess whether a burden imposed on a product or an individual is proportionate, the Court will have regard to the way other related products or individuals are treated even if they are not in a strictly comparable situation.[8] The participatory character of proportionality was particularly evident in the skimmed-milk powder cases. It will be remembered that in annulling the contested regulation, the Court declared that the obligation on feeding-stuff producers to purchase milk powder at a disproportionate price amounted to a discriminatory distribution of burdens between different agricultural sectors.[9] A central point in the reasoning of the Court was that the measure in issue made a particular group of producers to bear unevenly the economic burden of an unfavourable situation which had developed in another economic sector.

A further area where the interaction between equality and proportionality is vividly illustrated is the imposition of flat-rate charges. Claims that such charges infringe equal treatment and proportionality have been countered by the Court by the use of virtually identical reasoning irrespective of the breach of principle which is pleaded.[10]

---

[7] See above, 5.4.2. and 3.6.

[8] See e.g. Case C–24/90 *Werner Faust* [1991] ECR I–4905; Case C–25/90 *Wünsche* [1991] ECR I–4939; Case 122/78 *Buitoni* v. *Forma* [1979] ECR 677; Case C–256/90 *Mignini* [1992] ECR I–2651, cf. Opinion of Jacobs AG.

[9] Case 114/76 *Bela-Mühle* v. *Grows-Farm* [1977] ECR 1211. See above 3.4.2.4.

[10] See e.g. Joined Cases C–267 to C–285/88 *Wuidart and Others* [1990] ECR I–435; Case C–27/90 *SITPA* [1994] ECR I–133; Joined Cases C–133, C–300 and C–363/93 *Crispoltoni II* [1994] ECR I–4863; Case 5/73 *Balkan Import-Export* v. *Hauptzollamt Berlin-Packhof* [1973] ECR 1091.

The link between equal treatment and legitimate expectations is also evident in the case law. Examples abound. In *Spagl*,[11] the Court and the Advocate General were at odds as to which principle was applicable. The Court found an infringement of the principle of respect for legitimate expectation which, in the circumstances, it understood as a principle of participation, namely as dictating the equitable allocation of burdens among different classes of producers. The Advocate General, on the other hand, saw the issue as one of equal treatment between returning producers and continuing ones and found that objective justification existed. In *Spagl* the issue could justly be seen as involving the application of both principles but in *Meiko*[12] the Court was less exacting by establishing a legitimate expectation where none should exist: the issue there was clearly one of equal treatment.[13] Finally, in *Ruckdeschel*[14] the claim of the applicants that the principle of equality was breached was helped by the fact that an existing advantage had been withdrawn.

This fusion of general principles is not surprising given that they share common ideological foundations and pursue common objectives. Their functional equivalence denotes their character as methodological tools facilitating the judicial inquiry. In a word, these general principles are the primary tools for the enforcement of negative rights against public authorities.

In substantive terms, the reasoning of the Court is not always convincing. The preceding chapters identified certain cases where, in the view of this author, consistency is lacking[15] or the result reached is not supported by compelling arguments.[16] It may not be coincidental that the general principles of law is an area characterized by a relatively high proportion of cases where the Court has disagreed with the Advocate General. This may be explained by the fact that the application of general principles, especially the principle of proportionality, sometimes involves a subjective evaluation, and also by the fact that the Court invokes general principles of law to exercize an equitable jurisdiction. A notable example of disagreement is provided by the *Staff Salaries* case.[17] In a number of other cases, the Court applied the principle of legitimate expectations and reached a result more favourable to the individual than the Advocate General.[18] In other cases, by contrast, the Advocate General has found an infringement of a general principle but

[11] Case C–189/89 [1990] ECR I–4539. See also Case C–217/89 *Pastatter* [1990] ECR I–4585 and above 5.4.2.

[12] Case 224/82 *Meiko-Konservenfabrik* v. *Germany* [1983] ECR 2539.

[13] See above 5.3.3.

[14] Joined Cases 117/76 and 16/77 *Ruckdeschel* v. *Hauptzollamt Hamburg-St.Annen* [1977] ECR 1753.

[15] See e.g. the rules governing the retroactive application of laws.

[16] See e.g. Case 127/80 *Grogan* v. *Commission* [1982] ECR 869, above 5.7; Case C–312/93 *Peterbroeck* v. *Belgian State* [1995] ECR I–4599, above 8.5.

[17] Case 81/72 *Commission* v. *Council* [1973] ECR 575.

[18] See e.g. Case 74/74 *CNTA* v. *Commission* [1975] ECR 533 (Trabucchi AG); Case 5/75 *Deuka* v. *Einfuhr- und Vorratsstelle Getreide* [1975] ECR 759 (Trabucchi AG); Case 127/80 *Grogan* v. *Commission* [1982] ECR 869 (Capotorti AG); Joined Cases C–260 and C–261/91 *Diversinte and Iberlacta* [1993] ECR I–1885 (Gulmann AG).

the Court has disagreed.[19] In general, it may be said that Opinions are distinguished by a more compelling reasoning but are not necessarily more generous to the individual than the Court.

To some extent, consistency of reasoning is inhibited by the collegiate character of the judgment. The inherent limitations imposed by collegiality have led at least one former member of the Court of Justice to suggest that dissenting judgments should be allowed; as is the case in the European Court of Human Rights.[20] It is true that in recent years the Court employs more expansive reasoning. This is partly owing to the fact that, as the Community expanded and more legal cultures came to be reflected in the composition of the Court, the French influence on the style of the judgment waned and the output became more international. It has also been necessitated by the growing importance of the case law for the legal community and the public in general, and the national courts in particular. As more and more disputes at national level raise issues of Community law, national courts increasingly need to rely on the case law of the Court for their solution. It therefore becomes necessary for the Court to explain its reasoning in more detail.

It has become obvious from the preceding chapters that the relationship between Community law and the laws of Member States is a dialectical one. On the one hand, Community law borrows elements from national laws in order to fill the gaps in the Treaties and provide solutions to questions left unanswered by Community written law. On the other hand, Community law feeds back into the national legal systems principally through the national courts. This dialectical relationship deserves to be examined in more detail.

In the early stages of the development of Community law, the Court sought inspiration from national laws to cover the lacunae of written Community law. Thus in the early years, the general principles of law fulfilled a dual function: they provided a unifying theme adding cohesiveness and rationality to solutions of disparate legal problems. Also, they ensured that Community law was the legal and ideological continuum from the laws of the Member States, acting as a force of legitimacy. As the case law developed and the Community legal order reached a stage of relative maturity, the general principles came to embody constitutional values attuned to the special needs of the Community polity. It should be stressed that, even nowadays, the Community judicature continues to heed to, and seek inspiration from, the laws of the Member States on procedural and substantive issues. National law influences are sometimes overt but more often covert and indirect. We saw for example above,[21] how in *Technische Universität München* calls by the German judiciary for greater substantive scrutiny of the decisions of the

---

[19] See e.g. *Cehave* v. *Hoofdproduktschap voor Akkerbouwprodukten* [1989] ECR 2219 (equality, Tesauro AG); Case C–345/88 *Butterabsatz Osnabrück-Emsland* [1990] ECR I–159 (proportionality, Jacobs AG).

[20] See the evidence presented by Lord Slynn to the House of Lords Select Committee on the European Communities, Sub-committee on the 1996 Inter-Governmental Conference, *1996 Inter-Governmental Conference, Minutes of Evidence, House of Lords, Session 1994–95, 18th Report*, p. 246.

[21] Above, 7.2.

Community administration led to the elaboration by the Court of Justice of stricter procedural requirements.

In turn, the principles elaborated at Community level feed back to the national legal systems. Community law influences national laws in two ways. First, there is direct influence. Where national authorities act within the scope of Community law, they are bound to comply with Community principles and standards. National courts acquire powers to review national measures on the basis of grounds which may not be accepted under purely domestic law. Such direct influence is aptly illustrated in the Court's case law on fundamental rights. Following the judgment in *ERT*,[22] the national courts have jurisdiction to review the compatibility with fundamental rights of national measures which fall within the scope of Community law. Thus the case law of the Court of Justice has effectively let the European Convention of Human Rights into the English legal system by the back door and precipitated a shift in the balance of power between the judiciary and the executive in favour of the former. It may be thought that the influence of Community law on English law is particularly pervasive because the latter shares neither the ideological underpinnings nor the methodological tools of the former. But as already stated in the first chapter, it would be wrong to divide national law between borrowers and lenders. The Court's case law has had far-reaching and penetrating influence on the laws of all Member States. Its net effect has been to raise the standards of accountability of national public authorities through the introduction of new remedies and higher standards of judicial scrutiny.

Apart from its direct influence, Community law bears also indirect influence on national laws. By indirect influence, it is meant that the case law of the Court of Justice influences the development of national laws in areas unconnected with Community law. Such spillover effect is inevitable for two reasons. First, to a good extent, the courts of all European countries face similar problems. It is natural for the judges of one Member State to turn to the Community courts and, to the extent that it is practically possible, to their brethren in other Member States, with a view to gaining inspiration. Cross-fertilization between national and supranational legal systems is a sign of our times, perhaps more so than of other eras, and can be expected to increase.[23] That is especially so in areas where domestic law does not provide a clear answer or is perceived as suffering from deficiencies. The second reason is more powerful. Once different standards of judicial scrutiny are infused into a legal system, it is difficult to restrict their application only to certain areas of law unless such restriction can be justified not only on grounds of doctrinal reasoning but also on grounds of fairness. The expanding presence of Community law in the area of remedies and the higher standards introduced by the Court have led in many a case to reverse discrimination, namely, the situation

[22] Case C–160/89 [1991] ECR I–2925.
[23] See Beatson and Tridimas (eds.), *New Directions in European Public Law*, Ch. 1. For a judge's perspective, see Lord Justice Schiemann, The Application of General Principles of Community Law by English Courts', in Andenas and Jacobs, *European Community Law in the English Courts*, pp. 136–48.

where claims based on purely domestic law are treated less favourably than claims based on Community law. Such reverse discrimination flies in the face of justice. That is particularly so since often the intrinsic value of Community rights which enjoy superior protection is less than the intrinsic value that rights governed by domestic law possess. How, for example, can it be justified that action by a public authority which restricts the free movement of goods is reviewable on grounds of proportionality but public action which restricts fundamental rights in areas unconnected with Community law is not? In English law, the indirect influence of Community law is clearly illustrated in cases like *M* v. *Home Office*[24] and *Woolwich Equitable Building Society* v. *Inland Revenue Commissioners*.[25] Overall, it may be said that, so far, English courts have followed a cautious approach and have been selectively receptive to such indirect influences.[26] It may be argued, in fact, that the indirect influence of Community law, where visible, is not based on a genuine effort on the part of the national judiciary to follow the lead of Community law. Rather Community law is used as a catalyst to promote solutions which the national judiciary favours in terms of policy but feels unable to endorse being constrained by the principle of binding precedent or, more generally, by traditional ideas and concepts underpinning the legal system. Viewed in that light, reliance on Community law is nothing but a pretext, a concocted alibi. Whichever way it is seen, the influence of the case law on the public laws of the Member States has been extensive, pervasive and, at times, subversive. It has been described by a member of the French Constitutional court as 'a peaceful revolution in the law'. Such indirect influences and cross-fertilization, it is submitted, should not be viewed with consternation but be welcomed as an enrichment of the national legal traditions.[27]

One of the most important judicial developments of the last decade has been the gradual transformation of the principle of primacy from a general principle of constitutional law to a specific obligation on national courts to provide full and effective remedies for the protection of Community rights. The Court's leitmotiv can be encapsulated in the dictum *ubi jus, ibi remedium*. The culmination of this trend has been the establishment of State liability in damages for breach of Community law, which has marked a new stage in the evolution of the law of remedies. Overall, it is submitted that the judgments of the Court in this area are balanced. Liability is easy to establish where a Member State fails to take implementing measures but much more difficult to establish in any other case. The test of serious

---

[24] [1994] 1 AC 377.

[25] [1992] 3 WLR 366. See further Schiemann LJ, op.cit., at pp. 143 *et seq*. and the discussion in De Smith, Woolf and Jowell, pp. 897–9.

[26] See, e.g. for a rejection of Community standards regarding the principle of legitimate expectations, the judgment of the Court of Appeal in *R* v. *Secretary of State for the Home Department, ex parte Hargreaves* [1997] 1 All ER 397. Cf. *R* v. *Ministry for Agriculture, Fisheries and Food, ex parte Hamble (Offshore) Fisheries Limited* [1995] 2 All ER 714 and *R* v. *Secretary of State for Transport, ex parte Richmond upon Thames London BC* [1994] 1 WLR 74. For a more positive approach, see *Percy* v. *Hall* [1996] 4 All ER 523 at 545.

[27] A leading member of the English judiciary has described extrajudicially the growing direct and indirect influence of Community law as 'eminently sensible'. See Schiemann LJ, op.cit., at p. 140.

breach is a flexible formula which enables liability to be assessed in the light of the nature of the breach and the discretion enjoyed by the national authorities in the circumstances of the case. The future of the remedy will depend to a large extent on the way that it is applied by national courts. The interaction between Community law and national law is surrounded by uncertainty. Although the conditions of liability are governed by Community law, the remedy of reparation is a matter for national law subject to the limitations imposed by the Court's jurisprudence. The case law in this area seeks to strike a balance between the need to ensure the effective protection of Community rights and respect for the autonomy of national legal systems.[28] The resulting uncertainty is an inevitable consequence of the fragmentary development of the law inherent in the process of judicial harmonization.

[28] Joined Cases C–430 and C–431/93 *Van Schijndel and Van Veen* v. *SPF* [1995] ECR I–4705, at 4713 per Jacobs AG.

Bibliography

Adamovich, L., 'Marge d'appréciation du législateur et principe de proportionnalité dans l'appréciation des "restrictions prévues par la loi" au regard de la Convention européenne des droits de l'homme' (1991) R Trim.Dr. Homme 291

Alexander, W., 'Perte de la caution en droit agricole communautaire' (1988) CDE 384

Allan, T. R. S., 'The Limits of Parliamentary Sovereignty' [1985] PL 614

—— *Law, Liberty and Justice* (Oxford, 1993)

Allot, P. [1996] 55 CLJ 409

Arnull, A., *The General Principles of EEC Law and the Individual* (1990)

—— 'Does the Court of Justice have inherent jurisdiction?' (1990) 27 CMLRev. 683

—— 'Opinion 2/94 and its Implications for the future Constitution of the Union', in *The Human Rights Opinion of the ECJ and its Constitutional Implications* (CELS Occasional Paper No. 1, University of Cambridge, 1996), 7

Association européenne des avocats, Colloquium of 24/25 Jan. 1994, 'Droits de la défense et droits de la Commission dans le droit communautaire de la concurrence' (Bruylant, 1994)

Bailey, S. H., Harris, D. J., and Jones, B. L., *Civil Liberties, Cases and Materials* (4th edn., 1995)

Barents, R., *The Agricultural Law of the EC* (Kluwer, 1994)

Barnard, C., *EC Employment Law* (Wiley, 1995)

—— '*P* v. *S*: Kite Flying or a New Constitutional Approach?', in Dashwood, A., and O'Leary, S. (eds.), *The Principles of Equal Treatment in E.C. Law* (Sweet and Maxwell, 1997), 59–79

—— (1997) 22 ELRev. 451

Beatson, J., and Tridimas, T. (eds.), *New Directions in European Public Law* (1998)

Bellamy and Child, *Common Market Law of Competition* (Sweet and Maxwell, 4th Ed., 1993, Supplement, 1996)

Bercusson, B., *European Labour Law*, Part IV (Butterworths, 1996)

Bernard, N., 'Discrimination and Free Movement in EC Law' (1996) 45 ICLQ 82

Boulois, B. J., *Droit Institutionnel des Communautés Européennes* (Paris, 1984)

Boyron, S., 'Proportionality in English Administrative Law: A Faulty Translation?' (1992) 12 OJLS 237

Braun, A., 'Les droits de la défense devant la Commission et la Cour de justice des Communautés européennes' (1980) 141 IRCL 2

Brown, N., 'The First Five Years of the Court of First Instance and Appeals to the Court of Justice: Assessment and Statistics' (1995) 32 CMLRev. 743

Brown & Jacobs, *The Court of Justice of the European Communities* (4th edn. Sweet & Maxwell, 1995)

Brownlie, I., *Principles of Public International Law* (4th edn. OUP, 1990)

Campbell-White, F., 'Property rights: A Forgotten Issue under the Union', in Neuwahl, N., and Rosas, A. (eds.), *The European Union and Human Rights* (Kluwer, 1995), 249–63

Caranta, R., 'Judicial Protection Against Member States: A New *Jus Commune* Takes Shape' (1997) 34 CMLRev. 703

Cardwell, M., *Milk Quotas* (OUP, 1996)

Cassese, A., Clapham, A., and Weiler, J. (eds.), *Human Rights and the European Community*, Vols. II–III (1991)

CELS, *The Human Rights Opinion of the ECJ and its Constitutional Implications* (CELS Occasional Paper No. 1, University of Cambridge, 1996)

Chalmers, D., 'The Single Market: From Prima Donna to Journeyman', in Shaw, J., and More, G. (eds.), *New Legal Dynamics of the European Union*, (OUP, 1995), 55

Clapham, A., 'A Human Rights Policy for the European Community' (1990) 10 YEL 309

—— *Human Rights in the Private Sphere* (OUP, 1993)

Constantinesco, V., Kovar, R., and Simon, D., *Traité sur l'Union Européenne* (Economica Paris, 1995)

Coppel, J., and O'Neill, A., 'The European Court of Justice: Taking Rights Seriously' (1992) 29 CMLRev. 669

Craig, P., 'Legitimate Expectations: A Conceptual Analysis' (1992) 108 LQR 79

—— '*Francovich*, Remedies and the Scope of Damages Liability' (1993) 109 LQR 595

—— 'Substantive Legitimate Expectations in Domestic and Community Law' (1996) 55 CLJ 289

—— 'Once More unto the Breach: The Community, the State and Damages Liability' (1997) 113 LQR 67

—— *Administrative Law*, (3rd edn., Sweet & Maxwell, 1994)

Curtin, D., 'The Decentralised Enforcement of Community Law Rights: Judicial Snakes and Ladders', in Curtin, D., and O'Keeffe, D., *Constitutional Adjudication in European Community and National Law* (1992), 33–49

—— 'The Constitutional Structure of the Union: A Europe of Bits and Pieces' (1993) 30 CMLRev. 17

—— and Heukels, T. (eds.), *Institutional Dynamics of European Integrations, Essays in Honour of H. G. Schermers*, Vols. I–III (Kluwer)

—— and Meijers, H., 'Access to European Union Information: An Element of Citizenship and a Neglected Constitutional Right', in Neuwahl, N., and Rosas, A. (eds.), *The European Union and Human Rights* (Kluwer, 1995), 77–104

—— —— 'The Principle of Open Government in Schengen and the European Union: Democratic Retrogression?' (1995) 32 CMLRev. 391

Dallen jun., R. M., 'An Overview of European Community Protection of Human Rights, with some special references to the UK' (1990) 27 CMLRev. 761

Daniele, L., 'Non-Discriminatory Restrictions to the Free Movement of Persons' (1997) 22 ELRev. 191

Dashwood, A., 'The Limits of European Community Powers' (1996) 21 ELRev. 113, 114

—— and O'Leary, S. (eds.), *The Principle of Equal Treatment in E.C. Law* (Sweet & Maxwell, 1997)

Dauses, M., 'The Protection of Human Rights in the Community Legal Order' (1985) ELRev. 398

de Bùrca, G., 'Fundamental Human Rights and the Reach of European Law' (1992) 13 OJLS 283

—— 'The Principle of Proportionality and its Application in EC Law' (1993) 13 YEL 105

—— 'The Language of Rights in European Integration', in Shaw, J., and More, G. (eds.), *New Legal Dynamics of European Union*, (OUP, 1995) 29

de Smith, Woolf and Jowell, *Judicial Review of Administrative Action* (5th edn. 1995; First Supplement, 1998)

Downes, T., 'Trawling for a Remedy: State Liability under Community Law' (1997) 17 LS 286

Drzemczewski, A., 'The Domestic Application of the European Human Rights Convention as European Community Law' (1981) 30 ICLQ 118

Due, O., 'Le respect des droits de la défense dans le droit administratif communautaire' (1987) CDE 383

Duparc, C., *The European Community and Human Rights* (EC Commission, 1992)

Dworkin, R., *Taking Rights Seriously* (London, Duckworth, 1978)

EC Commission, 'The Protection of Fundamental Rights as Community Law is Created and Developed', EC Bull. Suppl. 5/76

—— 'Accession of the European Communities to the European Convention on Human Rights', EC Bull. Suppl. 2/79

—— 'The Development and Future of the Common Agriculture Policy', EC Bull. Suppl. 5/91

—— 'Public Access to Information', COM(93)191, OJ 1993 C 156/5

—— Communication 93/C 166/04, 'Openness in the Community', OJ 1993 C 166/4

Eeckhout, P., 'Liability of Member States in Damages and the Community System of Remedies', in Beatson, J., and Tridimas, T. (eds.), *New Directions in European Public Law* (1998), 63

Egger, 'The Principle of Proportionality in Community Anti-Dumping Law' (1993) 18 ELRev. 367

Ehlermann and Drijber, 'Legal Protection of Enterprises: Administrative Procedure, in particular Access to File and Confidentiality' (1996) ECLR 375

Elias, P., 'Legitimate Expectation and Judicial Review', in Jowell and Oliver (eds.),
    New Directions on Judicial Review (CLP Special Issue, (1988)), 37–50
Ellis, E., *European Community Sex Equality Law* (2nd edn., Clarendon Press, 1998)
Emiliou, N., *The Principle of Proportionality in European Law* (Kluwer, 1996)

Faull, J., 'Legal Professional Privilege (AM & S): The Commission Proposes
    International Negotiations' (1985) 10 ELRev. 119
Fennelly, N., 'Reflections of an Irish Advocate General' (1996) Irish J Eur.L 5
Fitzmaurice, Sir Gerald, 'The General Principles of International Law' (1957) 92
    Collected Courses of the Hague Academy of International Law
Forrester, I. S., 'Legal Professional Privilege: Limitations on the Commission's
    Powers of Inspection Following the AM & S Judgment' (1983) 20 CMLR 75
Forsyth, C., 'The Provenance and Protection of Legitimate Expectations' (1988)
    47 CLJ 238
—— '*Wednesbury* Protection of Substantive Legitimate Expectations' [1997] PL
    375
Fuss, E.-W., 'La responsabilité des Communautés européennes pour le comporte-
    ment illégal de leur organes' (1981) RTDE 1

Galmot, Y., 'L'apport des principes généraux du droit communautaire à la garantie
    des droits dans l'ordre juridique français' (1997) 33 CDE 67
Goffin, L., 'La jurisprudence de la Cour de justice sur les droits de défense' (1980)
    16 CDE 127
Grondman, F., 'La notion de violation suffisamment charactérisée en matière de
    responsabilité non contractuelle' (1979) 1 CDE 86
Guerrin and Kyriazis, 'Cartels: Proof and Procedural Issues', 16 Fordham Int.LJ
    266

Hall, S., 'Loss of Union Citizenship in Breach of Fundamental Rights' (1996) 21
    ELRev. 129
Hamson, C., *Executive Discretion and Judicial Control* (1954)
Harlow, C., 'Codification of EC Administrative Procedures? Fitting the Foot to
    the Shoe or the Shoe to the Foot?' (1996) 2 ELJ 3
—— 'Francovich and the Problem of the Disobedient State' (1996) 2 Eur.LJ 199
—— 'Back to Basics: Reinventing Administrative Law' (1997) PL 245
Harris, O'Boyle and Warbrick, *Law of the European Convention on Human Rights*
    (Butterworths, 1995)
Hartley, T. C., 'The European Court and the EEA' (1992) 41 ICLQ 841
—— *The Foundations of European Community Law* (4th edn., Oxford, 1998)
Heukels, T., and McDonell, A. (eds.), *The Action for Damages in Community Law*
    (Kluwer, 1997)
Himsworth, C., 'Things Fall Apart: The Harmonization of Community Judicial
    Procedural Protection Revisited' (1997) 22 ELR 291

Hoskins, M., 'Tilting the Balance: Supremacy and National Procedural Rules' (1996) 21 ELRev. 365

Issac, G., *Droit Communautaire Général* (3rd edn., Masson, 1992)

Jachtenfuchs, 'Theoretical Perspectives on European Governance' (1995) 1 ELJ 115

Jacobs, F. G., (ed.), *European Law and the Individual* (1976)
—— 'Human Rights in Europe: New Dimensions' (1992) 3 King's College LJ 49
—— 'European Community Law and the European Convention on Human Rights', in Curtin, D., and Heukels, T. (eds.), *Institutional Dynamics of European Integrations, Essays in Honour of H. G. Schermers*, Vol. II (Kluwer), 561–72

Joliet, R., 'La Libre Circulation des Merchandises: L'arrêt *Keck et Mithouard* et les nouvelles orientations de la jurisprudence' (1994) *Journal des tribunaux, Droit Européen* 145

Joshua, J. M., 'Balancing the Public Interests: Confidentiality, Trade Secrets and Disclosure of Evidence in EC Competition Procedures' (1994) 2 ECLR 68

Jowell, J., 'Is Equality a Constitutional Principle?' (1994) 47 CLP 1
—— and Lester, 'Proportionality: neither novel nor dangerous', in Jowell and Oliver (eds.), *New Directions in Judicial Review* (CLP Special Issue, (1988)), 51

Kakouris, C., 'Do the Member States possess judicial procedural autonomy?' (1997) 34 CMLRev. 1389

Kapteyn and Verloren van Themaat, *Introduction to the Law of the European Communities* (3rd edn., Kluwer, 1998)

Kerse, C. S., *EC Anti-Trust Procedure* (Sweet & Maxwell, 1994)
—— 'The Complainant in Competition Cases: A Progress Report' (1997) 34 CMLRev. 213

Koopmans, T., 'The Birth of European Law at the CrossRoads of Legal Traditions' (1991) 39 AJCL 493

Koopmans, T., 'Comparative Law and the Courts' (1996) 45 ICLQ 545

Korah, V., *EC Competition Law and Practice* (Hart Publishing, 6th Ed, 1997)
—— 'The Rights of the Defence in Administrative Proceedings Under Community Law' (1980) 33 CLP 73

Krogsgaard, L. B., 'Fundamental Rights in the European Community after Maastricht' (1993) LIEI 99

Lafay, F., 'L'accès aux documents du Conseil de l'Union: contribution à une problématique de la transparence en droit communautaire' (1997) 33 RTDE 37

Lamoureux, F., 'The Retroactivity of Community Acts in the Case Law of the Court of Justice' (1983) 20 CMLRev. 269

Lasok, 'The Privilege Against Self-incrimination in Competition Cases' (1990) II ECLR 90

Law Commission Consultation Paper No. 126

Lee, P., 'The Irish Report', 17 *FIDE Congress*, Vol. III (Berlin, 1996), 204–48

Lenaerts, K., *Le Juge et la Constitution aux États-Unis d'Amérique et dans l'Ordre Juridique Européen* (1988)

—— 'Fundamental Rights to be Included in a Community Catalogue' (1991) 16 ELRev. 367

—— 'L'Egalité de Traitement en Droit Communautaire' (1991) 27 CDE 3

—— General Report, in 'Procedures and Sanctions in Economic Administrative Law', 17 *FIDE Congress*, Vol. III (Berlin, 1996), 34

—— and Van Ypersele, P., 'Le principe de subsidiarité et son contexte: Étude de l'article 3B du traité CE' (1994) 30 CDE 3

—— and Vanhamme, J., 'Procedural Rights of Private Parties in the Community Administrative Process' (1997) 34 CMLRev. 531

Levitt, M., 'Access to the File: The Commission's Administrative Procedures in Cases under Articles 85 and 86' (1997) 34 CMLRev. 1413

Lewis, C. and Moore, S., 'Duties, Directives and Damages in European Community Law' (1993) PL 151

McBride, J., and Brown, L. N., 'The United Kingdom, The European Community and the European Convention of Human Rights' (1981) 1 YEL 167

McCrudden, C. (ed.), *Women, Employment and European Equality Law* (Eclipse, 1987)

McKean, *Equality and Discrimination under International Law* (1983)

Mancini and Keeling, 'Democracy and the European Court of Justice' (1994) 57 MLR 175

Mendelson, M. H., 'The European Court of Justice and Human Rights' (1981) 1 YEL 125

—— 'The Impact of European Community Law on the Implementation of the European Convention on Human Rights' (1983) 3 YEL 99

Moore, S., 'Nothing Positive from the Court of Justice' (1996) 21 ELRev. 156

Neil, Sir Patrick, QC, 'The European Court of Justice: a Case Study in Judicial Activism', *1996 Inter-Governmental Conference, Minutes of Evidence, House of Lords, Session 1994–95, 18th Report,* 218

Neri, S., 'Le principe de proportionnalité dans la jurisprudence de la Court relative au droit communautaire agricole' (1981) 17 RTDE 652

Neuwahl, N., and Rosas, A. (eds.), *The European Union and Human Rights* (Kluwer, 1995)

Neville Brown, L., 'State Liability to Individuals in Damages: An Emerging Doctrine of EU Law' (1996) 3 Ir.Jur. 7

Nolte, G., 'General Principles of German and European Administrative Law— A Comparison in Historical Perspective' (1994) 57 MLR 191

O'Leary, S., 'Aspects of the Relationship between Community Law and National Law', in Neuwahl, N., and Rosas, A. (eds.), *The European Union and Human Rights* (Kluwer, 1995), 23

Oliver, P., 'Enforcing Community Rights in the English Courts' (1987) 50 MLR 881

—— *Free Movement of Goods in the European Community* (3rd Edition, Sweet and Maxwell, 1996)

—— 'State Liability in Damages Following *Factortame III*: A Remedy Seen in Context', in Beatson, J., and Tridimas, T. (eds.), *New Directions in European Public Law* (1998), 49

Papadopoulou, R. E., *Principes Généraux du Droit et Droit Communautaire* (Bruylant, 1996)

Pescatore, P., 'Les objectifs de la CEE comme principes d'interprétation dans la jurisprudence de la Cour de justice', in *Miscellanea Ganshof van der Meersch*, II (Bruxelles, Bruylant, 1972), 325

—— 'La Cour de justice des Communautés européennes et la Convention européenne des droits de l'Homme', in Matscher and Petzold (eds.), *Protecting Human Rights and Freedoms: The European Dimension* (1988), 441

Picheral, C., and Olinga, A. D., 'La théorie de la marge d'appréciation dans la jurisprudence récente de la Cour européenne des droits de l'homme' (1995) R Trim.Dr. Homme 567

Plender, R., 'Equality and Non-discrimination in the Law of the European Union' (1995) 7 Pace Internl. LR 57

Poiares Maduro, Miguel, 'Reforming the Market or the State? Article 30 and the European Constitution: Economic Freedom and Political Rights' (1997) 3 ELJ 55

—— *We, the Court: The European Court of Justice and the European Economic Constitution* (Hart Publishing, 1998)

Posner, R. A., *The Problems of Jurisprudence* (Harvard University Press, 1990)

—— *Law and Legal Theory in the UK and USA* (OUP, 1996)

Prechal, S., and Burrows, N., *Gender Discrimination Law of the European Community* (Dartmouth, 1990)

Rasmussen, H., *On Law and Policy in the European Court of Justice* (Martinus Nijhoff 1986)

Rawls, J., *A Theory of Justice* (Clarendon Press, 1972)

Reich, N., 'The "November Revolution" of the European Court of Justice' (1994) 31 CMLRev. 459

Ruffert, M., 'Rights and Remedies in European Community Law: A Comparative View' (1997) 34 CMLRev. 307

Sauter, W., *Competition Law and Industrial Policy in the EU* (OUP, 1997)

Schermers, H. G., 'The Communities under the European Convention of Human Rights' (1978) 1 LIEI 1

Schermers, H. G., 'The European Community bound by Fundamental Human Rights' (1990) 27 CMLRev. 249

—— 'The Eleventh Protocol to the European Convention on Human Rights' (1994) 19 ELRev. 367

—— and Waelbroeck, *Judicial Protection in the European Communities* (Kluwer, 1992 5th edn.)

Schiemann, Lord Justice, 'The Application of General Principles of Community Law by English Courts', in Andenas and Jacobs, *European Community Law in the English Courts*, 136–48

Schwarze, J., *European Administrative Law* (1992)

—— (ed.), *European Influences in Administrative Law* (Sweet and Maxwell, 1998)

Shapiro, M., 'The Giving Reasons Requirement', in *The University of Chicago Legal Forum: Europe and America in 1992 and Beyond: Common Problems . . . Common Solutions?* (1992), 179

—— 'Codification of Administrative Law: The US and the Union' (1996) 2 ELJ 26

Sharpston, E., 'Legitimate Expectations and Economic Reality' (1990) 15 ELRev. 103

Simon, D., 'Y a-t-il des principes généraux du droit communautaire?' (1991) 14 *Droits* 73

Soulier, G., *L'Europe* (Colin, Paris 1994)

Spielmann, D., *L'effet potentiel de la Convention européenne des droits de l'homme entre personnes privées* (Bruylant, 1995)

Steiner, J., 'From Direct effects to Francovich: shifting means of enforcement of Community law' (1993) 18 ELRev. 3

Strozzi, G., 'Le principe de subsidiarité dans la perspective de l'intégration européenne: une énigme et beaucoup d'attentes' (1994) 30 RTDE 373

Szyszczak, E., 'Making Europe More Relevant To Its Citizens: Effective Judicial Process' (1996) 21 ELRev. 351

Thirlway, H., 'The Law and Procedure of the International Court of Justice 1960–1989' (1990) 61 BYIL 1, 110

Tomuschat, C., 'Le principle de proportionnalité: Quis iudicabit?' (1977) 13 CDE 97

Toth, A. G., *The Oxford Encyclopaedia of European Community Law*, Vol. I (1990)

—— 'The European Union and Human Rights: The Way Forward' (1997) 34 CMLRev. 491

Tridimas, T., 'The European Court of Justice and Judicial Activism' (1996) 21 ELRev. 199

—— 'The Principle of Proportionality in Community Law: From the Rule of Law to Market Integration' (1996) 31 *The Irish Jurist* 83

—— 'The Role of the Advocate General in the Development of Community Law: Some Reflections' (1997) 34 CMLRev. 1349

—— and Eeckhout, 'The External Competence of the Community and the Case-Law of the Court of Justice: Principle versus Pragmatism' (1994) 14 YEL 143

Usher, J. A., *General Principles of EC Law* (Longman, 1998)

Van Gerven, W., 'Non-Contractual Liability of Member States, Community Institutions and Individuals for Breaches of Community Law with a View to Common Law for Europe' (1994) 1 MJ 6
—— 'Bridging the Gap Between Community and National Laws: Towards a Principle of Homogeneity in the Field of Legal Remedies?' (1995) 32 CMLRev. 679
—— 'Bridging the Unbridgeable: Community and National Tort Laws after *Francovich* and *Brasserie*' (1996) 45 ICLQ 507
—— 'Taking Article 215 EC Seriously', in Beatson, J., and Tridimas, T. (eds.), *New Directions in European Public Law* (1998), 35
Vesterdof, 'Complaints concerning infringements of competition law within the context of European Community Law' (1994) 31 CMLRev. 77
Von Heydebrand und der Lasa, 'Confidential Information in Anti-dumping Proceedings before United States Courts and the European Court' (1986) 11 ELRev. 331

Wade, H. W. R. (1991) 107 LQR 1
Ward, A., 'Effective Sanctions in EC Law: A Moving Boundary in the Division of Competence' (1995) 1 ELJ 205
Wathelet, M., and Van Raepenbusch, S., 'La responsabilité des États Membres en cas de violation du droit Communautaire. Vers un alignement de la responsbilité de l'État sur celle de la Communauté ou l'inverse?' (1997) 33 CDE 13
Weatherill, *Law and Integration in the European Union* (OUP, 1995)
—— and Beaumont, *EC Law* (2nd Edition, Penguin, 1995
Weiler, J. H. H., 'The European Court at a Crossroads: Community Human Rights and Member State Action', in Capotorti, F., Ehlermann, C.-D., *et al.*, *Du droit international au droit de l'intégration*, Liber Amicorum Pierre Pescatore (Nomos, 1987), 821
—— 'Does Europe Need a Constitution? Demos, Telos and the German Maastricht Decision' (1995) 1 ELJ 219
—— 'Fundamental Rights and Fundamental Boundaries: On Standards and Values in the Protection of Human Rights', in Neuwahl, N., and Rosas, A. (eds.), *The European Union and Human Rights* (Kluwer, 1995), 51–76
Weiler, J. H. H. and Lockhart, N. J. S., ' "Taking Rights Seriously" Seriously: The European Court and its Fundamental Rights Jurisprudence' (1995) 32 CMLRev. 51
Westen, P., 'The Empty Idea of Equality' (1982) 95 HLR 537
Wyatt, D., 'European Community Law and Public Law in the United Kingdom', in Markesinis, B. S., *The Gradual Convergence*, 188–201

Index